THE APPLAUSE

PERFORMING ARTS GUIDE
TO
LOS ANGELES &
SOUTHERN CALIFORNIA

Including San Diego, Orange County, Santa Barbara & Palm Springs

by
CAREY SIMON

APPLAUSE
BOOKS
211 WEST 71 STREET • NEW YORK NY • 10023

An Applause Original

**The APPLAUSE Performing Arts Guide to Los Angeles &
Southern California**

Library of Congress Cataloging-in-Publication Data

Simon, Carey.
    The Applause performing arts guide to Los Angeles &
Southern California : including San Diego, Orange County,
Santa Barbara & Palm Springs / by Carey Simon.
        p.   cm.
    ISBN 1-55783-153-X : $15.95
    1. Performing arts--California--Los Angeles Metropolitan
Region--Directories. 2. Performing arts--California, Southern--
Directories. I. Title. II. Title: Performing arts guide to Los
Angeles & Southern California.
PN2277.L59S53 1994
791'.025'79494--dc20   94-6990
                                                                CIP

Production Assistant: Andrew Pontious

Applause Theatre Book Publishers
211 West 71st Street
New York, NY 10023
Phone: (212) 595-4735
Fax: 212-721-2856

First Applause Printing: 1994

DEDICATION

With gratitude to

Loretta Barrett
Shelley List
and
Sharon Gedan

Three wise and wonderful women.

ACKNOWLEDGMENTS

As I began to compile reams of faxes, boxes of background information, and tons of press releases for this project, I discovered I needed help!

Among the many professionals in the arts community, my gratitude goes first and foremost to Aaron Paley of the California Arts Resource Council (CARS). I also got immediate help from Rachel Cohen of Cadence, Alan Ziter and Rick Prickett of the San Diego Theater League, Daniel Hening of the Blank Theatre Co., Don Shirley, Peter Levinson, Joe McBride, James Burkes, and the staff of Actors Equity.

I was privileged to have such a fine group of writers contributing their expertise to the book: T.H. (Tom) McCulloh, Richard Ginnell, Kirk Silsbee, Jan Breslauer, Nancy Churnin, Janice Steinberg, Leslie Westbrook, Heather Holmberg, and David Groves. Collectively, their credits include the *Los Angeles Times*, *Los Angeles Times San Diego edition*, *LA Weekly*, *The Reader*, *Jazz Review*, *Daily Variety*, *Santa Barbara Magazine*, and *Westways*.

I am especially grateful for the support of those experts and artists who agreed to pen the introductions to the chapters that follow. My sincere thanks go to Bella Lewitzky, Esa-Pekka Salonen, Al Nodal, Ken Wlaschin, Don Shirley, and Mitzi Shore.

There should be a special award that goes to friends who stick by you and listen to you no matter what nonsense you spout. As usual, my dear friend Helen Hawkeotte listened always. I also treasure the wisdom, friendship, and editorial expertise of Marilyn Zeitlin, Charlene Solomon, and Peggy Norris.

Several people treated my computer phobia, and without them, I surely would have perished. First my thanks go to Sue Knopf. Locally, I was assisted by, Cecile Epstein, Debbie Ross, and Jonathan Simon.

One special reward of working on this book was being reunited with my friend Stephen Dolainski whose writing, researching, editing, and organizing abilities were invaluable. Many thanks go to Allegra Yust for her skill and perseverance through the months of ups and downs. Special thanks, too, to Erica Zeitlin for hours and hours of editorial assistance.

And of course my thanks and love go to my daughter Janey who helped research the **CHILDREN** chapter, and to my husband Danny, who, as usual, put everything into proper perspective.

CONTENTS

INTRODUCTION

If there remains a single naysayer who still thinks Southern California is a cultural wasteland, one look through the **Applause Guide** should convince that benighted individual otherwise. After researching performing arts groups, festivals, art film houses, and performance spaces from Solvang to San Diego, I discovered nearly 1,000 active organizations covering every category of the performing arts.

Entries describe each group in terms of forms of entertainment or genre, place and space, price, seating, and specialties of the house. You'll get directions, be advised where to park, and have addresses and phone numbers at your fingertips. There's a little history, a few anecdotes, and instructions on how to get tickets and special discounts. You'll even get restaurant ideas so you can plan your entire evening. What you won't get is a calendar of events; however, you will get a list of resources that publish specific times and dates.

Open your eyes to what Southern California has to offer. Check out the possibilities, grab the local papers for dates, and you're on your way.

WHAT'S HERE, WHAT'S NOT

No stone was left unturned in identifying all of Southern California's performing arts companies and venues. I sought out resident as well as nomadic performance groups who performed, if not regularly, at least annually. Theaters, churches, amphitheaters, coffeehouses, any place that served as a performing venue became a target for the **Applause Guide**.

Each chapter is comprised of one form of entertainment. Venues and groups (i.e., theater buildings and theater groups without permanent homes) are listed together alphabetically within those chapters. They are not separated by city. If you're not sure what genre a group appears under, consult the **INDEX**. Most performing arts series (a combination series of music, theater, and dance productions) are listed in **THEATER**.

The **MUSIC** chapter includes opera, chamber, orchestral, choral, contemporary, and rock concert halls.

In the **CLUBS** chapter, you'll find spots specializing in comedy, jazz, country, pop/rock, and blues, plus coffeehouses (which often schedule readings and performance art as well as music). For the most part, dance clubs are not included, although some of the spots listed do allow dancing.

If you're wondering how **ART FILMS** found their way into a book of live performing arts, all I can say is—this is Hollywood!

The **FESTIVAL** chapter includes celebrations for nearly every interest, every culture, and every age group, and those celebrations spread from Solvang's Hans Christian Anderson Fairy Tale Festival to San Diego's Mainly Mozart Festival. They are divided into seasons. When available, there is information about how to get on mailing lists allowing you to plan your calendar in advance. And don't forget the **FREE** events, listed in a separate chapter.

SEATING CHARTS for establishments with 400 seats or more are found in the back of the book.

If I've missed a group or a performing space (hard to believe!), please let me know, and so I may include it in the next edition.

The evaluations in these listings are formed from a consensus of local experts. Some viewpoints you'll agree with, some you won't. Several of us are 5'2" and under and are most conscious of viewing obstructions, others are more attuned to acoustics. But if commentary isn't what you're after, this book is set up so that you can go right to the ticket information, address, phone number, parking instructions, and directions.

AUDIENCE ETIQUETTE

To remind you of what you know already:

*Jangling jewelry is out.

*If you're coughing and sneezing, do us all a favor and stay home!

*Beepers should be put on "vibrate" if possible, or should be buried in your pocket or purse for the least possible disturbance. Cellular phones should be parked in holding cells!

*Please be considerate of others—don't whisper—and for heaven's sake, don't repeat everything said on stage to the person next to you who's having trouble hearing. Look for the 𝄞 symbol in the listings which indicates the availability of hearing devices.

*Children should be taken out of the theater immediately if they begin to cry. Don't let them stand up or kick the seat in front of them. (For more information on introducing children to live performances, see the chapter **CHILDREN**.)

*Heavy perfume or cologne can cause allergy attacks for some people. Please spritz it on later.

HOW TO FIND OUT WHAT'S GOING ON

After you've looked through the **Applause Guide**—something you'll do over and over again—you'll want to find specific performance dates and coming events. There are numerous resources including:

Daily News
Drama-Logue
LA Jazz Scene
LA Parent
LA Weekly
Los Angeles Magazine
Los Angeles Times (all city editions)
Orange County Register
Palm Springs Desert Sun
The Reader
San Diego Union Tribune

Guide to the Performing Arts in Santa Barbara is published by the Santa Barbara Theatre Alliance and the Santa Barbara Conference and Visitors Bureau. Call (800) 398-0722 to be put on the mailing list.

CARS (California Arts Resources) sells two helpful guides: **ARTS Inc. Directory**, which lists more than 500 nonprofit arts organizations, programs, technical assistance providers ($10); and **Southern California Performing Arts Venues**, a resource for directors, producers, writers, and event planners who want to rent theaters of all sizes, nightclubs, galleries, churches, and parks ($12.95). Write or stop by CARS, 1653 18th Street, Ste. #1, Santa Monica, CA 90404, or call (310) 315-9444. (Prices do not include shipping and mailing.) The publications are also available at Samuel French's Theatre & Film Bookshop.

The Los Angeles Cultural Affairs Department publishes an annual festival guide available by calling the Department at (213) 485-2433.

The San Diego Performing Arts Guide is a bi-monthly calendar listing of theater, music, dance, and children's performances. It's published by the San Diego Theatre League and is available for an annual subscription price of $6. Call (619) 238-0700. The League also sells Arts Pass gift certificates, which are coupons in increments of $10 redeemable at a number of San Diego theaters, allowing the recipient to choose the performance and date.

Santa Barbara also has its own **Performing Arts Guide**, which is printed quarterly by the Santa Barbara Theatre Alliance. For a copy, contact them at 21 East Canon Perdido Street, Suite 201, Santa Barbara, CA 93101; (805) 966-0190. They also sponsor a 24-hour Info Line of current events. During business hours, callers are connected to individual box offices to make ticket reservations. Call: (805) 962-4636.

For $15, you can order one year of *Hotline*, Theatre LA's newsletter, with news on current arts issues and events in Los Angeles theatre. For $20 you'll get *The Opening Night Calendar*, a monthly list of current productions. Write Theatre LA, 644 S. Figueroa St., Los Angeles, CA 90017. Phone (213) 614-0556.

Join The Dance Resource Center in Los Angeles and receive **The Dance Resource Newsletter**, a calendar of events, classes, and issues relating to dance. ($35 buys the full membership and includes the newsletter; $20 gets a subscription to the newsletter only.) Write The Dance Resource Center, P.O. Box 6299, Los Angeles, CA 90055, or phone (213) 622-0815.

The San Diego Convention & Visitors Bureau publishes the **San Diego Official Visitors Guide**, a directory which includes a calendar of arts events. It's free of charge. Write San Diego Convention & Visitors Bureau, 401B Street, Ste. 1400, San Diego, CA 92101-4237, or call (619) 236-1212.

HOTLINES

Call the following phone numbers for concert information:

*(619) 594-6020 24-hour music line for San Diego State University Department of Music concerts.

*(213) 688-ARTS sponsored by Theatre LA, this hotline gives 24-hour a day information on current theater, dance, music, film, museum, family programs, and festival schedules, plus information on how to get discount tickets.

*(800) 426-7779 Jazz FM 103.1 Concert Connection, 24 hour information on LA and Orange County.

*(310) 597-LIVE for the KLON Radio Jazz Hotline.

*(310) 498-8052 for the KLON Radio Blues Hotline.

*(619) 458-9898 for San Diego's KIFM 98.1 jazz information line, Thursday through Thursday.

Special arts-related programs and discounts

The Westin Century City and the J.W. Marriott, both in Los Angeles, often offer special theater packages that include room and tickets to the Shubert. The Best Western Pepper Tree Inn in Santa Barbara advertises group deals that include restaurant, theater, and party packages. The Westin South Coast Plaza in Orange County is another hotel with occasional room/ticket specials for performances at the Orange County Center for the Performing Arts.

Radio station KLON FM 88.1 has more than a decade of mainstream jazz programming under its belt. The member-supported station, broadcasting from Cal State Long Beach, offers commercial-free programming. As a member, you are eligible for a variety of discounts (usually about 10% or two-for-one) from a number of clubs listed in the **Applause Guide**. Contact them for further information at (310) 985-5566.

Entertainment Publications publishes an annual discount book for a number of Southern California cities. In addition to dining and sightseeing discounts, it offers coupons good for two-for-one tickets, or a percentage off the ticket price, to variety of local theaters, comedy clubs, and cinemas. Call (310) 396-5595.

HOW TO GET TICKETS

Outlined here are some explanations and guidelines to help you get a handle on ticket-buying options. The **Applause Guide** provides you with specific information about buying tickets for each particular performance group or venue in the chapter listings.

Box Office

All venues—whether the 17,000-seat Great Western Forum or a 99-seat theater in downtown San Diego—maintain limited box office hours.

Some venues contract with a ticket agency such as TicketMaster to handle sales. In some cases, you can't purchase tickets through the theater's box office until a few days before—or the night of—a performance. Even if you call the box office, you're likely to hear a recorded referral to the ticket agency's phone number. Some venues only publish the phone number of the ticket agency handling their particular performance.

In the case of many 99-Seat Plan theaters, community groups, studio playhouses, and workshop spaces, an answering machine will pick up your call. You'll be asked to leave a message with your name and phone number, the date of the performance you wish to attend, and the number of tickets you want. Your call may or may not be acknowledged. There's a growing trend among those venues to call back only if your reservation request can't be honored. The theaters assure us that because they deal in such small numbers of patrons, there's rarely a problem tracking a reservation.

Subscription Programs

If you're able to plan ahead, purchasing a season subscription to your favorite performing arts group is the most convenient and economical approach.

The advantages of a season subscription are obvious: You're guaranteed preferential seating at a pre-selected performance, at a discount off single ticket prices. To lure season subscribers, producers often offer bonuses: VIP passes to selected opening nights, champagne receptions with the artists, free parking, souvenir programs, and other inducements.

Most organizations offering regular season subscriptions also offer a variety of prearranged series options—Plan "ABC" on Thursday evenings, plan "XYZ" on Saturdays, and so on. The UCLA Center for the Performing Arts, for example, offers some 14 season subscription options, ranging in price from $45 to $169 for between two and six shows with a selection of theater, music, and dance. Similarly, the Los Angeles Philharmonic offers 16 different subscription series.

Aside from traditional season subscriptions, a variety of other programs are available. The Philharmonic's "A la Carte" series and UCLA's "Choose Your Own" series allow you to personalize your choice of which performances to see and when. The Music Center's "In the Wings" series lets you "sample" three events, one at each of the Music Center venues. Optional events are then offered, but those tickets are extra. Theatre LA, a theater service organization, offers a sampler series to several different Los Angeles theaters. In fact, the sampler-type subscription seems to be growing in popularity throughout Southern California among multifaceted performing arts organizations.

As you would expect, most major theater, music and dance organizations as well as venues in Southern California offer some sort of season subscription plan. But subscription plans are not the exclusive domain of the big guys. Many of the small 99-Seat Plan theaters, civic light operas, and community theater groups also provide season subscriptions. (The **Applause Guide** listings note whenever a subscription series is available.)

Brochures describing the subscription choices usually contain seating charts to show you where your seats are located. Seating charts for most of the venues listed in the **Applause Guide** with more than 400 seats can be found in the back of the book.

Ticket Services

If you're looking for front-row seats to a Lakers game or the A section for a U2 concert at Universal Amphitheatre, don't call one of the ticket services listed here. Unlike ticket brokers, who can come up with the best seats in town at the last minute (often for an extraordinary price), the following ticket services don't buy blocks of tickets to be resold at above-face-value prices. Instead, TicketMaster, Theatix, Tickets LA and Theater LA contract with the venue (or a show's producer) to handle the majority of their ticket sales. Consumers pay a service or "convenience" fee that typically ranges from $1 to $4.50 per ticket. A few of the LA theaters use Telecharge exclusively: (800) 447-7400. Even film tickets can be purchased in LA in advance by calling 777-FILM (use either 213 or 310 area code).

TicketMaster

Information/Charge Lines:
(213) 480-3232
(213) 365-3500
(619) 278-8497
(714) 740-2000
(805) 538-8700

TicketMaster is the largest ticket company in the nation. Its computerized service sells 48 million tickets to theater, music, and sporting events each year. The Los Angeles-based company has 180 walk-in outlets in Southern California, most prominently in Music Plus and Tower Records stores, Smith's Food King grocery stores and Robinson's-May Co. department stores.

TicketMaster's computer automatically selects the "best" seats, from the front of the house to the back. Service charges vary, from $1.25 to $4.50 per ticket, depending on the event.

It's cash only at TicketMaster's walk-in locations, and you can't exchange tickets once you've left the outlet. But unlike ordering by phone, the walk-in services have seating diagrams of the venues for you to check the location of your seats.

To purchase tickets with a credit card through TicketMaster, you must call the charge/information line. TicketMaster provides toll-free prefixes in the 213, 619, 714 and 805 calling areas.

You can purchase tickets through TicketMaster by credit card up to 3 pm the day of the performance, and then pick up the tickets at the venue box office. TicketMaster will mail your tickets to you with 11 days advance purchase.

Theatix

(213) 466-1767 (information and tickets)
Fax: (213) 466-6922

Besides theatrical productions, Theatix handles tickets for film festivals, fund-raisers, literary events and many other cultural activities in Los Angeles. Service charges on tickets ordered through Theatix range from $1 to $2.50 per ticket, depending on the ticket price. With a 10-day advance purchase, Theatix will mail you your tickets. Personal service is the key to Theatix. They'll give you advice on which restaurants are near the theater, where to park and what to wear, if you ask. And they've even called ticket holders personally to let them know of the cancellation of a show.

Tickets LA

4655 Kingswell Ave., Ste. 217
Los Angeles, CA 90027
(213) 660-TKTS (8587)

Now in its fourth year of operation, Tickets LA handles only theatrical events, usually in the smaller venues around town. A $2 per ticket service charge is added to telephone credit card purchases; there's no service charge if you pick up tickets at the walk-in location on Kingswell Avenue, off Vermont near Chatterton's Bookstore in the Los Feliz district. Tickets LA can mail your tickets and give you information about show content, parking, and restaurants.

Ticket Outlet

Theatre LA
(213) 688-ARTS

Theatre LA, an association of commercial, nonprofit, educational and community theaters in LA, has a same-day discount ticket service called Ticket Outlet. When you call between noon and 5 pm, Tuesday through Saturday, you'll be told what shows are available. Prices are discounted at least 40 per cent. The cost of the discounted tickets (which includes a $1.50 service charge per ticket) is charged to your credit card, and your ticket order is faxed to the theater box office. Call on Saturday for Sunday show discounts.

Times Art Tix

Horton Plaza, Broadway and Third
San Diego
(619) 238-3810 (recorded listing of shows)
(619) 238-0700 (San Diego Theatre League office)

Operated as a public service by the San Diego Theatre League and known primarily for offering half-price same-day tickets to San Diego's arts events, Times Art Tix also offers full-price advance purchase tickets. It is also downtown San Diego's TicketMaster outlet, selling tickets to events throughout Southern California.

To find out what shows are available at half-price, call the information line or check the show board at the booth itself. As you would expect, this is a first-come, first-served, cash-only operation. The booth is open Tuesday through Saturday, 10 am to 7 pm. Tickets for Sunday and Monday shows are available Saturday.

The Foundation offers other discount ticket programs, including its $5 Sneak Preview series, a family theater program (buy one adult, get one free kid's ticket), and an annual (June) cash-only pay-what-can Bargain Arts Day that attracts thousands of ticket buyers.

Its bimonthly guide listing all current performances of its members is available at restaurants, theaters, and coffeehouses.

Discount Tickets

As a rule, seniors, students and children are entitled to discounts at a large number of performances in the Southland. Many of the smaller theaters, community groups, and most all college and university events are available at a discount to seniors and students (with ID). Other traditional discounts apply to season subscribers and groups (varying in minimum size from 6 to 20).

Discount programs of one kind or another abound, so be sure to ask when you call for information. Among LA's larger theater organizations, for example, Center Theatre Group (Mark Taper Forum) offers a daily (except Saturday) Public Rush, when tickets are sold on a first-come, first-served basis ten minutes before curtain for $10. The Center Theatre Group also offers a Frequent Playgoer discount, as well as a periodic Pay What You Can program.

The San Diego Theatre Foundation supports a similar pay-what-you-can program each year.

HOW TO USE THIS GUIDE

Performing arts groups (and organizations) and performance spaces are listed alphabetically according to their main emphasis (theater, music, dance, etc.) in their corresponding chapters. The exception is the **FESTIVALS & SEASONAL EVENTS** chapter which lists items alphabetically according to the season of the year.

There are numerous cross-references throughout the book to guide you to the right chapter. For instance, if you look for the Gindi Auditorium in **MUSIC**, you'll be referred to the **THEATER** chapter.

Cross-references to another chapter are indicated with the chapter name in bold capital letters:

GINDI AUDITORIUM See **THEATER**

Cross-references to another heading in the same chapter are indicated with that heading in bold upper and lower case letters rather than capitals:

EL CAMINO COLLEGE/MARSEE AUDITORIUM See **South Bay Center for the Arts**

Cross-references to another heading in a *different* chapter are shown first with the different heading in upper and lower case bold letters, then with the chapter in upper case bold letters:

BECKMAN AUDITORIUM See **Caltech Public Events** in **THEATER**

Companies and performing spaces named for people will be found alphabetically under that person's *first* name:

STELLA ADLER THEATRE (S)

Some theater companies perform in one location. The company and venue may have different names. Those companies will be found under the name of the theater, but will be cross-referenced so the reader can locate them if the theater name is unknown:

ACTORS CONSERVATORY ENSEMBLE (ACE) See **Lex Theater**

In each chapter, there is practical information (address, phone, performance times, ticket information, directions) located just beneath and to the right of each listing, and general information in paragraph form.

SOME JARGON USED IN THIS GUIDE

VENUE

The place where a performance takes place. Performance spaces are designed in three basic shapes, which determine how the audience sees the action.

Proscenium Refers to the border above and at the sides of the stage (which often has a curtain going up and down to show you when the action is over). In a proscenium house, the audience sits in front of the stage.

Thrust The stage literally "thrusts" out into the auditorium and the audience sits around the stage on three sides.

Theater-in-the-Round The playing area is in the middle and the audience surrounds it on all sides. Most entrances and exits are made through the audience. No curtains here; the play is over when the lights go up and everybody bows.

BLACK BOX

A room (sometimes but not always painted black) which becomes a performance venue by the addition of lights and chairs. Chairs are sometimes arranged on risers (the theater term for platforms or bleachers).

RAKE

Refers to the slope of the auditorium floor. The more incline (or rake) from the back of the auditorium to the stage, the better the sightlines. For spaces not originally designed as performance venues, the easiest and cheapest way to provide rake is to put the seats on risers.

KEY TO SYMBOLS

	Air conditioning (Only in ART FILMS)		Hearing device available
	Snack bar		Binoculars availabe
	Full bar		All OK for kids
	Restaurant on premises		Some OK for kids
	Restaurant nearby		See seating plans
	Fully handicap accessible	RIP	Obituary—entity no longer exists or is no longer in operation
	Handicap seats only		

THEATER

Introduction to Theater

By Don Shirley

The supply of theater in LA is staggering. Take a gander at the listings to follow, as well as at the theater listings in the "Calendar" section of the Sunday *Los Angeles Times*. The list goes on and on. Compare it to corresponding lists in the newspapers of other cities—yes, even the New York papers—and you can hardly avoid concluding that Los Angeles may just be the most prolific theater town in the United States. LA is, in fact, the second most lucrative commercial theater market in the nation.

Because the audiences are smaller and more far-flung than in New York and because few tourists come to LA just for its theater, the city generally can't offer an entire repertoire of long-running productions in large theaters at any one time. Many of the mega-Broadway productions do pass through LA and reap handsome financial rewards—and a few, like *Phantom of the Opera* stay for years and make a fortune. *Tamara*, an off-Broadway sensation, kept theatergoers running through the many rooms of a Hollywood mansion for a decade. But the bulk of the hundreds of productions in LA each year occur in sub-100-seat theaters where they play for a few weeks or months, often on a schedule of only three or four performances a week.

It has been this way since 1972, when Actors Equity, the stage actors' union, allowed their members to waive all compensation when performing in 99-seat theaters inside Los Angeles County. While the "Waiver" system was modified in 1988, (Equity members must now be paid token fees), the flood of productions generated by the system—which is now known as the "99-Seat Theater Plan"—continues unabated.

For audiences, the result is a shoppers' (or viewers') paradise akin to that other LA institution, the swap meet: there's a lot out there, but you have to know where to look. If you keep well informed, you can get close-up seats—at relatively low prices—to a vast range of plays and musicals and performance pieces.

Indeed, the oft-heard cliche that LA is "not a theater town" is a canard from the point of view of the savvy audience member. It's true only from the perspective of the small-time suppliers—the minor producers who seldom make a profit and the actors who barely make enough in those intimate theaters to cover their expenses.

In normal environs, this lack of moolah might be reason enough for the theater scene to dry up. But in LA, it doesn't work that way. Because the center of the nation's film and TV industry is in LA, the talent keeps gravitating here, no matter how small the financial rewards for theater—and so do the shows. Most of the actors, writers, directors and designers who make the pilgrimage don't make it big in the movies or TV, and many of them practice theater in order to exercise their craft. Some who *do* make it big on the screen also remain devoted to the stage in order to maintain contact with their creative roots. Whatever the motivation, a lot of theater can be seen here.

There is always the danger that a given production is primarily a showcase to get the leading actor cast in a sitcom. But showcases and vanity productions abound off-off Broadway in New York, too. And like New York, you may well catch the ascent of a rising star in one of these hole-in-the-wall productions.

The listings in the *Times* are one source of current information on shows in Los Angeles. The *LA Weekly*, which is available for free throughout the city, also carries fairly comprehensive listings, though it doesn't venture as far outside Los Angeles County as do the *Times* listings. Other local newspapers and city magazines carry listings on their own regions. Generally, however, the *Times* and the *Weekly* listings have the edge not only in thoroughness, but also by including a precis from a review. (See more about resources in the Introduction to the **Applause Guide**.)

Theatre LA, an organization of theaters and individual producers, offers some information over its (213) 688-ARTS phone line. It's also a good number to keep handy for its same-day discounted tickets service, which has begun to function in decentralized LA as half-priced tickets booths do in other cities. (See more about tickets and hot lines in the Introduction to the **Applause Guide**.)

That decentralization can be a problem for theatergoers, particularly if they lack transportation. There is no single "theater district." The area that comes closest to that description is the neighborhood around the legendary intersection of Hollywood Boulevard and Vine Street. As many as three larger theaters (the Pantages, the Henry Fonda, the Doolittle, plus the Ivar and the Las Palmas) and at least as many sub-100-seat ventures operate simultaneously, within easy walking distance of each other.

A couple of small fledgling districts have begun to emerge: Theatre Row Hollywood, along two blocks of Santa Monica Boulevard, roughly one mile south of Hollywood and Vine, and the somewhat less intensive NoHo district centered around Magnolia and Lankershim boulevards in North Hollywood. Unfortunately, the city's busiest and most vibrant "Theater district" folded in 1991, when the downtown Los Angeles Theatre Center— where four or five stages were often occupied at once—collapsed under the weight of its fiscal burden.

When most people think of Los Angeles theater, they think of the Music Center, the downtown culture palace. Certainly everyone should keep tabs on what's happening at the Music Center's Mark Taper Forum, the city's most prominent theater company for more than 25 years. The same management also runs a separate, more conventional subscription season at the Music Center's larger Ahmanson Theatre or at the Doolittle Theatre in Hollywood (if the Ahmanson is otherwise occupied by a long-running hit such as *Phantom* or by the current renovations).

Many casual theatergoers think only of the Music Center and the major Broadway tours. They never venture into the hundreds of other venues you'll discover in this guide. These people miss the remarkably polished and often exciting seasons at the South Coast Repertory in Costa Mesa. Or the crowd-pleasers at the elegant old Pasadena Playhouse. Or the new takes on old musicals at the Long Beach Civic Light Opera. Or the popular shows at the Canon in Beverly Hills. Or the alfresco productions of Shakespeare Festival/LA, which operates in several neighborhoods each summer, or the Will Geer Theatricum Botanicum in Topanga Canyon.

Most Angelenos also skip the San Diego scene, unaware that taking the train or the freeway to the border city for its theater is one of the best weekend getaways in Southern California. Not many cities host professional companies of the stature of the Old Globe, La Jolla Playhouse, and the struggling San Diego Repertory Theatre.

Point yourself in almost any direction and you'll find a performing arts center with full seasons of not only theater, but music and dance, as well. Cerritos, the Norris, Poway, and the McCallum come to mind.

There is also a host of smaller civic light opera companies in the area, which bring at least a few professional actors from LA to large auditoriums in towns such as San Bernardino, San Gabriel, Redondo Beach, and Santa Barbara. The Orange County Performing Arts Center books in touring musicals, and a number of other civic or campus venues are favorite tour stops for smaller shows.

Then, of course, there are the multitudes of shows in the sub-100-seat arena. The professionalism of the best of them is startling, considering the average amount of remuneration. The programming ranges from large-cast revivals of classics to cutting-edge solo performances, featuring ethnic groups and sexual orientations that are all over the map.

There are hardly ever any bad seats in these theaters—you're always close enough to feel connected, provided the performers know how to connect with you. Sometimes, the experience is so gratifying, the house so tiny, and the ticket price so reasonable that it feels as if a performance has been done just for you. You're not likely to feel this way on Broadway. Cherish it.

Don Shirley is a theater reporter for the Los Angeles Times. *His "Stage Watch" column is the first thing many of us turn to in Sunday's "Calendar" section. Prior to joining the* Times, *Shirley created and broadcast the "Thoughts on Theater" program at KCRW-FM in Santa Monica for three years. He came to Los Angeles from Washington D.C., where he covered theater and other subjects for* The Washington Post.

ABRAHAM LINCOLN CABIN THEATER

8758 Desert Willow Trail
Morongo Valley, CA 92256
Info: (619) 363-6126   **Rsvn:** (619) 363-6126
Artistic Director: William Groves
48-seat desert theater specializing in works about Lincoln.

  In a small log cabin no bigger than Abe's Illinois birthplace, actor Bill Groves and his Lincoln Players stage short plays based on incidents in the life of the President. And all is done in California's Morongo Valley, near Palm Springs! A far cry from Lincoln-land.

  Groves, who bears a strong resemblance to Lincoln, writes all the plays, which usually run about an hour. His fascination with the 16th president began many years ago when, as a drama student at Ohio State, he memorized the Gettysburg Address for a class assignment.

  The audience, many of whom make the pilgrimage from the Palm Springs area, sits in a horseshoe configuration around the cabin while the actors perform on the floor. Needless to say, it's a highly intimate theater experience.

  Aside from a two-month hiatus during July and August, Groves and his players perform every Sunday afternoon. There's no admission charge, but at the end of the show, Mr. Lincoln's generous-sized hat is passed around.

Performances
 Sun 2:30 pm
Tickets
 $5 donation
Discounts
 Call BO
BO
 Open 24 hrs a day, call; check/reservations needed a week in advance
Location
 In the Palm Springs area; off Hwy 62; off Int-10 to Palm Springs
Parking
 On premises, free

ACME PLAYERS AT THE ACME COMEDY THEATRE

5124 Lankershim Boulevard
North Hollywood, CA 91601
Info: (818) 753-0650   **Rsvn:** (818) 753-0630
Artistic Director: M.D Sweeney
50-seat theater for improvisational comedy.

  You may remember them as the Tujunga Group at the Two Roads Theatre. As the Acme Players, the group's reputation has carried over to their new spiffy 50-seat Acme Comedy Theatre. (In fact, they've also recently been referred to as the "new Groundlings.") Group members pen the sketches—more character driven than political or social—although much is invented as they go along. In addition to the Friday and Saturday night 8 pm shows, a 10:30 Saturday night spot features the Acme Players and special guests in an all-improv show. The 7:30 pm Sunday slot goes to The Acme Sunday Players—The Next Generation.

Performances
 Fri-Sat 8:30 pm; Sat 10:30 pm; Sun 7:30 pm, 8 pm
Tickets
 $10-15
Discounts
 Groups of 10, call BO
BO
 Mon-Sun 9 am-9 pm check/reserve by mail, fax, TicketMaster
Location
 1 block S of Magnolia Blvd
Parking
 Street parking

ACTORS ALLEY REPERTORY THEATRE

5269 Lankershim Boulevard
North Hollywood, CA 91601
Info: (818) 508-4200   **Rsvn:** (818) 508-4200
Artistic Director: Jeremiah Morris
99- and 199-seat theaters featuring mainstage dramas and musicals; improv, free public theater, and staged readings.
The quake-shake shook up the El Portal, but efforts are being made to reopen as soon as possible. In the meantime, a tape recording will let you know where performances will be.

  Actors Alley just moved into new digs at the El Portal Theater, a silent movie theater dating from the '20s, which is being renovated with the aid of a Community Redevelopment Agency loan. With this move, Actors Alley

Performances
 Vary
Tickets
 Call
Discounts
 Previews/children/ seniors/students/groups of 10, call BO
BO
 Check/AE/MC/V/no exchanges made for the same night of the week; subscription program

has temporarily turned the space into two stages—one with 199-seats; the other, 99. Ultimately, the goal is to grow into a full theater-arts facility with 600 seats, making it the only Equity contract house in the Valley (performers get paid union scale).

ACTORS ALLEY REPERTORY THEATRE CO.—Resident Co.

With more than 150 productions under their collective belts, AART has expanded into other areas, including a Playwrights Workshop, New Works Staged Readings, and an educational and teen/senior program. Under current artistic director Jeremiah Morris, the fare at AART is toward familiar audience pleasers.

Now in its 20th year, AART has seen a successful season of performances such as *Crossing Delancey* and Ira Levin's *Cantorial*, both produced in association with the University of Judaism and staged at the Gindi Auditorium. An ensemble production is announced at the last minute (to the subscribers) each year.

The group's move to the El Portal gave it the chance to open Peter Lefcourt's *The Audit* in the larger theater, and the chance to use the smaller space for new plays.

Location
At Weddington and Lankershim
Parking
City lot within 1/2 block of venue; street parking

ACTORS ALLIANCE PLAYREADING SERIES AND ACTORS' FESTIVAL

See press listings for performance locations.
Info: (619) 238-7396
Artistic Director: Philip C. Sneed

Actors Alliance, a 200-member support group for San Diego artists, sponsors a year-round playreading series OnBook-OnStage, which features readings of original and lesser-known works.

Actors are the force behind The Actors' Annual Festival, selecting the material (none longer than 45 minutes), casting it, and otherwise directing its development. Three to five pieces are assembled for each evening of the two-week festival in February, held at the 200-seat St. Cecelia's Theater (formerly the 6th Avenue Playhouse). (For more information, see **FESTIVALS**.)

Performances
Oct-June; Mon 7:30 pm
Tickets
$5
Discounts
Students/groups of 5+
BO
Check/tickets held at door on the evening of the performance
Parking
Varies with location

ACTORS COMPANY See Burbank Little Theater

ACTORS CONSERVATORY ENSEMBLE (ACE) See Lex Theater

ACTORS CO-OP See Crossley Theatre

ACTORS' FESTIVAL See FESTIVALS & SEASONAL EVENTS

ACTORS FORUM THEATRE

3365 1/2 Cahuenga Boulevard West
Studio City, CA 90068
Info: (213) 850-9016   **Rsvn:** (213) 850-9016
Artistic Directors: Audrey Marlyn Singer and Shawn Michaels
Seats 49; features original and newly-adapted plays.

Not far away from this small, intimate space are good restaurants such as La Loggia, the Daily Grill, and Il Mito.

Performances
Fri-Sun
Tickets
$10-12.50
Discounts
Previews/children/ seniors/students/ Theatre LA/groups of 10+, call BO

ACTORS FORUM THEATRE COMPANY—Resident Co.

Established in 1975, this troupe presents original drama and fresh adaptations, as well as revivals, such as the recent *Come Back, Little Sheba*. A post-modernist production of Odets' *Awake and Sing* was a much celebrated event.

Occasionally, audiences are invited to meet the actors in an informal setting at the Forum's cast and crew parties.

BO
9 am-7:30 pm; check/AE/MC/V/reserve by mail, Theatix
Location
Between Barham and Lankershim in Studio City, near 101 and 134 Fwys
Parking
On premises, FREE; street parking

ACTORS' GANG

6209 Santa Monica Boulevard
Hollywood, CA 90038
Info: (213) 465-0566
Artistic Director: Tim Robbins
Theater seats 99 for new plays and classics, with a focus on socially- and politically-conscious themes.

This decade-old company utilizes a bold, raw style that will get you hooked for the long haul.

The Gang was co-founded by Tim Robbins (*Bob Roberts*, *The Player*), then part of a UCLA student contingency looking for a home of their own. Robbins, who remains the Artistic Director, routinely returns to the Actors' Gang along with the other founding members (also with outside careers) to regenerate and recommit themselves to the theater.

Don't expect sitcom or film fluff here—count on a moving, emotional theater experience. And while the Actors' Gang is known for addressing politically and socially conscious issues, they won't preach at you during your evening out. They average four shows a year, including new plays and classics.

Performances
Vary
Tickets
$10-12
Discounts
Groups/students, call BO
BO
Open days of performance, 1 hr prior of show; phone Theatix
Parking
On street

ACTORS REPERTORY THEATRE See **Courtyard Playhouse**

ACTORS' REPERTORY THEATER COMPANY See **Santa Monica Playhouse**

ADAM HILL THEATRE

8517 Santa Monica Boulevard
West Hollywood, CA 90069
Info: (310) 854-3988   **Rsvn:** (310) 854-3989
Artistic Director: Adam Hill
Seats 50 for traditional and contemporary mainstream plays.

The entrance to this modern, upper-level playhouse is around the back. Folks happily schmooze in the plushly carpeted, roomy entryway. During showtime, avoid the seats closest to the lobby in the last two rows, as one of the walls blocks your stage view.   Hugo's, a popular casual restaurant, is several blocks east. For after-theater play, several dance clubs lay in wait mere minutes away. You can find parking at either the Sports Connection lot across from the playhouse or at the nearby Ramada Inn.

Performances
Fri-Sun
Tickets
$10-20
Discounts
Children/seniors/ students/groups of 10+, call
BO
1-6 pm, showdays 1-9 pm; check/reserve by mail; exchanges with 48 hr notice
Location
Santa Monica Blvd near La Cienega

(More . . .)

ADAM HILL THEATER COMPANY—Resident Co.

This company of students and professionals performs original plays as showcases for the film and theater community. Call the studio for show dates and times.

Parking
On street; parking lots nearby

AHMANSON AT THE DOOLITTLE AND AHMANSON THEATRE See **Music Center of Los Angeles County**

ALEX THEATRE

216 North Brand Boulevard
Glendale, CA 91203
Info: (818) 792-8672   **Rsvn:** (800) 883-PLAY
Fax: (818) 792-7343
1,452-seat renovated theater for musicals and dramas; home to the Glendale Symphony.

Just out of the gate is the LA area's newest major theater venture. This former 1920s movie palace now hosts large-scale productions such as *Sayonara*, *Mame*, and *Fame*. Fairly-priced subscription tickets are available for two seasons of three plays each. The Alexander Terrace is the seating of choice. Musicals which originate here will go on to the Spreckels Theatre in San Diego.

Single tickets become available at box office or through Telecharge two weeks before—and during—performance.

Performances
Wed-Sun 8 pm, Sat-Sun matinee 2 pm
Tickets
$30-114 subscriptions; $10-42.50 individual
Discounts
Previews
BO
Daily noon-6 pm (till showtime when show begins); Alex Store (2nd level Glendale Galleria) Mon-Fri 10 am-9 pm, Sat to 8 pm, Sun 11 am-7 pm; check/AE/MC/V/ reserve by mail; subscription program; subscription tickets by phone (800) 883-PLAY, at Alex Store; single tickets Telecharge (800) 223-3123 or at BO
Location
Between California and Wilson
Parking
On premises, metered; street

ALLIANCE REPERTORY COMPANY

3204 West Magnolia Boulevard
Burbank, CA 91505
Info: (818) 566-7935   **Rsvn:** (818) 566-7935
48-seat theater.

The theater entrance and patio are in the rear of the building. Seats in this newly renovated space are raked and all have excellent sightlines. There's plenty of parking space nearby.

ALLIANCE REPERTORY COMPANY—Resident Co.

Alliance has garnered numerous LA honors and awards in the seven years since its inception. Its 70 actors, directors, and writers are dedicated to new or little-seen material relevant to contemporary society.

This company is not afraid to take chances to achieve fresh and imaginative results. *Thanksgiving* by Michael Slade was first produced (and first acclaimed) as part of its One Act Festival. The critically lauded, award-winning *Iron City* was staged in 1986. *Rage! Or, I'll Be Home for Christmas*, a biting look at a dysfunctional family,

Performances
Tues-Sun 8 pm
Tickets
$15
Discounts
Seniors/students/groups of 10+, call
BO
Check/MC/V/reserve by phone
Location
N of 134 Fwy on Magnolia between Hollywood Way and Buena Vista
Parking
On premises, no charge

by Kevin Armold and Gus Buktenica, was extended and played to sold out audiences.

ALTERNATIVE REPERTORY THEATER

1636 South Grand Avenue
Santa Ana, CA 92705
Info: (714) 836-7929   **Rsvn:** (714) 836-7929
Fax: (714) 836-7582
Artistic Director: Patricia L. Terry
61-seat theater-in-the-round staging classical revivals.

Imagine a personal, even profound theater experience in a tiny 61-seat theater-in-the-round tucked into a small industrial mall space. Sure, it's stuck between an exterminator and an auto body shop, but it's worth seeking out—it's even worth the drive from LA or San Diego.

ALTERNATIVE REPERTORY THEATER COMPANY— Resident Co.

This four-year-old non-Equity company's steadfast dedication to presenting stimulating, thought-provoking theater has finally paid off with a substantial increase in season subscribers. Alternative Repertory concentrates on plays with concepts and issues that are pertinent today, though they may have been written hundreds of years ago. This company has a love affair with words, regardless of when they were written.

The season might include *The Glass Menagerie*, excerpts of Brecht's poetry, prose, and drama in *Brecht on Brecht*, or Shakespeare's *The Tempest*. They also produce Pinter, Beckett, and even Aristophanes. Each year's traditional Christmas readings are memorable discoveries.

The company pays attention to detail: sets, costumes, and lighting are all carefully planned to make the most of the tiny stage space.

AMERICAN LIVING HISTORY THEATER

See press listings for performance locations.
Info: (213) 876-2202
Artistic Director: Doreen Ludwig

If you've never heard of ALHT, you might be surprised to read that it has presented thousands of performances throughout the area in spaces as diverse as the Jet Propulsion Labs and the Valley Hunt Club of Pasadena. Less obscure venues have included UCLA, Arco Plaza, and The Huntington Library.

Doreen Ludwig's performances, almost entirely one-person presentations, focus on the great characters and events in our nation's history and literature, including the contributions of women and minorities. The fully-costumed plays, running 35 to 60 minutes, are followed by question-and-answer sessions. Although ALHT plays to adult audiences, there are special programs for young people and children.

AMERICAN NEW THEATRE See **Mojo Ensemble**

Performances
Thurs-Sat 8 pm, Sun 7 pm
Tickets
$12.50-15
Discounts
Previews/groups of 15+, call
BO
Thurs-Sun 6:30-9:30 pm; MC/V/check; subscription program
Location
Off 55 Fwy at Grand and Edinger
Parking
On premises, no charge

THE AMERICAN RENEGADE THEATRE

11305 Magnolia Boulevard
North Hollywood, CA 91601
Info: (818) 763-4430 **Fax:** (818) 985-3084
Artistic Director: David A. Cox
Stage I seats 72, Stage II, 50. From classic revivals to avant-garde and one-acts.
While quake repairs are being made to Stage One, Stage Two is intact and performing at full force.
This new playhouse in North Hollywood used to be a mortuary, so its actors may be understandably stiff at times (sorry). Thankfully renovated, it is now a comfortable venue with good sightlines.
Members of AFTRA, SAG, and A & A should ask about special discounts.

THE AMERICAN RENEGADE THEATRE COMPANY—Resident Co.
Established to showcase new playwrights and recreate classic Broadway plays, this young company brings us a full, rich range of theater. These theatrical renegades operate two stages, a front space presenting traditional and more commercial, mainstream productions, and a back stage for one-acts and some avant-garde originals. On the mainstage, classic comedic and dramatic revivals for those with traditional tastes are the norm.

Performances
Thurs-Sat 8 pm; Sun 2 pm, or 7 pm
Tickets
$10-12
Discounts
Previews/seniors/students/groups of 15+, call
BO
Mon-Sat noon-6 pm; check/reserve by mail; exchanges with 24 hr notice; subscription program
Location
170 Fwy and Magnolia Blvd at Tujunga St
Parking
On premises, FREE; street parking

ANNENBERG THEATER

101 Museum Drive
Palm Springs, CA 92262
Info: (619) 325-7186 **Rsvn:** (619) 325-4490
Fax: (619) 327-5069
Performance series takes place in 450-seat theater in the Palm Springs Desert Museum.
A scalding hot season of theater, dance, music, and film keeps this desert theater, located in the Palm Springs Desert Museum, far from deserted November through May. A variety of performers is scheduled—perhaps not as glitzy as at the McCallum, but popular enough to attract a following. Past performances by acts such as The 5th Dimension, The Lettermen, and Lainie Kazan have alternated on the schedule with hot-footed visiting dance troupes—Lines Contemporary Ballet was one, the Alberta Ballet another. The Montana Repertory Theatre paid a visit, as did the Billy Taylor Trio. A film series, offered Saturday and Sunday afternoons at 1 pm, presents black-and-white classics, art films, and Academy-Award winners.
Single tickets are available, or you can build your own series. Sunday afternoon concerts are seductively priced at $8 for nonmembers ($6 for members), and there are student rush seats. And never fear, both the air-conditioning and the seating are state-of-the-art in this contemporary theater.

Performances
Tues-Sun 8 pm; Sat-Sun 1 pm, 2:30 pm
Tickets
$5-25
Discounts
Children/students/groups of 10+, call BO
BO
Hrs 10 am-4 pm Tues-Sun; 1 hr prior to performance; AE/MC/V/check/reserve by mail, fax, TicketMaster; exchanges for subscribers only; subscription program
Location
(from Los Angeles) Int-10 E to Hwy 111, Palm Springs exit, to center of town (Hwy 111 becomes Palm Canyon Dr), turn right on Tahquitz Canyon Way, go 1 block, turn right on Museum Dr
Parking
On premises, FREE; street parking

AT THE GROVE PRODUCTIONS

276 East 9th Street
Upland, CA 91786
Info: (714) 920-4343   **Rsvn:** (714) 920-4343
Fax: (714) 920-4342
Artistic Director: David Masterson
Musicals and concerts presented in a 1940s art deco theater seating 457.

A February-to-December season of six mainstream musicals and dramas on the order of *One Flew Over the Cuckoo's Nest*, *Annie*, and *Quilters*, is typical of the presentations in Upland's renovated 1940s cinema-turned-theater. The four-year-old group also performs a four-show series of children's musicals. Occasionally, artists such as Leon Russell are booked to fill holes in the schedule.

Fair Warning: Seats are NOT reserved, which occasionally makes pre-curtain time pretty dramatic.

Performances
Fri-Sun 7:29 pm, Sun 3 pm
Tickets
$10-50 (subscriptions)
Discounts
Children/seniors/ students/groups of 20+, call BO
BO
Open 1 hr before show; check/MC/V/reserve by phone, mail; no refunds, no exchanges; subscription program
Location
Off San Bernandino (10) Fwy, Euclid exit, 1 mile N of exit, right on 9th; on corner of 9th and 3rd
Parking
On premises, FREE; street parking

ATTIC THEATRE

6562 1/2 Santa Monica Boulevard
Hollywood, CA 90038
Info: (213) 462-9720   **Rsvn:** (213) 462-9720
Artistic Director: James Carey
Mainstage seats 53, second stage, 31; produces and rents out for original, contemporary and classic plays.

This Theatre Row playhouse sits upstairs with its little sibling, the Attic Too.

Seating in both theaters won't kill you, and the sightlines are good. Watch for the "free theater project" every few months, when the company performs gratis. Neither the Attic nor Attic Too is handicap-accessible due to their walk-up only location.

Only soft drinks and juices are available at a small lobby bar. For more substantial fare, try Marino's Restaurant on Melrose near Cole.

ATTIC THEATRE ENSEMBLE—Resident Co.

For more than five seasons, this resident troupe has played the theatrical gamut from modern, mainstream plays to Shakespeare to more experimental choices. *The Diviners*, *Our Town*, and *All My Sons* are typical efforts. You never know what the night will hold, but it's worth the gamble to find out.

Performances
Thurs-Sun 8 pm
Tickets
$12-15
Discounts
Previews/children/ seniors/students/groups of 8, call BO
BO
Call for reservations
Location
Between Cahuenga and Highland on Theatre Row
Parking
Near premises (security parking at 1141 N Seward), $2

AUDREY SKIRBALL-KENIS THEATRE

Info: (310) 284-8965   **Rsvn:** (310) 284-9027
Fax: (310) 203-8067

If you'd like to read the minds of LA's new playwrights, make a point of attending this group's weekly playreading series. About six years ago, LA arts patrons Audrey Skirball-Kenis and Charles Kenis set up this nonprofit organization to nurture the talents of new playwrights. A number of programs were designed around that goal, including the Monday night readings (which sometimes come very close to being full productions), thrice

Performances
Mon 7 pm
Tickets
FREE
BO
Reserve by phone
Parking
Varies with location

yearly workshop productions, and an annual New Works Festival (which is produced in association with the Mark Taper Forum).

Of late, free readings are performed at the Odyssey Theatre at 2055 South Sepulveda Boulevard on the Westside. For the most up-to-date info, ask that your name be put on the mailing list.

AVIATION PARK AUDITORIUM

1935 Manhattan Beach Boulevard
Redondo Beach, CA 90278
Info: (310) 372-1171   **Rsvn:** (310) 318-0610
South Bay community theater seating 1,464 and hosting the Civic Light Opera of South Bay Cities and the Redondo Beach City Theater Group.

The South Bay, it seems, has the upstanding habit of converting former school auditoriums into community theaters. If we must lose schools, how laudable to keep the buildings working to educate and entertain our citizens. Don't let the term "school auditorium" turn you off. The sightlines give you a clear shot at the principal.

This school auditorium became home base for the Redondo Beach City Theatre Group, a community theater company that stages adult and children's shows here (and at Perry Park Playhouse on Grant Avenue in Redondo Beach). (See Redondo Beach City Theatre Group for more information.) The Civic Light Opera of South Bay Cities also produces four shows a year here. (See the listing **Civic Light Opera of South Bay Cities** for further information.)

BACKSTAGE THEATRE AND COMPANY

1599 Superior Avenue, Suite B-2
Costa Mesa, CA 92627
Info: (714) 646-0333   **Rsvn:** (714) 646-5887
Artistic Director: Al Valletta
A 45-seat theater producing contemporary dramas, musicals, and one-person shows.

At Backstage, one of Orange County's smallest non-Equity theaters, you can almost reach out and touch the actors. Like *The Little Engine Who Could*, founder Al Valletta persevered to find space for his critically acclaimed performances. After being forced to vacate his original tiny location (it wasn't up to code), he managed to find a space just as small as his first, where his company currently performs.

BACKSTAGE THEATRE AND COMPANY—Resident Co.

Backstage began its career with a hit in 1990. *Jacques Brel Is Alive and Well and Living in Paris* opened to rave reviews and sold-out performances. *Deathtrap, The Belle of Amherst,* and *K2,* the story of two stranded mountaineers, followed and sustained their early promises.

Performances
Thurs-Sun 8 pm, Sun 2:30 pm
Tickets
$12.50-20
Discounts
Seniors/students/groups
BO
Check/MC/V/reserve by mail; subscription program
Location
Off 55 Fwy at W 16th and Superior Ave
Parking
On premises, no charge

BARNSDALL ARTISTS CAFE

Gallery Theatre
Barnsdall Art Park
4800 Hollywood Boulevard
Los Angeles, CA 90027
Info: (213) 485-8667   **Rsvn:** (213) 485-4587
Fax: (213) 485-8396
299-seat theater in Barnsdall Art Park; eclectic entertainment.

Bob Dale, in charge of calling the shots and the spots for this young program sponsored by the Los Angeles

Performances
Vary
Tickets
FREE- $10
Parking
On premises, FREE; street parking

Cultural Affairs Department, is open to just about anything. As a result, Barnsdall books in as wide-ranging a program of artists as you'll find in LA. Past performances have ranged from staged readings about the legacy of colonialism to a multimedia, hip-hop musical tribute to women. About an hour before the performances, which are usually on Tuesday evenings (twice a month) at 8 pm, the lobby of the Gallery Theatre is opened up for the "cafe" portion of the event. Cafe tables and chairs are set up, and light pastries, coffee, and other refreshments are available at reasonable prices. It's an inviting atmosphere for informal discussions on arts issues in a coffeehouse-like setting.

Some events are free, others charge a variety of admission prices. The best way to find out what's going on is to call to be put on the mailing list.

BASEMENT THEATRE

464 East Walnut
Pasadena, CA 91101
Info: (818) 397-1651   **Rsvn:** (818) 397-1651
Accommodates 75-99 seats in the basement of the 1st Congregational Church. Stages nearly every genre.

This isn't just a room recently offered to a group of actors for occasional performances. Company members have discovered backstage graffiti dating back to the 1930s. Audiences sit on cushioned seats on tiers of risers. The present company has been performing here for the past seven years. They will gladly accommodate handicapped patrons if notified in advance.

LA CANADA PLAYERS—Resident Co.

This troupe, newly operating under Equity's 99-seat theater plan, puts on an ambitious season of five to eight productions a year. Regular audiences, most of whom are from the Pasadena area, tend to expect the unexpected from this company. With the staging of original works, innovative interpretations of the classics, experimental dramas, and at least one traditional classic, the company strives to promote new writers, directors, and actors. Professional caliber productions at reasonable prices.

Performances
Fri-Sat 8 pm, Sun 2 pm (sometimes)
Tickets
$8-12
Discounts
Children/seniors/groups of 10+, call
BO
Check/reserve by mail; exchanges flexible; subscription program
Location
Corner of Walnut and Los Robles
Parking
On premises or street, no charge

BEVERLY HILLS LIBRARY AUDITORIUM

444 North Rexford
Beverly Hills, CA 90210
Info: (310) 288-2201
Space in the Beverly Hills Library devoted to theater and poetry readings, storytelling, and music. Accommodates 190.

The controversial Beverly Hills Civic Center, designed by Charles Moore, is the setting for the elegant Beverly Hills Library. Above the library itself, a wedge-shaped community room offers a platform stage, sculpture exhibit, and padded chairs to accommodate numerous public programs.

The handsome salon welcomes dramatic storytelling for kids and parents, monologues, and mime. You might also catch a local theater company trying out new material, or the Los Angeles Women in Theatre group presenting dramatic readings. Professional and amateur talent performs.

Much of the entertainment is free, but once in a while a $5 donation is requested. The parking lot is free for the first two hours.

Performances
Vary
Tickets
FREE-$5
Location
Between Santa Monica Blvd and Burton Way
Parking
On premises, 2 hrs free

BEVERLY HILLS PLAYHOUSE

254 South Robertson Boulevard
Beverly Hills, CA 90211
Info: (310) 855-1556
99-seat theater; sometimes American classics, sometimes musicals.

    A bronze bust of Tennessee Williams greets you in the lobby, a testimony to several of the playwright's big successes produced here. A wide range of subject matter and genres are presented, however, including original musicals.

    Owned by director and celebrated acting coach Milton Katselas, the theater presents high-caliber works. Although the plays are often not under Mr. Katselas's guidance, but rather produced through a rental contract, the track record here is laudable.

    This theater is not your typical backdoor black box; it's a small theater with lots of class. Seating is comfortable with good raking.

    You won't get snacks here, so I suggest either a pre- or post stop at Kate Mantilini, or a ride into nearby downtown Beverly Hills.

Performances
  Vary
Tickets
  $10-20
BO
  Hrs vary; TicketMaster
Location
  Between Olympic and Wilshire Blvds
Parking
  On street

BEYOND BAROQUE LITERARY/ARTS CENTER

681 Venice Boulevard
Venice, CA 90291
Info: (310) 822-3006   **Rsvn:** (310) 822-3006
Fax: (310) 827-7432
A literary arts center hosting theater, readings, performance art, film presentations, and music.

    You're heading towards the ocean driving down wide Venice Boulevard. You look north and what do you see but two strikingly beautiful sculptures by Luis Jimenez gracing the front of the SPARCS building just next door to Beyond Baroque (at what used to be the Venice City Hall). You park in the 10-hour-free parking lot, then walk through two large open doors into Southern California's only literary arts center, a place where risk-taking is the norm, where programming is innovative and determined to inspire.

    For close to 25 years the center has focused on promoting, presenting, publishing, and distributing the writing of contemporary living artists. To this end are a profusion of performances in the traditional 99-seat black box theater. One of the most popular events is The Friday Night Reading and Performance Series, a mix of local and visiting authors and yet-to-be published writers, all of whom represent disparate literary perspectives. Invited authors have included Amy Tan, Ishmael Reed, Hanif Kureishi, and Allen Ginsberg. Raymond Carver gave his last "performance" at Beyond Baroque. Some of the readings are presented at Barnsdall Art Park in Hollywood.

    Free Wednesday night poetry workshops have been led by local poets Bob Flanagan and Mark Robin since the opening of the center. Its graduates have included Exene Cervenka, Sandra Bernhard, Dennis Cooper, and Amy Gerstler. The free monthly Sunday Night Open Readings complement this workshop by providing audiences for these emerging writers.

    Regular art film showings and theatrical productions are offered every month. Most nights, the music program offers an unusual innovative lineup of performers who are more often than not experimenting with new methods or instruments. A gallery upstairs houses work by local artists, and the Small Press Bookstore and Library stocks more than 12,000 titles in all genres.

Performances
  Vary; call for current schedule
Tickets
  $3-10
Discounts
  Children/seniors/ students
BO
  At the door on evening of event; 45 minutes before curtain; check/MC/V
Location
  On Venice Blvd 1/2 mile W of Lincoln Blvd
Parking
  On premises, FREE; street parking

Among the most popular annual events are the Surrealist Manifesto Night, Night of Erotica, and Ghost and Horror Story Night. Call for dates.

Phone to get on the mailing list, but expect only a couple months' worth of calendars. You will be asked to become a member to continue receiving the schedule. Or call Tuesday through Friday for current performance information.

BFA'S LITTLE THEATRE

421 North Avenue 19
Los Angeles, CA 90039
Info: (213) 225-4044   **Rsvn:** (213) 225-4044
Fax: (213) 225-1250
Half in the round, 99-seat theater.

The Bilingual Foundation of the Arts is the supporting parent of Theatre/Teatro, the producing company. Under the guidance of actress Carmen Zapata (with most productions directed by Margarita Galban), the group opens an English version one night followed by its Spanish cousin the next—of classic plays by Lorca and others, as well as new plays such as *Kiss of the Spider Woman* (its American premiere!). No matter what your native tongue, these performances will speak to you.

BFA also offers nine staged readings a year of Hispanic plays as part of Teatro Leido. Readings are free to the public.

Seating is limited to 99 seats, three rows deep, with a wonderful view of the wide stage, which is always put to full use.

Currently, BFA is part of a group of theaters performing at LATC. Be sure to confirm where current performances are taking place.

Performances
Wed-Sat 8 pm, Sun 3 pm
Tickets
$10-15
Discounts
Previews/seniors/students/groups of 15+,call
BO
Wed-Sat 6:30-7:30 pm, Sun 1:30-2:30 pm; check/AE/MC/V/reserve by fax, mail; no refunds, no exchanges; subscription program
Location
Off Golden State (5) Fwy at Broadway; off Pasadena (110) Fwy at Solano-Academy Rd; corner of San Fernando Rd and Pasadena Ave
Parking
On premises or street, no charge
Special Features
Free Reader's Theatre on selected Mondays at 8 pm

BILINGUAL FOUNDATION FOR THE ARTS See BFA's Little Theatre

BIRDCAGE THEATRE

Knotts Berry Farm
8039 Beach Boulevard
Buena Park, CA 90620
Info: (714) 220-5215
300-seat melodrama theater at Knotts Berry Farm

You wouldn't normally think of going to the theater at an amusement park, and yet amusement isn't a bad point of departure for theater, is it? This proscenium venue, with seating for 300, is an ideal stage for watching lively melodrama—and it's included in the admission price to Knotts Berry Farm. The shows tend to be wonderfully old-fashioned plots with plenty of comedy and enthusiastic, colorful casts. Who doesn't love to cheer for the hero and hiss for the villain? Look for the Birdcage in the park's Ghost Town section. Performances fill up quickly.

Performances
Mon-Sun matinees and evenings; call for hrs
Tickets
Admission to theatre included in admission to Knotts; adults $25.95, kids $15.95; no reserved seating
BO
Call for hrs; at the gate
Parking
On premises, $5

BLACKFRIARS THEATRE COMPANY

See press listings for performance locations
Info: (619) 232-4088
Artistic Director: Ralph Elias

San Diego's only "homeless" Equity theater gets high marks from discerning theatergoers for its passionate productions of quality work.

The company, which changed its name from the Bowery Theatre under the direction of current artistic director Ralph Elias, specializes in contemporary small-cast productions. Its biggest hits have been love stories such as John Patrick Shanley's *Danny and the Deep Blue Sea* and *Italian-American Reconciliation*, Isaac Bashevis Singer's *Teibele and her Demon*, and its much-extended Joe Orton farce, *What the Butler Saw*. It also did a riveting production of Beth Henley's *Abundance*. The company draws you into the action and makes you think.

While they recently transformed the Hahn Cosmopolitan into a thrust theater for Sam Shepard's *Unseen Hand*, it's unknown where the company will perform in the future. Call for information, and pay attention to announcements in the press.

Performances
Thurs-Sat 8 pm; Sun 2 pm; sometimes Sun 7 pm, Wed 8 pm
Tickets
$10-18
Discounts
Previews/groups/students/seniors, call BO
BO
Call for reservations; check/AE/MC/V; exchanges with 24 hrs notice; subscription program
Location
Varies
Parking
Varies with location

THE BLANK THEATRE COMPANY

See press listings for performance locations.
Info: (213) 662-7734   **Rsvn:** (213) 660-TKTS
Artistic Director: Daniel Henning

The Blank Theater Company was formed just over four years ago by 24-year theater veteran Daniel Henning with a workshop production of a Harold Pinter play. Since then, this popular group has performed a wide variety of works ranging from plays by Shakespeare, David Mamet, Wendy Wasserstein (who is also on the Board of Advisors), Hemingway (who is not), and Christopher Durang. New plays by new writers have also been added to the season. The dedicated group often comes up with a winner. Blank's Young Playwrights Festival, open to budding writers 19 years old and under, made its mark last season with 13 one-acts performed over four evenings in June. This season promises to be as big.

Plays and venues vary greatly depending on the type and size of the production. Past performances have found homes in the Canon, Gardner Stage, and Attic theaters.

Henning also has created "The Living Room Series," a 39-week series of readings by very talented artists performed at The Lost Studio at 130 South La Brea. Although only rehearsed for two weeks, these highly successful plays are missing nothing but the staging.

Performances
Varies
Tickets
$6-22
Discounts
Groups of 15+, call
BO
1 hr before performance; check/MC/V/by phone; cash, check at door
Parking
Varies with location

BLUE LINE THEATRE COMPANY See **The Complex**

BREA CIVIC & CULTURAL CENTER—CURTIS THEATRE

1 Civic Center Circle
Brea, CA 92621
Info: (714) 990-7727   **Rsvn:** (714) 990-7722
Fax: (714) 990-2258
199-seat theater, part of the Brea Civic & Cultural Center.

The City of Brea had the right idea by creating an intimate 199-seat theater as part of their cultural center. Built in 1980, the Curtis is unusual in that the stage is actually larger than the seating area, making the back row

Performances
Wed-Sun evenings; Sat and Sun matinees
Tickets
$5-14
Discounts
Children/groups of 20+, call BO

only 35 feet from the stage front. This wonderful setting for live theater and music has 199 seats that are raked dramatically, insuring excellent sightlines from any seat. The sound and lighting equipment is state-of-the-art, and the state of mind is intimate. The lobby features the talent of local artists. Most appealing are the ticket prices (ranging from $4 to $13), and the free parking. The facility is also rentable for conferences.

If time permits, walk around the complex itself. There's an art gallery and library, and restaurants are within easy striking distance. Next door, in the Embassy Suites Hotel, Tut's Bar & Grill serves a pre-theater lunch or dinner. Dining packages are available, which include lunch or dinner and a theater ticket. Call the Curtis to find out more about these. The Cultural Center itself is located in an area filled with Brea night life, including the Improv directly across the street.

Three companies under contract pepper the season with rich, diversified entertainment. The new Civic Light Opera is fast becoming known for their well-executed productions of traditional musicals, of which they produce two a year. A community volunteer organization, the Brea Theatre League, has been producing at the Curtis for more than a decade. While community theater may have a reputation as just that, this theater benefits from the influx of talent from nearby Disneyland. Young talented actors, will put aside Mickey and Minnie to take on more challenging roles (if less challenging costumes). Still, the League primarily taps mainstream "heartwarming" selections for its conservative theater-going audience except for the occasional "outre" Sweeney Todd-type production. Exercise your traditional family values here, and be sure to call weeks in advance for tickets.

The Brea City Orchestra is a volunteer assemblage of 40 to 50 members who annually perform, under Leon Guide's guiding hand, two pop concerts, two holiday concerts and two children's concerts—Klassy Koncerts for Kids 1 and 2, where children are allowed to chime in.

BREA YOUTH THEATRE See **CHILDREN**
YOUTH ACTOR'S THEATRE See **CHILDREN**

BRIDGES AUDITORIUM

450 North College Way
Claremont, CA 91711
Info: (714) 621-8031   **Rsvn:** (714) 621-8032
Fax: (714) 621-8484
A 2,500-seat theater hosting an annual performing arts series.

Bridges Auditorium (its full name is Mabel Shaw Bridges Auditorium) was a gift of the Bridges family in 1931 to memorialize their daughter who died in 1907.

This Northern Italian Renaissance structure is beautiful. Just to give you an idea of the size of this magnificent structure, the 60,000-square-foot interior is surrounding by 14,000-square-feet of porches and walks. A dramatic 22,000-square-foot ceiling in blue, silver, and gold portrays signs of the zodiac.

Culturally, Bridges attracts everyone from violin soloist Nigel Kennedy to the Minnesota Orchestra to Chile's "balladeers" Inti-Illimani. There's generally something for everyone each year, as well as a family event or two (though there's no family series per se).

Some folks have remarked that sightlines aren't very good. On the other hand, those who have heard

BO
Mon-Fri 11 am-2 pm; check/MC/V/Disc/ reserve by mail; exchanges available; subscription program
Location
Off 57 Fwy at Imperial Hwy and Randolph St
Parking
On premises, FREE

Performances
Vary
Tickets
$ varies
Discounts
Students/children/ groups of 10+, call BO
BO
Mon-Fri 10 am-5 pm; AE/check/MC/V/reserve by mail, fax, TicketMaster; exchanges, but no refunds; subscription program
Location
Near Hwy 10, exit N on Indian Hill Blvd (4th and College Way), right on 4th St
Parking
On premises, FREE

musical performances at Bridges think the acoustics are great!

A variety of series with several discount ticket packages are offered.

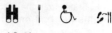

BURBAGE THEATRE

2330 Sawtelle Boulevard
Los Angeles, CA 90064
Info: (310) 478-0897   **Rsvn:** (310) 478-0897
49-and 99-seat theaters; often featuring experimental theater productions; West Coast or Los Angeles premieres.

Some of you may remember this group from the years it spent at the Century City Playhouse. Still guided by Ivan Spiegel, the group's performances are high quality, albeit with minimum production values. Their work, mostly by American playwrights, runs from Sam Shepard and David Mamet to Woody Allen and Tom Lehrer. *Bleacher Bums* was awarded numerous accolades when it opened in 1980, and went on to become the longest running professional production in the history of Los Angeles theater (at that time), closing in 1991.

You might drive right past the place, between Pico and Olympic, as it's housed in a brick structure looking not unlike the manufacturing companies nearby. There are two spaces, a commodious front theater with sofas and ever-changing artwork, and a small black box space in the rear; each has good tiered seating and fine sightlines. Often a number of different shows are running concurrently on different nights at different hours.

Performances
Thurs-Sun, sometimes Mon-Wed, times vary
Tickets
$12-17
Discounts
Previews/seniors/ students/groups of 10+, call BO
BO
Wed 2-5:30 pm; Thurs 2-8:30 pm; Fri-Sat 2-9:30 pm; Sun 4-7:30 pm; MC/V/check/reserve by mail; exchanges with 24 hr notice
Location
One block W of San Diego (405) Fwy; between Pico and Olympic Blvds
Parking
On premises, FREE

BURBANK CIVIC LIGHT OPERA

See press listings for performance locations.
Rsvn: (818) 953-8763
Artistic Director: Paul Van Bloem

Utilizing the talents of retired professionals, semi-professionals, and young would-be actors, BCLO puts on five plays a year. Since 1947, this energetic group has been performing musical comedies, revues, and operettas.

Performances
Fri-Sat 8:15 pm, Sun 2:30 pm
Tickets
$6-10
Discounts
Children/seniors/ students/groups of 25-49, call (818) 842-8060; 50+, $5 per ticket
BO
Check/reserve by mail (P.O. Box 201, Burbank, CA 91503); subscription program
Parking
Varies with location
Special Features
Open rehearsals

BURBANK LITTLE THEATER

George Izay Park
1111 West Olive
Burbank, CA 91506
Info: (818) 954-9858   **Rsvn:** (818) 954-9858
Fax: (818) 954-9138
Artistic Director: Lance Roberts
99-seat theater.
    The city of Burbank owns this 99-seater located in George Izay Park. The playhouse, which is rented and operated by The Actors Company, boasts a free lighted parking lot, central air and heat, a comfortable lobby, and brand-new seats—impressive attributes for one so diminutive. Long and narrow, the space can lend itself to imaginative set designs.

THE ACTORS COMPANY—Resident Co.

    In its five years, this troupe has performed about 15 widely divergent plays. The company includes anywhere from 40 to 60 professional acting members who perform some classics and revivals, but prefer new, original works (when they find one they like). So far, their tastes have been seconded by local critics.
    Recent productions include a one-woman Italian play about sexuality, *Orgasmo Adulto Escapes From The Zoo*; the Pulitzer prize-winning *Driving Miss Daisy*, the area premiere of Andrew Lloyd Webber's *Tell Me on a Sunday*, and an original audience-participated educational play about citizens' rights and responsibilities in a democracy. Shakespeare's rarely-seen drama, *Coriolanus*, was updated to the April '92 unrest in LA.
    On Sunday evenings, the Actors Company travels to the Hollywood Methodist Church to present "Living Newspaper," an ever-changing series of skits revolving around topical events. On Sunday days, Imagination Station takes over. Kids are treated to storytelling and readings by various members of the company. (See **CHILDREN** for more information). The Actors Company has a commendable track record of community outreach projects.

Performances
Fri-Sat 8 pm; Sun 3 pm
Tickets
$12-15
Discounts
Previews/children/
seniors/students/groups
of 24, call BO
BO
24 hrs answering
machine; subscription
program
Location
On Olive (in the George
Izay Park) near Victory
and Olive; near the
Olive exit off of Int-5
Parking
On premises, FREE;
street parking
Special Features
FREE play readings
throughout the year

CALIFORNIA COTTAGE THEATRE

5220 Sylmar Avenue
Sherman Oaks, CA 91401
Info: (818) 990-5773   **Rsvn:** (818) 990-5773
    New plays, performed in a private home, at no charge, with cookies and coffee served before the performance! A new theater experience? Well, California Cottage Theatre has been presenting its fare since 1987, when it began with a one-character, one-act play. Since then, the group has received numerous "critics choice" designations. Works have included tragedies, musicals, and comedies.
    Call and ask for an "invitation," which includes a map to that performance's location. The premise is: "Surprise is the cornerstone of entertainment!" How can you miss?

Performances
4 per month, Thurs-Fri 8
pm, Sat 7 and 9:30 pm
Tickets
FREE
BO
Reserve by phone
Location
Off Ventura (101) Fwy at
Van Nuys, 2 blocks E of
Van Nuys Blvd, N of
Magnolia
Parking
On street

THE CALIFORNIA MUSIC THEATRE

Former resident company of Pasadena's Raymond Theatre.

    Following on the departing heels of the LATC, 1992 saw the end of The California Music Theatre, the resident company of Pasadena's Raymond Theatre. The five-year-old company strove to present lavish musical theater. While their final season may have reflected poor play selections, myriad reasons for closure surfaced, primarily a debt reportedly between $1 and $2 million. The company grew from the Long Beach Civic Light Opera, born in 1979, and then invited to be "the" resident company of the Pasadena Civic Auditorium in 1986. But the company was plagued with a deficit from its opening strains. Even in the end, the money for an awareness campaign was unavailable to save the day. Unfortunately, this is an age old fact of theater life. The show must go on—as long as it's paid for.

CALIFORNIA REPERTORY COMPANY

1250 Bellflower Boulevard
Long Beach, CA 90840
Info: (310) 985-5356   **Rsvn:** (310) 985-5527
Fax: (310) 985-2263
Artistic Director: Howard Burman
Performances are staged in the 90-seat CalRep Theatre, the 220-seat Studio Theatre, and the 390-seat University Theatre.

Also known as CalRep, this is the semi-professional branch of the Department of Theater Arts at California State University, Long Beach. Like its famous cousins—Yale Repertory Theater and Harvard's American Repertory Theater—CalRep attempts to bond the profession of theater with its educational mission.

Each season four plays are presented with the goal of introducing audiences to international theatrical works with universal themes. They certainly hit their target with *Breaker Morant* and *Night Rehearsal*. During each season audiences will see at least one American or English-language premiere as well as one genuine world premiere.

When the company uses the CalRep Theatre (which it does most of the time), it's a comfortable experience in an attractive place; the large theater next door cannot boast those virtues.

Performances
Wed-Sat, Wed and Sat matinees
Tickets
$12-16
Discounts
Previews/seniors/students/groups, call (310) 985-2262
BO
Tues-Sat 11 am-3 pm and 6:30-9 pm; check/Disc/MC/V/reserve by mail, fax; exchanges with 24 hr notice; subscription program
Location
Off of the San Diego (405) Fwy at Bellflower Blvd
Parking
On premises, $2

CALIFORNIA YOUTH THEATRE

Twilight Theatre
Paramount Studios
5555 Melrose Avenue
Hollywood, CA
Info: (213) 956-2503   **Fax:** (310) 657-3272
Artistic Director: Jack Nakano

The three-decades-old CYT does, in fact, consist of a company of "youths" who train and team up with professional actors to present free summer performances at the new Twilight Theatre on the Paramount Studios lot. The company consists of teens and young adults—not young children. But a look at one recent season's offering (*The Robber Bridegroom*) leads me to believe these are not necessarily G-rated selections chosen for kids. On the other hand, the farce *Scapino* was the play of choice on last summer's schedule, along with *Rock Theatre's In Concert*, a music and dance spectacular, each geared toward the teen-and-older set.

My suggestion: Be sure you know what this season's performance is all about before you put that stroller in the trunk.

Performances
Summer: Wed-Sat 8 pm; Sun 7 pm
Tickets
$7.50-15
Discounts
Seniors/students/groups of 15+, call
BO
Mon-Sun 1 pm to curtain time; check/reserve by mail, fax; exchanges one day before performance
Parking
On premises

CALTECH PUBLIC EVENTS

Michigan Avenue South of Del Mar Boulevard
Pasadena, CA 91125
Info: (818) 356-3834   **Rsvn:** (800) 423-8849
Fax: (818) 577-0130
Performing arts program under the California Institute of Technology banner. Three venues for theater, music, dance, and family shows: Beckman seats 1,165; Ramo, 423; Dabney Lounge, up to 230.

California's Institute of Technology is home to more than the state's "infamous" seismology lab and 21 Nobel-prize-winning faculty and alumni. It also houses three important performing arts venues: the Beckman and Ramo auditoriums and Dabney Lounge. All are reached by entering the campus on Michigan Avenue, south of Del Mar Boulevard Park immediately in the lot as you enter, just behind Beckman Auditorium. The performance season for all the theaters more or less follows the academic year, October through May. Single tickets are usually to be had.

BECKMAN AUDITORIUM
You can't miss this circular building with its conical shaped roof. A colonnade of slender, diamond-shaped columns encircles the white African-looking building, which, aside from the brass hanging lamps in the colonnade, is unadorned.

Built in the early 1960s as a lecture hall, Beckman today hosts the Caltech Public Events performing arts series. Subscriptions and single tickets can be purchased for diverse music groups (Ladysmith Black Mambazo, Vienna Boys Choir), comedy (Mark Russell, The Capitol Steps), drama (California Shakespeare Festival), and even circus (the Flying Karamazov Brothers). The 90-year-old Coleman Chamber Music Association gives its season of Sunday performances in Beckman. Tickets can be ordered directly from that association (See **Coleman** in **MUSIC**). The 1,165-seat theater occasionally hosts lectures as well as a travel film series. The annual Family Faire series is also presented here (see **CHILDREN**).

The small stage actually rises only three steps above the auditorium floor. Little or no wing space prohibits big shows with lots of sets and fancy scenery. The house is gently raked, so dance performances don't work too well here either. But other than these logistical inconveniences, seats are never more than 90 feet from the stage and sightlines are no problem. The circular walls in the auditorium are covered in a white and gold quatrefoil pattern, and overhead small anodized metal disks in the conical shaped ceiling take on the look of a faux tent canopy.

Although there's separate wheelchair seating, it's limited to four spaces. CalTech promises to make every effort to accommodate the handicapped if given advance notice. The college will also arrange for lectures to be signed for the hearing impaired.

RAMO AUDITORIUM
At the south end of Baxter Hall, a short walk from Beckman, is Ramo Auditorium, a standard college auditorium with raked amphitheater-style and wood-frame cushioned seating. The stark theater is used for student performances, storytelling, lectures, and conferences. The auditorium itself is wheelchair accessible, though the restrooms at this end of the building are not; handicapped patrons will have to travel to the north end.

(More. . .)

Performances
Fri-Sun, matinees Sat-Sun
Tickets
$8.50-30
Discounts
Children/seniors/students/groups of 20+, call
BO
Mon-Fri 10 am-4:30 pm, Sat 1-4:30 pm (Sept.-May), 1 hr before performance; check/AE/Disc/MC/V/reserve by mail, fax, TicketMaster; exchanges before performance; subscription program
Location
1 mile S of Foothill (210) Fwy, S of Del Mar Blvd between Wilson and Hill
Parking
On premises, FREE; street

DABNEY LOUNGE

This stunning performance hall is a Spanish Renaissance beauty with magnificent French doors that open on to a garden of olive trees. Expansive hardwood floors also elegantly complement the free monthly chamber music series. The lounge is located in Dabney Hall, immediately south of Ramo Auditorium.

THE CANDLELIGHT PAVILION

555 West Foothill Boulevard
Claremont, CA 91711
Info: (714) 626-2411 ext. 200   **Rsvn:** (714) 626-1254
Fax: (714) 624-0756
380-seat dinner theater.

Since 1985, Candlelight has been serving up popular musicals, comedies, and revues accompanied by dinner and drinks. These lavish presentations are offered to guests in a large banquet-hall-like room. Dinner and a play—not a bad way to spend an evening. A season might include such sure pleasers as *Man of La Mancha*, *Show Boat*, or *Nunsense*. The traditional Christmas presentation is totally new every year and perfect for families.

The price includes one of three entrees, beverage, show, and tax. Appetizers, alcohol, desserts and tips are extra. Leave your tennis shoes at home; men have to wear jackets. The most expensive seating is on the upper tier, called the Terrace. The banquet tables are the cheapest, but the view's not the best and you'll have to share a table.

Performances
Wed, Thurs and Sat 8:15 pm, Fri 8:45 pm, Sun 7:15 pm, Sat and Sun 12:45 pm; dinner seating 2 hrs before performances
Tickets
$28-50
Discounts
Children/groups of 16+, call
BO
Tues-Sun 9 am-8 pm; check/AE/Disc/MC/V/ Diners' Club; exchanges with 48 hr notice; no refunds; subscription program
Location
N of San Bernandino (10) Fwy at intersection of Indian Hill and Foothill
Parking
On premises, FREE

CANON THEATER

205 North Canon
Beverly Hills, CA 90210
Info: (310) 859-8001 **Rsvn:** (310) 859-2830
Fax: (310) 859-8024
Beverly Hills theater seats 382 for musicals, dramas, and one-person shows.

We all know about the hundreds of legit theaters that were converted to screens. Well in the case of the Canon, a movie house was turned into a theater instead. Successful productions frequently move to the Canon, many from out of town. A.R. Gurney's *Love Letters* ran for over a year with a revolving cast of popular stars. *Forever Plaid* put in its appearance straight from the Pasadena Playhouse. Jackie Mason and Dick Shawn have graced the stage with their one-man crowd-pleasers.

At this moderately-sized Beverly Hills space, every seat offers good sightlines and leg room. Snacks can be bought in the lobby, but head for any number of Beverly Hills restaurants for before- or after-theater dining: delicious European-style bistro dining at Il Fornaio; New York-supper-club dining at The Grill in the Alley.

Performances
Vary
Tickets
$25-35
Discounts
Previews/children/ seniors/students/groups of 15, call BO
BO
Mon 10 am-6 pm; 10 am-showtime other days; check/AE/MC/ V/reserve by mail, TicketMaster
Location
1 block N of Wilshire
Parking
On premises (next door), $1 (after 6 pm); street parking

CARLSBAD CULTURAL ARTS CENTER See **Carlsbad Youth Theatre** in **CHILDREN**

CASSIUS CARTER CENTER STAGE See **Simon Edison Centre for Performing Arts**

CAST-AT-THE-CIRCLE (AND CAST THEATRE)

800 North El Centro Avenue
Hollywood, CA 90038
Info: (213) 462-9872   **Rsvn:** (213) 462-0265
Artistic Director: Diana Gibson
The Circle seats 99, the Cast, 65.
    Cast is one of the oldest theaters in the city, with a history that includes Charlie Chaplin, among other local names in lights, who directed here during the '40s. For years, Cast-at-the-Circle and its smaller sibling, the Cast, concentrated on imaginative new works directed by the esteemed Ted Schmitt. Diana Gibson took over after Schmitt's death but has kept alive his special innovative, avant-garde thrust. In addition to the regular evening performances, two late-night shows are offered on weekends. Justin Tanner's *Zombie Attack* has been drawing the crowds of lovers-of-the-weird for several years now (and more than 300 performances).
    The Cast recently walked away with numerous awards from *LA Weekly*'s annual theater awards presentation.

Performances
Thurs-Sat 8 pm, 10:30 pm; Sun 7 pm
Tickets
$12
Discounts
Groups call BO
BO
Tues-Sun 1 pm-7 pm; AE/MC/V
Location
Between Santa Monica Blvd and Melrose Ave, 1 block E of Vine
Parking
On street

CELEBRATION THEATRE

7051B Santa Monica Boulevard
West Hollywood, CA 90038
Info: (213) 957-1884   **Rsvn:** (213) 660-TKTS
Artistic Director: Robert Schrock
55-seat space dedicated to gay and lesbian theater.
    Not long ago, Celebration increased its seating capacity by a whopping 40 percent in its new well-designed West Hollywood house. Yes, that's 17 seats more than its first house in Hollywood. Parking isn't a problem because of the convenient location.
    In its new space the number of weekly performances has been expanded to four, and there's a play reading series as well as "off-night" stagings. Productions include one-acts, full-lengths, and performance art; comics and musicians are also showcased.
    As the only (openly) gay and lesbian professional, Equity signatory theater, the first-rate productions create a positive environment in which to explore the gay and lesbian experience. The group has received numerous awards including several from *LA Weekly* and *Drama-Logue*. Extraordinary that for ten-plus years Celebration has existed solely on ticket sales.

Performances
Thurs-Sat 8 pm, Sun 4 pm and 7 pm
Tickets
$12-15
Discounts
Previews/groups of 10+, call
BO
Phone reservations Mon-Sun noon-7 pm; 1 hr before curtain; check/ reserve by phone; subscription program
Location
1/2 block E of La Brea on Santa Monica Blvd
Parking
On premises or street, no charge

CELEBRITY CENTRE INTERNATIONAL

5930 Franklin Avenue
Hollywood, CA 90028
Info: (213) 960-3100   **Rsvn:** (213) 760-3100
Fax: (213) 960-3232
Artistic Director: Gary Allen Shay
Includes two rental spaces; seats 46 and 400 respectively.

CELEBRITY CENTRE THEATRE
    One of Hollywood's landmark residential buildings, Chateau Elysee was acquired by the Church of Scientology many years ago. Now known as the Manor Hotel, it houses the small 46-seat Celebrity Centre Theatre,

Performances
Mon-Sun 10 am-12 am
Tickets
$5-25
Discounts
Previews/children/group discounts negotiated, call BO
BO
10 am-11 pm; call (213) 960-3100 ext. 21603; check/AE/Disc/MC/V/ reserve by mail, fax

which has for the last 15 years staged readings and other small theatrical events.

You'll find an extremely comfortable venue with good sightlines and production values.

GARDEN PAVILION

Brand new at a cost of about $1 million, this state-of-the-art theater space seats 400 for musical theater.

Location
Off Hollywood (101) Fwy, Gower exit in Hollywood, corner of Bronson and Franklin

Parking
On premises, $ varies; valet, free; street parking also available

CELTIC ARTS CENTER/AN CLAIDHEAMH SOLUIS

Info: (213) 462-6844
Artistic Director: Sean Walsh
Note: As of this writing, a new home has not yet been found to replace the one that burned down.

Betcha didn't pronounce the name of this theater right! It sounds like "On Clive Solish." The center offers an ongoing artistic revival of Gaelic culture and history by presenting all forms of Celtic literature, music, theater, dance, crafts, and the fine arts.

An unfortunate fire closed the Center not long ago (although plans were already afoot for a move), and as of this writing, a new location has not been secured. Some performances are being farmed out to other locations. Call the number above to find out what's happening.

CENTER GREEN THEATRE AT PACIFIC DESIGN CENTER

Pacific Design Center
8687 Melrose Avenue
Los Angeles, CA 90069
Info: (310) 657-0800
Small specialty theater seating 382 for readings, music events, and film festivals.

Ask a hundred Angelenos if they've ever been to an event at the Center Green Theatre, and I'll bet you only one or two have had the pleasure. Few locals know about this plush well-appointed space located in the Cesar Pelli-designed Pacific Design Center. If nothing else, the 220 design showrooms and galleries provide what may be LA's most interesting theater "lobby."

The intimate, tasteful room, filled with 382 plush red-velour seats, is perfect for a select bill of readings (see the **Lannan Foundation**), film festivals, jazz, and other small music events. Audiences are, not surprisingly, upscale, and that's not by accident. Events staged in this venue are screened carefully so as not to conflict with the well-tonded image of the Center and its tony tenants. An adjacent outdoor amphitheater comes alive in the summer with the Summer Sound Series sponsored by the City of West Hollywood (see **FESTIVALS & SEASONAL EVENTS** for more information).

Performances
Mon-Sun
Tickets
$ varies
BO
Call
Location
On Melrose Ave, between San Vicente and La Cienega, and between Melrose and Santa Monica; entrances on Melrose and San Vicente
Parking
Parking on premises, $1.50 per half-hr, $6 max, $1.50 after 5 pm; street parking also available

CENTER STAGE THEATER

751 Paseo Nuevo, 2nd level
Santa Barbara, CA 93101
Info: (805) 963-8198   **Rsvn:** (805) 963-0408
160-seat theater for comedies, dramas, improv, dance, and music.

When the recent Paseo Nuevo Shopping Center went up in downtown Santa Barbara, one of the developer's

Performances
Thurs-Sun 8 pm; Sat-Sun 2 pm;
Tickets
$6.50-25

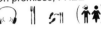

requirements was the inclusion of a small theater and art gallery. Hence the 160-seat Center Stage Theater was born.

The second-level space may not be roomy, but it's sure busy almost every night. Performances range from a Haitian family-life drama to a rendition of *Alice in Wonderland*. And if that's not enough to distract you from the boutiques, there's often a dance concert, lectures, poetry readings, performance art, and children's theater. It's best to call the box office to find out what's what. Ambitious future plans call for shopping around for three small theater companies, each with a different emphasis, to take up residence in the new space.

BO
Wed-Sat noon-6 pm; also 1 hr before performance; AE/MC/V

Parking
On premises, FREE

CENTER THEATER

300 East Ocean Boulevard
Long Beach, CA 90802
Info: (310) 436-3636   **Rsvn:** (310) 436-3661
Fax: (310) 436-9491
862-seat theater, part of the Long Beach Convention Center.

The smallest of the three Long Beach Convention and Entertainment Center venues, the Center Theater was built in 1977. The 862-seat thrust space, which was modeled after the Mark Taper Forum but with a more ample backstage and lobby areas, hosts a number of events throughout the year from educational seminars to mayor's forums. Most notable, however, are smaller productions mounted by the Long Beach Civic Light Opera and the Long Beach Opera, as well as visiting productions such as National Theatre for Children.

Critics have lauded the Center Theater for its suitability for the spoken word, while lamenting that no one seems to know of its existence.

Performances
Tues-Sat 8 pm; Sat-Sun 2 pm

Tickets
$14-34

Discounts
Seniors/students/groups of 29; group sales (213) 741-0821

BO
Mon-Sat 10 am-6 pm; AE/MC/V/reserve by mail,TicketMaster; subscription program

Location
Follow Long Beach (710) S until it ends; located off Shoreline Dr

Parking
On premises, $5; street parking limited

CERRITOS CENTER FOR THE PERFORMING ARTS

12700 Center Court Drive
Cerritos, CA 90701
Info: (310) 916-8510   **Rsvn:** (800) 300-4345 or (310) 916-8500
Fax: (310) 916-8514
Performing arts center accommodating from 950 to 1,863 for theater, music, dance, and children's entertainment.

Where, you may ask, is Cerritos? Isn't Cerritos the home of the Cerritos Auto Square? Well, yes, but it's also home to this elegant and innovative cultural arts center only 30 minutes from downtown LA, and 15 minutes from Orange County.

This brand-new performance space is the star feature of a 120-acre development project in Cerritos. The $60-million arts center, which opened in '92, entered its second season with a diverse group of entertainers: Whitney Houston, George Benson, American Ballroom Theater, Peter, Paul & Mary, Vienna Boys Choir, and Mstislav Rostropovich were just some of the names on its schedule. Theater presentations have included *Breaking Legs*, *City of Angels*, and *Cats*.

With its state-of-the-art architecture, this venue attempts to compete with long-established, world-class

Performances
Sept-June; Mon-Sun evenings and matinees

Tickets
$10-100

Discounts
Children/groups of 25+, call BO

BO
Mon-Sat 10 am-6 pm; check/AE/MC/V/reserve by mail, fax; exchanges for subscribers only; subscription program

Location
Directly off Riverside (91) Fwy

Parking
On premises, FREE

facilities for shrinking ticket purchases. On site is an office park, a hotel, and a 75-acre shopping and dining center.

The auditorium seats move on air casters and can be configured into five different seating arrangements to accommodate a variety of types of performances: arena, concert hall, lyric theater, Vegas-style cabaret room, and recital hall. Seating ranges from 950 in its smallest configuration to 1,863 in its largest. The jury is still out, though, on a verdict regarding the acoustics for classical music presentations.

The exterior was fashioned after the building designs in San Diego's Balboa Park—colorful tile, cream-colored stucco, and red granite. The interiors were modeled after the great theaters in Amsterdam and Vienna and Boston Symphony Hall.

There is a snack bar in the facility, but if you're looking for a full menu, consider The Grille 91 at the nearby Sheraton Hotel, or the restaurants in the new nearby shopping center. The Sheraton Cerritos Hotel, adjacent to the Center, offers a moderately-priced theater package.

The center is directly off the 91 Freeway.

CHAMBER THEATRE/CHAMBER THEATRE ANNEX

3759 Cahuenga Boulevard West
Studio City, CA 91604
Info: (310) 472-0525
50-seat theater for a variety of plays.

Way back at the beginning of the Chamber Theatre, in the 1950s, Vic Morrow directed a production starring Richard Chamberlain and Vic Tayback. Today the Chamber Theatre is employed as a rental space, so the quality depends on who's staying the night.

The foliage-shaded, garden-like entrance off Ventura Boulevard affords the only bucolic sight around. Walk through the gate and onto a patio leading to two separate performance spaces to the side and rear, one even smaller than the other's. Seating is commensurately close-quartered in both theaters, but the lobbies are comfortable.

Performances
Vary
Tickets
$10-20
Discounts
Previews/children/seniors/students/groups of 10, call BO
BO
Hrs vary; call
Location
Near the Hollywood (101) Fwy, N of the Hollywood Bowl
Parking
On premises (across the street), FREE

CHRISTIAN COMMUNITY THEATER

See press listings for performance locations.
Info: (619) 588-0206   **Rsvn:** (619) 588-0206 or (800) 696-1929
Fax: (619) 588-4384
Artistic Director: Paul Russell
Community theater presenting a summer outdoors series at Mount Helix in La Mesa, and the Kit Carson Amphitheatre in Escondido; winter productions are in a variety of San Diego locations.

The words "community theater" many conjure up an image of a tiny company in a tiny space on a shoestring budget serving a tiny community. That doesn't at all describe the Christian Community Theater, which is far and away San Diego County's largest and most rapidly growing community theater.

But it did start tiny in 1980; in the garage, in fact, of its artistic director, Paul Russell, who founded the company with his wife, Sheryl Russell. CCT now produces summer musicals under the stars at the top of scenic Mount Helix in La Mesa, at the Kit Carson Amphitheatre in Escondido, and a winter season of musicals and dramas in a variety of other San Diego locations, reaching a total

Performances
Thurs-Sun 8 pm
Tickets
$5-16
Discounts
Children/seniors/groups of 15+, call office for details
BO
Mon-Fri 9 am-5 pm; check/MC/V/reserve by mail (1545 Pioneer Way, El Cajon, CA 92020); exchange privileges guaranteed; subscription program
Location
Call

audience of over 60,000 annually. The La Mesa location, East County San Diego's highest peak, can accommodate 1,500 patrons; the Escondido site has seating for 1,100.

Despite its popularity, the CCT proudly remains very much a community theater. All of its performers, musicians, costumers, and stage crews are dedicated amateurs. Even refreshments and parking are managed by volunteers. Occasionally a performer of talent will rise up through the ranks and break through to work in San Diego's professional theaters.

Despite the Christian designation, the company is not overtly religious. But it does draw much of its support from San Diego churches and church-affiliated schools. The Russells also discuss their personal Christian ethics in their brochure and take pride in promoting work that "exerts a positive influence on today's youth." You can assume there will be nothing on the program that could possibly offend any member of the family. Past productions include such crowd pleasers as *Joseph and the Amazing Technicolor Dreamcoat*, *The Wizard of Oz*, and *Fiddler on the Roof*. The company scored its most successful season ever with *Singin' in the Rain* and *South Pacific*.

CCT also attracts school children from across San Diego to its Christian Youth Theater, which trains children ages 6 to 18. It presents such shows as *Anne of Green Gables*, *Robin Hood*, and *Charlotte's Web* at schools and theaters across the county.

If you are attending one of the open-air productions, dress warmly. Blankets and baskets of goodies are also advised.

Parking
Varies with location
Special Features
All rehearsals open

CHURCH IN OCEAN PARK

235 Hill Street
Santa Monica, CA 90405
Info: (310) 399-1631   **Rsvn:** (310) 399-1631
Fax: (310) 399-5823
250-seat venue used mostly for rentals.

An intimate spot for small theater, performance art, acoustic concerts, and poetry readings. The unraked floor makes it difficult to see if you're stuck behind Godzilla.

Look for press information regarding upcoming performances. Ticket information varies with each production company.

Performances
Fri-Sun
Tickets
Varies
Location
1 block E of Main St, 1 block S of Ocean Park Blvd
Parking
On street; public lot on Main St (six quarters)

CIVIC LIGHT OPERA OF SOUTH BAY CITIES

1721 Artesia Boulevard, Suite D
Manhattan Beach, CA 90266
Info: (310) 372-4477   **Rsvn:** (310) 372-4477
Fax: (310) 372-3198
Artistic Director: Irv Kimber
Productions are staged in the Aviation Park Auditorium, 1935 Manhattan Beach Boulevard, in Redondo Beach.

This relatively new organization played a successful first season in 1992 to loud applause. The recent season of *Evita*, *Singin' in the Rain*, *Pirates of Penzance*, and *Fiddler on the Roof* also proved popular.

Redondo Beach's Aviation Park facility houses the eager-to-please new CLO, the only professional musical theater company for miles. Major improvements in lighting, sound, and overall wattage at the venue have made professional-level production standards the norm.

Local performers fill most CLO supporting roles, while leads go to top names. For instance, Noel Harrison, Teri Ralston and Tom Hatten have been featured stars. The

Performances
March, May, Sept, Dec; Tues-Sun 8 pm; Sat-Sun 2 pm
Tickets
$18.50-27.50
Discounts
Previews/groups of 15+
BO
Call Mon-Fri 10 am-6 pm; Sat 10 am-2 pm; in person during performances; Mon-Sat noon-showtime; AE/MC/V/check/reserve by mail, fax; exchanges with 72 hrs notice; subscription program

season of four Broadway-style musicals runs March through December.

COAST PLAYHOUSE

8325 Santa Monica Boulevard
West Hollywood, CA 90069
Info: (213) 962-9092   **Rsvn:** (213) 650-8507
99-seat theater offering most theater genres.

The Coast has been both a producing and renting space for more than 30 years. The stage plays host to musicals, dramas, one-acts and performance artists (such as John Fleck). Under co-owners Gregory Harrison and his late partner, Frank Levy, this theater produced high-concept plays with high financing. Of late, the marquee has advertised *Naked at the Coast*, *Miss Vagina Pageant*, and *Not Without My Nipples!* Certainly the titles have attracted attention, and the presentations have attracted audiences.

Theater amenities include a roomy lobby and excellent seating and sightlines in a comfortable, air-conditioned space. There's no end to the dining possibilities nearby. Hugo's is in walking distance and nearby Barney's Beanery is a theatrical performance unto itself.

Performances
Vary
Tickets
$10-25
Discounts
Groups, call BO
Location
Between Sweetzer and Flores
Parking
On street

THE COLONY STUDIO THEATER

1944 Riverside Drive
Los Angeles, CA 90039
Info: (213) 665-0280   **Rsvn:** (213) 665-3011
Fax: (213) 660-2070
Producing Director: Barbara Beckley
99-seat theater producing classics, an annual musical, and original plays.

There's a ghost in the old Elysian Theater, but he/she doesn't seem to bother the actors and technicians—too much. Built to play silent movies in the 1920s, the old Elysian sat in decay while the freeways were built around it some 30 years later. The Colony Theater Company moved in, and the Elysian turned into the Colony Studio Theater replete with excellent acoustics, high ceilings, and comfortable seats.

THE COLONY—Resident Co.

One of LA's best long-lasting small companies, the Colony is high class and professional. The company has been playing to repeat audiences for years.

The 60-plus actors, with film, TV, and lots of theater background, revere one primary goal: to entertain. Their repertoire is positive and enlightening—mildly adventurous. Choices have included *Could I Have This Dance*, *The Last Metro*, and *Baby with the Bathwater*.

While they do not neglect the classics and they oblige with an annual musical, their first aim is toward new plays. In 1991, they received the Margaret Harford Award from the Los Angeles Drama Critics Circles. Two years ago, one of their original plays, Doug Haverty's *Could I Have This Dance?*, was chosen to be included in the annual "Best Plays of the Year" volume, one of three plays chosen from

Performances
Fall/winter: Thurs-Sat 8 pm, Sun 2 pm; spring/summer: Sun 3 pm
Tickets
$15-20
Discounts
Previews/children/seniors/students/groups of 20+, call BO
BO
Wed-Sat 2 pm-6 pm; tickets by reservation only; check/AE/MC/V/ reserve by phone; mail exchanges with 48 hr notice; subscription program
Location
Near intersection of Glendale (2) Fwy and Golden State (5) Fwy; on Riverside Dr between Fletcher Dr and Stadium Way
Parking
On street

outside New York. Not long ago they were honored by *LA Weekly* for *The Front Page* (Revival of the year), and *Candide* (Musical of the year). Stop by and give them your own award.

Special Features
Free bonus productions
for subscription
members

COMEDY SPORTZ

Tamarind Theatre
5919 Franklin Avenue
Hollywood, CA 90028
Info: (213) 871-1193   **Rsvn:** (213) 856-4796
Fax: (213) 462-6741
Artistic Director: James Thomas Bailey
Improvisational comedy late night Saturdays at the Tamarind Theatre.

If you like improv, check out this group. Not content to merely allow the audience to throw out suggestions for every skit (as do most improvisational groups), the Sportz stars instead go for the newest trick: competition between improv groups. Two opposing teams go at each other sporting-event style, with referees, scores, penalties, etc. The audience ultimately decides which side has been more entertaining, and it's the audience which also throws out the "first ball" (a.k.a., suggestions).

The team players change nightly, so you may not watch the same competition twice. Because of the time-clock, skits can be disappointingly short (but at least that beats out excruciatingly long!).

The parent company must be winning big: branches of Comedy Sportz have been franchised all over the country. Check them out!

Performances
Sat 10:30 pm
Tickets
$7.50
Discounts
Groups of 20+, call
BO
All tickets handled
through reservation line;
check/MC/V
Parking
Valet (sometimes);
street parking

COMEDY STORE PLAYHOUSE See **Richard Pryor Playhouse**

COMPANY OF ANGELS THEATRE

2106 Hyperion Avenue
Los Angeles, CA 90027
Info: (213) 666-6789   **Rsvn:** (213) 466-1767
49-seat theater with a focus on American classics.

This playhouse (also known as Angeles Theatre) in fun, arty Silver Lake, hosts one of the city's oldest theater troupes, Company of Angels. The group was forced to move here after 29 years in one location. Keep your eyes open for it—now that they're housed on highway-like Hyperion Avenue, it's easy to race past. This casual place is down-to-earth as theatrical venues go—it's comfortable, although the seats seem made more for sardines that humans. Sightlines are good from all seats. At the front entrance a refreshment bar fronts a modest socializing area.

There is security parking adjacent.

COMPANY OF ANGELS—Resident Co.

This professional group concentrates on heavy-hitting, socially-conscious American classics in the vein of *Requiem for a Heavyweight* and *Twelve Angry Men*. Often its productions are the *LA Times* Critic's Choice, or the *LA Weekly's* Pick of the Week.

Performances
Fri-Sat 8 pm; Sun 4 pm
Tickets
$10-15
Discounts
Groups of 10, call Don
Oscar Smith (818) 505-
0644 or Tony Maggio
(213) 661-8834
BO
Tues-Sun 11 am-7 pm;
AE/Disc/MC/V/Theatix
Location
From Hollywood: take
Fountain Ave E, cross
Sunset Blvd, bear left
where Fountain
becomes Hyperion,
continue to next traffic
light at Hyperion and
Lyric where you will find
the Angels Theatre
Parking
On premises, $3; street
parking

COMPANY OF CHARACTORS THEATRE

12655 Ventura Boulevard
Studio City, CA 91604
Info: (818) 508-4538   **Rsvn:** (818) 508-8838
Artistic Director: Herb Mitchell
Seats 70.

Yes, you will reach the CharActors' theater space, but you'll have to travel through the bowling alley and video arcade, and up the stairs to get there. Once you do, you'll find a comfortable theater with good sightlines everywhere. In addition to performances by its resident company, the theater is rented out to other producing companies. There's plenty of parking in the adjacent parking lot and sufficient soundproofing in the bowling alley's ceiling.

Jerry's Deli, open 24 hours, seven days a week, dishes out great deli food next door. Or try a late dinner and a set of Brazilian jazz at La Ve Lee, about a block or two east.

Performances
Thurs-Sat 8 pm; Sun 2 pm or 5 pm
Tickets
$10-15
Discounts
Children/seniors/students/groups of 10, call BO
BO
24 hr answering machine (818) 508-8838; or call Theatix
Parking
On premises

♿🍴

COMPANY OF CHARACTORS—Resident Co.

This four-year-old 65-member company works and plays down the hall from Theatre East. They put on about three or four shows per year, which so far have consisted mainly of familiar playwright's familiar plays. But the group is hoping to bowl over audiences with original works soon.

THE COMPLEX

6476 Santa Monica Boulevard
Los Angeles, CA 90038
Info: (213) 465-0383   **Rsvn:** (213) 464-2124
Five stages including the Ruby (45 seats), the Dorie (49), the Flight (40), Theatre 6470 (42), and The East (49).

This theater complex sits smack in the heart of true movieland, cheek-by-jowl to an array of film processing companies, set and prop rental houses, and sound-stage rentals. It's no coincidence that the Complex, part of the emerging "theatre row," has sprung up on these moviemaking blocks. In this town, actors, overwhelmingly struggling and unknown, strut their stuff on small stages like these to be seen by the "industry" powers that be. But this is not showcase theater. Most of these are serious performances staged by a variety of production companies. So if you see something you don't like, don't give up.

Choices have included everything from Randy Kagan's one-man alternative comedy, *Watering the Grass in the Rain*, to Harold Pinter's *The Dumbwaiter*.

Built loosely on the multiplex plan, the five separate theaters are all clean and well-maintained, complete with air conditioning and even, if needed, heat. The stages are owned by actor/producer/teacher Matt Chait, who rents three spaces out, the Ruby, Dorie and Flight theaters, on a per-production basis. The Theatre 6470 and The East (formerly the Blue Line) are rented annually to theater companies. Theatre 6470 is experiencing a sort of metamorphosis through a recent company reorganization, and has subsequently presented new plays as well as Chekhov's *Uncle Vanya*, staged by Peggy Shannon, and *An Evening With Edgar Poe*, by puppeteer Steven Ritz.

The Flight is the only space located above street level, up a long flight of stairs—ergo the name. All have raked theater-style seating, which is vintage but not shabby, and though all are small spaces, only Theatre 6470 feels meager. With its black, enclosing walls, it's The Complex's only real "black box." All five have proscenium-style stages

Performances
Thurs-Sun, matinee Sun
Tickets
$10-15
Discounts
Depends on production
BO
1 hr before performance; reserve by phone
Location
W off Hollywood (101) Fwy at Santa Monica Blvd, 4 blocks W of Vine
Parking
Valet, $2; street

♿🍴 (🚺🚹)

that are hip high, except the Flight, whose stage is closer to toes-high and is also more expansive.

Restrooms are located on street level in the lobby shared by the Ruby and Dorie, and also upstairs down the hall from the Flight. Wheelchair access is possible (though perhaps a bit tight) only in the Ruby.

The Complex offers valet parking across the street at Honda of Hollywood and self-parking at the post office. A security guard patrols the boulevard on performance nights (Thursday through Sunday).

For treats after the show, there's a little coffeehouse, the InBetween Cafe, in the nearby Hudson Theatre. But you're not far from Marino's Restaurant at Cole and Melrose for an outstanding complete Italian menu.

CONEJO PLAYERS THEATER

351 South Moorpark Road
Thousand Oaks, CA 91360
Info: (805) 495-3715   **Rsvn:** (805) 495-3715
188-seat community theater.

For 35 years this community theater has been showcasing comedies, musicals, and dramas. Open auditions are held for each show, and Thousand Oaks residents are encouraged to do everything from acting to set-building to costume-designing. In addition to its regular season of everything from *Bleacher Bums*, to *The Boys Next Door*, the theater offers CAT—Conejo Afternoon Theater—with excellent choices such as *Stop the World I Want To Get Off* and *The Gin Game*. Tickets for CAT are available only at the door for $5.

Performances
8:30 pm, Sun matinee 2:30 pm
Tickets
$8-13
Discounts
Children/seniors/ students/groups
BO
Check/MC/V/reserve by phone, mail (4135 W Potero Rd, Newbury Park, CA 91320); exchanges made up to two weeks prior to performance; subscription program
Parking
On premises or street, no charge
Special Features
Open dress rehearsals

CORNERSTONE THEATER COMPANY

See press listings for performance locations.
Info: (310) 449-1700
Artistic Director: Bill Rauch

It's no wonder Cornerstone has made multicultural Los Angeles its home base. The company has built a critically celebrated reputation by catering to decidedly non-elitist, non-discriminating audiences.

Established in 1986 as an alternative to college and profit-minded theater companies, the professional troupe currently consists of eight ensemble members. After graduating Harvard in 1986, the friends formed a company that would reach out to America's most secluded communities.

The company lived the following five years like Bedouins, traveling from one rural place to another for months on end. To get the communities involved in their shows, Cornerstone has always cast roles from a local pool of volunteers.

In 1992, the group decided to find a permanent home but one that wouldn't jeopardize the integrity of their original aims. The group chose LA as the most likely spot.

Nowadays, Cornerstone continues to promote "inclusive" theater by focusing on mutually-isolated groups among the city's cultural and racial kaleidoscope.

Performances
Thurs-Sun, times vary
Tickets
Donations accepted
BO
Call
Parking
Varies with location

Their intentions are admirable, but the bottom line of any theatrical company is the entertainment value and quality of its shows. Here the group gets another two thumbs up. Cornerstone now has over a dozen cleverly readapted classics to its name. The plays of writers from Moliere to Shakespeare to Chekhov are mounted in timely contexts and culturally-relevant settings and circumstances to draw the audiences intimately into the action. Cornerstone has also begun to add original plays to its far-ranging repertoire. Senior citizens from downtown's Angelus Plaza tried their acting wings in *The Toy Truck*. Pacoima's mixed bag of denizens added their skills to *Rushing Waters*, a bilingual musical history of the area written by Bronx, New York playwright Migdalia Cruz. Cornerstone participated with the Arab community in the '93 Los Angeles Festival with a production of *Ghurba*.

Shunning the glamour of Hollywood, this group deserves the brightest spotlight for continuing to embrace untraditional audiences. They play at a variety of venues throughout the year—usually outdoor ones—in ensemble performances, or in the community productions. Look for their show announcements and locations in press listings or call to be added to their mailing list.

CORONADO PLAYHOUSE

1775 Strand Way
Coronado, CA 92118
Rsvn: (619) 435-4856
Artistic Director: J. Sherwood Montgomery
Community theater set on Glorietta Bay in Coronado; dinner packages available; seats 104.

Probably the most famous tourist destination in Coronado is the Hotel Del Coronado, the lavish, luxurious resort on the water where it is said that Edward VII first met Mrs. Wallis Simpson, the American divorcee for whom he would later abdicate the British throne.

While you're hobnobbing, you might just want to check out one of only two Coronado theaters, the Coronado Playhouse, which will celebrate its 50th anniversary in 1996. (The other is Lamb's Players Theatre.)

The Coronado Playhouse is an unassuming 104-seat community theater in an unassuming space that once served as a WACs barracks. Seating is cabaret-style at round tables with four chairs.

When everything comes together, little gems unearth themselves during the course of a season. The Coronado poked fun at Andrew Lloyd Webber's *Phantom of the Opera* with *The Pinchpenny Phantom of the Opera* by Dave Reiser and Jack Sharkey, in which the famous chandelier is operated by an offstage fishing pole.

The theater presents five shows a year and for three years has produced an annual children's show based on the Beatrix Potter story, "The Tailor of Gloucester."

Dinner packages with Chez Loma restaurant are available. Full bar and snack food; no table service. Free on-premise parking.

Performances
Year-round; Thurs-Sat 8 pm; Sun 7 pm
Tickets
$8-16
Discounts
Children/seniors/ students/groups of 8+, call BO; active-duty military discounts
BO
Call Tues-Fri 9 am-5 pm; 1 hr prior to curtain; MC/V/check/reserve by mail,TicketMaster, Art Tix (619) 238-3810; Post-Tix mailings by S.D. Theatre League; exchanges made prior to 4 pm Thurs-Sat; and prior to 3 pm Sunday; subscription program
Location
3 blocks S of Hotel del Coronado
Parking
On premises, FREE; street parking

CORONET THEATRE See **Serendipity Theatre** in **CHILDREN**

THE COSTA MESA CIVIC PLAYHOUSE

661 Hamilton Street
Costa Mesa, CA 92627
Info: (714) 650-5269   **Rsvn:** (714) 650-5269
90-seat community theater.
Established under the auspices of the municipality of Costa Mesa, this community theater was the first in Orange County to be fully subsidized and governed under city programming. For nearly two decades, the theater shared its home with recreation facilities and programs in a converted World War II auditorium. Relocated to a remodeled schoolhouse, the theater now operates autonomously as a not-for-profit corporation. Its Board of Directors participates actively in the American Association of Community Theater Competitions, and in 1989 represented the United States in Barcelona.

The playhouse season includes four adult plays, one musical, a youth theater presentation and a Christmas pageant. A special August show is offered by the Theater of Contemporary Issue; its presentations deal with such topics as drugs, gang violence, and the homeless. No admission is charged for these performances.

Performances
Thurs-Sun 8 pm, Sun 2 pm
Tickets
$8.50-15
Discounts
Children/students/ groups of 20+, call
BO
Tues-Sat 11 am-4 pm; check/MC/V/reserve by mail; exchanges with 48 hr notice; subscription program
Location
S of San Diego (405) Fwy, 3 blocks W of Harbor Blvd
Parking
On premises or street, FREE

COURT THEATRE

722 North La Cienega Boulevard
Los Angeles, CA 90067
Info: (213) 652-4035   **Rsvn:** (213) 854-5495
Fax: (213) 854-5495
75-seats; outside producers.
This bucolic, ivy-covered venue offers audiences "artistically and socially provocative and entertaining" new works. It's also a house of world premieres by outside producers. 1991, for instance, saw the premiere of *Lady-Like* by Laura Shamas.

The Court, named in honor of its trademark courtyard and rustic feel, has also co-produced plays with Woody Harrelson and Susan Tyrrell and hosted the LA premiere of Arthur Miller's *A Memory of Two Mondays*.

The stage is large for a small theater and can hold a full second-story set. Great designers are brought in making what is really a small stage appear even bigger. As with most of the small venues, sightlines are good.

Performances
Thurs-Sun, matinee Sat and Sun
Tickets
$15-22
Discounts
Previews/seniors/ students
BO
Reserve by phone, Theatix
Location
At Melrose and La Cienega
Parking
Valet, $3.50; street

COURTYARD PLAYHOUSE

550 Deep Valley Drive
Rolling Hills Estates
Palos Verdes Peninsula, CA 90274
Info: (310) 378-3606   **Rsvn:** (310) 544-6555
40-seat theater.
This small playhouse sits on the third level of The Shops at Palos Verdes shopping center—next to Robinson's-May Company and a pleasant cafe and courtyard. As the center of the town's recreation and culture, the shopping mall is the late 20th century equivalent of Main Street. And since "Main Street" wouldn't be complete without a local playhouse or opera house, a former jewelry store was transformed into this matchbox theater. The floor is the stage so don't expect a Founders Circle. Fair warning: the bathrooms are located in the mall, not the theater.

Performances
Thurs-Sat 8 pm; Sun 7 pm
Tickets
$8, Sun $6
Discounts
Seniors/students
BO
Answering service 24 hrs; check/reserve by mail for 5 or more tickets

(More. . .)

ACTORS REPERTORY THEATRE—Resident Co.

Mainstream plays and romantic comedies a la Neil Simon. The actors are so close to the audience, you may earn your Equity card by sitting in the front row.

CROSSLEY THEATRE

1760 North Gower Street
Hollywood, CA 90028
Info: (213) 462-8460 **Rsvn:** (213) 964-3586
Fax: (213) 462-3199
Artistic Director: Robin Strand
80-seat theater located in the First Presbyterian Church.
The First Presbyterian Church of Hollywood is the venue for the Crossley Theatre, but that's as far as the religious connection goes. This is a comfortable space with good sightlines, air conditioning, and a proscenium stage. Refreshments are served at the snack bar. Parking is safe and secure in the adjacent guarded lot.

ACTORS CO-OP—Resident Co.

This 60-member group has been working together for more than five years, and producing together for the past three. Often cheerful musicals and holiday shows are on the schedule, but they've also produced such dark comedies as Paul Osborn's *Tomorrow's Monday*, and *Edith Stein*, the story of a nun who became a Holocaust victim. The musical comedy *Into the Woods* was the most recent offering, counterpointed by Hugh Whitemore's *Pack of Lies*.

A brunch/theatre package is offered before certain performances. In the past two years alone the group has garnered numerous awards and Critic's Choice notices.

Performances
Thurs-Sat 8 pm; Sun 2:30 pm
Tickets
$12
Discounts
Groups/children/seniors, call BO
BO
Call 24 hrs answering machine; MC/V/check/reserve by mail, fax, phone; subscription program
Location
Gower at Carlos
Parking
On premises, FREE
Special Features
Selected Sunday Brunch/Theatre packages; lunch on site

CULTURAL AFFAIRS DEPARTMENT, CITY OF LOS ANGELES

433 South Spring Street
Los Angeles, CA 90013
Info: (213) 485-2433
Los Angeles' arts centers around the city are all marvelous, culturally diverse resources of visual and performing arts offered through a number of programs including performance art, music, dance, theater (for children, teenagers, and adults), classes, workshops, and exhibitions. Some offerings are ongoing, some are one-time events; some are offered city-wide. Each art center director, however, works independently to create programs of interest to the local community.

Call the center in your area for information:
Art in the Park, 5568 Via Marisol, LA 90042 (213) 259-0861
Barnsdall Arts Center, 4800 Hollywood Boulevard, LA 90027 (213) 485-2116
Junior Arts Center, 4814 Hollywood Boulevard, LA 90027 (213) 485-4474
Lankershim Arts Center, 5108 Lankershim Boulevard, North Hollywood 91602 (818) 989-8066
Los Angeles Theatre Center (see separate listing)
McGroarty Arts Center, 7570 McGroarty Terrace, Tujunga 91042 (818) 352-5285
Watts Towers Arts Center, 1727 East 107th Street, LA 90002 (213) 569-8181
Wm. Grant Still Arts Center, 2520 West View Street, LA 90016 (213) 734-1164

CURTIS THEATRE See **Brea Civic & Cultural Center**

CYPRESS CIVIC THEATRE GUILD, INC.

Cypress Cultural Arts Center
5172 Orange Avenue
Cypress, CA
Info: (714) 229-6796   **Rsvn:** (714) 229-6796
Community theater seating 120 people for mysteries, comedies, and dramas.
    Founded in 1976, this community theater manages four mainstage productions a year consisting of dramas, comedies, and mysteries, along with one or two children's shows.

Performances
  Fri-Sat 8 pm
Tickets
  $7-10
Discounts
  Children/seniors/
  students/groups of 10+,
  call
BO
  Performance days 6:30-
  8:30 pm; check/reserve
  by mail (P.O. Box 2212,
  Cypress, CA 90630);
  exchanges before
  performance;
  subscription program

DANCING DOG THEATRE COMPANY

See press listings for performance locations
Info: (213) 739-3910
Artistic Director: Brian Van Dusen
    Twelfth Night set in pre-Nazi Germany? The artistic possibilities seem endless with this seven-year-old mostly itinerant company. Late of the Whitefire Theater and other venues around town, Dancing Dog is currently seeking a permanent home for its classical and neo-classical productions. Once they settle down, perhaps the local theatergoers will pay them the attention they deserve. Recent productions of Michael Frayn's *Wild Honey* and a successful *Frankenstein* have drawn audiences. Their lively newsletter, called Dancing Dog Dispatch, keeps subscribers and other interested parties in the know. Call for a spot on the list.

Performances
  Thurs-Sun evenings
Tickets
  $10-15
Discounts
  Seniors/previews/
  children/groups of 10+,
  call BO
BO
  Call for recorded
  information
Parking
  Varies with location

DEAF WEST THEATRE COMPANY

660 North Heliotrope Drive
Los Angeles, CA 90004
Info: (213) 660-0877   **Rsvn:** (213) 660-4673
99-seat theater in the former Heliotrope Theatre.
    The only resident company of deaf theater artists in the Western United States, this troupe offers a theater experience both compelling and original. Directed by former National Theatre of the Deaf member Ed Waterstreet, Deaf West presented its first production in the May of 1991, a rendition of *The Gin Game* starring Tony-award winner Phyllis Frelich.
    With only a few plays under its belt, Deaf West has managed to secure a huge grant from the United States Department of Education to continue producing its own plays. It will also create theater activities for area children with a three-year grant from the Department of Education. Locally it received *LA Weekly*'s Humanitarian Theatre Award in 1993.
    Performances by the young company are signed in American Sign Language. A simultaneous vocal rendition is piped through free headsets. Originally hosted by the Fountain Theatre, the company has set up shop in its own quarters in what was the Heliotrope Theatre, once home to

Performances
  Thurs-Sun 8 pm; Sat 2
  pm; Sun 3 pm;
Tickets
  $10-15
Discounts
  Previews/seniors/
  students/children/groups
  of 25+, call BO
BO
  Mon-Fri 11 am-6 pm;
  MC/V/check/reserve by
  mail; exchanges made
  with 24 hrs notice; no
  refunds
Location
  Off Hollywood (101)
  Fwy; 3 blocks E of
  Normandie, 1/2 block S
  of Melrose
Parking
  On premises, $2; street
  parking

an eclectic mix of folk music, unusual dramatic work, and comedy improv.

Nearby Cafe Mambo or Rincon Chileno are good tips for a bite to eat.

DISCAFE BOHEM CLUB & THEATER See **CLUBS**

DIVERSIONARY PLAYHOUSE

4545 Park Boulevard
San Diego, CA 92102
Info: (619) 574-1060
Artistic Director: Robert Joseph
San Diego playhouse dedicated to presenting gay and lesbian works.

San Diego's longest-running gay and lesbian theater focuses on musicals and dramas with—you guessed it—gay and/or lesbian themes. It presents about five shows a year.

Diversionary recently moved to a new 112-seat state-of-the-art theater in University Heights.

DIVERSIONARY THEATRE COMPANY—Resident Co.

DTC stages contemporary work in which a gay and lesbian presence actually is taken for granted. Not that in their rousing musicals and sensitive dramas the stories might not also have something universal to say about the nature of love and loss.

Performances
Year-round Thurs-Sat 8 pm
Tickets
$10 Thurs, $12 Fri-Sat
Discounts
Previews/seniors/ students/groups of 10+, call
BO
1/2 hr prior to show time; Art Tix, Blue Door Bookstore; exchange through the bookstore, up to one day before performance
Location
University Heights between Meade and Monroe
Parking
Street parking

DORIE THEATRE See **The Complex**

DOWNEY CIVIC LIGHT OPERA ASSOCIATION

Downey Theatre
8435 Firestone Boulevard
Downey, CA 90241
Info: (310) 923-8061   **Rsvn:** (310) 923-1714
Fax: (310) 923-8061
Presents Broadway musicals in a three-play series at the Downey Theatre.

Established in the mid-Fifties, this theater company is dedicated to presenting colorful musicals to its surrounding community. In residence at the Downey Theater from October through June, it mounts three Broadway musicals per season. Special features of DCLOA include the Happy Holidays Christmas musical, especially delightful for children, and the "Be a Star" drawing, which awards a cameo role in an upcoming DCLOA performance.

Although this is a subscription series, single tickets are usually available.

Performances
Thurs-Sat 8 pm; Sat-Sun 2:30 pm
Tickets
$18-22
Discounts
Previews/students/ groups of 11+, call BO
BO
Mon-Fri noon-4 pm; check/MC/V/reserve by mail, by phone; exchanges with 24 hr notice; subscription program
Location
S of Santa Ana (5) Fwy, between Long Beach (710) Fwy and San Gabriel River (605) Fwy; Firestone Blvd at Brookshire, between Paramount Blvd and Lakewood Blvd

(More. . .)

Parking
On premises, FREE;
street parking

DOWNEY THEATRE

8435 Firestone Boulevard
Downey, CA 90241
Info: (310) 904-7230 **Rsvn:** (310) 861-8211
Theater seats 748 for theater, music, and a travel film series.

    The Downey was rated one of the top ten new theaters in the country when it opened its doors in 1970. It has served as a forerunner of the recent bumper crop of 750-seat theaters in Southern California. The theater's continental orchestra section seats 526 and its tripartite balcony 222.

    The stage is given over to a variety of dance, theater, and music events. A main draw is the Downey Civic Light Opera, which performs a subscription series of three Broadway musicals October through June (Father's Day is the last performance each year). A travel film series, Irish musical groups such as the Rovers and the Chieftains, and a five-show celebrity performance series are sample attractions here during the year.

    For nearby pre-theater dining, try Gregory's Restaurant in the adjacent Embassy Suites Hotel, or Mimi's Cafe in the parking lot.

Performances
Mon-Sun evenings; Sat-Sun matinee
Tickets
$4.50-20
Discounts
Seniors/groups of 20+, call BO Mon-Fri 12 pm-4 pm
BO
Mon-Fri 1 hr prior to curtain; check/MC/V/ reserve by mail; no refunds or exchanges; subscription program
Parking
On premises, FREE

EAST WEST PLAYERS

4424 Santa Monica Boulevard
Los Angeles, CA 90029
Info: (213) 660-0366 **Rsvn:** (213) 660-8587
Fax: (213) 666-1929
Artistic Director: Tim Dang

    Under the tutelage of new artistic director Tim Dang, East West Players is experiencing a rebirth of sorts. The country's oldest Asian Pacific Theatre company (formed in 1965) moved boldly into nontraditional casting. It crossed the multicultural line in almost every other area: from its board, to its actors, to its audience. Now, under this new directorship, it plans to cross generational lines as well.

    East West projects powerfully poignant perspectives on Asian Pacific American life. Then it throws in some well-known crowd-pleasers, like *Into the Woods*, cast (primarily) with Asian actors. It also is willing to spend an entire season producing plays largely written by women or with women in lead roles. East West draws crowds from North and South and all other ethnic directions, in addition to its supportive Asian Pacific audience.

    As we go to press, Dang and his group are looking for a new home.

Performances
Fri-Sat, 8 pm, Sat-Sun 2 pm
Tickets
$16-25
BO
Reserve by mail, phone
Discounts
Previews/seniors/ students/groups of 10+, call BO
Location
Between Vermont and Sunset
Parking
On premises, $3; street

18TH STREET ARTS COMPLEX See **Highways Performance Space**

EL CAMINO COLLEGE/MARSEE AUDITORIUM See **South Bay Center for the Arts** and **MUSIC**

EMBASSY THEATRE

851 South Grand Avenue
Los Angeles, CA 90017
Info: (213) 743-1565   **Rsvn:** (213) 743-1565
Seats 1600 people; used mostly as a rental house.
 The oldest concert hall in Los Angeles, the Embassy was designated a historical monument in 1983. Debuting in 1914 with the Los Angeles Symphony Orchestra (precursor to the Los Angeles Philharmonic), the stage has since been graced by Sergei Prokofiev, the New York Symphony Orchestra, Alma Gluck, John McCormack, Efrem Zimbalist, Sr., and Gregor Piatigorsky, among other musical legends. Evangelist Aimee Semple Macpherson preached in the baroque, stained-glass-domed theater in the '20s; the sounds of jazz great Count Basie and Big Band leader Duke Ellington filled the hall in the '40s.
 Built without artificial amplification, the acoustics are natural and quite good throughout the auditorium.
 These days, the Embassy usually hosts non-Equity performances—and not very often. It is used for fashion shows, corporate conventions, political meetings and the like.

Performances
 Mon-Sun
Tickets
 $10-50
BO
 Reserve by phone, TicketMaster
Location
 Near Santa Monica (10) Fwy and Harbor (110) Fwy, downtown
Parking
 Parking lot nearby, $2.50; street

ENSEMBLE ARTS THEATRE

See press listings for performance locations.
Info: (619) 696-0458
Artistic Director: Glynn Bedington
 One of San Diego's best respected "gypsy" theater companies, Ensemble Arts Theatre has visited a variety of venues to present American premieres of new American, British, and Scottish plays. The schedule is limited to one or two plays each year.
 Founded by its artistic director, Glynn Bedington—a fine actress herself—the company has made an art form of staging plays that pose questions about the human condition rather than offering pat self-satisfying answers. When you leave, you'll be thinking about the world beyond the theater; but you won't wonder why you came.
 The technical facility of Ensemble Arts is surprisingly high, especially considering its nomadic existence. The acting, too, is invariably fine. Inevitably, however, budget and venues do at times shortchange the company, particularly in sets, original music, and lighting.

Performances
 Thurs-Sat 8 pm, Sun 7 pm
Tickets
 $14-16
Discounts
 Previews/children/seniors/students/groups of 8+, call
BO
 Call; varies with venue; Art Tix

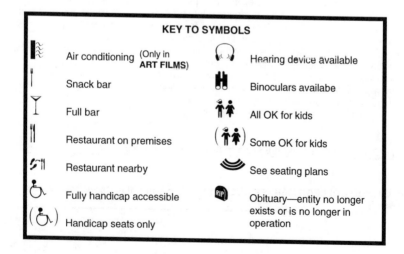

KEY TO SYMBOLS			
Air conditioning (Only in **ART FILMS**)		Hearing device available	
Snack bar		Binoculars availabe	
Full bar		All OK for kids	
Restaurant on premises		Some OK for kids	
Restaurant nearby		See seating plans	
Fully handicap accessible		Obituary—entity no longer exists or is no longer in operation	
Handicap seats only			

ENSEMBLE THEATRE COMPANY

Ensemble Theatre Company
914 Santa Barbara Street
Santa Barbara, CA 93101
Info: (805) 965-6252   **Rsvn:** (805) 962-8606
Artistic Director: Robert G. Weiss
Since its birth in 1979, the Ensemble Theatre Company has steadily built up a loyal following for their repertoire of classics such as *Death of a Salesman* and *The Homecoming*. Future plans for ETC include more innovative material.

Performances
Year-round; Wed-Sat 8 pm; Sun 2 pm first and last Sun of the run; and 7 pm any other Sun
Tickets
$10-14
Discounts
Students/groups of 10+, call group sales (805) 965-6252
BO
Mon-Sun hrs vary; and until showtime on day of performance; check/AE/reserve by mail; liberal exchange policy with 24 hr notice; subscription program
Parking
Parking lot, Santa Barbara St and Carrillo, FREE

FIRST STAGE

6817 Franklin Avenue
Hollywood, CA 90028
Info: (213) 850-6271   **Fax:** (213) 850-6295
Artistic Director: Denis Safren
Utilizes the stage at the United Methodist Church in Hollywood.
This respected nonprofit organization was founded in 1983 by members of Robert Redford's Sundance Institute. Its *raison d'etre* is staged readings of works-in-progress in a noncritical atmosphere, away from commercial considerations and reviews.
Professional actors and directors bring rehearsed readings to the stage, followed by intensive discussion about what flies and what doesn't. In addition, selected works are revamped as workshop presentations, a good system, no doubt, because many of the more successful plays which premiere here in their nascent form go on to Broadway or the silver screen. John Patrick Shanley's *Danny and the Deep Blue Sea* went on to Off-Broadway from First Stage and then served as the genesis for *Moonstruck*, which won a best screenplay Oscar for the writer.
All performed readings take place on a stage at the First United Methodist Church on Franklin Avenue at Highland. Ticket prices at the door are just five bucks. Witness theater bloom!

Performances
Mon 7 pm
Tickets
$5 donation at door
BO
At the door
Location
Corner of Highland and Franklin Aves in the United Methodist Church
Parking
On premises, FREE; street parking

FLIGHT THEATRE See **The Complex**

FORUM THEATER OF YORBA LINDA

4175 Fairmont Boulevard
Yorba Linda, CA 92686
Info: (714) 779-8591   **Rsvn:** (714) 779-8591
Fax: (714) 970-9267
A 315-seat community theater.
The Forum, one of four facilities that comprise the Yorba Linda Education Center, is a popular venue for

Performances
Fri-Sat 8 pm; Sun 2 pm
Tickets
$8-15
Discounts
Groups of 20+, call BO

theater, music, and dance. The space provides a home for the Yorba Linda Civic Light Opera, plus concerts by the

Forum Pops Orchestra, and a number of outside performers.

BO
Mon-Fri 9 am-3 pm, 1 1/2 hrs before show time; check/MC/V/ reserve by mail; tickets may be exchanged one week prior to performance; subscription program

Location
From the 91 Fwy take the Imperial Hwy exit, head N on Imperial about 1 1/2 miles, turn right on Yorba Linda, travel 1 1/2 miles, turn left on Fairmont Blvd, venue is on the left side of street

Parking
On premises, FREE

FOUND THEATRE

251 East 7th Street
Long Beach, CA 90813
Info: (310) 433-3363   **Rsvn:** (310) 433-3363
Artistic Director: Cynthia Galles
40-seat theater existing just on the edge of avant-garde.
    While downtown Long Beach attempts to revitalize itself, the corner of 7th and Long Beach Boulevard consistently draws a crowd. This black box space seats 40 in the round on comfortable, cushioned seats. Several restaurants serve dinner in the neighborhood: try Mumm's on Pine, 555 East, or the Ramada Renaissance.

FOUND THEATRE—Resident Co.
    After 19 years of production, the Found Theatre still hates definition. Pin them down and they'll admit they consider themselves the avant-garde arm of the Long Beach theater scene, being the only area theater producing an alternative theatrical experience. Using video, sound effects, and music, their work skirts the outrageous. The production quality may reflect limited resources, but the objective is laughter and healing as they slip some social commentary between the covers (and the lines).
    Ideas for the company-created pieces come from anywhere—props, characters, costumes—and after scripting and rehearsals, the seed grows into a full night of theater.

Performances
Fri-Sat 8:30 pm
Tickets
$10
Discounts
Groups of 10+, call
BO
Check/reserve by phone, pay at door
Location
Off Long Beach (710) Fwy, 6th St exit, at 7th St and Long Beach Blvd
Parking
On street; pay lots nearby
Special Features
Sign language interpretation of 1 or 2 performances per production

FOUNTAINHEAD THEATRE

1110 North Hudson Avenue
Los Angeles, CA 90038
Info: (213) 962-8185   **Rsvn:** (213) 962-8185
Artistic Director: Andrew Shaifer
Seats 74 for original adaptations and West Coast premieres.
    Around the corner from the Hudson and the World theaters, this compact performing space offers a small but efficient lobby and good sightlines. The stage is somewhere between thrust-style and theater-in-the-round. The concession stand opens at intermission. Park in the security lot on Seward. Arrange handicap seating in advance.

Performances
Thurs-Sun 8 pm
Tickets
$10
Discounts
Previews/groups of 10+, call BO

(More. . .)

FOUNTAINHEAD THEATRE COMPANY—Resident Co.

Adaptations of familiar works, as well as West Coast premieres, are the bread-and-butter of this young company. *Cock and Bull Story*, directed by Billy Hayes (author of *Midnight Express*), proved deeply satisfying. A loosely-structured series of issue-oriented pieces called "Uncensored" announced the troupe's debut. They present a one-night annual mini-festival called "Topics of Our Time," with a different theme each year. In today's puritan-beleaguered art world, Fountainhead's mission is most refreshing.

BO
Open 1 hr before performance; 24 hr answering machine; check/MC/V/reserve by mail, Theatix (213) 466-1767; subscription program

Location
On Theater Row in Hollywood; 3 blocks E of Highland Ave, on the corner of Santa Monica Blvd

Parking
On premises (security lot on Seward); street parking

FOUNTAIN THEATRE

5060 Fountain Avenue
Los Angeles, CA 90029
Info: (213) 663-2235   **Rsvn:** (213) 663-1525
Fax: (213) 666-0904
80 seats for plays, dance, and performance art.

The Fountain serves as the permanent home of the Barbara Culver Foundation, a nonprofit group directed by Deborah Lawlor, dedicated to pumping out small, but first-rate, theater and dance works. Culver Foundation productions have garnered numerous awards since the organization's inception in 1977.

More impressive yet, not long ago the LA City Council thanked Lawlor and Fountain Theater Artistic Director Stephen Sachs for their combined efforts to establish their theater as a forum for "the ethnic diversity and varied citizenry of Los Angeles."

Indeed, a listing of the theater's first year of performances reads like Disneyland's "It's a Small World After All." There was a dance drama based on a Japanese fable, a children's play in Spanish, and an Armenian chronicle of poetry and song, as well as a performance written and starring persons with physical disabilities. But then, you might expect such an admirable track record from a theater which also gave the first home to one of the country's very few resident deaf companies, the Deaf West Theatre Company.

In addition to its regular schedule of good works (and good deeds), the Fountain features a Sunday afternoon series entitled "Dance at the Fountain" boasting the finest dancers and artistic directors such as Roberto Amaral. Flamenco at the Fountain is an often-scheduled passionate afternoon of Spanish dance.

Fountain season tickets are available and include five plays and an evening of dance or a sixth play for the double-take price of of $60 to $110. (Note: there's a hefty $5 service charge per subscription when ordering with a credit card.)

The Fountain, a comfortable two-story complex in Hollywood, has been operating for over 40 years. It houses an 80-seat mainstage, a 25-seat theater lab, a dance studio and an outdoor patio—with fountain.

Performances
Fri-Sun 8 pm, Sun 3 pm

Tickets
$15-18

Discounts
Previews/children/seniors/students/groups of 10+, call

BO
Mon-Fri 10 am-5 pm, Sat 2-5 pm; check/MC/V/AE/reserve by mail, phone; no exchanges; subscription program

Location
Off Hollywood (101) Fwy, 1/2 block E of Normandy, 1 block S of Sunset Blvd

Parking
On premises or street, no charge

FRIENDS & ARTISTS THEATRE ENSEMBLE

1761 North Vermont Avenue
Los Angeles, CA 90027
Info: (213) 664-0680   **Rsvn:** (213) 664-0689
Artistic Director: Sal Romeo
53-seat theater presenting original and classic works of social conscience.

This tiny but comfortable playhouse lies appropriately in the Los Feliz area. Just like its eclectic surroundings, F.A.T.E. is an eclectic theater group.

The lobby is small, but the patio at the entrance (in the back of the building) expands the space for pre- and post-performance schmoozing. Complimentary cake, coffee, and wine are served before the show, during intermission, and after the shows, making spirited conversation inevitable.

FRIENDS & ARTISTS THEATRE ENSEMBLE—Resident Co.

Artistic Director Sal Romeo makes theater that's as exciting as it is rewarding. It's also avant-garde; yes, but powerful and rich in execution. Designer Robert Zentis designs all of the sets, sometimes making the narrow, lengthy stage look four times its size. Several of the group's productions have won critical praise from *LA Weekly*, as well as awards for set and costume design.

Occasionally, with advance notice—and with Romeo's permission—there are open rehearsals.

Performances
Mid-Jan-mid-Nov; Fri-Sat 8 pm; Tues and Sun 7:30 pm; Sat and Sun matinee (occasionally)
Tickets
$12-15
Discounts
Children/seniors/students/previews/Theatre LA/groups of 10+, call BO
BO
24 hrs, call; check/AE/Disc/MC/V/reserve by phone; mail; exchanges with 24 hrs notice
Location
Between Franklin and Hollywood Blvd, W side of street
Parking
On premises, FREE

FULLERTON CIVIC LIGHT OPERA

Plummer Auditorium
201 East Chapman
Fullerton, CA 92632
Info: (714) 526-3832   **Rsvn:** (714) 879-1732
Fax: (714) 992-1193
Artistic Directors: Jan Duncan and Griff Duncan
1,300-seat theater.

Founders Griff Duncan and Jan Duncan remain at the helm of this 21-year-old community group, which has amassed many favorable critical notices over the years. Summer shows are performed on the nearby Theatre-on-the-Green, while the rest of the season's excitement can be seen in the spiffed up Plummer Auditorium.

Performances
Thurs-Sat 8 pm; Sun 2 pm and 7 pm
Tickets
$12-24
Discounts
Seniors/students/groups of 20+, call BO
BO
Mon-Fri 10 am-5 pm; check/Disc/MC/V/reserve by mail; exchanges for subscribers only with 24 hr notice; subscription program
Location
Near Riverside (91) Fwy, Orange (57) Fwy, and Santa Ana (5) Fwy at Lemon and Chapman Sts
Parking
On premises, $3; street parking

GARDEN GROVE COMMUNITY THEATRE

Eastgate Park, 1001 St. Mark Street
Garden Grove, CA 92645
Info: (714) 897-5122   **Rsvn:** (714) 897-5122
75-seat community theater.

This community group has been active in tiny Garden Grove for 20 years. Its season consists of five

Performances
Fri-Sat 8 pm, Sun 2 pm (on second Sun of production)
Tickets
$7-10

annual shows, including a musical performed in an intimate theater. Shows generally run five weekends during the February through December season. The Thursday evening performance before opening is free.

Discounts
Previews/children/seniors/students/groups of 15+, call

BO
1/2 hr before performance; reserve by phone; exchanges OK; subscription progr am

Location
Off 22 Fwy near Valley View and Chapman in Eastgate Park

Parking
On street

Special Features
FREE preview on Thursday before opening

GARDEN PAVILION See **Celebrity Centre Theatre**

GARDNER STAGES

1501 North Gardner Street
Los Angeles, CA 90046
Info: (818) 767-4576 **Rsvn:** (213) 876-2870
Two spaces: one seats 40, the other 30.
This rental theater houses two tiny performance spaces in a back alley.

Performances
Fri-Sun, Sun matinee

Tickets
$10-15

Discounts
Previews/groups

BO
Reserve by phone

Location
Off Hollywood (101) Fwy at Sunset Blvd, between La Brea and Fairfax Aves

Parking
On street

KEY TO SYMBOLS

▒	Air conditioning (Only in **ART FILMS**)	🎧	Hearing device available
▮	Snack bar	▟	Binoculars availabe
▽	Full bar	👫	All OK for kids
‖	Restaurant on premises	(👫)	Some OK for kids
🍴	Restaurant nearby	〰	See seating plans
♿	Fully handicap accessible	RIP	Obituary—entity no longer exists or is no longer in operation
(♿)	Handicap seats only		

GARVIN THEATRE
STUDIO THEATRE
SANTA BARBARA CITY COLLEGE THEATRE GROUP

800 Block of Cliff Drive
Santa Barbara, CA 93109
Info: (805) 965-5935 **Rsvn:** (805) 965-5935
Fax: (805) 963-7222
Chairman of Theatre Arts Department: Tom Garey
College theaters staging a variety of performances; Garvin seats 400, Studio 100.

High marks go to this group for their outstanding productions mounted in an above-average setting high atop a coastal cliff in an above-average facility.

A recent production of *Biloxi Blues* gained a spot in the American College Theater Festival. Occasional professional guest artists, lured from the show-biz-heavy Santa Barbara community, add to the quality, as well as the night's receipts.

The Garvin is the bigger of the two spaces with 400 seats set in 14 well-raked rows. The black-box Studio Theatre provides 100 flexible seats.

Performances
Vary
Tickets
$4-14 (depending on show)
Discounts
Previews/children/ seniors/students/groups of 10+, call BO
BO
Mon-Fri 10 am-5 pm; check/AE/MC/V/reserve by mail; exchanges within same production, subject to availability; subscription program
Location
On West Campus of Santa Barbara City College
Parking
On premises, FREE

GASCON INSTITUTE FOR SPORT EDUCATION AND THE ARTS

8735 Washington Boulevard
Culver City, CA 90230
Info: (310) 204-2688
Artistic Director: John Camera
99-seat theater.

The Gascon Institute for Sport Education and the Arts is already known as the source for fencing instruction by Ted Katzoff, who choreographs sword fights in many feature films. It was natural for this company's evolution to include a dance center. Now the next stage of its ambition: a 200-seat Equity theater on the Washington Boulevard side of the Helms Bakery building in Culver City.

Gascon aims at a broad spectrum of new plays, new musicals, and classics selected by a group of literary agents, managers, and dramatists from all over the country.

"Sundays at Six" will offer readings of new plays in progress at no charge. The "Twenty Minute Play Competition" has no other restrictions than—guess what? Four of these are produced annually (for a total of 80 minutes).

When the Gascon Center grows some more, look for its new lounge and cafe in the Helms building.

Performances
Fri-Sat 8 pm (varies with performer)
Tickets
$7-15
Discounts
Children/seniors/ students
BO
Mon-Thurs 5 pm-10 pm check/reserve by mail
Location
In the Old Helm's Bakery Building; Washington Blvd near National Blvd; near the Santa Monica (10) Fwy;
Parking
On premises, FREE; street parking

GASLAMP QUARTER THEATRE COMPANY See **Hahn Cosmopolitan Theatre**

GEM THEATER AND GROVE SHAKESPEARE FESTIVAL

Sadly, what was formerly the second largest professional theater in Orange County has closed its doors. And strong doors they were. The Gem, in its comfortable 170-seat renovated Art Deco movie theater, presented contemporary American classics, classical plays, and small musicals for more than a decade. Each December we looked forward to *A Child's Christmas in Wales*, which squeezed out seven Christmases. On the schedule was everything from *Little Shop of Horrors* to *Long Day's Journey into Night*.

The 500-seat outdoor Grove Shakespeare Festival Amphitheater reached 15 seasons of fine classical plays. It was a wonderful spot to see Shakespeare done with imagination, insight, and an eye on modern audiences.

These two stages will be sorely missed.

GENE DYNARSKI THEATER

5600 Sunset Boulevard
Los Angeles, CA 90028
Info: (213) 467-6474　**Rsvn:** (213) 465-5600
Artistic Director: Gene Dynarski
Theater seats 99.

An extremely comfortable theater, tushy friendly and well-designed with good sightlines. The seats are properly raked, so you won't have to struggle to see. One only wonders why the theater is so often dark.

The performances vary depending on what company rents the space. It's a good idea to call to be placed on the mailing list.

Located on a corner of Sunset one block west of Western, the neighborhood ain't glamorous or glitzy. The consolation prize?—there's usually ample parking around.

Performances
　Vary
Tickets
　Donation up to $20
Discounts
　Previews/seniors/
　students/groups, call BO
BO
　Hrs vary; subscription
　program
Location
　2 blocks E of Hollywood
　(101) Fwy
Parking
　On premises (adjacent
　lots), FREE; street
　parking

GILBERT & SULLIVAN COMPANY OF SANTA BARBARA

Lobero Theatre
33 East Canon Perdido Street
Santa Barbara, CA 93101
Info: (805) 962-1458　**Rsvn:** (805) 963-0761
Artistic Director: Bill Budd

This volunteer organization has mounted over 125 full-length productions in its 10-year history. Every G & S comic operetta has been spotlighted here. The company sets-sail from Santa Barbara's Lobero Theatre.

Performances
　April, Sept; Fri-Sat 8 pm;
　Sun 2 pm
Tickets
　$6.75- 10.75
Discounts
　Children/seniors/
　students/groups of 10+,
　call Bill Budd
BO
　Mon-Fri 10 am-5:30 pm;
　Sat-Sun on performance
　days; check/AE/MC/V/
　reserve by mail
Parking
　Behind premises in city
　lot, FREE
Special Features
　Open rehearsals

GINDI AUDITORIUM AT THE UNIVERSITY OF JUDAISM

15600 Mulholland Drive
Los Angeles, CA 90077
Info: (310) 476-9777 ext. 302   **Rsvn:**(310) 476-9777 ext. 203
Fax: (310) 471-1278
Seats 479 for theater, music, and dance performances. The entire University of Judaism got hit severely in the January quake. The Gini expects to recover any day. Give them a call to find out whether "the show goes on."

This University auditorium is a pleasant enough place to watch a performance—if it's a good one. If not, you'll be distracted by clicking lights overhead. Avoid seats on the extreme sides where the sound system seems to throw the sound not from the actors' mouths, but from somewhere else. But the upholstered salmon-colored seats are comfortable, there's plenty of leg room, and the sightlines are excellent. The rows are configured continental-style (no middle aisle).

The annual performing arts series is a potpourri of dance, theater, music, and comedy from around the world and involving performers—and performances—representing all cultural walks of life. A collaboration between the University and Actors Alley Repertory brought to the stage the well-received *Cantorial* by Ira Levin. Names such as Bella Lewitzky, Mort Sahl, and the Klezmer Conservatory Band have been hosted on the Gindi stage. As with every performing arts series, subscription tickets are suggested to assure a seat, but single tickets are usually available.

Snacks are served at intermission in the large, light lobby. The art gallery is kept open for intermission browsing, and the university's gift shop stays open as well (there's plenty of reasonably-priced Judaica for sale.)

There's nowhere nearby to eat. As you are smack in between the San Fernando Valley and LA's Westside—you can take your pick of restaurants.

Performances
Mon-Thurs, Sat-Sun evenings; some Mon-Thurs matinees, Sun matinee
Tickets
$10-20
Discounts
Groups of 20+, call BO
BO
Mon-Fri 9 am-4 pm; Sat-Sun call (213) 472-6140 and leave message; check/MC/V/reserve by mail; no refunds, no exchanges; subscription program
Location
Off the San Diego (405) Fwy, exit off Mulholland
Parking
On premises,FREE

GLENDALE CENTRE THEATRE

324 North Orange Street
Glendale, CA 91203
Info: (818) 244-8481   **Rsvn:** (818) 244-8481
Fax: (818) 244-5042
430-seat community theater presenting family-oriented comedies and musicals in-the-round.

This theater bills itself as the "oldest continuously running center stage theater in America." And indeed, its history is a long one. Joe and Liz Kerr, and Nathan and Ruth Hale, began their dream theater in 1947. They trooped from site to site until settling in their New Orleans-style building in 1965, designed by their son-in-law Allan Dietlein. The Dietlein family now runs the theater.

Fans fill the large, comfortable lobby and settle into relaxing seats inside, which are steeply raked for good views.

A typical season might include: *Oliver, The Happiest Millionaire, Damn Yankees*, and *You Can't Take it With You*. Saturday matinees are devoted to children's performances.

Seating is open—not reserved—so arrive early.

Performances
Tues-Sat 8 pm, Sun 3 pm (12:00 children's show, Feb-Nov)
Tickets
$8.50-13
Discounts
Previews/seniors/groups/children, call; Wed night and Sun noon kids' show—$5 for kids, $7 for adults
BO
Mon-Sat 9:30 am-6 pm; AE/MC/V/check; exchanges up to 24 hrs before performance; subscription program
Location
S of 134 Fwy at California and Lexington
Parking
On street

GLOBE PLAYHOUSE

1107 North Kings Road
West Hollywood, CA 90069
Info: (213) 654-5623   **Rsvn:** (213) 654-5623
99-seat facsimile of a Shakespearean playhouse; mostly rentals.

Hark! Los Angeles Bardomanes, methinks thou art blessed. This 99-seat playhouse is the world's most legitimate replica of the historical Shakespearean playhouse, according to R. Thad Taylor, founder of the Shakespeare Society of America, and owner of this one-half-scale replica of the original Globe.

For years Taylor's mission has been to ensure that all, not just the most familiar, of Shakespeare's works are preserved on the stage. However, more and more this Shakespearean stage is seeing non-classical pieces from other producers. Still, a small museum and library are on site, where artifacts, rare works and a number of first editions of the playwright are proudly displayed. Any self-respecting English major will want to visit, extra credit or not.

There are numerous discounted tickets, and sometimes half-price preview tickets.

You probably won't find proper English food anywhere nearby, but Hugo's is just steps away, and within blocks east and west, or north to Sunset, south down La Cienega, are hundreds of restaurants.

Performances
Mon-Sun 8 pm; Sun 2 pm
Tickets
$10-25
Discounts
Previews/children/seniors/students/groups of 20, call BO
BO
Mon-Sun 9 am-7 pm when performing; check/reserve by mail, TicketMaster (sometimes)
Location
On Kings Rd 1/2 block N of Santa Monica Blvd
Parking
On premises, FREE; street parking

GNU THEATRE

We must report the demise of Gnu, one of the top professional small theaters in town. Artistic Director Jeff Seymour has moved on to work on other projects. It's possible the facility might reopen under another name and with another group. Stay tuned.

GRANADA THEATRE

18167 Chatsworth Street
Granada Hills, CA 91344
Info: (818) 363-3796   **Rsvn:** (818) 363-6887
Dinner theater seating 120 for a variety of performances.

Musicals, comedies, and mysteries have fared well for this 15-year-old community-based group, which converted a former health club into its new home in 1991. Granada Theatre performs nearly year-round with a four-show season, plus an annual holiday show.

Performances
Thurs-Fri 8 pm; Sat 7 pm; Sun 11:30 am, 5:30 pm
Tickets
$13.50-23.50
Discounts
Groups of 20+; Thurs evening and Sun matinee only, call Jo
BO
Check/MC/V; no exchanges; subscription program
Location
Near Simi (118) Fwy; between Balboa and Reseda
Parking
On premises, FREE; street parking

GRANADA THEATRE See **Santa Barbara Civic Light Opera**

GREAT LEAP INC.

See press listings for performance locations.
Info: (310) 392-7937 **Fax:** (310) 452-2552
Artistic Director: Nobuko Miyamoto

Performances
Vary

    In a way, Great Leap defies classification. The best description might be "touring performing arts organization dedicated to giving voice to the Asian American experience." To that end, Great Leap reaches out to an Asian audience that might not otherwise have the opportunity to see themselves reflected artistically. The multifaceted arts organization stages live entertainment in one- to five-person shows, or in huge concerts like the one they gave at the Anaheim Convention Center to an audience of more than 8,000. These bright, energetic actors, dancers, singers/songwriters manage to spread their talents, in every performing arts medium, to greater audiences and deep appreciation.

    Look for their performances at colleges and universities throughout the Southland. Or call the office to find out when they will perform next.

THE GROUNDLINGS THEATRE

7307 Melrose Avenue
Los Angeles, CA 90046
Info: (213) 934-4747 **Rsvn:** (213) 934-9700
Fax: (213) 934-8143
Artistic Director: John Gidcomb
99-seat improvisational theater; open seating.

Performances
Fri and Sat 8 pm and 10 pm; Sun 7:30 pm
Tickets
$10-17.50
Discounts
Groups of 11+, call BO
BO
Mon-Thurs 10 am-6 pm; Fri and Sat 10 am-10 pm; Sun noon-7:30 pm; check/AE/MC/V/fax, mail; subscription program
Location
4 blocks W of La Brea Ave on Melrose Ave
Parking
On street

    Most of the seats are good in this 99-seat theater, although none is reserved.

    Before or after-performance meals are available anywhere up and down Melrose. Parking is the usual problem—there isn't any! Try for street parking; read the parking restriction signs carefully.

THE GROUNDLINGS—Resident Co.

    For the past 18 years, The Groundlings has been a Los Angeles institution for comedy and improvisation. Many of today's best known performers made it their home base away from "Saturday Night Live" including Laraine Newman, Julia Sweeney, Cassandra (Elvira) Peterson, Phil Hartman, and Edie McClurg. Recently the Groundlings joined the move toward family performances with its long-running *Big Tush, Little Tush* on Sunday afternoons, and it made news by welcoming Light Flashes, the first deaf improv group, to its stage.

    Some people argue that the scripted portions of the show are funnier than the improv. But if you like improv and audience participation, you won't be disappointed. If you're like me, you'll be elated each time you return.

GROUP REPERTORY THEATRE

10900 Burbank Boulevard
North Hollywood, CA 91604
Info: (818) 761-1622 **Rsvn:** (818) 769-7529
Artistic Director: Lonny Chapman
92-seats; stages a variety of types of plays.

Performances
Fri-Sun 8 pm, Sat-Sun 2 pm and 5 pm
Tickets
$10-15
Discounts
Previews/children/ seniors/students/groups of 60+, call BO

    The GRT performance space was a motorcycle shop before its transformation into a theater ten years ago. Harleys and Suzukis are long gone, but theater continues to rev up at GRT. Its downstairs stage boasts sophisticated lighting and acoustics. The 92 practically antique seats, dating from 1922, come complete with an old-fashioned rim underneath for men's hats. Seats were donated and previously used by the LA Philharmonic. The first eight of these seats are reserved for the disabled.

GROUP REPERTORY THEATRE COMPANY—Resident Co.

With 100 productions under their collective belt, company member Erma Dean Chapman has no desire to limit the scope of drama presented. "We do the old and the new...we're always alternating." The 20th anniversary season was celebrated with Stephen Crane's *The Red Badge of Courage*. The 120 actors, writers, and directors are all professionals in various fields of the entertainment industry.

Although tickets are necessary for the polished, full-scale performances, many works in progress—often 20 to 30 per year—are open to the public free of charge.

BO
Thurs-Sun 1 pm-8 pm; check/reserve by phone; subscription program
Location
Near Hollywood (101) Fwy and Ventura (134) Fwy at Vineland and Burbank
Parking
On premises,FREE; street parking
Special Features
FREE admission to "project performances" (20-30 per year)

GROVE THEATRE See **Octad-One Productions**

GYPSY PLAYHOUSE

3321 West Olive Avenue
Burbank, CA 91505
Info: (818) 954-8458   **Rsvn:** (818) 563-3111
Fax: (818) 563-1174
Artistic Director: Lee Scott
68-seat theater.

The comfortable 68-seat playhouse serves as a venue for mainly comedy and musical comedy. Theater director Lee Scott is a former Tony Award nominee.

Bob Hope donated the space to the Professional Dancers Society, a nonprofit organization providing support to active and retired dancers.

Snacks are available at the theater, but for full meals try nearby Chadney's (and stay for the jazz), or Acapulco's.

Performances
Thurs-Sat
Tickets
$10-12.50
Discounts
Children/seniors/ students/groups of 10+, call
BO
Mon-Sun noon-5 pm; check/reserve by mail, fax, TicketMaster

HAHN COSMOPOLITAN THEATRE

---

444 4th Avenue
San Diego, CA 92101
Info: (619) 232-9608   **Rsvn:** (619) 234-9583
Fax: (619) 235-9359
Artistic Directors: Kit Goldman, Adleane Hunter, Will Simpson, Rosina Widdowson-Reynolds
Theater seats 250.

The Hahn Cosmopolitan is a handsome structure, built with the old-world elegance of a much larger theater. The bad news—there's no center row so you'll have to be patient if you're seated in the middle. The good news: there are no sight obstructions. Leave your evening gowns and tuxes in the closet. Parking is an ongoing problem in this area, so your best bet is to come early and hunt for free space on the adjacent streets.

GASLAMP QUARTER THEATRE COMPANY—Resident Co.

In its early years, Gaslamp became known for the high gloss and stylish spins it put on British works by the likes of Noel Coward and Harold Pinter. But as its success grew, so did its ambitions. Under the leadership of Will Simpson, Robert Earl, and Kit Goldman, who founded it in

Performances
Tues-Sun 8 pm, Sun 2 pm
Tickets
$15-22
Discounts
Students/seniors/groups of 15+, call (619) 232-9608
BO
Daily noon-6 pm; check/AE/MC/V/reserve by mail (subscription only), TicketMaster; exchanges OK; subscription program
Location
At Island and 4th in downtown San Diego
Parking
On street

1981, the company moved from a 99-seat theater to this special 250-seat site, a costly move. In the last few years it's been struggling to maintain the large venue.

Its founders moved on to other projects and left behind an artistic cooperative which redefined its goal as multicultural diversity. The newly inspired group presented a hugely successful interracial production of *Frankie and Johnny in the Clair de Lune*, with Pam Grier and local favorite William Anton. Recently it has taken to booking in a variety of shows to keep costs down.

Whatever its future, the theater has been a pioneer in settling the historic, but not yet gentrified Gaslamp Quarter area.

HARMAN AVENUE THEATER
HARMAN ALLEY THEATER

522 North La Brea Avenue
Los Angeles, CA 90036
Info: (213) 931-8137   **Rsvn:** (213) 931-8130
Fax: (213) 931-2436
Harman Avenue seats 86, while the Alley seats 40.

At least once a year the Harmon comes up aces—a terrific record for any theater connected with even a good acting school such as Estelle Harmon's Studio. Watch for plays, musicals, and showcases.

Performances
Thurs-Sun 8 pm; Sat-Sun 3 pm
Tickets
Varies
Discounts
Previews/children/seniors/students/groups of 8+, call BO
BO
Check/AE/MC/V
Location
Melrose and La Brea
Parking
On street

HAUGH PERFORMING ARTS CENTER

Citrus College
1000 West Foothill Boulevard
Glendora, CA 91740
Info: (818) 914-8847   **Rsvn:** (818) 963-9411
Fax: (818) 335-4715
Hosts musical and theatrical performances, a film series, and children's performances. Seats 1,469.

Located in San Gabriel Valley on the Citrus College campus, the Haugh Performing Arts Center was built to serve the community as well as the students of this two-year college.

You can't miss the building. It's a massive white concrete and cinder block structure that might be mistaken for a nuclear research facility. It's located at the far (north) end of the parking lot on Citrus Avenue and Foothill Boulevard.

The continental seating (no middle aisle) contributes to the sense of massiveness, as does the high ceiling and overhead space unbroken by a balcony. Seats in Section I are best; there are no obstructed seats anywhere.

The three "mini-series" which are offered annually provide something for everyone. Poland's Mazowsze dance company has graced the stage, as have comedians, big bands, and lavish stage productions such as *Peter Pan* and *Ain't Misbehavin*.

The theater is dark (closed) in summer, when school is out. Although there's a strong subscriber base, single tickets are almost always available. Plan to dine before or after the performances, as there's no snack or drink bar. Try out the Derby East, Fenderbenders, or The Golden Spur.

Performances
Wed, Fri-Sun 7 pm, 7:30 pm, 8 pm; Sun 2 pm
Tickets
$12-30
Discounts
Seniors/students/groups
BO
Mon-Sat 11 am-4 pm; and 1 hr prior to performance time; MC/V/check/order by mail; no refunds or exchanges; subscription program
Location
Off the Foothill (210) Fwy at Citrus Ave exit; head N 1 mile to the corner of Citrus Ave and Foothill Blvd
Parking
On premises, FREE; street parking

HAUNTED STUDIOS See **Haunted Cabaret** in **CLUBS**

HELIOTROPE THEATRE See **Deaf West Theatre Company**

HENRY FONDA THEATRE

6126 Hollywood Boulevard
Hollywood, CA 90028
Rsvn: (213) 480-3232
Seats 863 for theater, concerts, and benefits.
      One of Hollywood's early movie theaters, the Henry Fonda went legit as part of the 1970s revitalization effort to introduce more live theater to Hollywood. Located across Hollywood Boulevard from the Pantages but slightly farther east, and around the corner from the James A. Doolittle on Vine Street, the Fonda has, in recent years, hosted performances such as *Driving Miss Daisy* and *Lend Me A Tenor*. It is also booked for concerts, rock groups, and benefit shows.

Performances
  Vary
Tickets
  $20-45
Discounts
  Previews/groups of 20, call (213) 464-7521
BO
  Hrs vary; AE/MC/V/ reserve by mail, TicketMaster
Location
  Off Hollywood (101) Fwy, Gower St exit
Parking
  Public lots, street parking

HIGHWAYS PERFORMANCE SPACE

1651 18th Street
Santa Monica, CA 90404
Info: (310) 453-1755   **Rsvn:** (213) 660-8587
Fax: (310) 453-4347
Theater, dance, varied performances, visual exhibitions.
      Highways sped to the forefront of avant-garde venues in just three short years, and is now into its fifth performance season. Co-founders Linda Frye Burnham, who recently left, and Tim Miller, the sole artistic director, drew together a staff that serves an audience that has grown to 10,000 to 20,000 annually—many of whom aren't typically arts patrons.
      Recently Highways made the unprecedented move (unprecedented based on today's wanting arts economy) of combining with High Performance magazine to create a five-building 18th Street Arts Complex, an umbrella to shelter rental rehearsal studios, gallery, artists' studios, the Electronic Cafe International, the Empowerment Project, Community Arts Resources, Tearsheet Productions, Sidestreet Projects, and others. (Keep your eyes open for the complex in a light industrial area of Santa Monica, just off Olympic.)
      Highways presents more than 200 performances each year, four to five nights each week, in its simple black box space, and exhibits visual arts that are often coordinated with the theme of its "live" art. The range of presentations is awesome. The best way to find your way about is to get on the mailing list. As example: events have included evenings of short works by emerging and established LA area performers Annie Sprinkle, performance artist and former porn star whose work focuses on women's sexuality; lesbian comics Lea DeLaria and Kate Clinton who have gained much national attention; and Tim Miller, performance artist and co-founder of Highways,

Performances
  Thurs-Sun 8:30 pm
Tickets
  $10-12
Discounts
  Students
BO
  1 hr prior to performance; MC/V(call 660-TKTS)/reserve by mail, check or cash at door, call
Location
  1/2 block N of Olympic Blvd; near Santa Monica (10) Fwy
Parking
  On premises, FREE; street parking
Special Features
  Workshops—call (310) 315-9633

whose "My Queer Body" explored every centimeter of his subject.

Highways also presents numerous festivals, dance programming every month, and collaborations with the Virginia Avenue Project and a teen street youth group.

HOLLYWOOD ACTORS' THEATER

1157 North McCadden Place
Hollywood, CA 90038
Info: (310) 962-8557 **Rsvn:** (310) 982-6567
Artistic Director: Gabe Cohen
Seats 49 for original plays.

This 30-member rep company bounced back after a disastrous 1991 fire to produce a mostly original bill of comedies and dramas. They're currently renting space at the McCadden Place Theatre.

Performances
Thurs-Sun
Tickets
$10-15
Discounts
Seniors/students/groups of 8+, call BO
BO
Reserve by phone, mail; subscription program
Location
Off Hollywood (101) Fwy at Highland Ave; 1 block E of Highland Ave between Hollywood Blvd and Santa Monica Blvd
Parking
On street

HOLLYWOOD COURT THEATER

Hollywood United Methodist Church
6817 Franklin Avenue
Hollywood, CA 90028
Info: (213) 874-2104
65-seat rental facility.

Most churches welcome converts, of course. This one converted a large Sunday-school room into a theater for their theatrically active congregants. A blinding revelation followed: by renting it out to other groups, the church could earn additional revenue for their myriad worthwhile programs. It's been a popular venue ever since for many types of performances.

Enter the church grounds through the gates on Franklin Avenue, walk through the courtyard and up the stairs to the popular second floor theater containing a raised stage and 65 raised, upholstered seats.

Performances
Vary
Tickets
$ varies
BO
Call
Location
On Franklin Ave; enter through gates on Franklin Ave; enter courtyard; stairs to 2nd level; no elevator
Parking
On premises, FREE (limited); street parking (limited)

HOLLYWOOD MOGULS See CLUBS

HOLLYWOOD PLAYHOUSE See Richard Pryor Playhouse

HOLLYWOOD REPERTORY COMPANY

See press listings for performance locations
Info: (310) 281-3172

Keep your eyes and ears open for this young nomad group as it seeks performance spaces for its contemporary and avant-garde productions.

HOLLYWOOD THEATER COMPANY

See press listings for performance locations.
Info: (818) 984-1867
Artistic Director: Rai Tasco

This community based company is determined to bring professional-quality drama to stages throughout the city. Past pieces include *Anna Lucasta*, *Take a Giant Step*, *The Sign in Sidney Brustein's Window*, and *The Reckoning*, among other contemporary classics. HTC was founded about 20 years ago by actor/director Rai Tasco.

Performances
Fri-Sun 8 pm; Sun matinees
Tickets
$10-12
Discounts
Previews/students/ groups
BO
Check/reserve by mail
Parking
Varies with location
Special Features
Occasional open rehearsals

HUDSON THEATRE

6539 Santa Monica Boulevard
Hollywood, CA 90038
Info: (213) 856-4249 **Rsvn:** (213) 856-4249
99-seat Theatre Row space specializing in American plays.

Hard to believe this used to be a hole in the wall space called the Fig Tree Theatre. Now like the other theaters on Theatre Row, it's been completely redone—into a gorgeous space with an elegant (albeit small) lobby. Go figure. Once you ascend the stairs to the theater itself, its deep rake makes viewing a joy. All the production values, like sound, lighting, and set design, are topnotch.

The Hudson is devoted to developing new American plays, staged readings and creative workshops. The stage is also occasionally grabbed as a showcase for emerging musicians, storytellers, and visual artists.

Hudson members have won considerable recognition for their work, including an NAACP Award, a Media Access Award for portraying handicapped people in positive roles, and numerous LA Drama Critics Circle Awards.

In 1992, the Hudson Theatre opened a more flexible second space, dubbing it Hudson Backstage. This 99-seater allows for a variety of seating configurations and follows the Hudson's focus on socio-political themes; although polished, the shows tend to be a bit more experimental.

Performances
Mon-Sun
Tickets
$15-20
Discounts
Previews/seniors/ students/groups of 15+, call BO
BO
Call; MC/V/check/Disc/ AE/reserve by phone, Tickets LA, pay at BO
Location
Off Hollywood (101) Fwy between Highland Ave and Cahuenga Blvd at Santa Monica Blvd and Hudson Ave
Parking
Valet, $2; street parking

KEY TO SYMBOLS

Air conditioning (Only in **ART FILMS**)		Hearing device available	
Snack bar		Binoculars availabe	
Full bar		All OK for kids	
Restaurant on premises		Some OK for kids	
Restaurant nearby		See seating plans	
Fully handicap accessible		Obituary—entity no longer exists or is no longer in operation	
Handicap seats only			

HUNTINGTON BEACH PLAYHOUSE

7111 Talbert Avenue
Huntington Beach, CA 92648
Info: (714) 375-0696 **Rsvn:** (714) 832-1405
South Bay community theater.
    The Huntington Beach Playhouse has been staffed by volunteers since 1963. Anyone in the community is welcome to try out for the performances, now in its new 317-seat location, which range from serious dramas, to comedies, musicals, and mysteries.
    In addition to fare such as *Stalag 17*, *Prelude to a Kiss*, and *A Streetcar Named Desire*, the group performs Shakespeare in nearby Huntington Beach Central Park (in July), and offers an annual children's program during the Christmas holidays.

Performances
    Thurs-Sat 8 pm, Sun 7 pm
Tickets
    $10-18
Discounts
    Children/seniors/students/groups of 20+, call BO
BO
    Wed-Sat 2:30 pm-7 pm, Sun 10 am-4 pm (until showtime on performance days); check/MC/AE/V; exchanges made; subscription program
Location
    Off San Diego (405) Fwy, exit Golden W, W to Talbert
Parking
    On premises, FREE
Special Features
    Open final dress rehearsal (donation requested), call first

INCLINE, THE THEATRE GROUP

See press listings or call for performance locations.
Info: (310) 837-7014
Artistic Director: Colleen Flynn
    A still-rising company of talented and committed artists whose debut performances garnered critical praise, Incline's "inclinations" point in the right direction. The young company is dedicated to championing innovative and socially conscientious works. In its very brief history, the ensemble has earned a reputation for performing in enigmatic venues. Operating on the theory that a performance space should lend itself inevitably to the theme and logic of the play, the group was once seen "on stage" in a refurbished car-body shop. The brick warehouse-studio with skylights indeed enhanced the urban context of their play. Readings have been produced with well-known actors such as Dana Delany and staged at the Hudson Theatre and Coast Playhouse, with proceeds to finance a school tour of *Raft of the Medusa*, their AIDS education presentation.
    Producing socially conscious drama has always been an uphill battle. Incline has the traction now to keep moving.

Performances
    Spring and fall, Thurs-Sat 8 pm
Tickets
    $8.50-12.50
Discounts
    Seniors/students/groups of 10+, call
BO
    Check/AE/Disc/MC/V/ Tickets LA; exchanges OK
Parking
    Varies with location

INNER CITY CULTURAL CENTER

1605 North Ivar Street
Hollywood, CA 90028
Info: (213) 962-2102 **Rsvn:** (213) 962-2102
Fax: (213) 386-9017
Performances at the 300-seat New Ivar Theatre.
    C. Bernard Jackson was practicing "multiculturalism" long before it became the catchword of LA. From the ashes of the Watts riots, ICCC was formed in

Performances
    Mon-Sun 8 pm, Sun 3 pm
Tickets
    $15-25

1965 "as a tool for bridging the cultural gap between America's diverse communities." Perhaps if more people had paid attention in 1965, we wouldn't have had the ashes—or the catchwords—of 1992, which contributed to ICCC's move out of its 22-year old home down on New Hampshire Avenue, near Pico and Vermont. The reason for the move was the expensive renovations needed to bring the 1925-structure up to earthquake codes, as well as the security fears brought about by the "unrest." Although ICCC executive director Jackson has promised a return to the New Hampshire Avenue site, nobody at ICCC will comment officially on when. So for the foreseeable future, at least, this vital organization is in residence at the New Ivar Theater in Hollywood, which it owns. The Ivar, long-infamous as a burlesque (striptease) theater, has been dressed up to give ICCC a larger house in which to present its acclaimed programming. Although classes and workshops have been postponed for the moment, there are no plans to curtail the organization's regular output.

Many of LA's most-respected theater groups (Teatro Campesino, Bilingual Foundation of the Arts, East-West Players, for example) got a start years ago under the auspices of ICCC. Paul Winfield, Danny Glover, Edward James Olmos, Lou Gossett, Jr., and Nobu McCarthy are just a few of the greats whose careers were in some way spawned or nurtured at ICCC.

The local papers are your best bet for news on the current schedule and competitions. The Sunday Family Performances are great opportunities to introduce the kids to a variety of types of entertainment. There are two family shows, at 11 and noon; a modest donation is usually requested.

A dance series, "Voices in Motion" is a new addition that provides an opportunity to see a wide range of dance companies, most, African-American in focus. Tickets are $12.50 in advance. Call for details.

Discounts
Previews/children/ seniors/students/groups of 25+, call
BO
Mon-Sun 1-6 pm; check/MC/V/reserve by mail; exchanges with 72 hr notice
Location
1 block W of Hollywood and Vine, near Hollywood (101) Fwy
Parking
Valet, $5; street parking
Special Features
Special performances for members

INTERACT THEATRE CO. See **Theatre Exchange**

INTERNATIONAL CITY THEATRE

Corner of Clark and Harvey Way
Long Beach, CA 90808
Info: (310) 420-4051   **Rsvn:** (310) 420-4128
Fax: (310) 420-4118
Artistic Director: Shashin Desai
Flexible seating for 99. Plays of all kinds.
Patrons from Orange County and Los Angeles won't regret making the drive to ICT's very comfortable and appealing space on the campus of Long Beach City College. There's no lobby (while you wait you can feed carrots to the rabbit residents outside), but seating is good and the parking is simple.

INTERNATIONAL CITY THEATRE COMPANY—Resident Co.
Inching toward a decade of performances, ICT continues its ascent to high artistic achievement led by artistic director, Shashin Desai, who produces a four-play season. A high level of production values is constantly in evidence, and reviews are nearly always positive. Desai often stages new plays or Los Angeles area premieres—from dramatic comedies to classical satire to comedy-mysteries. ICT's Discovery Series brings to the stage something for everyone through readings and workshops.
Consider ICT a "must go."

Performances
Fri-Sat 8 pm, Sun 2 and 7 pm
Tickets
$13-15
Discounts
Previews/seniors/ students/groups of 15+, call
BO
Mon-Fri noon-5 pm and 1 hr before performance; check/MC/V/reserve by mail, fax, TicketMaster; exchanges flexible for subscribers; subscription program
Location
Near 405, 91 and 605 Fwys at Lakewood and Carson
Parking
On premises, FREE; street parking

THEATER

IRVINE BARCLAY THEATRE See MUSIC

IRVINE COMMUNITY THEATER GROUP

1 Sunnyhill
Irvine, CA 92715
Rsvn: (714) 857-5496
Community theater group usually performs at the Turtle Rock Community Park Auditorium.

This two-decade-plus Orange County group mounts a four-show season of comedies and dramas, favoring American works such as *The Odd Couple* (the female version), *All My Sons, Death of a Salesman*, and *Who's Afraid of Virginia Woolf?*

Performances are held at the Turtle Rock Community Park Auditorium. The 250 cushioned folding chairs rarely fill up. Lucky thing for audiences, since there's no reserved seating. Refreshments are served at intermission.

Performances
Fri-Sat 8 pm; Sun 2 pm
Tickets
$6-8
Discounts
Children/seniors/ students/groups of 20, call BO
BO
Buy tickets at door; check evening of performance; subscription program
Location
San Diego (405) Fwy to University
Parking
On premises, FREE

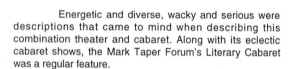

ITCHEY FOOT

Energetic and diverse, wacky and serious were descriptions that came to mind when describing this combination theater and cabaret. Along with its eclectic cabaret shows, the Mark Taper Forum's Literary Cabaret was a regular feature.

Sadly it is no more.

JAMES A. DOOLITTLE See Music Center of Los Angeles County

JAPAN AMERICA THEATRE

244 South San Pedro Street
Los Angeles, CA 90012
Info: (213) 628-2725   **Rsvn:** (213) 680-3700
Fax: (213) 617-8576
841-seat variety theater.

Kabuki, the highly-stylized, traditional Japanese theater, opened the Japan America Theatre 1983 and ever since the theater has been host to numerous native Japanese guests artists, traditional and contemporary. The assortment of performances in this intimate setting all reflects some aspect of either Californian or Japanese culture.

The fan-shaped seats are roomy, offer lots of leg room, and are so well-raked there's (practically) not a bad one in the house. Avoid row one, and if you're short, decline row two. For those of you at all noise sensitive, be sure your seats are NOT extreme right or left end seats in the first five rows, where the speakers are liable to blast you to Hokkaido. Don't plan on drinks and schmoozing during intermission—the bar is bonsai dimensions. But most everyone steps outside on the plaza for a look at the restful, award-winning James Irvine Garden.

The Celebrate California season showcases the music and theater of fine LA artists. Kokoro Concerts offer a series of Japanese American artists such as saxophone great Sadao Watanabe. Guests of the International Series

Performances
Vary
Tickets
FREE-$100
Discounts
Previews/children/ seniors/students/groups of 15-20+, call
BO
Daily noon-5 pm; check/MC/V/reserve by mail; no refunds, no exchanges; subscription program
Location
Near Hollywood (101) Fwy and Harbor (110) Fwy on San Pedro between 2nd and 3rd
Parking
On street; pay lots across the street $2.50

see some of Asia's finest traditional musicians, dancers, and performers. There's always something for the kids in The Family Series, and they love it.

Nearby awaits Little Tokyo, tailor-made for a before-theater dinner. There's a parking lot directly across the street from the theater.

JOHN ANSON FORD AMPHITHEATRE

2580 Cahuenga Boulevard East
Hollywood, CA 90068
Info: (213) 850-2060
1,200-seat outdoor stage used for theater and summer music presentations.

Built in 1920 as the site of an annual religious "Pilgrimage Play," this amphitheater is set in a hillside canyon just across the freeway from the Hollywood Bowl. Now operated by the LA County Department of Parks and Recreation, the ample space is rented out to groups. Performers from Shakespeare Festival/LA to dance, jazz, and opera concerts appear (See **FESTIVALS** for information on "Summer Nights at the Ford.") Its rustic locale makes for great scenery before the show begins. The technical quality of each show varies, since the companies renting are responsible for bringing in their own equipment.

Park in the lots at the base of the hill and walk up to the amphitheater. Special arrangements for car transport up the hill can be made for the physically disabled.

Performances
Vary
Tickets
$ varies
BO
Varies; reserve by mail, fax, TicketMaster
Location
Off of Hollywood (101) Fwy
Parking
On premises, $ 5

KCRW-FM See **LA Theatre Works**

KECK THEATER See **Occidental College Performing Arts Series** in **MUSIC**

LACE (LOS ANGELES CONTEMPORARY EXHIBITIONS)

6522 Hollywood Boulevard
Los Angeles, CA 90028
Info: (213) 624-5650   **Rsvn:** (213) 624-5650
Fax: (213) 624-6679
An interdisciplinary nonprofit artists' organization presenting a variety of performances.

LACE is a major presenter of innovative, contemporary art in all its many unexplored and underexplored manifestations.

Expect to see just about anything that defies artistic convention, like Poland's leading performance art troupe, Akademia Ruchu, portraying its perception of modern Polish life through symbolic commentary. Or you could catch an ensemble presentation previously performed on the streets featuring homeless and formerly homeless people exploring the causes of their nomadic lifestyles and destitution. Maybe you'll catch a video screening of promotional tapes, pseudo-documentaries, computer animation and video art called "Cyberspatial Intersections," a cross-section of works about "virtual reality," artificial intelligence, and computer animation.

LACE is truly a front-runner of cutting-edge art organizations. Close to 15 years old, LACE recently left its downtown location for Hollywood digs, between Hudson and Wilcox, and near what will be the new Metro Rail stop. There is secured parking in back of the building; during the five years planned for the Metro Rail construction, LACE will still be accessible via valet and nearby validated parking.

Performances
Thurs-Sun 8 pm; Sun 4 pm
Tickets
$ varies
BO
Check/reserve by mail, fax, TicketMaster
Location
Hollywood, between Hudson and Wilcox
Parking
Secured parking rear of building; valet; nearby validated parking lot

LA CONNECTION COMEDY THEATRE

13442 Ventura Boulevard
Sherman Oaks, CA 91423
Info: (818) 784-1868 **Rsvn:** (818) 784-1868
Fax: (818) 710-8666
99-seat comedy theater.

Just shy of 20 years old, this Valley nightspot is virtually an institution, presenting original comedy sketches and improv routines. The theater is well designed to maximize sightlines. Seating is "L" shaped, with half the chairs fixed theater seats, the other half unfixed chairs. The only refreshments served in the lobby are lollipops. You can bring in your own nonalcoholic beverages.

There are tons of restaurants nearby—if you can get in: try Mistral or Bistro Garden for starters. Want bagels and cream cheese instead? Jerry's Deli isn't far away.

LA CONNECTION COMEDY THEATRE—Resident Co.

If you're not already connected to comedy and improv, these people will plug you in. Their "new soundtracks" of campy, "B" movies are 90-minute shows redubbed live by the company. Playing every Friday at midnight, following the group's regular improv performances, is *Reefer Madness;* Saturdays you can see the midnight dubbing of Adam West's *Batman* movie.

The LA Connection Kids are a resident group of very young performers, ages 8 to 13, who test their comedy/improv wings on stage the last Sunday of every month.

Performances
Fri-Sat 7:30 pm, 9 pm, 10:30 pm; Sun 7 pm, 8:30 pm; last Sun of each month 4:30 pm
Tickets
$5-12
BO
Call; check/MC/V/ reserve by mail, fax, TicketMaster; exchanges made; subscription program
Parking
On premises, FREE; street parking

LAGUNA PLAYHOUSE

606 Laguna Canyon Road
Laguna Beach, CA 92651
Info: (714) 497-9244 **Rsvn:** (714) 494-8021
Artistic Director: Andrew Barnicle
Popular classics and original works.

Orange County's Laguna Playhouse has been in operation since 1920, making it the oldest continuously operating theater on the West Coast. The Playhouse draws a consistent pool of experienced LA area actors. While it generally elects proven off-Broadway successes and classic moneymakers, audiences are also exposed to original daring and thought-provoking works. This well-rounded combination has, in the past couple of years, boosted subscribership to 8,800.

A five-year-old fund-raising campaign was started to establish a smaller theater for challenging new works and as a part-time home for a Youth Theatre. The additional space, at 32356 Pacific Coast Highway, is planning its inaugural summer season for 1994.

The Playhouse's Moulton Theatre, located in "the village," has excellent sightlines and acoustics.

See **CHILDREN** for further information on the offerings for young people.

Playhouse Singles meets on pre-arranged nights during a run with a social prior to the performance for area singles to meet and share their common interest in the arts. Stage Talks are post-show discussions about the plays and generally occur on four specified nights during each run.

Performances
Tues-Sat 8 pm; Sun 7 pm; Sat-Sun 2 pm
Tickets
$11-22
Discounts
Previews/groups of 20+, call BO
BO
Tues-Sat noon-5 pm; check/MC/V/reserve by mail
Location
Near 133 Fwy (from 5 or 405 Fwys) or Pacific Coast Hwy
Parking
On premises or street, FREE

LA JOLLA PLAYHOUSE

2910 La Jolla Village Drive
La Jolla, CA 92037
Info: (619) 534-6760 **Rsvn:** (619) 534-3960
Fax: (619) 534-7870
Two spaces: the 500-seat Mandell Weiss Theatre and the 400-seat Mandell Weiss Forum.

    The nationally acclaimed La Jolla Playhouse is renowned for an eclectic blend of challenging, controversial theater concocted by some of the leading artists on the national and international scene. An indicative short list: Athol Fugard, often called the conscience of white South Africa; Stephen Sondheim and James Lapine, one of the great musical composing teams of our time; silent masterclown Bill Irwin; Tony-award-winning designer Heidi Landesman; eloquent actress Amanda Plummer; wunderkind director Peter Sellars; those wild and crazy Flying Karamazov Brothers; and rock legend Peter Townshend.

    The Playhouse was founded in 1947 by Hollywood stars Gregory Peck (a La Jolla boy), Dorothy McGuire, and Mel Ferrer as a summer place for movie actors to perform the classics in front of people other than film technicians. It closed down in 1965 and reopened in 1983 as an altogether new entity in a new home. Today, it's a fully professional theater (until recently under the artistic leadership of playwright/director and one-time rock musician Des McAnuff) and operates out of two new state-of-the-art facilities on the campus of the University of California at San Diego—the Mandell Weiss Theatre, a 500-seat proscenium stage and the Mandell Weiss Forum, a 400-seat thrust stage. McAnuff, who took time off to work on the Broadway production of *Tommy*, will remain Director-in-Residence.

    One of the playhouse's biggest hits was *Big River*, which went to Broadway in 1986, winning seven Tony awards, one for McAnuff's direction. (He also captured that award for *Tommy*.) Another enormous hit was Lee Blessing's *A Walk in the Woods*, a tale about an American and a Soviet arms negotiator. That too went to Broadway, and then London and Russia. In 1989, the playhouse sent Steppenwolf Theatre's version of *The Grapes of Wrath* to Broadway and London. Tony-award nominee *Tommy* later went on to New York to make one of the biggest splashes the Great White Way has seen in a long time. Just recently the challenging three-hour *Children of Paradise: Shooting a Dream*, by Theatre de la Jeune Lune, opened the theater's season.

    Each year, the Playhouse has incorporated an increasing amount of UCSD talent into its productions. It's hard to imagine a more positive synergy among academics, artists and the community. As for the productions themselves, they are consistently and consummately professional, ranking with the best in the country. This, after all, is the theater that built a river on stage for its migrant farmers to swim in *The Grapes of Wrath*! The Playhouse was rewarded for its excellence with the 1993 Tony award for Excellence in Regional Theatre, giving San Diego two Regional Theater award-winners (the Old Globe being the second).

    There isn't a bad seat in the house in the Forum. The best seats in the Mandell Weiss Theatre are rows E through K and 7 through 25. But there are really no obstructions from any seat.

    There's plenty of parking in the theater's on-campus lots, but UCSD does charge a nominal fee. You'll see a more tweedy, academic crowd here because of the

Performances
  Tues-Sat 8 pm; Sat-Sun 2 pm
Tickets
  $19.75-32.75
Discounts
  Previews/seniors/ students/groups of 15+, call Paula Herring (619) 534-6760
BO
  Mon 11 am-6 pm; Tues-Sun 11 am-8 pm; check/AE/Disc/MC/V/ reserve by mail, TicketMaster; exchanges for subscribers only, including exchange by fax; subscription program
Location
  On the UCSD campus, off Int-5 at La Jolla Village Dr
Parking
  On premises, $1; street parking

UCSD association. Intermission refreshments consist of pastries and nonalcoholic beverages.

Dinner spots are numerous: the first class George's Cafe & Ocean Terrace, with its breathtaking view of La Jolla Cove; Sammy's California Woodfired Pizza (gourmet pizzas); the conveniently located J.W.'s Sea Grill in the La Jolla Marriott; another is the inexpensive Soup Exchange where you can load up on an array of healthy and hip salads, soups, and breads.

LA JOLLA STAGE COMPANY

Parker Community Auditorium
750 Nautilus Street
La Jolla, CA 92037
Info: (619) 459-7773
Artistic Director: Walter Stewart
Community theater performances at the 474-seat Parker Auditorium.

When the community raised money to build a stage for La Jolla High School in 1980, Walter Stewart, an undoubtedly ambitious drama teacher at the school, conceived of a semiprofessional company to share the space.

Under Stewart's continuous leadership, La Jolla Stage has presented three shows a year at the Parker Auditorium, at roughly half the price of professional theater. (This has made the company especially appealing to senior citizens on fixed incomes.) The stage is clearly reminiscent of the classic high school auditorium. But the work on that stage surpasses anything you'll remember from high school, making it an ideal bridge between educational and professional theater. The repertoire is contemporary and eclectic, ranging from musicals such as *How to Succeed in Business Without Really Trying* to dramas such as *The Diviners*.

There's free on-street parking near the theater and a corner lot at Fay and Nautilus.

Performances
Oct-May
Tickets
$11-13
Discounts
Seniors/students/groups of 10+, call BO
BO
Mon-Fri noon-4 pm, 2 hrs before performances; Sat 2 pm-4 pm on performance days; check/MC/V/ reserve by mail; exchanges made only for season subscribers; subscription program
Parking
Street, FREE; nearby lot

LA MIRADA THEATRE FOR THE PERFORMING ARTS

14900 La Mirada Boulevard
La Mirada, CA 90638
Info: (714) 994-6150   **Rsvn:** (714) 994-6310 or (310) 944-9801
Fax: (714) 994-5796
A 1300-seat theater for musical theater, drama, symphony, and children's performances.

Built by the city of La Mirada in 1977, this civic theater has been compared to LA's Doolittle and has been dubbed "a Broadway theater in the suburbs." Watch for new programming in the 1994-5 season as the helm is turned over to a new production team, McCoy Rigby Entertainment. The team of Tom McCoy and Cathy Rigby plans solid audience-pleasing productions and family-fare. The contemporary architecture provides excellent sightlines (no one is more than 80 feet from the stage) in continental-style seating. Parking spaces circle the theater, so even they're not far away.

Discounts
Children/seniors/ students/groups of 20, call BO
BO
Mon-Thurs 10 am-5 pm; Fri 10 am-8 pm; Sat-Sun noon-5 pm, and 1 hr prior to curtain; MC/V/ check/AE/Disc/reserve mail or phone; $1 per ticket change; 24 hrs prior to date on original ticket; subscription program
Location
Rosecrans exit off Santa Ana (Int-5) Fwy
Parking
On premises, FREE; street parking

LA MIRADA CIVIC LIGHT OPERA (WHITTIER-LA MIRADA MUSICAL THEATRE ASSOCIATION)

This CLO can boast more than 40 seasons of musical hits supported by elaborate sets, full orchestras, and top talent. Normal subscription series tickets are the norm here as well.

Performances
Thurs-Sat 8 pm; Sat-Sun 2:30 pm
Tickets
$18-20

LA MIRADA PLAYHOUSE

The Playhouse performances have been going strong for more than 30 seasons. Comedy, drama, and mystery usually make up the season. Season tickets assure you of discounts. One series day always includes an interpreter for the deaf.

Performances
Fri-Sat 8 pm; Sun 2:30 pm, 7:30 pm
Tickets
$20

LA MIRADA JUNIOR PROGRAMS See CHILDREN

LA MIRADA SYMPHONY ORCHESTRA See MUSIC

LAMB'S PLAYERS THEATRE

Lamb's Players Theatre
1142 Orange Avenue
Coronado, CA 92118
Info: (619) 474-3385 **Rsvn:** (619) 474-4542
Fax: (619) 474-6156
Artistic Director: Robert Smyth
340-seat theater in Coronado.

Lamb's began life as street theater in Minnesota. Realizing (by Thanksgiving!) that the season for outdoor street theater in Minnesota was not terribly long, the company migrated to the mellow climate of San Diego in 1972. When Producing Artistic Director Robert Smyth joined up in 1976, he shepherded the company towards the purchase of a former Christian Scientist church in National City, which it renovated into a cozy 200-seat theater-in-the-round.

The lambs are on the move again. By the time you read this, they will have moved to their new state-of-the-art theater in a renovated opera house in Coronado. They promise the thrust stage and additional 140 seats won't compromise the intimate theater the company is known for.

The new location is within walking distance of the dramatic Hotel Del Coronado; there are also plenty of restaurants in the area. If you're coming from across the Bay, the bridge toll will be paid by Lamb's Theatre. Dress is still casual, except, traditionally for the annual Christmas shows.

Performances
Year-round Wed-Thurs 7:30 pm; Fri-Sat 8 pm; Sat-Sun 2 pm
Tickets
$16-21
Discounts
Children/seniors/students/groups of 15+, call BO
BO
Mon-Fri 10 am-5 pm; check/AE/Disc/MC/V/reserve by mail, fax, Art Tix; refunds and exchanges to subscribers only; subscription program
Parking
On street

LAMB'S PLAYERS THEATRE—Resident Co.

One of the San Diego area's best-kept secrets is the consistent, low-key excellence of the Lamb's Players, the area's only true repertory theater. Lamb's employs a staff of 19, about 16 of whom perform on stage in addition to other duties. The familiarity of faces fosters a sense of community in this highly professional little company. It's not uncommon for one's favorite Lamb's performer to be taking ticket orders at the box office, constructing sets or designing the lights.

The Lambs are bound together by "a commonality of Christian faith," and devotion to high-quality theater. The company has done wonderful missionary work for the secular likes of Shakespeare, Shaw, and Sheridan. Original and contemporary New York hits include *Steel Magnolias*, *Amadeus*, and *The Boys Next Door*.

Though the company leans toward the uplifting or enlightening, choices can range from *The Diary of Anne Frank* to Ionesco's *Rhinoceros* to Lanford Wilson's *Talley's Folly*. Still, Lamb's does pack in the faithful of all faiths with its holiday-oriented shows (sold separately from its season). *St. John's Gospel* is new to the Easter schedule. The company's annual hit, *A Festival of Christmas*, an original script, penned annually by Lamb's associate artistic producer, actress and resident playwright, Kerry Cederberg Meads, also includes much singing of Christmas carols. In recent years, the popularity of this show, which sometimes runs as often as three times a day, has led Lamb's to offer a second holiday show served after a sumptuous Victorian family-style feast.

Two or three times a year, the Lamb's Players venture downtown to play the Lyceum—and to entice new audiences to its home, which is just five minutes from downtown San Diego. Watch for info about the former National City location, which the company is using for other projects.

LANCASTER PERFORMING ARTS CENTER

750 West Lancaster Boulevard
Lancaster, CA 93534
Info: (805) 723-5940 **Rsvn:** (805) 723-5950
Fax: (805) 723-5945
Center for music, dance, theater, and variety shows; seats 758 in the main stage theater, 100 in the black box.

Eight years of planning and $10.5 million later, the town of Lancaster (90 miles northeast of Los Angeles) is in the theater biz. The neonate, high-tech facility serves this community of only 100,000 in grand style. Even Los Angeles residents are making the trek to the new complex in the Antelope Valley. Ticket prices are affordable; there's free parking and good local restaurants. Sounds like Mecca to me!

The center presents a wide spectrum of entertainment. Dance has included Lar Lubovitch Dance Co. It's also hosted Vienna Boys Choir, Chinese Magic Revue, and Emmylou Harris and Band, among others. Touring stage productions make the scene, and the center's new community theater, Cedar Street, mounts productions on the main stage as well as in the smaller facility.

The arts center was designed to accommodate "packaged" professional shows in the 758-seat main stage theater. Already the space has proven to be perfect for producers' rehearsals and tryouts of star-studded shows before they move on to the major markets.

The theater itself is wide, and the back row is only 96 feet from the stage. The front row is a favorite for some shows (especially for the comedy shows), but not recommended for dance programs—you can't see the feet! The other facility is the 100-seat black box theater.

Series tickets can be purchased for dance, classical music, theater, family, or children's performances. Single tickets are plentiful.

Performances
Mon-Sun 7:30 or 8 pm,
Sat-Sun 2 or 3 pm
Tickets
$5-75
Discounts
Children/students/
groups of 20+, call
BO
Tues-Sat noon-6 pm
and 1 hr before
performance through
intermission; check/MC/
V/reserve by mail, fax;
no refunds, no
exchanges; subscription
program
Location
Adjacent to Hwy 14 on
10th St W of Lancaster
Blvd
Parking
On premises; street
parking

LANDIS AUDITORIUM

4800 Magnolia Avenue
Riverside, CA 92506
Info: (714) 684-3240 ext. 325 **Rsvn:** (714) 684-9337
Fax: (714) 275-0651
Artistic Director: Gary D. Schultz
Seats 1,378 patrons for theater, music, and dance.

Set on the campus of Riverside Community College, Landis is home to Performance/Riverside, which encompasses Riverside Civic Light Opera, the Pops, Celebrity Series, and Conservatory Series (see those headings for more information), as well as some outside performances by organizations like the Riverside Ballet Theatre. Usual community-theater fare also takes to the mainstage: *Evita*, *Into the Woods* and *The Wiz*, as well as plays such as *The Crucible* and *Our Town*. Community support is broad-based, and both casting and audience subscriptions draw heavily from the surrounding neighborhoods.

As a structure, the Landis Auditorium is quite serviceable and fairly comfortable. The stage is larger than most and easily converted from proscenium to thrust. But sit at least 10 rows from the orchestra pit for a better view. In fact, the better sound is also to the rear of the house.

Adjacent to the mainstage is a small backstage studio theater seating 100.

Candy, cookies, coffee and soft drinks are offered in the lobby.

Also see **Performance/Riverside** for:

Riverside Civic Light Opera
Riverside Celebrity Series
Riverside Conservatory Series

Riverside Pops See **MUSIC**

Performances
Thurs-Sat 8 pm; Sat-Sun 2 pm
Tickets
$10.50- 13
Discounts
Groups of 20+, call Mike at (714) 684-5917
BO
Mon-Fri 12:30-5:30; MC/V/check/reserve by mail, fax (714) 684-5917; TicketMaster; exchanges made with 24 hrs notice for subscribers only; subscription program
Location
Between 14th and Magnolia; S of the 60 Fwy and W of the 91 Fwy
Parking
On premises, FREE; street parking

LANNAN FOUNDATION

See press listings for performance locations.
Info: (310) 306-1004 **Fax:** (310) 578-6445
Director of Literary Programs: Meg Brazill
Poetry and prose readings by distinguished authors; readings at the Center Green Theatre at the Pacific Design Center, 8687 Melrose Avenue, West Hollywood.

A surprisingly under-publicized multi-arts organization, the Lannan Foundation hosts a literary series that often performs to packed houses. Acclaimed authors read their works aloud followed by a discussion with Michael Silverblatt, the radio host of KCRW's "Bookworm."

The Tuesday and Thursday evening event, titled "Readings and Conversations," takes place at the Center Green Theatre inside the dazzling Pacific Design Center. With an annual schedule that reads like a Who's Who of the literary world, you can expect the 382-seat theater to fill up year after year. Poetry and fiction writers William H. Gass, Jimmy Santiago Baca, George Evans, and Amy Tan headed a recent line-up. I recommend you make reservations well in advance.

Occasionally, there are free events in the foundation's Poetry Garden, which also require reservations.

Performances
Sept-May
Tickets
$5 general, $2.50 seniors/students
Discounts
Seniors/students
BO
Tues-Sat; AE/MC/V/ check/reserve by mail, Tickets LA (213) 660-8587; no exchanges
Parking
On premises, $1.50; street parking

LAS PALMAS THEATER

1642 Las Palmas Avenue
Hollywood, CA 90028
Info: (213) 957-5728 **Rsvn:** (213) 957-5728
Seats 375 for plays, musicals, dance, comedy, and concerts.

    The original home of Susan Dietz's LA Stage Company, the Las Palmas has recently played host to *Together Again* (with Sid Caesar and Imogene Coca), *Quilters*, *The Normal Heart*, and an intimately staged *A Chorus Line*.

    The theater affords fine unobstructed sightlines even from the back of the house.

Location
Off Hollywood (101) Fwy, 2 blocks E of Highland Ave, 1/2 block S of Hollywood Blvd
Parking
Nearby, $4.50; street parking

LA THEATRE WORKS

Guest Quarters Suite Hotel
1707 4th Street
Santa Monica, CA 90401
Info: (310) 827-0808 **Rsvn:** (213) 660-8587
Fax: (310) 827-4949
Produces the new plays of established and emerging playwrights in a variety of venues; Radio Drama is recorded in-studio and broadcast over KCRW radio (89.9 FM); Radio Theatre Series for New Plays.

    It has been quite a long time since LATW surfaced with a stage play, and it's possible that they may never return to the stage, what with the sagging arts market. But if they do, you'll have an opportunity to watch one of the most dynamic companies in Los Angeles. Committed to the "discovery and development" of contemporary theater, LATW produced new plays of unknown and known writers from the U.S. and abroad. Its track record in premiering arresting new works is mighty impressive. Highly visible actors and directors are recruited to bring their work to life.

    Wooman Lovely Wooman, What A Sex You Are! starring Miriam Margolyes finished an SRO run at the Tiffany Theater in 1990. *Bouncers*, by John Godber, won seven LA Drama Critics' Circle Awards before moving to Off-Broadway in 1987. Numerous international, national, and local drama awards have gone to the company over the years.

    Equally electric is the LATW commitment to Radio Dramas. Begun in 1987 with high-voltage talent such as Marsha Mason, Edward Asner, and Amy Irving, Radio Dramas delivers full-length novels, short stories, and classic American plays as close as your nearest radio. The in-studio recordings can be heard over National Public Radio's KCRW radio.

    LATW's recent "The Play's the Thing" Radio Theatre Series for New Plays offers live-in-performance recordings staged before an audience and broadcast later over KCRW. These special performances, which also utilize top-name talent such as Jason Alexander, Judith Ivey, and Joe Mantegna, are usually sold out, so be sure to get your tickets early. (Call to be put on the mailing list.)

    Here's an idea: Make dining reservations at the 4th Street Grille in the Guest Quarters Suite Hotel (310/395-3332 or 395-7800) and receive preferred seating for the radio performance. You must be able to show your theater tickets to get those reserved seats.

Performances
Wed-Thurs 8 pm
Tickets
$20
Discounts
Groups of 20+, $2 off
BO
Mon-Sun noon-7 pm, performance days 6 pm-8 pm; check/AE/MC/V; mail (call); Theatix (213) 466-1767; no refunds, no exchanges; subscription program
Parking
On premises, $3

LAWRENCE WELK RESORT THEATRE

8860 Lawrence Welk Drive
Escondido, CA 92026
Info: (619) 749-3000   **Rsvn:** (619) 749-3448
Fax: (619) 749-6182
Artistic Director: Frank Wayne
Dinner-theater (restaurant in separate location) seating 331 for Broadway-style musicals.

For people who grew up loving the music of Lawrence Welk, going to the Lawrence Welk Resort Theatre is a lot like going to Disneyland: it's clean, it's neat—and that's meant literally and figuratively. Lawrence Welk hailed from North Dakota with a fourth-grade education. He created a television world in which everything was "wunnerful"—no poverty, no crime, no hemlines above the knee. He achieved that same safe, clean feeling in the nearly 1,000-acre Lawrence Welk Village, primarily designed as a retirement community. The theater opened in 1981 with Dorothy Lamour in Neil Simon's *Barefoot in the Park*, but it has since concentrated primarily on musicals like *The Sound of Music*, *Oliver*, and *Cabaret*, adapted for the Welk's continental-style 331-seat auditorium stage.

For some, the LWRT is not so "wunnerful." Critics harp mercilessly on the "orchestra"—three musicians who play synthesizers along with a trumpet and a piano. The sets are minimal, mostly paint and fabric, and the cast of most shows have been severely scaled down to fit the shallow stage. But the Welk is a professional theater, actually the only fully professional for-profit theater in Southern California. And at times artistic director Frank Wayne pulls all the pieces together with remarkable aplomb. The Welk can and does bomb, but its productions of *She Loves Me* and *The Unsinkable Molly Brown* were standouts. Wayne, artistic director since 1987, is trying to get the theater to stretch a bit. Recently he offered *A Chorus Line*—after taking out the four-letter words in the dialogue of course. The jury is still out as to whether people who go to the Lawrence Welk Resort Theatre want good theater, or just want the world that Welk built. Perhaps Wayne will prove that we can have both. This dinner theater not only serves its meal before the show, it serves it at a nearby restaurant on the resort grounds two hours before performances. An open-air tram transports you to the theater and back again. The delicious buffet adds as little as $3 to $6 to your ticket depending on the performance date. Parking is free at the resort.

The regular patrons, mostly senior citizens, *kvell* over the legendary Lawrence Welk as they pass his life-size bronze statue, the bronze musical notes in the ground, the giant paper cut-out of Welk, the huge crystal Champagne Glass and the museum dedicated to the story of his life inside the theater itself.

Avoid jeans, cut-offs, and minis; in deference to the Welk devotees, you should try to dress as if you were going to audition for The Man himself.

There are special packages for those who wish to combine theatergoing with a stay at the Lawrence Welk Hotel and work in some golf or tennis on the side.

Performances
Tues, Thurs-Sat 8 pm
(dinner buffet 5:30 pm-
7:30 pm); Tues-Thurs,
Sun 1:45 pm (luncheon
buffet 11 am- 1:15 pm)
Tickets
$26-36
Discounts
Children/students/
groups of 15+, call (619)
749-8501
BO
Mon-Sun 9 am-5 pm;
AE/MC/V/reserve by
mail; subscription
program; no exchanges
Location
N from San Diego, take
Int-15, Gopher Canyon
Rd exit; from Int-5 take
78 E at Oceanside, to
15 N at Escondido
Parking
On premises, FREE;
street parking

LEX THEATER

6760 Lexington Avenue
Hollywood, CA 90038
Info: (213) 463-6244   **Rsvn:** (213) 463-6244
Artistic Director: Jill C. Klein
49-seat theater staging new plays, classics and everything in between.

Home base for the Actors Conservatory Ensemble, this little theater in the heart of Hollywood has an accommodating lobby and a concession counter serving up coffee, beer, wine, sodas, and homemade sweets. The sightlines and acoustics are both good.

The location is convenient to after- or before-theater eats for Thai food at Chan Dara (Cahuenga and Sunset) or to my personal favorite Italian restaurant, Marino's on Melrose near Cole.

Performances
Fri-Tues 8 pm, Sun 2 pm
Tickets
$10
Discounts
Seniors/groups of 10+, call BO
BO
Check/reserve by phone
Location
Off Hollywood (101) Fwy at Highland; 1 block N of Santa Monica, 1 block E of Highland Ave
Parking
On street
Special Features
Occasional discussions after performances

ACTORS CONSERVATORY ENSEMBLE (ACE)— Resident Co.

ACE's core group of actors first convened 15 years ago while studying at the famous Loft Studio of Peggy Feury and Bill Traylor. When their master teachers passed away, the disciples formed this West Coast ensemble and now perform at The Lex.

The performances range from new plays to classics to late-night reviews. A pocket-book friendly theater, all preview performances are free. But this is a happy instance of not getting what you pay for, as the cast is an ace bunch to be sure.

THE LIMELIGHT THEATER

10634 Magnolia Boulevard
North Hollywood, CA 91601
Info: (818) 990-2324   **Rsvn:** (818) 990-2324
Theater seats 44.

North Hollywood is fast becoming the cultural hub of the San Fernando Valley. Its Limelight Theater, one block west of Cahuenga, is one of the Northern Lights to start up shop in NoHo's Arts District.

Up until now a rental space, the Limelight is home to Onstage Company, which has at its head director/playwright Mel Shapiro. Onstage premiered with *Misanthrope*, and set it in a ubiquitous LA gym.

Parking is available out back and on the street.

Entre Nous and Val's are two restaurant selections in nearby Toluca Lake.

Performances
Fri-Sat 8 pm; Sun 7 pm
Tickets
$ varies
Discounts
Vary from show to show
BO
Call theatre
Location
1 block W of Cahuenga about 1/2 mile N of Ventura (134) Fwy
Parking
On premises (limited), FREE; street parking

LINDHURST THEATRE See **Pepperdine University Center for the Arts**

LITTLE VICTORY THEATRE See **Victory Theatre**

LOBERO THEATRE

33 East Canon Perdido Street
Santa Barbara, CA 93101
Info: (805) 962-1458   **Rsvn:** (805) 963-0761
Fax: (805) 962-4857
Seats 680 for performances by the Santa Barbara Chamber Orchestra, Santa Barbara Dance Theater, the Pasadena Playhouse, and Gilbert & Sullivan Company.

The Lobero is California's oldest continuously operating theater, built in 1873 by an Italian immigrant as the state's first opera house south of San Francisco. By 1924, the old Lobero (which had at various times been known as Lobero's Theatre and the New Opera House), was torn down and rebuilt. The present theater stands on the original site but now hosts much more than opera. The Lobero Foundation sponsors a performing arts series that includes plays, musicals, dance, travel films, and music in a five-event Great Performances subscription series. The Family Series brings the Missoula Childrens' Theatre, the Santa Barbara Dance Theater and others to the Lobero stage.

In addition to its principal tenants, the Santa Barbara Chamber Orchestra and the Santa Barbara Dance Theater, the Lobero recently welcomed the Pasadena Playhouse after the Santa Barbara Civic Light Opera departed. The Playhouse (which also does a stint in Poway) brings with it six shows each year. Tickets for these shows are available by calling (800) 883-PLAY; at the Lobero Theatre box office two weeks prior to opening; or through TicketMaster.

P.S.: Don't believe the rumors about the Lobero shutting down for a year to make seismic safety improvements to the structure. The Lobero is going to undergo an earthquake code upgrade, but it'll still be business as usual at this historic theater. To make this work, the renovations will only shake up the theater's schedule for six weeks a year for three years starting in 1994.

Performances
 Mon-Sun
Tickets
 $12-30
Discounts
 Previews/children/ seniors/students/groups of 12+, call BO
BO
 Mon-Fri noon-5:30 pm; check/AE/MC/V/reserve by mail; subscription program
Location
 Between State and Anacapa Sts
Parking
 Behind premises in city lot, FREE

LONG BEACH CIVIC LIGHT OPERA See **Terrace Theater**

LONG BEACH COMMUNITY PLAYHOUSE—MAINSTAGE THEATRE AND STUDIO THEATRE

5021 East Anaheim Street
Long Beach, CA 90804
Info: (310) 494-1014   **Rsvn:** (310) 494-1616
Community theater seating 200; presents an annual season of two musicals, and six contemporary and classic dramas and comedies; Studio Theatre is a 99-seat plan performance space offering new, experimental and adult-oriented works, plus traditional plays and musicals.

In a city where houses and buildings get torn down and built up faster than you can drive crosstown in rush hour, anything that's been around for a decade counts as an historical monument. At 63 years old, then, the Long Beach Playhouse deserves the reverence accorded the pyramids.

The Mainstage forms a thrust stage with horseshoe seating for 200. In its "ancient" past, it has hosted more than 467 plays. But then, a theater doesn't stay around for 60-some-odd years because of its nice upholstery and accessible restrooms. Speaking of interiors, this one is comfortable (the air conditioning is not in its 60s) with unobstructed sightlines. Live music plays every Friday

Performances
 Fri-Sat 8 pm; selected Sun 2 pm
Tickets
 $9-14
Discounts
 Groups of 200+, call (groups can buy out a house)
BO
 Mon, Tues and Thurs 3 pm-8 pm, Wed 3-6 pm, Fri-Sat 3:30-8 pm, Sun 1:30-2 pm; check/MC/V/ reserve by phone, mail, box office exchanges with 12 hrs notice; subscription program

and Saturday night before curtain time and at intermission in the Playhouse Gallery. Its rotating exhibit of local artists' paintings helps make the theater complex a sort of holistic arts center.

From the middle-of-the-road to practically off the road, the Long Beach Playhouse will go the distance with just about any kind of theater.

Performances are held in the Studio and Mainstage simultaneously. Seating is good in the Studio, with only seven rows of seats facing the proscenium stage.

Dress rehearsals are open for handicapped patrons. Call for information.

Coffee, soft drinks, and wine are served at intermission in the Gallery. For pre-theater eats, you might want to grab a pastrami on rye at neighboring Jay's Deli.

Location
Off Pacific Coast Hwy on Anaheim St between Clark and Ximeno

Parking
On premises, FREE; street parking

Special Features
Dress rehearsals for handicapped

LONG BEACH CONVENTION & ENTERTAINMENT CENTER See **Center Theater** and **Terrace Theater** Also **Long Beach Arena** in **MUSIC**

LOS ANGELES CIVIC LIGHT OPERA

LACLO is a presenting organization that imports national touring companies such as *Guys and Dolls*, *Camelot*, and *Cole!* to suitable local theaters, including the Pantages, the Henry Fonda, and the Wilshire.

LOS ANGELES CONTEMPORARY EXHIBITIONS See **LACE**

LOS ANGELES MUSIC CENTER See **Music Center of Los Angeles County**

LOS ANGELES PIERCE COLLEGE PERFORMING ARTS BUILDING

6201 Winnetka Avenue
Woodland Hills, CA 92128
Info: (818) 719-6488   **Rsvn:** (818) 719-6488
Main Stage holds 375, Arena stage can seat 95.

One of many campuses in the Los Angeles Community College system, Pierce sits atop a hill in the West Valley, offering a pastoral setting that belies its urban location. The Performing Arts Building, built in 1981, is called upon primarily for the Theater Department's productions and classes.

Full-scale Theater Department student productions see life on the Main Stage each year (two each in the fall and spring semesters), plus one production for children (during either semester). Two recent productions, *The Heidi Chronicles* and *Green Card* (not the movie), achieved high enough marks to carry them all the way into the American College Theater Festival. Besides the Main Stage shows, Pierce presents an annual fall TheaterFest in its smaller Arena Stage. The weekend festival of student-produced (as well as directed and acted) one-acts is usually held in December.

Music, dance, and other performing arts events are also on the schedule. Los Angeles' Music Guild has expanded to offer an annual series here, as well.

Parking is FREE and plentiful.

Performances
Thurs-Sat 8 pm; Sun 2 pm

Tickets
$5-6

Discounts
Children/seniors/students/groups of 10+, contact theatre manager

BO
Mon-Fri 10 am-4 pm; open one hr prior to curtain; check/reserve by mail; exchanges made on availability; subscription program

Location
Between Victory and Ventura; near the Ventura (101) Fwy, exit Winnetka

Parking
On premises, FREE

Special Features
Free preview performances for student groups

LOS ANGELES THEATRE ACADEMY

Los Angeles City College
855 North Vermont Avenue
Los Angeles, CA 90029
Info: (213) 953-4337 **Rsvn:** (213) 953-4528
Fax: (213) 666-4294
Chairman: Winston Butler
Made up of the 299-seat Camino, 99-seat Caminito, and 75-seat Cameo stages.

This professional theater school located at Los Angeles Community College consistently offers the public outstanding, top-caliber productions. Established in 1929, it's one of the older drama academies in the U.S. Its productions have won a "consistently high standards" from the LA Drama Critics Circle. A recent performance of *The Grapes of Wrath*, a City Playhouse production (see below), garnered accolades from the *LA Times* and was so popular it was brought back in the fall.

Second- and third-year students act as a resident company on the Academy's three in-house performance spaces: the main Camino stage and the smaller Caminito and Cameo stages. Past students include Alan Arkin, James Coburn, Jose Quintero, Donna Reed, Robert Vaughn, Paul Winfield, Cindy Williams, and Hugh O'Brien.

Parking on campus is advised, as this is not the safest of neighborhoods. There's a well-lighted school parking lot on Heliotrope Avenue, west of Vermont, just above Melrose. All but the Cameo are handicap accessible.

New to the Academy is a relationship with the emerging City Playhouse, a professional company that will do one show each semester with the Academy, casting professional actors, alumni, and some students. Watch for it.

Performances
Oct-June; Wed-Sat 8 pm; Sat 2 pm
Tickets
$10
Discounts
Seniors/students/children/groups of 10+, call BO
BO
Mon-Fri 9 am-7 pm; phone reservations Mon-Fri 9 am-5 pm; check/AE/MC/V/reserve by mail; exchanges made upon availability; subscription series
Location
Corner Melrose and Vermont; Melrose exit off Hollywood (101) Fwy
Parking
On premises, FREE; street
Special Features
Open rehearsals

LOS ANGELES THEATRE CENTER

514 South Spring Street
Los Angeles, CA 90013
Info: (213) 627-6500 **Fax:** (213) 847-3169
Multi-stage theater, home to a dozen local theater groups.

In the heady days of the mid-'80s, an arts-happy Los Angeles ballyhooed the coming of its own municipal theater which would be housed in a renovated historic downtown bank building. When it finally hit town, critics, actors, and audiences swarmed over it. The shows were exciting, new and original. They ushered in the birth of the term "multicultural" in terms of themes, performers—and perhaps more importantly—audiences. Reportedly, 38 percent of the annual quarter-million people attending LATC were non-white.

Now, only eight years after its arrival, "audacious, controversial" LATC as we knew it, is gone, like many a victim of shrinking funding sources, economic malaise, and controversial decisions. To protect the substantial public investment in LATC, the City has taken over the facility while evaluating operations options and exploring the best means to maximize its value as a shared resource among the City's artistic communities and general population. For now, its stages have been turned into rental spaces with a cooperative of performing arts organizations given first call on the five-theater venue. The 10-member coop includes Will & Co., Airshow (Phyllis Frelich's deaf theater group), Bilingual Foundation of the Arts, Cold Tofu (an Asian-American comedy theater group), Co/Real Artists (an African-American performing arts company), LA Directors

Performances
Vary
Tickets
$10-18
Discounts
Vary from production to production
BO
Hrs vary
Location
E of Harbor (110) Fwy, between 5th and 6th on Spring St; N of Santa Monica (10) Fwy
Parking
On premises (lot next door), $5; limited street parking

Project, Music Center Opera, Mark Taper Forum, and Artists' Collective (a 10-member group of smaller, emerging theater companies and former LATC education and training labs).

As we go to press, four of these groups have not actually performed at LATC under the new arrangement (which is why you won't be reading about some of them in this book). Until on-site box office services are restored, each producer is responsible for promotion and ticket sales of its own programs. Calls to the main LATC number will result in a referral to the appropriate group.

LOST STUDIO

130 South La Brea Avenue
Los Angeles, CA 90036
Info: (213) 933-6944
Artistic Director: Cinda Jackson
75-seat theater.

Though busy with two or three annual in-house productions and some six or eight rentals, this stage is primarily an acting studio with ongoing classes and important workshops such as Circus Minimus. It was originally The Loft Studio, founded some two decades ago by Peggy Feury and William Traylor. The Blank Theatre uses it for its 39-week reading series.

Performances
Mon-Sun 8 pm; Sun matinee time varies
Tickets
$6-15
Discounts
Previews/children/ seniors/students/groups, depends on production
BO
1 hr before performance; check/AE
Location
2 blocks S of Beverly Blvd; 7 blocks N of Wilshire Blvd
Parking
On street

LOWELL DAVIES FESTIVAL THEATRE See **Simon Edison Centre for Performing Arts**

LOYOLA MARYMOUNT UNIVERSITY THEATRE ARTS AND DANCE DEPARTMENT

7101 West 80th Street
Los Angeles, CA 90045
Info: (310) 338-2837   **Rsvn:** (310) 338-7588
The University's Strub Theater seats 174 for department performances.

The Strub (pronounced "Strewb") theater is the main stage of Loyola's theater arts and dance department. The shows are student-performed and faculty-directed. Occasionally, guest directors and choreographers from the professional world are invited to work with the students.

Major productions each year in the Strub include a three-play series and two dance concerts, usually held in April. At least one solid family show is featured each year.

Performances
Wed-Sat 8 pm
Tickets
$5-7
Discounts
Students/groups of 20+, call BO
BO
Mon-Fri 9 am-5 pm check/reserve by mail
Location
Between Manchester and 80th, and Sepulveda and Lincoln; near San Diego (405) Fwy
Parking
On premises, FREE

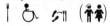

LYCEUM SPACE/LYCEUM STAGE See **San Diego Repertory Theatre**

MAGIC MASK See **Teatro Mascara Magica**

MAGNIFICENT MOORPARK MELODRAMA & VAUDEVILLE THEATRE

45 East High Street
Moorpark, CA 93021
Info: (805) 529-2599   **Rsvn:** (805) 529-1212
Fax: (805) 529-9412
A 306-seat professional vaudeville and melodrama theater.

Looking for some G-rated entertainment? Want to add some "mellow" drama to your life? Well, bear with me anyway.

In this Victorian-era theater in Moorpark (that's in Simi Valley for those who never drive north—or south—of Studio City), you'll be taught the "ancient" art of booing, hissing, and of course cheering. Performers in costume act as greeters, snack bar servers, and ushers. Just before the show begins, an MC lists the few rules (no projectiles, is one) and instructs you in how to "boo" the villain, "cheer" the hero, and "hummina" the heroine (in today's world, that probably means sexual harassment). Next you get a two-act musical comedy—maybe *Beauty & the Beast*, *Connecticut Yankee*, or *Dracula*. A third act is reserved for vaudeville performances by comedians, dancers, and songsters.

There are seven comedies a year running Thursday through Sunday evenings, plus a 3 pm Saturday performance and a Sunday matinee.

If you've schlepped out here and want to stoke up first, try the nearby Hunan Gourmet Inn or the Coffee Grinder. But no hissing these waiters!

Performances
Thurs 7 pm; Fri 8 pm; Sat 3 pm, 8 pm; Sun 7 pm, and 2 pm once every 8 weeks
Tickets
$9.50-12
Discounts
Children/seniors/students/groups of 20+, call reservation desk
BO
Mon-Sun noon-5 pm, and during performances; MC/V/check/reserve by mail, fax; 24 hr notice needed to cancel or exchange; subscription program
Location
At the W end of the 118 Fwy—go straight for 4 miles to "Old Town" Moorpark; Ventura (101) Fwy. to 23 Fwy N to the end—straight 3 lights to Moorpark Ave, right to High St, right
Parking
On premises, FREE; street parking

MARK TAPER FORUM See **Music Center of Los Angeles County**

MASCARA MAGICA See **Teatro Mascara Magica**

MATRIX THEATER

7657 Melrose Avenue
Los Angeles, CA 90046
Info: (213) 653-3279   **Rsvn:** (213) 852-1445
99-seat Melrose Avenue theater.

Joe Stern is living proof that you can come home again. Stern is owner of West Hollywood's Matrix, which has been a rental house since 1989. During that period, Stern was producing TV's "Law & Order" in New York.

Joseph Stern was the producing artistic director of Actors for Themselves from 1975 to 1989. Under his guidance, the company netted 19 Drama Critics Awards and 31 *LA Weekly* awards. He birthed *Harry Chapin Lies and Legends*, which enjoyed profitable runs nationwide and premiered the explosive *Orphans* by Lyle Kessler.

Now he's back to his prime Melrose Avenue location amid the trendiest of shops in the theater that, during his absence, provided local groups with a "hot spot" for their productions. Before returning to LA, Stern

Performances
Thurs-Sat 8 pm; Sun 2:30 pm, 7 pm
Tickets
$18
BO
Daily 10 am-6 pm; reserve by phone; MC/V/AE
Location
On Melrose Ave between La Brea and Fairfax Aves
Parking
On street

announced "a surprise" for local audiences, and indeed his production of George M. Cohan's *The Tavern* fulfilled that promise with its revolving cast of well-known local actors and went on to garner the most nominations from the 1993 Los Angeles Drama Critics.

THE MCCALLUM THEATRE FOR THE PERFORMING ARTS AT THE BOB HOPE CULTURAL CENTER

73000 Fred Waring Drive
Palm Desert, CA 92260
Info: (619) 346-6505   **Rsvn:** (619) 340-ARTS
Fax: (619) 341-9508
Seats 1,125 for plays, concerts, dance, and variety shows.

The Palm Springs area, long known as a retirement base for the over-60 set, will spring a few surprises on you if you haven't been lately. Its active, vital population, always looking for things to do and spend its big bucks on, supports international talent in a lavish way. The lovely contemporary McCallum Theatre bursts with activity year-round. Whether you live in the area or drive in often, you'll want to know about the variety of scheduled events. (Want to known how to get in good with the retired in-laws? Buy them tickets to the McCallum as birthday and anniversary gifts.)

The talent spans generations of ticket-buyers: from Leontyne Price to Penn & Teller, Hubbard Street Dance to Mummenschanz, The Four Tops to World Cup Figure Skating Champions to *The Will Rogers Follies*. Along with the full schedule of drama and musical theater, jazz and symphony performances are family programs. The Showstoppers Series packages a season of hoofers like The Rockettes, or nightingales like Dionne Warwick with showstoppers like Tommy Tune and Liza Minelli.

The theater seats are continental style (no center aisle). The front-row Founder's Level is ideal, but center rear orchestra wasn't bad for one recent musical. (If you're attending with children, they'll probably end up on your lap from back there.) Note that Founder's Level seats are sold only on a single ticket basis—no season subscribers. On the other hand, you'll have a tough time getting single tickets to the Showstoppers Series.

Performances
Mon-Sun (show time varies with artists); closed in Aug
Tickets
$20-80 (varies with artist)
BO
Mon-Sun 9 am-curtain on performance days; 9 am-5 pm non-performance days; AE/MC/V/check/reserve by mail, fax, TicketMaster; returns or exchanges made when possible; subscription program
Location
Off San Bernandino (10) Fwy, exit Monterey to Fred Waring Dr, corner of Monterey and Fred Waring Dr
Parking
On premises, FREE; valet, FREE but tips encouraged

MELROSE THEATER

733 North Seward Avenue
Hollywood, CA 90038
Info: (213) 465-1885   **Rsvn:** (213) 465-1885
Seats 82 for new plays, revivals, improvisation.

For 26 years the Melrose operated its own lively resident company. Now it contents itself with presenting outside work ranging from original plays (last year's *One Last Ride* garnered rave reviews), to revivals (Noel Coward's *Present Laughter* received three LA Drama Critics Awards), to comedy-improvisational shows (*Funny You Should Ask* proved a popular hit).

Located on a peaceful residential street just off busy Melrose Avenue, the only negative prospect is finding parking. The 82 seats are well situated without obstructions. Actually, this is one of the roomier "small" theaters in town.

Performances
Thurs-Sat 8 pm, Sun 3 and 7 pm
Tickets
$ varies
Discounts
Previews/children/seniors/students/groups of 10+, call
BO
1/2 hr before performance; varies from show to show
Location
S of Hollywood (101) Fwy, 5 blocks E of Highland Ave and 1/2 block N of Melrose
Parking
On premises, FREE

THE MET THEATRE

1089 North Oxford Street
Los Angeles, CA 90029
Info: (213) 957-1831   **Rsvn:** (213) 957-1152
99-seat space; stage can be transformed into proscenium, thrust, or in-the-round.

 Originally this Oxford Street space housed the Los Angeles Actors Theatre, which moved downtown to become the late Los Angeles Theatre Center. Later it became home to the West Coast branch of Ensemble Studio Theatre. The Met took it over and created a spacious venue with very good, very raked seating. One geographical note: the box office is on the street, the lobby upstairs.

 If past history is any indication, the Met has a great future. Their production of *East Texas Hot Links* was a bell-ringer. Its Great Writer Series has become very popular and sells out quickly. The Radio Plays Series returns every so often with live performances of radio dramas and comedies of the '30s, and '40s performed by stars of stage and screen. Big names play its stage: Beth Henley brought her *Control Freaks* here, and placed Holly Hunter in the lead; Peter Fonda directed *Southern Rapture*, with Sally Kirkland scheduled in the cast.

 Given the location of the theater, I'd either opt for before- or after-dinner fare in Hollywood (Musso & Frank's), Cha Cha Cha in Los Feliz, or farther southwest at Marino's on Melrose.

Performances
Vary
Tickets
$15
Discounts
Previews/seniors/
students/groups of 20+,
call
BO
Varies; MC/V/
TicketMaster
(depending on producer)
Location
1 block E of Western
Ave; 1/2 block S of
Santa Monica Blvd
Parking
On premises, $3; valet,
$3; street parking

MOJO ENSEMBLE

1540 North Cahuenga Boulevard
Hollywood, CA 90028
Info: (213) 957-0690   **Rsvn:** (213) 960-1604
Artistic Director: Michele Martin
Seats 64.

 In a world of rising costs and diminishing grants, Mojo offers a dramatic look at theater behind the scenes as well as in front. Mojo Ensemble performs in the former American New Theatre, a comfortable, well-appointed small theater reached through a parking courtyard off Cahuenga Boulevard in Hollywood.

 In its brief history, the group has made a name for itself and garnered numerous awards. It will be remembered for its award-winning production of Judi Ann Mason's *Indigo Blues*.

 Although the company takes risks and likes to exhibit its "we do it our way" sensibility, upon closer inspection it's obvious there are some bright thinkers and marketers in the company who reduce any potential risk with some neck-saving research. Regular patrons are invited to the yearly work-in-progress festival where they view a potential mainstage piece produced with minimal sets and minimal rehearsal. Following the performance is an open discussion. Given a fairly set audience, this is no doubt both a prudent and considerate mode of operation.

 Nonetheless, Mojo attracts new and established playwrights who write with a message in mind. The themes often hug the headlines, from spiritual hypocrisy, to homelessness, often with a multicultural bent.

 The company has expanded its regular season of four plays to include Family Theatre productions Sunday afternoons and Youth Theatre productions Saturday afternoons (see **CHILDREN** for further information). Stage of Grace, across the street, is the company's second stage, used primarily for the Festival of New Works. Look for the Mojo Ensemble sign above the American New Theatre sign.

Performances
Thurs-Sun 8 pm, 11 pm;
Sat-Sun 3 pm
Tickets
$4-15
Discounts
Previews/children/
seniors/students/groups
of 10+, call BO
BO
Open 45 min. before
performance; 24 hr
message machine;
check/AE/reserve by
mail; exchanges with 24
hrs notice
Location
Between Sunset and
Hollywood Blvds
Parking
Parking lot, $2.50; street
parking

Parking is quite convenient—just across the street in an attended lot.

MOONLIGHT AMPHITHEATRE
MOONLIGHT WINTER PLAYHOUSE

1200 Vale Terrace Drive
Vista, CA 92084
Info: (619) 724-6017   **Rsvn:** (619) 724-2110
Fax: (619) 945-7859
Artistic Director: Kathy M. Brombacher
Community theater presenting in summer at the amphitheater (450 reserved seats, 1,300 lawn seats), and in winter in the playhouse (175 seats on risers).

One of the most remarkable success stories in Vista has been the growth of the Moonlight Amphitheatre.

In 1981, high school drama teacher Kathy Brombacher persuaded the City of Vista to let her stage one musical in Brengle Terrace Park at 1200 Vale Terrace Drive. The surroundings and the facilities were primitive, but patrons flocked to the theater under the stars. The grassy sloped, seatless amphitheater proved perfect for reclining with food and drinks while the music played. Over the years, Brombacher worked with the Vista Parks and Community Services Department, and a small group of generous patrons, to add seats alongside the picnic areas, a formal stage, lighting, a fully loaded snack bar, indoor rest room facilities, and other such niceties. But many families, particularly those with young children, still seem to enjoy spreading out on the grass with a blanket, picnic basket, and car seats for the babies.

Today, Brombacher is artistic director of an organization that presents four musicals and one Youth Theatre production during the summer, and a mixture of four dramas, a musical, and a Youth Theatre selection in its adjoining Moonlight Winter Playhouse (a makeshift recreation area with folding chairs and a stage). She still has ambitions to build a permanent cover over the stage, increase the seating, upgrade the backstage areas, improve the orchestra pit and replace Moonlight's Winter Playhouse with a new and improved facility.

Each year, the quality of the shows seems to improve. But despite the occasional inclusion of professional actors, Moonlight is still a community theater, produced as a cultural arts program by the City of Vista. That sometimes detracts from the overall polish, but it also keeps the cost of production down, which in turn keeps the cost of tickets down. (One good turn deserves another.)

You can either purchase tickets for seats or for picnic-style seating, you can bring your own low-back beach chairs (the backs can be no higher than 25 inches). Parking is free. Full dinners and box lunches are available from "Felicia's Under the Moonlight," an Italian restaurant which will deliver your orders phoned in 24 hours in advance: (619) 726-2057.

If you're in need of special assistance, don't let the description of the amphitheater keep you away: a special golf cart, The Moonlight Express, is at your service from 6 pm until curtain time to whisk you to your seat.

Dress for the outdoors.

Performances
Wed-Sun 8 pm; Sun 2 pm (Winter Playhouse only)
Tickets
$6-12
Discounts
Children/seniors/ students/groups of 20+, call BO
BO
Hrs vary during season; call BO (619) 724-2110 for further information; check/MC/ V/reserve by mail; subscription program
Location
Accessible from Hwy 78, Int-5 or 15; the major cross street from Vale Terrace Way is East Vista Way
Parking
On premises, FREE

MORGAN-WIXSON THEATER

2627 Pico Boulevard
Santa Monica, CA 90405
Info: (310) 828-7510   **Rsvn:** (310) 828-7519
Fax: (310) 393-9560
200-seat community theater.

    This picturesque community theater offers seven to eight shows a year and 200 seats a night. One of the West Coast's longest running community theaters, the Santa Monica Theatre Guild's space has presented some fine shows with professional-level talent and has brought us everything from musicals to *Cyrano de Bergerac*. Yet you'll find more than standard commercial fare. Past performances of *Ma Rainey's Black Bottom*, *Quilters*, and *Buried Child* have had good runs for the money here.

    This is also a popular spot for performances by local dance troupes.

Performances
Fri-Sat 8 pm; Sun 2 pm
Tickets
$7-10
Discounts
Children/seniors/
students/groups of 20+,
call BO
BO
Wed-Sat 4 pm-8 pm;
MC/V/reserve by mail;
exchanges up to 24 hrs
before performance;
subscription program
Location
Between 26th and Pico;
near Santa Monica (10)
Fwy
Parking
On street

MUSIC CENTER OF LOS ANGELES COUNTY

135 North Grand Avenue
Los Angeles, CA 90012
Info: (213) 972-7211

    Los Angeles' major performing arts complex sits on seven acres in the Bunker Hill area of downtown Los Angeles. The Music Center's birth dates back to 1964 when Dorothy Buffum Chandler spearheaded a drive to raise nearly $20 million in private and business contributions toward the $34.5 million needed to build the Center. The County of Los Angeles and the private sector came together and the Music Center became a reality.

    The Music Center Operating Company is the umbrella organization which actually manages the complex, while each of the resident companies is its own producing company.

    The Music Center Plaza is one of the only places in the city where you can get a true feeling of an arts complex. It's at once a place to stroll, listen to pre-theater entertainment, catch a free concert in the afternoon (fall and spring), grab a snack, watch the children tempt the pulsating fountain, and take a peek into the Center's gift shop.

    Three performance stages make up the Music Center: The Ahmanson, Dorothy Chandler Pavilion, and the Mark Taper Forum. Ground has been broken for the addition of the Walt Disney Concert Hall, a 2,380-seat space which will become the permanent home of the Los Angeles Philharmonic.

    The Center puts out a fine Community Guide that offers information, in English and Spanish, about what goes on at the Music Center and which community outreach programs are available. It also gives directions, parking and public transportation information, and box office phone numbers. Call to have a copy sent to you.

    Parking for the Music Center has been complicated by the commencement of building for Disney Hall. For now, the only parking available is at the outdoor lot at Temple and Grand, under the Music Center itself, or via the valet. For popular shows, don't wait till the last minute and expect to zip into a parking space.

Location
Off Santa Ana (5) Fwy N
take Hollywood (101) N,
exit Grand Ave, turn
right; from Santa Ana (5)
Fwy S, take Harbor
(110) Fwy S, exit Hill St,
at Temple turn right, at
Grand, turn left; located
between 1st and Temple
Sts and Hope St and
Grand Ave
Parking
Evenings, weekend
evenings, and matinees,
$6 beneath Music
Center (enter Grand
Ave); weekdays, $14
maximum; valet $15
(enter Hope St)

For information about the following Music Center resident companies and festivals:

Annual Holiday Celebration See **FESTIVALS & SEASONAL EVENTS**

Los Angeles Philharmonic See **MUSIC**

Hollywood Bowl Orchestra See **MUSIC**

Open House at the Hollywood Bowl See **CHILDREN**

Open House at the Music Center See **CHILDREN**

Symphonies for Youth See **CHILDREN**

Los Angeles Master Chorale See **MUSIC**

Los Angeles Music Center Opera See **MUSIC**

P.L.A.Y. (formerly Improvisational Theatre Project) See **CHILDREN**

Taper Lab New Work Festival See **FESTIVALS & SEASONAL EVENTS**

TGIF Noontime Concerts See **FESTIVALS & SEASONAL EVENTS**

Viva LA! See **FESTIVALS & SEASONAL EVENTS**

AHMANSON THEATRE

Info: (213) 972-7401   **Rsvn:** (800) 762-7666

As we go to press, the long-running *Phantom of the Opera* has closed and work has begun to reconfigure the Ahmanson to allow for flexible seating capable of changing from 1,250 to 2,000, depending on the performance, and thus improving its ability to host drama. The lobby and box office areas will also undergo massive facelifts to make the final product more harmonious with the Dorothy Chandler. In the meantime, the regular Ahmanson series will continue at the Doolittle Theatre in Hollywood.

Performances
Tues-Sat 8 pm; Sun 7:30 pm; Sat-Sun 2 pm

Tickets
$ varies

Discounts
Seniors/students/groups of 20+, call (213) 972-7539

BO
Sun 12 pm-6 pm; Mon 10 am-6 pm; Tues-Sat 10 am-8:30 pm; check/AE/MC/V/reserve by mail; subscription program

AHMANSON AT THE DOOLITTLE

1615 North Vine Street
Hollywood, CA 90028
Info: (213) 972-7401   **Rsvn:** (213) 365-3500
Fax: (213) 972-7431
Broadway-style theater seating 1,021.

The Doolittle is the closest thing we have to a Broadway theater. It's easy to get to, the parking is simple, and you don't have to drive miles afterwards for a late-night snack. Because of its size, it makes a nice theater experience. I only wish the seats were more comfortable. While I've been granted leg room in the first row of the balcony—just short of the nosebleed section—most folks over five-feet tall will agree that's not the case in the rest of the theater. You don't want to sit downstairs in the orchestra section underneath the overhang, either, where the sound is less than satisfactory.

Like the Music Center's sister theaters, the Ahmanson at the Doolittle has a Pay What You Can program for two designated performances of each production. There is also a Public Rush plan offering tickets (limit two) for $10, 10 minutes before curtain for every performance except Saturday evening. Senior Rush tickets can be purchased for a 50% discount 30 minutes before curtain (limit two tickets) with an appropriate ID.

Performances
Tues-Sat 8 pm; Sat-Sun 2 pm; sometimes Sun 7 pm and Thurs 2 pm

Tickets
$31-42

Discounts
Previews/seniors/students/groups of 20+, call (213) 972-7372

BO
Sun noon-6 pm; Mon 10 am-6 pm; Tues-Sat 10 am-8:30 pm; check/AE/MC/V/reserve by mail (135 N Grand Ave, Los Angeles, CA 90012), fax (213) 962-2936, TicketMaster; no refunds or exchanges; subscription program

Location
Near Hollywood (101) Fwy; between Hollywood Blvd and Sunset Blvd

(More. . .)

CENTER THEATRE GROUP—AHMANSON—Resident Co.

Ahmanson at the Doolittle: Don't let this imprimatur confuse you—all it means is that while *Phantom* was the sole play at the Ahmanson Theatre at the Music Center, the regular Ahmanson series of plays were—and are—taking place at the James A. Doolittle Theatre in Hollywood.

For the past four years, Gordon Davidson, who has been the Mark Taper's Artistic Director for a quarter of a century, has been the Producing Director of the Ahmanson at the Doolittle, scheduling seasons of dramas, comedies, classic revivals, musicals, and world premieres. This will continue until the construction on the Ahmanson at the Music Center is completed. In the meantime, the Doolittle series will proceed with its four play schedule. Over the years, the Ahmanson has featured such examples as *Jake's Women* by Neil Simon, Elizabeth Taylor and Maureen Stapleton in *The Little Foxes*, Robert Anderson's *I Never Sang for My Father*, and August Wilson's *The Piano Lesson*.

DOROTHY CHANDLER PAVILION 〰

Seats 3,000 for music and dance performances.

See **MUSIC** for more information.

The Dorothy Chandler Pavilion, which hosts numerous music performances, including, of course, the Los Angeles Philharmonic, the Music Center Opera, and the Master Chorale, can accommodate just over 3,000 people. Seats are comfortable, but I'm not a fan of continental seating—theaters without center aisles—no matter how much leg room there is. The information in the Music Chapter on the best seats for listening to the Los Angeles Philharmonic bears repeating here: On the Main Floor, it is best to find seats around the region of left-center (that's where most critics like to sit), away from the overhanging tiers. The Founders' Circle gives you the best-focused blend available, with the Loge and Balcony also being pretty good. Lately (Music Director) Salonen has been experimenting with new risers for the orchestra, and the results have been brighter and a bit more strident thus far.

Even for music groups and soloists, the Founders' Circle is still the best. Seating on the main floor is tricky, and you may have to experiment from performance to performance—not an inexpensive experiment! No matter what the concert, I don't recommend seats on the extreme ends and under the balcony.

MARK TAPER FORUM 〰

Info: (213) 972-7353 **Rsvn:** (213) 365-3500
Fax: (213) 972-0746

760-seat theater with a 3/4 thrust stage.

The Taper is considered the experimental theater in the group, and it's a wonderful space. Fourteen rows of seats rise from the floor in a semi-oval around the stage, and there's not a bad seat in the house.

Ask about Public Rush tickets, low-priced tickets available for purchase 10 minutes prior to curtain, and the Pay What You Can program, which offers a limited number of tickets to patrons who are on the honor system to determine their own ticket price (cash only). These tickets, limit of two, can be purchased beginning one week before performance day. Seniors can buy half-price tickets on the day of the performance as long as they have their Medicare card with them (cash only and subject to availability). There is also a Frequent Playgoer card that is used like a frequent flier mileage card; this one will eventually allow you to buy discount tickets.

Parking
Parking in lots across from and near premises, $3.50-5.50; street parking

Special Features
Public Rush Tickets $10, 10 minutes before curtain, subject to availability

Performances
Tues-Sun 8 pm; Sat-Sun 2:30 pm

Tickets
$26-32

Discounts
Previews/seniors/groups, call (213) 972-7231

BO
Tues-Sat 10 am-8 pm; Sun noon-7:30 pm; check/AE/MC/V/reserve by mail, TicketMaster; exchange policy for season subscribers only ($1.50 charge); subscription program

CENTER THEATRE GROUP-MARK TAPER FORUM— Resident Co.

In its 25-year history, the Taper has presented over 250 plays which have included contemporary American, European, and classic titles. Its award record is copious, and many of the plays first produced at the Taper have gone on to Broadway. It is safe to say the Taper has won just about every theatrical award given, including a special Tony in 1977.

Don't let the "experimental" mantle scare you away. While some patrons feel you need to be lucky with what you pick to see, that is, after all, the nature of experimental theater.

In response to the need for programming to serve our large Latino community, the Taper Latino Theatre Initiative has been created. The four-year program will commission works by Latino playwrights, and seek Latino audiences.

D.A.T.E. (Deaf Audience Theatre Experience) provides a sign language interpreter for one designated Saturday matinee for each production.

TAPER, TOO

As of this writing, The Taper, Too series has not found funding for a current season through it's still being used for occasional workshops and the New Work Festival. (Free; reservations required.) It is a shame, as the group, which used the lower 90-seat space under the John Anson Ford Amphitheatre, did everything from fully-staged productions to developmental workshops and readings. They often worked on experimental pieces that might include new ways to approach known works and new works from other places.

Call—or watch the press listings—to see whether they come back.

Special Features
"Pay What You Can Performances", "2 for 1", and Public Rush Tickets $10

MYSTERY CAFE DINNER THEATRE

The Imperial House Restaurant
505 Kalmia
San Diego, CA 92103
Info: (619) 544-1600   **Rsvn:** (619) 544-1600
Fax: (619) 544-9226
Interactive mystery dinner theater accommodating 130 at the Imperial House Restaurant. Also appearing at the 128-seat Lake San Marcos Resort, 1121 La Bonita, San Marcos, CA 92069.

A little murder with your dinner? Since 1990, the Mystery Cafe has been making a little mint from mixing mayhem and a four-course meal. Ever more popular, it now boasts two locations to mix it up in.

There's nothing highbrow about this Boston-based franchise outlet. The scenarios may change, but the puns stay broad, the acting broader. The ever-present aim is to keep the audience laughing as they try to figure out whodunnit, whydunnit, and who's gonna get it next.

This is no place for the chronically shy; the actors don't need much encouragement to pull audience members into the action. The actors also double as waiters, so if you liked your murderer/victim/femme fatale, you get the chance to show your cultural appreciation at tip time.

Ticket price includes a full meal; beverages and gratuities are extra (in cash, please). The Imperial Restaurant location offers valet parking. Parking is free at the Lake San Marcos Resort Conference Center. The dress is weekend casual, although some people like to dress with an air of mystery. Call one phone number for both locations.

Performances
Fri 8 pm; Sat 5 pm and 8:30 pm
Tickets
$33-37
Discounts
Seniors/students/groups of 20+, call Group Sales (619) 544-1664
BO
Mon-Thurs 9 am-5 pm; Fri 9 am-7 pm; Sat 10 am-4 pm; AE/MC/V/ reserve by mail, fax; non-refundable; exchanges made 3 days prior to performance date
Location
Call for directions
Parking
Valet, FREE; street parking

THE NEW IVAR THEATER See **Inner City Cultural Center**

NEWPORT THEATRE ARTS CENTER

2501 Cliff Drive
Newport Beach, CA 92663
Info: (714) 631-0288   **Rsvn:** (714) 631-0288
93-seat community theater.
       Once upon a time (14 years ago), a little half-century-old church in a cliff-top residential neighborhood above the bay was converted to a theater to house a community theater group. Pews gave way to raked theater-style seating, and the altar was transformed into a stage.
       Today, the "theater on the cliff" produces a September through June season of plays and musicals such as *Picnic*, *Irma La Douce*, and *Fiddler on the Roof*.
       Refreshments are served at intermission. Make arrangements in advance for handicap accessibility.

Performances
Thurs-Sat 8 pm; Sun 2:30 pm
Tickets
$13-15
Discounts
Children/seniors/students/groups of 20+, call BO
BO
Call for reservations; open 2hrs prior to show; MC/V/check/reserve by mail; exchanges with 24 hrs notice; subscription program
Location
Take San Diego (405) Fwy to 73 Corona del Mar, exit Campus Dr/Irvine Ave to Cliff, right on Cliff; in a residential neighborhood
Parking
On premises, FREE; street parking

NEW STARLIGHT Look Under **Starlight**

NEWWORKS THEATRE

See press listings for performance locations.
Info: (619) 262-6162   **Rsvn:** (619) 298-0880
       This San Diego group got into the act about 11 years ago as a playwrights' workshop that met at the Coronado Playhouse. Next came the theater company, set up to perform original material from the workshop. Recent home-grown productions have included dramas based on the lives of Emily Dickinson and Edgar Allan Poe, plus a condensed version of *Antigone*.
       Although the group does not have a permanent home, performing wherever it can, it manages to produce about 10 shows each year, many of which are only staged readings. An offspring of NewWorks is the two-year-old program Vintage Theatre, which offers plays dealing with senior issues and aging.
       For you new playwrights, NewWorks considers new scripts.

Performances
Wed-Sat 8 pm; Sun 2:30 pm
Tickets
$10-15
Discounts
Previews/groups of 10+, call (619) 298-0880
BO
Reserve by phone; exchanges made up to 24 hrs in advance
Parking
Varies with location
Special Features
Open rehearsals

A NOISE WITHIN

Glendale Masonic Temple
234 South Brand Boulevard
Glendale, CA 91204
Info: (818) 353-2935   **Rsvn:** (818) 753-7750
Fax: (818) 353-2935
Artistic Directors: Geoff Elliott/Art Manke
Most performances are held in the Glendale Masonic Temple.

Behold, Los Angelenos, we have another resident classical repertory company in our midst. And let's hope they stay. And grow. And have success.

Just three years old, this company has already made noise (within and without) in the LA theatrical community. The troupe has attracted a following from the outset to its performances in the old Glendale Masonic Temple.

Audiences make it a point to attend because of the company they keep. The talented members hail from the San Francisco's American Conservatory Theatre, Julliard, and Yale. While some of the actors live that double LA TV/theater life, guest actors and directors shuttle in as needed. Everyone involved, though, shares a commitment to the classics.

A different work is staged each night in its season, not an easy accomplishment for any company.

A Noise Within currently occupies a third-floor, 99-seat space, but they are hoping to move to bigger digs. Future plans include touring with the productions. Coffee and treats are served in the little lounge.

Performances
Fall-spring; Wed-Sat 8 pm; Sun 2 pm, 7 pm
Tickets
$12-20
Discounts
Seniors/students/groups of 10+, call BO
BO
1 hr prior to performances; check/reserve by mail; subscription program
Parking
On premises

NORRIS THEATRE FOR THE PERFORMING ARTS

27570 Crossfield Drive
Rolling Hills Estates, CA 90274
Info: (310) 373-8417   **Rsvn:** (310) 544-0403
Fax: (310) 544-2473
Artistic Director: Dr. Frances Steiner
Performing arts center seating 450 for a variety of live events.

Here's another of those LA surprises. For "in towners," the drive out to Palos Verdes along Hawthorne or Crenshaw Boulevards, past endless strip malls and traffic lights, is something of an endurance test. But once you cross Pacific Coast Highway, the change from South Bay sprawl to Marin-like hills and fresh air is dramatic in itself.

The Norris Theatre for the Performing Arts lies in the commercial center of affluent Rolling Hills Estates. The lines of the stucco, boxy theater structure are softened by rounded corners and sidewalk planters brimming with flowers. The 450-seat theater is intimate and well-appointed, with comfy continental-style seating and wood everywhere. There are no bad seats, though you may suffer a slight sight line obstruction in the box section.

The Chamber Orchestra of the South Bay is resident, despite the less than accommodating acoustics. This venue was built for theater, not music. In addition to the concerts, the Norris presents about 20 different theater productions a season, ranging from dramas to dance concerts to other musical performances. For big music engagements, the theater hauls in an expensive sound system.

The Norris offers several series, from which subscribers can create their own. The Celebrity Series draws the likes of Mort Sahl and Ann Jillian. The Nouveau Series is an assemblage of everything from illusionists to comedians to quartets. There's also a two-season group of

Performances
Mon-Sun 8 pm, Sat-Sun matinee 1 pm and 4 pm
Tickets
$12-35
BO
Mon-Fri 10 am-6 pm, Sat noon-4 pm; check/MC/ V/reserve by mail (P.O. Box 2465, Palos Verdes Peninsula, CA 90274); TicketMaster; subscription program
Location
At Crossfield and Indian Peak
Parking
On premises, FREE

children's performances of plays and performers for youngsters over the age of 5.

P.S.: The drive in along the coast, through Hermosa Beach and Redondo Beach, is considerably less trying, yet the change once you hit the peninsula is just as dramatic.

NORTH COAST REPERTORY THEATRE

987-D Lomas Santa Fe Drive
Solano Beach, CA 92075
Info: (619) 481-1055 **Rsvn:** (619) 481-1055
Artistic Director: Olive Blakistone
194-seat community playhouse.

You go to the North Coast Repertory Theatre not expecting this tiny non-Equity company to make it up the artistic hill, but its dedicated troupe of actors, designers, and directors pull together to make it to the top of the mountain. Next thing you know, you're finding their version of Neil Simon's *Rumors* funnier than the Old Globe's just three years back.

Much of the North Coast Rep's success is owed to founder and artistic director Olive Blakistone. Blakistone knows what she likes and goes for it, but her tastes are eclectic and sometimes provocative. She'll grant her audiences Neil Simon, but she'll also feed them Jon Robin Baitz (before he wrote *The Substance of Fire*), Stephen Metcalfe, Alan Ayckbourn, and Harvey Fierstein. She also has a knack for timing. One of her big hits was a play by Vaclav Havel called *The Memorandum*. Few had heard of Havel or his play when she scheduled it, but by the time it opened, Havel, a playwright and often-jailed Czechoslovakian dissident, had become president of Czechoslovakia. Blakistone was the most surprised of all. She just liked the play.

Nearly a half-dozen years after the first 99-seater was built, Blakistone built a new theater, twice the size of the old, out of two adjoining store spaces in the same shopping center as the original (now bustling and busy), with comfortable, plush red seating and an ample stage.

The choices remain eclectic, with all the good and bad that entails. Blakistone is always looking for previously unproduced plays by new playwrights or lesser-known plays by well-known playwrights that may also take audiences by surprise.

Terrific homemade desserts are served during intermission. Before you dine, you may want to call the theater to find out about which restaurants are currently offering discounts for North Coast Rep patrons. But for sheer convenience, you can't beat Samurai Japanese Restaurant right in the shopping plaza. It boasts one of the largest sushi bars in California. Reservations are recommended.

Performances
Thurs-Sat 8 pm; Sun 2 pm, 7 pm
Tickets
$ varies
Discounts
Previews/seniors/ students/groups of 20+, call BO
BO
Mon-Sun 11 am-7 pm; MC/V/check/reserve by mail; exchanges made with 48 hr notice; subscription program
Location
1 block E of Int-5 at the Lomas Santa Fe Dr exit, in the Lomas Santa Fe Plaza, Solano Beach
Parking
On premises, FREE; street parking
Special Features
Acting classes for children; Forum Fridays: open discussions post performance

NOSOTROS THEATER

1314 North Wilton Place
Hollywood, CA 90028
Info: (213) 465-4167 **Rsvn:** (213) 465-4167
61-seat theater.

Established in 1970, this little space in Hollywood presents all kinds of Latino theater on weekends, including dramas, comedies, short plays, and musical showcases with stars such as Edward James Olmos and comedian Paul Rodriguez.

There's a modest lobby with refreshments served. The seats are a little cramped, but the sightlines aren't. And

Performances
Fri-Sat 8 pm; Sun 7 pm
Tickets
$10
Discounts
Seniors/students/ groups, call BO
BO
Call
Parking
On street

it may be worth a little discomfort to see the work of a neglected pool of artists. Strictly street parking.

OCCIDENTAL COLLEGE PERFORMING ARTS SERIES See MUSIC

OCTAD-ONE PRODUCTIONS

Grove Playhouse
3450 College Avenue
San Diego, CA 92115
Info: (619) 466-3987   **Rsvn:** (619) 466-3987
Artistic Director: Martin F. Gerrish
Performances in the 40-seat Grove Theatre.
    Tucked away in a tiny little shopping center, next to a Pic-n-Save, is the 40-plus-seat Grove Theatre, home of Octad-One. Octad-One is community theater—but for a community willing to take chances. Founded by retired Grossmont College drama professor Martin Gerrish, Octad-One mounts artistically ambitious seasons and, to the surprise of many, delivers with the likes of *Joe Turner's Come and Gone*, *Les Liaisons Dangereuses*, and *Artist Descending a Staircase*.
    For many summers, Octad-One has also presented free Shakespeare-by-the-Lake at the El Cajon Plaza Amphitheatre, the small semi-amphitheater outside Theatre East in El Cajon. This may not be where you seek the ultimate impassioned exploration of Shakespeare's depths. But the unjaded and the Shakespeare-shy may well find poignancy in *Romeo and Juliet* played by bona fide teenagers.
    The lighting is minimal, but well timed to coordinate with the setting sun and rising moon shimmering on the small lake just behind the stage. Props are minimal, too.
    The atmosphere is unpretentious almost to a fault. Parents and young children sip their drinks, munch on McNuggets and Kentucky Fried Chicken and stare wide-eyed at the stage. Purists beware: the plays are cut by Gerrish to simplify and shorten the experience for those audiences.
    Dress is casual for both venues. Bring blankets, goodies and warm clothing for the outdoor Shakespeare presentations. Restaurants and fast-food places come and go at the Grove shopping center, but you can always find something. There's ample free parking at both the shopping center and at Theatre East.

Performances
    Fri-Sat 8 pm; Sun 2 pm
Tickets
    $9-10
Discounts
    Seniors/students/groups of 20+, call BO
BO
    Call (619) 466-3987; check/reserve by mail, Art Tix; subscription program
Parking
    On premises, FREE

ODYSSEY THEATRE

2055 South Sepulveda Boulevard
Los Angeles, CA 90025
Info: (310) 477-2055   **Rsvn:** (310) 477-2055
Fax: (310) 444-0455
Artistic Director: Ron Sossi
Three spaces of 99 seats each.
    Founded in Hollywood in 1969, the Odyssey now fills this former Westside warehouse with three roomy, comfortable, and well-raked 99-seat theater spaces. Refreshments are served in the large lobby all evening. Parking is plentiful.

ODYSSEY THEATRE ENSEMBLE—Resident Co.
    The Odyssey's generally superior quality productions include the long-running hit *Kvetch* by Steven Berkoff. Even the rare outside production (e.g., the cutting

Performances
    Wed-Sun, matinées Sun
Tickets
    $17.50-21.50
Discounts
    Previews/children/ seniors/students/groups of 12+, call BO
BO
    Sat 10 am-6 pm, Sun 2-6 pm; check/AE/MC/V/ reserve by mail; exchanges OK; subscription program

edge Chicano Secret Service) is carefully chosen by artistic director Ron Sossi.

The Odyssey has accumulated numerous awards, including the LA Drama Critics Circle's most prestigious honor, the Margaret Harford Award. Its original plays (such as *Tracers* and *Chicago Conspiracy Trial*) and world premieres have been revived in productions around the world.

Sossi produces exciting theater with a company that is not afraid to experiment. This is truly one of LA's top theaters—if you've never been, get with it and go!

See the **CHILDREN** Chapter for information on the professional performances for youngsters.

Location
Off San Diego (405) Fwy at Olympic and Sepulveda Blvds
Parking
On premises, $2; street parking

OFF RAMP THEATRE

1953 North Cahuenga
Hollywood, CA 90028
Fax: (213) 469-4343
Seats 60 at the Off Ramp, 30 in the Play Box.

Nearly ten years ago, director Ken Rose took a nasty-looking factory and converted it into a small, 60-seat theater. Over the years, original works, revivals, and an occasional classic have gone up on the small proscenium stage. If you don't get a good seat here, have your eyes checked.

Next door is the Play Box Theater, a sibling space in-the-round, with only 30 seats. It's usually used for rehearsals and experiments, though it has hosted a very competent and entertaining production of *Candida*, and made its audience feel it was sitting in Rev. Morrell's parlor.

Performances
Thurs-Sun 8 pm; Sun 3 pm
Tickets
$12-20
Discounts
Children/seniors/ students/groups flexible, call BO
BO
Call and leave message; AE/MC/V/check
Location
Off the Hollywood (101) Fwy; Cahuenga exit
Parking
On premises (across the street), $3; street parking

OLD GLOBE THEATRE See Simon Edison Centre for Performing Arts

OLIO

3709 Sunset Boulevard
Los Angeles, CA 90026
Info: (213) 667-9556   **Rsvn:** (213) 667-9556
70-seat theater with an eclectic schedule.

Walk in the front door and you're smack-dab in the theater! The seating is a bit novel in this storefront space. Some is on risers or church-pew-like benches, some at tables in the front of the stage. The stage itself is unusually spaced, permitting great leeway for different types of performances.

Lately the fare has generally been imaginative presentations of new works in a variety of genres.

Performances
Vary
Tickets
$10-20
BO
Hrs vary; call answering machine 24 hrs; TicketMaster (sometimes)
Parking
On premises, FREE (limited); street parking

ONBOOK-ONSTAGE PLAYREADING SERIES See Actors Alliance

ON STAGE PRODUCTIONS

310 Third Avenue, Ste. B-9
Chula Vista, CA 91910
Info: (619) 426-0488 **Rsvn:** (619) 427-3672
Seats 47 at this community theater.
    This nonprofit, volunteer organization has been producing in this storefront theater since 1985. Each year they feature six plays; recent season offerings included *Harold & Maude*, *The Diviners*, and *Private Lives*.

Performances
    July-June; Thurs-Sat 8 pm; Sun 2 pm
Tickets
    $8-10
Discounts
    Seniors/students/groups of 20+, call BO
BO
    Mon-Sun 24 hrs answering service (619) 422-7787; check/MC/ reserve by mail, Art Tix, BO; subscription program
Parking
    On premises, FREE

OPEN FIST THEATRE COMPANY

1625-27 North La Brea Avenue
Hollywood, CA 90028
Info: (213) 882-6912 **Rsvn:** (213) 882-6912
Artistic Director: Ziad H. Hamzeh
99-seat space offering plays from the classical to the experimental.
    Set in a somewhat imposing black building in Hollywood, the Open Fist's large space can be reconfigured to fit the shape of its current production. Seats on risers are neither plush nor uncomfortable.

OPEN FIST THEATRE COMPANY—Resident Co.
    Not afraid to take risks, artistic director Ziad Hamzeh aims to produce fresh and imaginative works. Expect intelligent avant-garde as well as classical theater.
    One great way to get to know them better: attend a FREE preview two days before an opening.

Performances
    Thurs-Sun 8 pm
Tickets
    $10-15
Discounts
    Previews/children/ seniors/students/groups of 30+, call BO
BO
    Daily 10 am-6 pm; check/AE/reserve by mail; subscription program
Location
    On La Brea between Hollywood Blvd and Sunset Blvd
Parking
    On premises, $3; street
Special Features
    Free previews two days before opening

ORANGE COUNTY PERFORMING ARTS CENTER Also See MUSIC

600 Town Center Drive
Costa Mesa, CA 92626
Info: (714) 556-2121 **Rsvn:** (714) 740-2000
Fax: (714) 556-0156
    In addition to the dance, opera, symphony, chorale, and jazz featured in Segerstrom Hall, touring Broadway musicals such as *Guys and Dolls* and *Annie Get Your Gun* are on the schedule. OCPAC has quite a complete arts line that will give you up-to-date info.
    Call the nearby Westin South Coast Plaza (714) 540-2500 for information on theater packages that include accommodations and tickets.

Performances
    Oct-June, July-Sept
Tickets
    $ varies
Discounts
    Groups of 20+, call

(More. . .)

BO
Mon-Sat 10 am-6 pm; Sun noon-6 pm; performance days 10 am-8:309 pm; check/ AE/MC/V/reserve by mail; TicketMaster exchanges for subscribers only; subscription program

Location
Between Bristol and Town Center Dr near 405 and 55 Fwys

Parking
On premises, $4

PCPA THEATERFEST

Allan Hancock College
800 South College Drive
Santa Maria, CA 93466
Info: (805) 928-7731 **Rsvn:** (805) 922-8313
Fax: (805) 928-7506
Managing Artistic Director: Jack Shouse
Performances set in the Marian (448 seats) and Severson (200 seats) theaters on campus of Allan Hancock College in Santa Maria, and at the outdoor Solvang Festival Theatre (712 seats).

Touted as the only major theater between Los Angeles and San Francisco, PCPA's (Pacific Conservatory of the Performing Arts) producing efforts are a notable undertaking especially in these economic times. As part of Santa Maria's Allan Hancock College, the "Conservatory" uses an artist-in-residence program to teach while executing the hectic year-round production schedule at the campus-based Marian and Severson Theaters.

The Marian, a 448-seat thrust house, boasts no bad seats and free parking. While the standard season fare of Broadway and off-Broadway hits such as *Noises Off* fills the eight-show playbill, they seem to know what works and will even bring back for the third time a lavish production of *Joseph and the Amazing Technicolor Dreamcoat*, which they know will keep "packin' 'em in." Recent performances included *Cyrano de Bergerac* and *South Pacific*.

Go with what works, is the motto. But the beauty in the theater biz lies in flexibility. The 199-seat Severson Theatre, neighboring the Marian (and brand new as of January '93), affords PCPA an additional space for extended runs, workshops, and performance space for developing works. Not long ago it was the site of a new adaptation of *Great Expectations* by Charles Dickens, completed by the industrious artists-in-residence who teach by day and write or perform by night. The Severson is a theater-in-the-round that conforms specifically to each show.

The theatrical experience of the outdoor Theaterfest in Solvang is worth the trip. For those who have never been: 45 minutes north of Santa Maria, Solvang is a Danish tourist town complete with windmills, quaint architecture, and plenty of pastries and souvenir shops. In the summer, the company performs on a three week rotation schedule with the Marian. Performances are held nightly under the stars in a comfortable 712-seat amphitheater. Remember to bring a jacket or blanket for

Performances
Vary

Tickets
$11-17

Discounts
Children/seniors/ students/groups of 15+, call (800) PCPA-123

BO
Mon-Sun 12 pm-7 pm; or call (805) 922-8313, (800) 549-PCPA; MC/V/check/reserve by mail,TicketMaster (summer only); exchanges for subscribers only; subscription program

Location
For Santa Maria: Ventura (101) Fwy, exit Stowell; for Solvang: Ventura (101) Fwy, exit Buelton (Hwy 246) to Solvang

Parking
On premises, FREE; street parking

cool evenings. Pre-show picnicking is encouraged, but restaurants are close by. Call ahead for the production schedule.

PCPA offers a discounted Passport which gives you five tickets to selected PCPA productions any time, any location, matinee or evening. The company also offers half-price advance children's tickets to certain performances when you purchase an adult ticket. (Happily, they restrict attendance to children over the age of five, allowing everyone—kids and adults—a good time.) Many of the season's performances are perfect for the whole family. A separately sponsored Family Series offers Saturday performances of dance, music, and puppetry by visiting artists.

PACIFIC RESIDENT ENSEMBLE THEATRE

8780 Venice Boulevard
Los Angeles, CA 90026
Info: (213) 484-9757 **Rsvn:** (310) 306-3943 **and** (310) 838-9146
Artistic Director: Stephanie Shroyer
Mainstage at 8780 Venice Boulevard seats 60 to 80; workshop at 705-1/2 Venice holds 35.

This exciting theater group became well-known for staging large cast plays in nontraditional settings, with the audience frequently in the middle of the action. Now that it has found a home in a building across from Helms Bakery in Culver City, the integration of audience and actors hasn't changed. If you're not comfortable being right in the middle of the action—because that's literally where the audience may be seated at one of these productions—then you might want to stick to more traditional theater groups.

PRET is well-known for large-cast "environmental" theater: That means breaking the audience up into small groups and staging the action of the play all around them. One of its most successful shows was set up as the old Hollywood nightclub, Romanoff's, where the audience was seated at small round tables just as if they were patrons of the club.

If awards mean something to you, then you should know that PRET has received many, particularly from the LA Drama Critics Circle, including the most recent Margaret Harford Award. Memorable productions have included *Slaughterhouse on Tanners Close* (about 19th-Century grave-robbers), and John Gay's *Beggar's Opera*. The company's founding members come from PCPA-Theaterfest and San Francisco's American Conservatory Theatre.

PRET productions can be seen in two locations: one is its small storefront theater in Venice called the Coop, where workshop productions and staged readings—about 4 to 10 each year—are produced and directed by PRET members, but not under the artistic direction of PRET. Mainstage productions are handled at the Culver City location. PRET's mainstage may be moving into Helms Bakery (now it's in the same complex), so be sure to ask when you call for tickets. The mainstage season is generally from August to June, when between two to five plays are offered.

Besides its ongoing educational/conservatory role for young adult actors through UCLA's Extension program, PRET inaugurated a new program with Next Stage to acknowledge and serve the many ethnic groups that comprise LA's cultural community. If you're a budding playwright, you should know that the theater is always on the lookout for new works and gladly accepts submissions.

Performances
Vary
Tickets
$15-20 (tickets to Coop performances, donation only)
Discounts
Previews/children/seniors/students/groups of 10+, call BO
BO
Check/MC/V/reserve by phone; subscription program
Location
Between National and La Cienega Blvds
Parking
On premises; street
Special Features
Offers frequent workshop productions

PALOS VERDES PLAYERS

2433 Moreton
Torrance, CA 90505
Info: (310) 326-2287 **Rsvn:** (310) 326-2287
Fax: (310) 378-0246
Artistic Director: David DiAngelo
150-seat theater for all types of plays.

The home of the PVP is a converted warehouse with a recent full-body makeover. Its new interior and sound and lighting capability make this a place worth looking for. The auditorium seats 150 and offers dramas, musicals, comedies and classics, plus a series of experimental works.

At 60-plus, it is reportedly the oldest drama venue in the South Bay area. It's certainly one of the busiest nonprofessional theater companies. The space mounts eight mainstage shows each year and produces another eight in the experimental series. The PVP also recently began a Black Theater Workshop.

Performances
Fri-Sat 8 pm; Sun 7 pm; Sat-Sun 2 pm
Tickets
$9-12
Discounts
Seniors/children/ students/groups of 20+, call BO
BO
Call; open 1 hr before performance
Location
Off Crenshaw Blvd between Lomita Blvd and Pacific Coast Hwy
Parking
Lot, FREE; street

PANTAGES THEATER

6233 Hollywood Boulevard
Hollywood, CA 90028
Info: (213) 468-1700 **Rsvn:** (213) 480-3232
2,705-seat theater for Broadway productions, concerts, dance, and awards shows.

One of Hollywood's glorious movie palaces, the landmark Pantages opened in June 1930 with the premiere of *Floradora Girl* starring Marion Davies. Even Hollywood must have been stunned by the size and grandeur of the vaulted grand lobby, flanked by twin staircases and elaborate decorations and the vast interior devoted to public lobbies, lounges, and restrooms.

Since the Pantages was built to screen movies with the companion live shows that were so popular in those days, the theater has a huge stage space.

In 1940, Leopold Stokowski conducted an entire season of the LA Philharmonic at the Pantages. From 1949 to 1959, the Academy Awards were held here. (Yul Brynner accepted the Best Actor award for *The King And I* on stage in 1956 and 30 years later was back on its stage starring in a revival of the musical.) In 1977, after the Nederlander organization took over, the Pantages was converted into a full-time theatrical venue for touring Broadway musicals, such as *Les Miserables*, *Camelot*, and *Joseph and the Amazing Technicolor Dreamcoat*, as well as dance extravaganzas and major awards shows.

The auditorium is still breathtaking, so seeing (and staging) a show at the Pantages can be a bit overwhelming. The installation of a new sound system a few years ago seems to have eliminated past audio problems; however, a recent visit led me to wonder: is it the orchestra or the sound system that sometimes overwhelms the performers? Although it shouldn't stop you from seeing a play here, I wonder why I have to spend so much money on tickets then struggle to understand the words of miked performers. (Perhaps an FM simulcast is the answer.) The seats are comfortable (although leg room isn't generous), the sightlines are good, and the production values are first-class. First row balcony offers the fullest value of the staging.

I'd suggest parking close by, especially in the evening. There are convenient lots within one or two blocks

Performances
Vary
Tickets
$ varies
Discounts
Previews/groups of 20+, call (213) 464-7521
BO
Hrs vary; check/AE/MC/ V/reserve by mail, TicketMaster; no refunds, no exchanges; subscription program
Location
Off of Hollywood (101) Fwy, Vine St or Gower St exits
Parking
Lots nearby, $4-7; street parking

of the theater, as well as directly across the street. Call in advance to arrange handicap seating.

PARLOR PERFORMANCES See CLUBS

PASADENA CIVIC AUDITORIUM Also See MUSIC

300 East Green Street
Pasadena, CA 91101
Info: (818) 793-2122   **Rsvn:** (818) 449-7360
Fax: (818) 793-8014

The Pasadena Civic now offers a full season of musical theater. Patrons can see road shows of *Fiddler on the Roof*, *The Sound of Music*, and other popular large-scale productions.

Performances
Vary
Tickets
$15-47
BO
Mon-Sat 10 am-5 pm; check/MC/V/reserve by mail, TicketMaster
Parking
On premises, $5; street

PASADENA PLAYHOUSE

39 South El Molino
Pasadena, CA 91101
Info: (818) 792-8672   **Rsvn:** (818) 356-PLAY or (800) 883-PLAY
Fax: (818) 792-7343
Traditional theater; 701 seats.

Founded in 1917 by Gilmor Brown, the Pasadena Playhouse is not only a registered historic landmark, it is the official State Theatre of California.

In its history, The Pasadena Playhouse initiated numerous landmark plays including Eugene O'Neill's *Lazarus Laughed*, and Brecht's *Galileo*, produced by John Houseman and starring Charles Laughton. It was also home to one of the major theater schools in the country. Many stage and film stars, such as Raymond Burr, Tyrone Power, Elaine May, Victor Mature, and Jean Arthur performed or received training at the playhouse. The school and theater closed in the early '70s, then reopened much to our cultural advantage in the '80s.

Refurbished in its original mission-style design, its beautiful patio (and outdoor bar) becomes a very popular watering hole during intermission and before the show. Check out the classy gift shop while you're there.

Seats are all good. The 18 orchestra rows and 6 mezzanine rows aren't far from the stage. The rake, however, could be a bit steeper. What can I say—if you get stuck behind a tall person, you're stuck!

The past couple of years have seen successes such as *Lend Me a Tenor* and *Forever Plaid* move on to the Henry Fonda and the Canon in Beverly Hills, and beyond.

The Playhouse has instituted a rather experimental approach: in cooperation with the Poway Center for the Performing Arts and the Lobero Theatre in Santa Barbara, the same productions of shows that play in Pasadena are sent on to those locations after their local run. The success of this method of building audiences, and, of course selling tickets, seems to be working, resulting in the probability that even more theaters will be added to the mix.

Performances
Tues-Fri 8 pm; Sat 5 pm and 9 pm, Sun 2 pm and 7 pm
Tickets
$31.50
Discounts
Previews/groups of 15+, call (818) 797-8019
BO
Mon-Sat 10 am-showtime, Sun noon-showtime; AE/MC/V/ TicketMaster; subscriptions by mail; exchanges for subscribers only; subscription program
Location
Off Foothill (210) Fwy at Lake Ave; corner of El Molino Ave and Colorado Blvd
Parking
Nearby, $3; street parking

PEARSON PARK AMPHITHEATRE See CHILDREN

PEPPERDINE UNIVERSITY CENTER FOR THE ARTS

24255 Pacific Coast Highway
Malibu, CA 90263
Info: (310) 456-4558 **Rsvn:** (310) 456-4522
Fax: (310) 456-4556
College-supported arts center incorporating Lindhurst Theatre (100 seats), Smothers Theatre (456 seats), Raitt Recital Hall (118 seats), and an art gallery.

Just getting to Pepperdine is dramatic. The drive up Pacific Coast Highway from Santa Monica takes you along one of the most famous stretches of coastline in the world. Once you've parked your car, you'll have to tear yourself away from the spectacular Pacific panorama, as the well-endowed university sits perfectly perched on the hillside above Malibu and the ocean.

All three stages are housed in very contemporary "Malibu-modern" pale yellow-stucco structures across the parking lot from the main administration building. The bill of fare is rather middle-of-the-road, with the likes of the Kingston Trio, Bob McGrath (*Sesame Street*) singing his favorite songs, Dave Brubeck, Diane Schuur, plus various dance troupes, music groups, and theatrical shows put on by the college theater department. A Family Series, and a separate Kids Series for very young children, have proven popular.

Look to Malibu for a meal at the Adobe Cafe.

LINDHURST THEATRE

The Lindhurst, with its movable seating and platforms, is a free-form space serving student productions, acting classes, and rehearsals.

RAITT RECITAL HALL

This brand new, intimate 118-seat hall, in the same building as the Lindhurst, is perfect for lectures and recitals.

SMOTHERS THEATRE

The oldest of the three, the Smothers is the (so-called) mainstage, complete with scene and paint shop, elevator pit, dressing rooms, and green room. Cushioned seats in three sections make for an enjoyable evening.

Performances
Mon-Sun 8 pm, Wed 3 pm, Sat-Sun 3 pm
Tickets
$8-30
Discounts
Students/groups, call BO
BO
Mon-Fri 10 am-5 pm; check/AE/V/MC/reserve by mail, fax; subscription program
Location
Pacific Coast Hwy and Malibu Canyon Rd
Parking
On premises, $3; street parking

PERFORMANCE/RIVERSIDE

Landis Auditorium
4800 Magnolia Avenue
Riverside, CA 92506
Info: (909) 684-3240 x325 **Rsvn:** (909) 684-9337
Fax: (909) 275-0651
Artistic Director: Gary D. Schultz
Shows are performed at the 1,378-seat Landis Auditorium, Riverside Community College.

Performance/Riverside is the umbrella organization that produces the Riverside Celebrity Series, Conservatory, Civic Light Opera, and Riverside Pops. Each appears in the 1,378-seat Landis Auditorium on the campus of Riverside Community College (see **Landis Auditorium** listing).

Responding to the surrounding working-class community, Performance/Riverside attempts to bring "low-cost, family entertainment... to the workingman and his children." (Perhaps they have forgotten about the

Performances
Thurs-Sat 8 pm; Sat-Sun 2 pm
Tickets
$10.50-13
Discounts
Groups of 20+, call Michael Charles at (714) 684-5917
BO
Tues-Sat 12:30 pm-5:30 pm; check/MC/V/ reserve by mail, fax, TicketMaster; exchanges made 24 hrs in advance for season ticket holders only; subscription program

workingwoman and her children!) The use of amateurs and professionals together no doubt abets this cost-consciousness. The box office staff advises you to place a note on your dashboard indicating to security that you are attending a performance.

RIVERSIDE CELEBRITY SERIES

The Celebrity Series presents three or four shows a year, drawing such well-known entertainers as Mel Torme, Rita Moreno, and Shirley Jones. Its goal is mass entertainment.

RIVERSIDE CIVIC LIGHT OPERA

Not only does the CLO strive to produce large-cast, entertaining, and recognizable musicals, it also chooses what will be presentable to children ages six and up as well. The group will adapt a play to make it suitable to that age group if it isn't already. Its season includes four to six plays annually.

RIVERSIDE CONSERVATORY

As you can probably guess, this subgroup offers the non-musicals, usually with recognizable titles. Performances by the Conservatory always include a young member of its Actors' Conservatory program. These plays, too, are chosen for their presentability to youngsters (from the adults' point of view of course), in this case, adolescents in grades 6 to 12.

RIVERSIDE POPS See **MUSIC**

PIERSON PLAYHOUSE

Parking
On premises, FREE

841 Temescal Canyon Road
Pacific Palisades, CA 90272
Info: (310) 454-8040   **Rsvn:** (310) 454-1970
Seats 125 for American classics and children's plays.

Pierson Playhouse Theatre Palisades does not play up to anybody. It's content being strictly a community theater offering a season of five American standards. A sixth play is offered through an exchange arrangement with the Morgan Wixson Theater and the Santa Monica Theatre Guild.

The theater sits overlooking Temescal Canyon in Pacific Palisades. It can boast a pretty lobby, 125 comfortable seats and good sightlines.

The children's theater group is called Theatre Palisades Kids, and a teen group performs each fall. Every spring 50 to 80 younger children perform a play generally written by the director.

Performances
Fri-Sat 8 pm, Sun 3 pm
Tickets
$8-12
Discounts
Seniors/students/ children/groups of 10+, call (310) 559-9338
BO
Wed-Sat 3:30-7 pm 1/2 hr before showtime; check/MC/V/reserve by mail; exchanges up to 24 hrs before performance; subscription program
Location
Between Pacific Coast Hwy and Sunset Blvd on Temescal Canyon Rd
Parking
On premises or street, FREE

PINE HILLS PLAYERS

Pine Hills Lodge Dinner Theatre
2960 La Posada Way
Julian, CA 92036
Info: (619) 765-1100   **Rsvn:** (619) 765-1100
Artistic Director: Scott Kinney
Contemporary plays are performed dinner-theater-style in Pine Hills Lodge.

A journey to see the Pine Hills Players may begin as an excuse to sample the pleasures of rustic Julian. But chances are you'll be pleasantly surprised by the quality of the dinner theater show.

Out of three productions of *The Nerd* in San Diego, The Pine Hills Players dished up the funniest (or nerdiest). Still with all the limitations in the actor base that community theater implies, PHP aims high under the watchful eye of Dave Goodman, the owner of the Pine Hills Lodge (which lodges the theater), and his artistic director, Scott Kinney.

Audiences tend to be in a good mood anyway after traipsing around the hills of Julian. Those staying overnight at the Lodge don't even have to worry about the return traffic.

The Pine Hills Players have their own niche in San Diego dinner theater. The Lawrence Welk does musicals and the mystery dinner theaters do mysteries, but Pine Hills does dinner with contemporary theater, usually comedies.

The dinner at Pine Hills is packaged with the theater ticket. The food is of the "hearty" variety, good and ample. You'll sit at tables for eight and munch on barbecue baby-back pork ribs or chicken served buffet-style preceding the show. Most important, parking is free.

If you're not staying the night at the lodge, come early enough to sample Julian in the daytime. Julian is particularly famous for its homemade apple pies.

Performances
Fri-Sat 7 pm
Tickets
$27.50 (includes dinner)
Discounts
Children/groups of 12+, call BO
BO
Mon-Sun 9 am-6 pm; check/AE/MC/V/DC/ reserve by mail; subscription program
Location
Int-5 S to Oceanside, E on Hwy 78 to Ramona, 21 miles to Pine Hills Rd, 3 miles S to Lodge
Parking
On premises, FREE

PLAY BOX THEATRE See **Off Ramp Theatre**

PLAYHOUSE WEST

4250 Lankershim Boulevard
North Hollywood, CA 91602
Info: (310) 285-3311   **Rsvn:** (310) 285-3311
Director: Robert Carnegie
45-seat theater presenting socially-relevant pieces.

Playhouse West was founded by actor Jeff Goldblum and other Sanford Meisner acting grads. Goldblum still teaches at this school where the students, professional actors themselves, have written many of their own productions. Their long-running drama about Vietnam veterans, *Welcome Home, Soldier*, garnered the critical success that pushed its run into its third year.

Theater work here is often original and well-done and always socially relevant. All the box office donations go to veterans', police benevolent and other charities, and police officers, veterans, and their families get in free as a gesture of good will.

Performances
Sat 8 pm
Tickets
$7 donation requested
Discounts
Veterans and their families and police officers and their families admitted free
BO
Sat 7-8 pm check/ reserve by phone
Location
Off Hollywood (101) Fwy on Lankershim, 3 blocks N of Universal Studios
Parking
On street
Special Features
Special after-show discussions with cast

PLAYWRIGHTS' ARENA

5262 West Pico Boulevard
Los Angeles, CA 90019
Info: (213) 469-7156   **Rsvn:** (213) 466-1767
Fax: (818) 761-1664
35-seat theater featuring LA-based writers, directors, designers, and actors.

While all of the 99-seat plan theaters can be called small, this one is truly lilliputian. In fact, when someone is purchasing their ticket at the box office, you may have to squeeze in to the theater! But with just 35 raked seats, you'll certainly have no trouble seeing or hearing.

Formerly the Carpet Company Theater, the Playwrights' Arena is run by Jon Lawrence Rivera and Steve Tyler, who are putting on a season of four plays on weekend evenings. Most of the works are original, and the focus here is on LA-area artists. They've even managed to put musicals on this tiny stage!

The theater sits between Fairfax and La Brea, so you can head north up La Brea to City, Farfalla, or Campanile for dinner (ok, I didn't say you could get reservations—just that these are your nearest restaurant options!)

Performances
 Fri-Sat 8 pm
Tickets
 $ varies
BO
 Theatix (213) 466-1767
Location
 Near Santa Monica (10) Fwy; on Pico Blvd between Fairfax and La Brea Aves
Parking
 On premises, FREE; street parking

PLAYWRIGHTS PROJECT

See press listings for performance locations.
Info: (619) 232-6188
Artistic Director: Deborah Salzer

Every year, the Playwrights Project showcases three to six scripts from its annual contest for young writers in California, ages 18 and younger. Even those who don't win receive a detailed evaluation letter from the project.

Playwrights Project is one of the best programs for young writers in California and is one that has made a difference. One winner, Josefina Lopez, was an undocumented teenager living in fear in Los Angeles when she submitted her first play, a thinly disguised autobiographical story called *Simply Maria, or the American Dream*. Her play was later produced by KPBS-TV and by theaters all across the country, giving her the confidence to pursue her dreams of college and becoming a writer.

Founder and executive director Deborah Salzer modeled the Playwrights Project on New York's Young Playwright's Festival. Each year, Salzer and her troupe of teachers go into schools to teach children in grades 5 through 12 how to write plays. The project gives all students the opportunity to submit their work for a professional production in a professional theater.

Playwrights Project recently moved its festival to a December slot at the Old Globe Theatre's Cassius Carter Centre Stage in San Diego. Call for current dates.

Performances
 Dec or Jan; Wed-Sun 8 pm; Sat-Sun 2 pm
Tickets
 $7-9
Discounts
 Seniors/students/groups of 12+, call
BO
 Varies with theatre/box office
Parking
 Varies with location

THE PLAYWRIGHTS THEATRE

Westwood Playhouse
10886 Le Conte Avenue
Los Angeles, CA 90024
Info: (310) 208-6288
Artistic Director: Richard Polak

A developmental organization seemingly more on the run than having lengthy runs, Playwrights Theatre in its seven-year history has performed occasionally in venues as diverse as the Mark Taper Forum and for the UCLA Alumni Association. In addition to performing regionally, they're allied with New York's Helen Hayes Theatre and other off-Broadway theaters.

What sets the 17-member playwright organization apart from other playwrights' groups is that their work doesn't stop at writing plays. Putting their time and money where their mouths are, they actively pursue producers or finance productions themselves.

POETRY SOCIETY OF AMERICA IN LOS ANGELES

See press listings for performance locations.
Info: (213) 656-2215

A few years ago, this national society decided to branch out with a West Coast office. Apparently that was the right move because the success of PSA West far exceeded expectations.

Upwards of 400 people are turning out for the monthly Sunday readings at West Hollywood's charming Chateau Marmont. The group is currently reorganizing its resources so it can meet the popular demand for its Act of the Poet series. Actors read a selection of great poetry—either his/her choice—or a piece chosen by the society. The emphasis here is on great. The actors are not there to showcase their talents or try out new work—only writings of classical to contemporary poets with a couple of books to their names need apply. No new, up-and-coming writers. On the other hand, the selections are accessible, even to the uninitiated. On the same program are readings by poets of their own material. Sometimes an actor and the poet read a piece together.

But you'll have to call for information on times and days of other performances, as there's no regular printed schedule. Look for flyers at bookstores and libraries around town. At every reading a schedule for the next month is handed out.

Currently, readings are free. But by the time you read this, they may have started to request donations.

Performances
Vary
Tickets
FREE; possibly in the future a donation will be requested
Location
Varies

POWAY CENTER FOR THE PERFORMING ARTS

15498 Espola Road
Poway, CA 92064
Info: (619) 679-4211   **Rsvn:** (619) 748-0505
Fax: (619) 748-0286
815-seat performing arts center.

Well hidden in the heart of Poway, the beautiful, state-of-the-art Poway Center for the Performing Arts opened in May of 1990. This presenting organization, owned and operated by the City of Poway, signed a producing agreement with the acclaimed Pasadena Playhouse, which began its first six-play season at Poway in September of 1992. Each play, which is first seen at the theater in Pasadena, has a three-week run with 22 performances in each run at Poway.

Poway still books in touring shows, but its 815 seats are too few to attract national touring companies. It does, however, entice smaller touring shows as well as regional theater companies. Case in point: it scored a big hit with a one-night presentation of Andrew Lloyd Webber's *Song & Dance.*

The seats are comfy, the acoustics are fine, and the sightlines are good from the orchestra and the balcony. The two-story lobby is all open glass overlooking a tree-lined patio area.

Don't assume that every offering at the theater is professional. Local schools also use the space. It's best to call and check it out.

Performances
Vary
Tickets
$ varies
Discounts
Students/seniors/ children/previews/ groups of 20+, call (619) 679-4211
BO
Tues-Sat; MC/V/check/ reserve by mail; subscription program
Location
6 miles E of Int-15
Parking
On premises, FREE

Parking is free and adjacent to the theater. Unless you're familiar enough with Poway not to get lost, you're better off dining at your point of departure. The local eateries are okay, they're just hard to find.

THE POWERHOUSE

3116 2nd Street
Santa Monica, CA 90405
Info: (310) 392-6529 **Rsvn:** (310) 392-6529
Artistic Director: Eric Zane
Theater seats 86.

More history—and on the Westside, yet! Back in the early 1900's, this building was home to the generator that ran the trolleys along Santa Monica's Main Street. As a theater, Powerhouse is comfortable, and has an enclosed patio for pre-show and intermission gatherings. You're within walking distance of all the trendy Main Street shops and restaurants. Park in the lot or on the streets around the theater—sometimes it isn't so easy, so allow time for the search. (And forget about catching that trolley!)

THE POWERHOUSE THEATER REPERTORY CO.—
Resident Co.

Having gotten off to "an uneven if promising start," the company tries hard. It can trace its bloodline back to the Company Theatre, one of the most prolific and innovative groups to come out of LA's small theater scene in the late '60s and '70s. If the genes have been passed on, this could be a powerhouse group for the '90s. Its goal is original, entertaining, thought-provoking "theater, dance, music, comedy, film, improv, and other performance arts." There's certainly no lack of ambition.

Performances
Tues-Sun, matinees
Sat-Sun (Sun Children's
Theatre)
Tickets
$10-12
Discounts
Groups
BO
1/2 hr before
performance; 24 hr
answering machine for
reservations;
subscription program
Location
Off Santa Monica (10)
Fwy at 4th St S; 1 block
N of Rose, 1 block E of
Main
Parking
On premises, FREE;
street parking

PROFESSIONAL DANCERS SOCIETY GYPSIES See **Gypsy Playhouse**

PROJECT THEATER/FERN STREET CIRCUS

See press listings for performance locations.
Info: (619) 235-9756

Professional theater doesn't get more intimate than the Project Theater productions at The Big Kitchen Cafe. Since 1989, Project Theater co-founders Eric Grischkat, John Highkin, and Kevin O'Neill have adapted short, high-quality one-act plays to present in these tiny culinary confines in Golden Hill.

Their first show, Bertolt Brecht's *Conversations in Exile*, conveniently took place at a restaurant counter. Every show since has been unique. To compensate for the lack of lighting in Edward Albee's *Counting the Ways*, they finessed scene changes by asking the audience to shut their eyes at the first ring of a bell and open them at the second ring. (If only critics were so accommodating!) They've also sweetened the evening (and assured compliance) by serving each patron one of The Big Kitchen's decadently rich, gooey pies before the show.

The company has done work by Slowomir Mrozek, Maria Irene Fornes, David Mamet, and Vaclav Havel. The colorful props in Mamet's *Bobby Gould in Hell*, reflected co-founder John Highkin's other life, as creator and designer of the Fern Street Circus, San Diego's only community based one-ring circus, also based in Golden Hill.

The Fern Street Circus is a large, colorful affair featuring acrobats, jugglers, unicyclists, clowns, and performers who can tell stories with comedic skill. It usually takes place in the Fall and somewhere in the festivities is a parade open to all comers. Call for dates and details.

The Big Kitchen, which is famous for its lavish and cozy breakfasts, is best known in San Diego for Whoopi Goldberg's former waitressing. Her picture is now enshrined, and there's even a breakfast special named for her. Autographed pictures of such celebrities as rockers Jackson Browne and Jerry Garcia and pro basketball great Bill Walton also adorn the walls. (No, they never waited tables.)

Dress is ultra casual. Street parking is ultra free. You can eat downtown before going to Golden Hill or you can just save room for the scrumptious desserts at the Project Theatre. If you're planning to catch a matinee of the Fern Street Circus, eating at The Big Kitchen is highly recommended. But be forewarned: the lines on a Saturday or Sunday morning are usually quite impressive.

PUBLIC WORKS IMPROVISATIONAL THEATER COMPANY

650 North Berendo Avenue
Los Angeles, CA 90004
Info: (213) 661-0524   **Rsvn:** (213) 660-1110
Artistic Director: Marlene Resnick
Presents at the Trinity Episcopal Church, 650 North Berendo Avenue, and other area venues.

Self-described as "stylistically innovative," this theater company offers original music and improvisation designed to put audiences in touch with contemporary political events. Their works are cabaret-style, blending theater games, poetry, performance art, and music. A recent offering looked at the aftermath of the Los Angeles "unrest" in Second Summer, a play based on a retirement home for free-thinking Los Angeles elders.

Listings in the press are infrequent, so it's best to call.

Performances
Fri-Sun 8 pm, matinees
10:30 am and 1:30 pm
Tickets
$5-12.50
Discounts
Previews/children/
seniors/students/groups
of 5+, call info #
BO
Check/reserve by mail;
exchanges flexible
Special Features
Open rehearsals

RAYMOND THEATER

129 North Raymond Avenue
Pasadena, CA 91103
Info: (213) 722-3992
1900-seat restored 1920's theater presenting musicals.

A vaudeville house in the 1920s and a rock concert venue later, the restored Raymond Theater was the final home of the California Music Theater (prior to that, most of the CMT productions were at Pasadena Civic Auditorium). Its elegant narrow interior and 1900 seats have all been refurbished, and a state-of-the-art sound system has been installed. But currently it's only used occasionally for concerts or other programs.

REDONDO BEACH CITY THEATER GROUP

1935 Manhattan Beach Boulevard
Redondo Beach, CA 90278
Info: (310) 372-1171 ext. 2213   **Rsvn:** (310) 318-0610 ext. 0
Fax: (310) 316-6467
Performances at Aviation Park Auditorium, 1935 Manhattan Beach Boulevard, Redondo Beach, and Perry Park Playhouse, 2301 Grant Avenue, Redondo Beach.

Residents and nonresidents alike have fun performing in this community theater company. Musicals are the mainstay of the adult offerings. Children's performances are appropriate for many age ranges. Unless you're cozy

Performances
Fri-Sat 8 pm, Sun 2 pm
Tickets
$3-8
Discounts
Children/seniors/
students/previews/
groups of 20+, call BO
BO
Mon-Fri 8 am-5 pm;
check/MC/V; exchanges
prior to performance;
subscription program

with one of the actors, tickets for Perry Park Playhouse will have to be purchased at the door.

Location
Off San Diego (405) Fwy at Inglewood; W on Manhattan Beach Blvd to Aviation Blvd

Parking
On premises, no charge

RICHARD PRYOR PLAYHOUSE

1445 North Las Palmas Avenue
Los Angeles, CA 90028
Info: (213) 466-2222   **Rsvn:** (213) 466-2222
Fax: (213) 466-8179
A 227-seat theater devoted to comedy.

Here's some Los Angeles history to brag about. Today's audiences might be familiar with this theater for having hosted a five-year run of *The Fantasticks*. But back in the 1930's, it was the "A-List" haven, social club, and private performing venue of the legendary "Writer's Club," with a membership including Eric von Stroheim, Douglas Fairbanks, Jr., Joan Crawford, Jackie Cooper, Charlie Chaplin, Bela Lugosi, Mary Pickford, Clark Gable, Arthur Lake, and Randolph Scott, to name, as they say, a few.

After taking on another life as a USO stop during World War II, it's now owned by Mitzi Shore, who also owns Sunset Boulevard's legendary Comedy Store, and who first called it the Comedy Store Playhouse. In its next incarnation, it was called the Hollywood Playhouse and was used mostly as a rental house.

Recently, owner Shore renamed the theater the Richard Pryor Playhouse and is devoting the space to plays, staged readings, dance, and one-person shows. The emphasis is on bringing in as many groups as possible, including minority productions. But this has not turned into a nightclub; the performers use the stage environment to showcase their talent. Today's refurbished version is large enough to feature good sound and light, and small enough to remain friendly and intimate. Seats are cozy.

Parking is available across the street. You're right in the heart of Hollywood, so try Hollywood's oldest restaurant, also filled with history, Musso and Frank.

Performances
Tues-Sat 8 pm; Sun 3 pm

Tickets
$15-30

Discounts
Previews/children/ groups of 20, call BO

BO
Tues-Sun 1 pm-7 pm; check/AE/MC/V/ TicketMaster

Location
2 blocks E of Highland; 1 door S of Sunset

Parking
On premises (security lot across street), $3-5; valet, $5-7; street parking

---

KEY TO SYMBOLS

![]	Air conditioning (Only in **ART FILMS**)	🎧	Hearing device available
	Snack bar	🔭	Binoculars availabe
Y	Full bar	👫	All OK for kids
‖	Restaurant on premises	(👫)	Some OK for kids
⌇‖	Restaurant nearby	〰	See seating plans
♿	Fully handicap accessible	🆁🅸🅿	Obituary—entity no longer exists or is no longer in operation
(♿)	Handicap seats only		

RIVERSIDE CELEBRITY SERIES See **Performance/Riverside**

RIVERSIDE CIVIC LIGHT OPERA See **Performance/Riverside**

RIVERSIDE CONSERVATORY See **Performance/Riverside**

THE ROAD THEATER COMPANY

14141 Covello Street #9-D
Van Nuys, CA 91405
Info: (818) 785-6175
Artistic Directors: Brad Hills, Ch'rae Adams, Dan Butler, Taylor Gilbert
49 seat space.
  The new home for this group is located in a Van Nuys industrial park; there's plenty of secure, free parking. Press the intercom button for access.

THE ROAD THEATER COMPANY—Resident Co.
  This troupe is completing its second year and has moved to a new location. It opened with a challenging Lanford Wilson play, *Balm in Gilead*, then went on to present *In The Name of the People* by Tim Boland and *I-Land*, written by Sonia Pilcer. The first play in its new home was *Vig*, which dealt with abuse and victimization. The company's mission is "to produce new works, new voices, and world premieres that deal with social and political issues."

Performances
 Thurs-Sun 8 pm
Tickets
 $10-12.50
Discounts
 Previews/seniors/
 students/groups of 5+,
 call
BO
 1 hr prior to
 performance; call and
 leave message; check/
 MC/V/mail; exchanges
 made; subscription
 program
Parking
 On premises, FREE

ROSE THEATER

318 Lincoln Boulevard
Venice, CA 90291
Info: (310) 392-4911 **Rsvn:** (310) 392-6963
Seats 49 for a variety of theater company productions.
  As of now, the Rose is strictly a rental facility, as comfortable as it is hard to find. The entrance is in the rear of the building, and there's ample parking.
  Generally, this is a place where interesting groups start out, moving on to better work and more accessible venues. But look for a renaissance when management begins to produce in-house.

Performances
 Vary
Tickets
 $7-10
BO
 Mon-Fri 9 am-5 pm;
 check/MC/V/reserve by
 mail; refunds available
Location
 At Santa Monica (10)
 Fwy; Lincoln Blvd exit
Parking
 On premises, FREE

THE ROUGH THEATER

See press listings for performance locations.
Info: (213) 388-7860
Fax: (213) 387-6969
Artistic Director: Brent Morris
  Formed in 1987, this group debuted with a post-apocalyptic comedy performed on the Venice beach boardwalk and the Santa Monica bluffs. A people's theater group, their productions are performed by a loosely connected group of actors, writers, and directors. Shows are often free. The company likes to experiment with original works and alternative venues. They emphasize socially relevant pieces, such as one dark comedy about the sad shape of the environment—mounted inside a mortar-shell bunker in San Pedro.

Performances
 Vary
Tickets
 $10-20
Discounts
 Previews/children/
 seniors/students/groups
 of 5+, call
Parking
 Varies with location

As they have no permanent home (or bunker), you'll have to look for notices in the press.

ROYCE HALL See UCLA

RUBY THEATRE See The Complex

ST. GENESIUS THEATRE

1047-1051 North Havenhurst
West Hollywood, CA 90069
Info: (213) 650-8823   **Rsvn:** (213) 962-3422
A 53-seat theater with an eclectic line-up.
    The best looking little theater in West Hollywood! St. Genesius spent $100,000 on remodeling their 50-plus-seat building not long ago. The rows are raked with plenty of leg room and while the lobby isn't prestigious, the name St. Genesius Theatre is heard with much frequency. As a rental, this house attracts the outrageous, the campy, the politically outspoken, and even the classics. Artistic quality may vary, but the production values are usually good. Performances run Friday through Sunday.

Performances
  Fri-Sun 8 pm
Tickets
  $8-15
Discounts
  Varies from production to production
BO
  Varies
Location
  1 block W of Crescent Heights, 20 ft S of Santa Monica Blvd
Parking
  On street; metered lot

SAN DIEGO ACTORS THEATRE

See press listings for performance locations.
Info: (619) 268-4494
    This highly regarded "homeless" San Diego theater is run by its founder and artistic director Patricia Elmore. The nomadic company presents one or two high-quality productions during the year at a variety of venues.
    Among the company's triumphs: the San Diego premieres of Beth Henley's *The Miss Firecracker Contest*, at the old Bowery Theatre site, which has since burned down (though not from the fireworks), and Lee Blessing's *Eleeomosynary* at the old Gaslamp Quarter Theatre Company venue, which has since been overtaken by a restaurant, Cafe Sevilla.
    Recently, the San Diego Actors Theatre found a quasi-home for its staged reading series, sharing digs with Mary Pappas's Athens Market Restaurant at 109 West F Street in downtown San Diego. Tickets for the staged readings of such works as Terrence McNally's *Lips Together, Teeth Apart* and Paul Rudnick's *I Hate Hamlet* are just $5 at the door. But you can also get complete dinner theater packages for $25, including tax and gratuity, at the Athens Market Restaurant. Not a bad deal, considering the Athens Market is one of San Diego's best Greek restaurants. For other production information, call the theater company directly, or keep a lookout in the press.
    For Athens Market, parking is free if you can find it on the street. If you're willing to park at Horton Plaza, any purchase buys you three hours validation on your parking.
    Call for information about the Children's Classics series of four shows per season, rotating every three months.

SAN DIEGO CONCOURSE/SAN DIEGO CIVIC THEATRE

202 C Street
San Diego, CA 92101
Info: (619) 236-6500 **Rsvn:** (619) 236-6510

The Civic Theatre, operated by the city-owned San Diego Concourse, hosts the San Diego Opera series and most of the San Diego Playgoers series, plus select Celebrity Series presentations by the La Jolla Chamber Music Society. You've got to be big—really big—to play the Civic Theatre. Small, intimate performances merely drown in its vast reaches.

The seats are civic-mindedly comfortable. Veteran arts-lovers prefer the front section of the orchestra, the front row mezzanine, or the boxes that swoop out towards the stage front. You'll feel cheated at the back of the orchestra. For the upper reaches of the balcony, you're definitely going to need binoculars (for rent in the lobby).

For an impress-your-companion style of dining, try Mister A's with its breathtaking view of the city, the elegance of the Westgate (at the Little America Westgate Hotel), the Grant Grill (at the U.S. Grant Hotel), or Dobson's (for all-around terrific continental food in an intimate setting). Nearby Athens Market is one of the best Greek restaurants in town (see S.D. Actors Theatre for more of the theater menu). Cafe Bravo offers authentic Portuguese cooking, Reidy O'Neil's specializes in Irish fare and Cafe Sevilla is great fun for a casual dining experience with live music and Spanish food. With all these culinary options, you may want to pass up the more sedate fare available at the Civic.

Opening nights require the most formal attire always. Opening night at the opera, for instance, is a (fashion) show in itself.

If you arrive early, park in the Ace lot across the street. If you're running late, don't despair, there are several more Ace lots nearby, and the farther you go, the less they cost. There are always spaces at Third and C, but feed the designated slot (if an attendant is not on duty), unless you're prepared to pay the price.

Performances
Vary
Tickets
$ varies
BO
Mon-Fri 9 am-5:30 pm; phone
Location
S on the 5 Fwy, exit Front St; N, exit Center City
Parking
Parking lots nearby

SAN DIEGO REPERTORY THEATRE

Lyceum Theatre
79 Horton Plaza
San Diego, CA 92101
Info: (619) 231-3586 **Fax:** (619) 235-0939
Producing Director: Sam Woodhouse

The San Diego Rep launched this town's longest running hit, *Six Women With Brain Death or Expiring Minds Want to Know*, which ran from 1987 to 1989.

The company operates fall to spring in the Lyceum Space and the Lyceum Theatre in Horton Plaza downtown. In addition to producing shows, the Rep manages the space for the city and takes seriously its mandate to keep it profitably occupied. Lamb's Players Theatre has been a regular tenant a couple times a year; the Rep also sometimes books in touring shows, such as *Ain't Misbehavin'* and *Greater Tuna*.

The theater has been hard-hit by the recession holdover, and is scaling their previous ambitious offerings down to meet the shrinking budgets.

The Rep has a proud history of being multicultural before the trend was hip. Many years ago, a mixed-race cast of *A Christmas Carol* included a then-unknown Whoopi Goldberg. Goldberg has come back to do more than one Rep benefit.

Recently, they offered an excellent revisionist look at *Uncle Tom's Cabin*, titled *I Ain't Yo Uncle*, by the San

Performances
Oct-May; Tues- Sat 8 pm; Sun 2 pm, 7 pm
Tickets
$16-22
Discounts
Students/seniors/ children/previews/ groups of 15+, call BO
BO
Tues-Sun noon-8 pm; check/AE/Disc/MC/V/ reserve by mail, fax, TicketMaster; subscription program
Parking
Horton Plaza, FREE with validation

Francisco Mime Troupe. For years, the company has offered a bilingual Teatro Sin Fronteras program of various shows. The company boldly tackles classics such as Shakespeare's *Cymbeline* or Dickens' *Hard Times*. They show strength with contemporary works as well, as with David Mamet's *Glengarry Glen Ross* and Lanford Wilson's *Burn This*.

One constant remains its annual *A Christmas Carol*, adapted by artistic director Doug Jacobs but done differently each year by a different director. Some of these have been quite offbeat, but the shows popularity is evergreen.

All seats are good in both theaters, although in the large Lyceum Stage the front orchestra sections are best. The Lyceum Space is a black box theater that configures itself for each show.

Dress a step or two above casual. Park for free in Horton Plaza, where your ticket stub validates you for three hours. Dine in Horton Plaza itself—either on fast foods, at the California Cafe Bar & Grill, or at the Panda Inn.

SAN DIEGO STATE UNIVERSITY DEPARTMENT OF DRAMA

San Diego, CA 92182
Info: (619) 594-6363 **Rsvn:** (619) 594-6884
University theater series performed in two theaters: 500-seat Don Powell Theatre, and 175-seat Experimental Theatre.

Once upon a time, before San Diego became a thriving theater town, San Diego State University provided local residents with some of the best theater around. It still does but no longer has ambitions of reaching a large commercial audience. Instead, it focuses on developing the talent that has been making over the San Diego theater scene over the years, producing performers of national stature such as Julie Kavner, Marion Ross, Cleavon Little, and rising star Kathy Najimy, not to mention such local talent as William Anton and Kandis Chappell.

Under the leadership of Paula Kalustian, musical theater department chairperson, San Diego State has also promoted newer theater works. Recently it produced a well-received work based on the life of Lewis Carroll and then the San Diego premiere of Stephen Sondheim's *Assassins*.

Performances are held in the Don Powell Theatre and the smaller Experimental Theatre. Season subscriptions entitle you to either series, or a combination of both.

You'll need a parking pass from the San Diego State Information Booth on the way in.

Rubio's Fish Tacos on College Avenue right across the street from campus provides a spicy, tasty quick place to eat right before the show. College Restaurant, also near the school, is nothing fancy, but serves plentiful fresh food for people on a budget.

Performances
Tues-Sat 8 pm; Sat-Sun 2 pm
Tickets
$5-12
Discounts
Children/seniors/ students/groups of 10+, call (619) 594-6365
BO
Mon-Fri 8:30 am-4 pm; check/MC/V/reserve by mail (season only), TicketMaster; exchanges only; subscription program
Location
Take Int-8, exit at College Ave
Parking
On premises, FREE; street parking
Special Features
Open dress rehearsals, lectures and tours for groups

SAN GABRIEL VALLEY CIVIC AUDITORIUM

320 South Mission Drive
San Gabriel, CA 91776
Info: (818) 281-9444 **Rsvn:** (818) 308-2868
A 1,450-seat theater hosting the San Gabriel Valley Civic Light Opera.

For more than 65 years, this playhouse has reveled in all its Spanish glory in the central San Gabriel Valley. Built as the Mission Playhouse, its sole theatrical mission was to host the *Mission Play*, a story of the California Missions and their founding by the Franciscan Fathers written by John Stevens McGroarty. The playhouse was so constructed as to accommodate the play's 150-

Performances
Thurs-Sat 8:15 pm, Sat-Sun 2:15 pm
Tickets
$15-30
Discounts
Students/groups of 15+, call BO

member cast. After 1932, the building went through a variety of transformations, from movie theater to converted apartments. Finally in 1945 it was purchased by the City of San Gabriel which also hunted down and snatched up many of the original furnishings and art works. Major refurbishment followed so that today the auditorium can show off its Spanish, Mexican, Indian heritage. It still boasts one of the largest stages on the West Coast, great sightlines, and excellent acoustics..

SAN GABRIEL CIVIC LIGHT OPERA—Resident Co.

The award-winning SGCLO produces three or four full-scale musical productions a year, in addition to celebrity gigs which have showcased major international stars over the years.

BO
Mon-Fri 10 am-5 pm; check/MC/V/reserve by mail; exchanges for subscribers only; subscription program
Location
Near the 210 or 10 Fwys; San Gabriel Blvd is the nearest large cross street
Parking
On premises, $3; street parking also available

SANTA BARBARA CITY COLLEGE THEATRE GROUP See **Garvin Theatre**

SANTA BARBARA CIVIC LIGHT OPERA

Granada Theatre
1216 State Street
Santa Barbara, CA 93101
Info: (805) 962-1922   **Rsvn:** (805) 966-2324
Fax: (805) 963-3510

The SBCLO claims to be the "largest, independent performing arts organization between Los Angeles and San Jose." They've backed up their own and their librettist's words with productions that have broken box office records over and over again, and with numerous awards to their credit. In short, they're a company worth keeping company with.

Their annual four-play series of American musicals are produced at the renovated Granada Theatre. Since 1984, local performers and professionals from around the country have belted out hits such as *Guys and Dolls*, *Gypsy*, *The Mystery of Edwin Drood*, and *The Pirates of Penzance*. In addition to the regular series and an outreach program, the SBCLO spices up a variety of area events with abbreviated performances of its full-bodied stage fare.

Performances
Sept-June; Wed-Sat 8 pm; Sun 7 pm; Sat-Sun 2 pm
Tickets
$26-28
Discounts
Previews/children/seniors/students/groups of 15+, call (800) 549-1922
BO
Mon-Fri 10 am-5 pm; check/AE/Disc/MC/V/reserve by mail; exchanges for subscribers only; subscription program
Parking
Behind theater, FREE (after 7:30 pm and Sun)

SANTA MONICA COLLEGE MAIN STAGE & STUDIO STAGE See **MUSIC**

SANTA MONICA PLAYHOUSE

1211 4th Street
Santa Monica, CA 90401
Info: (310) 394-9779   **Rsvn:** (310) 394-9779
Artistic Directors: Chris DeCarlo & Evelyn Rudie
Westside theater seating 88; presents adult and children's plays—comedies, musicals, original plays.

It would be surprising if a Los Angeleno theatergoer hadn't been to the Santa Monica Playhouse at least once. Over a 30-year existence, the numbers are exponentially mind-boggling—more than 350 productions and over 10,000 performances!

Home to the Actors' Repertory Theater Company, the playhouse itself is a little jewel box tucked away off Wilshire Boulevard (with its entrance on 4th Street). There's

Performances
Mon 8 pm; Tues-Wed 7:30 pm; Thurs-Fri 8 pm; Sat 6:30 and 9:15 pm; Sun 7:30 pm
Tickets
$15-20
Discounts
Previews/seniors/students/groups of 20+, call BO

a small courtyard leading to the decorative building. Indoors, sightlines are good and seats comfy.

If you haven't been for the adult performances, its possible you've attended a child's birthday party on the weekend. The theater is one of the most popular spots in town for children's birthday parties.

For dinner, try any of the eateries on the Third Street Promenade.

ACTORS' REPERTORY THEATER COMPANY—Resident Co.

What more could you want? Very entertaining theater at affordable prices. Their success shows. Actors' Rep is entirely box-office supported.

All genres from the Absurd, farce, comedy, dramas, have seen the light of the stage here. Plays also have long runs: *Author! Author!* a poignant evening with Sholom Aleichem, ran 4 1/2 years; *Almost Perfect*, the first of Jerry Mayer's touching plays, ran nearly 14 months, while his *Aspirin & Elephants* lasted more than two years.

The theater has won numerous awards including the Los Angeles Drama Critics Circle's Margaret Harford Award and Drama-Logue's Publisher's Award "for exceptional achievement in theater."

Be sure to turn to the **CHILDREN** chapter for information about the numerous presentations for kids.

BO
Mon-Sun 11 am-6 pm; MC/V/check/reserve by mail, phone; no refunds, emergency exchanges with 10% charge

Location
Off Santa Monica (10) Fwy, exit 4th St

Parking
On street , $.50/hr

SANTA PAULA THEATER CENTER

125 South 7th Street
Santa Paula, CA 93060
Info: (805) 525-3073   **Rsvn:** (805) 525-4645
Fax: (805) 933-2548
Community theater seating 97.

Physically, Ventura County's community theater has it all over most modern West Coast cultural arts buildings. Built for the Ebell Women's Club in 1917 to bring the arts to Santa Paula, the center boasts the Craftsman style hardwood maple floors, beamed ceilings, and character indicative of that architecture so popular in the early 1900s.

In 1988 it became the Santa Paula Theater Center, opening its first season with Shaw's *Major Barbara*. In 1989 it made the National Register of Historic Places.

The word is out that this is one of the most progressive theater companies in Ventura County. The main stage is popular for its traditional theater fare, but waiting in the new 50-seat Wiegand Backstage Theatre you'll find a series of new works, reader's theater, poetry readings, and musical comedy reviews (and will pay a nominal admission price of only $5). While most of the current audience is over 35, the staff seeks to become more well-rounded and attract a younger audience.

The company is attempting to rise above the image of "community" theater by hiring costume and set designers and fostering a professional image in all of their productions. If a volunteer theater wasn't effort enough, this company has been known to produce a bilingual version to run simultaneously with the current production. Two separate casts, two separate directors—they will do a Spanish version to draw the large nearby Hispanic community.

Performances
Thurs-Sat 8 pm, Sun 2:30 pm

Tickets
$11-12.50

Discounts
Previews/seniors/ students/groups of 10+, call

BO
Tues-Fri 9:30 am-1:30 pm, Thurs-Sat 4-8 pm, Sun 12-2:30 pm; check/MC/V/reserve by mail; exchanges with 24 hr notice; subscription program

Location
Off 126 Fwy at intersection of 7th and Main St

Parking
On street

2ND STAGE THEATRE

6500 Santa Monica Boulevard
Hollywood, CA 90038
Info: (213) 465-6029   **Rsvn:** (213) 466-1767
Fax: (213) 466-6972
50-seat theater.
   Having completed a decade in West Hollywood, 2nd Stage is still operating double-time as a rental space, with LA Theatre Unit and other "wandering" companies taking their turns in this 50-seat black box. The August Strindberg Society of Los Angeles has made itself at home at 2nd Stage, offering at least one full production each year, plus periodic readings from the Swedish playwright's oeuvre.

Performances
 Wed-Sun evenings
Tickets
 $7-16
Discounts
 Previews/groups of 15+, call BO
BO
 Tues-Sun 11 am-7 pm
 AE/MC/V/check/reserve
 by mail, fax, Theatix
Location
 On SW corner of Santa
 Monica Blvd and Wilcox
Parking
 Valet; street parking

SHAKESPEARE FESTIVAL/LA See FESTIVALS & SEASONAL EVENTS

SHAKESPEARE—ORANGE COUNTY

Chapman University, 333 North Glassell
Orange, CA 92666
Info: (714) 744-7016   **Rsvn:** (714) 744-7016
Fax: (714) 744-7015
Artistic Director: Thomas F. Bradac
Professional productions of the classics.
   Shakespeare—Orange County began its premiere seven-week season in the summer of 1992. Thomas Bradac, formerly the artistic director of the Grove Shakespeare Festival, formed the company with a number of actors from the Grove to present professional productions of the classics. The emphasis, of course, is on Shakespeare. They started out OK on the stage of the Waltmar Theatre at Chapman University, which is where they will continue their residency.

Performances
 June-Sept, Thurs-Sat
 8:00 pm, Sun 3 and 7:30
 pm
Tickets
 $16-23
Discounts
 Previews/children/
 seniors/students/
 groups of 15+, call BO
BO
 Noon-5 pm; 1 hr prior to
 curtain; check/MC/V/
 reserve by mail (P.O.
 Box 923, Orange, CA
 92666), fax; exchanges
 with 48 hrs notice;
 subscription program

SHOWBOAT DINNER THEATRE

Swedish Inn
19817 Ventura Boulevard
Woodland Hills, CA 91364
Info: (818) 222-7239   **Rsvn:** (818) 884-7461
Music Director: Bob Brandzel and Richard Kiley
100-seat dinner theater.
   Just over one decade-old, this dinner theater continues to thrive in its west Valley location. It runs a near year-round schedule, with a new show up and running every two to three months.
   Management has taken a banquet room in the Swedish Inn and turned it into a Vegas-style showroom, with booths and tables on risers. As you'd expect, the theatrical fare is from the light musical menu, a la *Damn Yankees*, *My Fair Lady*, and *Oklahoma!*

Performances
 Fri-Sat 8 pm, Sun
 matinee
Tickets
 $15-25
Discounts
 Children/seniors/
 students/groups of 20
BO
 Call Mon-Sun; 11 am-9
 pm; AE/MC/V/reserve
 by mail
Parking
 On premises, FREE;
 street parking

Dinner is served buffet-style, and the price includes everything but the beverage.

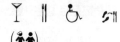

SHRINE AUDITORIUM See MUSIC

SHUBERT THEATRE

2020 Avenue of the Stars
Los Angeles, CA 90067
Info: (310) 201-1500   **Rsvn:** (800) 233-3123
Fax: (310) 201-1585
Westside theater seating 2,150; mostly Broadway-scale national tours of musicals.

The Shubert Theatre, ensconced in the ABC Entertainment Center, is a swanky rental space, usually reserved for large-scale musicals. The big Broadway touring productions look (and do) fine here, but when the powers that be book in a nonmusical play, it's inevitably dwarfed by the space.

The Shubert is not unlike a Westside Ahmanson. You can run races in the huge lobby. The theater has been reconfigured for the long-awaited Andrew Lloyd Webber version of *Sunset Boulevard* among other improvements. The management agreed to redo the balcony seats and change their grading. For this we cheer them.

Be picky about your seats; you may even want to make your reservations in person at the box office (as we go to press the new seating chart is not available). The underground self-parking is convenient, or there is the advantage of valet parking out front.

As for dining, the ABC Center is indeed entertaining. If a show is particularly popular, reserve a table at Harry's Bar for post-theater dining and wait until the parking lot empties. Also check with the Century Plaza Hotel and the J.W. Marriott, both across the street for possible early dining specials. They may also have a theater package of room and tickets, so you can make a weekend of it.

Performances
Tues-Sat 8 pm, Sun 7:30 pm; Wed, Sat-Sun 2 pm
Tickets
$35-65
Discounts
Previews/groups of 20+, call group sales (800) 432-7780
BO
Mon 10 am-6 pm, Tues-Sat 10 am-8:30 pm, Sun noon-8 pm; check/AE/Disc/MC/V/reserve by mail, Telecharge (800) 233-3123; subscription program
Location
Near the Santa Monica (10) Fwy and San Diego (405) Fwy; between Olympic and Santa Monica Blvds on Ave of the Stars
Parking
On premises, $3.50; valet

SIMON EDISON CENTRE FOR PERFORMING ARTS

CASSIUS CARTER CENTER STAGE
LOWELL DAVIES FESTIVAL THEATRE
OLD GLOBE THEATRE
1363 Old Globe Way
Balboa Park, CA
Info: (619) 231-1941   **Rsvn:** (619) 230 2255
Fax: (619) 231-5879
Artistic Director: Jack O'Brien
Three stages: Cassius Carter seats 225 in-the-round, Lowell Davies is an outdoor space seating 612, the Old Globe can handle 581.

Nestled in beautiful downtown Balboa Park (one of the country's most beautiful parks), the Simon Edison Centre for Performing Arts is usually known just as The Old Globe. It's San Diego's flagship theater and definitely its pride and its handsomely-funded joy.

The Old Globe began in the 1930s as a community theater nurtured by a young actor turned director named Craig Noel. More than half a century later, the gnomish Noel still presides as executive producer and frequent director. In 1981, he gave the Globe a transfusion

Performances
Generally Tues-Sat 8 pm; Sun 7 pm, but vary with venue
Tickets
$17-29.50
Discounts
Previews/seniors/students/groups of 15+, contact Diane Willcox (619) 231-1941

of fresh theatrical blood in the form of artistic director Jack O'Brien and managing director Thomas Hall. Under O'Brien's leadership, the theater won a Tony for best regional theater in 1984.

Today, the Globe produces a dozen shows a year in two seasons on a budget of just under $8-million. It serves just under 50,000 subscribers (one of the nation's largest subscription bases), as well as makes its spaces available to other groups, from The Playwrights Project to the Malashock Dance & Company. During November and December it fills the house with outside theatrical events from the Moscow Circus to the presentation of the hit musical *Forever Plaid*.

True to its old London namesake, this Old Globe includes two Shakespeare productions each summer season. The company's take on Shakespeare ranges from the gently conventional to the cuttingly contemporary: in John Hirsch's extraordinary *Coriolanus,* Coriolanus rode on stage in a WWII jeep wearing a U.S. Army uniform to address TV reporters.

O'Brien, who has earned two Tony nominations for best director, has spun the Globe into the orbit of new work. The Old Globe premiered Stephen Sondheim's *Into the Woods*, Neil Simon's *Rumors* and *Jake's Women*, all of which graduated to Broadway, as well as A.R. Gurney's *The Cocktail Hour*, which subsequently hit it off well, Off Broadway. The Globe has become a West Coast must-stop for pre-Broadway runs of two-time Pulitzer Prize winner August Wilson.

America's top playwrights, directors, and performers consider it a coup to work at the Globe. Each year its Play Discovery Program—a series of Monday night readings spread throughout the year—is flooded with promising new material.

There really isn't a bad seat in any of the Globe houses, although the floor seating in the mainstage Old Globe space is preferable to the balcony. One never gets too far from the stage in the theater-in-the-round Cassius Carter Centre Stage. In Lanie Robertson's *Lady Day at Emerson's Bar & Grill*, some of the seats were actually on the stage.

The seats are also inclined in the Lowell Davies, so vision isn't obstructed. But it can get cool outside in summertime; you'd be well advised to dress warmly. Blankets are for rent at the theater for a few dollars.

If you've never had the pleasure of visiting Balboa Park, take the time to sample some of the wonderful museums including the San Diego Museum of Art, the Timken Art Gallery, the Museum of Man, the Reuben H. Fleet Space Center, the Hall of Champions, and the Museum of Natural History. Or simply walk around and check out the park life: clowns make animal balloons for the kids; jugglers, dancers, and other troubadours may be encountered. On summer weekends, look for a free community theater production of Shakespeare by San Diego's Naked Shakespeare Festival (they're fully clothed) in Zorro Gardens near the Reuben H. Fleet.

Restaurants and snack areas abound. Right in the park itself the Sculpture Garden Cafe serves brunch and adjoins the Globe; the Cafe del Rey Moro serves brunch, lunch, or dinner. Or, if you leave enough time, there are also numerous restaurants to choose from in the surrounding Hillcrest and downtown areas: Stefano's or Busalacchi's for Italian food, the Corvette Diner for '50s style chow, Calliope's Greek Cafe and San Diego's famous Mr. A's, a rooftop restaurant overlooking the city.

Park parking is free; if that's full, try the Naval Hospital lot across the street. A trolley shuttles patrons from

BO
Mon 10 am-5 pm; Tues-Sat 10 am-8:30 pm; Sun 10 am-7:30 pm; check/AE/Disc/MC/V/ reserve by mail, fax (619) 231-1037, Art Tix (619) 238-3810; exchanges made 24 hrs prior to performance; return tickets in person, by mail or fax—no phone exchanges; subscription program

Location
Balboa Park, near downtown San Diego, off Hwy 163

Parking
5-10 minute walk from farthest lot in the park

Special Features
Post-Performance Forums (selected evenings), in-depth seminars on selected Monday nights, play discovery program readings

the Naval Hospital to the Globe every 15 minutes from 9:30 am to 5:30 pm from April 5 through October 4. The winter hours are 10 am to 4 pm.

On opening night, the Globe Guilders, volunteer Globe supporters, don their tuxes and best duds. You'll feel most comfortable if you dress up for the evening shows, warmly for the outdoor shows. The theater gift shop sells children's illustrated books on Shakespeare, handcrafted jewelry, posters and other knickknacks from intermission to 10 pm. The lavish snack bar and actual bar offer wine and beer as well as pastries, cappuccino, and hot cider during intermission.

SKYLIGHT THEATER

1816 1/2 North Vermont Avenue
Los Angeles, CA 90027
Info: (213) 666-2202
99-seat theater used by a variety of theater companies.

The Skylight presents some terrific shows, including the long-running Milton Katselas-directed *Romeo and Juliet* starring Tom Harrison and, count 'em, five Juliets to play opposite him, including Mary Crosby and Linda Purl. Along with the Beverly Hills Playhouse, the Skylight is owned by theater bigwig Milton Katselas.

You make your entrance through a walkway between buildings on Vermont. A tiny lobby somehow defies its size and provides comfortable standing room. Seating is raked for easy viewing.

This is a rental house, so performances depend on who rents, but it seems to draw numerous *LA Weekly* "Picks of the Week."

Performances
Fri-Sun 8 pm, Sun matinee
Tickets
$10-15
Parking
On premises, FREE (limited); valet, FREE; street parking

SLEDGEHAMMER THEATRE

St. Cecilia Theater
1620 6th Avenue
San Diego, CA 92101
Info: (619) 544-1484   **Rsvn:** (619) 544-1484
Fax: (619) 544-1485
Artistic Director: Scott Feldsher
Seats 150 for new American works and new interpretations of classics.

True to its name, Sledgehammer Theatre does not aim to please, but it's aiming for you.

It aims to shock, to challenge and to push the edge of the artistic envelope.

From a three-hour, intermissionless version of Beckett's *Endgame* (Samuel and Werner Erhard would be pleased) to a five-hour *Hamlet*, in which Hamlet urinates on stage, this is a company that is the target for equal amounts of kudos and tomatoes.

Sledgehammer co-founders Scott Feldsher and Ethan Feerst have ingeniously carved stages out of old abandoned warehouses. In one production, *Blow Out The Sun*, audiences were ushered from one scenic area to the next. At one point everyone had to stand back for a car zooming through the factory—another scene in the piece.

In 1992, Sledgehammer permanently settled into what had long been known as the Sixth Avenue Playhouse, the San Diego Repertory Theatre's original stage. Sledgehammer restored the name it had before the Rep took it over—St. Cecilia's, which was once a funeral parlor. The stage is high and the seating area long and narrow. The whole effect is Gothic (read dungeonesque) in style.

St. Cecilia's is still haunted by hits from its old Rep days—such as the long-running *Six Women With Brain Death or Expiring Minds Want to Know*, *Rap Master Ronnie*,

Performances
Thurs-Sun 8 pm
Tickets
$10-15
Discounts
Previews/children/ seniors/students/groups of 10+, call administrative office
BO
Call 24 hrs; BO opens 15 minutes prior to performance; check/MC/ V/reserve by mail, fax, Art Tix Booth; exchanges must be made 24 hrs in advance; subscription program
Parking
Adjacent lot, FREE; street
Special Features
There are usually 2 "pay what you can" performances per run

Working—but you're not likely to see such populist fare under the Sledgehammer. Recently the company segued from obscure classicists to new American playwrights such as Mac Wellman and Erik Ehn, whose works have split the critics into camps of wild enthusiasm and utter disdain. The Sledgehammer artistic directors couldn't be happier.

There are many eating establishments nearby, but the best place for getting into the Sledgehammer "swing" of things would be the Java Cafe, a coffee and brie sort of place. If you're determined to have a full, sit-down meal, Croce's is cool.

SMOTHERS THEATRE See **Pepperdine University Center for the Arts**

SOUTH BAY CENTER FOR THE ARTS Also See **MUSIC**

El Camino College/Marsee Auditorium
16007 Crenshaw Boulevard
Torrance, CA 90506
Info: (310) 715-3715   **Rsvn:** (310) 329-5345
Fax: (310) 715-7734
This performing arts center, adorning the campus of El Camino College, offers a wide selection of events, including theater, music, dance, and celebrity speakers.

Performances
Tue-Sun evenings 8 pm, matinee 2 pm
Tickets
$12-33 (depending on event)
Discounts
Children/seniors/students/groups of 20+, through BO
BO
Mon-Fri 9:30 am-7 pm; check/MC/V/reserve by mail, phone; no exchanges or refunds; subscription program
Location
Between Redondo Beach Blvd and Manhattan Beach Blvd; near San Diego (405) Fwy, Artesia (91) Fwy, Harbor (110) Fwy
Parking
On premises, $1 weeknights, FREE weekends;

SOUTH COAST REPERTORY

655 Town Center Drive
Costa Mesa, CA 92626
Info: (714) 957-2602   **Rsvn:** (714) 957-4033
Fax: (714) 545-0391
Producing Artistic Director: David Emmes
Artistic Director: Martin Benson
Two spaces: 507-seat Mainstage, and 161-seat Second Stage.
Founded in 1964, South Coast Repertory is the largest company of professionals in Orange County. Its 10-month, 12-production season is mounted on two stages—the 507-seat Mainstage, and on the more intimate 161-seat Second Stage, with seating on three sides.

Both theaters are elegant and extremely comfortable. A full bar in the lobby, fine restaurants at nearby South Coast Plaza, and a large parking structure

Performances
Tues-Sat 8 pm, Sun 7:30 pm, Sat and Sun 2:30 pm
Tickets
$14-34
Discounts
Previews/children/seniors/students/groups of 15+, call Group Sales Manager, ext. 269

across the street, make it a convenient, not-to-be-missed theater experience.

Awards seem to be the mainstay here, including the 1988 Tony award for Distinguished Achievement in Regional Theatre.

The Mainstage concentrates on classics, but high-powered new plays are not uncommon. The recent season saw plays by Shaw, Steinbeck, and Ibsen, for instance. The Second Stage leans more to the avant-garde and dramas (and comedies) that intelligently inspect the human condition. Some of America's top playwrights are commissioned for new plays by this highly regarded LORT (League of Resident Theatres) theater.

Season subscription tickets offer a considerable discount over single tickets and each subscription comes with a monthly newspaper.

Call for information about the annual *Christmas Carol*, and other family performances during the season.

BO
Mon 10 am-6 pm; Tues-Sat 10 am-8:30 pm; Sun noon-8 pm; check/AE/MC/V; exchanges for subscribers only, with 24 hrs notice; subscription program
Location
Off San Diego (405) Fwy. at Bristol St N
Parking
Nearby, $4

SPRECKELS THEATRE

121 Broadway
San Diego, CA 92101
Info: (619) 235-0494 **Rsvn:** (619) 235-9500
Fax: (619) 233-4524
Seats 1,480 for theater, music, film, and dance.

Few theaters can claim a past full-scale production of *Ben Hur* complete with horse-drawn chariot. But the Spreckels is not just another theater. Now a registered National Historic Site, it was built in 1912 as a small opera house by sugar magnate John D. Spreckels. And Mr. Spreckels did not skimp. The lobby and auditorium abound with Baroque elegance, allegorical paintings, frescoes, and murals.

The 1,480-seat site has presented Enrico Caruso (whose signature is preserved on the basement wall), Eva La Galliene, the Barrymores (John, Lionel, and Ethel), Hepburn, Jolson, Rachmananoff, Martha Graham and countless other legends in their own right.

Today, it presents performances by the Starlight Musical Theatre and touring companies looking for a more intimate setting than the cavernous San Diego Civic Theatre.

You'll want to dress up for this theater. There's no free downtown parking, so your best bet here is to sigh and cough up the going rate at the parking lot under the building, or find another nearby lot and hoof it. You can also arrange to park in a shopping center where a trolley shuttles back and forth from the theater.

Eat at any number of Horton Plaza's sit-down and fast food eateries. Or make a night of it at Dobson's, where chef Debra Schneider has a way with French and international cuisine, or at the elegant Grant Grill & Lounge at the Grant Hotel just across the street, or La Gran Tapa for Spanish specialties.

Performances
Vary
Tickets
$ varies
BO
Call for current hrs; MC/V/TicketMaster
Location
Downtown San Diego, on Broadway between 1st and 2nd; near Int-5, 8 and 163
Parking
On premises, $5; valet, $5; street parking

STAGE DOOR THEATRE

28311 Agoura Road
Agoura, CA 91301
Info: (818) 889-5209 **Rsvn:** (818) 889-5209
50-seat playhouse.

Neil Simon and Agatha Christie get a lot of wear at this rustic, cottage-like space in Agoura. There's a homey, summer-stock feel to the 50-seat playhouse, but you won't find renowned actors or fancy productions here. The plays are tried and true, nothing original, heavy, or

Performances
Thurs 8 pm; Fri-Sat 8:30 pm
Tickets
$8-9
Discounts
Students/seniors/groups of 20+, call BO

avant-garde. SDT offers a six-show season of comedies and mysteries (and occasionally comedies that are mysteries). A Thursday evening dinner package is available in conjunction with Casa Rea restaurant, directly behind the theater.

BO
Answering machine 24 hrs; check/reserve by mail
Location
Cheseboro Rd; Ventura (101) Fwy
Parking
On premises, FREE; street parking

STAGES THEATRE CENTER

1540 North McCadden Place
Hollywood, CA 90028
Info: (213) 463-5356   **Rsvn:** (213) 466-1767
Theater seats 49 for important international plays, some presented in other languages.

Formerly billed as the Stages Trilingual, the Stages Theatre Center has been performing intriguing, high-quality, multi-lingual work for over a decade. Playwrights from Europe, North and South America, many unfamiliar to local audiences, have been produced here. Two Eugene Ionesco Festivals have taken over the stage; works by French writer Marguerite Duras have been surveyed; the entire Eduardo Pavlovsky company from Argentina has performed; other important playwrights from Italy, Quebec, and around the world have been featured. Some of the above have been performed in their native tongue, some bilingually with English.

All told, the past ten years have garnered STC dozens of awards including a recent Los Angeles Drama Critics' Circle Margaret Harford Award for excellence in small theater, four Critic's Circle nominations, and consistent plaudits from apparently fearless audiences.

In addition to the 49-seat theater, there's an outdoor stage, used infrequently, as weather permits, and a 30-seat Laboratory theater sometimes used for readings.

Park across the street in the lot; Le Cafe des Artistes is right next door for those making an evening of it.

Performances
Mon-Sat 8 pm
Tickets
$10-18
Discounts
Previews/children/ seniors/Theatre LA/ groups of 10+, call BO
BO
Call Tues-Sun 11 am-7 pm; open 1 hr before performance; check/AE/ MC/ V/reserve by Theatix (213) 466-1767; no refunds, no exchanges
Location
Off Hollywood (101) Fwy, exit Highland Ave; 1 block E of Highland Ave and 1 block N of Sunset Blvd
Parking
In designated lot across street

NEW STARLIGHT THEATER

Starlight Bowl
1549 El Prado Balboa Park
San Diego, CA 92101
Info: (619) 544-7800   **Rsvn:** (800) 883-PLAY
Fax: (619) 633-1523
In addition to performances at the Starlight Bowl, shows are presented at the Spreckels Theatre in downtown San Diego.

Formerly known as the Starlight Musical Theatre and responsible for 48 seasons of summer outdoor musicals, the New Starlight has been taken over by Theatre Corp. of America, the same organization responsible for the resurgence of Glendale's Alex Theatre.

During those many seasons, Starlight offered up a steady stream of *Sound of Music*, *West Side Story*, and *Camelot* under the stars and the tutelage of then-co-artistic directors Don and Bonnie Ward, who are now producing directors of the New Starlight. The Wards were once a professional dance team and so come by their love of musicals honestly. In fact, they met doing a Starlight musical and eventually it even became a family affair when their children made their appearances.

Performances
Tues-Sun 8 pm; Spreckels matinee Sat 2 pm, Sun 2 pm, 7 pm
Tickets
$12-32, Bowl; $15-37.50, Spreckels
Discounts
Children/seniors/ students/groups of 15+
BO
AE/MC/V/TicketMaster, Art Tix, mail (P.O. Box 3519, San Diego, CA 92101); Starlight Bowl BO, summer Tues-Sat 11 am-6 pm; call Spreckels for current hrs; exchanges for subscribers only; subscription program

The Wards' strengths are the big song and dance numbers, charm, and sheer entertainment. They were instrumental in building up the professionalism (as well as the cast) of the Starlight productions. In recent years, they attempted to gently nudge the conservative Starlight audiences toward newer works, such as *La Cage Aux Folles*, *Dreamgirls*, *Follies*, and *Jesus Christ Superstar*. The first three, noble efforts all, nudged most of them out of the theater. But *Jesus Christ Superstar*, done in a spirit of reverence, proved one of the Starlight's biggest grossing shows ever.

Theatre Corp.'s plans include circulating big productions such as *Fame*, *Sayonara*, and *Mame* from the Alex in Glendale, to Starlight Bowl, to the Warren in Fresno. A six-show series is set for the Spreckels location, and three more large-scale musicals are scheduled for the outdoor Starlight Bowl. Some shows will originate in San Diego, some at the Alex.

In the past, Starlight's biggest challenge was overcoming the limitations of its venue. Patrons have repeatedly told Starlight that they want shows in the open-air Starlight Bowl in Balboa Park, despite the 40-plus airplanes a night zooming overhead (and for which the action expertly and curiously stopped in a freeze frame until the buzz fades). It used to be a scramble nightly to try to make quick scene changes on a backstage where there wasn't much room for the actors to squeeze between the props. But the city of San Diego has come to the rescue with a million dollars-plus for renovation costs. And Theatre Corp.'s management has alluded to many positive future plans, such as special reception areas for new members and updated concession areas.

So the audiences that for years loved sitting outdoors, eating their popcorn, and sipping their drinks while the orchestra played and the tappers tapped, can still do so. The winter season is entirely indoors at the Spreckels Theatre.

Dress warmly and comfortably at the Starlight Bowl; blankets are recommended. Balboa Park parking is free. You can buy hot dogs, popcorn, and desserts at Starlight, or you can dine in the park at the Cafe Del Rey Moro. But most Starlight patrons prefer to picnic it on a nice grassy area in the park before the show.

For information about parking for the Spreckels and San Diego Civic Theatres, see those individual listings.

Location
Bowl, Balboa Park enter off 12th Ave on Presidents Way; Spreckels, see listing
Parking
On premises, FREE (Bowl)

STARMAX PRODUCTIONS

See press listings for performance locations.
Info: (310) 278-7712   **Fax:** (310) 278-8731
Artistic Director: Carole Kean
Mystery dinner theater solvable in a variety of area restaurants.

Where can you go for dinner, drinks, and a murder? Elementary, my dear Watson. For the past eight years, this theater troupe has specialized in putting you smack in the middle of a mystery. *Murder by Night* and *A Case of Medium Murder* are two parlor-type whodunits Starmax plays out as you dine.

Someone (onstage) is slain, and it's up to you to help track down the villain. Both plays were devised by actress Carole Kean and her actor-husband, Earl Boen (of *Terminator* and *Who's The Boss?* repute). With limited seating, the experience unfailingly proves intimate and you're bound to befriend the neighboring table. Plan to expend three hours. Guests are encouraged to dress appropriately for a murder, so have a ball in a black velvet

Performances
Year round; Fri 8 pm; Sat 7 pm
Tickets
$45-55 (includes dinner, tax, tip, show)
Discounts
Children/previews/ seniors/students/groups of 10+, call info
BO
Hrs by arrangement; call info; check/reserve by mail (P.O. Box 11086, Beverly Hills, CA 90213), fax; no refunds; exchange fees $10 per ticket
Parking
Varies with location

gown or a menacing motorcycle jacket. One price buys you dinner (including tax and tip), and the show.

Starmax also presents an audience-participation cabaret of songs and comedy starring Kean herself. The show, *All That Glitz*, has celebrated its first year as we speak.

Each play is held at a cozy restaurant. Though the scene of the crime changes all the time, many of the murder mysteries are performed at Taix Restaurant and the Cat & Fiddle Pub and Restaurant, both on Sunset Boulevard.

Be sure to call for location information.

STELLA ADLER THEATRE & ACADEMY

6773 Hollywood Boulevard
Hollywood, CA 90028
Info: (213) 465-4446   **Rsvn:** (213) 465-4446
Fax: (213) 469-6049
Artistic Director: Irene Gilbert
Home of the 99-seat professional stage, and the Stella Adler Academy Theatre seating 66.

The legendary Stella Adler, who died in December of 1992, left behind a legacy of acting pupils whose works have dazzled us almost as much as she did: Robert De Niro, Marlon Brando, Ellen Burstyn, Harvey Keitel and on and on. Born of two great actors of the Yiddish theater, Jacob and Sarah Adler, Stella Adler became one of the foremost teachers of acting in the world.

While the original Stella Adler Theater has been torn down, her theater foundation lives on. A new theater is now operational. The Theatre is rented out for professional performances offered Thursday through Sunday, while the Academy stage is used for student productions scheduled Friday through Sunday. The Columbia Bar & Grill is a good dinner choice.

Performances
Fri-Sun 8 pm
Tickets
$6-20
Discounts
Students/groups of 20+
BO
Opens at 7:30 pm; check/reserve by phone, mail, fax; call to see if possible to exchange tickets for another date
Location
1/2 block E of Highland, above Hollywood Wax Museum; near the Hollywood (101) Fwy
Parking
On street; 3 parking lots in the vicinity

STRUB THEATRE See **Loyola Marymount University**

STUDIO THEATRE See **Long Beach Community Playhouse**

STUDIO THEATRE (SANTA BARBARA) See **Garvin Theatre**

SUSHI

See press listings for performance locations.
Info: (619) 235-8466   **Rsvn:** (619) 235-8466

San Diego's innovative and bold presenter is nearing its 15th birthday (see **DANCE** for more background). While it searches for a new permanent home, it continues to schedule performance artists in addition to its dance series. Recently Emmy-award-winner Carla Kirkwood brought her "Bodies of Evidence" to Sushi patrons, and New York solo performer Reno tackled current politics, democracy, and relationships on the St. Cecilia stage, where, to date, the performance series takes place. Be sure to find out what's on tap for the upcoming season, and whether shows will still be at St. Cecilia's, 1620 Sixth Avenue at Cedar.

Performances
Vary
Tickets
$15
Discounts
Members/students
BO
Phone; Art Tix
Location
Varies with performance

SWEETOOTH COMEDY THEATRE

Maryland Hotel
630 F Street
San Diego, CA 92101
Info: (619) 265-0471 **Rsvn:** (619) 265-0471
Artistic Director: Thomas Overland

This small theater company, operating out of downtown San Diego's Maryland Hotel, got its name from the toothsomely sweet desserts it serves during intermission.

Over the years this company has shown a taste for an eclectic smorgasbord from *Gertrude Stein and a Companion* to the female version of Neil Simon's *The Odd Couple* to Cynthia Heimel's *A Girl's Guide to Chaos*. Sweetooth also produces an annual December holiday show that intermixes Hanukkah tales and Christmas stories. The company's stated goal is to emphasize shows by or for women.

Special shows for the hearing-impaired are offered; call for details. If you can find street parking, grab it. Otherwise, bring single bills to feed the nearby Ace Parking slots.

Performances
Thurs-Sun 8 pm; Sun 2 pm
Tickets
$10-12
Discounts
Children/seniors/students/groups of 20+, call 265-0471 arrange date and pre-payment
BO
1 hr prior to show; call for reservations; check/reserve by mail, Art Tix; subscription program
Location
Downtown San Diego, on "F" St, between 6th and 7th
Parking
On premises, $2; street parking also available
Special Features
Special performances for the hearing impaired

SYNTHAXIS THEATRE COMPANY

See press listings for performance locations.
Info: (213) 877-4726
Executive Director: Estelle Busch

This small non-Equity company performs for everyone from kindergartners to octogenarians, as example: two one-woman shows, *A Woman's Place*, the study of seven courageous women who helped to change history, and *Window Panes*, a look at five older women in today's youth-oriented society. Youth performances have included adaptations of the classics, music, and original contemporary plays.

Synthaxis has performed at the Museum of Science and Industry, the Children's Museum, and other local venues.

Performances
Vary
Tickets
$ varies

TAMARIND THEATER

5919 Franklin Avenue
Hollywood, CA 90028
Info: (213) 465-7980 **Rsvn:** (213) 466-9714
Fax: (213) 465-8093
Seats 99 to 125 for contemporary plays.

Out-of-towners who think LA theater is out-to-lunch should drop by the Tamarind. One of the busiest houses in town, it concentrates on upbeat contemporary theater. The past few years a slate of productions has kept the theater open almost seven days a week. Theater producers Max Croft and Jody Kiel know how to get audiences in, and name actors are also frequently landed. Productions have been directed by Charles Nelson Reilly and Don ("Happy Days") Most. "Picks of the Week" and Critics Choice awards often favor this lively venue.

Built in the '20s, the building is recognized as a historical site (according to one of the theater producers). The seating, fortunately, is not as venerable, and the

Performances
Mon-Sun, late night Fri-Sun, matinees Sat-Sun
Tickets
$10-20
Discounts
Previews/seniors/children/students/groups of 10+, call BO
BO
7 pm; check/MC/V/reserve by phone
Location
Near Hollywood (101) Fwy; on Franklin Ave 3 blocks E of Gower St

viewing is good. The Tamarind lies due south of the hillside Hollywood sign in "Little Greenwich Village," itself an entertaining revitalized neighborhood of coffeehouses, restaurants and memorabilia shops.

Parking
Valet (sometimes); street parking

TAPER, TOO See **Music Center of Los Angeles County**

TEATRO MASCARA MAGICA—A COMMON GROUND THEATRE

See press listings for performance locations.
Info: (619) 474-6784   **Rsvn:** (619) 474-5270
Fax: (619) 474-5035
Artistic Director: William A. Virchis

Performing at various sites around San Diego, this 15-year old theater group strives for a "consistent forum for multi-ethnic expressions of cultural diversity." That translates into five shows a year, each drawing on a different cultural tradition—American, Hispanic, African-American, and Asian theater—or some combination of these.

Mascara Magica started out at San Diego's Old Globe and still presents its annual Christmas *La Pastorale* there. At least two Mascara Magica productions tour nationally each year.

They're not easy to reach by phone, but be persistent.

Performances
Jan-Dec: Th-Sun 8 pm; Sat-Sun 2 pm
Tickets
$5-15
Discounts
Previews/children/ seniors/students/groups of 10+, call office
BO
Mon-Sun 10 am-5 pm; check/AE/Disc/MC/V/ reserve by mail (140 W 16th St, National City, CA 91950), fax, Art Tix; subscription program
Parking
Varies with location
Special Features
Open rehearsals depending on director

TERRACE THEATER

300 East Ocean Boulevard
Long Beach, CA 90802
Info: (310) 436-3636   **Rsvn:** (310) 436-3661
Fax: (310) 437-6396
Seats 3,141 for theater, music, and dance performances.

Some patrons don't realize that the Terrace, the Center Theater, and the Long Beach Arena are all part of the Long Beach Convention and Entertainment Center. The Center and the Terrace are just steps away from each other.

Like a mini-Dorothy Chandler Pavilion, the Terrace is a comfortable performance space (except that there's no center aisle and getting out at intermission and final curtain can take an eternity). Red is the primary color here, in the carpeting, the lobbies, the theater itself, the seats, and the upholstery.

The main lobby sports a sort of sunken "bullpen" bar. From the main lobby, an open staircase leads to the loge-balcony level offering another lobby (with limited rest room facilities).

The Terrace is home to the Long Beach Civic Light Opera, the Long Beach Symphony, and ballet and opera performances. Usually the LBCLO offers family fare. I would suggest, however, you check the seating chart carefully if you're bringing children—or anyone else short of stature. Without a seating chart I was left at the mercy of a reservationist who repeatedly assured me the seats she chose were perfect for the two children in our group.

Performances
Oct-July; Tues-Sat evening; Sat-Sun matinees
Tickets
$14-34
Discounts
Previews/children/ seniors/students/groups of 20+, call BO
BO
Mon-Sat 10 am-6 pm; check/AE/MC/V/reserve by mail, fax, TicketMaster; subscription program
Parking
On premises, $5

Needless to say, two adults ended up with two children on their laps for the duration of the show. You won't always get perfect seats, but patrons should be told if there are sight obstructions.

Parking is available in the adjacent structure as well as in other nearby lots.

LONG BEACH CIVIC LIGHT OPERA—Resident Co.

In addition to performances at the Terrace, the LBCLO uses the more intimate Center Theater at the same location for its smaller productions. Top stars do their civic duty here (i.e., Tyne Daly and Charles Durning in *Queen of the Stardust Ballroom* and Carol Burnett in *From the Top!*).

Subscription series tickets entitle ticket holders to performances at both theaters. Call (310) 435-7605 for information, and TicketMaster or (310) 432-7926 for single tickets, (800) 659-9899 for season tickets.

THEATER OF ARTS

4128 Wilshire Boulevard
Los Angeles, CA 90010
Info: (213) 380-0511   (213) 380-0513
Fax: (213) 380-0543
Artistic Director: Jeremy Whelan
A 90-seat theater for outside producers.

Inhabiting an old acting school on Wilshire Boulevard, this is room and board theater, period. Still, this place is a good starting point for those whose talent and determination will eventually drive them to more glamorous surroundings. Though seats are on permanent risers, sightlines are poor in certain areas, so expect to lean left or right to see.

Performances
 Mon, Wed, Fri-Sun 5
 pm, 7 pm or 8 pm
Tickets
 $10-20
Discounts
 Previews/children/
 seniors/students/groups
 of 8+, call BO
BO
 Mon-Sun 10 am-10 pm
 check/reserve by mail,
 phone, TicketMaster;
 exchanges made
Location
 Mid Wilshire district
Parking
 On premises, FREE;
 street parking

THEATER 6470 See **The Complex**

THEATRE AMERICANA

568 East Mt. Curve
Altadena, CA 91001
Info: (818) 397-1740   **Rsvn:** (818) 397-1740
Community theater producing original scripts; seats 150.

Established in 1934, Theatre Americana claims to be the oldest small playhouse in the United States dedicated to producing original American plays and musicals. Of the 100 or so scripts submitted each year for production, four are selected to go on its community stage. The rotating actors, directors, writers, and crews generously offer their talents and skills without charge.

Truly a community theater, T.A. offers groups of handicapped audiences special free previews of all their plays.

Performances
 Fri-Sat 8 pm
Tickets
 $6-10
Discounts
 Children/seniors/
 students/groups of 10+,
 call
BO
 Tickets at performances
 only, check/cash;
 subscription program
Location
 N off Foothill (210) Fwy
 at Lake to Mt. Curve
 Ave
Parking
 On premises, FREE;
 street parking

THEATRE EAST

12655 Ventura Boulevard
Studio City, CA 91604
Rsvn: (818) 760-4160
95-seat theater for workshop performances.

Producer Tom Patchett, writer Danny Simon, and actors Theodore Bikel and Mariette Hartley are past or present members of Theatre East, which touts itself as LA's oldest workshop and is certainly one of the oldest theater companies in town. The professional group of actors, writers, directors, casting directors and others workshop their original projects in the theater's "gymnasium atmosphere." They are dedicated to "growing, and to failing...in a setting that has no one technique or way of working," according to Elaine Welton Hill, a ten-year veteran, as well as current president.

There's no regular performance schedule, but audiences are occasionally invited to watch these works-in-progress free of charge. Much of their original work has been critically acclaimed and subsequently published. The workshop that subsequently became George Furth's *Company* was developed at Theatre East.

Look for the bright red awning over Jerry's Deli on Ventura Boulevard. The theater is just to the right, through the bowling alley and video arcade doors, and up the stairs. Hill assures that (most) performances are not the least bowled over by the noise. On non-tournament nights, there's plenty of parking in the adjacent lot.

If you need a pre-theater food-fix, Jerry's, open 24 hours seven days a week, serves up good deli food, and the favorite Daily Grill has a spot at Laurel Canyon and Ventura Boulevard. An alternative choice might be a late set of Brazilian jazz at La Ve Lee, just east of the theater.

Performances
Vary
Tickets
$5-12
Discounts
Depend on type of show
BO
Check/reserve by phone
Location
Off Ventura (101) Fwy; between Coldwater Canyon and Whitsett; above Jerry's Famous Deli
Parking
On street; lot parking adjacent nearby
Special Features
Open dress rehearsals sometimes; free admission to labs

THEATRE EAST

210 East Main Street
El Cajon, CA 92020
Info: (619) 440-0372   **Rsvn:** (619) 440-2277
Fax: (619) 440-6429
Seats 1,218 for touring theater companies, music, and dance events.

This presenting house is still finding its identity and focus. Formerly known as the East County Performing Arts Center, or ECPAC, Theatre East (part of the Grossmont College system) provides a venue for college shows. It also books commercial tour groups and shows from other regional theaters, as well as music and dance events.

The facility is big and barnlike. One goes for the individual show rather than for the atmosphere. Just outside, however, is the charming El Cajon Plaza Amphitheatre, a tiny jewel backed by a small lake. The El Cajon is where Octad-One presents its annual free Shakespeare-by-the-lake shows.

Don't dress up. There's lots of parking in the nearby lots. Fast food and franchise restaurants abound; Marie Callender's is a popular choice.

Performances
Mon-Sun
Tickets
$ varies
Discounts
Children/seniors/ students/groups
BO
Mon-Fri noon-4 pm; Sat 11 am-3 pm; MC/V/ check/reserve by mail; no refunds, no exchanges
Location
Hwy (8) E; Magnolia Civic Center exit; Intersection of Main St and W.D. Hall
Parking
On premises, FREE; street parking

THEATRE EXCHANGE

11855 Hart Street
North Hollywood, CA 91605
Info: (818) 773-7862   **Rsvn:** (818) 773-7862
Seats 57.

    Back in the days when the San Fernando Valley was ranch country, ranchers auctioned off their livestock in Theatre Exchange's circular building. (An early form of California summer stock?) Later it served as the land office for Mr. Lankershim, he of Lankershim Boulevard fame. Nowadays it's cheek-by-jowl with the residential and industrial areas of North Hollywood. Some patrons may think they're traveling to Oregon to get there, but it's worth the effort.

    With worn but cushy seats, the pie-shaped theater fits 57 with more breathing room than most storefront spaces. In winter, favor the back row—it's a bit cramped but warm.

INTERACT—Resident Co.

    The company of seasoned well-trained actors apply classical acting technique to unusual literary material. They've received exceptional response to their staged treatments of actual short stories. These are not dramatic adaptations; the author's descriptive prose is spoken as well as the dialogue. It's a treat to see and hear Hemingway and Dylan Thomas meaningfully brought to life.

    Call the hotline number for the latest events (818) 773-7862; it's updated weekly. For a small donation, the public is invited to Interact's Monday night cold readings, the Tuesday evening Playwrights Lab, or the current workshop production.

Performances
    Thurs-Sat 8 pm, Sun 3 pm, 7:30 pm
Tickets
    $10-15
Discounts
    Previews/seniors/ students/groups of 10+, call BO
BO
    1 hr prior to performance; call 24 hr hotline (818) 773-7862; check; no exchanges
Location
    Two blocks S of Sherman Way between Laurel Canyon and Lankershim Blvds
Parking
    Street

THEATRE 40

241 Moreno Drive
Beverly Hills, CA 90212
Info: (310) 277-4221
Fax: (213) 876-0227
Artistic Director: Charles Arthur
99-seat theater offering a variety of theater genres.

    A favorite of the city's theater troupes, the productions these thespians render are always professional and their accommodations, obliging. They have presented wonderful versions of *The Shadow Box, Under Milkwood,* as well as an on-track record of Shakespeare. The theater's annual Festival of One-Acts often garners rave reviews.

    Running the gamut of genres, Theatre 40 performs on the campus of Beverly Hills High School (yes, the famed home of Fox's "Beverly Hills 90210"), in one of the most comfortable 99-seat theaters in town. A generous season ticket policy insures easy reservations; parking is free.

Performances
    Mon-Sun evenings; Sun 2 pm
Tickets
    $10-17
Discounts
    Previews/students/ groups
BO
    Open 1 hr before performances; AE/MC/ V/check/Theatix; exchanges made thru Theatix; subscription program
Location
    San Diego (405) Fwy; Santa Monica Blvd exit; 1 block E of Santa Monica (Little) Blvd; right, in Beverly Hills High School, next to Century City
Parking
    On premises (a huge school lot), FREE

THEATRE IN OLD TOWN

4040 Twiggs Street
San Diego, CA 92110
Info: (619) 688-2496   **Rsvn:** (619) 688-2494
Fax: (619) 569-0621
Artistic Director: Paula Kalustian
A 244-seat theater for professional as well as school-sponsored plays.

The Theatre in Old Town is a lovely theater nestled in the heart of picturesque Old Town.

The Francis Parker High School performs here, but most of the schedule is taken up by professional performances. Judging from the track record of new artistic director Paula Kalustian, the theater will continue to present small-scale, high-quality contemporary musicals.

Kalustian's first effort, *Beehive*, a five-woman show that romped from the songs of the '50s (and those mandatory beehive hairdos) to the end of the '60s, was the biggest hit the theater had ever seen, selling out in one week in advance for a February to Labor Day run.

In fact, it was the sweet success of *Beehive* that secured Kalustian the queen-bee post as artistic director. Kalustian, the chair of the San Diego State University musical theater department, had originally been hired to direct *Beehive*. At a time when the Old Town theater was undergoing a crisis of identity, Kalustian came in, hired faculty members at SDSU to do the design work, called on old actress friends to fly in from various assignments in other cities, and produced the kind of runaway hit that produces industry buzz.

The theater is currently experimenting with its first season.

Parking is free at the lot across the street, but it fills up quickly—arrive early. There is parking on the street, but again, that's often hard to find because Old Town is such a popular tourist destination. Old Town is known for its Mexican restaurants, particularly Casa De Bandini and the Old Town Mexican Cafe.

Performances
Thurs-Sat 8 pm; Sat 5 pm; Sun 7 pm;
Tickets
$10-18
Discounts
Children/seniors/ students/groups of 20+, call BO; military discounts also given
BO
Tues-Sat 10 am-6 pm; Sun for performance only; check/MC/V/ reserve by mail, Art Tix; exchanges for subscribers only; no ticket exchanges on single ticket sales; subscription program
Location
In Old Town, San Diego; 5 S to Old Town Ave exit, left on San Diego Ave, right on Twiggs; or 8 W to Taylor St, left on Juan, right on Twiggs
Parking
On premises, FREE; street parking

THEATRE OF N.O.T.E.

Info: (213) 666-5550

N.O.T.E. stands for New One Act Theatre Ensemble, the playhouse so named for its resident company's immersion in original shorts. The January trembler trembled this former coffeehouse, and it has permanently shut down. The crew is scrambling for new digs—preferably in Hollywood—where they were before being so rudely shaken up.

NEW ONE-ACT THEATRE ENSEMBLE (N.O.T.E.)— Resident Co.

With a penchant for performing outlandish, innovative, avant-garde theater, this playful troupe is usually intriguing. It's an ensemble willing to take chances; they were recently nominated for six *LA Weekly* awards. It's a group definitely worth watching—and looking for. Now that they are "homeless," you'll have to keep checking the calendar listings for news. Also see information in **FESTIVALS** about **Festival of N.O.T.E.**

THEATRE PALISADES See **Pierson Playhouse**

THEATRE/THEATER

1713 Cahuenga Boulevard
Hollywood, CA 90028
Info: (213) 850-6941 **Rsvn:** (213) 871-0210
Mainstage seats 71, backstage, 26.

Despite the redundancy of the name, consider this a "must attend"—I repeat "must attend" theater—a chance to see work truly out of the ordinary in a local theater setting. Established in 1981, and, according to artistic director Jeff Murray, "... conceived as a theater space committed to eclectic performances," emphasizing original and unfamiliar works, Theatre/Theater has kept up its act as a critically and commercially successful small production house. Its opening work, *Creeps*, ran for 22 months and won not only four Los Angeles Drama Critics Circle Awards but every major Los Angeles theatrical award.

Other offerings have captured the *LA Weekly* Production of the Year award. The same newspaper not long ago distinguished it as "the hottest theatrical venue around for wild, shocking, fresh new work." Recently, the theater won enthusiastic reviews and Critics Choice awards in the *LA Times*, *LA Reader*, and *Variety*, among others.

With no resident company, Murray and his wife Nicolette Chaffey cast about for each project. Then they either produce themselves or co-produce.

In any case, everything they pick fills the two stages (the tiny backstage seats 26, the front a grand total of 71) here five nights a week, including performance artists, ensemble plays, music and comedy. TheaterSports, which was described by the *LA Reader* as "simply the best Improv group in LA," keeps its lockers here. (In case you don't know about TheaterSports: two improvisational teams compete in front of a live audience—Saturday and Monday evenings for adults, Saturday afternoons for kids. See the **CHILDREN** chapter for more information on TheaterSports Kidprov at Theatre/Theater.)

The building's pretty much the heart of Hollywood, so cough up the $3.50 and park in the theater's parking lot.

Performances
Mon-Thurs 8 pm; Fri - Sat 8 pm and 10 pm; Sun 7 pm; Sat-Sun 2 pm
Tickets
$10-20
Discounts
Previews/children/ seniors/students/groups of 10+, call BO
BO
1 hr before performance; check/reserve by phone, mail; exchanges made
Location
S off Hollywood (101) Fwy, exit at Cahuenga Blvd; 1/2 block N of Hollywood Blvd
Parking
On premises, $3.50; street parking

THEATRE WEST

3333 Cahuenga Boulevard West
Los Angeles, CA 90068
Info: (213) 851-4839 **Rsvn:** (213) 851-7977
Artistic Moderator: Norman Cohen
Seats 180 for all sorts of plays; children's performances on weekends.

Trusting to honesty as the best theater policy, managing director Doug Marney courageously describes his theater as "... not spectacularly adorable; but I wouldn't call it ugly. I'd like to lie and say it's nestled in the Hollywood Hills somewhere, but it's just a nondescript box in front of Hanna Barbera Studios." It's an apt description, but you do get to park in the Hanna Barbera lot across the street.

THEATRE WEST—Resident Co.

Once upon a time, an assortment of actor friends met in New York to work (or rather play) together. Their creative efforts led to *Spoon River Anthology* and then to Broadway. When these actors moved West one by one, their Los Angeles company came to life.

"We present Shakespeare to musical-comedy to filthy plays," relates one of the 300 members of this

Performances
Fri-Sun, matinees Sat-Sun
Tickets
$10-15
Discounts
Children/seniors/ students/groups of 15+, call BO
BO
Call; check/MC/V/AE; no exchanges; subscription program
Location
On Cahuenga Blvd (parallel to Hollywood (101) Fwy) between Barham and Lankershim
Parking
Lot across street, FREE; street parking

cooperative of actors, designers, directors, and others who assemble to brainstorm material. There's no artistic director and no executive board in Theatre West, which takes pride in being "a total democracy." The company's finished shows are first born and nurtured in ongoing rehearsal workshops. At 30 years old, Theatre West is one of the city's oldest operating acting companies. Their annual performance schedule is erratic, featuring anywhere from zero to ten shows. It depends on the number of plays they feel are presentable. Recently launched was an ambitious series of nine plays entitled Theatre West Works, most naturally developed in-house.

Check out the **CHILDREN** chapter for information on the company's Storybook Theatre.

THIRD RAIL THEATRE COMPANY

See press listings for performance locations.
Info: (818) 501-3729   **Rsvn:** (818) 501-3729
Artistic Director: Susan Hirschman

Many of the company's members are transplanted from New York, where the subway sign, "DANGER, THE THIRD RAIL IS ELECTRIC, DO NOT TOUCH," inspired their name.

Artistic Director Susan Hirschman likes to be eclectic as well as electric. She spurns a single performance format, interweaving various presentational art-forms. Some of the company's performances, for instance, have included live musicians on stage. "Pre-sets," sometimes precede the main show to introduce the motifs and themes to come later. The cast promises to bring the electric voltage of New York's third rail to the Los Angeles small theater experience.

Performances
  Thurs-Sun 8 pm,
  readings Mon 8 pm
Tickets
  $10-12
BO
  Mon-Sun 10 am-6 pm;
  check/MC/V; exchanges
  with 24 hr notice
Parking
  Varies with location

THIRD STAGE THEATER

2811 West Magnolia Boulevard
Burbank, CA 91505
Info: (818) 842-4755   **Rsvn:** (818) 842-4755
50-seats, rental productions.

This small Burbank space has a large track record of hosting good plays. You can't miss its blue facade on an otherwise pretty unremarkable portion of Magnolia Boulevard. The appointments within are not glamorous, what with well-worn seats and a cramped lobby area. Also, the public bathroom is unstrategically located backstage where the actors wait for their cues, so pray that nature calls after the curtain calls, or you may have to disrupt the performance.

For inexpensive Italian cuisine served in generous portions, you may want to try Pinocchio's Deli down the block. After the fact, head for Chadney's nearby for late-night music.

Performances
  Fri-Sun 8 pm; Sun 2 pm
Tickets
  $10-15
Discounts
  Previews/children/
  seniors/students/groups
  of 15+, call BO
BO
  Varies with production
Location
  Between Hollywood
  Way and Buena Vista; N
  of Ventura (101) Fwy; W
  of Golden State (5) Fwy
Parking
  On street

THE TIFFANY THEATERS

8532 Sunset Boulevard
West Hollywood, CA 90069
Info: (310) 854-3684   **Rsvn:** (310) 289-2999
Fax: (310) 289-2989
Two 99-seat stages.

The Tiffany has been a popular Sunset Strip venue for live theater since its conversion from a movie house (which years ago fostered repeated midnight pilgrimages to its presentation of *The Rocky Horror Picture Show*).

Performances
  Thurs-Sun
Tickets
  $15-24
Discounts
  Previews/seniors/
  students/groups of 10+,
  call

Since 1985, its two 99-seat theaters have been offering the usual TV-familiar casts (Tracy Scoggins, Susan Anton, et al) in entertaining shows that seem to be a little more expensive than most non-Equity houses. Numerous shows hit a popular nerve—*Bouncers* and *Nite Club Confidential* surface to mind—and take off for longer runs (no syndication, darn it!). *Wooman Lovely Wooman, What A Sex You Are!* enjoyed an SRO run here.

BO
Tues-Wed 1-5 pm, Thurs-Sun 1 pm-showtime; check/MC/V; no refunds, no exchanges
Location
On Sunset 1/2 block W of La Cienega Blvd
Parking
On premises, $3

TRACY ROBERTS THEATER

141 South Robertson Boulevard
Los Angeles, CA 90048
Info: (310) 271-2730 **Rsvn:** (310) 271-1478
Artistic Director: Tracy Roberts

The fare here varies from student showcases to professional productions of Sartre's *The Respectful Prostitute* and the West Coast premiere of Tina Howe's *The Art of Dining*. Located in the Tracy Roberts Actors Studio, this small theater doubles as a classroom for Miss Roberts' acting students, who range from beginning to professional working actors.

Performances
Fri-Sun 8 pm, Sun 2 pm
Tickets
$10 donation
BO
Noon-8 pm; check/MC/V
Location
Just N of 3rd St
Parking
Nearby, $1; street parking

TWO ROADS THEATRE CO.

4348 Tujunga Avenue
Studio City, CA 91604
Info: (818) 766-9381 **Rsvn:** (818) 766-9381
48-seat theater offering contemporary plays.

Two Roads is, literally, a storefront space on a spiffy strip of Tujunga Avenue adjacent to a very pleasant residential area. Ragtag furniture sits in the lobby, but the seats are fine and, like many of these small places, the sightlines are good.

If you're famished, there is an Armenian restaurant right next door called El Nejme, Italian food across the street at Vitello's, and barbecue around the corner at Village BBQ.

TWO ROADS THEATRE CO.—Resident Co.

This new group likes contemporary fun. *Stay Carl Stay* was a comedy not long ago about a dog (played by a human actor) who breaks up a relationship.

The company is open to just about anything. Dramas, one-acts, original and published works, are all on their menu. Musicals are about the only genre they don't do.

Performances
Thurs-Sun 8 pm, Sun 2 pm
Tickets
$8-15
Discounts
Previews/children/ seniors/students/groups of 10+, call
BO
Check/reserve by phone; exchanges flexible; subscription program
Location
At Hollywood and Ventura (101) Fwys, 1/2 block S of Moorpark
Parking
On street

UCI SCHOOL OF FINE ARTS

Corner of Campus Drive and Bridge Road
University of California, Irvine
Irvine, CA 92717
Info: (714) 856-8748 **Rsvn:** (714) 856-6616
Fax: (714) 725-2450
University performances are held in the Village Theater (seating 420) and Studio Theatre (90 seats).

Sheer numbers here would seem to promise some talented productions. Even classy ones. There are some 45,000 students enrolled at the University of California at Irvine. Of these, hundreds pursue degrees in the

Performances
Vary
Tickets
$6-15
Discounts
Seniors/students/groups of 15+, call BO

performing arts. Over 200 student performances are given each year!

Besides the regular subscription series of dance, drama, and orchestra, there are many free music events and recitals. Some are scheduled, such as the quarterly concerts by jazz, wind, and percussion groups, and the twice-yearly opera workshop performances. Others, like the noon and evening student recitals, bloom at a variety of times during the year.

The box office dispenses information on the regular series, the scheduled free performances, and the student recitals.

All the venues used for student works are small, from the main stage Village Theatre of 420 seats to the 90-seat black box Studio Theatre.

Check out the Market Place across the street from the University for a variety of dining choices.

BO
Oct-June, Mon-Fri 10 am-3 pm; MC/V/ reserve by mail, TicketMaster, UCI Bren Events Center (714) 856-5000; exchanges made 24 hr in advance, subject to availability; subscription program

Location
Off the San Diego (405) Fwy; between Jamboree on the North and Culver Dr on the South

Parking
On premises, $3; street parking

UCLA (ROYCE, SCHOENBERG, WADSWORTH 〰)

The scope of music, theater, and dance events during a year at UCLA is extraordinary. Hundreds of performances are staged in at least half a dozen venues, including Wadsworth Theater, Schoenberg Hall, Ralph Freud Playhouse, the Little Theater, Pauley Pavilion, and Melnitz Theater. Artists and programs represent just about every performance style, discipline, persuasion, and trend. The range of expertise begins with acting student projects (which can be very good!) to the most renowned professionals. And let's not forget the classic film series.

The January 1994 earthquake in Los Angeles did its terrible deed on Royce Hall. At last word, the damage was repairable, but UCLA decided to go ahead with previous plans to make the historic building earthquake-safe. Therefore, it's not yet known whether the building will open for the 1994-5 UCLA Performing Arts Series on time. If it doesn't, peformances will be scheduled in alternate venues such as Wadsworth. It's best to call the box office if you're unsure about a Royce Hall performance.

UCLA CENTER FOR THE PERFORMING ARTS
See press listings for performance locations.
Rsvn: (310) 825-2101
Artistic Director: Michael Blachly

How to figure it all out? Where do you go first in Paradise? First request a free brochure of events by calling (310) 825-6879. Then put your name on the mailing list; call (310) 825-2101. The Center issues an exemplary season brochure. It's easy to follow and facilitates ordering from the gaggle of series.

The UCLA Center presents such major artists as soprano Kathleen Battle, cellist Yo-Yo Ma, Britain's Royal National Theatre, Alvin Ailey American Dance Theater, Children's Theatre Company of Minneapolis, and other bill toppers who combined can draw more than 200,000 patrons to some 200 performances on the Westwood campus each year. The main season is September through June. Only a scattering of events take place during the summer.

Don't be confused by the term "center." That's a title for the umbrella organization, not a location. Performances are usually held in UCLA's main venues: Royce Hall, Schoenberg Hall, or Wadsworth Theater (as well as at other locations mentioned above). This is a high-profile, well-publicized, money-making operation that dukes it out with the Kennedy Center, the Los Angeles Music

Performances
Vary

Tickets
$10-40

Discounts
Students/children/ seniors/groups of 25+, call BO

BO
Mon-Fri 9 am-5 pm; Sat 9 am-1 pm; Sun 10 am-3 pm; check/AE/MC/V/ reserve by phone, mail (UCLA Central Ticket Office, P.O. Box 24607, CA 90024-0607), TicketMaster; exchanges or cancellations for subscribers only; subscription program

Location
Call for individual performance locations

Center, and Carnegie Hall as one of the nation's leading culture conveyors.

The Center offers a spectrum of classical music, jazz, dance, and theater series subscriptions options. At last count, 14 in all, ranging from $45 to $169 for between two and six performances per series. All series subscriptions are discounted 10% off single-ticket prices. Subscribers get at least a six-week jump on ticket sales over the general public, as well as the same seat at each performance (or a similar seat if at different venues).

Speaking of seats, this is my only hesitation when it comes to ordering by phone or mail. I was told my seats at Royce Hall and Wadsworth were "terrific," only to land directly in front of the huge speakers at Wadsworth, and in extreme side balcony seats at a near-empty dance performance in Royce Hall. Whenever possible, use your seating charts.

Anybody who's ever griped about buying a pre-selected series can opt for the "Choose Your Own Series." It allows you to personalize at least four events from among all the series and still receive the 10% discount. Certain performances may be blacked out for this option, and this option is offered after the regular series subscription offers.

If you buy two series (other than Choose Your Own and the LA Chamber Orchestra), you'll receive free parking. That's a pretty fair offer considering the $5 per space fee. Depending on the series, you could save up to $50 just on parking.

Series subscribers account for a majority of ticket sales. Still, singles, from $10 to $40, are usually available for most events. But no refunds—on any tickets—except for cancelled events. Series subscribers may exchange tickets; single ticket buyers, no way.

Two-dollar discounts to many events are available to members of the UCLA Alumni Association. Full-time students (from any school) and seniors can pick up discounted tickets on a "rush" basis at the venue's ticket office a half hour before showtime (if the event isn't sold out). One caveat—this is a cash-only deal. Always call the Central Ticket Office first to find out if "rush" tickets are available.

Pre-concert forums, with faculty, artists and critics, add enlightening background, historical perspective, and cultural commentary to many of the events. These popular forums are held one hour prior to curtain.

A free jazz series is presented by the UCLA Student Committee on the first Sunday of each month at 7 pm in Wadsworth Theater. Trust the students to invite such greats as Branford Marsalis, Tuck and Patti, Buddy Collette, and Freddie Hubbard. Tickets are not issued for these events; seating is on a first-come basis, so show up early for a good show. Call the Central Ticket Office for artist info.

The Central Ticket Office (CTO) is located in James West Center near Ackerman Union. (Call 310-825-2101.) CTO operating hours are 9 am to 5 pm Monday through Friday; 9 am to 1 pm Saturday; 10 am to 3 pm Sunday. CTO is closed Saturday and Sunday during the summer.

SCHOOL OF THE ARTS AND SCHOOL OF THEATER, FILM AND TELEVISION
See press listings for performance locations.
Info: (310) 206-6465   **Rsvn:** (310) 825-2101
Fax: (310) 206-8504

The performing arts academic departments are divided between the School of the Arts (which includes music and dance) and the School of Theater, Film and Television. These schools sponsor the student and faculty

Parking
On premises, $5;
(parking is free if 2
series are purchased)

Performances
Sept-June
Tickets
$ varies
Discounts
Children/seniors/
students/groups of 25+

productions. Occasional outside professional groups perform independently or as part of a school-sponsored event.

If you've never attended a student-faculty production at UCLA, don't get the wrong idea about the caliber of performance—it's quite high. The faculty numbers many highly regarded professional artists. In the music department, for instance, Johana Harris is an internationally acclaimed pianist and RCA recording artist; Gary Gray (clarinet/saxophone) is a Grammy award winner; composer Roger Bourland recently composed the critically acclaimed AIDS cantata, *Hidden Legacies*. The dance department is the nation's oldest state university dance arts program.

On the theater, film and TV side, Tony award winning director Mel Shapiro leads the school's acting program. Gilbert Cates, who in 1990 was appointed Dean of the School of Theater, Film and Television, produced the original Broadway production of *I Never Sang for My Father*, and later produced and directed the 1970 film version (which received three Academy Award nominations).

The School of Theater, Film and Television sponsors its own play subscription series November through June. You can create your own lineup by choosing five out of nine plays for about $50 (seniors get away for less). Single tickets, almost always available, run about $10; students and seniors get a break.

About one-third of the presentations are thesis productions by graduate students in directing. All shows are produced in the Ralph Freud (pronounced "frude") Playhouse in Macgowan Hall (at the northeast end of the campus). The comfortable playhouse seats 500, (orchestra seating only, continental style). Acoustics don't get high honors.

Just across a courtyard from Freud is the cozy, 175-seat Little Theater ("everybody's favorite" according to a long-time department staffer) used for classes as well as student productions.

Two other notable but under-publicized theater department events are the two bills of one-acts put on each quarter, and Noon Miracles. The one-acts, all student produced and directed, are presented free, usually in the evening at one of the studio theaters (1330 or 1340 Macgowan Hall) or in the Little Theater. Noon Miracles occur each Friday (at noon) in 1340 Macgowan Hall. These theater projects are so completely student-generated, the students get to do just about anything they want, from monologues to rock-band musicals. Most of the work is original. The results are sometimes unfathomable but always imaginative. And remember, they're free.

The annual UCLA Festival spotlights student accomplishment in film, video, and theater. For one week in June, films and videos, many final thesis productions, are screened, and an evening of acting competition is held (the latter by invitation only). Most of the screenings shine in Melnitz Theater (in Melnitz Hall) and are well attended; tickets are reasonably priced at about $5.

Call the Central Ticket Office at (310) 825-2101 for information on the UCLA Festival and theater subscription series. Call (310) 206-0426 to find out more about the one-acts, Noon Miracles, other Theater Department events, or to put your name on the mailing list. Park in Lot 3 for events at Macgowan and Melnitz.

Last but by no means least in the UCLA performing arts pantheon is the Film and Television Archive. See **ART FILMS** and **MUSIC** for further information.

BO
Mon-Fri 9 am-5 pm; Sat 9 am-1 pm; Sun 10 am-3 pm; AE/MC/V/ TicketMaster; no exchanges or single tickets; subscription progr am

UCSD DEPARTMENT OF DRAMA

Mandell Weiss Theatre, UCSD
9500 Gilman Drive
La Jolla, CA 92093-0344
Info: (619) 534-3793   **Rsvn:** (619) 534-4574
Fax: (619) 534-1080
Artistic Director: Frantisek Deak, Department Chair

Generally acknowledged as having one of the finest graduate acting programs in the country, the University of California at San Diego often provides an inexpensive preview of tomorrow's potential stars.

The company performs in the technically sumptuous Mandell Weiss Theatre and the Mandell Weiss Forum, facilities it shares with the La Jolla Playhouse. It also shares its budding talent with the Playhouse. All the students appear in Playhouse shows at some point during the season, usually when the school session overlaps with the Playhouse's fall tenancy.

UCSD's theatrical choices for its season are relentlessly avant-garde, of the sort that sends academics into ecstasy and the general population into the parking lot. But stay in your seats. These often prove to be very stimulating theatrical exercises. And look for new works by student playwrights, some of whose promise (and promise) is actually kept. The university's annual guest artist director production also often delivers the goods. The guest artist production, usually a spring affair, attracts some of the country's best and most adventurous directors and often results in work of great impact. Local people still talk about Anne Bogart's *1941* and the way it dealt with the McCarthy hearings, as well as her *Strindberg Sonata*, a poetic, mystical exploration inside August Strindberg's mind.

Like most state-funded complexes, there's ample parking, but you must pay your way at the information booth before proceeding on to the campus parking lot. Dress is collegiate casual. If you want to eat like a student, too—quickly and inexpensively—pull in first to nearby Samson's Deli or the Soup Plantation.

Performances
Nov-May; Wed-Sat 8 pm; Sat 2 pm; Sun 7 pm
Tickets
$6-12
Discounts
Seniors/students/groups of 10, call BO
BO
Mon-Fri 11 am-6 pm; check/AE/Disc/MC/V/ reserve by mail, fax; exchanges for subscribers only; subscription program

UC SAN DIEGO UNIVERSITY EVENTS

UCSD, Mandeville Auditorium, off Gilman Drive
La Jolla, CA 92093-0078
Info: (619) 534-4090   **Rsvn:** (619) 534-6467
Fax: (619) 534-1505

This annual on-campus performing arts series unfolds in Mandeville Auditorium from fall to spring. The great variety of performers and performances are booked here generally assures something for all tastes. A Chamber Music Series is one option; a Dance Series another. The Music program has offered Ondekoza, the demon drummers of Japan, Kulintang Arts, a program of dance and music from the Philippines, and Clarence Fountain & The Blind Boys of Alabama. Theater presentations number family shows as well as grown up fare. Special events range from lectures to an International Film Festival.

Order single tickets or save your bucks for tuition by creating a discounted series of five events of your choice. Tickets are sold by mail (call for an order form and season brochure), or through TicketMaster outlets.

Performances
Tues-Sun 8 pm
Tickets
$6-25
Discounts
Children/seniors/ students/groups of 20+, call BO
BO
Tues-Fri 10 am-5 pm; 1 hr before performance; check/MC/V/reserve by mail, by phone, Ticket-Master; no exchanges; subscription program
Location
Take Int-5 to La Jolla Village Dr; go W to Gilman Dr exit; take a right turn onto Gilman Dr; the visitor's information stand will be to the right side
Parking
On premises, $3

UPFRONT COMEDY SHOWCASE See **CLUBS**

VICTORY THEATRE
LITTLE VICTORY

3324 West Victory Boulevard
Burbank, CA 91505
Info: (818) 841-4404   **Rsvn:** (818) 841-5421
Fax: (818) 766-7065
Artistic Directors: Maria Gobetti/Tom Ormeny
The Victory seats 91, the LV, 48.
     This two-theater complex produces three or four shows each year, subsisting or feasting, as the case may be, on original plays and world or West Coast premieres. When they score a direct hit (i.e., *On the Money* or *Miss Firecracker Contest*) they extend the show for months beyond the usual six-week run.
     Facing a raised proscenium stage, the 91 seats rake steeply, so expect few sightline problems (other than man-made ones).
     The Little Victory Theatre next door seats 48 and is the usual spot for children's programs of the *Sleeping Beauty* ilk.

Performances
  Thurs-Sun evenings;
  Thurs-Sat matinees
Tickets
  $10-17
Discounts
  Children/seniors/
  students/groups of 10,
  call BO
BO
  Mon-Fri 1 pm-6 pm; Sat-
  Sun 2 pm-7 pm; MC/V/
  reserve by mail;
  exchanges made 24 hrs
  in advance
Location
  1 block E of Hollywood
  Way in Burbank
Parking
  On premises, FREE;
  street parking

VOX BOX ARTS COLLECTIVE

See press listings for performance locations.
Info: (213) 954-1971
Artistic Directors: Janice Mautner/Keith Mitchell
     Definitions blur when attempting to pin down multimedia companies such as Vox Box. This developing group mounts small productions based on traditional forms of theater and narrative, but infused with abstract poetry, prose, music, sculpture, light, and film. Its multicultural artists' goal, in fact, is to blur the edges of the artistic disciplines. "What?" you ask. Watch for them at venues such as the Los Angeles Children's Museum, the Westside Arts Center, and other small performance spaces.

Performances
  Vary
Tickets
  $ varies
BO
  Hrs vary
Parking
  Varies with location
Special features
  Open rehearsals

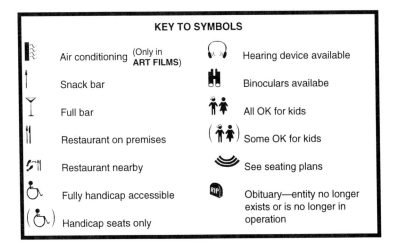

KEY TO SYMBOLS

Air conditioning (Only in **ART FILMS**)		Hearing device available
Snack bar		Binoculars availabe
Full bar		All OK for kids
Restaurant on premises		Some OK for kids
Restaurant nearby		See seating plans
Fully handicap accessible		Obituary—entity no longer exists or is no longer in operation
Handicap seats only		

THEATER

WADSWORTH THEATER See UCLA

WALNUT DIAMOND BAR THEATRE

See press listings for performance locations.
Info: (714) 861-3653   **Rsvn:** (714) 865-8329
Fax: (213) 388-0569
Artistic Director: Mack Gilliland

 Entering its fourth season, the Walnut's work consists of crowd-pleasers on the order of *Plaza Suite* and *You Can't Take it With You*, with some classics thrown into the mix. The group of about 50 members performs in area school auditoriums. For community theater, they do somewhat astonish with elaborate set designs and costuming. Performances usually run weekends only, four months annually.

Performances
 Aug, Dec, March/April;
 Fri-Sun 8 pm; Sat-Sun
 2:30 pm
Tickets
 $5-7
Discounts
 Children/seniors/
 students/groups of 10,
 call BO
BO
 24 hr answering
 machine; check/ reserve
 by mail, fax; exchanges
 made for another
 performance
Parking
 Varies with location
Special Features
 Open rehearsals

WAY OFF BROADWAY PLAYHOUSE

1058 East 1st Street
Santa Ana, CA 92701
Info: (714) 547-8997   **Rsvn:** (714) 547-8997
Artistic Director: Tony Reverditto
Seats 70 for comedies and improv sketches, and full-length plays.

 You really can't get much farther off Broadway than this basement theater in Santa Ana. There's no front access, so don't be discouraged if you can't find your way in right off. Though the address is 1st Street, you'll gain entrance on Walnut (one block south of 1st) off Grand (the last driveway on the right), in the basement of the Advertising Arts Building. Sounds more like directions to a drug drop than a theater, but you can't say it's not dramatic.

 The six-year-old troupe seems to know its way about at least, drawing audiences from age 16 to 80. Each year it produces four full-length plays (such as *Women of Manhattan*) and four comedy shows (a mix of stand-up, sketches, and improv). Artistic Director Tony Reverditto best sums up the group's approach with, "If we ever did *Steel Magnolias*, we'd do it in drag."

Performances
 Fri-Sat 8 pm; Sun 2 pm
Tickets
 $12.50-15
Discounts
 Seniors/students/groups
 of 10, call BO
BO
 Phone orders or pay at
 the door; subscription
 program
Location
 On Walnut 1 block S of
 1st St; off Grand last
 driveway on right; in the
 basement suite of
 Advertising Arts
 Building; no front access
Parking
 On premises, FREE

WEST COAST ENSEMBLE THEATER

6240 Hollywood Boulevard
Hollywood, CA 90028
Info: (213) 871-8673   **Rsvn:** (213) 871-1052
Fax: (213) 462-6741
Artistic Director: Les Hanson
A 60- and a 99-seat performance space; one-acts, old and modern classics.

 Located in a prime theater neighborhood in Hollywood, with the Pantages and the Doolittle close by and new Theatre Row in the vicinity, this playhouse keeps good company. However, before artists moved in, the two-and-a-half story Spanish-style building hosted far less animated

Performances
 Fri-Sat 8 pm, Sun 3 pm
Tickets
 $10-20
Discounts
 Previews/children/
 seniors/students/groups
 of 10+, call BO

folks as it did duty as a mortuary. But theater history prevailed, and before the WCE took it over, it was home to the American Theatre Arts company who staged the world premiere of D.L. Coburn's Pulitzer-prize-winning *The Gin Game*. Seating is—appropriately—church-pew-style, but padded and comfortable.

WEST COAST ENSEMBLE—Resident Co.

Each time the company makes a move, it becomes more successful. It consistently garners awards and critical acclaim, including last year's Margaret Harford Award and three Drama Critics Awards for its production of *Cloud Nine*.

The repertory includes old and modern classics and an annual Celebration of One-Acts, soon to enter its 10th season. Theater co-founder Les Hanson is committed to introducing Los Angelenos to unknown playwrights (and vice versa) through this popular one-act festival, which has presented over 70 such plays to appreciative audiences.

The two spaces here are always busy, always worthwhile attending.

BO
Daily, 1 hr before curtain; check/MC/V/ reserve by phone (24 hr), mail; no exchanges or refunds; subscription program
Location
At Hollywood and Argyle, 1 block E of Vine
Parking
Nearby lots; street

WEST END PLAYHOUSE

7446 Van Nuys Boulevard
Van Nuys, CA 91405
Info: (818) 996-0505   **Rsvn:** (818) 904-0444
Seats 83 people for musicals.

Productions here currently concentrate on musicals. "Broadway Sings Out," with 63 songs from 52 Broadway musicals, is one example. *Crazy Words, Crazy Tunes* has enjoyed a long run of more than 150 shows, seeing the light first at the Center Stage before it moved to the West End. The quality of these tuneful smorgasbords varies, but they are generally worth watching and hearing.

The theater and its lobby are spacious and the seats have good sightlines.

Performances
Vary
Tickets
$12.50-20
Discounts
Children/seniors/ students/groups of 15+, call
BO
Before performance; check/AE/ MC/V/reserve by phone, mail; exchanges OK; subscription program
Location
Near San Diego (405) Fwy and Ventura (101) Fwy, on Van Nuys Blvd 1 1/2 blocks N of Sherman Way
Parking
On premises, FREE; street parking

WESTWOOD PLAYHOUSE

10886 Le Conte Avenue
Westwood, CA 90024
Info: (310) 208-6500   **Rsvn:** (310) 208-5454
Fax: (310) 206-1686
498-seat theater presenting UCLA School of Theater plays and UCLA Film and Television Archive screenings.

The sale of the Westwood Playhouse to UCLA will enable UCLA's School of Theater, Film and Television to expand its already remarkable arts offerings. The theater school's dean, Gilbert Cates, is managing the venue as a professional stage and an educational resource. The

Location
Three blocks N of Wilshire Blvd, 1/2 block E of Westwood Blvd
Parking
Street; nearby lots

Playhouse will also be the site for UCLA Film and Television Archive screenings.

UCLA expects to introduce its own programming in late 1994, in order to allow time for renovation on the 1929 building. A season of three to five plays is planned. In the interim, however, an outside producer continues to program the theater.

The Westwood Playhouse has played host to some significant theater: The opening show was Lillian Hellman's *Little Foxes*. O'Neill's *Hughie* with Jason Robards was also presented. More recently Avery Brooks gave a wonderful performance in Phillip Hayes Dean's *Paul Robeson*.

The Westwood Playhouse, tucked behind lush greenery in a Mediterranean-style building reminiscent of UCLA's first buildings, is ideally placed in the center of Westwood Village near UCLA, adjacent to Bullock's department store (where you can park for the show), and amid little shops and cafes. Before- or after-theater dining is varied.

Call the theater for information on current performances; watch for the UCLA announcement regarding its premiere season.

WHITEFIRE THEATER

13500 Ventura Boulevard
Sherman Oaks, CA 91423
Info: (818) 990-2324 **Rsvn:** (818) 990-2324
65 seats; outside productions.

A 65-seat black box, the Whitefire is an air-conditioned, well-raked, and comfortable theatrical space. Numerous companies strut their stuff on its stage.

Whitefire is at the corner of Sunnyslope and Ventura Boulevard, in the heart of Sherman Oaks' "restaurant row."

Performances
Thurs-Sat 8 pm; Sun 7 pm
Tickets
$10-15
Discounts
Vary from show to show
BO
Varies from show to show
Location
Off Ventura (101) Fwy between Coldwater Cyn and Woodman
Parking
On street

WHITTIER COMMUNITY THEATRE

Center Theatre
Whittier Community Center
7360 Washington Avenue
Whittier, CA 90600
Info: (310) 692-6163 **Rsvn:** (310) 693-1105
400-seat community theater.

This community theater can accommodate 430 in its recently renovated space. Sightlines are good, parking is free, and refreshments are served at intermission.

WHITTIER COMMUNITY THEATRE—Resident Co.

Now in its 72nd season, WCT is an all-volunteer group putting on four plays and/or musicals September through June. Most shows run for three weekends.

Performances
Fri-Sat 8 pm; Sun 2:30 pm
Tickets
$8-10
Discounts
Children/seniors/students/groups, call BO
BO
Phone; MC/V/check
Location
605 Fwy exit Whittier Blvd E to Mar Vista N to Washington Ave
Parking
Lot, FREE; street

WHITTIER-LA MIRADA MUSICAL THEATRE See **La Mirada Theatre for the Performing Arts**

WILD SIDE THEATRE

10945 Camarillo
North Hollywood, CA 91602
Info: (818) 506-8838   **Rsvn:** (818) 506-8838
Fax: (818) 506-8838 #8
Seats 50 for improv performances.

Artistic director Sam Langoria swears the Wild Side was founded by actress Susan Hayward "as a home for Hayward Girls." Kidding aside, the theater is a fairly cramped black box space. Miscellaneous framed posters and novelties do the adorning. The seats are frowsy and torn, but not uncomfortable.

Just across the street, Little Toni's, according to one noted LA theater critic, tosses up "the best pizza in the Valley."

WILD SIDE THEATRE COMPANY—Resident Co.

The company members present six weekly improv shows with alternating casts. Sometimes up to 15 performers jam (and jam on) the itty-bitty stage. Occasionally, scripted shows (written by Langoria and other members) are trundled out. While they rarely get reviewed, the place is always packed. Is there a connection someplace?

Performances
Fri-Sat 7:30 pm, 9 pm, 10:30 pm
Tickets
$10
BO
Check/Disc/MC/V/ reserve by phone, mail
Location
At corner of Lankershim, Vineland, Camarillo; 1 mile N of Universal Studios; 4 lights N of Vineland exit off Ventura (134) Fwy or Hollywood (101) Fwy
Parking
On premises, FREE; valet, $1; street parking

WILL & COMPANY

See press listings for performance locations.
Info: (310) 798-6290   **Rsvn:** (310) 798-6290

Known widely throughout California among the school-age set for kid-sized versions of Shakespeare and other classics, Will & Company put on long pants recently with the January 1993 debut of its full-blown adult series as one of the 10 cooperative members at newly incarnated LATC (Los Angeles Theater Center). This doesn't mean Will & Company will be giving up its children's programs. Rather, it means the 12-member professional ensemble will be busier than ever, performing more than 450 shows a year, including its statewide tours of schools and other kiddie venues, adult productions of English and Spanish versions of *The Three Musketeers* and *Taming of the Shrew* at LATC, as well as its annual 24-hour "Shakespeare 'Til You Drop" marathon. Its brand-new classics series, Quicktakes, has taken off with one-hour versions of classic stories such as *The Odyssey* and *Great Expectations*, adapted with the entire family in mind. Will & Company also presents signed performances (60 percent of the troupe signs for the hearing-impaired).

Performances
Sept-June; Thurs-Sun 8 pm; Sun 2:30 pm
Tickets
$5-15
Discounts
Children/seniors/ students/groups of 10+, call BO
BO
Call and leave message; exchanges made
Parking
Varies with location

WILL GEER THEATRICUM BOTANICUM

1419 Topanga Canyon
Topanga, CA 90290
Info: (310) 455-2322   **Rsvn:** (310) 455-3723
Artistic Director: Ellen Geer
350-seat outdoor theater.

Fans of TV's *The Waltons* place the name Will Geer right off, but even they may not know that Will Geer performed with some of Broadway's and films' greatest stars, treading the Broadway boards in *The Merry Wives of Windsor* and revving it up with Steve McQueen in *The Reivers*. In the early 1950s Geer "...carved Theatricum

Performances
June-Sept-Fri and Sat 8 pm, Sun 1 pm and 4 pm
Tickets
$4-11.50
Discounts
Children/seniors/ students/groups of 10+, call BO

Botanicum out of the side of a mountain." In those early days, Woody Guthrie lived on the grounds. Some years later, when the rustic theater was hammered into a nonprofit organization, free performances, Shakespeare workshops and musical concerts began to flourish in the Botanicum garden. Well known musicians and singers such as Arlo Guthrie, Pete Seeger, and Della Reese have helped cultivate the outdoor amphitheater.

Nestled in rocky and woodsy Topanga Canyon, replete with Greek-style amphitheater seating, the Will Geer Memorial Shakespearean Garden is landscaped in the style of a Tudor pleasure ground. Volunteers tend to the flower beds and plants, many of which are cited in Shakespeare's works. Plans now are to turn Woody Guthrie's little red shack into a museum for Geer's memorabilia.

Pack a picnic basket with wine and cheese for a pre-show supper and drink in the loveliness of the five-acre grounds. But also pack a cushion, as the "railroad-tie" seating is not tushy-friendly.

Dining beside a gentle creek to a background of classical music at The Inn of the Seventh Ray nearby is also sure to put you in the mood.

The season runs from June to September; call to be put on the mailing list for future schedules.

WILL GEER THEATRICUM BOTANICUM THEATER CO.—Resident Co.

This is a superb venue for Shakespeare-watching, especially those bucolic comedies. The theater company can also whip up modern classics, such as the recent *The Caucasian Chalk Circle*, and counts five original plays in its repertoire.

The company supports a busy outreach program of in-school programs, youth and adult classes, seminars, workshops, and a summer youth drama camp, as well as frequent special musical concerts (like blues and reggae).

WILSHIRE EBELL THEATRE See **MUSIC**

BO
Fri-Sun; check/reserve by mail; subscription program
Location
Topanga Canyon between Ventura (101) Fwy and Pacific Coast (1) Hwy
Parking
On premises, FREE; street parking

WILSHIRE THEATRE

8440 Wilshire Boulevard
Beverly Hills, CA 90211
Rsvn: (213) 480-3232
1,910-seat production house; touring Broadway productions and celebrity concerts.

Built in the '20s as a movie theater, the Wilshire is now operated by the Nederlander organization, which trucks in big musicals (like *Stardust*), children's theater, celebrity concerts, and plays. The theater even doubles as a synagogue during the High Holy Days.

This is one of LA's larger legit venues, so mind where you sit. Acoustics aren't terrific, and you may find yourself leaning forward to hear. Many shows here are miked to try and help the situation. As specific seat selection can't be guaranteed by phone, go to the box office (with our handy seating chart) if you can. The orchestra section is short, with a maximum of 27 rows. The first eight cover an orchestra pit and can be removed. Avoid, if possible, the extreme sides. I like Orchestra rows E or F in the center. If you sit too close, you have to look up during the performance. The front of the Mezzanine is good; the Rear Balcony is the nosebleed section. Let the theater know in advance if handicap seating in needed.

Performances
Vary
Tickets
$20-45
Discounts
Previews/groups of 20, call (213) 464-7521
BO
Hrs vary; AE/MC/V/ TicketMaster
Location
N of Santa Monica (10) Fwy; E of La Cienaga Blvd
Parking
Lots nearby, street parking

WILTERN THEATRE See **MUSIC**

WOODEN-O-THEATRE STUDIO

2207 Federal Avenue
Los Angeles, CA 90064
Info: (310) 470-6027   **Rsvn:** (310) 477-2199
Artistic Director: Jonathan Luria
50-seat theater space presenting original, first-run plays and revivals.

This 50-seat theater used to be a garage before founder Jonathan Luria remodeled and soundproofed it with the help of fellow company members. There are far too few playhouses on the Westside, so this intimate space is a welcome vehicle.

The Wooden-O manages to hold a full-sized stage equipped with a complete light and sound system impressive for such a small venue.

WOODEN-O-THEATRE COMPANY—Resident Co.

Only a few years old, this company of 20 ensemble members occasionally welcomes a name guest star to its ranks. The troupe performs both revivals and first-run plays, but are always eager to produce original material. In the past year, two Mac Wellman plays have occupied the stage, including the well-received *7 Blowjobs*.

The theater and company are named in honor of Shakespeare's prologue from *Henry V*, in which the narrator exhorts the audience to imagine vast armies and other spectacles unfolding on his "wooden O," a circular stage. The same advice amply applies to this ex-garage.

Performances
Thurs-Sun 8 pm
Tickets
$ varies
Discounts
Groups of 10+, call BO
BO
Reserve by mail; exchanges made
Location
Near the San Diego (405) Fwy and Santa Monica (10) Fwy
Parking
On premises, FREE; street parking

WOODLAND HILLS COMMUNITY THEATRE

22700 Sherman Way
Canoga Park, CA 91307
Info: (818) 884-1907   **Rsvn:** (818) 884-1907
Seats 107.

This community group produces four shows each year—a musical, a mystery, a comedy, and a classic (although not necessarily in that order). At least one performance of each show (except the musical) is signed for the hearing impaired.

Performances
Fri-Sat
Tickets
$15
Discounts
Seniors/students/groups of 10+
BO
Check/reserve by phone, pay by mail; exchanges up to 24 hrs before performance (if available); subscription program
Location
N off Ventura (101) Fwy at Shoup Ave, SE corner of Sherman Way and Fallbrook
Parking
On premises, FREE
Special Features
One performance is sign language interpreted

WORLD THEATER

6543 Santa Monica Boulevard
Hollywood, CA 90038
Info: (213) 669-1625   **Rsvn:** (213) 960-5596
Fax: (310) 559-0433
Artistic Director: Dan Piburn
Original pieces and translations; 70 seats.

Born of the demise of the Theatre IgLoo at the end of 1991, the World sees itself as "trying to take some chances." It premieres original works and original translations that you'd usually see performed for mainstream audiences. The World revolves around its newly renovated 70-seat space, with a tiny stage, on Hollywood's Theatre Row.

Performances
Mon-Sun evenings; Sun matinee
Tickets
$8-15
Discounts
Previews/children/ seniors/students/groups of 8+, call BO
BO
Phone reservations; check/reserve by mail, fax
Location
On Theatre Row Hollywood, between Highland Ave and Cahuenga Blvd
Parking
On premises, $3; valet; street parking

YORBA LINDA CIVIC LIGHT OPERA

The Forum Theater of Yorba Linda
4175 Fairmont Boulevard
Yorba Linda, CA 92686
Info: (714) 779-8591

This community-based theater group, founded in 1985, mounts four fully staged musicals per annum, plus a summer musical revue, in Yorba Linda's Forum Theater.

Performances
Sept-June; Fri-Sat 8 pm; Sun 2 pm
Tickets
$10-15
Discounts
Children/seniors/groups of 20+, call BO
BO
Mon-Fri 9 am-3 pm, 1 1/2 hrs before show time; check/MC/V/ reserve by mail; tickets may be exchanged one week prior to performance; subscription program

ZEPHYR THEATER

7456 Melrose Avenue
Hollywood, CA 90046
Info: (213) 653-4667   **Rsvn:** (213) 852-9069
Fax: (213) 852-9633
99-seat house.

The Zephyr is an oasis of culture amid the Melrose—let me be polite—eclecticism. One of the oldest Equity theaters in Hollywood, it dates back to the '50s when it was called the Horseshoe Stage, named for the semi-round configuration still used today.

The current owner, Lee Sankowich (also Artistic Director of Mill Valley's Marin Theater Company), hopes to renovate to create more leg room. But for now, the 99-seat theater comes with well-worn blue velveteen chairs that are older than the theater itself. The courtyard entrance is

Performances
Mon-Sat 8 pm; Sun 2 pm, 7 pm
Tickets
$8-20
BO
1/2 hr before show time; Tickets LA
Location
Between Fairfax and La Brea Aves at Vista St
Parking
On street

inviting and the perfect atmosphere for pre-theater mixing and intermission discussions. The Zephyr rents out its space Thursday through Sunday. Musicals, dramas, and a few children's productions are the regular fare, but the theater is usually compared to an "off-off-Broadway" house. Notable as well as typical productions in the past have included *A Paper Rose* by Richard Lortz, *Durante* by Richard Wolf and Frank Spiering, and *Berlin to Broadway with Kurt Weill*, winner of several Drama Critics awards in the mid-'80s.

Parking is the usual Melrose dilemma. It's available on side streets after 6 pm or at the meters on Melrose. But be sure to read the signs for parking restrictions. Once you've claimed your spot, there are some great restaurants on Melrose within walking distance of the Zephyr. Try Rosso and Nero, Cocina, Cafe Luna, or Antonio's.

MUSIC

INTRODUCTION TO MUSIC

By Esa-Pekka Salonen

As a European, I am fascinated with the musical possibilities of Los Angeles—an almost unbelievable mixture of cultures which can, when brought together, stimulate unexpected collaborations, create unique styles, sometimes clash but never bore. This is a city with so many traditions that one is utterly free to choose from among them, or, better yet, to create a new one.

I am very optimistic about music-making in Los Angeles. Things are possible here precisely because of the lack of weighty "tradition." I like the openness here, the fact that you seldom hear somebody define something by saying "this is the way we always do it."

We at the Los Angeles Philharmonic are eager to broaden the audience for classical music. Cultural differences aren't the problem, because the music ultimately speaks for itself. Our job is to get the music out there, to show everyone that it pertains to them and their lives. In addition to our concerts at the Music Center and at the Hollywood Bowl, we are now giving regular neighborhood concerts, taking musicians to high schools, churches, any place where people gather in a neighborhood. We are even introducing classical music to children as young as three in our Saturday programs. All it takes is a chance to hear tho music.

I've often been asked "what makes music good?" Good music is able to move us, to communicate with us on a level that is different from either verbal or visual communication. I would like to say that music reaches us on a higher level. A great human masterpiece, whether it is a classic such as a Beethoven symphony or a new work like Ligeti's Requiem, has a tremendous richness which can reach us at so many different levels. These pieces can move us, scare us, give us sensual pleasure, stimulate us, give us a kick, raise questions, give answers, satisfy and irritate us.

Although we live in a media-dominated age, in a media-dominated city, I continue to believe in the essential vitality of live music. Like everyone else, I delight in the pleasures of Walkmans, CD's, car stereos, and every new techno-innovation. But the music-making immortalized on record is inevitably a mere echo of that experienced by a listener seated in the same room as the musician. Even at its very best, a recording can only produce a skeleton, which the concert clothes in the flesh of social energy.

Southern California is bursting with music. I invite you to listen.

In October of 1992, Esa-Pekka Salonen officially took the post of music director of the Los Angeles Philharmonic. The 10th conductor in the Philharmonic's 73-plus history, Salonen had served as music director-designate since 1989. Salonen debuted with the Finnish Radio Symphony Orchestra in 1979, and soon after became a much sought-after artist after a widely acclaimed debut with the Philharmonia Orchestra in London in 1983. Salonen is also a composer in his own right.

AFRO-AMERICAN CHAMBER MUSIC SOCIETY

See press listings for performance locations.
Info: (213) 292-6547
Music Director: Janise White-McRae
Performs at Kinsey Auditorium.

Determined to make up for the general lack of attention paid to classical music by African-American composers, the AACMS has devoted itself to research and performance in this area since 1986.

Founder Janise White-McRae, a pianist and educator by trade, and librarian Valencia Mitchell have been assembling a library of scores—now numbering over 100—that date back to the 18th century and which range from chamber music and art songs to blues and ragtime. They are also taking care that their collection of new work extends into the 21st century by sponsoring an annual composer's competition, the first of which took place during the 1991/92 season.

AACMS' holds court in Exposition Park's Kinsey Auditorium and Bing Auditorium at the Los Angeles County Museum of Art. They also perform concerts at various colleges as well as broadcast live on LA's classical radio stations. White-McRae draws upon a pool of local studio and concert musicians for these concerts, which often include displays of modern and African-American dance as a bonus.

Performances
Feb-June, Sun 2:30 pm
Tickets
$5 donation
BO
Check/reserve by phone
Parking
Varies with location

AMBASSADOR AUDITORIUM

131 South Saint John Avenue
Pasadena, CA 91129
Info: (818) 304-6166   **Rsvn:** (818) 304-6161 or (800) 266-2378
Fax: (818) 356-0552
Music Director: Christof Perick
Seats 1,442 for classical music concerts, jazz performances, big band sounds, opera, and travel films.

Don't let the term "auditorium" fool you. Though the Ambassador began life in 1974 as a college auditorium (with a concert by the Vienna Symphony led by Carlo Maria Giulini), it has been justifiably called the Carnegie Hall of the West and is renowned for its superb acoustics. If you've never taken in a performance at the Ambassador, I suggest you put it on your list of things to do.

Arthur Rubinstein, Vladimir Horowitz, Luciano Pavarotti, and Leontyne Price have all put in appearances. The Los Angeles Chamber Orchestra calls the Ambassador home and has recorded the Brandenburg Concertos in this hall. The season offers, in addition to the LACO, soloists, a "Stars of Opera" series, world-renowned orchestras, a Festival of Early Music, a pops series, and much more. In summer, there is a new jazz festival. In all, more than 100 concerts (30 subscription series) are played here each year.

You can't miss the glamorous hall. Come nightfall, the Ambassador's exterior and surrounding water works of pools and fountains resembles a glowing temple of glass and gilt. Inside, the drama intensifies, courtesy of the lobby's 2-1/2 ton, three-tier crystal chandelier. Underfoot lies a brilliant royal purple carpet designed to reflect the prismatic light of the chandelier. Up ahead rises an altar-like wall of rose onyx flanked by two seven-foot tall, 650-pound Baccarat crystal candelabra (originally commissioned by the Shah of Iran to commemorate the 2,500th anniversary of Persia!).

The auditorium walls within are lined with panels of rosewood inset with teak. One musician has likened the

Performances
Mon-Thurs 8 pm; Sat 8:30 pm, Sun 2 pm, 8 pm
Tickets
$5.50-$60
Discounts
Children/seniors students/groups of 20+, call (800) 266-2378
BO
Sun 12 pm-5 pm; Mon-Thurs 9 am-5 pm; Fri 9 am-4 pm; check/AE/MC/V/reserve by mail (P.O. Box 7004, Pasadena, CA 91109), fax; refunds or exchanges for subscribers only two business days before ticketed event; subscription program
Location
From Pasadena (110) Fwy exit Orange Grove Blvd, left, go six lights, right on Green St, right on South St. John; from 210 Westbound, exit Orange Grove Blvd, turn left, right on Green St
Parking
On premises, $2-7; street parking

effect to playing inside a giant guitar. Acoustical curtains in the walls and ceiling are manipulated to "tune the hall," making every seat a good one.

Single tickets are usually available for all performances. But your best bet for tickets is always the Gold Medal series of 12 chamber music and vocal performances, which has extremely low ticket prices and special student, teacher, and senior discounts. Bear in mind, however, that the Ambassador has an ironclad policy of no refunds and no exchanges on tickets except for subscribers.

Although you can walk to Old Town Pasadena if you're wearing your tennies, you'll probably prefer to drive there for after-theater fare.

Special Features
Pre-concert lectures

AMERICAN CHAMBER SYMPHONY

See press listings for performance locations.
Info: (310) 201-0045   **Fax:** (310) 277-3069
Music Director: Nelson Nirenberg
Performs regularly at the Gindi Auditorium in the University of Judaism, 15600 Mulhollard Drive

The 40-member chamber orchestra may not get as much attention as some of its rivals but it's often considerably more adventurous in its programming.

Though Brazilian-born conductor/founder Nelson Nirenberg gives the bread-and-butter staples of Mozart and his ilk their due, he also displays a healthy interest in contemporary music, as well as in unearthing older neglected pieces. In 1986, the ACS managed to pull off the serious coup of offering the North American premiere of Polish giant Krzysztof Penderecki's new *Viola Concerto*, a concert that won national attention.

This cohesive ensemble, founded in 1981, is equipped with skilled players and led by a maestro with a reputation for rousing fire. And the ACS enjoys the distinct advantage of a regular home in the University of Judaism's small but pleasant Gindi Auditorium.

Performances
Nov.-July, Mon 8 pm,
Sun 7:30 pm
Tickets
$8-100
Discounts
Previews/children
seniors/students/groups
of 20+, call
BO
Check/reserve by mail
(1801 Ave Of The Stars,
Los Angeles, CA
90067), TicketMaster;
no exchanges, no
refunds; subscription
program
Parking
Varies with location
Special Features
Open rehearsals

AMERICAN YOUTH SYMPHONY

See press listings for performance locations.
Info: (310) 476-2825
Music Director: Mehli Mehta
Classical symphony training group.

At 85 years young, Mehli Mehta is a civic treasure, still on the job, running, programming, prodding, and conducting this accomplished youth orchestra. The Bombay-born orchestra builder has been imparting his knowledge to talented young musicians here since 1964 and has no intentions of laying down the baton.

The orchestra's trainees (ages 16 to 25) get a rigorous grounding in the repertoire that major symphony orchestras play. But more often than not, these young kids on the classical block play with the same intensity, unity, and depth of understanding of long-seasoned professionals. In other words, they put on a great concert.

Mehta really works his young players, making few allowances for youth. He has shepherded his charges through some of the most difficult challenges in the repertoire—all of Richard Strauss' tone poems, all of Brahms' major orchestral and choral works, Mahler's gigantic Symphonies (Nos. 1, 2, 3, 5 and 9), Bruckner's sprawling Symphonies (Nos. 4 and 9). . . and the list—like Mehta—never quits. In fact, the only concession Mehta makes to his own advancing age is somewhat slower tempos. Otherwise, he still memorizes every performance

Performances
Oct-May; one concert
every month, Sun 8 pm
Tickets
FREE; tickets for annual
benefit concert $5-175
BO
Check/reserve by mail
(343 Church Lane,
Los Angeles, CA
90049)
Parking
Varies with venue
Special Features
Open rehearsals

score and conducts with the unflagging energy of his youngest pupil.

Each winter, the AYS treats itself to a gala benefit concert at the Dorothy Chandler Pavilion with a guest soloist as the drawing card. There you might catch struggling unknowns like Isaac Stern, Itzhak Perlman, Daniel Barenboim, Lynn Harrell, Pinchas Zukerman, Midori, Thomas Hampson, Sir Yehudi Menuhin, or even Zubin Mehta—all of whom donate their services.

Until the January earthquake, AYS had been performing free at Royce Hall. Call, or watch for press listings of scheduled performances.

ANAHEIM ARENA

2695 East Katella Avenue
Anaheim, CA 92806
Info: (714) 704-2400 **Rsvn:** (714) 704-2500
Fax: (714) 704-2443
Seats 19,400 for center stage entertainment; also hosts sporting events.

Anaheim Arena has made its entrance into the area's musical concert scene with a boast declaring it the largest arena in Southern California.

When it's not featuring Barry Manilow or Run DMC or Clint Black and Wynonna Judd, the Arena gets iced up for the Tour of World Figure Skating Champions, and, to the excitement of Hockey Fans, will be center stage to the National Hockey League's new Mighty Ducks.

Ticket prices range anywhere from $3 to $100 depending on the entertainment.

Performances
Vary
Tickets
$ varies
BO
Mon-Fri, 10am-6 pm;
Sat, 11am-4 pm; Sun
days of performance
only; AE/MC/V/
TicketMaster; no
exchanges
Location
Off of Santa Ana (5)
Fwy; or Orange (57)
Fwy
Parking
On premises, $6

Y &. (**††**)

ANNENBERG THEATER See THEATER

ARNOLD SCHOENBERG INSTITUTE See USC School of Music

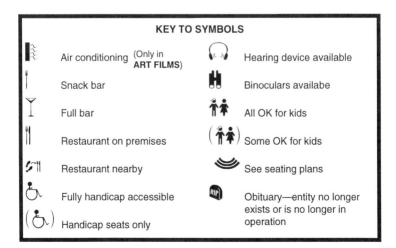

KEY TO SYMBOLS

▓≋	Air conditioning (Only in **ART FILMS**)	🎧	Hearing device available
⌇	Snack bar	👓	Binoculars availabe
Y	Full bar	**††**	All OK for kids
‖	Restaurant on premises	(**††**)	Some OK for kids
⸙‖	Restaurant nearby	≋	See seating plans
&.	Fully handicap accessible	RIP	Obituary—entity no longer exists or is no longer in operation
(&.)	Handicap seats only		

BACH CAMERATA

Lobero Theatre
33 East Canon Perdido Street
Santa Barbara, CA 93101
Info: (805) 684-2287   **Rsvn:** (805) 963-0761
Fax: (805) 687-9702
Performs at Lobero Theatre and other area venues.

     A recent arrival to the Santa Barbara musical family, the Bach Camerata has found a welcoming place in the community after three successful seasons.

     In addition to the Lobero Theatre, the chamber size orchestra also presents concerts in a variety of venues throughout the year. Some of the city's finest restaurants host the group's performances paired with special gourmet menus. Connoisseurs of fine food and music will wish this partnership a long run.

Performances
  Nov-Feb
Tickets
  $2.75-21
Discounts
  Children/seniors/
  students/groups of 20+,
  call
BO
  Mon-Fri 10am-5 pm; Sat
  noon-5 pm; check/AE/
  Disc/MC/V/reserve by
  mail; full price tickets
  when returned have a
  partial refund;
  subscription program
Parking
  Behind premises in city
  lot, FREE
Special Features
  Open rehearsals with
  restricted attendance

BECKMAN AUDITORIUM See **Caltech Public Events** in **THEATER**

BEVERLY HILLS LIVE! See **FESTIVALS & SEASONAL EVENTS**

BEYOND BAROQUE See **THEATER**

BLOCKBUSTER PAVILION

Colen Helen Regional Park
Devore, CA
Info: (909) 88-MUSIC
16,000-seat outdoor concert site.

     Brand new to Southern California, this Glen Helen facility opened with a bang. It started off with an oldies rock show, and went on with a schedule that included Lynyrd Skynyrd, Don Henley, and Rod Stewart. Although Anaheim Arena bills itself as the largest concert facility, Blockbuster is in fact the largest site to feature concerts exclusively (Anaheim Arena is booked mostly with sporting events).

     For those willing to drive the 60 or so miles from LA, Blockbuster gives them their time's—and money's—worth. People rave about the great sound, and everyone seems to be able to see. That's pretty good with 16,000 seats. It remains to be seen what will happen when the surrounding area is made available for another 60,000-plus lawn-seaters.

     No food, coolers, drinks, or lawn chairs may be brought in. Cameras should be left at home. Pillows and blanks are OK. Handicapped patrons must secure tickets by calling (909) 880-6500 (also discuss parking when you reserve your tickets).

Performances
  Vary
Tickets
  $ varies
BO
  Noon, day of show;
  announced day of "on-
  sale"; MC/V/reserve by
  phone, TicketMaster;
  subscription program
Location
  From LA, Int-10 E to 15
  N, exit Sierra, left on
  Devore Rd, right 3 miles
  to park road
Parking
  On premises, $5

BRAND LIBRARY AND ART GALLERIES See **DANCE**

BRIDGES AUDITORIUM See **THEATER**

CALARTS SPRING MUSIC FESTIVAL See **FESTIVALS & SEASONAL EVENTS**

CALIFORNIA PLAZA See **FESTIVALS & SEASONAL EVENTS**

CALIFORNIA TRADITIONAL MUSIC SOCIETY

See press listings for performance locations.
Info: (818) 342-7664 **Fax:** (818) 609-0106
Executive Director: Elaine Weisman
    CTMS gives folk-music lovers the Summer Solstice Folk Music & Dance Festival as well as two annual Folk Music Concert Series. One look at its semiannual journal and you'll be toe-tapping to a world of fiddles and dulcimers, banjos and tin whistles. Folk music aficionados will be familiar with the regular concerts and annual festival. Others may find a treasure trove of Irish ballads, bluegrass, Dixieland jazz, and Scottish harp tunes. Call or write to be put on the mailing list. (See **FESTIVALS** for more information on the Summer Solstice Festival.)

Performances
The weekend after Father's Day
Tickets
$13-18
BO
Call; check/reserve by mail (4401 Trancas Pl, Tarzana, CA 91358-5399)
Parking
Varies with location

CAMBRIDGE SINGERS

Info: (818) 842-7467 **Fax:** (818) 842-7467
Music Director: Alexander Ruggieri
Performances are held at the Pasadena Presbyterian Church, corner of Madison and Colorado Boulevard in Pasadena.
    The Cambridge Singers can be heard within the reverberant, architecturally sweeping Pasadena Presbyterian Church on Sunday afternoons. Performances at other locations are announced in a mailing (call to have your name placed on the list).
    Established in 1984, the Cambridge Singers are a mid-sized, semiprofessional group of some 45 members, a head count which gives them considerable flexibility. For instance thanks to the authenticity movement, they're right at home in numbers for replicating the original Dublin version of Handel's *Messiah*. Their strength in numbers also lets them do interesting offbeat programs like "1000 Years of Russian Choral Music" (Russian music being a specialty of founder/music director Alexander Ruggieri). They also offer workshops and outreach programs for the community.

Performances
Sept-June, Sun 4 pm
Tickets
$12.50-13.75
Discounts
Seniors/students/groups of 10+, call
BO
Before concerts only; check/MC/V/reserve by mail; Old Town Music Co., Pedrini Music; no exchanges; subscription program
Parking
On premises, FREE
Special Features
Some open rehearsals

I CANTORI

See press listings for performance locations.
Info: (818) 798-3208 **Fax:** (818) 791-0579
Music Director: Edward Cansino
Performs at Occidental College's Thorne Hall and other LA venues.
    Though the name I Cantori might conjure up the unappetizing image of solemn, retrograde musicologists, in practice these vocalizers are anything but. The core of I Cantori is its 11 voices—all accomplished soloists in their own right—capable of delivering a glistening, limpid collective tone quality in music of any period and almost any style. These singers have been put to use in high-quality performances of works as diverse as Haydn's *Lord Nelson Mass*, the early-music opera *Il Sant'Alessio,* and Japanese composer Yuji Takahashi's opera *Michi-Yuki*.

Performances
Sept-May, Sat 8 pm, Sun 3 or 3:30 pm
Tickets
$7-15
Discounts
Seniors/students/groups of 10+, call

Founder/director Edward Cansino also loves to put on a show, often semi-staging performances in a whimsical fashion (a flamboyance he may have picked up from his aunt actress Rita Hayworth). Once, during a Christmas show in a Pasadena church, he followed a lovely, floating, Renaissance-dominated set with a child-like "St. George and the Dragon" skit in which I Cantori's gifted mezzo-soprano Kerry Walsh performed a belly dance. Saints preserve us—in a church!

Moreover, Cansino is a composer himself and isn't afraid to sprinkle his group's repertoire with contemporary music and mores, ethnic music from anywhere you can name, and pertinent points about the human and environmental condition. In a recent season, Cansino combined many of these elements into his snazzy, multimedia theater piece, *Visit to a Small Planet*.

I Cantori likes to take its chances during the normal course of its regular season in Occidental College's Thorne Hall. The group also makes itself heard in the rotunda of Los Angeles' City Hall, in various other locales, and in summer festivals.

BO
1 hr before performance; check/AE/MC/V/reserve by mail (P.O. Box 94001, Pasadena, CA 91109); exchanges up to 24 hrs before performance; subscription program

Parking
Varies with location

CELEBRITY THEATRE

201 East Broadway
Anaheim, CA 92815
Info: (714) 535-2000   **Rsvn:** (714) 999-9536
Fax: (714) 999-9546
Seats 2,500 for music concerts.

This theater-in-the-round offers us reason beyond Disneyland for visiting Anaheim. Country music, R&B, rock, and comedy are regularly performed on the revolving stage.

The list of Celebrity's guest artists reads like a *Who's Who* in entertainment. There's something for everyone's musical taste, from Kansas to Chicago, the Pointer Sisters to the Oakridge Boys, Chris Isaak to B.B. King, Robert Townsend to Willie Nelson to the Psychedelic Furs.

Thanks to veteran funny people like Mort Sahl, Joan Rivers, and Bill Cosby, and to "newcomer" Jerry Seinfeld, there are a lot of laughs to be found here, too.

Try to avoid the sightline obstructions in the back seven rows of aisles 5 and 12. And for sensitive ears, try to stay away from aisle 15 where the sound board is located.

Tip (these go fast): The on-premises Unlisted Restaurant offers a special dinner package. For an extra $20 per person, you get a full dinner and guaranteed seats in the first four rows of the theater.

Performances
Vary
Tickets
$7-35
Discounts
Groups of 30+, call
BO
Mon-Fri 10am-6 pm, Sat noon-6 pm check/AE/5MC/V/reserve by TicketMaster; no refunds, no exchanges; Checks 3 weeks prior to show and only with check guarantee card
Location
Near Santa Ana (5) Fwy at Broadway and Anaheim, 1.5 miles E of Disneyland
Parking
On premises, $4-6; street parking

CENTER THEATER See **Long Beach Opera** and **THEATER**

CERRITOS CENTER FOR THE PERFORMING ARTS See **THEATER**

CHAMBER MUSIC IN HISTORIC SITES See **Da Camera Society**

CHAMBER MUSIC/LA FESTIVAL See **FESTIVALS & SEASONAL EVENTS**

CHAMBER ORCHESTRA OF THE SOUTH BAY

Info: (310) 373-3151   **Rsvn:** (310) 544-0403
Music Director: Dr. Francis Steiner
Performances take place at the Norris Theatre for the Performing Arts in Palos Verdes and the Torrance Cultural Arts Center in Torrance.

As led by Dr. Frances Steiner, the COSB serves as the resident orchestra of the Norris Theatre for the Performing Arts in what used to be culturally undernourished Palos Verdes Peninsula.

Future dates for the COSB promise an expanded schedule in the 500-seat James R. Armstrong Theatre of the Torrance Cultural Arts Center, and include a number of noted Los Angeles Philharmonic guest soloists.

Performances
Oct-May, Sat-Sun 8 pm
Tickets
$20-24
BO
Mon-Fri 10 am-6 pm; check/MC/V/reserve by mail (P.O. Box 2095, Palos Verdes Peninsula, CA 90274); subscription program
Special Features
Open rehearsals

CHORALE BEL CANTO

See press listings for performance locations.
Info: (310) 907-4233
Music Director: Stephen Gothold
Majority of performances at the Shannon Center for the Performing Arts at Whittier College, corner of Painter and Philadelphia in Whittier.

Based in Whittier College's brightly-colored, music hall-like Shannon Center for the Performing Arts, Chorale Bel Canto is an 80-voice choir comprised of Whittier residents and volunteers from 15 surrounding communities.

With more than 10 seasons to its credit, the Chorale concentrates upon the popular choral activities—the annual singalong *Messiah* (more than eight years running, to date), the Mozart bicentennial tribute, the Christmas carol show, etc. The Chorale also performs at the First Friends Church in Whittier.

Performances
Oct-Dec, March-June, Sat 8 pm, Sun 3 pm
Tickets
$12-15
Discounts
Seniors/students
BO
Before performance; reserve by mail (P.O. Box 451, Whittier, CA 90608); exchanges Sat for Sun and vice versa; subscription program
Parking
Varies with location
Special Features
Open rehearsals

THE COACH HOUSE See CLUBS

COLEMAN CHAMBER MUSIC ASSOCIATION

Beckman Auditorium
CalTech
South Michigan Avenue
Pasadena, CA 91125
Info: (818) 793-4191   **Rsvn:** (818) 356-4652
Fax: (818) 787-1294
Performances held in Beckman Auditorium on CalTech campus.

The Coleman Chamber Music Association has become more than an institution; it seems like a permanently chiseled fixture in the landscape. It has been around since 1904, making it the oldest continuously operating organization in America that is devoted to chamber music.

This hardy series came about as a result of the efforts of Alice Coleman Batchelder, a wealthy Pasadenan who was a noted local organist, pianist and teacher. The concerts were originally given in a variety of places—the Elks Hall, theaters, private homes and gardens, even Ms. Coleman's own home. By 1927, the concerts found a steady home at last in the then-newly-built Pasadena Playhouse.

Performances
Oct-May; Sun 3:30 pm
Tickets
$12-21
Discounts
Students/seniors/groups of 15+, call BO
BO
Check/AE/Disc/MC/V reserve by mail (202 S Lake St, Ste. 201, Pasadena, CA 91101); subscription program
Parking
On premises

There the concerts stayed for some 27 years before moving to the circular Beckman Auditorium on the CalTech campus in 1965.

Whisk ahead another 28 years, and the concerts are still in Beckman. The organization imports the best chamber music groups from around the globe six times per season. The intent is to limit the number of concerts in the series so that Coleman can present the finest that chamber music has to offer.

Over the decades, the Coleman series has been able to present the leading chamber music groups of the century, among them the Pro Arte, Guarneri, Juilliard, and Tokyo String quartets. The selection of material from these touring groups is generally conservative, grounded in the bedrock of European tradition, but several 20th-century works do show up, particularly whenever Juilliard pays a visit.

For over 47 years, the Coleman organization has also sponsored a Coleman Chamber Ensemble Competition, held in nearby Ramo Auditorium. The competition itself is open to the public free of charge, and a concert featuring the winners is presented the following afternoon.

CONCERTS IN THE PARK See FESTIVALS & SEASONAL EVENTS

COPLEY SYMPHONY HALL See San Diego Symphony

CYPRESS POPS ORCHESTRA

Cypress College
9400 Valley View Avenue
Cypress, CA 90630
Info: (714) 527-0964 **Fax:** (714) 236-0220
Music Director: John East Hall III
Most concerts are scheduled at Cypress College.

Performances
April-Dec; Sat-Sun 6 pm
or 7 pm; Sun 4 pm-6 pm
Tickets
FREE
Parking
On premises
Special Features
Open rehearsals

Cypress Pops Orchestra founder/music director John E. Hall III is refreshingly up front about his orchestra's agenda: "I give audiences what they want to hear, not what I want to hear."

The now venerable Boston Pops is the inspiration for Hall, a former trombonist. With his credo and the Bostonians in mind, he likes to program popular operatic arias, film, and Broadway show tunes, brief classical pieces, medleys, and marches. In the past, the CPO's programs have leaned toward concepts such as "Symphony of Holiday Favorites" (a mixed bag of tidbits from Haydn to Leroy Anderson), "Patriotic Showcase" (in the wake of the Persian Gulf War), and "Big Band Salute."

The Pops plays a dozen concerts from May to December, mostly at Cypress College and outdoors in the Cypress Civic Center, with run-out dates in Buena Park, Orange, and at the Annenberg Theatre in Palm Springs. Admission is free. Now that is something we want to hear!

THE DA CAMERA SOCIETY OF MOUNT ST. MARY'S COLLEGE

See press listings for performance locations.
Info: (310) 440-1351
Music Director: MaryAnn Bonino

Performances
Vary
Tickets
$5-55
Discounts
Students/groups of 10+, call

This is undoubtedly the most imaginative, permanent floating concert series in Southern California, if not the nation.

Founding director Dr. MaryAnn Bonino, a professor at Mount St. Mary's College, started the series in

1980 as a radical alternative to the usual concertgoing rituals. Actually, her new-fangled idea was an age-old one: To make chamber music the intimate salon experience it once was by staging concerts in private homes or architecturally interesting buildings around Southern California.

Within a decade, it evolved into something more—a free-spirited smorgasbord of musical styles and settings, with the effervescent Dr. Bonino as host and guide. She has led a growing army of subscribers into a plethora of places they'd have never visited otherwise—elegant homes, mansions and historic buildings, churches ornate and plain, hotel ballrooms, quiet public libraries, the merry-go-round at Griffith Park, a jailhouse in Pasadena, and even ancient Hangar #1 at LAX!

Before long, even chamber music itself proved to be too limiting a boundary for adventurous Dr. Bonino. The series scored some major musical coups by hosting the world premiere of Morton Subotnick's electronic homage to Halley's comet, *Return*, in 1986 at the Griffith Park Planetarium, and the U.S. premiere of Arvo Part's breathtaking *Berlin Mass* at St. Basil's Church in 1991. The program also spilled out of classical music in its Over the Edge and Now! series when the world music band Huayucaltia played the Mayan Theatre and Richie Cole and Alto Madness jazzed up the Museum of Flying. Most of the time, the combinations of music and locale are unerringly, even dazzlingly right.

At its peak in 1989, there was a mind-boggling variety of individual series from which to choose—over 50 concerts in over 30 locations. In addition, two or three times a year, CMIHS hightailed it out of town for a series of festivals in exotic places; earlier chamber music weekends occurred on Catalina Island, and 1991/92 patrons ended up in Lake Arrowhead and San Diego. However, in response to the chronically weak economy that still plagues the arts, Dr. Bonino slashed back the number of concerts in 1992/93 from 42 to 18, and temporarily eliminated the weekend festivals. Happily the 1993/94 season saw an addition of four more events. The children's concerts have not been cut, however (more in **CHILDREN** chapter).

BO
By phone Mon-Fri 8:30 am-5 pm; MC/V/reserve by mail (12001 Chalon Rd., Los Angeles, CA 90049), fax (310) 440-1363; no refunds, no exchanges; subscription program

Special Features
Open rehearsals

DOROTHY CHANDLER PAVILION See **Los Angeles Philharmonic, Los Angeles Master Chorale,** and **Music Center of Los Angeles County** in **THEATER**

EL CAMINO COLLEGE/MARSEE AUDITORIUM See **South Bay Center for the Arts**

eXINDIGO!

See press listings for performance locations.
Info: (818) 591-0687
Music Director: Ted Peterson

No, the name eXindigo! isn't quite as extreme as one might suppose. The group is actually a revival of a defunct outfit called the Ex Indigo Singers, and was formed in 1990 by composer/artistic director Ted Peterson and his wife, conductor Laurie Gurman.

This new music organization mixes contemporary subjects, idioms and mediums as freely as it does the upper and lower case letters in its name. Near the height of George Bush's popularity in 1991, eXindigo! gleefully took on Ed Bland's work for choir, piano and percussion, *The New World Order*—which contained movements with such titles as "President Quayle" and "Gimme That Tape." Video artist Stuart Bender and composer Angelo Funicelli

Performances
Nov through July; Sat 8 pm
Tickets
$7-12
Discounts
Seniors/students/groups of 10+, call
BO
Usually the night of performance only; check/reserve by mail (21724 Ventura Blvd, Ste. 232, Woodland Hills, CA 91364) or phone

combined forces with eXindigo! in a multimedia oratorio "Visitations" at the Long Beach Museum of Art in summer 1991. Minimalists, atonalists, synthesists, and any other "ists" imaginable are welcome under the eXindigo! tent.

eXindigo! has no permanent base; the locales exchange with every excursion. Call for the latest info.

Parking
Varies with location

GAY MEN'S CHORUS OF LONG BEACH

See press listings for performance locations.
Info: (310) 984-8330
Music Director: Paul Bodkin
Performs regularly at the Ebell Theatre in Long Beach, 290 Cerritos Avenue at 3rd.

Ten-year-old GMCLB presents a winter and a spring concert each year. The 22-member group draws a loyal cadre of supporters from not only Long Beach and the South Bay, but as far away as Los Angeles and Orange County.

The group performs a "smattering of all types" of music, from Orff's *Carmina Burana* to Lehar's *The Merry Widow* and Christmas choral selections. Most performances are given at the 500-seat Ebell Theatre in Long Beach.

Performances
Winter, spring Sat 8 pm, Sun, 4 pm
Tickets
$10-15
BO
Call; reserve by mail (P.O. Box 3566, Long Beach, CA 90803-3566)
Parking
Varies with location

GAY MEN'S CHORUS OF LOS ANGELES

Info: (213) 650-0756
Most performances at the Wiltern Theatre.

Founded in 1979, this accomplished 165-member choir has transcended its primary purpose—making music—by becoming a champion for the gay community. The toll on the group from AIDS-related illnesses has been frightening—more than 75 members to-date have died.

In 1990, GMCLA artistic director Jon Bailey commissioned UCLA composer Roger Bourland and librettist John Hall to write a cantata about the AIDS crisis. The result, *Hidden Legacies*— which roams freely through a wide variety of musical idioms—was unveiled by the chorus in spring 1992 and was immediately embraced by the gay community. The work has since been encored repeatedly by the chorus and by five other North American gay choirs.

While *Hidden Legacies* is the GMCLA's most visible project, the chorus has also commissioned or premiered works by such noted composers as Ned Rorem and Libby Larsen, as well as its resident composer Scott Henderson. Aside from three regular concerts per year, the chorus participates in many AIDS benefits and masses, and has traveled to New York City, Dallas, Denver, Prague, Budapest, and other major tour stops. Currently the chorus' base is the Wiltern Theatre.

GILBERT & SULLIVAN CO. OF SANTA BARBARA See THEATER

GINDI AUDITORIUM See THEATER

GLENDALE SYMPHONY ORCHESTRA

Alex Theatre
216 North Brand Boulevard
Glendale, CA 91203
Info: (818) 500-8720   **Rsvn:** (818) 500-8720
Fax: (818) 500-2484
Music Director: Lalo Schifrin
A resident company at the Alex Theatre.

Performances
Sat 8 pm
Tickets
$15

Active since 1924 and from 1965 until recently a resident of the Music Center, the Glendale Symphony is finally playing in its home city as it moves permanently to the renovated 1450-seat Alex Theatre beginning with its 1994-95 season.

For over two decades, the GSO was the vehicle for Carmen Dragon. In 1984-85 Daniel Lewis, the hero of the Pasadena Symphony, stepped in as artistic advisor. As in Pasadena, he started hiring crackerjack young musicians and freshened the repertoire. But Lewis left after one season, and the board, reading its audience, decided to pursue a pops-oriented direction.

Currently the music director is Lalo Schifrin, a dazzlingly versatile composer/arranger/pianist in the film, TV and jazz worlds. The programs contain mostly standard, undemanding classics and pops, with occasional guest star turns by celebrities such as Doc Severinsen or Tony Bennett.

On a given night, you might hear the local premiere of his latest, often pleasing concert work. The Argentine-born conductor has programmed some unusual pieces from south of the border.

BO
AE/MC/V/check/reserve by phone, mail (401 N Brand Blvd, #520, Glendale, CA 91203); subscription program
Location
Just off 134 Fwy
Parking
Nearby lots

THE GREAT WESTERN FORUM

3900 West Manchester Boulevard
Inglewood, CA 90301
Info: (310) 419-3100
Arena used for sporting events and concerts; seats between 16,000 and 18,000.

The blue-columned Forum, as it's known to most people, is more reminiscent of Caesar's Palace in Las Vegas than anything Rome ever erected. Now celebrating its 25th anniversary, the Forum is the home of Los Angeles's Kings, Lakers, and Strings. It also hosts up to 240 events each year, from rock concerts to ice-skating extravaganzas.

Depending on the event, the arena can seat 16,000 to 18,000 in two levels of seating—loge and colonnade. Special restrooms were built for handicap access; all others are accessible by stairs. There's wheelchair seating for 40, with parking immediately adjacent to entrance ramps. Parking is ample, but be sure to park in one of the secured parking lots.

Concession stands offer hard liquor, wine, and beer (depending on the event), and snacks such as pizza, nachos, and hot dogs. The Whistle Stop is a stand-up, cafeteria-style restaurant serving hot sandwiches; there's no table service.

Performances
Vary
Tickets
$ varies
Discounts
Groups of 30+, call
BO
Daily 10am-6 pm; AE/MC/V/reserve by mail, TicketMaster; no refunds, no exchanges; subscription program
Location
E of San Diego (405) Fwy at Manchester Blvd and Prairie Ave
Parking
On premises, $6; street parking

THE GREEK THEATRE

2700 North Vermont Avenue
Los Angeles, CA 90027
Info: (213) 665-1927   **Rsvn:** (213) 665-3156
Fax: (213) 666-8202
Outdoor amphitheater seating 6,187.

One of the main attractions in Griffith Park, the Greek is a landmark amphitheater featuring the hottest performers from Aerosmith to Bob Hope, Julio Iglesias and Bob Dylan. The Jethro Tull 25th anniversary was celebrated at the Greek, and the stage has rocked and rolled with Dan Fogelberg, Paul Taylor Dance Company, the Allman Brothers, and Kenny G.

The concert venue is named for its classical architectural facade. The structure has a history dating way back—at least by LA standards. Back in 1886, Griffith J. Griffith, a gold speculator and philanthropist, bestowed upon

Performances
May 1-Nov 1, days and times vary
Tickets
$ varies
Discounts
Groups of 20+, call
(213) 464-7521

the city 3,000 hilly, chaparral-covered acres to be converted into a city park. The natural acoustics of the canyon made it a perfect theater site. Thirtysomething years and a fundraising crusade later, the amphitheater was constructed and formally dedicated.

The setting is unsurpassed—from some seats, you can reach out and touch the trees and canyon walls. Unlike the Hollywood Bowl, which shows off its tremendous size immediately upon entering, the Greek feels much smaller and more intimate than its seating capacity would indicate.

Sightlines at the Greek are unobstructed from almost any location. The best seats, of course, are in Center Section A, and the view decreases by degree as you move farther away and upwards. If your seats are towards the back of Section B (rows L-W, or anywhere in C), you may want to rent binoculars (available at the theater for $5). Section B Left is also the non-smoking section. Along the extreme sides are the North and South Terraces. Although some Terrace seats along the middle aisles in Rows GG, HH, JJ, A and B are satisfactory, the Terrace sections closest to the stage rake off and away at a pretty sharp angle. The four rows at the very rear of the theater are bench seats. The sound is heavily amplified, overwhelming whatever natural acoustics that once existed. Wheelchair seating can be requested in advance.

Frequent "goers" join a Premiere Club: pick six attractions and get seat assignments first and advance notice for new attractions. Premiere Club Ltd. gives four choices, and tickets are processed right after Premiere Club. Consult the press listings to find out whether the "Create Your Own Concert Series" offer is still in effect.

The snack bar offers sports stadium fare—hot dogs, cheeseburgers, beer and wine—at prices around $3.50 to $4.50. Better yet, arrive early to avoid the nightmare of parking and enjoy a picnic meal on the grass while everyone else is fighting over spaces in the lot.

Parking and bathroom lines will test your patience. The lots are unpaved and stack-parked (cars are parked tightly on all four sides), and there's only one way out—plan to take your time getting home.

When you do get out, consider the following for after-concert eats: Farfalla or Katsu on Hillhurst, Louise's Trattoria at Los Feliz and Vermont.

BO
Mon-Fri noon-6 pm, Sat-Sun 10 am-4 pm, performance days noon-9 pm; check/AE/MC/V/ reserve by mail (pre-season only), TicketMaster; no refunds, no exchanges—rain or shine; subscription program
Location
W off Golden State (5) Fwy at Los Feliz Blvd, on Vermont Ave N of Los Feliz Blvd in Griffith Park
Parking
On premises, $5-7

GUILD OPERA CO. See **CHILDREN**

HAUGH PERFORMING ARTS CENTER See **THEATER**

HERMOSA CIVIC THEATRE

710 Pier Avenue
Hermosa Beach, CA 90254
Info: (310) 318-3452   **Rsvn:** (310) 318-3452
500-seat community theater highlighting jazz and classical guitar performances.

Just a few blocks from the ocean, Hermosa Beach's 500-seat Civic Theatre has survived earthquakes, the WPA, and the threat of demolition. The restored Art Deco theater is the focal point of the Hermosa Beach Community Center.

Numerous performances are scheduled including a Solo Series and Jazz Series, which have featured Woody Harrelson's Manly Moondog and The Three Kool Kats (funky R&B and socially conscious folk music); David

Performances
March-June; Fri-Sat 8 pm
Tickets
$10-40
Discounts
Groups of 50+, call
BO
Mon-Fri 1-6 pm check/MC/V/reserve by phone, mail; no refunds, no exchanges; subscription program

Richter, soloist; and Liona Boyd, one of the world's leading classical guitarists.

The folks here don't really call their lineup a performing arts series, instead they advertise the season as an Annual Theatre Gala. The revival film series is an on-again, off-again program—who knows, this year you may be in luck! Rainy night flicks like *Gaslight* and *The Three Faces of Eve* were recent offerings.

Location
At Pacific Coast Hwy
and Pier Ave
Parking
On premises, FREE;
street parking

HOLLYWOOD BOWL ORCHESTRA

(See Hollywood Bowl Summer Festival in FESTIVAL & SEASONAL EVENTS for further information.)

Usually, the procedure goes like this: an orchestra is born, it rehearses, it plays some concerts, and then it goes into the recording studio. But the Hollywood Bowl Orchestra gave its very first performance in a recording studio, and only several months later did it appear before the public for the first time.

Such was the birth of this unusual ensemble, the joint creation of the Philips record label and the Los Angeles Philharmonic Association. First heard on the fabled MGM scoring stage in February of 1991, the Bowl Orchestra made its public debut that July as the second resident orchestra of the Hollywood Bowl (the longtime resident LA Philharmonic is the other).

The Hollywood Bowl Orchestra is an old name dating as far back as the 1920s (some fascinating 78 RPM records were made under that name in 1928). But not since the end of World War II, when Leopold Stokowski was in charge of the Bowl, has there been a distinct ensemble under that title.

John Mauceri, the articulate, personable music director of the Bowl Orchestra, says that this orchestra should be capable of playing music of any era, any style—from Mozart to Mancini, as it were. He says he wants to break down the barriers between so-called "serious" music and so-called "pops," whose spheres of influence are clearly marked on the Bowl schedule (classics during the week, pops on weekends).

Be that as it may, in its first season, the Bowl Orchestra seemed very much in the mold of a conventional pops orchestra, playing Gershwin, film music, Rodgers and Hammerstein, and the perennially sold-out Bowl tradition, the "Tchaikovsky Spectacular." As the schedule expanded the following summer, though, Mauceri began to fulfill more of his original charter. In place of the Salzburg-bound Philharmonic, the Bowl Orchestra took over a week of classical programming and expanded its weekend pops agenda from five to seven programs.

Luckily, this is a cracking good pops orchestra, one that already is playing with a remarkable fizz and snap, led by one of those rare conductors who is as much at home in a Broadway theater as in a concert hall. Indeed, their level of ensemble is even more astounding when you consider that the Bowl Orchestra is made up from a fluctuating pool of studio pros, many of whom also play in other regional orchestras.

Not only that, but Mauceri is a wonderfully sardonic, mischievous emcee, entertaining and enlightening the audience, inventing new ways to shrug off those arch nemeses of the Bowl, buzzing helicopters and other nasty flying machines. And even within the tritest pops formats, Mauceri is breaking new ground; his first Gershwin date in 1991 uncovered valuable film music that had never been performed live in public before.

Eventually, the Bowl Orchestra will occupy all of the weekend slots, which should result in better music-making from everyone, especially the rested Philharmonic. And be advised; Mauceri and his Bowl Orchestra soon may be the hottest Bowl ticket of all.

HOLLYWOOD OPERA ENSEMBLE

See press listings for performance locations.
Info: (213) 851-0271
Music Director: Aida Monte
Performances take place at Immanuel Presbyterian Church in Los Angeles and Temple Beth Ami in West Covina.

The Hollywood Opera Ensemble exists thanks to the stubborn vision of a determined Italian-born, Juilliard-trained former violinist, Aida Monte. A legal secretary by day, she's been fulfilling her musical fantasies since 1975 by running her own opera company literally out of her downstairs apartment.

She is the producer, director, scenery-mover, costume-maker and prima donna for her company, which uses an assortment of amateur singers to purvey the bread-and-butter repertoire of Bizet, Puccini, Verdi, Lehar and friends. She finances her company on a shoestring but entirely by herself, never soliciting grants or donations beyond the admission fee.

Performances
3 times a year at different times
Tickets
$8-10
Discounts
Seniors/students/groups of 25
BO
Open 1/2 hr before performance time; check/reserve by mail (call for address)
Parking
Varies with location

HOLLYWOOD PALLADIUM

6215 Sunset Boulevard
Hollywood, CA 90028
Info: (213) 962-7600   **Fax:** (213) 962-0662
The concert hall can accommodate 3,750; there is no seating.

The Palladium is one of Los Angeles' few bona fide entertainment landmarks. A dream of Los Angeles Times Publisher Norman Chandler, the building was finished at a cost of $1 million-plus and opened as a ballroom in 1940 to the tunes of Frank Sinatra.

In its heyday, the 11,000-square-foot oval dance floor was a hotspot hosting entertainers such as Benny Goodman, Harry James, the Dorsey Brothers, Doris Day, Judy Garland, Glenn Miller, and Peggy Lee. Lawrence Welk effervesced here every Saturday night from 1961 to 1976. Today it's a rental house for rock concerts and private functions such as awards banquets.

Sadly, over the years the Palladium's star has paled. The neighborhood has faded along with it; the studios once across the street have moved across town. Although the ballroom's marquee was replaced in the 1950s, the interior has gone practically untouched—literally. The wooden dance floor (which was turned into a roller-rink one night a week during the '70s skating craze) is scarred and pockmarked with cigarette burns. The place reeks of stale smoke, and the ceiling plaster is cracked and stained.

The unruly crowds of recent years have given the Palladium a black eye as far as the community is concerned. At press time, the future of the Palladium as a concert facility is in some doubt. Rock will not be left out of the Palladium's future line-up, but management will attempt to book other types of entertainment, as well.

Performances
Mon-Sun 7 pm
Tickets
$10-35
BO
Mon-Fri noon-6 pm reserve by mail, TicketMaster
Location
Near the Hollywood (101) Fwy; near the corner of Sunset and Vine
Parking
On premises, $5; on street

I CANTORI See **Cantori**

INGLEWOOD PHILHARMONIC ASSOCIATION

See press listings for performance locations.
Info: (310) 674-1688
Music Director: Leroy Hurte
Performs mainly at Inglewood High School Auditorium, 231 South Grevillea Avenue, Inglewood, CA 90301 (310) 419-2585; also performs at El Camino College, various churches, Music Center.

Founded in 1949, the Inglewood Philharmonic pushes onward under current music director Leroy Hurte. Three decades ago, it was able to attract the likes of André Previn, Henri Temianka, Mehli Mehta, and film composer/conductor Miklos Rozsa. Today, the orchestra still makes a point of world premiering works by new composers.

In addition to its regular season, the Philharmonic presents an annual pops concert with the usual mix of film tunes, Broadway hits, operatic tidbits, and hummable overtures. There's also an annual young people's concert for the children of Inglewood Unified School District.

The Philharmonic can usually be found playing the Inglewood High School Auditorium, but has also performed at El Camino College, various churches in the area, and even the Music Center downtown.

Performances
Fall-spring, Sat-Sun 5 pm; annual youth concert
Tickets
$10
Discounts
Children/seniors/ students/groups of 6+, call
BO
Before performance check/reserve by mail (P.O. Box 2055, Inglewood, CA 90305); no exchanges; subscription program
Parking
Varies with location
Special Features
Open rehearsals

IRVINE BARCLAY THEATRE

UCI
4242 Campus Drive
Irvine, CA 92715
Info: (714) 854-4607   **Rsvn:** (714) 854-4646
Fax: (714) 854-4999
756-seat space for music, dance, and family programs.

Located on the campus of the University of California Irvine, the theater looks from the outside not unlike the hundreds of office buildings that dot Irvine. But inside, the two-story building is an all-business intimate space: 756 seats, none more than 60 feet from the stage, make it suitable for local organizations as well pros. A wide range of programming—ballet, theater, philharmonic and chamber music, children's and young adults' events—keeps this $17.6 million facility busy year-round.

The Irvine Barclay also stands as a local symbol of sorts, because it took 16 years and a unique partnership of local government, university, and private-sector interests to raise the dough and secure a site.

In addition to regular performances by Ballet Pacifica, the Irvine Civic Light Opera, Orange County Philharmonic, Laguna Chamber Music Society, and Orange County Chamber Orchestra, the Irvine Barclay hosts the UCI (University of California at Irvine) Lectures & Cultural Events series. As with most university performing arts series, this one includes dance, theater, film, and all kinds of music. Additionally, an authors series and other special lectures fill out the schedule. Season tickets are available.

The parking structure adjacent to the theater (and across from the Student Center) charges a nominal fee.

Performances
Mon-Sun
Tickets
$10-25
Discounts
Previews/children/ seniors/students/groups of 20+
BO
Mon-Sat 10 am-6 pm; Sun noon-6 pm MC/V/check/ TicketMaster; no exchanges or refunds
Location
Between Campus and Bridge; near San Diego (405) Fwy
Parking
On premises, $2

IRVINE MEADOWS AMPHITHEATRE

8808 Irvine Center Drive
Irvine, CA 92718
Info: (714) 855-8096   **Rsvn:** (714) 855-2863
Fax: (714) 855-9195
An outdoor concert amphitheater with reserved seating for 10,418 and lawn-seating capacity for 4,582.

Performances
March- Oct
Tickets
$17.50-30
Discounts
Groups of 25+, call

The hills of the Orange County community come alive with music March through October. The bill of fare includes everything from the Pacific Symphony Orchestra to Dan Fogelberg and other contemporary musical acts.

Tucked into a hillside and surrounded by agricultural fields, the open-air amphitheater acts as home to the Symphony all summer, when night time temperatures are a bit more agreeable for the gentry. The amplified sound is often surprisingly lifelike for classical music. Clearly these sound engineers know how to mike an orchestra.

Those with tickets for the lawn should bring along a blanket and binoculars. Picnics are allowed for the Symphony performances only. For the other concerts, you cannot bring in your own food or drink. Ticket prices are pretty steep, and so is parking at $6 per car.

BO
Performance days, noon-9 pm
MC/V/reserve by mail, TicketMaster; no exchanges; subscription program
Location
At San Diego (405) Fwy and Irvine Center Dr
Parking
On premises, $6

JAPAN AMERICA SYMPHONY ORCHESTRA OF LOS ANGELES

See press listings for performance locations.
Info: (213) 489-5660   **Rsvn:** (213) 680-3700
Fax: (213) 627-1353
Music Director: Heiichiro Ohyama
Performances are held at the Japan America Theatre and the Dorothy Chandler Pavilion.

Known for its first 30 years as the Japanese Philharmonic Orchestra of Los Angeles, in 1991 this orchestra underwent not only a name change but a musical face-lift as well.

After years of mediocre notices, the orchestra has been turned around by new music director, Heiichiro Ohyama, former Los Angeles Philharmonic principal violist/assistant conductor. The hard-working Ohyama has upgraded the musical standards of this ensemble, of which only about 40 percent of the members are of Japanese descent.

The programming policy couples standard repertoire pieces with rare contemporary works by Japanese composers. Hence, Beethoven's *Fifth Symphony* can rest cheek to jowl on a program with the U.S. premiere of a new Maki Ishii concerto for Japanese flute and orchestra. (To accommodate this range, the orchestra expands from chamber to symphonic size whenever events dictate.)

The orchestra also has the distinct advantage of playing most of its concerts in the Japan America Theatre, whose pleasing, not-too-dry acoustics flatter chamber-sized groups.

Performances
Vary
Tickets
$15-30
Discounts
Seniors/students/groups of 10+, call
BO
Japan America Theatre Mon-Sun noon-5 pm; Dorothy Chandler Pavilion (213) 972-7211; payment options vary with location; subscription program
Parking
Varies with location

JAZZ LIVE AT THE HYATT See FESTIVALS & SEASONAL EVENTS

JOHN ANSON FORD AMPHITHEATRE See THEATER and FESTIVALS & SEASONAL EVENTS

KECK THEATER See Occidental College Performing Arts Series

KOREAN PHILHARMONIC ORCHESTRA

See press listings for performance locations.
Info: (213) 387-4632   **Fax:** (213) 387-7025
Music Director: Raymond M. Cho
Most performances scheduled for the Wilshire Ebell Theatre.

Performances
Feb, May, Sept and Dec, Fri-Sat 8 pm
Tickets
$10

Founded in 1969 by its present music director, Raymond Cho, the Korean Philharmonic serenades the large LA Korean community—as well as other nationalities—with a four-concert series.

Cho, a Seoul native who emigrated in 1960, programs a mix of standard classics (Tchaikovsky, Brahms, Beethoven, etc.) with Oriental compositions. Cho also promotes racial harmony. In the spring of 1992, for instance, not long after the LA civil disturbances, he staged a concert with choir that harmoniously combined Korean-American and African-American music.

The 70-member orchestra—about half Korean, half "other"—is about 50 percent professional and fluctuates in number according to the program. Every few years, the Korean Philharmonic participates in an opera such as *La Boheme* or a less familiar work by a Korean composer.

The orchestra plays most of its season at the cozy Wilshire Ebell Theatre but delivers its Christmas program at the Korean Philadelphia Church of Los Angeles. In the past, the orchestra has played the Hollywood Bowl's famous Easter Sunrise service.

BO
Weekdays one week before performance, 10 am-5 pm check/reserve by mail (3123 W 8th St, Ste. 208, Los Angeles, CA 90005), fax; no exchanges; subscription program

Parking
Varies with location

KOROYAR FOLKLORE ENSEMBLE

See press listings for performance locations.
Info: (714) 736-9608
Folk dance and music ensemble, specializing in dance from Bulgaria, Greece, Turkey and Armenia.

You want unique? You want unfamiliar? You want a musical trip around the world in one performance? Then look for Koroyar at area fairs and festivals. Koroyar is both a dance troupe and musical ensemble presenting diverse musical arrangements with Balkan, Middle Eastern, Slavic, Gypsy, and Jewish influences, as well as totally original pieces integrating the sounds of these peoples. Programs include archaic and contemporary folk melodies and ornate and disparate rhythms.

You will hear instruments at Koroyar's concerts you've never heard (or heard of) before, for example, the two-string, mandolin-like *citelija*, popular among the Albanians in Yugoslavia. (By the way, Koroyar's citelija is the only one of its kind in the United States.) The ensemble has otherwise amassed a formidable repertoire of over 440 folk songs and melodies, which it has perfected over the course of hundreds of recital and festival appearances.

Performances
Vary
Tickets
$ varies
Parking
Varies with location
Special Features
Open rehearsals

LA JOLLA CHAMBER MUSIC SOCIETY

See press listings for performance locations.
Info: (619) 459-3724 **Fax:** (619) 459-3727
Executive Director: Neale Perl
Sherwood Series, the Discovery Series, and SummerFest take place at Sherwood Auditorium in the Museum of Contemporary Art, San Diego (in La Jolla); Celebrity Series is at San Diego Civic Theatre, downtown San Diego.

For nearly 25 years, the La Jolla Chamber Music Society has quietly slipped chamber music onto the calendar at Sherwood Auditorium. This small, intimate theater is interesting inside and out. Since it's located inside the Museum of Contemporary Art, the outside offers all varieties of visual expression. The museum also owns one of San Diego's best views of the Pacific coastline.

In the last decade, the Society has expanded beyond Sherwood, bringing YoYo Ma and André Watts, for example, to the downtown Civic Theatre for the annual Celebrity classical music series. This series, the new Discovery series, and the society's SummerFest (a week-

Performances
Begin at 8 pm on different days of the week, but usually Sat; 3 series in the winter and SummerFest in August
Tickets
$10-55
Discounts
Students/groups of 10+, call
BO
Mon-Fri 9am-5 pm check/AE/MC/V/reserve by mail (P.O. Box 2168, La Jolla, CA 92038), TicketMaster; Arti Tix Booth; no exchanges; subscription program

long chamber music festival at Sherwood that has André Previn among the international regulars) have enormously enhanced San Diego's classical music life.

As a special bonus, SummerFest holds open rehearsals.

Parking
Varies with location
Special Features
Open rehearsals during SummerFest only

LA JOLLA SYMPHONY AND CHORUS

Mandeville Auditorium
University of California, San Diego
La Jolla, CA 92093
Info: (619) 534-4637   **Rsvn:** (619) 534-4637
Fax: (619) 534-8502
Music Director: Thomas Nee
Performs at Mandeville Auditorium at the University of California, San Diego.

Any orchestra that plans Beethoven and something called *Boojum!* in the same season has the kind of approach you might want to follow. The La Jolla Symphony and Chorus turns on the talents of San Diego college students and musicians. Typical seasons include six concerts of classical and contemporary orchestral, choral, and music-theater works.

The 95 orchestra members and 125 choral musicians perform under the direction of Thomas Nee and choral conductor David Chase at Mandeville Auditorium on the UCSD campus. The symphonic ensemble, founded in 1954, is actually older than the university. As with the Playhouse, the university setting and affiliation has had an influence—innovative and alternative programming. They take risks.

The orchestra and chorus has, in the past few years, gained a reputation for presenting overlooked masterpieces, premieres by American composers, and giant works (as 300 musicians on-stage) that include idiosyncratic instruments.

(By the way, *Boojum!* is Australian composer Martin Wesley-Smith's theater-piece inspired by Lewis Carroll's writings.)

Performances
Nov through June; Sat 8 pm; Sun 3 pm
Tickets
$8-10
Discounts
Seniors/children/ students/groups of 10+, call
BO
MC/V/check/reserve by mail, TicketMaster; exchanges made on availability; subscription program
Parking
On premises
Special Features
Open rehearsals

LA MIRADA SYMPHONY ORCHESTRA

La Mirada Theatre for the Performing Arts
14900 La Mirada Boulevard
La Mirada, CA 90638
Info: (714) 521-2786   **Rsvn:** (714) 994-6310
Music Director: Leon Guide
Performs at La Mirada Theatre for the Performing Arts.

This community orchestra, now approaching its 30th season, concertizes four Saturday nights a year in La Mirada Theatre for the Performing Arts. Music Director Leon Guide gravitates toward the safe and the tuneful. A recent season featured an all-Tchaikovsky program, a "Best of Broadway" night and such familiar chestnuts as Rimsky-Korsakov's *Scheherazade* and Schumann's *Piano Concerto.*

Students, seniors, and children are admitted free; all others are asked for a "donation."

Performances
Sat 8:30 pm
Tickets
Donation
BO
At the door
Location
Rosecrans exit off Santa Ana (5) Fwy
Parking
On premises, FREE; street parking

LANCASTER PERFORMING ARTS CENTER See THEATER

LANDIS AUDITORIUM See Riverside Pops

LONG BEACH ARENA

300 East Ocean Boulevard
Long Beach, CA 90802
Info: (310) 436-3636   **Rsvn:** (310) 436-3661
Fax: (310) 436-9491
Seats 14,000-plus for variety shows and concerts.
    A multi-use facility built in 1963, the Long Beach Arena presents everything from Long Beach Symphony Pops concerts to heavy metal rock, "Disney on Ice" shows, the Ringling Bros. circus, and evangelical crusades. (But not all at once.) Floor seating is on both flats and risers in this 14,000-seat arena.

Performances
  Sat 8 pm
Tickets
  $ varies
BO
  Mon-Sat 10 am-6 pm;
  AE/MC/V/TicketMaster;
  subscription program
Location
  Off Long Beach (710)
  Fwy S, take to end and
  follow Shoreline Dr
Parking
  On premises, $5; on
  street (limited)

LONG BEACH BACH FESTIVAL See FESTIVALS & SEASONAL EVENTS

LONG BEACH OPERA (TERRACE, CENTER THEATERS   )

Terrace Theater and Center Theater
300 East Ocean Boulevard
Long Beach, CA 90802
Info: (310) 596-5556   **Rsvn:** (310) 436-3661
Fax: (310) 596-8380
Gereral Director: Michael Milenski
Resident opera company at the Terrace and Center theaters in Long Beach.
    If Opera Pacific is the conservative operatic stronghold of Metropolitan Los Angeles, and Music Center Opera straddles the middle while leaning left, Long Beach Opera stands out as the wild-eyed radicals down the freeway.
    Once a humdrum purveyor of bread-and-butter repertoire, Long Beach Opera suddenly started sizzling in 1983 with a stunningly stark production of Britten's *Death In Venice*. Egged on by its iconoclastic general director Michael Milenski, LBO soon became a laboratory for the mod, zany and/or macabre productions of the Alden twins, Christopher and David (who have gone on to some fame), along with other free-thinking directors.
    Whether you love 'em or loathe 'em—and it's either one or the other—there's no question Long Beach Opera has style. They use often strikingly threadbare sets (which fit in nicely with LBO's perennially strapped budgets), often in trendy black-and-white as if Mozart shopped on LA's Melrose Avenue. They can take outrageous liberties with standard repertoire; their S&M *Tales Of Hoffman* and rap sequence in *Ariadne auf Naxos* come to mind.
    The casts are generally young and full of energy, musical standards rigorously high, and though tamper they might with the settings, LBO always gives you the score perfectly straight. In the "pit"—or wherever they choose to place their orchestra (LBO once suspended the musicians overhead!)—such scrupulous maestros as Nicholas McGegan and Randall Behr could be found before their rise to renown.
    LBO has done some pioneering, nationally newsworthy productions of rare pieces such as Ernst Krenek's *Jonny spielt auf* and Karol Szymanowski's *King*

Performances
  Wed, Sat 8 pm; Sun 4
  pm
Tickets
  $22-55
Discounts
  Seniors/students/groups
  of 10+
BO
  Mon-Sat 10am-5 pm
  AE/MC/V/check/reserve
  by mail, fax,
  TicketMaster;
  subscribers only may
  exchange seats;
  subscription program
Parking
  On premises, $5

Roger. And they've probably helped drive Music Center Opera off center of the road.

Long Beach Opera comes off best in the dry, intimate Center Theatre, where the directors milk its thrust stage and the audience can clearly hear the words (almost always sung in English). Occasionally they take a grander production into neighboring Terrace Theatre, where things tend to get lost somewhere above the proscenium. Sometimes they even travel outside their home turf, turning up, for example, at the John Anson Ford Theatre. Tickets may initially be plentiful but when word gets out about a hot production, you'll wish you'd booked before.

LONG BEACH SYMPHONY ORCHESTRA

Terrace Theatre
300 East Ocean Boulevard
Long Beach, CA 90802
Info: (310) 436-3203 **Rsvn:** (310) 436-3203
Fax: (310) 491-3599
Music Director: JoAnn Falletta
Resident orchestra at Long Beach's Terrace Theatre.

Not long ago, the LBSO, a 60-year-old distinguished veteran, tottered on the brink of extinction, even having to cancel its 1984/85 season due to lack of funds. But since 1989, LBSO's subscription seasons have been SRO. What happened? JoAnn Falletta happened.

Falletta, a young dynamo, took over in 1989/90 and touched off a box-office stampede. And as of the last three seasons, the LBSO has become a hit.

This messianic rise becomes more mythic when you consider that Falletta was completely unknown in Southern California before she arrived. She has clearly and painstakingly established a personal link with the community, particularly with her packed concert previews.

She has a grand podium manner, full of wide, expansive arcs with the baton. As a programmer, Falletta fuses an enlightened balance between the 20th century and the more popular 19th, drawing from her staggering repertoire of more than 866 pieces. She has a particularly strong interest in women composers; thus, contemporary figures like Libby Larsen, Joan Tower, and Ellen Taaffe Zwilich are turning up on LBSO programs. She's also willing to try new approaches with established pieces, playing, for example, Mahler's *First Symphony* complete with its rare "Blumine" movement. For those with lighter tastes, Falletta also has a three-concert pops series, with occasional guest maestros like Cincinnati Pops conductor Erich Kunzel.

Important tip: if you're trying to rustle up LBSO tickets in the Terrace Theatre, go for the balcony, where the sound is much better focused than that of the orchestra floor.

Performances
Sept-June, Sat
8 pm
Tickets
$18-36
Discounts
Seniors/students/groups of 20+, call
BO
Mon-Fri 9am-5 pm; at theatre Mon-Sat 10 am-6 pm; check/MC/V/ reserve by mail, fax, TicketMaster; exchanges made on availability; subscription program
Parking
On premises, $5
Special Features
Open rehearsals

LOS ANGELES BACH FESTIVAL See FESTIVALS & SEASONAL EVENTS

LOS ANGELES BAROQUE ORCHESTRA

See press listings for performance locations.
Info: (310) 578-7698 **Fax:** (310) 578-7698
Music Director: Gregory M. Maldonado
Concerts given at churches in Santa Monica and Pasadena.

While performances of classical and baroque music on "authentic" instruments are all the rage in world concert halls and record shops, Los Angeles has lagged behind—until recently. The Los Angeles Baroque Orchestra was one of the first such ensembles to surface here, and it's

Performances
Sept-June, Fri-Sat 8 pm, Sun 4 pm
Tickets
$18
Discounts
Children/seniors/ students/groups of 10+, call

produced many handsome performances of music written roughly between the years 1600 and 1830.

This all-professional group, ranging from seven to about 40 members, uses only old instruments or authentic reproductions. Why go through the fuss and bother of using often recalcitrant old instruments? To get closer to the actual sounds of the instruments and ensembles for which Bach, Mozart, Beethoven, and their friends wrote their masterpieces. But beyond merely pleasing the academics, old instruments have softer, tangy, zestful sounds with a sensual appeal all their own. And, rather than use conventional concert halls, the LABO seeks out performance spaces that give old instruments a chance to bloom. Gregory Maldonado, founder/director of LABO, started in 1985 with Christmas concerts in local churches. He then floated a three-concert subscription series in the spring of 1986. Sensing the pent-up demand for a resident authentic instrument group, he launched a full-blown series the following year.

Currently the LABO carries a load of performances in over a dozen churches in Pasadena and Santa Monica. For six years running, the LABO has also been part of a summer series at the Getty Museum, giving anywhere from one to four concerts.

BO
Check/MC/V/reserve by phone, mail (2554 Lincoln Blvd, Ste. 344, Marina Del Rey, CA 90291); exchanges before performance; subscription program

Parking
Varies with location

LOS ANGELES CHAMBER ORCHESTRA

See press listings for performance locations.
Info: (213) 622-7001 **Fax:** (213) 955-2071
Music Director: Christof Perick
Performs at the Ambassador Auditorium, Royce Hall, and Japan America Theatre.

Player for player, this group has been for many years the best orchestra in Southern California—and it promises to get even better, assuming its current financial problems (which caused postponement of several recent concerts) are solved.

Christof Perick, a vigorous, versatile German conductor in his 40s, took over as music director for the 1992/93 season, succeeding Iona Brown who has stayed on as principal guest conductor. From his first appearances here back in 1985, when the LACO played for Deutsche Opera Berlin's production of Mozart's *Le Nozze di Figaro*, Perick and the orchestra hit it off, and he returned many times as a guest. Together they produce a warm, lyrical yet fluid and precise sound, always pressing inexorably forward.

In his first concert as music director in October of 1992, Perick chose to lead off the evening with a bold gesture—the world premiere of Mel Powell's thorny, uncompromising *Settings For Small Orchestra*. In another outing, he broke up an all-Vivaldi program by inserting Alban Berg's *Three Pieces from Lyric Suite* as a jarring interlude.

Indeed, Perick seems determined to take the LACO back to its Golden Age, the tenure of Gerard Schwarz (1978-86). Like Schwarz, Perick doesn't mind taking on a big symphonic challenge in small orchestra garb now and then. And Perick has revived the LACO's recording program that expanded tremendously under Schwarz only to peter out completely after he left.

The LACO's history is not long as world-class orchestras go, but plenty distinguished. Its first music director, Neville Marriner (1969-1978), instantly put the crack studio-centered players on the international map. Schwarz drove the level of precision and fire even higher during his tenure.

The LACO has a number of musical homes, fielding subscription seasons in Ambassador Auditorium (where it sounds warmest), Royce Hall (assuming it can be

Performances
Oct-May

Tickets
$27-34

Discounts
Children/seniors/ students/groups of 10+, call

BO
Check/MC/V/reserve by mail (315 W 9th St, Ste. 801, Los Angeles, CA 90015), fax, TicketMaster; exchanges on availability; subscription program

Parking
Varies with location

Special Features
Open rehearsals (by invitation only)

restored—where their playing has the highest definition), and the smaller Japan America Theatre. An expanded edition of the LACO also continues to serve as the superb regular pit orchestra for Music Center Opera at the Dorothy Chandler Pavilion.

The LACO has a Christmas tradition of presenting Bach's complete *Brandenburg Concertos*. In the summertime, you can often catch the group ladling good cheer from the vast expanses of the Hollywood Bowl.

LOS ANGELES COUNTY MUSEUM OF ART—BING THEATER

5905 Wilshire Boulevard
Los Angeles, CA 90036
Info:(213) 857-6115   **Rsvn:** (213) 857-6010
Fax: (213) 931-7347

While the venerable Monday Evening Concerts (see separate entry) is the flagship of the music program at the Los Angeles County Museum of Art's Bing Theater, it's not the only series of interest there; and season tickets are available for these series as well.

BING CONCERTS

These programs, presented by LACMA since 1965, follow the chamber music mainstream (all things being relative), presenting soloists such as pianist Robert Taub, and groups such as the Fine Arts Quartet, Francesco Trio, and the unorthodox quintet TASHI with superclarinetist Richard Stoltzman.

ENSEMBLE RESIDENCY

Established in 1987, the Ensemble Residency is a series devoted to a single group. In 1992/93, the versatile California E.A.R. Unit took on four programs, including a Terry Riley world premiere, a tribute to the late John Cage, and a collaboration with Lula Washington's Los Angeles Contemporary Dance Theater. The 1993 program chose Morton Feldman's "For Frank Ohara" and the world premiere of *Psychotropes* by Stephen L. Mosko.

PHILHARMONIA BAROQUE ORCHESTRA

Fairly new to the museum's schedule, this series features the Philharmonia Baroque Orchestra conducted by the lively classical/baroque expert Nicholas McGegan. Philharmonia Baroque, which specializes in music from the 18th century, is arguably the country's best-known authentic-instruments ensemble.

PRO MUSICIS RECITALS

Each year since 1965, Pro Musicis has sponsored recitals all over the world by exceptionally talented young and/or little-known performers, including the winners of the previous year's Pro Musicis Award.

SUNDAYS AT FOUR

This series of free chamber music concerts is presented by the City of Los Angeles Cultural Affairs Department and broadcast live over KUSC-FM (91.5). Included are the Dame Myra Hess Recitals (recently renamed the Los Angeles Virtuoso Concerts), appearances by local orchestras and chamber groups of many sizes, and various instrumental soloists.

The repertoire here varies, from the 18th- and 19th-century mainstream to thematic presentations (such as the February 1993 Black History Month programs), and some contemporary music.

And if you think 4 pm Sunday is an odd time to hold a concert, just remember it was Vladimir Horowitz's preferred hour to perform—and he didn't do too badly.

Performances
  Mon, Wed 8 pm
Tickets
  $8-25
Discounts
  Children/seniors/
  students/groups of 10+,
  call; members
BO
  Tues-Thurs 10am-5 pm,
  Fri 5-9 pm, Sat and Sun
  11am-6 pm; check/
  reserve by phone, mail,
  TicketMaster;
  subscription program
Location
  At Wilshire Blvd
  between La Brea Ave
  and Fairfax Ave
Parking
  On premises; on street

JAZZ PROGRAMS

Each Friday night, from 5:30 to 8:30 pm, the museum sponsors jazz concerts on the Plaza. The free programs are offered year-round. A recent schedule included saxophonist Kim Richmond, Bobby Bradford, Kei Akagi, and Thomas Tedesco Quartet.

From 1:30 to 3:30 pm, on alternate Sundays in summer, the museum presents free big band concerts (at the museum's Times Mirror Central Court).

LOS ANGELES HARBOR COLLEGE, MUSIC RECITAL HALL

1111 Figueroa Place
Wilmington, CA 90744
Info: (310) 522-8200   **Rsvn:** (310) 522-8247
Fax: (310) 834-1882
College-supported 204-seat recital hall.

Music Recital Hall (also known as MU 101) is the pride and joy of the LA Community College District. An intimate space, it's been dubbed a "live" hall for its excellent acoustics.

The South Bay Chamber Music Society and the Musicians' Collective each present ten monthly concerts in the hall throughout the year. Guest and student recitals are also given. With most ticket prices under $10, and many concerts free of charge, the Harbor College music program is worth checking out.

Performances
Wed-Mon 7 pm, 7:30 pm or 8 pm; Tues noon; Sun 3 pm or 5 pm
Tickets
FREE; $5-6 for benefits
BO
In Music Office or at the door; check/reserve by mail
Location
Off Harbor (110) Fwy S at Anaheim St, on "L" St N of Anaheim Blvd
Parking
On premises, FREE; school hrs, parking across "L" St, 75 cents

LOS ANGELES MASTER CHORALE AND SINFONIA ORCHESTRA

Music Center
Dorothy Chandler Pavilion
135 North Grand Avenue
Los Angeles, CA 90012
Info: (213) 972-7282   **Rsvn:** (213) 626-0910
Fax: (213) 626-0196
Artistic Director: Paul Salamunovich
Resident company of the Dorothy Chandler Pavilion.

Good news for choral music fans. The Los Angeles Master Chorale is clearly on the rebound, reclaiming its reputation as one of the world's best professional choral groups.

The late, redoubtable Roger Wagner created this chorale in 1964 as a resident company within the Music Center and whipped it into an amazingly flexible instrument. You could always sense a brightly lit, barely contained current of electricity in Wagner's chorales, with—wonder of wonders—every syllable enunciated clearly and precisely.

Alas, Wagner was forced to retire as music director in 1986 to make way for Scotland's John Currie, who dismantled the Wagner sound into an amorphous, less well-defined blend. But Currie's successor in 1991 was a savvy veteran local choir director, Paul Salamunovich, a disciple of Wagner who has effectively restored much of his mentor's sound while showing a cultivated interest in neglected, first-rate yet audience-friendly 20th-century music. He's even outdone Wagner in one key area, getting tighter, more focused playing from the Chorale's Sinfonia Orchestra (generally a pickup group).

The Master Chorale has its own subscription season at the Dorothy Chandler Pavilion. The Chorale can also be heard backing the Los Angeles Philharmonic

Performances
Oct-May; Sat 8 pm; Sun 7:30 pm
Tickets
$7-44
Discounts
Seniors/students/groups of 10+, call (213) 972-7231
BO
Mon-Sat 10 am-6 pm check/AE/MC/V/reserve by mail, fax, TicketMaster; $1/ticket exchange fee; subscription program
Parking
On premises, $6; nearby lot, $4

whenever it does major choral/orchestral pieces, and it gave Music Center Opera a first-rate house chorus from Day One of the latter's existence.

A perennial December treat is the *Messiah* Singalong, a Wagner innovation and always a sellout, where would-be Domingos and Sutherlands in the audience bring their own scores and bellow along with the chorus. Get your tickets (and perhaps earplugs) early for that one.

LOS ANGELES MOZART ORCHESTRA

Wilshire Ebell Theatre
4401 West 8th Street
Los Angeles, CA 90005
Info: (213) 851-4256   **Rsvn:** (213) 851-7100 and (213) 939-1128
Music Director: Lucinda Carver
Subscription series performances held at the Wilshire Ebell Theatre in Los Angeles; chamber music concerts held in a variety of local venues.

True to its name, this professional chamber ensemble concentrates upon the music of Wolfgang Amadeus, but not exclusively. Each season offers one all Mozart concert, while the remainder of the programs are a sprinkling of Mozart contemporaries and modern compositions based on the chamber orchestra style.

Most of the time, the orchestra offers generally shipshape, performances of baroque and classical-period repertoire. In the 1992/93 season, Lucinda Carver took the helm as music director and has since obtained lively, graceful results. One of her goals upon taking this role was to expand the orchestra with a full complement of winds, opening up new territory in the 19th and 20th centuries. Not content to stop there, she has added chamber music concerts to the season, and has initiated an outreach program into the Los Angeles public schools.

LAMO was founded by David Keith in 1975, who remained music director until the close of the 1990/91 season. Today, LAMO holds six to seven concerts a year, and offers separate subscription series to the orchestral and chamber music concerts.

Performances
Fall-spring; Sat 8 pm;
Sun 2 pm
Tickets
$15-28
Discounts
Seniors/students/groups of 10+, call LAMO office (213) 851-7100
BO
MC/V/check/reserve by mail, Theatix on individual basis; subscription program
Parking
Varies with location

LOS ANGELES MUSIC CENTER OPERA

Music Center
Dorothy Chandler Pavilion
135 North Grand Avenue
Los Angeles, CA 90012
Info: (213) 972-7219   **Rsvn:** (213) 972-7211
Fax: (213) 687-3490
General Director: Peter Hemmings
Resident opera company of the Dorothy Chandler Pavilion.

Who says LA is a cultural desert? Those who named it so used to point to the absence of a major resident opera company here as Exhibit A. They can't do that anymore.

From the moment the curtain went up for Music Center Opera's inaugural production of Verdi's *Otello* in October 1986, Los Angeles hit the operatic big leagues. But that's not all. The MCO has unexpectedly become one of the nation's more daring companies, often putting on bold, nationally newsworthy productions—and all the while satisfying the local appetite for imported stars.

In previous years, opera-starved LA made do with ill-fated local outfits, road companies from the Met, San Francisco Opera, and, most recently, New York City Opera. But in 1982, spurred by a successful Los Angeles

Performances
Sept-June
Tickets
$19-95
Discounts
Seniors/students/groups of 20+, call (213) 972-7231
BO
Mon-Sat 10 am-6 pm; check/AE/MC/V/reserve by mail, TicketMaster; exchanges for subscribers only; subscription program
Parking
On premises, $6; nearby lot $4

Philharmonic production of Verdi's *Falstaff,* the Music Center Opera Association finally decided to go to the mat. City Opera was thrown out of the Dorothy Chandler Pavilion, Peter Hemmings of the London Symphony was signed as general director of the projected company, supertenor Placido Domingo joined the board as an "artistic consultant," and after a three-year gestation period, a world-class company sprouted.

A good deal of the credit goes to Hemmings, whose erect, proper British bearing camouflages an open mind and adventurous eye and ear in selecting repertoire. He's not been afraid to engage strong stage directors—the dark, brooding visions of Goetz Friedrich, the literal yet vivid elegance of Sir Peter Hall, the reincarnations of Jonathan Miller, or the mod look of David Alden. Occasionally he'll reach for a rarity like Janacek's powerful *Katya Kabanova,* Weill's *The Rise and Fall of the City of Mahagonny* (whose scathing Brecht satire on capitalism must have charmed the board members), or Manuel Penella's 1916 *El Gato Montes.*

In a given year, you might see a budget-busting spectacular like Wagner's *Tristan und Isolde* (with David Hockney's stunning sets and Zubin Mehta in the pit) or the massive, sometimes bizarre staging of Berlioz's huge *Les Troyens.* Or you can catch the latest, such as John Adams' controversial *Nixon in China* or the world premiere of Aulis Sallinen's powerful *Kullervo.* All this and plenty of *La Bohemes, Butterflys,* and *Carmens* to appease the paying hordes.

The great Domingo graces one or two productions per year, usually drafting other international stars in his wake to perform with the company. The list of major singers who've roamed on the ample Pavilion stage is impressive—Sherrill Milnes, Frederica von Stade, Marilyn Horne, Jorma Hynninen, Maria Ewing, Arleen Auger, Benjamin Luxon, Carol Vaness, for starters. Top podium figures have also made pit stops here—among them Zubin Mehta, Simon Rattle, Charles Dutoit, Sir Neville Marriner and Kent Nagano—even occasionally Domingo himself, exercising his growing baton skills.

The company had two first-class components in place from Day One—the crack Los Angeles Chamber Orchestra in the pit and the precise Los Angeles Master Chorale as an on-stage chorus—and they remain there today. Hemmings has been careful to nurture a resident company of often brilliant local singers (Jonathan Mack, Louis Lebherz, Stephanie Vlahos, Michael Gallup, among others) who before MCO had to gain experience overseas. Occasionally the Philharmonic has done opera duty as well. For Kullervo, MCO brought in the entire Finnish National Opera.

No thanks to the sour economy, MCO may be entering a more conservative era; the 1992/93 season was noticeably short on adventure, retreating to the bread-and-butter repertoire, and the 1993/94 season scheduled seven, not eight operas. But the opera remains popular, often selling out the house and giving the lie to those who knew LA could not support an opera company. Indeed, any popular opera *(Traviata, Carmen,* etc.)—or anything with Domingo in it—is going to sell out quickly, so orchestrate your plans well in advance.

LOS ANGELES PHILHARMONIC

Music Center
Dorothy Chandler Pavilion
135 North Grand Avenue
Los Angeles, CA 90012
Info: (213) 850-2000 **Rsvn:** (213) 972-7398
Fax: (213) 617-3065
Music Director: Esa-Pekka Salonen
Performs at the Dorothy Chandler Pavilion and the Hollywood Bowl.

After the extraordinary growth of classical music throughout the region, the Philharmonic remains, as always, the biggest show in town, the flagship of Los Angeles concert life.

Founded in 1919, the orchestra was led by musical directors Artur Rodzinski and Otto Klemperer in the '30s, followed by Alfred Wallenstein's long, distinguished run in the '40s and '50s. Some Philharmonic veterans believe that Eduard van Beinum's brief reign in the '50s, cut short by his death in 1959, was the orchestra's Golden Age. Despite its remarkable history, few outside Los Angeles took the Philharmonic seriously until the coming of India's Zubin Mehta—then only a 26-year-old tyro—in 1962. Mehta rebuilt the orchestra, secured a major recording contract, took it on tour, and made a name for himself in the process. Mehta became known for his big Romantic canvases by the likes of Richard Strauss, Mahler and Bruckner. Under the Mehta regime, the orchestra also received a big glamorous boost in its move from the creaking Philharmonic Auditorium (now demolished) to the new Dorothy Chandler Pavilion in 1964.

Carlo Maria Giulini, the Italian aesthete, took over in 1978 when Mehta left for the New York Philharmonic. He was known for performances of weighty insight, and a memorable fully-staged opera, Verdi's *Falstaff* in 1982.

André Previn, Hollywood's musical whiz-kid, succeeded Giulini. Previn's tenure was marked by first-rate performances of the 20th-century English and Russian repertoires. Yet this marriage made in La-la-land Heaven was not to last. Perhaps audiences expected another John Williams—and got instead an affable, serious, low-key musician who wanted nothing to do with Tinseltown. Previn resigned in angry protest in April 1989.

In recent years, the Philharmonic has been like a chameleon, changing its colors and qualities before a parade of guest conductors. The Phil toiled without a real music director at the controls until Esa-Pekka Salonen, a young, dynamic Finn with a yen for adventure, took full command in 1992/93 after three seasons as Music Director-Designate. Already his tremendous abilities in Haydn, contemporary music and the Scandinavians have been fully displayed. He has done much to restore some needed glamour Downtown, and the notoriously conservative subscription audience has been sitting still for his progressive programming—programming which, by the way, earned Salonen and the Philharmonic the top 1993 American Society of Composers award for adventuresome programming of contemporary music.

While Salonen places his permanent stamp on the orchestra, the Philharmonic remains subject to the whims of its regular guests. For tried-and-true Germanic standard repertoire, they turn to veteran Kurt Sanderling, who gets a warm, polished, Central European sound from the orchestra that reminds some old-timers of the van Beinum days. Whenever Pierre Boulez comes to town— roughly every other year—the Phil becomes a precise, incisive, colorful instrument for the Impressionists, the

Performances
Oct-May (Music Center);
July-Sept (Hollywood
Bowl); Wed-Sat 8 pm;
Fri 1:30 pm; Sun 2:30
pm
Tickets
$5-52 (Music Center)
Discounts
Previews/children/
seniors/students/groups
of 10+, call BO, ask for
Group Sales
Depatrment
BO
Mon-Sat 10am-6 pm;
Sun noon-4 pm; and
through intermission on
all concert evenings;
check/AE/MC/V/reserve
by mail, TicketMaster
free of charge exchange
for same program;
service charge to
exchange for different
program; subscription
program
Location
Off Santa Ana (5) Fwy,
Temple St Exit
Parking
On premises, $6; nearby
lot $4
Special Features
Open rehearsals

Schoenberg/Berg/Webern axis, and lots of stimulating contemporary music.

Simon Rattle, formerly the principal guest conductor for over a decade now, is an innovative programmer in all centuries, while Yuri Temirkanov carves rough-hewn expertise out of the Russians. And when Mehta checks in, the Phil sounds almost exactly the way it did for him some 20 years ago—thick-textured, impulsive and exciting.

The winter subscription season is only the hub for a wide range of Philharmonic activities befitting the vast reach of this organization. During the season, musicians from the Philharmonic organize their own Philharmonic Chamber Music Society series in the acoustically mellow Gindi Auditorium at the University of Judaism. Devotees of the far-out can turn to the Philharmonic's New Music Group at the Japan America Theatre (see separate entry). Celebrity Concerts bring in soloists such as YoYo Ma, Isaac Stern, and Itzhak Perlman, as well as orchestras from around the world.

The Philharmonic holds court at the Pavilion from October through May. The 1993/94 saw an increase in subscription series options climb to 21. A three-concert Saturday afternoon family series was added, as was an additional four-concert Friday evening program. Over the years, the Pavilion has proven to be one of the more satisfactory modern halls in the country, though it has its isolated sonic quirks. On the Main Floor, it is best to find seats around the region of left-center (that's where most critics like to sit), away from the overhanging tiers. The Founders' Circle gives you the best-focused blend available, with the Loge and Balcony also being good. Salonen has experimented with new risers for the orchestra, producing brighter and a bit more strident results.

In the summer, the Philharmonic takes up residence in historic Hollywood Bowl, that vast 17,979-seat concrete amphitheater in what was once called Daisy Dell. There, the black penguin suits of the musicians turn white, the music is amplified, and the repertoire reflects the laid-back yet hardcore traditional mood of picnickers in the boxes and benches. The Bowl has become a gold mine for the Philharmonic, a chance to rack up revenues to underwrite the more idealistic ventures of the winter season.

Tuesdays and Thursdays at the Bowl are devoted mainly to the so-called "serious" classics, led mostly by guest conductors. On Fridays and Saturdays, the Philharmonic turns into a sometimes solid, yet often routine pops orchestra, sometimes accompanied by some truly spectacular fireworks displays. The new Hollywood Bowl Orchestra (see separate entry) is, however, increasingly giving the hard-working Philharmonic a needed breather on weekends.

On Wednesdays, the Phil offers a Virtuoso Series for touring soloists and orchestras, and a Jazz at the Bowl series for leading acts in the world of jazz. At the nearby John Anson Ford Theatre on occasional Mondays you'll discover Chamber Music Under the Stars, where touring chamber groups and members of the Philharmonic compete more-or-less successfully with the Hollywood Freeway.

Sunday nights used to be the preserve of the Los Angeles Philharmonic Institute Orchestra, the youthful performing arm of the UCLA-housed Philharmonic Institute. But a severe budget crisis caused the Phil to cancel the Institute in 1992 and its future remains in grave doubt.

Local wags say that the only way you can get box seat subscriptions for the Bowl these days is to inherit them (indeed, they have even become hotly contested items of joint property in divorce settlements). The only option for the newcomer is the bench seats, which have been completely overhauled in recent years. Bring or rent seat cushions anyway. The good news is 1,000 tickets are set aside for the general public at $1 each for the Tuesday, Thursday and Sunday concerts.

In December 1992, ground was broken on the ultramodern, Frank Gehry-designed Walt Disney Concert Hall opposite the Dorothy Chandler Pavilion on 1st Street, where the Phil will be the sole resident starting in 1997.

LOS ANGELES PHILHARMONIC NEW MUSIC GROUP (GREEN UMBRELLA)

Info: (213) 850-2000   **Rsvn:** (213) 480-3232
Resident company of the Japan America Theatre, 244 South San Pedro Street, Los Angeles.

Though the New Music Group is part of the vast Philharmonic empire, it's a different world when you enter the NMG's Little Tokyo home, the Japan America Theatre. The dress is defiantly more casual, and the lobby talk decidedly less frivolous. The person sitting next to you might be a distinguished gray-thatched composer, an enthusiastic CalArts music student, or a dyed-in-the-jeans rock 'n' roller. All are there in search of new sounds as various ad-hoc delegations from the Philharmonic explore the 20th century.

A logical outgrowth of previous Philharmonic new music ventures like Composer's Choice, the New Music Group series began in 1981 under the direction of composer/conductor/percussionist William Kraft. The concerts began in the acoustically dry Mark Taper Forum but switched to the warmer, more musical Japan America in 1983.

A witty raconteur, Kraft would speak between pieces, clarifying and humanizing some of the world's most difficult music. But Kraft gave way in 1985 to John Harbison, who makes his commentary pre-concert, favoring earlybirds. The 1987/88 season saw the beginning of an alliance with The New CalArts Twentieth Century Players, an expansion of the season, and a new name, the Green Umbrella Series. Since 1988, the series has been overseen by new-music advisor Steven Stucky.

Often, famous composer/conductors imported for the Philharmonic proper take time out to lead the New Music Group. Pierre Boulez has made several memorable appearances; Sir Michael Tippett wielded the baton a few days after his 80th birthday. Witold Lutoslawski, Oliver Knussen, and the Philharmonic's André Previn and Esa-Pekka Salonen have also conducted their own works.

Unfortunately, the Philharmonic's current budget woes have slashed the series back from seven concerts to five. One can only hope this brave, long-running project continues to elude the ax.

Performances
Vary
Tickets
$10-13
BO
In person at Dorothy Chandler; by mail (Philharmonic, c/o Dorothy Chandler, 135 N Grand Ave, Los Angeles, CA 90012); at door night of performance; TicketMaster
Location
On San Pedro between 2nd and 3rd
Parking
On street; pay lots across street, $2.50

LOS ANGELES PIERCE COLLEGE PERFORMING ARTS BUILDING See THEATER

MAINLY MOZART FESTIVAL See FESTIVALS & SEASONAL EVENTS

MALIBU STRAWBERRY CREEK MUSIC FESTIVAL See FESTIVALS & SEASONAL EVENTS

MARINA DEL REY-WESTCHESTER SYMPHONY ORCHESTRA

See press listings for performance locations.
Info: (310) 837-5757
Music Director: Frank Fetta

    This 69-member community orchestra got its start back in 1963 under George Berres as a 20-piece string ensemble. Three decades and several additions later, it continues to push onward under its talented maestro of the last several years, Frank Fetta.

    In addition to its symphonic schedule, the orchestra has occasionally ventured into opera under Fetta (who is also the conductor of Opera a la Carte). Among its concert performances was the West Coast premiere of Meyerbeer's rare *Gil Amori de Teolinda,* as well as standard fare like *The Magic Flute* and *La Boheme.*

    Once a year, the orchestra holds a gala benefit concert that helps fund its regular season of free concerts. This event has attracted some noted local musicians and celebrities as guest performers, including Music Center Opera bass Louis Lebherz and Los Angeles Rams owner and sometime soprano Georgia Frontiere. The orchestra also sponsors an annual Young Artists Competition, whose winners appear with the orchestra during its season.

Performances
  Sat 8 pm, Sun 3 pm
Tickets
  FREE
Parking
  Varies with location

MASTER CHORALE OF ORANGE COUNTY

Info: (714) 556-6262   **Rsvn:** (714) 556-6262
Fax: (714) 556-6341
Music Director: William D. Hall
Concerts held at the Orange County Performing Arts Center, 600 Town Center Drive, Costa Mesa.

    This 160-member choral group is the sum total of two organizations, both dating back to 1956. One was the Master Chorale of Orange County proper, which persevered long enough to open the Orange County Performing Arts Center's Segerstrom Hall with the Los Angeles Philharmonic 30 years later. The other is the famous William Hall Chorale—the creation of its energetic eponymous leader—which had its own distinguished, often adventurous season based in Pasadena, toured the world, and cut some interesting recordings.

    Together as of 1989, the combined Chorale now performs under the leadership of Hall in Segerstrom Hall. The programming is a diverse mix of traditional and contemporary, including major works like the Verdi *Requiem,* Brahms' *Ein Deutsche Requiem,* and a Hall specialty, the *Britten War Requiem.* Performances can be persuasive and powerful.

    The Chorale also collaborates with the Los Angeles Philharmonic whenever it hits town with orchestral/choral material. It has vocalized with the Joffrey Ballet and Bella Lewitzky Dance Companies as well. MCOC was also the first to present opera (*Amahl and the Night Visitors*) in Segerstrom, beating both the visiting New York City Opera and the resident Opera Pacific. The Chorale scored its biggest coup in October 1992, when it presented the West Coast premiere of Paul McCartney's first classical composition *Liverpool Oratorio,* which was enlivened immensely by Hall's propulsive approach.

Performances
  Oct, Dec, March, May;
  Sat 8 pm; Sun 7:30 pm
Tickets
  $15-40
Discounts
  Children/seniors/
  students/groups of 10+,
  call
BO
  Mon-Sun 10 am-6 pm;
  performance days 10
  am-curtain time;
  check/MC/V/reserve by
  mail (P.O. Box 2156,
  Costa Mesa, CA 92628),
  fax, TicketMaster;
  subscription program
Parking
  On premises, $4

MCCALLUM THEATRE FOR THE PERFORMING ARTS See **THEATER**

MINI-CONCERTS AT NOON

The Athenaeum Music and Arts Library
108 Wall Street
La Jolla, CA 92037
Info: (619) 454-5872

      The beautiful Athenaeum Music and Arts Library is a private library that befits the panache of La Jolla. Founded more than a century ago, the library evolved into a cultural center for a variety of arts. Every other Monday at noon, from fall to spring, the Athenaeum sponsors free one-hour classical music concerts performed by local and visiting duets, trios, and chamber orchestras. There are also Sunday chamber concerts featuring such musicians as the Elgart/Yates Guitar Duo, Elaine Thornburgh, and Aleck Karis. Admission is charged for these performances, and reservations should be made in advance. Call for information on upcoming concerts.

Performances
  Fall-spring
Tickets
  $12-15
BO
  Reserve by mail, phone; subscriptions
Location
  Downtown La Jolla
Parking
  FREE on street

MONDAY EVENING CONCERTS

At the Los Angeles County Museum of Art's Bing Theater.
      See listing under **Los Angeles County Museum of Art—Bing Theater** for ticket information.
      The oldest new music series in the city, dating back to 1939, Monday Evening Concerts still carries a legendary aura as it quietly goes about its business at the Leo S. Bing Theater of the LA County Art Museum. Known until 1954 as Evenings On The Roof under founder Peter Yates, MEC was a prime testing ground of the avant-garde, the in-place for a small but hugely influential circle of musicians and composers. Almost everyone agrees that MEC's Golden Age occurred under the late Lawrence Morton, a crusty, taciturn Minnesotan who programmed the series from 1954 to 1971 with a bracing mixture of the very old and the very new. Igor Stravinsky, then living just above the Sunset Strip, was a regular participant; so were local notables like Michael Tilson Thomas, André Previn, Lukas Foss, and Ingolf Dahl, and distinguished visitors like Aaron Copland and Pierre Boulez.
      But not long after Morton's retirement, new music's main thrust would pass to other organizations like CalArts and the Los Angeles Philharmonic New Music Group. Performance standards began to slip, and MEC gradually lost a good deal of its influence and its audience. Yet Monday Evening Concerts are still there pitching, hanging tough, reminding us there's still a great deal of interesting and even lasting new music to be heard. Leading contemporary music specialists like the New York New Music Ensemble and California E.A.R. Unit drop in; concept programs and tributes to renowned figures of past and present dot the schedule. Moreover, 1992-93 produced a quickening of the new music pulse with the world premiere of a new Terry Riley multimedia work, *St. Adolf Bing,* and two concerts in pianist Alan Feinberg's adventurous series, "Discover America."
      Occasionally there are starry reminders of the past when an MEC alumnus like Thomas drops in to conduct. And who knows, you might be lucky enough to catch a scandal in the making, as on that famous night in 1984 when the E.A.R. Unit mimed a difficult new chamber piece by Frank Zappa and no one knew the difference! Tickets are plentiful at the spacious, comfortable Bing Theater, and seating is open.

MUSIC

MUSIC AT THE MUSEUM See **Los Angeles County Museum of Art—Bing Theater**

THE MUSIC CIRCLE

See press listings for performance locations.
Info: (818) 449-6987   **Fax:** (818) 449-6987
Music Director: Harihar Rao

Founded in the early '70s by Ravi Shankar and Harihar Rao, The Music Circle has introduced the subtleties of Indian music and dance to scores of American audiences. Typically, an ambitious season of six to twelve concerts is performed in small halls at Occidental College and other intimate spaces. Indian food is served during intermission; following the break, performances go on sometimes for hours.

Performances
Sept-June, mostly Sat 8 pm
Tickets
$12-18
Discounts
Groups of 15+, call
BO
Reserve by phone; subscription program
Parking
Varies with location

MUSIC GUILD

See press listings for performance locations.
Info: (310) 275-9040   **Rsvn:** (310) 275-9040
Fax: (310) 275-8130
Music Director: Eugene Golden
Series of performances at the Wilshire Ebell in Los Angeles, at Pierce College in the San Fernando Valley, and Cal State Long Beach.

The Music Guild is nearing its 50th season of presenting international chamber music ensembles at the Wilshire Ebell. With its annual concert series of six performances, it claims to have the largest audience for chamber music outside of Manhattan.

Like its venerable rival to the north, the Coleman Chamber Music Association, the Music Guild leans toward meat-and-potatoes programming, attracting top-flight foursomes like the American and Borodin Quartets. But the Guild is somewhat less tradition-bound. In 1992-93, two-thirds of the programs contained at least one 20th-century work. The Guild also made inroads into the music-parched San Fernando Valley in 1991 with a four-concert series at Pierce College's 375-seat concert hall. The newest venture added the Gerald R. Daniel Recital Hall at Cal State Long Beach to its performance spaces.

Performances
Oct-April
Tickets
$18-22 single ticket; $30-78 subscription
Discounts
Children/seniors/ students/call
BO
Check; call BO; subscription program
Parking
Varies with location

THE NIGERIAN TALKING DRUM ENSEMBLE

See press listings for performance locations.
Info: (310) 398-2316
Music Director: Francis Awe

How many times in your life are you going to have an audience with a prince? Francis Awe, Master Talking Drummer and music director of this percussion ensemble, is a prince from the Yorba tribe of Nigeria. This particular prince prefers drumdom to a kingdom. His grandma discovered the little prince's affinity for the talking drum when the boy was still in diapers, and she presented him to the village drummers to be nurtured and raised by them.

If you've never seen a Talking Drum (Dundun), you may be amazed at its size and what it can do. The articulate instrument, according to varying degrees of pressure by the musician, emits a variety of tonal sounds which imitate the Yorba language.

The Nigerian Talking Drum Ensemble offers a special look at Nigerian culture at festivals, the Santa

Performances
Vary
Tickets
$ varies

Monica Pier, the African Marketplace, and at other spots throughout the Southland.

NORRIS THEATRE FOR THE PERFORMING ARTS See THEATER

OCCIDENTAL COLLEGE PERFORMING ARTS SERIES

1600 Campus Road
Los Angeles, CA 90041
Info: (213) 341-4920   **Rsvn:** (213) 341-4920
Fax: (213) 341-4983

Performances are held on the campus of Occidental College; Keck Theater (400 seats), Remsen Bird Hillside Theater (3,500-seat outdoor amphitheater), Thorne Hall (817 seats for musical performances).

To reach the Occidental campus (which is in the Eagle Rock district sandwiched by Pasadena and Glendale, perched on a hill in a residential area just off Eagle Rock Boulevard), turn east on Westdale Avenue off Eagle Rock Boulevard; from York Boulevard, turn north on Campus Road. Signs direct you to parking.

Performances
Sept-May, days vary
Tickets
$12
Discounts
Students/seniors
BO
Mon-Fri 8 am-5 pm; check/MC/V/reserve by mail, fax; no refunds; subscription program
Location
Between 134, 5 and 2 Fwys at Westdale and Eagle Rock
Parking
On premises, no charge

KECK THEATER

The Keck is Oxy's $9-million "Jewel on the Hill." The outside, modern and somewhat stark, doesn't really prepare you for the inside, which is inventively designed to blend Shakespeare's Globe Theatre with rococo architecture. Two horseshoe galleries look down upon a flexible main-floor seating system called the "Lambda system." The Keck is one of the first venues in the world to have the Lambda (not to be confused with the Lambada), which allows for nearly a dozen different configurations of seating by electronically storing or moving the seats according to the desired stage plan.

Dance, theater and some musical performances are held here as part of the performing arts series. The Bella Lewitzky Dance Company, the National Theater of the Deaf, and El Teatro Campesino are three top-notch examples. There's also a separate Keck Theater—College Season of plays performed by Department of Theater students. (The department's Summer Theater Festival started out as a one-year endeavor and recently celebrated its 30th.)

REMSEN BIRD HILLSIDE THEATER

This outdoor amphitheater, just across the parking lot from the Keck, presents a summer-only series of four programs in repertory. It may be a musical, Shakespeare, Gilbert & Sullivan, etc. Families often have pre-performance picnics on the grounds and then settle in on the concrete amphitheater seats—I'd suggest cushions and a blanket.

There is some wheelchair access, but it's best to call ahead to let them know you're coming.

THORNE HALL

In contrast to the Keck's modern appearance, Thorne Hall, which was built in 1938, is reminiscent of an elegant, old-world concert hall. Wainscoting covers the lower walls of the hall itself, theater doors are padded and covered in leather. The 817 seats are quite comfortable. While the hall is not big enough for a full orchestra, chamber orchestra and vocal performances fit it to a T. (It has been compared acoustically to UCLA's Royce Hall.)

Performing Arts Series performances include classical music concerts and "special events" (from Queen Ida and the Bon Temps Zydeco Band, to the blues, gospel, and buck dancing of Juke Joints & Jubilee). Seats for these and the other performing arts series programs are reserved.

The Concert Series, which is offered September through May, is general admission, unreserved seating.

OJAI MUSIC FESTIVAL See FESTIVALS & SEASONAL EVENTS

OPERA A LA CARTE

See press listings for performance locations.
Info: (818) 791-0844
Music Director: Richard Sheldon

Richard Sheldon, British expatriate and steel-willed founder and director of this lively troupe, has never lost touch with traditional approaches to Gilbert and Sullivan's delightfully wicked comic operas. He's a by-the-book Savoyard, an alumnus and devotee of the Gospel According to the D'Oyly Carte Opera Company of England, whose practices descend directly from G&S themselves. For decades now, this company has reliably dispensed deadpan delivery of Gilbert's outrageous lines, excellent singing, properly understated acting, and a real orchestra (stylishly led by Frank Fetta) playing exactly what Sullivan wrote. You can keep the hammy mugging and electronic "improvements" of so-called modern interpretations; Opera A La Carte proves time and time again that Gilbert and Sullivan is freshest and funniest when done the old-fashioned way.

Opera A La Carte usually holds down a number of showcase dates at Ambassador Auditorium but also touches down at other Southern Californian locales with complete works or programs of G&S excerpts. More often then not, the comic opera of choice is one of the Big Three (*The Mikado, H.M.S. Pinafore, The Pirates of Penzance*) but occasionally this group dips into something off the beaten path like Sullivan's *The Zoo*. Sheldon himself directs and also sings many of the leading patter roles.

To quote Mr. Gilbert, "This saucy ship's a beauty."

Performances
Vary
Tickets
$ varies
BO
Hrs vary

OPERA ON THE CONCOURSE See FESTIVALS & SEASONAL EVENTS

OPERA PACIFIC

Orange County Performing Arts Center
600 Town Center Drive
Costa Mesa, CA 92626
Info: (714) 546-7372 **Rsvn:** (714) 979-7000
Fax: (714) 662-2796
General Director: Dr. David DiChiera
Performances are given at the Orange County Performing Arts Center.

Granted, Orange County is not as daring as, say, New York, and it's unfair to compare Apples and Oranges. But Opera Pacific is an emphatically conservative company in a like-minded region, dedicated to the well-loved, well-known staples of the operatic diet and the Broadway theater. Still, one can't deny there's a place for such a company in the Los Angeles area, given the radical stance of Long Beach Opera and the more progressive impulses at the Music Center Opera.

Opera Pacific is even newer than the Los Angeles Music Center Opera, bobbing up in early 1987 just after the Orange County Performing Arts Center opened. It was the building of OCPAC that motivated the formation of Opera Pacific as its resident opera group, and David DiChiera has been its general director from the first overture.

Performances
Thurs-Sat 8 pm; Sun 2 pm
Tickets
$20-75
Discounts
Seniors/students/groups of 15+, call
BO
Performance days 10 am-8 pm; non-performance days 10 am-6 pm; call (714) 502-2787; check/AE/MC/V/reserve by mail, fax, TicketMaster; exchanges for subscribers only; subscription program
Location
San Diego (405) Fwy at Bristol St

Opera Pacific is thoroughly professional, capable of first-class productions (i.e., an opulently staged *Aïda* with Leona Mitchell) and, occasionally, of making news. It was able to host one of Dame Joan Sutherland's last operatic appearances in Bellini's *Norma*. It's also launched a major career for at least one high-flying soprano—Ealynn Voss in Puccini's *Turandot*.

Opera Pacific has occasionally been known to brave a relatively uncommon work such as Bizet's *The Pearl Fishers*. And despite the ongoing flap about opera companies slumming through Broadway, at least one of Opera Pacific's attempts—a *West Side Story* in its inaugural season—rang amazingly true.

Segerstrom Hall is a fine home for Opera Pacific; sightlines are excellent, there's plenty of room backstage and voices project well. Early on, it was thought voices projected a bit too well, because amplification was used in some productions, but we can testify that electronics aren't requisite for operatic-sized voices here.

Parking
On premises, $4

ORANGE COUNTY PERFORMING ARTS CENTER

600 Town Center Drive
Costa Mesa, CA 92626
Info: (714) 556-2121 **Rsvn:** (714) 740-2000
Fax: (714)556-0156
Music Director: Carl St. Clair
Home to the 3,000-seat Segerstrom Hall and 299-seat Founders Hall.

Out in the former wilds of Costa Mesa, where beans once flourished, now stands an imposing red granite concert hall framed by a huge 120-foot archway. On September 29, 1986, Zubin Mehta lifted his baton, Leontyne Price sang the National Anthem—and lo and behold, Orange County was no longer a cultural desert. Orange County denizens became the beneficiaries of the 3,000-seat Segerstrom Hall and the 299-seat Founders Hall (also called Black Box).

The Segerstrom family, which donated the land, has been involved with the center going back to 1956 when the Orange County Philharmonic Society hatched the idea for a serious concert facility. The land was formally obtained in 1979 followed by groundbreaking in 1983.

From its beginning, Segerstrom Hall has been the home base of the Pacific Symphony, the Pacific Chorale, the Master Chorale of Orange County, Opera Pacific, and the presenting Orange County Philharmonic Society. In addition, Segerstrom has hosted some important exclusive engagements including appearances by the New York City Opera and England's D'Oyly Carte Opera Company. The Joffrey Ballet, American Ballet Theatre, and New York City Ballet were among the companies headlining the 1993 dance series. Classical orchestras from around the world and touring musical theater are also scheduled during the year.

Segerstrom Hall seats its 3,000 concertgoers within a radical design of four massive interspersed trapezoid-shaped sections—an orchestra floor and three tiers. Founders Hall, its small, adjacent "black box" theater now plays host to chamber music, theatrical performances, and some children's events.

The odd-shaped tiers of Segerstrom Hall remind one of the famous Berlin Philharmonie; the maroon carpeting, upholstery and walls give the hall a high-tech feel. You can see the catwalks and lighting fixtures in the ceiling, creating the illusion of being in a giant television studio. Despite its size, the hall seems intimate, even from the uppermost reaches. The sound from top to bottom is rather

Performances
Tues-Sun 8 pm; Sat-Sun 2 pm
Tickets
$14-60
Discounts
Groups of 20+, call
BO
Mon-Sun 10 am-6 pm; Sun noon-6 pm; Performance days 10 am-8:30 pm; AE/MC/V/reserve by mail, TicketMaster; exchanges for subscribers only; subscription program
Location
Between Bristol and Town Center Dr; near the 405 and 55 Fwys
Parking
On premises, $4

warm, somewhat homogenized, and reassuringly uniform, with some variation underneath the tiers and additional brightness downstairs. In the case of orchestral music, there have been concerns with clarity, particularly in the bass. Yet one remembers that the Chicago Symphony had no trouble producing a rich, clear, satisfying bass here in 1987—without even an on-stage rehearsal.

For opera, though, Segerstrom is indisputably terrific, completely changing its sonic personality. Opera orchestras project with amazing clarity and point from the pit, and the voices shoot right out to the audience—yes, even without dreaded amplification. Sightlines are excellent from all points, and there is plenty of backstage room.

Though the grand stairways and hallways can be an asymmetrical maze to the newcomer, Segerstrom is a very comfortable hall overall—with plenty of legroom in front of each seat. Moreover, if you overdo it on culture, Southern California's largest shopping mall, South Coast Plaza, is a five-minute walk away. Angelenos wary of a punishing drive on gridlocked regional freeways will find Segerstrom often makes it worthwhile.

See also:
Opera Pacific
Orange County Philharmonic Society
Pacific Symphony Orchestra
Master Chorale
Pacific Chorale
Imagination Celebration in **CHILDREN**

ORANGE COUNTY PHILHARMONIC SOCIETY

Orange County Performing Arts Center
600 Town Center Drive
Costa Mesa, CA 92626
Info: (714) 553-2422   **Rsvn:** (714) 556-ARTS
Fax: (714) 553-2421
Executive Director: Erich A. Vollmer

This presenting organization imports world-class artists for the Orange County Performing Arts Center and the Irvine Barclay Theatre. The OCPS has been on the job since 1954, making it the oldest music organization in the county.

For decades, it has carried on the lonely missionary work of bringing classical music to a region where there was little or no history of such pursuits. Even before OCPAC's opening in 1986, the Society was able to proffer such blue-chip ensembles as the Philadelphia Orchestra and the Concertgebouw Orchestra of Amsterdam.

Now, with a first-class facility (Segerstrom Hall) at its disposal at last—not to mention the rise of other spanking new West Coast facilities that make it more feasible for out-of-state artists and orchestras to tour—the OCPS has entered high society.

The world's great orchestras now parade proudly through Costa Mesa on their U.S. tours—at times, the OCPS has even been able to score some scoops and finagle exclusive appearances. Frequently, ensembles like the Chicago Symphony and the Cleveland Orchestra play here before Los Angeles. A few years back, the hot recording conductor Eliahu Inbal and the Frankfurt Radio Symphony Orchestra stopped by—and skipped LA.

Through the OCPS, the Los Angeles Philharmonic continues to make frequent run-out appearances here, with the same star conductors and soloists in tow that perform at LA's Music Center. Celebrities like cellist YoYo Ma, soprano Jessye Norman, and flutist James Galway regularly hit town for concerts and recitals.

Performances
Sept-May 1; evenings
and Sat-Sun 3 pm
Tickets
$5-45
Discounts
Seniors/students/groups
of 10, call
BO
Mon-Fri 10 am-6 pm;
Sun noon-6 pm; AE/
'MC/V/check/reserve by
mail, fax; TicketMaster;
exchanges for
subscribers only;
subscription program
Parking
On premises, $4
O.C.P.A.C.; $2 Irving
Barclay

Ever on the move, the OCPS recently opened a Festival Series and a Chamber Music Series at the new, comfortable, acoustically marvelous Irvine Barclay Theatre on the UC Irvine campus. The former offers recitals by the likes of flutist Paula Robison and the piano/vocal team of Joan Morris and William Bolcom, while the latter touts touring chamber ensembles (the Juilliard, Tokyo and Cleveland Quartets) and small orchestras like the Los Angeles Chamber Orchestra.

Finally, there are youth outreach programs that present an eclectic assortment of 20 concerts in Segerstrom and music programs in the schools that reach some 300,000 kids a year.

PACIFIC AMPHITHEATRE

100 Fair Drive
Costa Mesa, CA 92626
Info: (714) 979-5944   **Rsvn:** (714) 546-4876
Fax: (714) 850-1157
Outdoor amphitheater with a capacity for 18,729. Usually open spring to fall.

Its capacity for over 18,000 cheering fans makes the PA a "must stop" on any artist's tour through Southern California. Until recently, the Pacific Amphitheatre got its share of performers from the Christian music of Sandi Patti to the disparaging vulgarity of Andrew "Dice" Clay. It has also presented such big timers as Madonna, Eric Clapton, Barbara Mandrell, and Diana Ross. A recent sale by the Nederlander organization to the Orange County Fair Board, will change the list of entertainers from rock 'n' rollers to family-oriented fare. Complaints by area residents about loud noise and traffic precipitated the new deal. Watch the papers for the schedule of events.

What can I say? This is a gigantic venue with three seating sections within the amphitheater itself. As you move back from the loge circle, loge, and terrace—to row Z in the Terrace, for example—you'll be a "mere" 195 feet from the stage. Binoculars are definitely advised. For lawn seating, which obviously begins even farther away, I suggest you bring blankets and/or your own cushions. But this isn't the Hollywood Bowl—you'll have to leave your picnic basket at home; the only food allowed is that which is sold on the premises. Too bad. As for the food service— attempts have been made to respond to customer requests. For the first time, you can order a chilled salad and cappuccino. Beer and wine are also available.

As with all Southern California concert venues, ticket prices are hefty and they don't include parking.

Performances
May 1-Nov 1, days and times vary
Tickets
$17-50
Discounts
Groups of 24+, call (213) 464-7521
BO
Mon-Fri 10 am-6 pm; Sat 10 am-4 pm; performance days 10 am-9 pm; check/AE/MC/V/reserve by TicketMaster; no exchanges or refunds; subscription program
Location
Off Newport (55) Fwy at Fair and Fairview
Parking
Nearby, $5

PACIFIC CHORALE

Orange County Performing Arts Center
600 Town Center Drive
Costa Mesa, CA 92626
Info: (714) 252-1234   **Rsvn:** (714) 252-1234
Fax: (714) 252-1885
Music Director: John Alexander
In residence at the Orange County Performing Arts Center.

The Pacific Chorale is part of the choral empire of ever-busy John Alexander, who also heads the Valley Master Chorale (which shares some personnel with the former group). A semi-professional group of some 170 singers in residence at the Orange County Performing Arts Center, the Chorale now claims to have the largest subscription audience of any chorus in the Western states.

Performances
Sun 7:30 pm
Tickets
$15-40
Discounts
Seniors/students/groups of 10+, call
BO
Mon-Sun 10am-6 pm; check/MC/V/reserve by mail, fax, Performing Arts Center (714) 556-2787, TicketMaster; subscription program

The Chorale produces a robust, vigorous choral sound and often imports impressive vocal guest soloists when called for. Alexander's direction comes up with some intriguing, even moving programming ideas, such as combining Haydn's implicitly anti-war *Mass in Time of War* with two rare nationalistic choral pieces by Dvorak. At Christmas time, there's the *Messiah,* a traditional concert rendering, and/or a singalong.

The Chorale also functions as a backing group for the Pacific Symphony, the visiting Los Angeles Philharmonic, and the Pasadena and Long Beach Symphonies on their home turf.

Location
Between Bristol and Town Center Dr; near the 405 and 55 Fwys
Parking
On premises, $4

PACIFIC SYMPHONY ORCHESTRA

Orange County Performing Arts Center
600 Town Center Drive
Costa Mesa, CA 92626
Info: (714) 474-2109 **Rsvn:** (714) 556-2787
Fax: (714) 474-2256
Music Director: Carl St. Clair
Segerstrom Hall is home to this group.

What a difference a new hall makes.

Prior to the opening of Segerstrom Hall in 1986, the Orange County Pacific Symphony was an orchestra in waiting, playing out its seasons patiently in the acoustically interesting but uncomfortable Santa Ana High School Auditorium. Now luxuriously "over-halled" in Segerstrom, PSY is gaining more respect and expanding its agenda faster than any U.S. orchestra. It's now the fourth largest orchestra in California after the Los Angeles Philharmonic, San Francisco Symphony, and San Diego Symphony.

Carl St. Clair followed Keith Clark as the music director in 1990, post-Segerstrom. Young and energetic, St. Clair is a protégé of the late Leonard Bernstein.

Entrusted to take the PSO into the big leagues, and personally the recipient of much critical acclaim, St. Clair veered his programming toward the cautious side in his first season, a pragmatic move in a region still developing a core audience for the classics. But more of the 20th century is beginning to infiltrate. New audience-friendly music by the likes of Michael Torke, John Corigliano, and Joan Tower dotted his recent agenda. In honor of the 20th anniversary, in 1995, of the end of the Vietnam War, a huge symphonic-choral work, sure to be the talk of many, has been commissioned to be composed by Elliot Goldenthal.

The orchestra itself is built around top-flight studio players, some of whom are members of other part-time orchestras in the region. While the PSO is capable of first-class performances, it's often hampered by factors such as the demands of Hollywood's film and recording industry on its members (a John Williams film date once deprived the orchestra of most of its regular brass section for a crucial concert). Consistency, then, is a sometime thing, but when it's on, the PSO can be right on.

The orchestra now plays nine subscription programs at Segerstrom—hardly a full load (the LA Philharmonic, for example, plays 21), but more than most regional groups—along with a series of pops concerts headlined by well-known performers. It also fills a five-concert summer season at the nearby Irvine Meadows Amphitheatre, where there are pops and Mozart programs, green spaces for picnicking, occasional fireworks displays, and surprisingly good amplified sound.

Performances
Oct-June, July-Sept
Tickets
$12-75
Discounts
Children/seniors/students/groups of 20+, call
BO
Check/AE/MC/V/reserve by mail (2151 Michelson Dr, Suite 216, Irvine, CA 92715), fax, TicketMaster; exchanges for subscribers only
Location
Between Bristol and Town Center Dr; near the 405 and 55 Fwys
Parking
On premises, $4

THE PALACE See CLUBS

PANTAGES See **THEATER**

PARLOR PERFORMANCES See **CLUBS**

PASADENA CIVIC AUDITORIUM

300 East Green Street
Pasadena, CA 91101
Info: (818) 793-2122   **Rsvn:** (818) 449-7360
Fax: (818) 793-7180
Music Director: Jorge Mester
Seats 3,059 for symphony performances, ballet, musical theater, and pops concerts.

The Pasadena Civic is the bull's eye of The Pasadena Center. Flanked by two structures that look more like concrete bunkers than convention/meeting facilities, the auditorium's Italian Renaissance facade stands out as a reminder of Pasadena's gentility. The 60-year-old building, one of the most beautiful "unrestored" buildings in Los Angeles, is well-groomed. The original ornate classic motifs and decorations still adorn the walls and ceilings throughout the entry, lobby, and theater. The only disappointment is the seating, which was "renovated" some years ago to economical plastic-molded auditorium seats out of sync with the otherwise lavish decor. (And, in what must have been another quirky bid for economy, the oversized rattan and vinyl California patio furniture in the restroom lounges deserves to be flushed altogether.)

This rental hall, which once hosted the California Music Theatre, now hosts the Ambassador Auditorium's Pops series, performances by the Pasadena Symphony, Broadway musicals, ballet, the Emmy Awards, and other TV specials.

There are five sections of seating in the Orchestra and Loge; four in the Balcony. The best seats are orchestra center, right and left center, and the front of the loge for viewing performances. But many a classical music aficionado would prefer the front end of the balcony. The sound is more clearly focused upstairs.

Old Town Pasadena beckons from not far away (you'll have to drive though).

Performances
  Oct-May; Sat 8:30 pm
Tickets
  $12.50-32.50
BO
  Mon-Sat 10 am-5 pm
  check/MC/V/reserve by
  TicketMaster; no
  refunds, no exchanges;
  subscription program
Location
  Take Pasadena (110)
  Fwy to end, becomes
  Arroyo Pkwy, to Green
  St, turn right
Parking
  On premises, $5
Special Features
  Open rehearsals

PASADENA COMMUNITY ORCHESTRA

First Church of the Nazarene
3700 East Sierra Madre
Pasadena, CA 91107
Info: (818) 445-6708
Concerts offered in the First Church of the Nazarene, 3700 East Sierra Madre, Pasadena.

Consisting of some 70 dedicated amateur musicians, the Pasadena Community Orchestra plays a series of four free concerts in Pasadena's First Church of the Nazarene. Wayne Reinecke (who also leads the Rio Hondo Symphony) music directs.

After its series in the church is over, the PCO also plays an annual free concert in Sierra Madre Memorial Park, where the programming is of the pops variety. The orchestra also does children's concerts, "Musical Chairs," at the Clairbourn School in San Gabriel, and sponsors a Young Artists Talent Competition, the winner of which receives a featured solo spot at a PSO concert.

Performances
  Oct-June, Fri 8 pm
Tickets
  FREE

PASADENA POPS ORCHESTRA

Ritz-Carlton Huntington Hotel
1401 South Oak Knoll
Pasadena, CA 91106
Info: (818) 792-7677 **Rsvn:** (818) 792-POPS
Music Director: Victor Vener
Scheduled concerts at Ritz-Carlton Huntington Hotel's Grand Ball Room.

The Pasadena Pops is dedicated to the notion, unfashionable in many circles, that orchestra concerts can be fun. The 45-50-member all-professional orchestra had been holding forth in the unlikely venue of the International Ballroom of the Pasadena Hilton since 1988. Currently, Pasadena's Ritz-Carlton Huntington Hotel is the site for this special blend of short familiar classics and popular music.

Two series cater to a variety of musical tastes. The Pops Ballroom Series is a mix of light classical selections with contemporary music—Stravinsky and Glenn Miller, for instance. There are four concerts scheduled each year. Guests (850 can be accommodated) can purchase a pre-concert three-course dinner with the maestro for $25 (includes tax and gratuity).

The Pasadena Pops also plays a series of outdoor concerts usually at the Courtyard of Champions at the Rose Bowl in the summer. In a convivial atmosphere of picnic dinners and evening dancing, the orchestra performs classical and popular music. On a given evening, the entire arroyo will rumble to the sounds of the *1812 Overture*. These single-concert tickets range in price from $10 to $35; a season subscription is available at $30 to $105. Picnic dinners can be ordered through the Pops. Be sure to call for this year's location—the sounds of World Cup Soccer have driven out the sounds of the trombone for this year.

Performances
Sat 8 pm
Tickets
$10, $25, $35; dinner is an additional $25
Discounts
Seniors/students/groups of 10+, call (818) 792-POPS
BO
Mon-Fri 3 pm-5 pm; answering machine on weekends check/MC/V/ reserve by mail, TicketMaster; subscription program
Parking
Valet, $5; limited self-parking

PASADENA PRO MUSICA

Neighborhood Church
301 North Orange Grove Boulevard
Pasadena, CA 91103
Info: (818) 449-3470 **Rsvn:** (818) 351-9795
Music Director: Edward Low

Edward Low has managed to keep this chamber chorus/orchestra program going since 1964, the year he founded the group. The 50-member volunteer chorus is accompanied by a pickup orchestra and guest vocal soloists.

Along the way, this group of semipros has presented a number of first performances by such noted American composers as William Kraft and Daniel Pinkham, as well as West Coast premieres of older, neglected works.

The Pro Musica makes its home at Pasadena's Neighborhood Church, with the "Carol Sing" taking place in CalTech's Dabney Lounge. There are anywhere from five to seven concerts per season.

Performances
Nov-June; Fri 7:30 pm, Sun 4:30 pm
Tickets
$10
Discounts
Children/seniors/ students
BO
Mon-Fri 10 am-5 pm check/reserve by mail (on special request); no exchanges; checks and cash only
Parking
On premises, on street
Special Features
Open final dress rehearsal; free reception following every concert

PASADENA SYMPHONY

Pasadena Civic Auditorium
300 East Green Street
Pasadena, CA 91101
Info: (818) 793-7172   **Rsvn:** (818) 449-7725
Fax: (818) 793-7180
Music Director: Jorge Mester
Concerts are given at Pasadena Civic Auditorium.

This is considered the finest regional orchestra in Southern California, able even to outplay the mighty Los Angeles Philharmonic on a given day. This is all the more remarkable considering PSO's mere five concerts a year—and long gaps of inactivity in between.

Though the PSO dates to 1928, the orchestra really began to blossom when Daniel Lewis took over the music director's job from Dr. Richard Lert in 1972. Lewis made the PSO a fully professional outfit, drawing upon a core of principal players from the Los Angeles Chamber Orchestra and adding scores of crack young musicians from LA's best youth orchestras and the studios. He also became known for innovative programming, taking on seldom-performed pieces like Nielsen's *Third Symphony* and Bartok's *Bluebeard's Castle* and making them shine.

Jorge Mester, Lewis's distinguished successor from Juilliard and Aspen, picked up the ball in 1984, maintaining and even sharpening the PSO's precise, passionate playing while adding showman-like flair. Mester has struck a satisfying compromise between tried-and-true and out-of-the-way.

Mester loves to program ambitious cycles that stretch over several seasons. Early in his tenure, he started a Berlioz cycle, playing outsized pieces such as *La Damnation de Faust* and *Romeo and Juliet*. He embarked upon a Shostakovich cycle, producing terrific, hell-bent performances of the Tenth, Eighth, Seventh, Sixth, and First Symphonies and even the rare, radical Fourth. Recently, he has been occupied with Mahler's giant emotionally turbulent symphonies, along with a well-received Verdi *Requiem*.

The PSO dwells in the venerable Pasadena Civic Auditorium, a large, wide, grandiose yet inviting edifice which you might recognize from various televised awards programs (see the **Pasadena Civic** listing above for more details on this site). PSO aficionados have long known that the best seats in the house by far occupy the front end of the balcony, where the sound carries beautifully in a way that the diffuse Main Floor cannot match. As a result, the upstairs is often packed solid on the PSO's Saturday evening concerts when there may be large gaps downstairs.

Performances
Oct-May, Sat 8:30 pm
Tickets
$12.50-32.50
BO
Mon-Fri 10 am-5 pm; check/MC/V/reserve by TicketMaster; no refunds, no exchanges; subscription program
Special Features
Open rehearsals

PASADENA YOUNG MUSICIANS ORCHESTRA

See press listings for performance locations.
Info: (818) 793-0701
Music Director: Christopher Russell

One of Southern California's oldest youth orchestras (founded back in 1942), the Pasadena Young Musicians Orchestra continues to train talented kids in grades ten through junior college.

Originally called the San Gabriel Valley Junior Symphony, the Orchestra culls members from some 18 school orchestras in 12 cities in the region. The orchestra maintains an association with the Pasadena Symphony, whose music director, Jorge Mester, occasionally stops by to coach rehearsals.

The 60-member orchestra plays from three to four free concerts per season under music director Christopher Russell in various Pasadena locales including the venerable

Performances
Nov, Dec, March, May; Tues 8 pm, Sun 3 pm
Tickets
FREE
Parking
Varies with location**Special features**
Open rehearsals

Ambassador Auditorium. In addition, there's an annual fundraising benefit dance called "A Night in Old Vienna," where Russell's young charges play appropriate waltzes and polkas for the contributors' happy feet. There are also PYMO chamber group spin-offs—string, brass and wind ensembles sent out to perform privately and publicly as part of an outreach program.

PEPPERDINE UNIVERSITY CENTER FOR THE ARTS See THEATER

PERFORMANCE/RIVERSIDE See Riverside Pops

RAITT RECITAL HALL See Pepperdine University Center for the Arts in THEATER

R.D. COLBURN SCHOOL OF PERFORMING ARTS

3131 South Figueroa Street
Los Angeles, CA 90007
Info: (213) 743-5252   **Rsvn:** (213) 743-5252
Fax: (213) 746-7017
Free music performances at the school and a variety of off-campus locations.

    The R.D. Colburn School trains precollege students (ages 3 1/2 to 18) for their futures in music and dance. The school has gained an international reputation for developing highly gifted students from around the world, including Michael Tilson Thomas and violinist Anne Akiko. Its visitors list reads like a *Who's Who* of the performing arts world: Wynton Marsalis, Leon Fleisher, Isaac Stern, Yehudi Menuhin, and Iona Brown are regulars.

    Students give numerous performances, including the informal "Friday Night Recitals." Several times each season, leading ensembles such as the Colburn Chamber Orchestra and the California Children's Choir offer major performances at various city sites. The concerts and recitals are free, and everyone is welcome.

    The best way to find out what's going on is to request to be put on the mailing list. Most important: get a free guest permit from the school to park in the USC lot.

Performances
  Weekly
Tickets
  FREE
Location
  At Figueroa and 32nd St
Parking
  On premises, obtain
  guest permit for USC;
  on street
Special Features
  Open classes and
  rehearsals periodically

RIO HONDO SYMPHONY ASSOCIATION

See press listings for performance locations.
Info: (310) 699-4640
Music Director: Wayne Reinecke
Concerts are scheduled at Whittier High School Auditorium.

    The Rio Hondo Symphony has been around for an astounding 60 years, beguiling the cities of Whittier, Pico Rivera, and Santa Fe Springs with a series of free concerts.

    Wayne Reinecke of Pasadena College (and the Pasadena Community Orchestra) has just completed his fifth year as music director. His programming proclivities lead him toward 18th- and 19th-century classics with cautious excursions into the 20th. A typical program might include Brahms, Mozart or Schubert standards linked with an acknowledged masterwork of this century like Stravinsky's *Pulcinella Suite* or Britten's Serenade for Tenor, Horn and Strings.

    The orchestra plays its four-concert season on occasional Sunday afternoons in the Whittier High School Auditorium. They welcome children to all the programs, but

Performances
  4 concerts, Oct-April;
  Sun 3 pm
Tickets
  FREE
Parking
  On premises
Special Features
  Open rehearsals

the fourth concert of the season is especially geared for them.

RIVERSIDE POPS

Performs at Landis Auditorium on the Riverside Community College Campus.

See **Performance/Riverside** in **THEATER** for more information.

The only professional band of its kind in the Inland Empire, this big-band orchestra performs under the auspices of Performance/Riverside. Three concerts a year are tendered by leader Richard Stover. Popular music is the norm; each concert of a different style. Guest stars figure prominently.

ROYCE HALL See **UCLA in THEATER**

SAN DIEGO CHAMBER ORCHESTRA

Parker Community Auditorium
750 Nautilus Street
La Jolla, CA
Info: (619) 753-6402   **Rsvn:** (619) 753-6402
Fax: (619) 753-2089
Music Director: Donald Barra

In 1983, conductor Donald Barra assembled a small orchestra for a Christmas program at a Rancho Santa Fe Church. In less than a year, the San Diego Chamber Orchestra was born and hosting such guest artists as pianist Misha Dichter. Before anyone could say "Dmitri Borisovich Kabalevsky," the ensemble of two dozen musicians had recorded the Russian composer's work!

Truthfully, it took a few years before the SDCO signed a recording contract with Koch International to put Kabalevsky's *The Comedians* on a disk with three other Russian composers' works. Nevertheless, the group has surprised everyone by knocking off four CDs since 1990, in addition to performing locally.

The orchestra can be heard live October through May (for at least the next two seasons) at Parker Community Auditorium in La Jolla, and in Fairbanks Ranch in Rancho Santa Fe. Other special concerts and events are performed at venues throughout San Diego County.

Performances
Oct-May; Mon, Tues 8 pm
Tickets
$18-40
Discounts
Children/seniors/ students/groups of 15+, call
BO
Mon-Fri 9 am-5 pm check/MC/V/reserve by mail (P.O. Box 3333, Rancho Santa Fe, CA 92067) or phone; tickets exchanged for another performance with at least 24 hrs advance notice; no refunds; subscription program
Parking
Varies with location

SAN DIEGO CHORAL ARTISTS

See press listings for performance locations.
Info: (619) 491-1940   **Fax:** (619) 437-0420
Music Director: Ron Gillis

Founded in only 1991, San Diego's new 32-voice choir is an all-pro unit, a stipulation founder/conductor Ron Gillis claims is essential to good choral music. The idea has been to provide a distinct alternative to the 100-voice-plus San Diego Master Chorale, the nonprofessional yet dominant symphony chorus of the San Diego region.

Thirty-two voices is still a lot of volume, capable of handling "authentic" Handel *Messiahs* at holiday time as well as a lot of contemporary and Renaissance music with ample sprinklings from less-heard-from centuries. And the pay, however modest, also provides incentive to sharpen one's skills, as opposed to the just-for-the-love-of-it bait.

The compact size of the group also means it can be corralled into a great variety of performance spaces. In its first season, the SDCA performed pairs of concerts in locales as diverse as Temple Beth Israel downtown, the

Performances
Sept, Dec, Feb, April; Sat 8 pm, Sun matinee
Tickets
$15
Discounts
Children/students/ seniors/groups of 10+, call
BO
Mon-Sun; check/MC/V/ reserve by mail (826 Orange Ave, #520, Coronado, CA 92118), pick up at performance; no refunds; exchanges made on availability; subscription program

Founders Hall Chapel at UCSD, the Mission San Luis Rey near Oceanside, and the La Mesa First United Methodist Church. Of special note that year was the holiday concert in the Mission, which—wonder of wonders—actually gave near-equal time to Hanukkah music.

Parking
Varies with location

SAN DIEGO COMIC OPERA COMPANY

Casa Del Prado Theatre
Balboa Park, CA 92101
Info: (619) 231-5714   **Rsvn:** (619) 239-8836
Fax: (619) 231-0662
Artistic Director: Leon Natker
Performances at Casa Del Prado Theatre in Balboa Park.

  Comic musical theater, acted and sung in English, with frolicsome dance and theatrical antics comprise the formula for this popular company. If you haven't guessed, we're talking Gilbert and Sullivan—*The Pirates of Penzance, H.M.S. Pinafore, The Mikado*...irreverence above *par excellence.*

  The San Diego Comic Opera loves its G&S, traditionally mounting operettas and musical reviews for the spring and summer seasons at Balboa Park's Casa del Prado Theatre.

  The organization's mission is to help develop San Diego's talent pool of young actors, stage directors, musicians, singers, and costume and scenic designers. They proudly state with appropriate Savoy bluster that theirs is family entertainment—musical theater for the broadest possible audience. Indubitably.

  Ticket prices are kept reasonable, preview performances free to high-schoolers.

Performances
March/April, June/July, Sept–Nov; Fri, Sat 8 pm; Sun 2:30 pm
Tickets
$12-18
Discounts
Children/seniors/ students/groups of 10+, contact Group Sales Coordinator
BO
Mon-Sun 10 am-4 pm; 6 pm-9 pm evenings of production; box office opens week before performance; MC/V/ check/reserve by mail,TicketMaster, Post Tix (Theatre League), Art Tix; subscription program
Location
Village Place entrance, E side of park next to zoo
Parking
On premises, FREE (park near Spanish village)

SAN DIEGO EARLY MUSIC SOCIETY

See press listings for performance locations.
Info: (619) 291-8246
Music Director: Evelyn Lakoff

  Period instruments. Those are fighting words in some circles. This Early Music Society banded together in 1981 to toot the horns of the Middle Ages, Renaissance, and Baroque eras, and believes early music "best reveals itself when played on instruments of the period."

  The scholars, performers, teachers, and instrument makers who for years had traveled all over to hear early music on recorder, lute, harpsichord, and viol da gamba (among others), decided to stop bumping into each other out of town and sponsor concerts right in San Diego.

  SDEMS's concerts feature local and international artists of both instrumental and vocal works. Such notables as Trevor Pinnock, Nicholas McGegan, and the Tallis Scholars have joined a variety of soloists, ensembles, and orchestras—and the Early Music ensemble of San Diego—in a series of concerts, many held in La Jolla's beautiful St. James by the Sea Episcopal Church.

Performances
8 pm
Tickets
$13-20
Discounts
Seniors/students
BO
Check/reserve by mail (3510 Dove Court, San Diego, CA 92103); exchanges made; subscription program
Parking
Varies with location

MUSIC

SAN DIEGO MINI-CONCERTS

The Lyceum Theatre
Horton Plaza
San Diego, CA 92101
Info: (619) 454-6522
Music Director: Glenna Hazelton
Free concerts performed by top professional musicians at the Lyceum Theater.

  Classical musicians from the San Diego Symphony, the San Diego Chamber Orchestra, as well as national touring artists, perform free noontime concerts at this popular biweekly bash. Every other Monday from October through May bring a bag lunch and feast on the one-hour concert in the Lyceum Theater.

  You have Glenna Hazelton, founder of the series, to thank for this musical beneficence. Twenty-one years ago, members of the Athenaeum Music and Arts Library in La Jolla had plans to sell the library piano in order to make more bookshelf space. The large instrument had been sitting neglected, taking up volume, not dispensing it. Hazleton pleaded for its life, swearing to put the piano to good use. Thus the mini-concerts were born. (Sounds like it would make a lovely children's story!) Before their present home at the Lyceum Theatre, the concerts took place in the foyer of Golden Hall and at the Grand Salon of the Civic Theatre. In 1986, the concerts settled into the Lyceum Theatre in Horton Plaza.

  What kind of music can you expect? Not only classical. Jazz and big band music sneak in, as well as dance from the likes of Malashock Dance & Company or Jazz Unlimited. Each season ends with an outdoor event called The Mayor's Concert.

  Audiences are a mixed bag of business people on their lunch break, tourists, senior citizens, and students. At only an hour long, and free at that, this is a great opportunity for children to wet their feet in an adult music program. Even better, you won't feel bad if you have to leave because of a bored child.

Performances
 Oct-May; every other Mon noon;
Tickets
 FREE
Parking
 On premises

SAN DIEGO OPERA

San Diego Civic Theatre
3rd Avenue and B Street
San Diego, CA 92101
Info: (619) 232-7636 **Rsvn:** (619) 236-6510
Fax: (619) 231-6915
General Director: Ian D. Campbell
Performances are held at the San Diego Civic Theatre.

  Listen up Los Angeles: San Diego has a grand opera company that's pushing 30.

  In fact, many of the San Diego Opera subscribers are from LA, opera fanatics who head south for the staples of Verdi and Puccini, but who also crave the less known. Recently, the company staged the West Coast premiere of Carlyle Floyd's *The Passion of Jonathan Wade,* set during Reconstruction, and mounted two smaller works by Benjamin Britten, *Albert Herring* and *The Rape of Lucretia.*

  Madame Butterfly? Carmen? The Barber of Seville? Yes, yes, yes. Most of the programming includes the big lovable works. And some big lovable stars have graced the stage now and then—Prey, Sutherland, Pavarotti—joining casts of international singers who perform at the Met and opera houses the world over. Daniel Catàn's *La Hija de Rappaccini* premiered in the 1993 season, and José Carreras's solo performance was part of the 1993 kickoff.

Performances
 Jan-April; Tues, Wed, Sat 7 pm; Fri 8 pm; Sun 2 pm
Tickets
 $15-80
Discounts
 Seniors/students/groups of 12+, call
BO
 Mon-Fri 9 am-5 pm; check/MC/V/reserve by mail, phone, TicketMaster; exchanges for subscribers only; subscription program
Parking
 Parking lot (1st and A Sts)) $4 after 5:30 pm weekdays

Five operas round out each season at the Civic Theatre; subscription packages are available for three, four, and five operas, each sung in its native tongue with English supertitles. Prior to Friday night performances, a free backstage tour of the Civic Theatre is sometimes available; call the Opera for information. The Civic boasts easy parking, nearby restaurants, comfortable seats, good sightlines, and a magnificent chandelier glittering above the Beverly Sills Salon. (Yes, she, too, has sung with the company.)

SAN DIEGO SUMMERPOPS See FESTIVALS & SEASONAL EVENTS

SAN DIEGO SYMPHONY ORCHESTRA

Copley Symphony Hall
750 B Street
San Diego, CA 92101
Info: (619) 685-1186   **Rsvn:** (619) 699-4205
Fax: (619) 699-4205
Music Director: Yoav Talmi
Performs at Copely Symphony Hall.

Performances
  Winter; Oct-May;
Tickets
  $14-42
BO
  Mon-Fri 10am-6 pm;
  Sat-Sun performance
  days noon-end of
  performance AE/MC/V/
  reserve by mail (1245
  Seventh Ave, San
  Diego, CA 92101), fax,
  phone, TicketMaster;
  exchanges made only to
  season subscribers 24
  hrs prior to purchased
  performance date
Parking
  On premises, $5; valet;
  on street

San Diego's oldest performing arts institution was created in the late '30s. The San Diego Symphony Orchestra currently works a 20- to 30-week season in the restored 2,255-seat Fox Theater, now called Copley Symphony Hall.

Yoav Talmi, made music director in 1990, leads the 80-plus musicians through serious classical repertoire, demonstrating a propensity, and critically noted acumen, for large Romantic symphonies. Premieres by composers from a variety of periods and cultural backgrounds figure large, as do guest appearances by artists of international stature.

Preeminent choral conductor Robert Shaw is principal guest conductor, said to have sought the post after a guest engagement featuring the impressive San Diego Master Chorale. The latter performs major choral works with the orchestra, and every other year, at holiday time, joins the orchestra for the irrepressible *Messiah*.

Just to make life a bit more complicated (and enjoyable), there is a variety of series to choose from in addition to (or in combination with) the regular season series. Classical Hits is especially appropriate for adults who, like many, would like to identify Rachmaninov from Tchaikovsky. In this series, commentary accompanies the orchestra's repertoire.

A Nickelodeon Series is a unique combination of live classical music and classic silent films. There are also Young People's Concerts for schoolchildren. And if you just can't get enough of the orchestra, sneak out of the office at 2 pm for the Afternoon Delights Series.

SAN DIEGO YOUTH SYMPHONY

See press listings for performance locations.
Info: (619) 233-3232
Music Director: Louis J. Campiglia

Performances
  Year-round
Tickets
  $10-25
Discounts
  Students/groups of 20+,
  call
BO
  Reserve by mail (Casa
  del Prado, Balboa Park,
  CA 92101)

The San Diego Youth Symphony is getting old, yet staying young. Forty-eight years ago it was founded to help young musicians, ages 6 to 23, gain performance experience in the classical symphonic music repertory. Now it's considered one of the world's best youth orchestras.

Currently under the direction of Louis Campiglia, the musicians get a view of that world every other year via a concert touring program any adult orchestra would envy. They've performed in numerous European countries and south of the border. In 1990, the orchestra performed at six music festivals in Spain. The summer of 1992 included music festival concerts throughout Italy.

At home, the group rehearses at Balboa Park. The organization now has a chamber orchestra, and both this ensemble and the full orchestra perform at city concerts and benefits. Each June through July and January, the group performs "Night in Vienna" in Balboa Park, and a special evening of Strauss waltzes and polkas. Guests often dress in the costumes of Strauss's time and dance and listen to the music, sip wine, nibble on hors d'oeuvres and dessert. Call for dates and special prices.

Parking
Varies with location
Special Features
Open rehearsals

SAN FERNANDO VALLEY COMMUNITY CONCERTS

14650 Albers Street
Van Nuys, CA 91411
Info: (818) 889-4953 **Rsvn:** (818) 886-3033
The concert series can be heard in the 848-seat auditorium at Van Nuys Junior High School, 14650 Albers Street in Van Nuys.

This organization operates in concert with the community concerts program of Columbia Artists Management in New York, probably the most prestigious of its kind on the globe. Columbia's program has been running for over 45 years—and, as a result, this local group can present an ever-changing, eclectic smorgasbord of touring performers at the Van Nuys Junior High School auditorium.

No, Itzhak Perlman isn't expected anytime soon, but you do get the likes of violin/guitar duo Clayton Haslop and Jack Sanders, or one of those proliferating brass ensembles, the Monumental Brass Quintet. Not only that, the SFVCC links up with other community concerts programs to allow you to attend events in neighboring areas at no additional charge. No single tickets, only a membership card that gives you access to the concerts and the "reciprocity list" of other concerts.

Performances
Sat 8 pm, Sun 3 pm
Tickets
$22 per season
Discounts
Students
BO
Check/reserve by phone, mail (32016 Allenby Ct, Westlake Village, CA 91361); subscription program
Location
Off Ventura (101) Fwy at Van Nuys Blvd; on Albers between Vesper and Cedros
Parking
On premises, no charge; on street

SANTA BARBARA CHAMBER ORCHESTRA

Lobero Theatre
33 East Canon Perdido
Santa Barbara, CA 93101
Info: (805) 564-8887 **Rsvn:** (805) 963-0761
Music Director: Heiichiro Ohyama
Performances scheduled at Lobero Theatre.

Currently under the directorship of Heiichiro Ohyama, the Santa Barbara Chamber Orchestra has been performing locally for more than a decade. Performances are offered in Lobero Theatre. In addition to the regular subscription season, the Orchestra mounts a Sunday afternoon mini-series of four performances reprised the following Tuesday evenings.

Performances
Oct-May; Tues 8 pm; Sun 4 pm
Tickets
$15-20
Discounts
Seniors/students/groups of 10+, call
BO
Mon-Fri 10 am-5:30 pm; Sat noon-5 pm
check/AE/MC/V/reserve by mail (P.O. Box 90903, Santa Barbara, CA 93190); no refunds or exchanges; subscription program
Parking
Behind premises in city lot, FREE

SANTA BARBARA SYMPHONY

Arlington Theatre
1317 State Street
Santa Barbara, CA 93101
Info: (805) 965-6596   **Rsvn:** (805) 963-4408
Fax: (805) 963-3510

Back in 1953, a pair of UC Santa Barbara faculty members, Stefan Krayk and Clayton Wilson, formed a core group of 35 musicians and put on a concert in small, historic Lobero Theatre under the baton of Adolph Frezin. There's been slow, steady progress ever since—interrupted by occasional financial setbacks—to the point where the Santa Barbara Symphony now presents eight pairs of weekend concerts per season (doubling its original quota) in 2,007-seat Arlington Theatre.

UCSB has maintained strong ties with the Symphony, giving its music directors from 1960 onward dual appointments on the faculty. From 1985 until his recent death, the symphony was in the hands of Varujan Kojian, formerly the music director of the internationally-respected Utah Symphony and whose emphatic podium manner reminded one of Zubin Mehta (indeed, Kojian was Mehta's assistant at the Los Angeles Philharmonic in 1970). As of this writing, a new conductor has not been named.

In 1992/93, the Symphony attracted pianists Horacio Gutierrez, Jerome Lowenthal, and Ruth Laredo and violinist Elmar Oliveira to the Arlington stage. It also gave a special summer outdoor family concert at the County Bowl.

Performances
Oct-May; Sat 8 pm; Sun 3 pm
Tickets
$10- 32
Discounts
Seniors/students/groups of 10+, call
BO
Mon-Fri 9 am-5:30 pm; Sat-Sun 9 pm-4 pm AE/MC/V/reserve by mail (214 E Victoria St, Santa Barbara, CA 93101); exchanges for subscribers only; subscription program
Location
Between Victoria and Sola
Parking
Nearby city lots, $1 per hr; on street

SANTA MARIA SYMPHONY SOCIETY

First Assembly of God Church, Corner of Bradley and Santa Maria Way, Santa Maria, CA 93456
Info: (805) 922-7748
Music Director: Patrick Howard Kelly

Since 1990/91, the Santa Maria Symphony Orchestra has been under the helm of the much ballyhooed Patrick Howard Kelly. One Santa Barbara critic labeled him "a dynamic new musical force," and another from Santa Maria wrote, "Look for the outrageous to continue." In any case, the Symphony plays its four-concert season in First Assembly of God Church Saturday evenings. Guests have included such soloists as the formidable violinist Endre Balogh and organist Dr. Samuel Swartz. The orchestra also performs Christmas and children's concerts. Speaking of children, the Society even offers childcare during concerts— what a concept!

Performances
Fall, winter, spring; a total of 4 concerts; Sat 7:30 pm
Tickets
$14-17
Discounts
Seniors/students
BO
MC/V/check/reserve by mail (P.O. Box 1216, Santa Maria, CA 93456); exchanges made; subscription program
Parking
On premises, on street

SANTA MONICA COLLEGE

1900 Pico Boulevard
Santa Monica, CA 90405
Info: (310) 452-9350   **Rsvn:** (310) 452-9396
Home of the 250-seat Concert Hall and 1,500-seat outdoor Amphitheatre for music, and the Studio Stage and Main Stage for theatrical performances.

This small, college-supported arts complex is found at the campus's northeast corner. You can't miss "Concert Hall" spelled out on the side of the boxy, single-story building. It's a cheerful if small hall filled with plastic-molded cushioned seats. Sans lobby, you enter through a closet-sized "foyer" directly into the hall itself. (Refreshments

Performances
Vary
Tickets
$5-12.50
BO
Mon-Thurs 9 pm-5 pm; Fri 9 pm-4 pm check/ MC/V/reserve by mail; subscription program
Location
Cloverfield exit off Santa Monica (10) Fwy

are set up alfresco.) Wheelchair seating is limited due to the hall's amphitheater style.

The Concert Hall, open year-round, features the Santa Monica College Orchestra, Santa Monica College Opera, and various jazz performances, in addition to family shows and art lectures. Most tickets are enticingly priced, while some Music Department series programs are gratis.

Seating in the outdoor Amphitheatre is on concrete, but for some college productions, cushions are provided; for the others—you're on your own. Bring sweaters or jackets to evening performances, as you're not far from the beach. The Summer Night series includes opera, symphony, dance, and special events. Series passes provide a nominal discount off single ticket prices.

Just across the walkway from the Amphitheater is the Studio Stage, the black box—or experimental theater—used largely for dance, rehearsals and some small theatrical pieces. Next door, in the same building, is the 330-seat Main Stage, lair of student productions.

Parking
On premises, $3; on street

SANTA MONICA SYMPHONY ORCHESTRA

See press listings for performance locations.
Info: (213) 850-5660   **Rsvn:** (310) 458-8551
Fax: (213) 874-6246
Music Director: Allen Gross
Performs mostly at Santa Monica Civic Auditorium, 1855 Main Street

Venerable and once quite renowned (thanks to some early recordings made not long after its beginnings in 1945), the SMSO has maintained a lower profile in recent years. But they needn't be underestimated anymore, for their music director, Allen Robert Gross, has proved to be a compelling presence.

Gross impressed in his first concert as music director, proving himself capable of sparking an orchestra, getting it to play to the peak of its capabilities. His programming hugged the basics in his opening season but did throw some modernish though accessible curves like William Schuman's *New England Triptych*.

The core orchestra is an amalgam of Santa Monica college music students and local musicians, with the addition of some savvy pros as stabilizers. Alas, they still play their concerts at the Santa Monica Civic Auditorium, not your most simpatico place for classical music, where a high ambient noise level from the outside world can drown out soft passages. But hey, like the street noise, the concerts are free.

Performances
Oct-May, Sun 7:30 pm
Tickets
FREE
Parking
On premises, $5

SCHOENBERG HALL See UCLA in THEATER

SEGERSTROM HALL See Orange County Performing Arts Center

SHRINE AUDITORIUM

649 West Jefferson Boulevard
Los Angeles, CA 90007
Info: (213) 748-5116   **Fax:** (213) 742-9922
6,300-seat auditorium featuring music, dance, variety shows, awards shows.

Built in 1924 at cost of $2 million (a fortune in those days), this mammoth 6,300-seat auditorium was recognized as a triumph of civil engineering and architecture. You may recognize it from having watched the Grammy Awards, Academy Awards, or the American Music

Performances
Vary
Tickets
$ varies
BO
Hrs vary; open only on days of performance; TicketMaster

Awards. Numerous concerts, ballets, and all types of other variety shows have graced its huge stage. The grand chandelier still gleams, and its ornate Moorish architecture is worth the trip. But this grand dame is a bit threadbare in places as evidenced by more than a few broken, albeit plush, seats.

Claiming to be America's largest theater, it has a proscenium stage which itself is able to accommodate more than 1,000 people! When the Opus 4446, the world's largest theater pipe organ is put to use, the sound is extraordinary.

If you want to watch hoofers hoof, skip the first few orchestra rows, which hide the dancers' feet.

The snacks are just that: cookies, potato chips, deli sandwiches, and beverages. There's lots of room for sit-down eating, but you'll have to climb a mountain of stairs to get there.

You may feel more secure parking in the lots surrounding the auditorium. Should you opt for street parking, be sure to walk back to your car with a crowd from the theater.

Location
1 block W of Figueroa, between Figueroa and Hoover; near the Harbor (110) Fwy or Santa Monica (10) Fwy
Parking
On premises, $5; on street

SMOTHERS THEATRE See **Pepperdine** in **THEATER**

SONOR

See press listings for performance locations.
Info: (619) 534-6467
Fax: (619) 534-8502
Performances are heard in Sherwood Hall in the Museum of Contemporary Art in La Jolla, and in Mandeville Auditorium.

San Diegans know their city is famous for the weather. What many don't know, at least until they get out of town, is that the city is internationally known for the sunny accomplishments of its living composers. Most of those composers create new music at UCSD using innovative techniques on traditional instruments alongside computers and electronic instruments.

SONOR performs both at the 500-seat Sherwood Hall at the Museum of Contemporary Art in La Jolla, and at their primary home, Mandeville Auditorium (also seating 500). Their quarterly performances give local audiences the chance to hear the music of their own contemporary composers such as Brian Ferneyhough, Rand Steiger, Joji Yuasa, Harvey Sollberger, and Pulitzer Prize-winner Roger Reynolds.

Much of the music is challenging, elegant, and even poignant, unlike any music ever experienced. Some stretches may prove intriguingly inscrutable to the uninitiated. Some of the most experimental work is also amusing, clever, even downright silly. (At one concert, the composer at the keyboard had to stop playing to shush his 2-year old son in the audience who got a severe case of the giggles over his dad's music!)

Call the Music Department to have your name put on a mailing list.

Performances
Vary
Tickets
$8
Discounts
Seniors/students/groups, ask Music Dept. for further details
BO
Located in Price Center, UCSD; Tues-Fri 10 am-5 pm; check/reserve by mail (call BO)
Parking
On premises

SOUTH BAY CENTER FOR THE ARTS

El Camino College/Marsee Auditorium
16007 Crenshaw Boulevard
Torrance, CA 90506
Info: (310) 715-3715 **Rsvn:** (310) 329-5345
Fax: (310) 715-7734

A college performing arts center with a 2,048-seat auditorium that presents the full spectrum of performing arts.

Classical music and dance, pop, jazz and country concerts are some of the ongoing performances you can catch at this spacious college auditorium, which fills up during popular engagements. Performances include big-name artists such as Mel Torme, Bobby McFerrin, Helen Reddy, Victor Borge, and Patty Loveless, in addition to a variety of arts ensembles and special lectures by prominent artists such as actress Claire Bloom. Local groups such as Lula Washington's LA Dance Theatre, and El Teatro Campesino are featured, as well.

As with most arts foundations and venues, economic cutbacks have affected the Marsee's lineup of guests and forced the South Bay Center for the Arts to reduce the number of performers for the year. But the quality and the artistic integrity of the performances has thankfully remained intact.

Weekdays, patrons can obtain complimentary parking permits if tickets are bought at least two hours in advance; otherwise there's a $1 charge. On weekends, parking is free.

Snacks, soft drinks, and coffee are served in the lobby. Before- or after-theater restaurants nearby include Benihana, the Velvet Turtle, and Red Lobster.

Performances
Tue-Sun evenings 8 pm, matinee 2 pm
Tickets
$12-33 (depending on event)
Discounts
Children/seniors/ students/groups of 20+
BO
Mon-Fri 9:30 am-7 pm check/MC/V/reserve by mail, phone; no exchanges or refunds; subscription program; no service charges
Location
Between Redondo Beach Blvd and Manhattan Beach Blvd; near San Diego (405) Fwy, Artesia (91) Fwy, Harbor (110) Fwy
Parking
On premises, $1 weeknights, FREE weekends and with advance ticket sales

SOUTHWEST CHAMBER MUSIC SOCIETY

See press listings or call for performance locations.
Info: (818) 794-4799 **Fax:** (818) 794-4799
Artistic Director: Jeff von der Schmidt
Concerts can be heard in Salmon Recital Hall, Chapman University, and in Pasadena at Pasadena Public Library.

The Southwest Chamber Music Society is an unusually enlightened chamber series, unafraid of the bold gesture. Artistic Director Jeff von der Schmidt—a fine French horn player himself—has gathered a core of first-rate professional LA players, along with spot guests. Often, sparks do fly; one remembers a passionate, expertly played pair of Haydn and Dvorak Trios in a recent season that went beyond normal polite chamber music.

The SCMS also goes beyond predictable repertoire, scheduling new and world music, as well as challenging contemporary works like Gyorgy Ligeti's *Horn Trio,* Charles Wuorinen's *Double Solo,* and music by Pierre Boulez, Mel Powell, and the late Olivier Messiaen. Those who want an exclusive diet of easy-listening salon music should apply elsewhere.

The guest list grows increasingly distinguished. Noted new music sopranos Phyllis Bryn-Julson and Lucy Shelton, composer/conductor Oliver Knussen, and organist Martin Haselböck are among those now on the books.

The Society shuttles between Chapman University's Salmon Recital Hall in Orange and the Pasadena Presbyterian Church. Nine programs per season are performed, starting out in Pasadena on Saturdays and moving to Chapman on Sundays. Salmon Recital Hall has the wide-open ambiance of a rehearsal hall, with more than

Performances
Sun 4 pm (Chapman), Sat 8 pm (Pasadena)
Tickets
$8-15
Discounts
Seniors/students/ groups, call
BO
Check/MC/V/reserve by phone, mail (P.O. Box 94474, Pasadena, CA 91109); no exchanges; subscription program
Parking
Varies with location
Special Features
Open rehearsals for donors and subscribers

ample space for the performers and fine acoustics. A reception with munchies and drinks follows each performance.

As for the Presbyterian Church, a sweeping, modern, nicely reverberant structure, this represents a shift in locale from SCMS's former base, the Pasadena Library. Four additional concerts will hail in various other venues.

SPRECKELS ORGAN PAVILION

Balboa Park Visitors Center
1549 El Prado
San Diego, CA 92101-1619
Info: (619) 239-0512
Located in Balboa Park.

Performances
Jan-Dec; Sun 2 pm;
July-Aug; Mon 8 pm
Tickets
FREE

San Diego boasts the largest outdoor pipe organ in the world, and you can hear it free, year-round. The 4,445-pipe organ is set in an ornate structure in Balboa Park. Lively concerts are performed by San Diego Civic Organist Robert Plimpton Sundays at 2 pm. The whole family is likely to enjoy the organ classics, marches, Broadway show tunes, and contemporary melodies. In summer there are special Monday evening concerts at 8. See **FESTIVALS** for information about the Annual Twilight in the Park Summer Concerts.

SPRECKELS THEATRE See **THEATER**

SUNDAYS AT FOUR See **Los Angeles County Museum of Art—Bing Theater**

TERRACE THEATER See **THEATER**

TGIF NOONTIME CONCERTS See **FESTIVALS & SEASONAL EVENTS**

THORNE HALL See **Occidental College Performing Arts Series**

UCI LECTURES & CULTURAL EVENTS SERIES See **Irvine Barclay Theatre**

UCLA SCHOOL OF THE ARTS See **UCLA** in **THEATER**

UCSB NEW MUSIC FESTIVAL See **FESTIVALS & SEASONAL EVENTS**

UNIVERSAL AMPHITHEATER

100 Universal City Plaza
Universal City, CA 91608
Info: (818) 777-4461   **Rsvn:** (818) 980-9421
Seats 6,251 for music concerts and award performances.

Performances
Vary
Tickets
$15-40
Discounts
Groups of 25+, call
(818) 777-4466

A little over a decade ago, when Universal was an open-air amphitheater (and had been for about 10 years), management kept hearing from its hillside neighbors about the "noise." Now that there's a roof over it, the musical artists who perform here (mostly contemporary acts, but also a good range of country, Latin, and comedy performers) can blow it off if they want. Bette Midler, Diana

Ross, Frank Sinatra, Linda Ronstadt, Three Dog Night, and many more of a similar constellation have appeared here. Even President Bush made an appearance on-stage once. The amphitheater is often used as a film location (*Wayne's World*) and annually hosts Comic Relief and the Academy of Country Music Awards.

Whatever performer, benefit, or awards show brings you out to Universal, be prepared for at least a five minute walk from the parking lot to the entrance turnstiles. Not that you're finished yet. You still have a few more minutes to go, up the ramp and across the bridge-like walkway over a pond before reaching your destination.

The concourse mini-bars, lobby bars, or two bar-lounges and snack counters should adequately refuel you, but don't expect much more than a hot dog, pizza, nachos, and a Coke. Should you need further treats, new CityWalk is just a walk away and offers plenty of nourishment. Despite the trek, you'll be glad you made it to Universal, one of the area's most popular concert spots.

The 70-foot stage overlooks 6,251 seats spread over a main orchestra level and mezzanine. Alas, the best seats, orchestra sections 1, 2, and 3, then 4 and 5, are chronically elusive. Your next try should be for mezzanine sections 10 through 13. Avoid the extreme sides in the mezzanine (sections 29 and 30), where you'd be at least 200 feet from the stage (unless, of course, you're taking the kiddies to a Twisted Sister concert). The good news is, however, that the acoustics are so good that you'll hear from anywhere even if you can't see optimally. This is a rare bird; a hall specifically built for amplified music with no reverberation—the electronics take care of everything.

Handicapped visitors will be relieved to learn their parking is closest to entrance turnstiles. In addition to wheelchair seating, Universal offers escorts for those on crutches or in need of someone to push a wheelchair. (This must be arranged in advance.)

BO
Tue-Sat 1 pm-9 pm check/MC/V/reserve by mail, TicketMaster; no exchanges or refunds; subscription program
Location
Off Hollywood (101) Fwy, Lankershim Blvd exit
Parking
On premises, $5

USC SCHOOL OF MUSIC—ARNOLD SCHOENBERG INSTITUTE

Info: (213) 746-4090

Arnold Schoenberg, the giant of 20th century music who made Los Angeles his home for his last 17 years, was pensioned exactly $38 a month by UCLA when forced to retire from its faculty at age 70. Since his death in 1951, however, the city's institutions have tried to make amends.

Hence, the Arnold Schoenberg Institute, a striking building on the USC campus that houses the largest collection of Schoenberg papers and artifacts in the world. Just inside the entrance awaits a fascinating mock-up of Schoenberg's Brentwood workroom as he left it.

The Institute's tiny 175-seat performance hall—actually a room that doubles as a gallery—has been home to a forward-looking concert series that takes on adventurous projects for 20th-century music connoisseurs. In recent years, the Institute played host to a long-term series, "The Pierrot Project," featuring newly commissioned works that paid homage to Schoenberg's pathbreaking song cycle, "Pierrot Lunaire."

Among the memorable single concerts have been a tribute to Ernst Krenek not long after his 90th birthday and an evening devoted to music composed in the Terezin concentration camp during World War II. Major artists such as baritone Thomas Hampson, sopranos Arleen Auger and Phyllis Bryn-Julson and singer Michael Feinstein have held forth in special programs in this room.

Unfortunately the Institute suspended its concert series in 1992/93, hoping to raise enough funds to strike it up again someday. Call the Institute for the latest.

VALLEY MASTER CHORALE AT NORTHRIDGE

See press listings for performance locations.
Info: (818) 885-3365 **Fax:** (818) 362-0212
Music Director: John Alexander

For a relatively young ensemble, the Valley Master Chorale already has a rather interesting history. For starters, it was founded in 1975 by the late Bill Lee—one of Hollywood's most noted singers and vocal directors—and his wife Ada Beth Lee. Then, under successors Alan Davies (till '81) and Gerald Eskelin (till '87), the Master Chorale veered down the pops and jazz path.

In 1987, Eskelin's replacement, John Alexander, the leader of the Masterworks Chorale at Cal State Northridge and Pacific Chorale, led the group back toward the choral mainstream. The VMC and the Masterworks Chorale then merged to form a formidable 150-voice organization. It's this super-charged group that now presents a four-concert subscription series under the name, Valley Master Chorale at Northridge. Got that? Good, because it won't be repeated here!

Currently the VMC presents an eclectic mix of major choral pieces, popular music, and a Christmas program, usually backed by a 60-piece orchestra. In addition, the VMC is frequently invited to back groups like the Glendale and Pasadena symphonies. Singers from the chorale also present mini-concerts at health care facilities and retirement homes. A Children's Chorus spin-off is in the nascent stage.

The biggest obstacle the VMC faces is the lack of an adequate performance space in the San Fernando Valley, a problem not likely to be soon solved. Call for current performance information.

Performances
Nov-May; Sat 8 pm
Tickets
$9-25
Discounts
Seniors/students/groups of 10+, call
BO
Call Mon-Fri 9:30 am-3:30 pm; or CSU Northridge BO (818) 885-3093; check/MC/V/ reserve by mail (P.O. Box 8347, Northridge, CA 91327), fax; subscription program
Parking
Varies with location
Special Features
Open rehearsals Wed evenings at CSU Northridge

VENTURA CONCERT THEATRE

26 South Chestnut Street
Ventura, CA 93001
Info: (805) 648-1888 **Rsvn:** (805) 648-1888
Fax: (805) 648-3689
Dinner/concert theater seats 850. All music varieties are performed.

One of Ventura County's oldest cultural sites, this theater was built in 1928 as a vaudeville showhouse at a time when the 975 seats were a sizable proportion of the total city population of 11,000. You won't catch vaudeville on the stage today, but you can enjoy live acts ranging from rock to reggae, blues, country and jazz, plus occasional comedy. Legends like Arlo Guthrie, The Neville Brothers, B.B. King, and the Byrds have graced—and still grace—its stage.

The building has since been renovated into a cross-section of Victorian and Spanish architecture. Long tables close to the stage cater to dining customers while the rear half seats general admission audiences. Two bars have been strategically placed to quench thirsts, and a sizable dance floor circumnavigates the stage.

If you don't live nearby, you might as well make it an evening of dinner and a show. The dinner menu is limited to chicken, steak, fish, and vegetables, but it serves its purpose.

Performances
Vary
Tickets
$13.50-25
BO
Mon-Fri 10 am-6 pm; Sat-Sun noon-6 pm; check/MC/V/reserve by phone, TicketMaster, "Videotyme" in Ventura; no exchanges
Location
Between Main and Santa Clara, on Chestnut St
Parking
On street

WADSWORTH THEATER See UCLA

WEST VALLEY SYMPHONY ORCHESTRA

Pierce College Performing Arts Theatre
6201 Winnetka Avenue
Woodlands Hills, CA
Info: (818) 883-6283
Fax: (818) 883-3148
Music Director: James Domine
Concerts scheduled at Pierce College Performing Arts Center.

Long accustomed to camping out in various public school buildings, this community orchestra recently moved into a permanent home at the Pierce College Performing Arts Center. WVSO has no doubt begun to enrich the relatively arid cultural soil of the San Fernando Valley, where residents often must find their live music on the other side of the Santa Monica Mountains.

The orchestra plays a six-concert season at Pierce, led by longtime music director James Domine. Recent programming relies on popular classics, with a touch of ambition in the form of Beethoven's *Ninth Symphony* and a season-ending four-concerto Mozart Marathon. But Domine has forayed into new works in the past and presumably will again.

Performances
Oct-June, Sat 8 pm
Tickets
$7.50-10.00
Discounts
Children/seniors/ students/groups of 6+, call
BO
Mon-Fri 8:30-6:00 pm; check/cash/reserve by mail (20113 Vanowen St, Winnetka, CA 91306); subscription program

WILSHIRE EBELL THEATRE

4401 West 8th Street
Los Angeles, CA 90005
Info: (213) 939-1128   **Rsvn:** (213) 939-1128
Rental facility with 1,270 seats.

The Wilshire Ebell may be a grand dame a bit down at the heel, a bit worn about the edges perhaps, but she retains her certain charm. This Renaissance-style, peach-colored structure was, in fact, originally built in 1927 as the clubhouse for the Ebell, a private ladies club still in existence.

Everybody loves this place, especially producers who know it's a non-union house which can be rented at alluring prices. The LA Mozart Orchestra and the Music Guild's chamber music series are regular tenants. The house also touts troupes of Russian singers, Armenian dancers, and gospel musical plays. It's commandeered regularly as a film and TV-special location.

Wine-colored velour draperies and heavy carved wood furniture decorate the lobby. In the theater itself, some new carpeting has been added and the padded seats are holding their own. The best seats are in the loge and front balcony. When choosing orchestra seats, stay away from those near the two support columns in the last four rows. Seats technically behind posts are not sold, but some adjacent seats still have slightly obstructed views. The acoustics are good, and amplification is never used.

Depending on the producer, snacks may be served outside, but there is never food service in the lobby. Nearby Larchmont Village, on Larchmont between Third and Beverly, has several fine eating spots to choose from, including La Luna. For more action, head the other way to the Atlas Bar & Grill in the Wiltern Building at Western and Wilshire.

Performances
Mon-Sun
Tickets
$ varies
BO
Mon-Fri 10 am-5 pm; Sat 1 pm-5 pm; check/TicketMaster
Location
4 blocks W of Crenshaw Blvd, 1 block S of Wilshire Blvd; N of the Santa Monica (10) Fwy
Parking
On premises, FREE; on street

WILTERN THEATRE

3790 Wilshire Boulevard
Los Angeles, CA 90010
Info: (213) 380-5005
Fax: (213) 388-0242
A 2,288-seat Art Deco Historical Landmark featuring concerts, plays, and dance.

Built in 1931, the Wiltern Theatre is a fine example of Art Deco architecture and art. This Historical Landmark was completely restored eight years ago to its current glory. It's such an elegant setting in which to see ballet and theater and to listen to music. It's too bad, though, that when they went to all that trouble—and money—to renovate, that they didn't do something about the sightlines. I suppose if you are over 5'5", you have nothing to worry about—except your legs. One recent performance was spent with a man's knee jabbed into my back. But the acoustics are natural and there is a customized sound system for electric shows.

As is the case in so many local theaters, the women's restrooms are inadequate—even for a non-sellout performance. Come prepared to cross your legs. Children's performances are sometimes booked here. Be forewarned: giant, messy chocolate candy bars are the snacks for those shows. Perhaps I should send in my cleaning bills?

Despite all the negatives, it is a grand setting for a performance. The hopping, trendy Atlas Bar and Grill is just steps away.

Performances
Mon-Sun 8 pm; Sat-Sun matinees
Tickets
$15-35
Discounts
Groups of 20+, call BO
BO
Mon-Fri noon-6 pm; MC/V/check/ TicketMaster
Location
At the corner of Wilshire Blvd and Western Ave; within 5 minutes of the Santa Monica (10) Fwy. and the Hollywood (101) Fwy.
Parking
On premises, $5; valet-sometimes; on street

XTET

See press listings for performance locations.
Info: (213) 257-4454   **Fax:** (213) 257-4454

XTET? Ten members? Perhaps an ex-group? Pre NC-17? Well, the X in XTET actually means "X" number of players may play a wide range of chamber music. (X usually equals 2 to 12 players.)

XTET was formulated (among other reasons) in 1986 to perform Schoenberg's ground-breaking *Pierrot Lunaire*—and the group has since become best-known as bold explorers of new music. Yet they're just as likely to program Brahms Clarinet Trio.

The core of XTET consists of violinists Elizabeth Baker, Jennifer Woodward and Kazi Pitelka; cellist Roger Lebow; flutist Gary Woodward; clarinetist David Ocker; bassoonist John Steinmetz; pianists Gloria Cheng and Vicki Ray; percussionist David Johnson; harpist JoAnn Turovsky and soprano Daisietta Kim. Sometimes XTET expands, if a work calls for it, but not often; these expert players are quite self-contained.

Though XTET has no permanent home base, they can be heard at the Monday Evening Concerts at the Los Angeles County Museum of Art, Occidental College, the South Bay Chamber Music Society, and various universities out of town. They generally put on about five LA area concerts per season, with an "X" number of others elsewhere in the state.

Performances
Vary
Tickets
$10-15
Discounts
Children/seniors/ students
BO
Call; also available at door day of performance

YOUNG ARTISTS PENINSULA MUSIC FESTIVAL See **FESTIVALS & SEASONAL EVENTS**

YOUNG MUSICIANS FOUNDATION DEBUT ORCHESTRA

See press listings for performance locations.
Info: (310) 859-7668 **Fax:** (310) 859-1365
Conductor: Daniel Hege

Performances
Dec-May; Sun 8 pm
Tickets
FREE
BO
Call
Parking
Varies with location

In true Medialand fashion, this excellent youth orchestra was actually spun off a television program. The program was called *Debut*, a live music competition (ah, the early days of television!) where young musicians competed before a judges' panel for prizes. When the show went off the air, Sylvia Kunin, a feisty, determined woman, decided this was too good an idea to abandon. And so, with some help from the likes of Gregor Piatigorsky and Bruno Walter, she started the Young Musicians Foundation in 1954.

The Debut Orchestra was formed the following year, led in its first concert by the young André Previn. It continues to give young talented musicians a chance to play symphonic repertoire. Unlike the huge American Youth Symphony, the YMF Debut Orchestra has varied in size over the years. Chamber-sized over a decade ago, it grew to some 90 members in the '80s then scaled back to 65, where it is today. The YMF players average 18 to 25, with the occasional wunderkind as young as 13.

The conductor of the YMF is selected through a national competition for a three-year term. The ranks of the alumni are filled with now-prominent folks who often served concurrently in assistant posts with the Los Angeles Philharmonic. Michael Tilson Thomas, Calvin Simmons, Myung-Whun Chung, Lawrence Foster, Neal Stulberg, Henry Lewis, and Leonard Slatkin comprise the distinguished gallery of YMF conductors. The current conductor, Laura Webber, is the first woman to lead this nearly four-decade-old institution.

You won't feel shortchanged at a Debut Orchestra concert, for like the AYS, this ensemble is capable of handling serious symphonic challenges. In addition, the Debut Orchestra performs at least one premiere work each year (that one being the winner of the BMI Foundation's Composer Competition).

For the last several years, the Debut Orchestra performed in Royce Hall. But escalating rent, plus a desire to expand out of its Westside base, now takes the ensemble elsewhere: Gindi Auditorium, the Japan America Theatre, the Dorothy Chandler Pavilion, and Thorne Hall at Occidental College. Performances are free, but donations are appreciated.

If you really like chipping in, there's the annual gala fund-raising benefit at the Beverly Hilton Hotel in which the Debut Orchestra plays the first half, leaving the second half to visiting celebrity performers like Anthony Newley and the Cleo Laine/Johnny Dankworth team.

DANCE

INTRODUCTION TO DANCE

By Bella Lewitzky

Dance in our nation has reached a level of maturity that places it in a rightful position alongside its sister arts. The creative vitality of dance is singular.

The West Coast forms the nation's second dance center. The legacy of dance in the West was formidable even in the days of the few valiant pioneers. In fact, the Western few included the mother of modern dance, Isadora Duncan. It is perhaps no accident that this nation's oldest ballet company was formed on the West Coast—that the Denishawn school was founded in Los Angeles—that the life work of my mentor, Lester Horton, existed here—that a formative part of Martha Graham's life was here—that much of Agnes De Mille's beginnings was here. There are others, too numerous to list, equal in quality and reputation.

Those of us nurtured in the Western climate treasure that which is special to our area: the open landscape, the towering mountains, the desert, the sea, the brilliance of colors which mark this geography. Our landscape is incredibly varied and has attracted a comparable variety of people. And so, our dance is broad in range.

Los Angeles—and indeed the entire Southern California area—boasts many classical dance companies: Korean, Chinese, Japanese, Philippine, Mexican, Spanish, American Indian, Indian, and African; folk ensembles such as AMAN and AVAZ, ballet companies such as the Los Angeles Chamber Ballet. There are tap masters and jazz dancers. There is an abundance of exciting and diverse modern dance companies which range from traditional to avant-garde. There is a dance service organization called Dance Resource Center. In addition, presenters bring both national and international dance companies to many of our Southern California cities.

We are all here for you to enjoy, and your attendance keeps the legacy alive and well.

Bella Lewitzky has been at the forefront of modern dance on the West Coast for more than five decades. Her contributions as a dancer and choreographer are legendary. Along with Lester Horton, she founded the Dance Theater of Los Angeles in 1946. In 1966, the Lewitzky Dance Company was born, the company that under Lewitzky's tutelage became one of the leading international modern dance companies performing all over the world.

Not only is her talent known worldwide, but Ms. Lewitzky is heralded for her activities on behalf of the development of dance in the U.S.

AISHA ALI DANCE CO.

See press listings for performance locations.
Info: (310) 474-4867
Artistic Director: Aisha Ali
Music and dance of the Middle East and North Africa.

Anyone who longs for the mysterious Middle East of fables and children's books—land of pashas, tents and seductive belly dancers—will be royally satisfied by an evening with Aisha Ali. Founded in 1973 at the since-departed Annual International Folkdance Festival, Aisha Ali's troupe specializes in the authentic dance and music of the Middle East and North Africa, including a variety of folk forms, from the joyful but contained rites of Egyptian wedding dances to the ever-popular jiggles and undulations of the classic belly dance. In 1984, artistic director Aisha Ali and Company represented the countries of Egypt, Tunisia and Morocco at the Olympic opening ceremonies and performed as part of the Olympic Arts Festival.

AMAN FOLK ENSEMBLE

See press listings for performance locations.
Info: (213) 629-8387   **Fax:** (213) 629-8396
Artistic Director: Barry Glass

Barry Glass's veteran group elevates international folk dancing out of the category of amateur kitsch back into the realm of serious dance (where it belongs). The disciplined movement and the cultural traditions that accompany the dances combine with striking costumes to create a remarkable spectacle.

For three decades, Aman has transported to the stage the long-preserved folk dances of Eastern European cultures and guest dancers from other countries. Recently Aman took its first steps into modern dance thanks to a grant-funded collaboration with New York choreographer-composer, Laura Dean.

For the uninitiated, an evening with Aman is a fine way to get a quick education in world dance.

AMERICAN BALLET ENSEMBLE See **Metropolitan Ballet of San Diego**

APSARA DANCERS OF CAMBODIA

See press listings for performance locations.
Info: (818) 785-1498
Artistic Director: Amy Catlin

These dancers present a fluid and delicate movement style resembling the less obscure Javanese dance. The members of this unique troupe range in age from seven to seventeen (plus the twenty-five-year-old professional lead dancer). You'll find them at the usual educational culture haunts such as museums, schools, special events, and festivals. Their big annual events are the Cambodian New Year in spring and the Cambodian "Thanksgiving" in late September, both community religious festivals.

The dance teachers acquired their expertise during extended stays in refugee camps on the Thai/Cambodian border. Project director and ethnomusicologist, Amy Catlin, narrates along with a slide show on Cambodian music and dance.

Performances
Mid-April (Cambodian New Year); late Sept (Cambodian "Thanksgiving")
Parking
Varies with location
Special Features
Open rehearsals

AVAZ INTERNATIONAL DANCE THEATRE

See press listings for performance locations.
Info: (818) 441-1630   **Fax:** (818) 441-4048
Artistic Director: Anthony Shay

       Shy young ladies ritually enter into maidenhood beneath crossed swords; young bucks flash their macho stunts in courtship dances; and peasants celebrate the harvest. Storybook narratives spring to life on the Avaz stage. Artistic director and founder Anthony Shay's company is one of the U.S.'s leading international folk troupes. There are yelps of joy at the sensual Middle Eastern undulations. Yet the result definitely isn't the corny stereotypes and generalized circle dances you might expect. Rich in ethno-specific detail and executed with the same rigor expected of classical footwork, Avaz's dances include traditional music and movement from Eastern Europe, the Middle East, central Asia, North Africa, and America.

       Among the company's fifty members are musicians who wring tunes from the most obscure instruments this side of the Smithsonian. Watch for performances throughout the Southland.

Performances
  Fri-Sun 7:30 pm or 8 pm; Sun 2 pm
Tickets
  $10-25
Discounts
  Children/seniors/ students/groups of 10+, call
BO
  Varies with location
Parking
  Varies with location

BALLET FOLKLORICO OLLIN

See press listings for performance locations.
Info: (818) 894-5858
Artistic Director: Virginia Diediker

       For the past 20 years, Virginia Diediker has taken her students, ranging in age from four to ninety, and molded them into an authentic, prolific Mexican dance company. Virginia is one of the only Anglos leading a Mexican folklorico dance company.

       You may have seen them perform in the 91st Tournament of Roses Parade, or annually at the Northridge Park "Salute to the Arts," the first weekend in June. That same weekend each year, the company appears in a fiesta in Apple Valley. Cinco de Mayo is celebrated in dance at Victor Valley Jr. College. The company performs year-round at fairs, during holidays, and in concerts. Diediker even has a senior citizen group from east Los Angeles, Los Hilos de Plata (the Silver Threads) which she incorporates into her regular performances.

       It was Diediker's degree in Mexican history and professional dance experience that led her to form this energetic company. She has painstakingly researched the dances of at least 12 regions in Mexico, and takes care that not only the dance steps, but the costumes reflect authenticity.

BALLET PACIFICA

Info: (714) 642-9275   **Rsvn:** (714) 854-4646
Fax: (714) 642-9277
Artistic Director: Molly Linch
Performs at the Laguna Moulton Playhouse, Irvine Barclay Theatre, and Festival Forum Theatre.

       Ballet Pacifica (formerly the Laguna Beach Civic Ballet), now approaching its 30th season, displays its graceful wares at the Laguna Moulton Playhouse in Orange County, as well as at the Irvine Barclay Theatre.

       For your seasonal fix of the *Nutcracker*'s sugar plums and evil Drosselmeyers, try Ballet Pacifica's annual crack at it. Their traditional repertoire also ventures—albeit cautiously—into the realm of new works, with selections from local and national choreographers such as Philip Jerry

Performances
  Oct-June, Fri-Sat 8 pm, Sat 2:30 pm
Tickets
  $6-15
Discounts
  Children/seniors/ students/groups of 15+, call

(former principal dancer with the Joffrey Ballet), Rick McCullough (former principal dancer with the Netherlands Dance Theatre), and Diane Coburn Bruning (the 1990 recipient of the Dewar's Young Artist's Award).

A Children's Series of familiar works is staged four weekends at the Festival Forum Theatre.

BO
Mon-Fri 10 am-4:30 pm; check/AE/MC/V/reserve by mail; exchanges for subscribers only; subscription program

BENITA BIKE'S DANCEART CO.

See press listings for performance locations.
Info: (818) 353-5734 **Fax:** (818) 353-5734
Artistic Director: Benita Bike

One of the newer players on the Los Angeles dance scene, Boston expatriate Benita Bike and her female company are known for woman-centric dances that evoke sensibilities ranging from the sweeping landscapes of Georgia O'Keeffe to the ethereal utterances of Bulgarian singing. The works are ambitious and often overtly feminine without lapsing into early feminism's mushy sentimentality. Choreographer Bike typically turns to a tribal or ritualistic movement basis, then crosses it with touches of American stage choreography. Sometimes her dancers are members of a generic tribe on the Native American plains, and sometimes they're caught up in an activity part spiritual and part aerobics. Bike also has her lighter moments, and although the dances aren't all equally original, hers is definitely a choreographic presence picking up its step.

In addition to her own major concerts, Bike offers a thought-provoking series of low-cost performances for mixed-age audiences entitled "Double Take." At the completion of the three dances in the program, the audience joins the choreographer and dancers in a Q & A session to explore the significance of the work. One of the more complicated dances of the three is then performed again, presumably to a more alert (and educated) audience.

Performances
Thurs-Sun 7 pm or 8 pm, Sun 2 pm or 3 pm (call to verify)
Tickets
FREE-$12
Discounts
Seniors/students
BO
Reserve by phone
Parking
Varies with location

BLACK MOUNTAIN DANCE THEATRE

See press listings for performance locations.
Info: (619) 674-1006
Artistic Director: Sylvia Palmer

Like the California Ballet, Black Mountain Dance Theatre follows a disciplined classical repertoire. Professional guest stars from other cities are lured in—a strategy that's a boon to ticket sales, and better yet, provides excellent exposure for the company.

Black Mountain beautifully fills a gap in San Diego's North County. Performances are held at the Poway Center for the Performing Arts, as well as at smaller venues. A *Nutcracker*? You bet.

Performances
Fri-Sun 8 pm; Sat-Sun 2 pm
Tickets
$10-22
Discounts
Children/seniors/ students/groups of 10+, call
BO
Varies with location
Parking
Varies with location

BLUE PALM

See press listings for performance locations.
Info: (213) 663-2683
Artistic Directors: J. Planeix / T. Crocker

Jackie Planeix and Tom Crocker, former soloists with Maurice Bejart's "Ballet of the 20th Century" and the Grand Theatre de Geneve, are the hippest, chichi, and yet ultra-smart dance duo this side of Paris. Their performances are fun-food for the intelligentsia executed with the finest dance and theater technique. Their style is a unique blend of narrative, theater, dance, and music. The sense of humor

Tickets
FREE- $15 depending on venue and performance
Special Features
Open rehearsals

ranges from bitter black to whipped cream, while the anecdotes they incorporate belie a sneakily sophisticated take on the modern condition. Best known for their dance-theater pieces on topics both existential and amorous, the sexy cerebralists have also turned their skills to the kiddie beat with equal aplomb (minus the sexy). They are also among the city's finest teachers, for young and old alike, in a variety of disciplines.

Check out their performances—in theaters, clubs, universities, art galleries, and coffeehouses.

BRAND LIBRARY AND ART GALLERIES

1601 West Mountain Street
Glendale, CA 91201
Info: (818) 548-2051 **Fax:** (818) 548-5079
Featuring an annual dance and music series.

The Brand Mansion, built in 1904 by Leslie C. Brand, who named his abode El Miradero, is reason enough to make a visit to Glendale. The exterior is a combination of Indian, Moorish, and Spanish architectures, inspired by the East Indian Pavilion at the Chicago 1893 Columbian World Exposition. The period Victorian interior is rather a jolt from the soothingly classical exterior. In 1956, the mansion was converted into Brand Library, currently housing more than 40,000 books on art and music. A gallery, concert hall, and exhibit space were added a decade later.

The cultural arts center hosts a dance series four times a year, and a music series of five programs annually in its 150-seat concert hall. An alternating Board of Directors decides on the performance format to keep the programs fresh and unpredictable. A recent dance program presented Collage Dance Theatre, Louise Reichlin & Dancers (Reichlin coordinates the dance programs), Carla Lubow, and Oguri, Steinberg and Ring.

One constant, thankfully, is the price—all shows are free. Call and ask to have your name placed on the mailing list.

Performances
  Sun 3 pm
Tickets
  FREE
Location
  Off Golden State (5) Fwy; Western exit; E to Mountain
Parking
  On premises, FREE; street parking

BRIDGES AUDITORIUM See THEATER

CALIFORNIA BALLET

San Diego Civic Theater,
202 'C' Street
San Diego, CA 92101
Info & Rsvn: (619) 560-6741   **Fax:** (619) 560-0072
Artistic Director: Maxine K. Mahon
Also performs at Theatre East and other locations throughout San Diego.

A classical ballet company is one of the staples of the cultural life of any city worth its salt. Right? So West Coast balletomanes have long been hard-pressed to explain why California's biggest city—LA—boasts no such beauty. The closest the Golden State comes to fulfilling this basic asset are the resident companies in the number two and three population centers, San Francisco and San Diego.

The California Ballet, which just celebrated its silver anniversary, is based in San Diego and embraces a basic repertoire. They perform at their home base, the San Diego Civic Theater, and elsewhere around town, including Spreckels Theatre, East County Performing Arts Center (Theatre East), the Lyceum Theatre, Poway Center for the Performing Arts, and in Ramona and El Cajon.

Performances
  Wed-Sun 8 pm; Fri-Sun 2:30 pm; Sept-May
Tickets
  $11.50-36
Discounts
  Seniors/students/groups of 15+; no exchanges or refunds; payment in advance
BO
  Mon-Fri 9 am-5 pm check/MC/V/reserve by mail, TicketMaster
Parking
  Varies with location

COLLAGE DANCE THEATRE

See press listings for performance locations.
Info: (818) 788-5113   **Fax:** (818) 981-4116
Artistic Director: Heidi Duckler

Heidi Duckler's enterprising troupe boldly goes where few performing companies dare to tread let alone leap and cavort. Inspired by the peculiarities and ironies of modern urban life, their efforts have taken them literally into a water fountain, onto a church pulpit, and onto the tops of unsuspecting washing and drying machines in a laundromat. Fun-spirited, satirical and full of flair, their multimedia site-specific dance-theater works are among the most inventive in the Los Angeles area. Thematically, Duckler typically mixes the metaphors of one or two common realms of experience to comment upon some aspect of our modern day alienation (i.e., high-hype evangelical religion crossed with the cult of food). Often, the work addresses the condition of women, but the bent is anything but humorless feminism. Instead, Duckler and her able dancers do a number on the society's deadening misogyny while having so much fun you can't help but see their point.

Accessible and energetic, Collage's shows are perfect for the (till now) dance-phobic and the uninitiated. Watch for their next dance landing site in the papers. Sometimes rehearsals are open to the public.

Performances
Thurs-Sun, usually 8 pm
Tickets
$8-15, often FREE
Discounts
Previews/seniors/ students
BO
Varies with location
Parking
Varies with location
Special features
Open rehearsals

DANCE AT THE FOUNTAIN THEATRE SERIES

5060 Fountain Avenue
Los Angeles, CA 90029
Info & Rsvn: (213) 663-1525

Every third Sunday of the month, look for a different dance group to grace the stage of the Fountain. Tina Gerstler and her company have appeared, as has Benita Bike's DanceArt, Ballet Folklorico Del Sur de California, Donna Sternberg & Dancers, and Viji Prakash, Virtuoso of Bharatanatyam. Flamenco dancing is also on the schedule, and in July and August, the Fuego Flamenco (see below) troupe of Roberto Amaral presents its heart-pumping movements. (Also see **Jazz Tap Ensemble** below.)

Performances
Third Sun of month, 3 pm
Tickets
$15
BO
Mon-Fri 10-5 pm, Sat 2-5; check/MC/V
Location
Off Hollywood (101) Fwy, 1/2 block E of Normandy, 1 block S of Sunset
Parking
Parking on premises, street, FREE

DANCE KALEIDOSCOPE See FESTIVALS & SEASONAL EVENTS

DANCE TRAFFIC SERIES

Highways Performance Space
1651 18th Street
Santa Monica, CA 90404
Info: (310) 453-1755   **Rsvn:** (213) 660-TKTS
Fax: (310) 453-4347

Highways Performance Space (of late the 18th Street Arts Complex) may be best-known as one of the infamous targets of the politically-weakened National Endowment for the Arts. This has not, however, slowed down this multi-use venue. It continues to program a wealth and variety of events, including the popular Dance Traffic series, with something on the schedule every month.

Emphasizing experimental, local, and performance-art oriented dance, this series presents an

Performances
Vary
Tickets
$ varies
BO
Noon-7 pm (by phone); 7:30 pm-8:30 pm; check/MC/V/reserve by phone; Tickets LA (213) 660-8587

array of artists both familiar and unfamiliar to local audiences. Typically, you find highly-politicized AIDS-inspired works that employ both movement and language side-by-side with archly abstract dances in the modernist vein. Also, there's a great deal of attention paid to the multicultural imperative, and the festival endeavors to present a variety of works that use dance to articulate the cultural and social perspectives of a wide range of creators, especially those from marginalized communities. It is well-attended and a good bet for discovering the unusual. It's also a venue for the best local choreographers and movement-based performance artists to experiment with new works and new directions, or simply to enjoy the all-too-scarce privilege of an enthusiastic audience.

Discounts
Students; Dance Resource Center Membership
Parking
On premises, FREE; on street

DANCE WAREHOUSE

1018 de la Vina Street
Santa Barbara, CA 93101
Info: (805) 963-2403
Space for classes, workshops, and performances.

It's not unusual to find Broadway hoofers showing their stuff at the Dance Warehouse. For example, Jon Engstrom, Dance Captain with the original Broadway company of *42nd Street*, along with Albert Reid, an instructor for Merce Cunningham, and Argentinean–trained tango dancers Loreen Arbus and Alberto Tolendano have all displayed their talents. Owner Julie McLeod was in the original company of *West Side Story*, *The King and I* and other Broadway hits. Founded in 1979, the Dance Warehouse is a Santa Barbara studio facility that offers classes, guest artists, performances, workshops and a home for resident companies Improv, Inc. and the new Taps Unlimited. Watch press listings for, or call about the Guest Artist Series, which draws upon talent from Los Angeles, nearby universities and touring arts.

Improv, Inc., the resident company, is an eight-member company that borders on the outrageous, with loosely set pieces performed (you guessed it) improvisationally. No two performances are alike. The company gives lecture/demonstrations, outdoor performances, studio concerts, and public openings.

Performances
Fri-Sun, 8 pm; Sat-Sun 2:30 pm
Tickets
$6-12
BO
Varies; check/reserve by mail
Location
On de la Vina near Carrillo
Parking
On premises, FREE

DANZA FLORICANTO/USA

Plaza De La Raza
3540 North Mission Road.
Los Angeles, CA 90031
Info: (213) 223-2475   **Rsvn:** (213) 223-2475
Fax: (213) 223-1804
Artistic Director: Gema Sandoval

Residing at Los Angeles' Plaza de la Raza, this company promotes Mexican culture and history to community audiences all over California. Founding artistic director Gema Sandoval introduces and comments bilingually on the performances, making them thought-provoking as well as entertaining.

Through the dances from Colima and Guerrero, or the spirited "Concheras" that Sandoval claims as Chicanismo incarnate, cultural pride inflates this unique celebration. From the symbolically romantic duets to the festival–style whirling of the group dances, all the pageantry of folklore is there for the ogling. Just click your heels together twice and say "Viva la Raza,' and you'll be transported to a world ablaze with color and emotion.

Performances
Vary
Tickets
$15-50
Discounts
Groups of 10+, call
BO
Check/reserve by mail
Parking
Street parking

DONNA STERNBERG & DANCERS

See press listings for performance locations.
Info: (310) 260-1198
Contemporary dance
Artistic Director: Donna Sternberg

Donna Sternberg is one of several talented local modern dance choreographers who, after paying her dues in the companies of Donald Byrd, Mary Jane Eisenberg, and others, stepped out on her own.

Sternberg's preference is for themes spiritual, although she manages to avoid the usual sentimentality of that terrain. The company guest-performs at locations such as Cal State LA, Pierce College, and the University of Redlands.

Performances
Late spring and fall (though varies), Fri-Sat 8 pm
Tickets
$10-12
Discounts
Children/seniors/ students/DRC member discount
BO
Check/reserve by phone
Parking
Varies with location
Special Features
Open rehearsals (by special arrangement only)

EL CAMINO COLLEGE/MARSEE AUDITORIUM See MUSIC

¡FLAMENCO TALAVERA!

See press listings for performance locations.
Info: (310) 699-7575
Artistic Director: Juan Talavera

Classical Spanish dance typically gets relegated to restaurants with fake bricks and wrought iron furniture. Or you might see it in grab-bag folk and international festivals, sandwiched between other acts that have nothing to do with each other. That's too bad, because a company as professional as Flamenco Talavera deserves a surer shot at broadbased attention. Disciplined and dedicated to the art despite the paucity of opportunities, Flamenco Talavera is a strong argument for the mainstreaming of culturally specific dance. Stiletto footstomping, dramatic teeth clenching, sexy partnering and all the red on black romance you want are yours at any outing of Juan Talavera's company. This is Spanish dancing the way you want to see it—full out and full of flourish. The 50-member company is known internationally for their lavish and rigorously executed group dances, as well as East LA-born Talavera's own star turns.

Watch the press listings for performances of this dynamic group.

Performances
Vary
Tickets
$22.50-26.50
Discounts
Groups of 25+, call
BO
Varies with location

FRANCISCO MARTINEZ DANCE THEATRE

Plaza de la Raza Cultural Center
3540 North Mission Road
Los Angeles, CA 90031
Info: (818) 988-2192
Artistic Director: Francisco Martinez

Mexican-born Francisco Martinez designs eclectic dance programs for his contemporary dance/ballet company that—most astonishingly—appeal to large audiences. On one night, expect a grouping of works that are classical, modern, avant-garde, and even comic. Martinez is known for his unusual music scores, and is currently undertaking dance based upon literature (recently, Chekhov's *Three Sisters*).

The primarily Hispanic seven-member company performs extensively in Southern California and recently began a series of national tours.

Performances
Vary
Tickets
$10-15
Discounts
Children/seniors/ students/groups of 20+
BO
Check; reserve by mail
Parking
Varies with location

FUEGO FLAMENCO

Fountain Theater
5060 Fountain Avenue
Hollywood, CA 90029
Info: (213) 663-2235 **Rsvn:** (213) 663-1525
Artistic Director: Roberto Amaral
  The father of the nascent troupe Fuego Flamenco, Roberto Amaral is a dazzling soloist and one of Los Angeles veteran Spanish artists. Too few people outside the Spanish dance community know his work. Since his return to California from Spain in the late '70s, his footwork has seldom graced general-audience stages, being more often limited to ethnic-specific festivals or small venues.
  Back in the late 1970s and early 1980s opportunities were more plentiful for specialists such as Amaral. He now concentrates on self-producing and teaching. But when he does go out, he goes all out, sometimes creating dramatic scenarios around the dances that showcase his and his dancers' classical technique.
  One good sign: The popularity of Flamenco has grown enormously. One scheduled three-week appearance at Hollywood's Fountain Theatre, two years ago, is still going!

Performances
 Winter, spring, summer
 Fri-Sat 8 pm; Sun 3 pm
Tickets
 $18-22
Discounts
 Groups of 20+
BO
 Check/MC/V
Parking
 FREE security

GINDI AUDITORIUM AT THE UNIVERSITY OF JUDAISM See **THEATER**

IMPROV, INC. See **Dance Warehouse**

IRVINE BARCLAY THEATRE See **Ballet Pacifica**

ISAACS, MCCALEB & DANCERS

See press listings for performance locations.
Info: (619) 296-9523
Artistic Directors: Nancy McCaleb, Jean Isaacs
  Artistic Director Jean Isaacs is a modern dance angel—an active force in San Diego for two decades teaching, producing, and presenting contemporary dance. The company she co-founded with Betzi Roe and Patrick Nollet in 1974 has not only survived but flourished—a near miracle for San Diego. Now with co-artistic director and choreographer Nancy McCaleb, Isaacs has built a professional modern dance company of seven dancers and three interns.
  Isaacs' choreography sidesteps the hard edge category, leaning more towards lyricism. McCaleb creates dance-theater pieces, often collaborating with musicians and visual artists.
  Home theater for the group is the Mandell Weiss Theater on the UCSD campus, where one major concert is presented annually. By contrast, their Fifth Avenue studio space has a community spirit—intimate, low-tech concerts have been successfully presented here for years.

Performances
 Thurs-Sun 8 pm
Tickets
 $10-15
Discounts
 Children/seniors/
 students/groups of 20+
BO
 Mon-Fri 9 am-5 pm;
 Sat 9 am-2 pm
 MC/V/check/reserve by
 mail; exchanges made
Parking
 Varies with location

JAZZ DANCERS, INC.

See press listings for performance locations.
Info: (310) 394-2805
Artistic Directors: Dennon Rawles, Sayhber Rawles
  Jazz dancing often seems to apply to everything but dancing to jazz. But Dennon and Sayhber Rawles and their nine-member company are committed to concert jazz dancing with jazz music. Whether it's the classical rhythms of Gershwin or the toe-tapping tunes of today's artists as

Performances
 Spring (May-June) and
 sometimes fall, Fri-Sat 8
 pm, sometimes Sun 2
 pm
Tickets
 $12-25

backdrop, the taut choreographies have the stuff of popular appeal as well as professional expertise. They hop and bop to Miles Davis as easily as to Pete Escovedo, with a healthy helping of jazz-influenced pop musicians such as Sting on the roster as well.

The Rawles are veterans of the showbiz circuit, having choreographed the Barry Levinson/Warren Beatty film *Bugsy*, the 1983 movie *Staying Alive* with John Travolta, and seven other feature films. Their television gigs have included "Baryshnikov on Broadway," "Baryshnikov in Hollywood" and several Academy Awards programs.

Locally, the Japan America Theatre and Idyllwild School of Music and the Arts are places to watch for the company's performances.

Discounts
Seniors/students/groups of 10+, call
BO
At Japan America Theatre; check/MC/V/ reserve by mail; no refunds, no exchanges
Parking
Varies with location
Special Features
Open rehearsals (for "supporters" only)

JAZZ TAP ENSEMBLE

See press listings for performance locations.
Info: (310) 475-4412 **Fax:** (310) 475-4412
Artistic Director: Lynn Dally

If you think jazz and tap can't dance together, you're definitely out of step. This winning combination has put Lynn Dally's Jazz Tap Ensemble in the vanguard of tap's renaissance. Now in its second triumphant decade, the ensemble of three dancers and four resident musicians is known for its spontaneity and imaginative spirit.

Even though it's an LA group, be sure to get those tix next time you see them scheduled in the area. They're in such great demand around the world, its rare to actually see them in their own backyard. When you're lucky, you can catch them in the "Dance at the Fountain Theatre" and "Summer Nights at the Ford" series, and at the Morgan-Wixson Theatre.

Dally's "Caravan Project" trains young jazz tap dancers who perform on occasion with the company.

THE JOFFREY BALLET

There are, after all, certain requisite components to the cultural life of any upstanding major American city, such as a resident ballet company. Unfortunately, LA has never quite been able to get its arts act together on this score. No sooner had long-suffering local balletomanes enthused over the idea that the Joffrey had become bicoastal—with a seasonal residence at the city's acropolis, The Los Angeles Music Center—than the deal was botched.

First there were the much-publicized battles over who held the production rights to the Gerald Arpino repertory. Then there were disagreements among top management over who controlled the operation. Then there were fusses between the company and the Music Center over financial matters. Then after signing a contract with the Wiltern Theatre, the group first cut its season in half, then cut out altogether, purportedly because of the "local unrest." In the end, what many perceive as an ill-advised battle of egos between local honchos and the Joffrey folks ended with the company pulling up stakes.

While they may not be the best American ballet company, they certainly are major-league. It's a shame to think a town the size of LA still can't support a resident dance company.

The above would have been the end of the story, except that suddenly the Joffrey is back—perhaps temporarily—and not as an LA company. Iowans were the first to see it rise up again like a Phoenix in the shape of Prince's rock ballet, "Billboards." Eventually the troupe came to Los Angeles where in just five performances, the presses screamed, the Joffrey had taken in nearly a half million dollars (a figure the company had not been familiar with for a long time). It remains to be seen whether the Joffrey will resume its old life, or whether we've seen their last *Nutcracker*.

KARPATOK HUNGARIAN FOLK ENSEMBLE

See press listings for performance location.
Info: (818) 363-2219　**Fax:** (818) 363-1349
Artistic Director: Tibor Toghia
　　　This 45-member group performs traditional Eastern European dance and music with lots of energy and flair. Dancers wear embroidered costumes collected from Hungarian villages, as well as reproductions of garments no longer available. The classic folk dances are in repertory with new works inspired by village folklore. The dancers are accompanied by musicians on wonderfully unique folk instruments like the *tekero* and *koboz*. Watch for this group in concert or at the various dance festivals throughout the year.

KATJA BIESANZ/ DANCE THEATER

See press listings for performance locations.
Info: (818) 507-0733　**Rsvn:** (818) 241-6169
Artistic Director: Katja Biesanz
　　　Modern dance's preoccupation with matters spiritual can spook you after a while. You know, those twisting, turning, arms-uplifted gyrations of those all too familiar works in which a group of women in filmy dresses enacts a vague analogy about enlightenment, isolation, and good and evil. Once in a while, though, you can take all those same ingredients, put them in the right hands, and come up with something extraordinary. That's the case with Katja Biesanz and her company of seven.
　　　Biesanz, who put in time with such masters as Bella Lewitzky, Alwin Nikolais, and Donald McKayle, has a background in theater as well as dance, most notably with Le Theatre du Soleil. She brings their sense of narrative drama to her creations, stepping up the standard modern dance idiom with an attention to human detail. She also enlivens the works with her knowledge from such diverse disciplines as martial arts and Eastern dance.
　　　Whenever possible, matinees are provided for families replete with bilingual lectures and demonstrations. Look for performances in LA and from Lancaster to San Diego. Add your name to the mailing list for advance notice.

Performances
　Vary
Tickets
　$5-12.50
Discounts
　Children/seniors/
　students/groups of 10+,
　call BO
BO
　Varies with location
Parking
　Varies with location
Special Features
　Matinees for families
　with lecture
　demonstrations in
　English and Spanish

KAYAMANAN NG LAHI—PHILIPPINE PERFORMING ARTS, INC.

See press listings for performance locations.
Info: (310) 821-5896
Artistic Director: Leonilo Angos
　　　For those of you whose knowledge of Philippine culture extends to, say, the voice of Miss Saigon star Lea Salonga, this group will be a much-valued introduction to the close but unknown island world's variety of arts. The name, according to the folks who ought to know, translates as "Treasures of Our People" and refers to their repertoire of folk arts. The bent is preservational, aiming as they do to keep alive the traditional Filipino forms of music and folk dance. Offerings include group dances and ritual, complete with traditional garb, as well as more Western-influenced selections. They're accompanied by a string ensemble like none you've ever heard: Brass gongs, bamboo instruments, and other simple music-making devices.

Performances
　Vary
Tickets
　$10-20
Previews
　Children/seniors/
　students/groups of 10+,
　call
BO
　Varies with location
Parking
　Varies with location
Special Features
　Open rehearsals

Leonilo "Boy" Angos who, along with Joel F. Jacinto, heads the company's executive staff, is a veteran of three world tours with the widely recognized Bayanihan Dance Company.

The group performs in a variety of venues throughout Southern California.

KECK THEATER See OCCIDENTAL PERFORMING ARTS SERIES in MUSIC

KESHET CHAIM DANCE ENSEMBLE

See press listings for performance locations.
Info: (818) 986-0125
Artistic Director: Eytan Avisar

"The Rainbow of Life," as the Hebrew name suggests, is dedicated to the dance history of Israeli culture and Jewish heritage. This young company is the only Israeli folk dance troupe in the city. The talented dancers have performed at the 1984 Olympics Celebration, the Music Center, and the Los Angeles Festival. Each year they dance in the Israeli Independence Day performance at the University of Judaism.

Performances
Vary
Tickets
$20-50
Discounts
Children/students/
groups
BO
Varies with location
Parking
Varies with location
Special Features
Open rehearsals

KOROYAR FOLKLORE ENSEMBLE See MUSIC

LEWITZKY DANCE CO.

See press listings for performance locations.
Info: (213) 627-5555   **Fax:** (213) 627-9249
Artistic Director: Bella Lewitzky

Lewitzky Dance Company is inarguably California's most famous dance troupe. Headed by the West's best known modern doyenne, whose name the company bears, the 25-year-old company simply means "the best." It is consistently touted among the top six or seven companies in the United States. That reputation was earned despite its lack of a New York address—considered by many not only a maverick choice, but a potentially suicidal one. Bella proved, against all odds, that it was possible to forge a major international career in modern dance independent of the New York scene. She has given Los Angeles a professional gauge for modern dance that was unthinkable before.

Bella Lewitzky was raised by Russian immigrant parents on a chicken ranch near San Bernardino. Those open spaces of her young years became inspiration for her early choreographies. Her energies were galvanized when she became the indispensable choreographic Girl Friday to modern dance pioneer Lester Horton. Lewitzky's trademark dances combine a perfectionist technical sensibility with precise Western athleticism and a compelling emotional core. Although she no longer performs herself, her dancers closely follow in her footsteps.

Lewitzky's is a landmark career also notable for commercial works (including schooling Agnes de Mille's dancers for *Oklahoma!*). Her outspoken political activism was not silenced by the House Unamerican Activities Committee nor, decades later, the National Endowment for the Arts.

The company performs at Occidental College, Japan America Theatre, Royce Hall, Pepperdine University, the University of Judaism and elsewhere throughout the Southland, and tours throughout the world.

LORETTA LIVINGSTON & DANCERS

See press listings for performance locations.
Info: (213) 484-9888
Artistic Director: Loretta Livingston

Sexy, smart, and packed full of provocative ideas, Loretta Livingston's works extend the frontiers of modern dance. Loretta Livingston, a ten-year Lewitzky troupe veteran, heads Los Angeles' next (or next to next) biggest and most important modern company. They're risk takers, both in technique and in substance, presenting work you can wrestle with emotionally and intellectually.

Livingston favors issues of community, whether the power dynamics of couples or the destruction of the global ecology or the ways in which those two seemingly distinct spheres interact with each other. Hers is a Western sensibility: full of love of space, human ambition and literal and psychological scope. In 1990, Livingston's work nabbed the prestigious first prize in the Dewars Young Artist Recognition Award program. Among her most recent projects is the multipart *A History of Restlessness*, which contains, among many other ingredients, images inspired by the choreographer's time on Navajo and Hopi Indian reservations in northern Arizona.

Although the company isn't officially resident, Livingston regards the Japan America Theatre as home. This is where she's premiered her new works for the past three seasons. The company also can be seen moonlighting at UCLA, Cal State LA, the Wilshire Ebell Theatre, and other area venues.

Performances
Fri-Sat 8 pm
Tickets
$11-23
Discounts
Seniors/students/groups of 15+, call
BO
Varies with location
Parking
Varies with location
Special Features
Open rehearsals

LOS ANGELES CHAMBER BALLET

See press listings for performance locations.
Info: (310) 453-4952   **Fax:** (310) 453-9555
Artistic Directors: Raiford Rogers/Victoria Koenig

This group's work articulates loud and clear that ballet never need be boring: one too many Sleeping Beauty(s) or Nutcrackers, after all, can turn off a would-be balletomane for life. And it's not like this art form can afford to lose any aficionados from the upcoming MTV-fed generation!

LACB has made its mark by collaborating with and using the works of popular contemporary artists from other fields. Eclectic in both taste and stylistic approach, artistic directors Victoria Koenig and Raiford Rogers have presented such confections as a silly ballet with a libretto by Woody Allen, a full-length please-the-kiddies-and-the-grownups version of *The Little Prince*, a rendition of Rudyard Kipling's *Just So Stories* to music by Bobby McFerrin as well as new works by Los Angeles choreographers.

The ballet company performs at least once a year at the Japan America Theatre. They may be found the rest of the year at area locations such as the Irvine Barclay Theatre, and in the "Summer Nights at the Ford" series at the John Anson Ford.

Performances
In spring and summer
Tickets
FREE- $20
Discounts
Previews/children/ seniors/students/groups
BO
Varies with location
Parking
Varies with location

LOS ANGELES CHOREOGRAPHERS & DANCERS

See press listings for performance locations.
Info: (213) 665-5628
Artistic Director: Louise Reichlin

The name may sound like a service organization, but Los Angeles Choreographers & Dancers is actually a dance company founded by artistic and managing director Louise Reichlin. Each year, the company presents 60

Performances
Vary
Tickets
$6-12

performances of both modern and tap dance in a variety of venues, from theaters to museums to the great outdoors. The roster includes 11 modern dancers in choreography by Reichlin and tap soloist Alfred Desio, who works in both traditional tap style and his own invented electronic tap style, aka TapTronics, as featured in the movie *Tap*.

Best known for its trademark The Tennis Dances—a multi-illusion work replete with rackets, nets and balls—the company's modern dance centers on folk themes and incorporates a variety of musical styles, including world, medieval, bluegrass, and more. Celtic Suite mixes the modern and tap idioms, while tapper Desio's work—hokey as the gadgetry may sound—actually allows the dancer to compose music with every step he takes. A veteran of appearances on *The Today Show*, *Two on the Town*, and even the usually more somber NBC News, Desio's routine includes an interactive high-tech finale in which audience members join the dancer in footing their own TapTronics rhythms.

Reichlin's group seems to perform everywhere: Japan America Theatre, Keck Theatre, Brand Art Gallery, Newport Harbor Art Museum, and Bing Theater at USC, to name some. Also look for her family performances at the Los Angeles Zoo, and the children's Imagination Celebration of the Orange County Performing Arts Center.

Discounts
Children/seniors/
students/groups of 15+,
call

LOS ANGELES CLASSICAL BALLET

See press listings for performance locations.
Info: (818) 564-0575   **Fax:** (213) 426-2622
Artistic Director: David Wilcox

The year 1991 was a turning point (so to speak) for the Long Beach Ballet, with its change of name to the Los Angeles Classical Ballet. Despite its new title, the Long Beach Terrace Theater will continue to host some of LACB's popular performances, as well as remain home base for the company's ballet school and studios.

This meat-and-potatoes company presents the canon albeit, with few surprises. If you're looking for the best local-based *Nutcracker* come Santa time, ounce for ounce this is the best bet. There are oodles of special effects with enough frills to please even the most recalcitrant kiddies. The largest native dance company in Southern California, its repertoire, including other classics like *Coppelia*, *A Midsummer Night's Dream* and *Petrushka*, tends to be elaborately designed, with lofty sets and grand costumes. (These ballets are presented in versions created and premiered in the '80s by David Wilcox, Terri Lewis, and Christopher Tabor.)

The minor repertoire boasts miscellaneous classical, neoclassical, and contemporary works ensemble, pas de deux, and solo. But when most folks think of LACB, they still see visions of sugar plums.

LACB has had as one of its most formidable members dancer Helena Ross, the young socially-conscious ballerina who's been as likely to take the *Nutcracker* lead as to teach free classes to underprivileged kids in MacArthur Park. With LACB's financial future in doubt, though, Ms. Ross has taken a leave of absence to join the Vienna Stage Opera Ballet. It is unknown at this time, whether there will be a new schedule for the struggling LACB.

Performances
Vary
Tickets
$14-32
Discounts
Children/seniors/groups
of 20+, call
BO
Varies with location

LOS ANGELES KOREAN FOLK DANCE GROUP

See press listings for performance locations.
Info: (213) 933-9661   **Fax:** (213) 382-7738
Artistic Director: Chang Rok Lee

     One of the great advantages of LA is that you can visit several cultures within a 10-mile radius. For instance, you may sample the Far East anytime this Korean dance and music group performs. Their traditional folk dances are performed in festivals and parades around the city.

     Especially interesting is their percussion selection which integrates the sounds of leather and metal instruments. Metal symbolizes heaven and leather symbolizes earth, while the musicians themselves represent the human element to complete a whole symbolic universe.

     Dancers and other performers include charming, serious youthful members, some as young as four or five.

Performances
  Vary
Tickets
  FREE-$10
BO
  Varies with location
Parking
  Varies with location

LULA WASHINGTON CONTEMPORARY DANCE THEATRE

5179 1/2 West Adams Boulevard
Los Angeles , CA 90016
Info: (213) 936-6591   **Fax:** (213) 671-4572
Artistic Director: Lula Washington
Resident co. in venue of same name—also performs statewide and throughout the U.S. (The January quake damaged their studio considerably. Call for an update.)

     Lula Washington's company is not only the most socially important African-American dance group in Los Angeles, it's the force behind a school that does as much for the future of dance as for its neighborhood. Washington also has the distinction of being the first modern company in LA to purchase its own studio building, a converted Masonic temple that houses several studios and offices. Inside there's a school of dance, a youth performing group called the Children's Jazz Dance Ensemble, and the professional troupe itself.

     In addition to Washington's choreography, the company performs works by such well-known artists as Donald McKayle and Rod Rogers, as well as younger black artists such as Raymond Johnson and Karen McDonald.

     Washington is a major force in African-American art in Los Angeles. Among many other credits, she coordinated the 1984 Olympic Black Dance Festival as part of the Olympic Arts Festival. She has toured her work extensively.

     Washington's dance company can be seen throughout the area; watch for announcements.

Performances
  Vary
Tickets
  $10-25
Discounts
  Groups of seniors/
  students/10+, call
BO
  Check/reserve by mail;
  no exchanges
Parking
  On street

MALASHOCK DANCE & COMPANY

See press listings for performance locations.
Info: (619) 298-3304   **Fax:** (619) 291-6652
Artistic Director: John Malashock

     Founded by former Twyla Tharp star John Malashock, this San Diego-based company may be the most interesting step California has taken in the past decade. The company of five to seven dancers presents a variety of works by Malashock, all of them splendidly theatrical and packing an emotional wallop seldom associated with modern dance. Whether it's a redux of a Carson McCullers-esque milieu or the more abstract postmodernism of one of Malashock's less narrative works, the mission here is to explore the human soul in its many realms.

     Malashock is an archly romantic choreographer in a dance age when romanticism has fallen from grace.

Performances
  Most often Thurs-Sun 8
  pm; Sun 2 pm; fall and
  spring premieres
Tickets
  $8-16
Discounts
  Seniors/students/groups
  of 25+, call the
  managing director at
  (619) 298-3304
BO
  Varies with location
Parking
  Varies with location

However, he has the genius to see that such human, and humane, work has in no way lost its power to touch both women and men.

When in San Diego, the troupe can be seen at the Old Globe and the Lyceum Theatres; they also tour regionally.

Special Features
Open rehearsals

MARGALIT DANCE THEATER COMPANY

See press listings for performance locations.
Info: (310) 471-4941 **Fax:** (310) 476-2538
Artistic Director: Margalit Oved

Margalit Oved creates "danced plays." Her shows are multifarious, emotionally intense and visionary. Formerly a principal dancer in Israel's Imbal Dance Company, and now the director, choreographer, and leading performer of her own touring troupe, her work draws heavily on Arab and Israeli traditions to develop a poetic autobiography of ideas which incorporate multiple forms of theatrical expressions, including modern dance, drums, songs, biblical stories and fairy tales. One of her numbers, "Besamin, the Beauty Without Shoes," tells a variation of the Cinderella story, expressed in movement and music, and combining Middle-Eastern, Mexican, and Flamenco harmonies.

Performances
Tues-Sun 8 pm; Sat-Sun 2 pm
Tickets
$22-30
Discounts
Previews/children/ seniors/students/groups of 10+, call
BO
Varies with location
Parking
Varies with location
Special Features
Open rehearsals

MARTIN DANCERS/DANCNICIANS

See press listings for performance locations.
Info: (213) 386-6299
Artistic Director: Shirley Martin

Shirley Martin's troupe combines elements of theater and bilingual dialogue with eclectic modern dance.

Frequent visitors to such venues as the Inner City Cultural Center (the troupe's home base of sorts for years) and the New Ivar Theatre (ICCC's new Hollywood acquisition), the Martin Dancers/Dancnicians play an important role in bringing disadvantaged youths into the arts. They also perform at the Wilshire Ebell Theater and at sundry schools and fundraisers throughout Southern California.

Performances
Thurs-Sun 7:30 pm, Sat-Sun 3 pm
Tickets
$6-12
Discounts
Previews/children/ seniors/students/groups of 15+, call
BO
Varies with location
Parking
Varies with location
Special Features
Open rehearsals; dancers can take company technique class

METROPOLITAN BALLET OF SAN DIEGO

See press listings for performance locations.
Info: (619) 792-1882
Artistic Director: Ken Nickel

The newest kid on the block in San Diego's dance community is Ken Nickel. In 1993, Nickel, a former principal dancer with the Pittsburgh and Dallas Ballets, joined forces with the American Ballet of San Diego to create the Metropolitan Ballet.

The Metropolitan, which bills itself as the only all-professional ballet company in town, offered its premier performance of *Cinderella* at the Spreckels Theatre in April, 1993. The choreography was by Nickel and the roster of guest artists included Vanessa Harwood, former principal of the National Ballet of Canada, and former Bolshoi principal Galina Shlyapina.

MEXICAN DANCE THEATRE

See press listings for performance locations.
Info: (213) 267-0140
Artistic Director: Miguel Delgado

Mixing it up for some high-spirited kicks, Miguel Delgado's energetic company combines traditional folk dance with contemporary work. The Chicano-Latino performance company, founded in the early '70s, is as comfortable with classic Mexican style as with modern modes that embrace various strains of Latino culture.

Delgado himself, the troupe's charismatic head, is familiar to audiences both as a choreographer and a veteran film-stage-television actor. An Emmy-nominated performer, his film credits include *La Bamba*, *In the Mood*, *Double Agent*, and *Zoot Suit*. He co-starred with Cheech Marin in *Born in East LA* and also showed up in the films *Stones for Ibarra* and *Flatliners*. When he's not on a movie set somewhere, he and his company set up in numerous local venues.

Performances
Thurs-Sat 8 pm, Sat-Sun 2 pm
Tickets
$8-12
Discounts
Previews/children/seniors/students/groups, call
BO
Varies with location
Parking
Varies with location
Special Features
Open rehearsals (with special permission)

MORE ZAP PRODUCTIONS

See press listings for performance locations.
Info: (310) 477-2118 **Fax:** (310) 470-2667
Artistic Director: Michelle Zeitlin

This freelance dance and musical theater company performs in public festivals and events throughout Southern California. A recent show, performed to raise money and consciousness for an environmental organization, included a breathtaking, futuristic ballet set in a toxic-free world of white shades and shapes.

Company director Michelle Zeitlin, a former Joffrey Ballet Concert member and veteran of Michael Bennett's Scandal workshop on Broadway, choreographs shows ranging in length, theme, and character according to the nature of the gala, from full-scale shows with dozens of performers, elaborate sets, lights, special effects and live music to a modest piano solo. The company has also toured in Vienna, Leningrad, Jerusalem, and Tokyo.

Performances
All year
Tickets
$ varies
Discounts
Seniors/groups of 15, call (213) 850-8665
BO
Call (213) 850-8665
Parking
Varies with location

NANNETTE BRODIE DANCE THEATRE

See press listings for performance locations.
Info: (310) 594-8003
Artistic Director: Nannette Brodie

Having narrowed her entourage down to a few choice dancers that included some new blood culled from auditions, Nannette Brodie has a future that bodes well. Focusing on what the choreographer describes as "the human physical reaction to life," Brodie's dances are shaped to many musical styles, traditional to contemporary. Bluegrass is the backdrop for her restaging of the familiar Americana of *The Auction*; Philip Glass's minimalist compositions score Brodie's *Islands of the Blessed*.

Primarily an educational outfit, with many performances in schools and colleges in Orange County and the surrounding area, Nannette Brodie Dance Theatre is among the most active outreach dance organizations in the greater Los Angeles area. She shoes in two to three other performances each year.

Performances
Vary
Tickets
$6-12
BO
Call company line for info
Parking
Varies with location
Special Features
Open rehearsals

ORANGE COUNTY PERFORMING ARTS CENTER See **MUSIC**

PACIFIC AMERICAN BALLET THEATRE, INC.

See press listings for performance locations.
Info: (310) 302-9361
Artistic Director: Mariko

One of a flock of fledgling performing arts groups to spring up in the cultural salad of contemporary Los Angeles, the Pacific American Ballet Theatre was founded expressly to address the still overwhelmingly white profile of ballet in America. A seven-year-old multiethnic ballet company, Pacific American teaches a strict Russian Vaganova curriculum at its resident studio, the Santa Monica Dance Center, and typically performs as a part of the Los Angeles Theatre Center Collaborative, and at the James Armstrong Theatre in the Torrance Civic Center. *Winter War*, a trilogy focusing on the Japanese-American experience, premiered at the Smithsonian Institute as part of a national tour. Other repertory numbers include *Proud Heritage*, a trilogy based on the history of the Southwest, as well as more classical pieces from the likes of *Don Quixote* and *Les Sylphides*. Old warhorses like *The Nutcracker*, *Sleeping Beauty* and *Swan Lake* also get their due.

Mariko, a dancer whose career reaches back to a principal part in Uncle Tom's Cabin and who has shown up in the *Who's Who of American Women*, is the Pacific American Ballet Theatre's artistic director. Cory-Jeanne Murakami, a widely traveled dancer/choreographer whose credits include a recent stint at Robert Redford's Sundance Institute, is the codirector and ballerina for the company.

Performances
Vary
Tickets
$ varies
Discounts
Children/seniors/ students/groups of 20+
BO
Varies with location
Parking
In Torrance, FREE; at LATC $3-5 in parking lot

PACIFIC DANCE ENSEMBLE

See press listings for performance listings.
Info: (310) 839-8083
Artistic Director: Danielle Shapiro

A young contemporary repertory company headed by Danielle Shapiro, Pacific Dance Ensemble is unique in the Los Angeles area in its mission to commission all its works from choreographers. In only a few years together, the group has already commissioned more than 15 pieces, as well as original scores by nearly a dozen composers. The company has also brought interdisciplinary types into its creative fold, encouraging and nurturing collaborations between the dancers and musicians, as well as among visual, literary and intermedia artists.

The goal of all this seed-sowing is to bring to California audiences a new crop of stimulating dances that reflect the varied local culture. If the dancers continue to be as successful in stimulating creators and audiences alike as they have been, the Pacific Dance Ensemble may be a true shot in the arm for local dance. Shapiro's ambition is considerable and her goals daunting, but so far she and her ensemble seem on their toes.

Performances
Vary
Tickets
$8-15
Discounts
Children/seniors/ students/groups of 10+, call
BO
Varies by location
Special Features
Open rehearsals

DANCE

PALOS VERDES BALLET

See press listings for performance locations.
Info: (310) 659-3223
Most performances at Norris Theatre.

With a classical repertoire that includes *Cinderella*, *Coppelia*, *Giselle*, and of course *The Nutcracker*, this decade-old company has lured Bolshoi Ballet stars Alla Khaniashvili-Artuishkina and Vitaly Artushkin to dance leading roles in its performances.

The group performs at the beautiful Norris Theatre and is sometimes seen at the South Bay Center for the Arts, El Camino College, the Wilshire Ebell Theatre, and Royce Hall at UCLA.

Performances
Fri-Sun evenings; Sat-Sun afternoons
Tickets
$10-25
Discounts
Children/seniors/groups
BO
Varies with location
Parking
Varies with location

PARACHEUTE DANCE THEATRE

See press listings for performance locations.
Info: (213) 931-6967 **Fax:** (213) 653-3034
Artistic Director: Jonathan Siegel

Given the vast number of Angelenos mesmerized by the entertainment industry, it's small wonder that even the dance in this company town plays to a Hollywood tune. Paracheute (their spelling) Dance Theatre is the perfect example of how the two worlds interconnect. Basically the vehicle of artistic director Jonathan Siegel and choreographer Cindera Che, this dozen-dancer group makes pop dance for the MTV generation. Hip-hoppin' and boppin' to the likes of Eurythmics, Janet Jackson, Iggy Pop and others, the movement steals from whatever works, be it jazz, funk or hypedup modern.

Siegal is an MTV editor and music-video director whose credits include MC Hammer's "You Can't Touch This," Warrant's "Cherry Pie," and Wilson Phillips' "The Dream Is Still Alive." Dancer/choreographer Che has had her stuff strutted with such notables as Stevie Wonder, Stephanie Mills, and Ben Vareen. She was also the principal dancer with Michael Jackson in "Smooth Criminal."

Performances
Vary
Tickets
$ varies
Special Features
Open rehearsals can be arranged.

PASACAT PHILIPPINE PERFORMING ARTS COMPANY
SAMAHAN PHILIPPINE DANCE COMPANY

See press listings for performance locations.

Pasacat:
Info: (619) 477-3383
Artistic Director: Anamaria Labao Cabato

Samahan:
Info: (619) 444-7528
Artistic Director: Lolita Carter

These rival companies probably won't like being listed together, but there's strength in numbers. Both troupes present the various traditional Filipino folk dances with live accompaniment on traditional instruments and in authentic costumes. Both are important to the preservation of folk dance traditions and to the continuing cultural education of young Filipinos (and young everybody).

Samahan's concerts, for example, have included southern Philippine stylized dances, which have a decided Spanish flavor, and rituals and ceremonials of the northern mountain tribes. The dances are exotic and colorful in both sight and sound, particularly in the use of reed instruments and gamelan gongs.

PERFUMES OF ARABY DANCE CO.

See press listings for performance locations.
Info: (818) 893-9019
Artistic Director: Diane Webber

  Okay, so the name is a little extravagant. On the other hand, what better way to set the tone for an art form that borders on high kitsch? Founded in the mid-1960s and still claiming to be the longest continuously extant troupe of belly dancers in the United States, this group of 12 certainly gets around. They're as likely to wiggle their way into the laps of the revelers at the annual Renaissance Pleasure Faire as to show up at an international dance festival or some Palm Spring private soiree. Combining traditional Middle Eastern belly dancing with more modern American interpretations of the form, the group puts on an annual concert and, in general, gives a gutsy performance.

Performances
 Sat-Sun 2 and 7:30 pm
Tickets
 $10-25
Discounts
 Previews/children/
 seniors/groups of 10+,
 call
BO
 Varies with location
Parking
 Varies with location
Special Features
 Open rehearsals

RHAPSODY IN TAPS

See press listings for performance locations.
Info: (714) 838-3318 **Fax:** (714) 838-4660
Artistic Director: Linda Sohl-Donnell

  Tap Master Eddie Brown heads this five-dancer, five-musician touring group specializing in rhythm tap and jazz music. Besides the venerable Brown, whose career spans five decades, the company has gigged with the likes of Sandman Sims, Bunny Briggs, Fred Strickler, Charles "Honi" Coles, Leon Collins, Steve Condos, and Jimmy Slyde. And, if all that name-dropping doesn't floor you, in 1990 Rhapsody in Taps got to work out with Gregory Hines, who created new choreography for the company.

  Among the premiere tap groups in the country, Rhapsody in Taps has been seen in LA at the Dorothy Chandler Pavilion and in New York at Lincoln Center's Out Of Doors festival. The group performs annual seasons in Los Angeles at the Japan America Theatre, and in Costa Mesa at Orange Coast College. Linda Sohl-Donnell, artistic director and choreographer, created the dance for Little Richard's music video Grand Slam and worked on the 1989 film *Tap* with Hines and Sammy Davis, Jr.

ROSE POLSKY AND DANCERS

See press listings for performance locations.
Info: (310) 542-3260
Artistic Director: Rose Polsky

  First establishing herself in Los Angeles as a soloist of note after moving here in 1985, Polsky went on to build a company to showcase her choreography. A relative purist, Polsky goes in for emotional and often visceral portraiture. She's a regular feature of the best festivals and most experimental venues, taking on large psychological or sociological topics and translating them into human scale. There's little evidence in Polsky's work of modern dance's recent preoccupation with cool and emotionless movement. She reaches both back and forward to a time when modern dance preferred to evoke feelings. She's also very in touch with the plagues of the modern age, from AIDS to the environment. Ask to be put on the mailing list.

Performances
 Fri-Sun 8 pm; Sun 2 pm
Tickets
 $8-12
Discounts
 Children/seniors/
 students
BO
 Varies with location
Parking
 Varies with location
Special Features
 Open rehearsals by
 invitation

RUDY PEREZ PERFORMANCE ENSEMBLE

See press listings for performance locations.
Info: (213) 931-3604
Artistic Director: Rudy Perez

Los Angeles has never properly appreciated the treasure represented by Rudy Perez. A veteran of New York's famous Judson Dance Theatre, Perez first became widely known during the '60s for his solo work and has often been credited as one of the first forces of postmodernist dance. In the early 1980s, he moved West and quickly established himself as a West Coast force while remaining a national performer.

Not only is Perez's choreography among the most vibrant contemporary work around, he is widely hailed as a master teacher. Mesmerizing, insightful and unfailingly rigorous in its technique, Perez's choreography incorporates elements of theater and performance art. Indeed, some of his more post-postmodern works would be more aptly called performance art, although precisely detailed movement is always integral to the creative whole.

An avid supporter of his fellow artists in other mediums—and known as an outspoken arts activist—Perez usually works in collaboration with prominent visual artists and musicians ordering original scores and sometimes performing to live music. The company has performed as part of the Los Angeles Festival and appeared at New York's Bessie Schoemberg Theatre.

When you see his performances announced, call immediately for tickets. Possibilities in LA are: the Japan America Theatre, UCLA, LACE (Los Angeles Contemporary Exhibitions), Highways, and the LA Photography Center.

Performances
Fri-Sun 8 pm, Sun 2 pm or 3 pm
Tickets
$10-15
Discounts
Children/seniors/ students
BO
Check/ reserve by phone; or purchase at the door
Parking
Varies with location
Special Features
Open rehearsals, classes, lecture-demos

SAMAHAN PHILIPPINE DANCE COMPANY See **Pasacat Philippine Performing Arts Company**

SAN DIEGO FOUNDATION FOR PERFORMING ARTS

It was a bleak day for San Diego in October, 1992, when the San Diego Foundation for Performing Arts announced that neither pleas to the community nor a benefit performance by the Lyon Opera Ballet had raised sufficient funds to cover the Foundation's shortfall, and thus the distinguished 11-year-old dance presenter was forced to close up shop.

The Foundation was the doyenne presenter of major dance companies from around the world, such as Martha Graham, Alvin Ailey, Twyla Tharp, Bill T. Jones and, on the classical side, the Kirov and American Ballet Theatre. Although other organizations picked up some of the Foundation's 1992-93 roster, none has emerged as the heir apparent in consistently presenting dance troupes of international renown. The Foundation is attempting to raise the money to get back on its toe shoes. All dance lovers must ardently hope that it succeeds. Perhaps you'd like to help. Better yet, perhaps by the time you read this, they'll be back on their feet!

SHIRLEY KIRKES BALLET CO.

See press listings for performance locations.
Info & Rsvn: (310) 820-5395
Artistic Director: Shirley Kirkes

Shirley Kirkes emphasizes a simple, straightforward storytelling ballet addressing themes even younger audiences (and dancers) can identify with, such as homelessness and fated love. SKBC performs at a number

Performances
Vary
Tickets
FREE-$15
Discounts
Seniors/students

of local colleges, auditoriums, and theaters, including the Morgan-Wixson. A recent video of their homelessness ballet, "Where Angels Live and Die," is available in schools and libraries nationwide.

BO
Varies with location
Parking
Varies with location

SHRINE AUDITORIUM See MUSIC

SILAYAN—PHILIPPINE AMERICAN DANCE CO.

See press listings for performance locations.
Info: (213) 384-9539
Artistic Director: Dulce Capadocia

The ethnic-specific performing groups in the Los Angeles area are too numerous even to begin to count. And even if you could begin, chances are you'd miss the majority of highly-trained and professional companies, simply because they seldom venture out of their home communities, let alone into the mainstream venues and press. Silayan, Philippine American Dance Company, unlike many of their peers, is an exception.

Performing traditional folk and other types of work, this group appears throughout the greater Los Angeles area and in Europe. They present an annual summer concert and are most likely to be spotted during such specialized celebrations as Asian Pacific Heritage Month.

Performances
Summer, Fri-Sun 8 pm, Sun 2 pm
Tickets
$10-25 (sometimes FREE)
Discounts
Children/seniors/ students/groups of 25+, call
BO
Varies with location
Parking
Varies with location

SINAY BALLET

See press listings for performance locations.
Info: (213) 654-8620 **Rsvn:** (213) 933-7069 **Fax:** (213) 380-1710
Artistic Director: Florence Sinay

Florence Tsu Sinay was born in China and trained in New York at, among other places, the Joffrey Ballet. She toured internationally with the Imperial Japanese Dancers, Le Ballet de Paris, and Le Grands Ballet Canadiens. Now the co-owner and ballet director of Danceworks Studio in West Hollywood, Sinay has choreographed more than 40 works in the past decade. Her ten-member contemporary ballet company performs these works, set either to familiar classical and jazz selections or new music. Her company can be seen at her own studio and other theaters such as the Morgan-Wixson or Barnsdall Gallery Theatre.

Performances
Fri-Sun 8 pm, Sat-Sun 2 pm
Tickets
$8-12
Discounts
Children/seniors/ students/groups, call
BO
Varies with location
Parking
Varies with location
Special Features
Open rehearsals for Donors only

SOLERA FLAMENCO

See press listings for performance locations.
Info: (619) 281-8605
Artistic Director: Yaelisa

Yaelisa (artistic director) and flamenco guitarist Bruce Patterson (musical director), debuted this small company in 1990. Yaelisa, who goes by one name, was the daughter of a flamenco artist and grew up amidst intense vocals and clicking heelwork.

Yaelisa has taken her company in new directions by combining traditional flamenco with dance theater. She has also created full length theater works with dance, theater, poetry, and contemporary themes at the core. A collaboration with John Malashock of Malashock Dance & Company produced a flamenco-based story-dance about a tragic jealousy between brothers. She and her band of dancers can be seen at special arts events as well as at the

Performances
Vary
Tickets
$8-20
Discounts
Children/seniors/ students
BO
Varies with location
Parking
Varies with location

Lyceum, local San Diego restaurants, in the dance series at the Fountain Theatre in Los Angeles, and at other small venues throughout Southern California.

SUSHI PERFORMANCE AND VISUAL ARTS

See press listings for performance locations.
Info & Rsvn: (619) 235-8466
A performing arts presenter for a variety of arts genres.

Lynn Schuette is the creative mind behind Sushi, a space where artists perform, dance, exhibit, create, and collaborate. Since its inception in 1980, Schuette has made Sushi a mainstay for out-of-the-mainstream expression in San Diego.

Sushi has steadily presented innovative and high quality contemporary dance from such talent as Bebe Miller, Joe Goode, Goat Island, and Molissa Fenley. The Danse Fraiche series brings several experimental troupes and soloists to the city within a few weeks; in April of 1992 and March of 1993, Sushi hosted the San Diego leg of the highly reputed Black Choreographers Moving project, a three-city effort in which black choreographers and companies participate in symposia, classes, and educational activities. Best of all, the participants, such as Donald Byrd and Joanna Haigood, performed in concert at the Lyceum Space at Horton Plaza.

In 1993, Sushi had to vacate its long-time downtown performance space. However, the indomitable Lynn Schuette has not cut back the new fall schedule of Danse Fraiche and a spring Neofest. Until it finds a new permanent home, Sushi will rent space at various venues throughout San Diego, including St. Cecilia's. Call for current performance locations.

Performances
Vary
Tickets
$12-15
Discounts
Groups of 20+, call
BO
Mon-Fri 9 am-4 pm; Sat noon-4 pm; AE/MC/V/ check/Art Tix; reserve by mail; flexible exchange policy; subscription program
Parking
Varies with location

SWINGBRAZIL DANCE COMPANY

See press listings for performance locations.
Info: (213) 957-4952
Owner: Max Junior

Brazilian dance means more than samba to the folks at SwingBrazil. Resplendent with the snazzy getups North Americans have come to associate with the hot-blooded hoofing of this tropical country, SwingBrazil delivers the entertainment goods without skimping on artistic or cultural authenticity. One dozen strong, this melange of Americans and Brazilians covers the Brazilian music and dance gamut. That means folk, jazz, and contemporary styles of choreography, from the *Xaxado* and *Lundun* to the *Candomble* to the *Maracatu* and the *Afoxe*. In addition to these northeastern social dances, Afro-Brazilian ritual dances, ceremonial, and *carnaval* dances, there's also the more familiar martial arts dance known as *Capoeira* and, lest we forget, the *Lambada*. And yes, this group also does a mean samba. It is, after all, the Brazilian national dance.

TERRI LEWIS DANCE ENSEMBLE

See press listings for performance locations.
Info: (818) 798-9853
Artistic Director: Terri Lewis

A chamber ballet company with six to eight dancers, the Terri Lewis Dance Ensemble follows in traditional footsteps. Their work ranges from simple storytelling interludes to slightly less narrative-bound classical on pointe pieces. Lewis, a former soloist with the Colorado Ballet and the Nuremberg Ballet, creates most of the choreography herself concentrating on new ballets centered on age-old themes and mythologies.

Performances
Sat 2:30 and 8 pm
Tickets
$6-10
Discounts
Children/seniors/ students/groups of 8+, call; also discounts through the Dance Resource Center
BO
Reserve by phone
Parking
Varies with location
Special Features
Open rehearsals

TEYE SA THIOSANNE AFRICAN DANCE COMPANY

See press listings for performance locations.
Info: (619) 975-0092   **Rsvn:** (619) 296-5224
Artistic Director: Bernard Thomas

Teye Sa Thiosanne, San Diego's African dance company, specializes in exuberant African dance and drumming. Performances feature infectious, pulsing polyrythmic beats, calls, and authentic costumes, along with high-energy dancing that reflects West African traditions of Gambia, Guinea, Senegal, and Liberia.

The troupe picked up the beat in 1989, with director Bernard Thomas and associate director Aminisha Cunningham. Besides performances, the group holds workshops for adults and kids. But dancing and drumming are the main gig.

Performances
Vary
Tickets
$12-15
Discounts
Children/seniors/ students/groups of 15+, call info
BO
Varies with location
Parking
Varies with location
Special Features
Open rehearsals

TINA GERSTLER / DANCEWORKS

See press listings for performance locations.
Info: (213) 930-0115
Artistic Director: Tina Gerstler

This local choreographer paints intelligent portraits of the modern woman in crisis. Trod upon by the usual vicissitudes of romance and weighed down by the ills of the universe, her anti-heroines exude a steely resolve. The sister of poet Amy, Tina Gerstler frequently choreographs feminist scenarios in which the woman-subject courageously slams the door, Nora-like, behind her.

Gerstler incorporates a variety of performance modes into her dances. The written/spoken word is used to oppose or counterpoint movement, just as performance-art like transitions provide bridges between pure dance segments. Gerstler leaps again and again into the breach, taking on the plight of her gender.

Performance sites vary but include the Japan America Theatre, Loyola Marymount, and UCLA.

Performances
Thurs-Sun 8 pm, Sun 2:30 pm
Tickets
$8-20
Discounts
Children/seniors/ students
BO
Reserve by phone
Parking
Varies with location
Special Features
Open rehearsals sometimes

UCLA DANCE DEPARTMENT

Dance Building
405 Hilgard, Room 200
Los Angeles, CA 90024
Info: (310) 825-3951 **Rsvn:** (310) 825-2101
     This is the premier non-company training ground for Los Angeles performers and choreographers, turning out a wide range of talent. The program follows an admirably diverse approach to dance, artistically and academically. Headed by scholar and one-time Los Angeles Festival mover and shaker Judy Mitoma, the disciplines range from contemporary Western styles to the so-called world dance. Not limited to the politically correct or ethnically-oriented disciplines, this enclave is also a force in producing modern dance and experimental practitioners. Witness the performance art antics of alums such as The Shrimps' Martin Kersels or the sly humor of dancer-performer Melinda Ring.
     Call (310) 825-3951 to request a Calendar of Events. Also see **UCLA School of the Arts** in **MUSIC**.

Performances
  Vary
Tickets
  $ varies
Discounts
  Seniors/students
BO
  Hrs call/AE/MC/V/ reserve by mail, TicketMaster
Location
  Enter off Sunset Blvd, between Veteran and Hilgard
Parking
  On premises, $5

UCSD UNIVERSITY EVENTS

See press listings for performance locations.
Info: (619) 534-4090   **Rsvn:** (619) 534-6467
     University Events was the first to foot Lar Lubovich and company on their bill before it became a household name. It was the same story for Paul Taylor and Twyla Tharp. Susan Marshall, David Gordon Pick-Up, Donald Byrd and numerous other contemporary choreographers of mid-size companies have toed the line for UE at Mandeville Auditorium on the UCSD campus.
     Each year you can count on University Events to enroll the best dance in town that's not being booked elsewhere. Over the past 20 years, they've sidestepped from major and up-and-coming ballet troupes to multidisciplinary and multicultural efforts along the lines of dance and world music and ethnic dance-theater productions.
     Following the demise of The Foundation for the Performing Arts, which was San Diego's foremost presenter of large dance companies, University Events picked up a portion of that series and will be presenting some concerts at the Spreckels Theatre in downtown San Diego.

Performances
  Vary
Tickets
  $12-25
Discounts
  children/seniors/ students/groups of 20+, call
BO
  Tues-Fri 10 am-5 pm; open 1 hr prior to show MC/V/check/ reserve by mail-call,TicketMaster; subscription program
Parking
  Varies with location

WESTSIDE ACADEMY OF DANCE

1711 Steward Street
Santa Monica, CA 90404
Info: (310) 828-2018 **Rsvn:** (310) 828-6211
Performance space and school.
     Why are there so few venues for dance in Los Angeles? Less than a decade ago, experimental houses flourished, creating a quasi-Bohemia filled with lofts and rehearsal rooms downtown. But recent hard times have driven all but a few into dormancy. Even at the best of times, there are too few spaces, making dance among the most poorly presented of the arts in LA.
     The Westside Academy of Dance is one of a small number of surviving facilities that successfully teach and present dance. The Academy showcases the work of local choreographers as well as their guest artists on mixed bill evenings.
     The airy studio setting boasts an accommodating floor with rudimentary theatrical lighting and reasonably comfortable risers—sort of an upscale recital setting. It's not

Performances
  Vary
Tickets
  Vary
Location
  Off Santa Monica (10) Fwy, exit Centinela; San Diego (405) Fwy, exit Olympic
Parking
  On premises, FREE after 5 pm; on street

luxury, but anybody who follows concert dance in California
has seen terpsichoreans take to far more rickety boards.

WILTERN THEATRE See **MUSIC**

CLUBS

INTRODUCTION TO CLUBS

By Mitzi Shore

During the 20 years I have been operating The Comedy Store on the Sunset Strip, clubs have opened and closed, coffeehouses have come and gone—and come back again. Rockabilly was The Next Big Thing for a nanosecond in 1983. Did punk rock last even that long? The Comedy Store opened in 1972 when hold-over hippies were still frequenting the shops and restaurants on the Strip, and music clubs like the Troubadour, the Whisky, and the Roxy flourished.

The Comedy Store had its beginning as a hangout for Vegas acts such as Redd Foxx, Flip Wilson, and Sammy Shore who would come to the club and work out between gigs. I realized that the new vanguard of fresh comics was being shut out because the old guard ruled the stage time. So I decided to initiate a new format. For the first time, a comedy club featured an all stand-up program. No musical acts, no variety acts, just pure continuous stand-up comedy all night long. Soon the Store began to attract young comics like Ed Begley Jr., Steve Landesberg, and Craig T. Nelson.

In 1972, Johnny Carson and "The Tonight Show" moved from New York to Burbank. A wave of talent coordinators, agents, and bookers soon followed to scour the music and comedy clubs for performers. Before long, the word was out. The Comedy Store was a hotbed of budding comic talent attracting fresh faced comics from all over the country—Jay Leno from Massachusetts, David Letterman from Indiana, and Jimmy Walker from New York, to name a few. On any given night Robin Williams, Garry Shandling, Andy Kaufman and Gabe Kaplan could be found holding court before sold out crowds.

The comedy world was exploding, and The Comedy Store had the names to prove it. There was Richard Pryor recording albums live from The Store; Whoopie Goldberg showcasing her unique talents for an audience which included Jack Nicholson, Barbra Streisand, Lily Tomlin, and Steven Spielberg; Howie Mandel, in LA for a carpet sales convention, going onstage on amateur night on a dare; David Letterman working seven nights a week as the M.C. of the Original Room shows; and Pauly Shore running the kitchen of the Westwood Comedy Store at age 14.

While all this was going on the comedy scene, the singer/songwriters who formed the so-called Southern California rock movement were hanging out and playing the music clubs. The list of pop and rock acts that have sprung from Los Angeles clubs seems endless—the Beach Boys, the Righteous Brothers, the Doors, the Kinks, Buffalo Springfield, The Eagles, Joni Mitchell, James Taylor, Randy Newman, and lots of other "new" groups.

Today at any one time, Los Angeles alone can boast about 250 clubs of all sorts, but that number doesn't adequately reflect the transitory quality of the club scene. Many clubs ride into town high on the crest of a trend, packed every night to the gills, even turning people away at the door. Six months later, some of them disappear. Coffeehouses are back with entertainment of all types—music both plugged-in and unplugged, poetry readings, performance art, you name it. LA also attracts its fair share of jazz and more eclectic forms, too. Big jazz names such as McCoy Tyner, Elvin Jones, and other artists of the first rank are constantly passing through, and local jazz artists such as Charlie Hayden and Branford Marsalis give audiences their best at Lunaria, Vine St. Bar & Grill, Catalina Bar & Grill, the Jazz Bakery.

Through the years, it's been the legendary clubs that have been able to ride the inevitable ups and downs that prevail in such a fickle business—The Comedy Store, the Improv, the Coach House, Vine St. Bar & Grill, the Whisky, the Roxy, the Palomino, and, of course, the Troubadour. The Comedy Store celebrated its 20th anniversary in 1992. Through those 20 years of change, certain things have remained constant. The Store provides a safe workshop environment for comedians to hone their craft. The Los Angeles audiences continue to encourage and support. The Sunset Strip is still exciting.

As for the next 20 years? "You ain't seen nothin' yet!"

Mitzi Shore, owner of the Los Angeles Comedy Store, has been called the "Queen of Comedy" and the "Godmother of Comics." Her Sunset Strip landmark club has several stages highlighting comics with varying levels of experience. She still watches every newcomer's act to determine which stage they are best suited to.

ALLIGATOR LOUNGE

3321 Pico Boulevard
Santa Monica, CA 90405
Info: (310) 449-1844 **Rsvn:** (310) 449-1844
Fax: (310) 449-1842
Restaurant/nightclub; seats 150: 100 at tables, 50 at bar; food served during sets; no reservations necessary; 21 and over.

Westside nightclub-goers might remember this space as "B.B.C.," a trendy, neo-'70s dance club *du jour* with mirrored walls, flashing disco lights, and a DJ spinning funky, top-40 mixes. Now under new ownership, and after major reconstructive surgery, this club is a whole 'nother reptile. The draw at the Alligator Lounge—at least on weeknights—is not the dance floor but the stage.

This comfortable bistro-like set up offers a varied menu of live music vacillating between easy-going, jazz/cabaret sounds and the "hard" stuff, Wednesday through Sunday.

There's nothing showy about the place, and the modest stage hugs a black curtain backdrop. Architecturally, the only attempts at a "decor" are red-painted walls and the "Don't feed or molest alligators" poster.

The acoustics come in loud (but thankfully, not too loud) and clear. Sightlines are obstructed by two wooden pillars in the center of the room, but if you can avoid these, you'll be sitting pretty.

Though both the ambiance and the crowd fluxes somewhat with the music, the space remains a comfortable listen-and-dine spot. A complete Cajun and "California cuisine" menu is offered in addition to the full bar. Sunday night is Cajun music night, when tables are cleared off the floor to make room for you to kick up your feet.

There's no trouble spotting this place on Pico, just West of Centinela. The entrance calls out loudly with a colorful mural.

Performances
Wed-Sun evenings; service during sets
Cost or Cover Charge
$ varies; checks
Dining
Cajun; food: $7-15; drinks: $3; individual tables
Reservations
At door
Location
Centinela exit off of Santa Monica (10) Fwy
Parking
On street

ANASTASIA'S ASYLUM

1028 Wilshire Boulevard
Santa Monica, CA 90401
Info: (310) 394-7113
Cafe/coffeehouse; seats 70 at tables, 4 at espresso bar; reservations not necessary; food served; all ages.

During the Russian Revolution the reigning Romanov family was executed, but, as the story goes, daughter Anastasia supposedly escaped. Some say she spent a number of years in an asylum, then came to LA (a natural enough progression!). So, a coffeehouse was opened for her royal highness.

Anastasia's Asylum makes a welcome change from spots charging covers and two-drink minimums. Here's a coffeehouse with free entertainment, lots of refreshments (yes, of course, coffee), a forest of vegetarian munchies—and all in a kind of quasi-European-style funky Santa Monica setting.

In spite of its small size, Anastasia's keeps three bands a night brewing seven nights a week. There are the ubiquitous open mike nights, acoustic R&B groups, country rock, and some folk, jazz, poetry, and performance art. Call to find out what's on tap.

All ages and types will feel comfortable here, even unescorted women. The "meat market" scene doesn't suit this vegetarian set up. When not providing entertainment, Anastasia's is still a welcome asylum for a peaceful breakfast and lunch.

Performances
Mon-Sun usually every hr beginning at 8 pm; service during sets
Cost or Cover Charge
No cover; 1 drink min; MC/V/check
Dining
Vegetarian continental; food: $4-7; drinks: $2-3.75; individual tables
Location
Off Santa Monica (10) Fwy; at 11th and Wilshire Blvd
Parking
On premises, FREE; valet, $3; on street

ART'S BAR

2611 De La Vina
Santa Barbara, CA 93105
Info: (805) 569-0052
Accommodates 50 for live blues and rock; seats 10 at the bar, 40 at tables; no reservations; snacks only; 21 and over.

       One of Santa Barbara's best kept secrets—an old-fashioned neighborhood joint, located away from the action of lower State Street—Art's features good local blues and rock bands. It's comfortable, it's casual, and on weekends, it's jumpin'! Find it near upper State Street going toward the Mission. Art's is most popular with the local over-21 crowd that comes to play pool and listen to the music.

Performances
  Wed-Sat 9 pm
Dining
  Complimentary snacks; drinks: $1-4; individual tables
Cost or Cover Charge
  No cover; MC/V
Location
  Between Constance and Alzmar
Parking
  On street

ATLAS BAR AND GRILL

3760 Wilshire Boulevard
Los Angeles, CA 90010
Rsvn: (213) 380-8400
Supper club seats 300 patrons; jazz, cabaret, performance art; reservations recommended; food served during performances; all ages.

       The first thing you'll notice at Atlas is the decor. Large and rectangular with a high ceiling and metal wall decorations (sunbursts smile down from the far ends of the room), Atlas resembles a gilded airplane hangar. At the eastern end of the building is a very long bar; to the west, the bandstand. In between east and west stretches a small football field of seating. This is a "to-be-seen" spot, although the lighting is too dim to be seeing much more than everyone dressed in requisite black.

       Atlas is essentially a restaurant with live background music and entertainment Tuesday through Saturday. The dinner menu changes constantly, riding the ebb and flow of city trends. Food alone will run you anywhere from $9.50 to $18 per person. Be prepared to wait a while for your table—even with a reservation.

       Perhaps the performers know they serve as human audio wallpaper for hungry diners. Nonetheless, an eclectic schedule that includes cabaret singers, small jazz bands, Latin outfits, light rock, and that nebulous "other category," gets subjected to one of the loudest and most distracting audiences anywhere. Black/Note is sort of the "resident" group performing Tuesdays and weekends. I'm not sure if it's the audience's fault, or the fault of the acoustics. In any event, this is not the best place for serious music fans. But those desserts...!

Performances
  Wed-Sat 9 pm; service during sets
Cost or Cover Charge
  Cover varies; no cover Tues and weekends; no min; AE/MC/V
Dining
  Food from around the world; $9.50-18; individual tables
Reservations
  Reserve at door, by phone
Location
  Adjacent to the Wiltern Theatre at Wilshire and Western
Parking
  On premises, $4

AT MY PLACE

       If you haven't hit town lately, and plan to head to this old Santa Monica haunt, you're out of luck. Owner Jim Arthur closed the decade-old music spot when artistic director Matt Kramer split. One of Santa Monica's most popular nightclubs, and one that predated the city's cultural and commercial renaissance of the past few years, At My Place offered diverse live music over the years from musical legends such as Stevie Wonder, Jackson Brown and Etta James, and comedy from the likes of Arsenio Hall, Joan Rivers, and Jerry Seinfeld. The jazz artists who played were usually too big (pop-oriented) for the average jazz club, but not big enough for the concert hall. Fusion players and purveyors of hyphenated jazz of every stripe populated and popularized the schedule.

At My Place will be missed. It remains to be seen how Nightwinds, the club now in this location, succeeds with jazz devotees in its place.

THE BAKED POTATO

3787 Cahuenga Boulevard
North Hollywood, CA 91604
Info: (818) 980-1615   **Rsvn:** (818) 980-1615
and
26 East Colorado Boulevard
Pasadena, CA 91105
Rsvn: (818) 564-1122 or 564-1720
Cafe/nightclub; North Hollywood location seats less than 100, Pasadena serves 150; reservations for six or more; food served during sets; all ages.

That's "potato" without an e. This funky little joint, owned by keyboardist Don Randi, is the LA capital of fusion and hyphenated jazz. In the original North Hollywood location, the walls are wood panelled but you'd never know it, buried as they are under a blizzard of 8 X 10 glossies of most of the entertainers who have incubated here. Lee Ritenour, Larry Carlton, and the Yellowjackets all got their jump starts here. One note of acoustical caution: the bands that play the BP like the music loud enough to jar the fillings in your teeth.

Joe, the garrulous doorman, claims the club seats 100 people—it's probably more like 80. If you're particularly sensitive to cigarette smoke, stay away. If you want to eat, come early; once the music has started and the cigarettes are lit, you won't be able to taste (or see) a thing.

So many Japanese visitors patron the BP that Randi will soon open a Tokyo arm of the club. In the meantime, he recently opened a branch somewhat closer to home—in Pasadena.

The larger Pasadena location is about three times the size of the original, and accommodates 150 at tables, booths, and barstools, none of which is more than 25 feet from the stage. Watch for Latin, salsa, R&B, and straight-ahead groups here.

Food is served at both locations. Guess what kind! There are 20 varieties of baked potatoes (from $4.75 to $12). They come in the size of small footballs and play home field to every combination of garnish known to man. In Pasadena, the menu is more extensive: pasta, salads, chicken, and steak can be ordered, and the prices aren't bad.

North Hollywood:
Performances
   Mon-Sun 9:30, 11:30;
   service during sets
Cost or Cover Charge
   $10; drink min at bar,
   enforced if not dining;
   check/AE/MC/V
Dining
   20 varieties of potato;
   $4.75-12
Reservations
   Reserve at door
Location
   Near Lankershim and
   Ventura Blvds
Parking
   On premises, FREE; on
   street

Pasadena:
Performances
   Sun, Mon-Thurs 8:30
   pm, 10:30 pm; Fri-Sat
   9:30 pm, 11 pm; Mon,
   Fri matinees
Cost or Cover Charge
   $5-10; AE/MC/V
Dining
   Extended menu; steak,
   chicken, salad; food:
   $4.75-12; drinks: $4+
Reservations
   At door, by phone
Location
   Old Town Pasadena
Parking
   On street; municipal
   structure on Green and
   Fairoaks, $2-3.50

THE BAKERY ON MELROSE

7261 Melrose Avenue
Los Angeles, CA 90046
Info: (213) 934-4493   **Rsvn:** (213) 934-4493
Bakery by day, jazz spot by weekend night; 28 seats; no reservations; no liquor; food served; all non-smoking; all ages.

Boy do I wish this place had been here when I lived around the corner! By day, it's a neighborhood bakery and coffee spot where the staff knows the customers by name. On Friday and Saturday nights the music begins and the place really starts cooking.

There's an upscale flavor to both nights, which (unfortunately for the bakers) are often populated by "dates

Performances
   Fri-Sat 9 pm-12 am;
   service during sets
Cost or Cover Charge
   $5 min, enforced if not
   dining; check/Disc/MC/V
Dining
   Bakery treats: European
   tortes, croissants and
   pastries, cookies,
   coffees; $.95-4.25;
   drinks: $.85-3; individual
   tables

on diets." For non-calorie counters, there are divine cakes, tortes, and cookies to order up with the house espresso (be sure to give in at least to the mocha cookie!).

The jazz solos, duos, and trios occasionally make room for "world-ethnic" and Brazilian music. There may even be a vocalist the night you go, or perhaps a traditional Peruvian folk trio.

Come by after dinner on Melrose, or even after the theater. The atmosphere is easy, the treats are scrumptious, and nothing costs much dough. No liquor, though—not even in the pastries. The only negative? The usual problem parking on Melrose—there is none! (What a good excuse to walk off the mocha cookie!) Read the parking restriction signs carefully.

Reservations
Not accepted
Location
On the Melrose Strip, 3 blocks W of La Brea
Parking
On street

BARNSDALL ARTISTS CAFE See THEATER

BIRDLAND WEST

105 West Broadway
Long Beach, CA 90802
Info: (310) 436-9341   **Rsvn:** (310) 436-9341 or (213) 432-2004
Fax: (310) 495-8498
Nightclub/bar seating 200 for jazz and blues; reservations recommended; food served during sets; separate non-smoking section; 18 and over.

Long Beach's major jazz club, Birdland West originally offered jazz and blues five nights a week, but now turns Tuesday nights over to comedians. Local blues players are scattered through the monthly calendar. This upstairs club is owned and operated by drummer Al Williams, who leads his own quintet Thursdays. A bebop drummer, Williams' bands are always straight ahead musically. Wednesday nights could be called Talent Deserving of Wider Recognition night. It's the time for local players on the way up, like the Black/Note Quintet (who are probably there by now) or singer Andrea Palm.

Friday and Saturday nights are reserved for the big guns. Fusioneers like Brandon Fields, pop-jazz players like Bernard Ighner, Wayne Henderson, Roy Ayers, and Fattburger all do a turn at BWest If you're lucky, you'll get to hear the occasional mainstream jazz artists like salsero Poncho Sanchez or Eddie Harris.

If you're coming for dinner (American, Cajun, and Italian specialties) be sure to make a reservation. The cover depends on who's playing.

Performances
Tues-Sun 8:30 pm-10:30 pm; service during sets
Cost or Cover Charge
$ varies; 2 drink min; MC
Dining
American, Italian, Cajun; $11.95- 17.95; individual tables; reserved tables; smoking/non-smoking
Reservations
Reserve at door, by phone, fax, TicketMaster
Location
S on Long Beach (710) Downtown exit Broadway; corner of Pine at Broadway
Parking
Valet; on street available

BLUE SALOON

4657 Lankersheim Boulevard
North Hollywood, CA 91602
Info: (818) 766-4644
Saloon; seating at bar and tables for 100; no food served; no reservations; 21 and over.

This North Hollywood saloon is one of the friendliest in town. You're bound to make new acquaintances in a jiffy, promises owner Blue Shaw. Shaw puts his money where your mouth is: If the bartender doesn't know your face, you get your first drink on the house. The country-like bar has been around since 1951 and a decidedly '50s coziness still predominates. Even the stage occasionally hosts names from that era, such as Sleepy LaBeef and Rose Maddox. But "cozy" doesn't mean dull and old-fashioned. This stage heats up with some '90s country, blues, and rock 'n' roll from some good bands. The

Performances
Mon-Sun 9:30 pm
Cost or Cover Charge
$5; no drink min
Location
At Riverside and Lankersheim
Parking
On premises, FREE; on street

crowd tends to be way under 35 and invariably jeans-clad. Between sets try a round of pool.

Parking is available both in the lot for free and on the street. The cover is about $5, and there's no drink minimum.

B STREET CALIFORNIA GRILL & JAZZ BAR

425 West B Street
San Diego, CA 92101
Info: (619) 236-1707
Restaurant and jazz club seats 250 at tables, 50 at the bar for jazz and blues; reservations recommended but not necessary; food and liquor served during sets; separate non-smoking section; 21 and over.

This local watering hole, frequented by single young professionals, was voted "Best Happy Hour in San Diego."

The entertainment line-up includes jazz in all its incarnations (played five nights a week), reggae, and blues. It's really more of a restaurant than a bar. The diverse menu announces salads, fish, pasta, gourmet pizza, and lots of appetizers. B Street is located near the train station downtown.

Performances
Mon-Thurs 7:30 pm-11:30 pm; Fri-Sat 9 pm-1 am; service during sets
Cost or Cover Charge
$2-5, 2 drink min, enforced if not dining; AE/MC/V
Dining
California cuisine; $8.95-18.95; drinks: $2-3.50; individual tables; reserved tables; smoking/non-smoking
Reservations
Reserve at door, by phone
Location
B St at Columbia; 1 block from train
Parking
On street

Y || (&)

CAFE BECKETT

Unfortunately this popular spot burned down in 1992; no information on a new location as of this writing. Call (213) 462-6844 to find out about performances being rerouted to other locations.

CANNIBAL BAR

Catamaran Resort Hotel
3999 Mission Boulevard
San Diego, CA 92609
Info: (619) 488-1081   **Rsvn:** (619) 488-1081
Fax: (619) 488-1619
Cabaret/bar, mostly rock 'n' roll; seats 350; reservations recommended; food served during sets; 21 and over.

San Diego's Cannibal Bar in the Catamaran Resort Hotel is not-for-tourists-only. This large room is set up cabaret-style for all breeds of rock 'n' rollers.

Or how about some Chicago R&B with Ruby and the Red Hots, or country tunes with Cowboys from Mars? There's always something special going on at least once a month. It might be a special Valentine's Day weekend featuring San Diego's Rockola, or Drive Feelgood and the Interns of Love on Superbowl weekend. Each New Year's Eve the Catamaran and its sister hotel the Bahia throw a major bash featuring—hold on to your old 45s—Gary Puckett and The Union Gap, The Young Rascals (*with* Felix Cavaliere), and The Buckinghams.

The cover for non-hotel guests varies, depending upon the performance, but it's not very expensive, and there's no drink minimum. Food is available—although

Performances
Wed 8 pm; Thurs 8:30 pm; Fri-Sat 9 pm; service during sets
Cost or Cover Charge
$3-5; AE/Disc/MC/V
Dining
Gourmet pizza; $6.50-11.95; drinks: $2.75-4.75; individual tables; reserved tables
Reservations
Reserve by phone
Location
Off Int-5 S to San Diego; Beaches exit; W on Garnet to Mission Blvd; left on Mission Blvd to 3999
Parking
On premises, $1/hr; valet, $2/hr; on street

Y || &

mostly on a pizza. Make reservations well in advance for New Year's—it's always a far-out sell-out.

CANTER'S KIBBITZ ROOM

419 North Fairfax Avenue
Los Angeles, CA 90036
Info: (213) 651-2030
Deli/performance bar; seats 75; food served during sets; no reservations; all ages.

LA's landmark 24-hour deli in the Fairfax district serves up something different, musically speaking, every night of the week. It's not surprising that this deli should decide to go to entertainment. In the "olden" days of the '60s it served up matzo balls and kreplach to hordes of rockers after the clubs closed.

In its small bar, which many locals may not know about if they're used to noshing in the other dining room, you get a *bisel* of this and a *bisel* of that. Monday, it's jazz, with the Bobby Sexton band; Tuesday is full-blown "club night," with a rock-blues jam session that's heavy on the '60s and '70s sounds and light on the metal; Wednesday ushers in song stylings reminiscent of Vegas-lounge type acts; Thursday is new act night, with folk, rock and blues performers; Friday and Saturday are scaled-down versions of Tuesday, with more jammin'; and on Sundays—(spare me!)—The Spareribs entertain with their version of the rock-blues.

The median age of Canter's deli dollies is about 70—but the dalliers out for some kitschy new entertainment average 20-something. How can you go wrong? There's no cover, and the parking is validated if you order food!

Performances
Mon-Sun 9 pm; service during sets
Cost or Cover Charge
No cover; MC/V
Dining
Delicatessen food: $5-11; drinks: $1.50-3
Reservations
None
Location
On Fairfax between Beverly and Wilshire Blvds; near Santa Monica (10) Fwy and Hollywood (101) Fwy
Parking
On premises, FREE; on street

CAT & FIDDLE PUB AND RESTAURANT

6530 Sunset Boulevard
Hollywood, CA 90028
Info: (213) 468-3800
Restaurant/jazz bar; seats 300 at tables, 15 at bar; food served during sets; all ages.

Enter through the iron-gated archway to the best of both worlds—a high-ceilinged English-style pub, and an outdoor patio filled with California weather. Jazz is offered only on Sunday night when alto saxophonist Pat Britt and tenor saxophonist Wilbur Brown co-lead a straight-ahead band that usually fills out with pianist Art Hillary, bassist Pat Senatore, and drummer Clarence Johnston (veteran of more than one old Blue Note recording date).

This is one of the city's best jazz bargains. There's no cover and the drinks won't bankrupt you. Square meals are served—Grovesner Square that is—like their palatable fish-and-chips. A meal will run you $10 to $12, hamburgers less. The crowd is casually dressed; at last check it was still a fairly international crowd, 20s through 40s.

In good weather, sit outside in the courtyard at an umbrella table, where you can also take your dinner (heaters are turned on when necessary). Inside, the bandstand isn't accessible to all of the dining tables, so you may want to eat early and sit at the bar when the band strikes up at 7 pm.

Parking isn't hard to find on the street Sunday nights or there's valet parking.

Performances
Sun 7 pm-11 pm; service during sets
Dining
Pub-style, pasta, hamburgers, fish; food: $9-12; drinks: $3.75; individual tables; smoking/non-smoking; AE/MC/V
Reservations
Reserve at door, by phone
Location
Between Cahuenga and Highland
Parking
Valet, $2.75; on street

CATALINA BAR & GRILL

1640 North Cahuenga Boulevard
Los Angeles, CA 90028
Info: (213) 466-2210   **Rsvn:** (213) 466-2210
Fax: (213) 466-9217
Restaurant seating 105 at tables, 20 at the bar; top jazz artists; reservations highly recommended; food served during sets; separate non-smoking section; all ages.

This is the major league of Southern California jazz clubs. What the Blue Note or the Vanguard or the Sweet Basil is to New York, Catalina is to LA. Originally a continental restaurant, proprietor Catalina Popescu one day added a bandstand and moved in a Steinway piano and the rest is history.

Catalina books the major players in jazz a downbeat away from concert hall stature. Those who work the week have recording contracts with the jazzier jazz labels. McCoy Tyner, Frank Morgan, Abbey Lincoln, Elvin Jones, Joe Henderson, and Tony Willams are prime examples. One memorable week saw Henderson, Charlie Haden, Eric Reed, and Joe Chambers together on one stage. If a musician can't make the full contract, Catalina will plug in local bands (like the Bill Holman Orchestra, Jack Sheldon, or Bobby Bradford) for a night or two.

The club features two shows a night, Tuesday through Sunday. Cover charges, hovering around $20 a head on weekends, come down during the rest of the week. There's also a two-drink minimum per show.

The continental menu remains unchanged from the days before they struck up the bands. Two people can eat very well in the neighborhood of $75. You don't have to order food to sit at the bar. The main dining area is on the left as you enter, or you can eat at the few tables on the other side. Except for a couple of booths near the kitchen exit, the bandstand can be seen and heard from almost every vantage point. The sound system ably accommodates acoustic bands as well as bands whose volume peels paint off the walls.

Park in the lot across the street. There's street parking on Cahuenga if you can find it; skip the side streets though.

Performances
Tues-Sun 9 pm-11 pm; service during sets
Cost or Cover Charge
$10-20 cover; 2 drink min at bar, enforced if not dining; AE/Disc/MC/V
Dining
Continental cuisine; fresh seafood; food: $10-20; drinks: $3.50-8; individual tables; reserved tables; smoking/non-smoking
Reservations
Reserve at door, by phone, mail
Location
Between Sunset and Hollywood Blvds; exit Cahuenga from Hollywood (101) Fwy
Parking
On premises, $2; on street also available

CHADNEY'S

3000 West Olive Avenue
Burbank, CA 91505
Info: (818) 843-5333
Restaurant/jazz bar seats 60 at individual tables, 10 at the bar; reservations recommended, reserved tables available; food served during sets; all ages.

Well-known to Valleyites, Chadney's switched from its popular country line up to a jazzy one about four years ago. Now the sounds of mainstream jazz fill the lounge six nights a week.

"No one is ugly after 2 am," reads the sign that greets visitors to the downstairs music lounge. A perfect setting: a nice long room, individual tables, that '60s lounge feeling—and no cover charge or minimum if you're dining; you need only choose one drink in the bar. For some reason, it offers the ideal setting and soundtrack for marital patchups and breakups. I've known many a couple that has retied or cut the knot during hours of otherwise special listening here. And one friend even found her second husband there! (Must be that '60s decor loosening everyone's libido again.)

Like any popular neighborhood bar, Chadney's draws its regulars. The restaurant caters to the NBC crowd

Performances
Tues-Sun 9:15 pm; service during sets
Cost or Cover Charge
No cover; 1 drink min, enforced if not dining; AE/Disc/MC/V
Dining
American-continental; Sunday-Monday food served until 9:30 pm; Tues-Sat until 10:30 pm
Reservations
Reserve at door, by phone
Location
Just off Fwy 134, exit Buena Vista; across from NBC Studios
Parking
On premises, FREE; valet, $1 min; on street

from next door. The menu is hearty, favoring steaks, chops, fish, and pasta—meals to chow down after cutting those tough network deals. Food can be ordered in the lounge or in the restaurant; dinners start at $10. If you want to save a few dollars, come for the "sunset" dinners served from 4:30 to 7 pm.

After dinner, the lounge is just the place to knock back some drinks and sample a workingperson's diet of mainstream jazz. The six-night schedule (Tuesday through Sunday) includes some of the finest straight-ahead small groups in LA jazz. A typical, eclectic week will find the likes of vibraphonist Gene Estes, pianist Billy Mitchell and his band, guitarist Sid Jacobs and singer Sandra Booker.

CINEGRILL

7000 Hollywood Boulevard
Hollywood, CA 90028
Info: (213) 466-7000   **Rsvn:** (213) 466-7000
Fax: (213) 462-8056
Lounge seats 125 for jazz, cabaret, pop; reservations recommended, reserved tables not available; no food served; separate non-smoking section, but no smoking allowed during the show; 21 and over.

Housed in the historic splendor of the Hollywood Roosevelt Hotel, the Cinegrill has become an important spot for established performers in many fields (jazz, blues, country, pop, even performance art) to showcase new work or jump-start careers. Under booker Jan Wellner, the Cinegrill quickly became a coveted place to catch Charles Brown, Jimmy Scott, Ruth Brown, Kinky Friedman, Jimmy Webb, Chuck Jackson, and a number of other top-draw singers and cabaret artists. Female impersonators and unclassifiables like Susan Tyrell's one woman tour-de-force, "My Rotten Life," also draw crowds.

The cover can be steep—around $20, plus a two-drink minimum—so it's best to arrive early to get the pick of seats. Various vertical supports in the room may obstruct your view.

There's one show weeknights, two shows weekends. A dinner package deal is available through the hotel's restaurant, Theodore's, and includes dinner, the Cinegrill cover charge and validated parking. The package adds up to $45 per person.

A monthly mailer lists upcoming performances; call to get on the list.

Performances
Tues-Thurs 9 pm; Fri-Sat 8:30 and 10:30
Cost or Cover Charge
$ varies; 2 drink min; AE/Disc/MC/V
Dining
Drinks only in Cinegrill; Hotel restaurant (Theodore's) in same building; food: $12.50-22.50 depending on artist appearing; dinner show package available; individual tables
Reservations
Reserve at door, by phone, TicketMaster
Location
Hollywood Blvd at Orange Dr; across from Mann's Chinese; inside the Hollywood Roosevelt Hotel
Parking
On premises; valet, $5.50; on street also available

CLUB BRASSERIE

1020 North San Vicente
Los Angeles, CA 90069
Info: (310) 854-1111   **Fax:** (310) 854-0926
Restaurant/jazz club; seats 100 at tables, 20 at bar; reservations required for dinner; food served during sets; non-smoking until 10 pm; all ages.

West Hollywood's hot Club Brasserie sits atop the elegant Bel Age Hotel, where the view from on high is special and provides a glamorous backdrop for the adventurous jazz groups in attendance. Guitarist Sid Jacobs has started booking the room with greats like Charles McPherson, Kenny Kirkland, and James Williams and Cedar Walton, and the response has been fabulous. This isn't a large space; drop-ins without reservations may have to sit at the bar. Jazz holds sway Tuesday through Saturday.

By day—and evening—this is a restaurant serving cuisine almost as *haute* as its altitude. On my last visit, sitting at the bar, I was in a great location to observe the room. The dining room holds tables and booths. The only

Performances
Tues-Sat evenings; service during sets
Cost or Cover Charge
No cover; 2 drink min; check/AE/MC/V
Dining
Food: $4-15; drinks: $5+; individual tables; reserved tables; non-smoking in dining room until 10 pm
Reservations
Reserve at door
Location
In the Bel Age Hotel

caveat? If more than two of you sit in one of the booths, someone won't get to see the musicians. The "sound lines" are great, but if sightlines are equally important to you, request a table. (If your request is granted, though, you must order food.) There's no cover, but there's a two-drink minimum.

CLUB LINGERIE

6507 Sunset Boulevard
Los Angeles, CA 90028
Info: (213) 466-8557
Rock club; tables and two bars seating 25; reservations not necessary; limited food items served; 21 and over.

    For a city that supposedly has no history, Club Lingerie actually has a substantial heritage dating all the way back to the late 1950s when it hosted Eddie Cochran and his guitar. As time went on, it evolved into the Red Velvet and scheduled the easy to remember names like Cher (and of course Sonny), the Kinks, and the Turtles. It turned soul in the '70s and became celebrated for both its music and its guests.

    Today, if you're looking for alternative bands, this place is a pretty good candidate. Club frequenters (lots of college students) laud the local bands.

    There are two full bars; even if you're just weeks under 21, don't even think about trying to pull the wool over the fastidious bouncer's eyes—he's got a reputation for eating false I.D.'s.

    Cover charge varies depending on the popularity of the act, and there's a not-too-strictly-enforced two drink minimum. Monday nights are free of a cover charge. If a nationally-touring band is lined up for the evening, you'll need to make reservations through TicketMaster (check the *LA Weekly*). Otherwise, just arrive for the show and pay at the door (cash only).

CLUB M See **Mancini's**

CLUB WITH NO NAME

836 North Highland Avenue
Hollywood, CA 90038
Info: (213) 461-8301
Rock club; no reservations; snack food served; 18 and over.

    Another 20-something place to see and be seen.

    If Orwell's *1984* had had a rock club, this would be it. There are two lines to get in: one for members and one for members-to-be. If you're not already a member, you have to fill out a short questionnaire. Once that's done, you're entitled to discounted Monday evenings or free Thursday evening entries. Then there's the routine I.D. check. Minors are welcome to everything but the alcohol; if you pass the I.D. check, you must wear an I.D. bracelet. Next you pay, and finally you are through the door. (Be sure to keep your membership card on you.) Once you're past the frustration of getting inside, however, this is a good place to listen to alternative and mainstream rock bands.

    Inside the club itself you're greeted by strobe lights, black lights, red flashing lights, and mirrors everywhere. It's a bit of Dante's *Inferno* mixed with Serling's *Twilight Zone*. Your final destination is a large room with high ceilings and a stage, two video screens, a disco globe, and an amazingly loud sound system. Despite the high decibel range, the audio portion of the program is clear,

---

Parking
  On premises, FREE;
  valet, FREE; on street

Performances
  Mon-Sun 9 pm-2 am
Cost or Cover Charge
  $ varies; 2 drink min;
  cash only
Dining
  Individual tables;
  reserved tables
Reservations
  Reserve at door; some
  through TicketMaster
Location
  Between Wilcox and
  Vine; near the
  Hollywood (101) Fwy
Parking
  On premises; on street
  available

Performances
  Mon, Thurs 9:30 pm
Cost or Cover Charge
  FREE-$8
Dining
  Junk food; festival
  seating
Location
  Between Willoughby
  and Melrose; near
  Hollywood (101) Fwy
Parking
  On street

even crisp, allowing the bands the luxury to sound the way they should.

Only snack food is served here so you might want to eat first. To that end, you're not far from Hampton's or from all the Melrose eateries.

It takes a lot of cruisin' to land a parking space around here; beware the permit parking signs on the surrounding streets and the meter people lurking around just waiting to write you up.

COACH HOUSE

33157 Camino Capistrano "c"
San Juan Capistrano, CA 92675
Info: (714) 496-8930   **Rsvn:** (714) 496-8930
Fax: (714) 496-2063
Restaurant/nightclub with 400 seats, 240 of which are reserved dinner seats; all sorts of music and comedy; reservations highly recommended; food served during sets; all ages.

The Coach House is not actually a club; it is Orange County's premiere concert-house, set in picturesque San Juan Capistrano. A venue this big can only survive by featuring all kinds of music and comedy. Although jazz is part of the menu, you won't hear it every night. The House books artists with sizeable followings like Ray Charles, Emmylou Harris, Wynton Marsalis, Robben Ford, and Richard Elliot. It's also a place to hear Adam Ant, Gregg Allman, Roseanne Arnold, or Etta James.

The best way to work this place is to check the papers for the schedules and book early.

The Coach House serves dinner consisting of four basic combinations and a nightly special. Complete dinners go for $8 to $15. Although the shows start at 8 and 10:30 pm, the doors open at 6. It's a good idea to get your meal out of the way before the music gets under way.

If you're there for just the music, the seating is best described as "cocktail and Vegas-style," which means small tables and space at the bar. The covers vary, and the two-drink minimum is ironclad and enforced whether you're eating or not.

Performances
Mon-Sun 8 pm, 10:30 pm; doors open at 6 pm; service during sets
Cost or Cover Charge
$ varies; 2 drink min at tables and bar; AE/MC/V
Dining
Food: $7.95-14.95; individual tables; reserved tables
Reservations
Reserve at door, by phone, mail, TicketMaster (selected shows)
Location
Off the 5 Fwy at Camino Capistrano and Aeropuerto
Parking
On premises; on street

COCK-N-BULL

2947 Lincoln Boulevard
Santa Monica, CA 90405
Info: (310) 399-9696
Nightclub seats 75 at tables, 18 at bar for live rock music three nights a week; no reservations; food served during shows; 21 and over.

A British pub on LA's Westside, this music and schmoozing space caters to a congenial crowd of Brits and Yanks. The folksy space is a conglomeration of dart boards, videos of soccer matches, and disparate U.K. accents. But the neon Budweiser signs above billiard tables, Levi's and plain T-shirts, and the countryish friendliness of the space suggest Texas. Live music plays Wednesdays, Thursdays and Saturdays only, and ranges from hardish rock to folksy acoustic.

Yorkshire potatoes and vegetable beef stew prevail. Share them at a table close to the small stage or sit at the bar with a beer—or the hard stuff.

Performances
Wed-Thurs, Sat 8:30 pm-12:30 am; service during sets
Cost or Cover Charge
$5; 2 drink min
Dining
Food: $4-7.25; drinks: $2.75-3.75
Reservations
No reservations
Parking
On premises, FREE; on street

COCONUT TEASZER

8117 Sunset Boulevard
Hollywood, CA 90046
Info: (213) 654-4887   **Rsvn:** (213) 654-4774
Rock club; holds 300 people; reserved tables by request; separate room for dancing; food served special days; 18 and over Friday- Sunday, 21 and over other nights.

It's hard to miss this bright purple building on the corner of Sunset and Crescent Heights Boulevards. The under-30 set comes to the Teaszer to hear some great (and some not-so-great) bands—often several in one evening. If you spot someone not fitting the under 30 description, it may be a corporate music mogul scouting out new bands. This is hunting ground for the industry.

A doorman checks I.D.'s; be sure to let them know which band you're coming to hear—bands that play this venue usually get paid only if they draw a certain amount of people.

On one side is a room of piped-in deejay music and strobe lights—it's usually empty. To the right is the main music room with sawdust on the floor and a step-up stage. If the music gets too loud, step outside to the patio set up with tables and chairs. Downstairs is the popular 8121 Room, a good spot to listen to acoustic tunes (see separate description).

Look for the new bar with the great drink specials. Some food is served. Park in the lot; most of the surrounding area requires a parking permit.

Performances
Mon-Sun 8 pm; service during sets
Cost or Cover Charge
$5-10; AE/MC/V
Dining
Free buffet with cover Thurs, Sun, alternate Tues; drinks specials; reserved tables
Reservations
Reserve by phone; TicketMaster (selected shows)
Location
At corner of Sunset Blvd and Crescent Heights
Parking
On premises, $3.50; valet, $3,50; on street

COFFEE EMPORIUM

4325 Glencoe Avenue
Marina del Rey, CA 90292
Info: (310) 823-4446
Coffeehouse seats 50 people; jazz and blues; food served during sets; no reservations; separate non-smoking section; all ages.

True to its name, this is, above all, a summit for heavenly brews. The Coffee Emporium is set in the unlikely spot of an upscale shopping center. Despite the external hubbub of frenzied consumerism, it is an oasis of tranquility.

Its jazz/blues program is confined to weekend evenings. You'll hear some excellent guitarists like that treasure trove of standards and arcana, Fred Socolow.

Comfortably furnished with a decor that's easy on the eye, the CE is a spot to relax in and indulge your java desires. About 30 different exotic samplings of international coffee beans are available while the staff whips up its own coffee exotica array of special drinks. For those whose creative juices are unleashed in such contemplative settings, crayons are provided for what Horace Silver called *doodlin'*.

Performances
Thurs-Fri 8 pm; service during sets
Cost or Cover Charge
No cover; AE/MC/V
Dining
American cuisine; food: $6; drinks: $1.75; individual tables; smoking/non-smoking
Reservations
None
Location
Off Marina (90) Fwy; cross streets: Maxella and Mindenao off Lincoln
Parking
On premises; street

COFFEE ROASTER CAFE

550 Washington Street
Marina del Rey, CA 90292
Info: (310) 305-7147
Cafe seats 55 for food and jazz; no reservations; food served during performances; alcohol served; separate non-smoking section; all ages.

You'll find this eclectic jazz cafe inside a modern and upscale shopping center in the Marina, where its mammoth coffee roaster grinds beans up fresh. Since the summer of 1990, the cafe has also served live acoustic jazz

Performances
Fri-Sat 8 pm-10 pm; service during sets
Cost or Cover Charge
$5

along with its custom-made roasts and sinful desserts, healthy salads, sandwiches and pastas. Most food items fall in the $4 to $8 dollar range and are served cafeteria-style—nothing fancy. Even the stage is simple. Light and airy, with two glass walls, 25 tables inside and a sidewalk cafe set up outside, this is a local hangout for jazz every Friday and Saturday evening. There's a $5 cover on Friday and Saturday, but no drink minimum. The laid-back decor includes movie posters and old photographs, a hanging buffalo head and an antique gas pump.

Dining
Breakfast, lunch, dinner; food: $5-10; drinks: cappucinos, lattes, espresso, custom coffee made to order; individual tables; reserved tables; smoking/non-smoking
Reservations
No reservations
Location
On Washington St W of Lincoln Blvd near PCH and Marina (90) Fwy; 5 blocks from beach
Parking
On premises

Y ‖ �&

COLD SPRING TAVERN

5995 Stagecoach Road
San Marcos Pass
Santa Barbara , CA 93105
Info: (805) 967-0066
Bar/restaurant featuring rock, blues, country; accommodates 100; no reservations; food served during sets; 21 and over evenings, all ages daytime.

Cold Spring, once a historic stagecoach stop off Highway 154, is now a hillbilly bar and restaurant that attracts a wide cross-section of humanity. *Real* Harley Davidson riders, college kids, Santa Ynez cowboys, and car club members converge on the tavern, especially on Sunday afternoons. Good local bands play rock 'n' roll, blues, and country music while guests chow down on chili dogs and tri-tip sandwiches at outdoor picnic tables. The music lasts from mid-afternoon to 9 or 10 pm.

The tavern itself is rustic and homey—if home to you means stuffed animal heads on the walls overlooking hunting and cowboy artifacts. Saturday night sounds range from 5 pm to 9 pm. There's no cover or drink minimum. If you intend to drink the maximum, however, be forewarned—it's quite a ride back down the mountain, so take along your designated driver.

Performances
Sat 5 pm-9 pm; Sun 1:30 pm-9 pm or 10 pm; service during sets
Cost or Cover Charge
No cover; MC/V
Dining
Chili, chili-dogs, tri-tip sandwiches; food: $4-6; drinks: $3.50-4; individual tables
Reservations
None
Location
Off San Marcos Pass; 8 miles N of 101 on Hwy 54
Parking
On premises, FREE; on street

Y ‖ �&

COMEDY ACT THEATRE

3339 West 43rd Street
Los Angeles, CA 90008
Info: (310) 677-4101   **Rsvn:** (310) 677-4101
Comedy club; seats 300 at tables; food served; reservations available for parties of 6 or more; 21 and over.

This is one of the city's better-known clubs that features African-American stand-up. It's said numerous established performers kicked off their careers here since the club's opening act in 1985. The roster of regular patrons who come for laughs is an "A list" of African-American celebrities: Magic Johnson, Wesley Snipes, and Denzel Washington, to name drop a few. The club's success has even engendered two spinoffs: one in Atlanta and another (in the works) in Chicago.

Only cash is accepted at the door. The menu includes hot wings, fries and other fast foods, and there's a no-nonsense full bar. Shows begin at 8:30 pm and run to about midnight. The lineup usually numbers five acts. If you plan on arriving with fewer than six people, you'll have to

Performances
Thurs-Sat 8:30 pm-12 midnight
Cost or Cover Charge
$10; cash only
Dining
Hors d'oeuvres and snacks: hot wings, french fries; individual tables
Reservations
Groups of 6+
Location
Santa Monica (10) Fwy to Crenshaw Blvd exit; S to 43rd St
Parking
On premises, FREE; on street

take your chances on a table, as they're only reserved for six or more. There's free parking in the lot.

COMEDY & MAGIC CLUB

1018 Hermosa Avenue
Hermosa Beach, CA 90254
Info: (310) 376-6914 **Rsvn:** (310) 372-1193
Fax: (310) 379-2806
Comedy club; 300 at tables, 65 at bar; food served; non-smoking section; 18 and over evenings, all ages matinees.

You're in store for a bag of tricks as well as a barrel of laughs at this nightclub. Top show business men and women appear (and disappear) on stage regularly. Even TV's big man Jay Leno was recently trying out his new material here. The magicians genuinely amaze, while the comedians are first class, and management insists their acts are "clean"! (Well PG-13, anyway.)

The less mysterious dinner menu stars steak, seafood, jumbalaya, salads and burgers. Or just order appetizers and drinks at the bar. There's a two-drink minimum aside from the hefty cover charge paid at the door, but ticket costs vary with the change of entertainment. The club's open every night of the week and on Sundays at noon for a special children's show. Call for the line up, and for performance times, which vary with the show.

Performances
Sun noon kids show with lunch; Sun-Thurs 8 pm (some Sun and Mon 7:30 pm); Fri-Sat 8 pm, 10:30 pm

Cost or Cover Charge
$8-15; 2 drink min; check/AE/MC/V

Dining
A variety of appetizers and full dinners; salads, sandwiches, burgers, steak, fresh fish and Jumbalaya; food: $3.50-13; individual tables; smoking/non-smoking

Reservations
Reserve at door, by phone

Location
Corner of 10th St and Hermosa Ave; off Pier Ave; 91 Fwy, straight down to Artesia, left on PCH, right on Pier and left on Hermosa Ave; close to the San Diego (405) Fwy also

Parking
On premises; on street

THE COMEDY CLUB

49 South Pine Avenue
Long Beach, CA 90802
Info: (310) 437-6709 **Rsvn:** (310) 437-5326
Comedy club; seats 200; no reservations accepted; food served before and during sets; front row non-smoking, Sunday nights entirely non-smoking; 18 and over.

This small Long Beach club would like to remind people why comedy clubs became so popular that they began popping up on every channel on the remote control—it's a fun, usually wild and always inexpensive night out. This is a club, in point: it's a cheerful place, parking is free, the cover is reasonable, and there's only a two-drink minimum. The crowd is diverse, although the 10:30 Friday night show draws a predominantly collegiate, 21-ish crowd.

If you follow the comedy-club circuit and tune in to the TV comedy shows, then you'll recognize some of the name comics who play here: Fred Greenlee, John Wing, Craig Shoemaker, Bob Nickman, Sheila Kay, and Carol Montgomery—all of whom have save some of their best material for this live show.

Performances
Tues-Sun 8:30 pm; Fri-Sat 8:30 pm, 10:30 pm; service during sets

Cost or Cover Charge
$6-8; 2 drink min; AE/MC/V

Dining
Dinner, sandwich, appetizers; food: $5-8; drinks: $2.75-3; individual tables; reserved tables; Sunday is non-smoking night

Reservations
None

Location
Downtown Long Beach

Parking
On premises, FREE

COMEDY ISLE

Bahia Hotel
998 West Mission Bay Drive
San Diego, CA 92109
Info: (619) 488-0551   **Rsvn:** (619) 488-6872
Fax: (619) 488-1512
Comedy club; 200 people can sit at tables for four; limited menu, served during shows; reservations necessary; 21 and over.

You can't miss the location of Comedy Isle; it's set in the Bahia Hotel overlooking Mission Bay, right near Belmont Park's wonderful wooden roller coaster.

Nationally known comics tease audiences and even get them into the act, so be prepared. The front row puts you practically on-stage with the comedians, so you're sure to catch their eye—and often their barbs—from here. However, being that it's kind of a dark, smokey nightclub, few people will see you turn red.

The crowd includes locals and hotel guests drawn to regular lineups of national stand-up comedians who have appeared on "Comedy Club Network," "The Tonight Show," and "The Arsenio Hall Show." (The lineup changes weekly.)

Buy a T-shirt and you're guaranteed free admission and free hors d'oeuvres on Sunday. Dinner in the Bahia Restaurant guarantees V.I.P. seating and half-price admission. Comedy Isle itself has a limited, reasonably priced menu vending pizzas, quesadillas, and hamburgers.

Performances
Wed-Thurs, Sun 8:30 pm; Fri-Sat 8:30, 10:30 pm; service during sets
Cost or Cover Charge
$7-10; 2 drink min; check/AE/Disc/MC/V
Dining
Pizzas, quesadillas, cheeseburgers; food: $6; drinks: $3.50; individual tables
Reservations
Reserve at door, by phone
Location
Near 5 and 8 Fwy; located on Mission Bay Dr near the Roller Coaster
Parking
On premises, FREE; on street

THE COMEDY STORE

8433 Sunset Boulevard
West Hollywood, CA 90069
Info: (213) 650-6268   **Rsvn:** (213) 656-6225
Fax: (213) 654-3176
Comedy club; seats 400 in Main Room, 200 in Original Room, 100 in Belly Room; reservations necessary; no food; 21 and over.

"The Store" has been around since 1972 (although with all its different comedy rooms, they should call it "The Mall"). To have lasted so long—even in star-studded Los Angeles—puts Mitzi Shore's venture in the company of only a few other legendary LA clubs.

Still housed in what was the popular Sunset Strip hot spot, Ciro's, The Comedy Club has launched the careers of some of entertainment's most entertaining names. After a divorce from husband and comedian Sammy Shore, Mitzi Shore took over and molded the club into a comedians' workshop where new talent was constantly nurtured along the way. Richard Pryor was one of the first. Comedy czars such as Garry Shandling, Robin Williams, Freddie Prinze, and David Letterman cut their teeth here. Comedians not only stood up and practiced their work, they worked the doors, sat the guests, and did "whatever." Shore launched the controversial Belly Room, the upstairs hideout originally set aside just for new female stand-ups.

The Comedy Store is like one big maze. Because the cover charges differ so greatly from nook to cranny, know where you want to be! The Main Room is the "Best of..." location where the greats and going-to-be-greats perform in Las Vegas-style shows. The Original Room is the granddaddy, the first space Mitzi Shore opened. This is also where the comedians workshop, cultivating their new material. Up to 14 comics each night perform in all of these showplaces. The upstairs Belly Room, with 10 to 12 performers each night, hosts a gay and lesbian night, Latina de la Noche, and a night for one-woman or one-man shows.

Performances
Mon-Sun 8 pm-2 am (continuous)
Cost or Cover Charge
$7-10; Mon no cover; 2 drink min; AE/MC/V
Reservations
Reserve by phone, TicketMaster; reserved tables
Location
On the Sunset Strip between La Cienega and Sweetzer
Parking
On street; parking lot behind the Hyatt Hotel

Because of its history and cachet, the Comedy Store still attracts the top talent. Often the best established comics just drop in.

The week's schedule comes out on Tuesday. Reservations are the best policy. There's a two-drink minimum in force. No food is served, but you're just minutes from all the Sunset Plaza cafes.

THE COMEDY STORE (LA JOLLA)

916 Pearl Street
La Jolla, CA 92037
Rsvn: (619) 454-9176
Comedy club seats 200 at individual tables; reservations are recommended; no food served; 21 and over.

In a cool and quiet-looking ivy-covered building in tony La Jolla, The Comedy Store serves up hot evening entertainment. This is Mitzi Shore's spot for comedians seeking a working vacation. The La Jolla branch of the famous Los Angeles Comedy Store features—and is run by—stand-up comedians. Negotiate the dimly lit front room bar—which doubles as the backstage through-way for completed acts—to the tightly-packed main room. The black walls are covered with posters of the Marx Brothers, Chaplin, Laurel & Hardy, Joey Brown and their peers.

The person who pours your drink may be the next act onstage. Or it might be the doorman or various bartenders or even the manager, Fred. There's always a varied menu of comics. Many of the same comedians who play the LA scene take this stage. Robin Williams, David Letterman, Jay Leno, and the late Sam Kinison all gained career momentum here. Some comics consider this the best road club in the country; they say the audiences are great, and the surroundings couldn't be better!

Food is not served, so chow down first. On Monday and Tuesday nights the cover charge is waived, but the two-drink minimum is still enforced.

Performances
Mon-Tues 8 pm-12 am; Wed 8 pm-10 pm; Thurs and Sun 8:30 pm-10:30 pm; Fri-Sat 8 pm and 10:30 pm

Cost or Cover Charge
$6-10; no cover on Mon and Tues; 2 drink min; AE/MC/V

Dining
No food; drinks: $3.25-4.50; reserved tables

Reservations
Reserve at door, by phone

Location
Between Fay and Girard

CONGO SQUARE

1238 3rd Street Promenade
Santa Monica, CA 90401
Info: (310) 395-5606
A coffeehouse with mellow entertainment; seating for 75 at tables; no reservations; desserts served during sets; no cover; all ages.

This espresso and tea house features a mix of live musical forms every weekend, including bebop, Brazilian jazz, and worldbeat. Weekly poetry readings are also scheduled. Instead of charging a cover, a $.50 per item surcharge automatically gets added during scheduled musical performances.

The atmosphere is congenial, hippie-Berkeley-esque. Among the amalgamated crowd of Santa Monicans, sleepy students with books linger over pick-me-up sandwiches, desserts and gourmet roasts. (The cafe's apricot-raisin cookie and caffe latte are favorite choices.) Tattered but homey (and comfy) living room furniture decorates an elongated lounge. The decor looks truly thrift shop, but maybe that's what keeps out the pretentious nouveau coffeehouse types. Its rotating gallery of eclectic paintings makes for an interesting sideshow.

Weekends are crowded, so grab a sofa early.

Performances
Mon, Fri-Sat 9 pm-midnight; service during sets

Cost or Cover Charge
No cover

Dining
Pastries, sandwiches, bagels, coffee delights; food: $2-5; drinks: $1.25-3; individual tables

Location
On 3rd St Promenade; 4th St exit on Santa Monica (10) Fwy; between Wilshire Blvd and Arizona Ave

Parking
On street; parking structures on 2nd and 4th Sts

CRAZY HORSE STEAK HOUSE

1580 Brookhollow Drive
Santa Ana, CA 92705
Info: (714) 549-8233   **Rsvn:** (714) 549-1512
Fax: (714) 850-9297
Nightclub specializing in country music; seats 250 at tables, 18 at bar; reservations required; food served during sets; first show all ages, second show 21 and over.

      In a region where live country music performed by name acts is hard to come by, the Crazy Horse stands virtually alone. Easily visible (and accessible) from the 55 Freeway, this Santa Ana treasure manages to attract top talent despite its tiny size (250 seats) and has even roped many Nightclub of the Year awards from Nashville's Academy of Country Music.

      Fred Reiser, now a highly respected figure in country music circles, opened the Crazy Horse in 1979 with a Western decor theme in mind and virtually no experience in booking music acts. After six months of using relative unknowns, he booked Ray Price for a successful benefit, followed two months later by Hoyt Axton—and by 1981, a regular flow of talent had begun.

      When North Hollywood's famous Palomino club dropped its exclusive country music diet in the '80s, the Crazy Horse became the only club in the region to regularly book big country acts. San Juan Capistrano's Coach House offers occasional competition.

      The list of performers who have stomped this wooden-floored Saloon Theatre is long and glittering. Many of today's hottest country stars—Garth Brooks, Mary Chapin Carpenter, Reba McEntire, Randy Travis—have stopped here on their way up. The club has also played host to super vets like Merle Haggard, Roger Miller, Mel Tillis, Bill Monroe, Roy Clark and Waylon Jennings. The roster also has included Southern rockabilly survivors like Jerry Lee Lewis and Carl Perkins; folk-era favorites like John Stewart, the Kingston Trio and the Limeliters; nostalgia rockers Chubby Checker and the Ventures; and the unclassifiable Ray Charles.

      Today's acts befit the "Country With Class" club slogan—nothing outrageous to incense more conservative clientele. Ray Price has come back, and the club has recently presented Marie Osmond, Ronnie Milsap, John Anderson, and Steve Wariner.

      The Crazy Horse is divided into two rooms, a family restaurant and the Saloon Theater. Steaks, naturally, are the house specialties, but prime ribs and chicken entrees also do a good business. (Don't let the name fool you—no horse steaks, crazy or otherwise, are served here.) Concert nights are Mondays and Tuesdays with shows at 7 and 10 pm. Local bands fill the rest of the week.

Performances
    Mon-Sun 7 pm, 10 pm; service during sets
Cost or Cover Charge
    $3-30
Dining
    Dining room separate from concert hall; full menu, table service; food: $14.50
Reservations
    Call BO
Location
    Costa Mesa/Newport Beach Fwy/Dyer Road (State Hwy 55)
Parking
    On premises, FREE

CROCE'S RESTAURANT & JAZZ BAR

802 Fifth Avenue
San Diego, CA 92101
Info: (619) 232-2891   **Rsvn:** (619) 233-4355
Fax: (619) 232-9836
Restaurant seats 75, bar seats 50 for traditional jazz; reservations not available in bar; priority seating available one hour in advance in restaurant; food and liquor served during sets; separate non-smoking section; 21 and over in bar.

      As you reach 5th and F Streets in San Diego's Gaslamp Quarter, you get an overall view of Ingrid Croce's dynasty. Ingrid, the widow of the late great Jim Croce,

Performances
    Call for performance schedules; service during sets
Cost or Cover Charge
    FREE-$3; $5 min at bar, enforced if not dining; Disc/MC/V

opened the first of her combination music clubs and restaurants in 1983 with Croce's Restaurant & Jazz Bar. On the corner is the restaurant, next door the Jazz Bar, followed by Croce's Top Hat Bar & Grille (see below for separate review), and then Ingrid's Cantina. Fronting these spaces is the outdoor Sidewalk Cafe.

A larger-than-wall-size black-and-white picture of the legendary Jim Croce holding his stogee smiles at you from the back wall of the Jazz Bar's long narrow room. Ingrid Croce opened this spot in tribute to her late husband, and consistently fills it with great traditional jazz artists from the surrounding areas and LA. It's an exceptional place to spend an evening, with the sounds of Hollis Gentry, Daniel Jackson, and Quarteto Agape, to name just a few regulars. Croce's son A.J., an R&B piano player, singer, and songwriter in his own right plays regularly.

There are just a dozen tables and bentwood chairs sitting on the big black-and-white tiles, and they're surrounded by a bar and walls filled with memorabilia of the late great songster. Both the Jazz Bar and Top Hat Bar & Grille seem to get appreciative and friendly crowds, a nice mix of tourists, conventioneers, and locals. The food fare is light and includes appetizers and salads.

Jazz can be heard seven nights a week, but if that's not enough, try this place for Jazz Lunch, Monday, Wednesday, Friday and Saturday; Champagne Jazz Brunch on Sunday; and Jazz Happy Hour Tuesday, Thursday, and Friday from 5:30 pm to 8:30 pm, Saturday and Sunday from 6 pm to 8 pm

No matter where you end up sitting, you'll find a casual, unpretentious atmosphere. And the food is good! Lunch and dinner are selected from an American-International menu with choices such as char-grilled swordfish (wrapped in grape leaves), deep dish vegetable lasagna and Thai chicken pasta.

Dining
American/international cuisine: fresh fish, creative salads, pastas, tender filets; food: $5-10 (lunch), $10-20 (dinner); drinks: $2.50 draft beers; individual tables; smoking/non-smoking

Reservations
Reservations for large groups; priority seating, call 1 hr in advance

Location
At the corner of Fifth Ave and F St; 1 block E of Horton Plaza in the Historic Gaslamp Quarter

Parking
Valet, $3; on street

CROCE'S TOP HAT BAR & GRILLE

818 Fifth Avenue
San Diego, CA 92101
Info: (619) 232-2891   **Rsvn:** (619) 233-6945
Fax: (619) 232-9836
Restaurant seats 75, bar seats 125 for live R&B; no reservations; food and liquor served during sets; separate non-smoking section; all ages.

Like its counterpart above, the Top Hat is young and fun, a sort of '90s speakeasy reminiscent of a New Orleans club. If jazz isn't your thing, grab a table here to catch the sexy R&B sounds from the likes of Earl Thomas, the Janiva Magness Band, Maggie Mayall's group, The Cash McCall Express, and, of course, A.J. Croce, who brings in his six-piece band for this gig.

Walls are of exposed brick; an old movie marquee rests above the musicians. Balcony seating (from which you can enter Ingrid's Cantina) is in addition to the tables below.

Lest you think the Hard Rock Cafe is the only restaurant that can cook up a rare T-shirt, Croce's storefront at Ingrid's Cantina is rich with Croce merchandise for sale, plus Ingrid's own cookbooks, gourmet food, coffee, cassettes and CDs.

Performances
Mon-Wed 8:30 pm-12:30 am; Thurs-Sat 9 pm-1 am; Sun 9:30 pm-1:30 am; service during sets

Cost or Cover Charge
FREE-$3; $5 min at bar, enforced if not dining; Disc/MC/V

Dining
Burgers, cheesecakes, pizza, sandwiches, salads; food: $3-8; drinks: $2.50; individual tables; reserved tables; smoking/non-smoking

Reservations
None

Location
At the corner of Fifth Ave and F St; 1 block E of Horton Plaza in the Historic Gaslamp Quarter

Parking
Valet, $3; on street

DICK'S LAST RESORT

345 Fourth Avenue
San Diego , CA 92101
Info: (619) 231-9100   **Fax:** (619) 231-6859
Accommodates 520 for jazz, R&B, Dixieland; no reservations; food and liquor served during sets; separate non-smoking section; 21 and over Friday and Saturday.

Even the management describes this place as a "joint." Well, if you're looking to be abused by rude waiters in a giant (10,000-square feet) warehouse setting, you've found your El Dorado.

The joint draws a young crowd as well as conventioneers. Folks who come here like to sit communal-style at big long tables on sawdust-covered floors and chomp on ribs—and everything else—served in buckets. (At least you don't have to worry about using the wrong fork.)

There's jazz and blues in the early evening, followed by loud Dixieland and R&B music seven nights a week. And, the food is cheap, there's no cover charge, and everyone wants to party.

Performances
Mon-Sun 5 pm-1 am
Cost or Cover Charge
No cover; AE/Disc/MC/V
Dining
Big sloppy ribs, BBQ chicken, crab legs, wimpy salads, best fries in town, catfish, coleslaw; food: $9.95-17.95; drinks: $2-3.50; reserved tables; smoking/non-smoking
Reservations
None
Location
Between J and K Sts; near Int-5

DISCAFE BOHEM CLUB & THEATER

4430 Fountain Avenue, 2nd floor
Hollywood, CA 90029
Info: (213) 662-1597   **Rsvn:** (213) 662-1597
A club and theater combo; 99 seats, some reserved; non-smoking policy; reservations necessary for some performances; food served; no age limit.

Defying traditional definitions, this ambitious spot aims to offer a complete evening of dining, dancing, and live entertainment. With its strict no-smoking policy and expansive carpeted space, the Discafe Bohem does not fit the atmospheric mold of Bohemian, dark coffeehouses. In fact, its minimalist decor resembles a modern art gallery with paintings by local artists on display.

The entertainment here varies from video screenings, improv, stand-up comedians and theater groups to groups playing jazz, blues, folk, European, and acoustic rock and roll.

Hot and cold food and drinks, beer and wine, are served. Prices are moderate.

Performances
Thurs-Sun at 7 pm; Sat-Sun noon (generally); music Sat 9 pm; call for details
Cost or Cover Charge
$5-10
Dining
Hot food, sandwiches, desserts, coffee, beer, wine; food and drinks: $2-5; individual tables; reserved tables; no smoking
Reservations
Reserve at door, by phone, mail
Location
In Hollywood E of Vermont between Sunset and Santa Monica Blvds
Parking
On premises; on street

DODSWORTH BAR & GRILL

2 West Colorado Boulevard
Pasadena, CA 91105
Info: (818) 578-1344
Jazz club; table seating for 225, 100 accommodated at bar; reservations necessary for the dining room; food served during sets; separate non-smoking section; 21 and over in the bar.

Located at a particularly busy corner of Pasadena's Old Town section, Dodsworth is jumping, especially in the separate music room just off the bar. Though not quite as frantic as a three-ring circus, don't expect a calm, laid-back atmosphere. The noisy diners are screened off, true, but the lounge's own patrons more than make up for any lost decibels.

Performances
Call for schedule; service during sets
Cost or Cover Charge
No cover; 2 drink min; check/MC/V
Dining
Continental cuisine; food: $12-16; drinks: $2.50-4; individual tables; smoking/non-smoking

Of course when you get an outfit like tenor saxophonist Benn Clatworthy and his band in the room, you won't hear the conversation at the next table. Dodsworth draws good talent such as Clatworthy or singers Shelly Moore and Toni Janotta. The trick is to find out who you want to hear and get there early. Space (and a couple of inconveniently located columns) is always a concern in this cramped room with its tiny tables and crowded bar.

Continental entrees and pasta are served in the restaurant ($12 to $16). The Saturday night crowd gets dressed up for dinner, but the bar scene sports a variety of costumes. Although there's no cover charge, the two-drink minimum (on Friday, Saturday, and Sunday nights) is enforced whether you're dining or not, and whether you're at the bar or a table; and each set means a new minimum.

Reservations
Reserve at door, by phone
Location
At corner of Fair Oaks and Colorado; near 210 and 134 Fwys
Parking
On premises; valet, $3; on street also available

DRESDEN ROOM

1760 North Vermont Avenue
Los Angeles, CA 90027
Info: (213) 665-4294
Lounge seats 50 at tables, 16 at the bar; jazz, show tunes, and easy-listening; reservations recommended; food served during sets; 21 and over.

There's a lounge revival going on in LA, and the Dresden Room tops the list.

The young, Hollywood crowd that drops in for live jazz and show tunes includes Michelle Pfeiffer, Nicholas Cage, Sean Penn, Julia Roberts, and Kiefer Sutherland. The dark, smokey lounge is otherwise filled with artsy types, maybe due in part to the 1950s-'60s ambience of the place, which has made such an enthusiastic comeback with '90s hipsters. But this is no replica, no neo- or pseudo- '50s hot spot. The Dresden has just been hanging out for 35 years, waiting to happen all over again.

Husband and wife duo Elayne and Marty Roberts sing at the piano bar and alternate playing bass, drums, flute, and organ. They perform cabaret numbers from 9 pm till 1 am Thursday through Saturday. Tuesdays are "open-mike" nights, offering patrons a chance to strut their musical stuff. Wednesdays the stage is handed over to the winning performer from the night before. There are also guest musicians and vocalists during the week.

The restaurant serves up Continental entrees; appetizers are available in the bar.

Get there early on weekends if you want to be assured of a seat—the place is packed.

Performances
Tues-Sat 8:30 pm-1 am; service during sets
Cost or Cover Charge
No cover; AE/MC/V
Dining
Continental cuisine; food: $11-19; drinks; $4; individual tables
Reservations
Reserve at door, by phone
Location
Between Hollywood Blvd and Franklin Ave; near Hollywood (101) Fwy
Parking
On premises; valet; on street

8121 ROOM

8117 Sunset Boulevard
Hollywood, CA 90046
Info: (213) 654-4887   **Rsvn:** (213) 654-4773
Mostly acoustic music; accommodates 8 to 16 at the bar, 8 tables; reservations not necessary; no food; 21 and over.

This dark cozy club is the antithesis of its upstairs neighbor, the Coconut Teaszer. The crowd here prefers the simplicity of acoustic music with some blues and country thrown in, over the loud, amplified sounds upstairs.

There's not much to see at first in this dark underground room. But then you spot the goofy twinkling year-round Christmas lights surrounding the bar, and you soon cotton to the amicable bartender. It's hard to believe the drinks can be so cheap in LA! Beers are $ .85 and well drinks a mere $1.85 during Happy Hour, which lasts more than its moniker (it goes to 10 pm).

Performances
Tues-Sat 8 pm-2 am
Cost or Cover Charge
$1.50-5
Dining
Drinks: 8 pm-10 pm $.85 beer, $1.85 well drinks; 10 pm on $3.75-4.75; individual tables
Reservations
Not necessary
Location
Corner of Laurel Canyon, Crescent Heights and Sunset Blvd

Black couches and tables and chairs take up most of the room with the stage smushed into one corner. (It's so small that sometimes the equipment blocks the performers.) Don't fret about "sound lines," though, as the sound at this casual spot is clean and comfortable.

The cover is just $1.50 at all times, except for Saturday night after 10 pm when the price jumps to $5. Showtimes are to be paid attention to; unlike most live music clubs, the acts here do go on as scheduled, with only a 5- or 10-minute delay; from 8 pm on, they go on every hour on the hour till midnight.

On the street, parking is a problem, especially on weekends. If you're feeling financially solvent, utilize the valet parking lot ($3 to $5) next door on Sunset Boulevard. Though there's no food served at 8121, you can pick and choose to your heart's delight from the nearby spots such as Jacopo's serving pizza across the street; The Source is down the street; Greenblatt's is for deli lovers; and the Gaucho Grill serves sizzling South American fare.

Parking
On premises, $3-5; valet, $3-5; on street

ELARIO'S

7955 La Jolla Shores Drive
La Jolla, CA 92037
Info: (619) 459-0261   **Rsvn:** (619) 459-0541
Fax: (619) 459-7644
Jazz club; seats 100; reservations not necessary; limited bar menu served during sets; 21 and over.

Here on the top floor of the Summer House Inn in La Jolla, top names in jazz blow their mellifluous horns in an acoustically pleasing, yet small and intimate, room. Talent like Hollis Gentry, Chuck McPherson, and many impressive others do their thing seven nights a week on the small raised stage.

Though Elario's draws an appreciative audience of regulars and hotel guests who get dressed up for dinner and come by later to listen to mellow mainstream jazz, don't worry about having to dress up as it's not required. It's just a nice place to spend a lazy night listening to good music. If you want a nibble, a limited bar menu is available. If you come between 5 pm and 7 pm, hors d'oeuvres and a sunset are complimentary.

Performances
Sun-Thurs 8:30 pm, 9:15 pm, 11 pm; Fri-Sat 8:30 pm, 9:45 pm, 10:30 pm; service during sets
Cost or Cover Charge
$ varies; 2 drink min, enforced if not dining; AE/Disc/MC/V
Dining
Hamburgers; food: $2.75-9.75; drinks: $2.50-4.25; individual tables
Reservations
Not necessary
Location
At La Jolla Shores Dr at Torrey Pines Road; off 5 Fwy
Parking
On premises, FREE; valet, FREE; on street

THE ESPRESSO BAR

34 South Raymond Avenue
Pasadena, CA 91105
Info: (818) 356-9095
Coffeehouse, poetry and music; seats 49 inside; no reservations; some food; all ages.

You'll reach the entrance to The Espresso Bar through an alleyway in Pasadena's "hot" Old Town. This very popular coffeehouse presents anything musical that you won't hear on a typical Top 40 radio station. There are also poetry readings and an open mike night on Tuesdays.

The comfort of the large living room-like space with its high ceilings, hardwood floors, and working fireplace attracts all sorts of people from the "kids" of the '60s, to the "kids" of the '90s. The indoors and outdoors are filled with tables and chairs, so grab a seat where you can. Desserts and, of course, coffee, are served. You'll need a $2 drink ticket on Tuesday nights.

Performances
Tues-Wed 9 pm
Cost or Cover Charge
$2 Tues
Reservations
None
Location
In alleyway behind 34 South Raymond
Parking
Structure across the street; on street

Park in the public parking structure across the street—it's pretty hard to find street parking in the evening.

FAHRENHEIT 451

540 South Coast Highway
Laguna Beach, CA 92651
(Watch for an upcoming move to 225 Forest Avenue in downtown Laguna.)
Info: (714) 494-5151
A bookstore-coffeehouse featuring "mellow" entertainment; seating at tables indoors for 82; reservations optional; limited menu of desserts and coffees served during sets; inside non-smoking; all ages.

If you're in, at, or on Laguna Beach, stop by this delightfully enigmatic performance space. The well-stocked bookstore doubles as a coffeehouse and triples as an entertainment venue. Besides featuring an impressive catalogue of titles, the space offers poetry readings, a variety of live music, including jazz and folk, monthly opera concerts, and whatever else strikes the fancy of owner Dorothy Ibsen (a distant relative of Henrik!).

The store, housed in a historical landmark, has been in business for 25 years. Ownership changed hands in 1988, and the bookstore has since flourished into a popular nightspot. Ibsen extended the bookstore to a space across the street and started brewing coffee. No sooner was cappuccino served than she began to book nightly entertainment.

Tenors, sopranos and mezzos take over on amateur opera night the third Tuesday each month, while afternoon and evening instrumentalists perform everything from harp to flamenco to string quartets. Enjoy the show and a gourmet dessert from tables and chairs arranged against the front picture windows inside, or take in the fresh sea air on the spacious outdoor patio.

Performances
Mon-Sun afternoons, weekend evenings 5 pm-8 pm, 9 pm-midnight
Cost or Cover Charge
No cover; check/AE/Disc/MC/V
Dining
Gourmet cakes, coffees, fruit bars, cookies, candies; food: $2-3; drinks: $2.75; individual tables; tables reserved for food and drink; non-smoking except patio and balcony
Reservations
None
Location
At Legion and Pacific Coast Hwy
Parking
On premises, 1 hr FREE with validation; on street

FESS PARKER'S RED LION INN

633 East Cabrillo Boulevard
Santa Barbara, CA 93103
Info: (805) 564-4333
Hotel's Barro Los Arcos features jazz and classical guitar and can seat 100; no reservations necessary; appetizers; 21 and over.

The pretty pink hotel, just across the street from the ocean, devotes its sedate lobby lounge bar to jazz on Sunday and Monday, classical guitar Tuesday and Wednesday, and dance music the rest of the week. The same jazz duo, Santa Barbara old-timers Hank & Wayne, has been playing there for about as long as the hotel has been open. Appetizers are served and there's a nightly Happy Hour. (The step-down lounge is near the check-in desk.)

Performances
Nightly
Cost or Cover Charge
No cover
Dining
Drinks: $3.25-3.50; individual tables
Reservations
Not necessary
Location
Near Hwy 101; across from the Pacific Ocean; cross street Puerto Vallarta
Parking
Valet, tip required; on street

FLUTES AT THE HORTON GRAND HOTEL

Horton Grand Hotel
311 Island Avenue
San Diego, CA 92101
Info: (619) 544-1886 **Fax:** (619) 239-3823
Bar/jazz club, seats 80 at tables, 8 at the bar for live jazz; reservations not necessary; food and liquor served during sets; all ages.

      Don't tell a soul! Flutes is a little-known San Diego secret. Few people are aware that really hip jazz is played here by Mike Wofford, San Diego's top jazz pianist (who has recorded in this room and appears from time to time), Red Holloway and his tenor sax, Harry Pickens at the piano, and Jeannie and Jimmy Cheatham, singer and arranger, respectively.

      The setting is a nostalgic, restored Victorian hotel, slightly off the beaten path in the Gaslamp Quarter. This hip room looks like a turn-of-the-century parlor, with seating on comfortable antique chairs. While the hotel guests benefit from the bar, naturally anyone is welcome. You won't find the typical tourist hotel setting; this is good, professional jazz.

      The sets are almost always free except for name acts, when the cover jumps to $5 or $10. Appetizers, soups, and sandwiches can be ordered in the bar.

Performances
  Thurs-Sat 8:30 pm; service during sets
Cost or Cover Charge
  FREE-$10, 2 drink min, enforced if not dining; AE/Disc/MC/V
Dining
  Hamburgers, sandwiches, desserts; individual tables
Reservations
  Not necessary
Location
  At 4th and Island; in the Gaslamp Quarter
Parking
  Valet, $5 + tip; on street

THE GARDENIA CLUB

7066 Santa Monica Boulevard
Los Angeles, CA 90038
Info: (213) 467-7444
Supper club; reservations recommended; food served during sets; all ages.

      This is an LA answer to a New York cabaret. Its weeknight and Saturday schedule ranges from variety acts to vocalists to comedians in an intimate environment, which often attracts the 40-and-older crowd. The small supper club has two dinner seatings a night (7 pm and 10:30 pm), and one show at 9. The menu leans toward Italian, though they bill it as continental. The cover varies depending on the entertainer. New York actress and songstress Andrea Marcovicci makes this a regular stop.

Performances
  Mon-Sat 9 pm; service during sets
Cost or Cover Charge
  $4-12; $8 drink min at bar; AE/MC/V
Dining
  Continental; food: $11-18
Reservations
  By phone
Location
  Just E of La Brea
Parking
  On street

GENGHIS COHEN CANTINA

740 North Fairfax Avenue
Los Angeles, CA 90046
Info: (213) 653-0640
Restaurant/club offering acoustic music; seats 60 at tables, 8 at bar; no reservations; appetizers available; all ages.

      Behind the black shiny walls of this excellent Chinese restaurant lies a long, narrow, light-blue room with a small stage, tables and chairs. Separated from the diners, the Cantina is its own popular nighttime party. The people who come here, and many are regulars, come for original acoustic music. The thread that connects all the performers is intensity. The audience is always given something passionate to take home. Don't be surprised if the crowd unanimously hushes for the slow ballad tune, or seems to know all the songs and their lyrics.

      Come early if you want seats. People do come and go between songs, so if you're persistent, you'll get to

Performances
  Sun-Thurs 8:30 pm; Fri-Sat 9 pm
Cost or Cover Charge
  $2 and up; AE/MC/V
Dining
  Chinese; appetizers and a few entrees; food: $4 and up; individual tables
Reservations
  None
Location
  Off Melrose
Parking
  On premises; on street

sit. Someone may even offer you a chair—the crowd, which ranges from 20 on up, is super mellow, happy, and polite.

The Chinese food in the restaurant is great, albeit expensive. Appetizers can be ordered in the Cantina, which has a full bar. The cover charge is minimal, and there's no drink minimum. Such a deal!

GIORGIO'S PLACE

300 Ocean Boulevard
Long Beach, CA 90802
Info: (310) 437-2119
Restaurant/jazz club; seats 65 at tables, 25 at bar; reservations usually not necessary; food served during sets; non-smoking section; all ages.

Not to be confused with that former yellow-striped boutique on ritzy Rodeo Drive, Giorgio's Place in Long Beach offers sweet, soft jazz for mellow moods. The little performing space, unlike the Beverly Hills store, is pocketbook-friendly.

No cover or drink minimum. Valet parking is available at—are you ready?—no cost. Jazz near the beach for nada? Sounds good to me! Friday and Saturday shows begin at 8 pm; appetizers, pastas, and full meals are served during sets.

Performances
Fri-Sat 8 pm-12 am; service during sets
Cost or Cover Charge
No cover; AE/Disc/MC/V
Dining
Riviera cuisine; food: $10-15; individual tables; reserved tables; smoking/non-smoking
Reservations
Reserve by phone
Location
Long Beach (710) off at Golden Shore exit; left to Ocean Blvd
Parking
On premises; valet, FREE

HARVELLE'S

1432 4th Street
Santa Monica, CA 90401
Info: (310) 395-1676 **Fax:** (310) 450-3782
A vintage Santa Monica bar seating 60 at tables, 30 at bar; no reservations; no food; 21 and over.

The oldest club in Santa Monica, this snug, Chicago-style bar features live music each night of the week. A different four- to seven-piece blues band plays nightly, except Wednesday, when Cajun-Zydeco style music gets the spotlight. Harvelle's attracts a downtown audience—shoppers from the nearby Santa Monica Place Mall, or people just looking for a place to sit down and chat. Weekends bring out the party animals. In either case, Harvelle's bands are either talented local musicians looking for a place to jam or getting their chops together before hitting the road. Larry Johnson's Sunday night blues jam is often congenial with the open mike policy.

The owner of the bar, Rainer Beck, is an environmental scientist by day who bought the place several years ago and transformed it from a rocker's bar into a pure blues sanctuary. Thanks to his profession, Beck is cognizant of atmospheric comfort and gauges the number of people allowed inside. So, you may have to wait outside a while, but once you get in, you'll appreciate the ample room on the dance floor. A new high-tech ventilation system ably handles the cigarette smoke. The room is one of those tunnel types, with entrance at one end, stage at the other. In between is a long bar on the left and a string of small tables along the right.

Cover prices are modest (usually $5 a head) and only apply Wednesday through Saturday; Sundays and Mondays are free. Harvelle's is kitchenless, but also so close to the Third Street Promenade's numerous restaurants, you can practically order while you're listening to music.

Performances
Mon-Sun 8:30 pm-1:30 am
Cost or Cover Charge
$5-7; 2 drink min
Reservations
None
Location
Downtown Santa Monica; at end of the Santa Monica 10 Fwy
Parking
On street, large parking structure next door

HAUNTED CABARET & HAUNTED STUDIOS

6417 Hollywood Boulevard
Hollywood, CA 90028
Info: (213) 465-5224
Music, "cabaret" shows, one-act plays; seats 50 at tables; limited snack menu; no reservations; all ages.

A ghost has a permanent table at this place, but no one seems to complain; after all, it was here first...

Located in the midst of Hollywood Boulevard's eccentric street life is the small haunted storefront. Following a "greeting room," the long rectangular main space contains the stage on one side, with spartan tables and chairs on the other.

A 12-person cast attempts to raise the spirits of old Hollywood legends with "Jimmy's Hollywood Spirits" cabaret show Friday and Saturday nights. For the faint of heart, there's live jazz and blues played by local and out-of-town bands on other nights.

Upstairs is the equally unusual Haunted Studios, a performance space out of an Anne Rice novel. Every late Saturday night the Theatre of the Vampires gets together to put on its act of live gothic music—don't forget your fangs! The rest of the nights are rented out to more or less normal mortal performance art groups.

The windowless walls are painted gray, sofas from '50s-style booths line one wall, and mirrors reflect you—and the vampires—from every direction.

No alcohol is served; but you can get coffee, juices, and snacks really cheap.

Parking is difficult and expensive (a parking lot is located just behind the place) especially weekends when Hollywood Boulevard is closed. Best bet: street parking on Cahuenga or Wilcox.

Performances
Wed-Sun evening; service during sets
Cost or Cover Charge
$3-10; check/MC/V
Dining
Gourmet snacks and deli sandwiches; food: $4-8; drinks: $1-3; individual tables; reserved tables
Location
On Hollywood Blvd near Cahuenga; near Hollywood (101) Fwy
Parking
On street and the Aloha parking lot behind club

HIGHLAND GROUNDS

742 North Highland Avenue
Los Angeles, CA 90038
Info: (213) 466-1507
Coffeehouse seating 56 at tables, 12 at the bar; no reserved tables; food served during sets; all ages.

Highland Grounds was one of the first half dozen pioneer coffeehouses to open in the early 1990s. It's found its mark as a popular stop for all age groups. Afternoons are busy with intimate conversations, take-out latte orders, and the occasional business meeting. Its eclectic design includes tables and chairs in all sorts of shapes, sizes and colors; indoor and outdoor seating.

As the sun sets, Highland Grounds picks up. It's less and less of a secret find now that every evening showcases some sort of entertainment. Starting at 8 pm (usually) you might find a poetry reading, open-mike acoustic night, scheduled blues, folk, rock 'n' roll bands, or one- (or more) person theater presentations.

Expect the unexpected—you never know who might show up to perform, or who might use this forum as a jumping off point to larger less-intimate venues. Be sure to get to the cafe before the show begins to get a seat. The cover charge is minimal ($2-$3), and a one or two drink minimum is enforced after 7 pm.

The service is always friendly and the staff has a good eye for remembering faces. Customers leave drawings on the bulletin board, and messages on the chalkboard. The food is good and filling—American style cuisine of sandwiches, salads, soups and desserts—and it's cheap.

Park on the street after 7 pm, but be sure to note parking restrictions.

Performances
Mon-Sun 8 pm; service during sets
Cost or Cover Charge
$2-3; 1 or 2 drink min at bar, enforced if not dining; MC/V
Dining
Sandwiches, salads; food: $3.50-5.75; drinks: $1.50-3.25; individual tables
Location
1/2 block N of Melrose
Parking
On premises; on street also available

HOLLY STREET BAR AND GRILL

175 East Holly Street
Pasadena , CA 91103
Info: (818) 440-1421
Bar/jazz club; seats 90 at tables; reservations recommended; food served during sets; restaurant non-smoking; all ages.

Five nights a week, mellow jazz or classical piano serenade dinner guests here. The music runs from 6:30 to 10:30 p.m, and can be heard from both the outdoor patio and main dining room.

The atmosphere heats up on weekends when local bands and studio musicians work out. To accommodate the diners, the music starts conservatively then shoots off in more progressive tangents as the night wears on (don't want to disturb that "dinner vibe"). Fusion players, usually no more than five to a band, flock here. Music is played from 8:30 to 12:30 on weekends. There's no cover any night.

California/continental cuisine is the dining theme. Pastas, seafood, and salads dominate the menu, and have a distinctive Pacific Rim patina. Reservations are a good idea.

Performances
Mon-Thurs 6:30 pm-
10:30 pm; weekends
8:30 pm-12:30 am;
service during sets
Cost or Cover Charge
No cover
Dining
California Continental—
pasta, seafood, salads;
food: $12 ; drinks
$2.50; individual tables;
reserved tables;
restaurant non-smoking
Reservations
Reserve at door, by
phone
Location
Between Arroyo
Parkway and Marango
Parking
On premises, FREE;
valet, $1.50; on street

HOLLYWOOD MOGULS

1650 North Hudson
Hollywood, CA 90028
Info: (213) 465-7449   **Rsvn:** (213) 465-7449
Fax: (213) 465-7449
Club/theater; seats 150 in the cafe at tables, 12 at bar; reservations not necessary; limited menu served during sets; all ages.

What used to be the Young Moguls has grown up into the Hollywood Moguls, a multi-use space that combines a 99-seat theater on one side of a renovated warehouse with a big performance space on the other.

The club, a mixed bag of acoustic music and performance art, is a great place to hear music, meet musicians, mind your own business, or let loose your extroverted side. The schedule is ever-changing—one night you might walk in on a film, another on a performance artist. In the evening, a recording lists the current schedule. Comfy chairs and sofas are plentiful, and there are even writing tables to be found in this spacious room decorated with quality art.

A brand new Equity space has been set up for live theater. This 99-seater can also be transformed into a screening room for the scheduled film presentations. Patrons have only to travel a few steps from the theater to the restaurant for an intermission snack. Speaking of snacks, there's an odd menu with choices such as turkey tacos and pimp chicken wings—don't ask! Liquor isn't served, but there are plenty of beverages on tap.

Attended parking lot is available, or seek a spot on the street.

Performances
Call for schedule;
service during sets
Cost or Cover Charge
$3-5; check/AE/Disc/
MC/V
Dining
Snacks and light foods;
food: $3-7; drinks:
$1.50-3; reserved tables
Reservations
Not necessary
Location
1/2 block S of Hollywood
Blvd
Parking
On street; parking lot,
$3.50

HOUSE OF BLUES

Sunset Boulevard and Olive Avenue
Info: (310) 650-0235

This new on the Strip blues club/restaurant had not opened as we went to press, but it's being eagerly awaited—all 29,000 square feet of it! The restaurant alone seats nearly 400 hungry customers, and about 1,000 music fans can cover the music club. Boston and New Orleans each have their own House of Blues already. Management promises every kind of blues available, plus other non-blues bands.

THE ICE HOUSE

24 North Mentor Avenue
Pasadena, CA 91106
Info: (818) 449-4053 **Rsvn:** (818) 577-1894
Comedy nightclub; seating for 200 at tables; reservations necessary; full menu; Tuesday is non-smoking night; 17 and older.

This Pasadena venue, long ago a renowned folk club, serves up comedy and dinner to a faithful following. While the menu features entrees named after famous comedians, the likes of Rosie O'Donnell, Dennis Miller, and Stephanie Hodge are a few of the delicious headliners not yet immortalized on the menu.

But you don't have to mix your dinner salads with your jokes. Dinner is served in Comics restaurant, while the comedy club itself is set up in the basic table and chair configuration facing a step up stage. Preferred seating is given to customers who purchase the dinner/show package. The package also includes a coupon for a free night of comedy for your next visit. If you're compulsive about comedy, it's the way to go.

Since its opening in 1960, the Ice House has featured such talent as Robin Williams, Lily Tomlin, and David Letterman. Thirty-plus years of photos, capturing them all, fill the warmly decorated restaurant walls.

Based upon their reputation, the Ice House draws a substantial crowd from the San Gabriel Valley with a significant number of people who travel from other areas.

Saturday nights feature three shows in the main showroom, Fridays two, and weekdays and Sunday there is one show per evening.

Valet parking is available in the alleyway, in the parking structure across the street for $2.50 Friday and Saturday only, or on the street.

Performances
Tues-Sun; call for times; service during sets
Cost or Cover Charge
$7.50 weeknights and Sun, $10.50 Fri-Sat; 2 drink min; extra charge for extra sets; AE/MC/V
Dining
Food: dining room $10-20; showrrom $3-8; drinks: $3.50-5
Reservations
Reserve at door, by phone
Location
Just S of the 210 Fwy; major intersection is Lake Ave and Colorado Blvd 1 bock NE
Parking
On premises, FREE; valet (Fri-Sat only), $2.50; on street

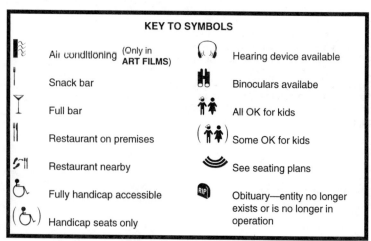

KEY TO SYMBOLS

Air conditioning (Only in ART FILMS)		Hearing device available	
Snack bar		Binoculars availabe	
Full bar		All OK for kids	
Restaurant on premises		Some OK for kids	
Restaurant nearby		See seating plans	
Fully handicap accessible		Obituary—entity no longer exists or is no longer in operation	
Handicap seats only			

THE ICE HOUSE ANNEX

24 North Mentor Avenue
Pasadena, CA 91106
Info: (818) 577-1895 **Rsvn:** (818) 577-9133
Comedy/blues club; seats 70 at tables, 10 at bar; reservations required; food served during sets; 17 and over.

Located in the same, near-historic building as the Ice House, The Annex is an 80-seat, intimate dinner theater and performing space that plays it cool for its own crowds. Originally designed for music but now cleanly redecorated, the new look seems more suitable to the one-person shows, improv, intimate comedy, an "almost" open mike night, and small jazz bands. It's working. The space is small, and every seat has a great view of the stage. Call for info on performance times and ticket availability.

Performances
Wed-Sun evenings; service during sets
Cost or Cover Charge
$5; AE/MC/V
Dining
American cuisine; food: $4.75-7.50; drinks $3-8
Reservations
Reserve at door, by phone
Location
2 blocks S of the 210 Fwy; Lake Street exit; at the corners of Lake and Colorado
Parking
On premises, FREE; valet, $2.50; on street

IGBY'S COMEDY CABARET

11637 Pico Boulevard
Los Angeles, CA 90064
Rsvn: (310) 477-3553
Comedy nightclub; seating for 165 at tables; reservations necessary; separate non-smoking sections; Thursday non-smoking night; 18 and over.

4 blocks east of Bundy

Igby's isn't a biggy—size-wise. But although this may be a small club, it has featured big names in comedy such as Dennis Wolfberg, Pam Stone, Carrie Snow, and Gilbert Gottfried (the voice of the parrot in _Aladdin_). If you need a good laugh on the Westside, you should check out this place.

In addition to serving up chuckles and bellylaughs, Igby's serves up killer nachos. Dinner is also on the menu here. Show nights are Tuesday through Sunday. (Monday is set aside for the comic's relief.)

Performances
Tues-Sun 8 pm; Fri-Sat 8 pm and 10:30 pm
Cost or Cover Charge
$ varies; 2 drink min; AE/Disc/MC/V
Dining
California cuisine; food: $2.75-9.50; individual tables
Reservations
Reserve at door, by phone
Location
Near the San Diego (405) and Santa Monica (10) Fwys
Parking
On premises, FREE; on street

IGUANA CAFE

10943 Camarillo Street
North Hollywood, CA 91602
Info: (818) 763-7735
Coffeehouse offering eclectic entertainment; seats 50; no reservations; no food; no smoking throughout; all ages.

Don't bother dressing up for this funky, living room-like coffeehouse with its menagerie of sofas and chairs, and menagerie of entertainment: performance art, poetry readings, or music. By day, regulars hang out reading the used books that line the shelves, some of which are for sale, as are the old records that line the opposite wall. Paintings of local struggling artists are always on exhibit at this friendly, super casual hangout. Today's off-beat generation of mellow anti-conformists can get off even their own beat path in this place.

Performances
Tues-Sun 9 pm; service during sets
Cost or Cover Charge
$3-4
Reservations
None
Location
Off the Hollywood (101) Fwy, exit Lankershim; where Lankershim, Vineland and Camarillo meet

You'll track down the elusive Iguana adjacent to a tiny theater on Camarillo Street, smack in the center North Hollywood's busy Lankershim/Vineland intersection. Eat well before you come, since the most substantial "meal" you can order here is a muffin. But a rainbow of sodas, soft drinks and juices sell for a buck apiece, and a coffee (plain coffee) and tea counter offers drinks for an optional donation.

Parking
On premises (across the street Hughes lot), FREE; on street

THE IMPROV

8162 Melrose Avenue
Los Angeles, CA 90046
Info: (213) 651-2583   **Rsvn:** (213) 651-2583

Brea Marketplace Shopping Center
945 East Birch Street, Ste. A
Brea, CA 92621
Info: (714) 529-7878   **Rsvn:** (714) 529-7878
Fax: (714) 529-5823

4255 Campus Drive, Ste. 138
Irvine, CA 92621
Info: (714) 854-5459   **Rsvn:** (714) 854-5455
Fax: (714) 854-6507

Comedy club with locations in LA, Brea, Irvine, and San Diego. (For San Diego, see next listing.) LA seats 220; reservations recommended; food served during sets; non-smoking section; 16 and over. Brea and Irvine: seat 300; reservations recommended; food served during sets; non-smoking nights, Wednesday and Sunday; 18 and over Monday, 21 and over other nights.

You can hardly turn around nowadays without bumping into something with the Improv name on it. At last count there were 15 Improv comedy showcase/restaurants scattered around the country from Washington, D.C. to Dallas. There are four clubs right here in Southern California: Los Angeles, San Diego, Brea, and Irvine. Besides the clubs, there's the A&E cable show, "An Evening at the Improv," a board game in the planning stages, plus a chain of Improv driving schools. (For those of you with different driving laws: in California you can opt for driving school instead of having a speeding ticket on your record. Being Los Angeles...we have driving schools hosted by comedians! All the better to laugh than to cry!) Improv founder Budd Friedman even teaches a stand-up comedy class at UCLA.

The Improv is an LA institution. It's still flourishing in its Melrose Avenue digs of nearly 20 years on the site of the old super-popular folk and blues spot, the Ash Grove. But the Improv was actually born in New York, in 1963, when Budd Friedman, then a hopeful Broadway producer, opened up a little theater district coffeehouse for singers (and anyone else who wanted to get up and make a fool of him- or herself) as a way to pay the rent until his Broadway career took off. Friedman's Broadway dreams never got off Ninth Avenue, but his little cafe became a long-running hit with show people. It wasn't long before the likes of Judy Garland, Liza Minnelli and Peter Allen were dropping by to entertain with improvised encores.

Singers gave way to comedians (Richard Pryor was the first), and in the mid '70s, Friedman headed west with the idea of opening up an Improv in Los Angeles. The Melrose Avenue site of the old folk-hippie music club, the Ash Grove, was selected. Before the decade was out, Friedman partnered himself with Mark Lonow, and since then the two men have marketed a comedy

Los Angeles:
Performances
Sun-Thurs 8 pm; Fri 8 pm, 10:30 pm; Sat 7:30 pm, 9:45 pm, 11:45 pm; service during sets
Cost or Cover Charge
$8-11; 2 drink min, enforced if not dining; AE/Disc/MC/V
Dining
Italian cuisine; pasta, pizza, salads, burgers; food: $8-18; drinks $3-$6; individual tables
Reservations
Reserve at door, by phone
Location
Between Crescent Heights and La Cienega Blvds
Parking
Valet, $3; on street

Brea:
Performances
Sun 8 pm; Mon-Thurs 8:30 pm; Fri 8:30 pm/10:30 pm; Sat 8 pm, 10:30 pm
Cost or Cover Charge
$7-10; 2 item min, enforced if not dining; AE/MC/V
Dining
7 entrees; prime rib, chicken cordon bleu, daily fresh catch; appetizers; food: dinners $9-12, appetizers $3-7; drinks $3.50-5; non-smoking Sun and/or Wed
Reservations
At door, by phone; no refunds, credits or exchanges
Location
Just W of the 57 Fwy, between the 60 and 91 Fwys; across the street from the Brea Mall

showcase/restaurant format that packs 'em in seven nights a week.

Over the years, the Improv has established itself as a launching pad for superstar comics. Freddie Prinze, Jimmy Walker, Elayne Boosler, Robin Williams, David Letterman, Richard Pryor, Andy Kaufman, and Rodney Dangerfield are all Improv alumni. (You will have read many of these same names in the Comedy Store profile. Obviously, these are competing clubs—to put the best face on the long rivalry.)

Today's comics have a lot more media exposure—MTV, late night TV, cable comedy networks and shows—so you're more likely to catch the act of a comic you've seen perform on TV. The Melrose location has jazz and cabaret, too. There are two or three show times a night, except for Sunday and Monday when those alternative forms of entertainment fill the bills. It wouldn't be unusual to see Jay Leno, Jerry Seinfeld, or Roseanne and Tom Arnold stop by and try out some new material at the Melrose location.

All the Southern California clubs operate more or less under the same set-up. They aren't big venues—350 seats max (not all in one room, and not at all clubs), usually at tables accommodating four persons. At least one night a week (Sunday and/or Wednesday) is a no-smoking night; dinner reservations guarantee seating, and cover charges range from $7 to $11. There's a two-item minimum, meaning you can choose one food item and one drink, or two drinks, or two food items, etc. Mark Lonow stresses that those drinks don't have to be alcoholic. With the purchase of a $10 Improv T-shirt, you're entitled to free admission every Tuesday night for the rest of your life, at the Brea, Irvine, and San Diego locations.

Parking

On premises (Marketplace parking structure and lot), FREE

Irvine:
Performances

Sun 8 pm; Mon-Thurs 8:30 pm; Fri 8:30, 10:30; Sat 8 pm, 10:30 pm

Cost or Cover Charge

$7-10; 2 item min, enforced if not dining; AE/MC/V

Dining

Pasta, fresh fish, prime rib, chicken; appetizers; dinners $9.95-11.95; drinks $1.75-5; non-smoking Sun and/or Wed

Reservations

Reserve at door, by phone

Location

Across from UCI, in the Irvine Marketplace Shopping Center; exit San Diego (405) Fwy at Jamboree

---

THE IMPROV (SAN DIEGO)

832 Grand Avenue
San Diego, CA 92109
Info: (619) 483-4522   **Rsvn:** (619) 483-4522
Fax: (619) 483-8624
Comedy club; accommodates 280; comedy acts; reservations are recommended; serves dinner during the first half-hour of the show; separate non-smoking section; 21 and over.

Young college kids make up the usual crowd at this Improv, and *crowd* is the operative word here. The audience is packed liked lemmings into one giant black room chock full of individual tables. Dinner is served during the first half hour at small tables. Comics from all over the country stand up and do their thing on the attractive, well-lit stage. Some have already had national exposure on "Late Night with David Letterman" or the "Tonight Show" (old and new), and some are on their way there.

On Tuesday nights, when the cover charge is $8, you can purchase a $10 Improv T-shirt and get in any subsequent Tuesday free. The two-item minimum is conveniently flexible: you don't have to order two drinks, you can get one food item and one drink to make it work (and they don't have to be alcoholic). Every Sunday night constitutes a non-smoking night for the entire room. Special package deals are available. Dinner reservations entitle you to guaranteed priority seating (whatever that means in such a tightly packed room) and two cover charges. Dinner entrees range in price from $10 to $14; appetizers are $5 to $8.

This locale features its standup downstairs, and a bar and cabaret upstairs.

Performances

Sun 8 pm; Mon-Thurs 8:30 pm; Fri 8:30 pm, 10:30 pm; Sat 8 pm, 10:30 pm; service during sets

Cost or Cover Charge

$8-10; 2 item min, enforced if not dining; AE/MC/V

Dining

Dinner: pasta, fresh fish, prime rib, chicken; appetizers: taquitos, chicken wings, potato skins, shrimp cocktail; dinner: $9.95-11.95; drinks: $1.75-5; non-smoking Sun

Reservations

Reserve at door, by phone

Location

Between Mission Blvd and Garnet; 1 block E of the beach

Parking

On premises, FREE; on street

INN ARTY'S

36 East Holly Street
Pasadena, CA 91103
Info: (818) 793-3723
Restaurant/jazz club; seats 40 at tables, 10 at bar; reservations recommended; food served; all non-smoking; all ages.

Set in the busy Old Town area of downtown Pasadena, Inn Arty's is one of those deceptive little bistros from the outside. But one listen to the sounds inside will change your mind.

Many local Pasadena players work this place, some quite good, such as tenor saxophonist Chuck Manning and his band. The high ceilings and long narrow room encourage the musicians to play acoustically. The bar is on one side with booths on the other and in back. The industrial gray interior is clean, unobtrusive and shows off the rotating visual art on the walls.

The menu at Inn Arty's is French, all entrees costing $13. If you've come just to listen, an extensive wine list ($50 a bottle tops) and some fine, obscure beers should slake you. There's an occasional cover charge (depending on who's playing) and a two-drink minimum.

Like the Dodsworth Bar & Grill a couple of blocks away, Inn Arty's isn't always parking-accessible. A public lot on Prospect, two blocks south and parallel, is worth investigating.

Performances
Thurs 8 pm-12 am; Fri-Sat 9 pm-1 am
Cost or Cover Charge
$ varies; 2 drink min; MC/V
Dining
Bistro; generous portions, home-style traditonal French food; food: entrees $13, appetizers, salads and desserts $4-6.95; non-smoking
Reservations
Reserve at door, by phone
Location
2 blocks S of Pasadena's 210 Fwy; 2 blocks N of Colorado Blvd; between Raymond and Fair Oaks
Parking
On street

JAX

338 North Brand Boulevard
Glendale, CA 91203
Info: (818) 500-1604   **Fax:** (818) 500-1945
Supper club; seats 110, 75 at the bar; reservations recommended; food served; 21 and over at the bar, all ages in restaurant.

Jax is a stylish Glendale supper club featuring jazz seven nights a week. A happy hour with pianists Arlette McCoy and Jim Selogy alternating hits at 5:30 Monday through Friday.

This club might be a serious contender for Noisiest Music Venue. In fact, the moderately priced continental dinners are the main attraction, as any musician who's ever worked here knows. The long and narrow room's bandstand isn't always accessible to everyone there.

Despite these drawbacks, Jax books some very respectable talent. Saxophonists Bill Perkins, Med Flory, Lanny Morgan, and Benn Clatworthy are regulars. Pianists Frank Strazzerri and Cecilia Coleman also add to the musical fabric. Every July Jax has its anniversary celebration night, where an impressive display of all-star bands made up of regulars and alumni alternate taking the stand.

Performances
Mon-Thurs 9 pm-1 am; Fri-Sat 9 pm-1:30 am; Sun 7:30 pm-midnight
Cost or Cover Charge
No cover; AE/MC/V
Dining
Lunch and dinner; contemporary California cuisine; food: lunch: $4.95-9.95; dinner: $6.95-13.95; individual tables
Reservations
Reserve at door, by phone
Location
Off 134 Fwy, Central-Brand exit, located 1/2 block on Brand S of Lexington
Parking
On premises, FREE; valet, FREE (in rear alley); on street

THE JAZZ BAKERY PERFORMANCE SPACE

3221 Hutchison Avenue
Los Angeles, CA 90034
Rsvn: (310) 271-9039
85-seat studio devoted to jazz performances; reservations a must; no liquor, snacks only; no smoking; all ages.

Pianist and songwriter Dave Frishberg called The Jazz Bakery "the best place to work in at least the Western Hemisphere." Pianist Mike Wofford, when on tour in Europe, overheard conversations in Paris and Rome extolling the Bakery's virtues!

Vocalist Ruth Price and photographer Jim Britt, who began the Bakery next door to the Helms Bakery in 1991, operate it on weekend evenings and Sunday afternoons. (During the week it functions as Britt's studio.)

Unlike some clubs, which are actually restaurants with a piano, the JB is set up specifically for listening. Folding chairs are set up in neat rows, and no one speaks during the performances. Furthermore, Price's booking policy is to provide a place for deserving artists and unknowns.

The room is essentially a square box with blank walls and a high ceiling. This configuration, plus discreet sound reinforcement, results in the most acoustically perfect room in town. Two great pianos supplied by David L. Abel are kept tuned and make duet programs possible. The pin-drop quiet audiences make it a place where performers love to work. Imaginative pairings like duets between pianists Wofford and Bill Mays, or Horace Tapscott and Nate Morgan, couldn't happen anywhere else.

Another unique feature—the subscription program. With a $250 membership, subscribers get 10 double or 20 single admissions, or that can be doubled. Single tickets are available, beginning at $15. Tickets include dessert and coffee or cold beverages, which are served before—not during—the performances.

Performances
Thurs-Sat 8 pm; Sun matinee, 7 pm
Cost or Cover Charge
$15-20; cash or check at door
Dining
Coffee, soft drinks, dessert
Reservations
Reserve by phone
Location
Between Washington and Venice Blvds; and National and La Cienega; near Santa Monica (10) and San Diego (405) Fwys
Parking
On premises, FREE; on street

JAZZ LIVE AT THE HYATT See **FESTIVALS & SEASONAL EVENTS**

JP'S MONEY TREE

10149 Riverside Drive
Toluca Lake, CA 91602
Info: (818) 769-8800
Jazz supper club; seats 70 at tables; reservations highly recommended; food served; 21 and over.

The dining/listening room of this classy club is quite cozy with its low lighting, black leather banquettes, crisp tablecloths and romantic flowers on every table. The long, narrow room ends at the small stage, making the acts harder to see from the street-side tables. But it's a small enough room so you can hear the music everywhere.

JP's draws the likes of Burt Reynolds and Lily Tomlin, as well as members of popular rock groups sneaking in to hear their favorite jazz artists. Karen Hernandez and Frank Wilson are regular performers, as is Jimmy Spencer. Page Cavanaugh and Trio do Thursday through Saturday nights. Tuesday is open mike night, and Wednesday is a different featured performer. The music—and kitchen—begin at 9 pm and go to 1:30. You can order dinner until 11 on weeknights, till midnight on weekends. Featured are steaks, pasta, chicken and house specials. Full dinners range from $10.50 to $16.50.

Performances
Mon-Sun 9 pm
Cost or Cover Charge
No cover; MC/V
Dining
Dinner served Mon-Sat; steaks, chicken, pastas, salads; food: $10.50-16.50; booths and tables
Reservations
Reserve by phone
Location
Between Pass Ave and Cahuenga Blvd; near the 134 Fwy
Parking
Valet; street parking

Make your reservations in advance; weekends are especially jam-packed. Evenings, a valet works the front, or there's street parking.

LARGO (THE PUB ON FAIRFAX)

432 North Fairfax
Los Angeles, CA 90036
Info: (213) 852-1073   **Rsvn:** (213) 852-1851
Fax: (213) 852-1073
Pub/nightclub with eclectic lineup; seats 113 at tables, 10 at the bar; reservations highly recommended; food and liquor served during performances; 21 and over after 9 pm.

Ireland comes to Fairfax Avenue. Well, that's what it seems like at first when you meet owner/booker Mark Flanagan, who has renovated and revamped the old Cafe Largo into a pub-like atmosphere and imported into it a friendly, laissez-faire attitude. All that's missing is the mist and the fireplace. In terms of performing artists, however, this place is as far from shamrocks and Blarney stones as you can imagine.

A full range of entertainment is served up nightly: classical, jazz and blues, rock-and-roll, acoustic and folk bands, country music, poetry readings, story telling, stand-up comedy and small theatrical presentations. Thursday night is blues night, while cabaret plays on Sunday. Men at Work's Colin Hay has appeared to sing and play his guitar on the small corner stage, as has John Stewart, once a member of the Kingston Trio. Timothy Leary's spoken word presentations are *tres* popular, and Jim Carroll's poetry readings are immediate sell-outs.

The large room is more intimate than it seems at first glance. Seating is at very-close-together tables in the middle of the room, or at the few black leather banquettes along one wall. An extra long bar accommodates ten, with several tall tables and stools along another wall.

Suggested dinner entrees, served during sets: Irish stew, shepherd's pie, or pasta. Dinners range from $6.50 to $12.50; appetizers go for $2.50 to $7. Drinks will run you $2.75 to $6.50.

Park on the street or in the attended municipal lot on the northeast corner at Fairfax and Rosewood.

Performances
7:30 pm; service during sets

Cost or Cover Charge
$3-15; 2 drink min, enforced if not dining; AE/MC/V

Dining
European cuisine; fresh chicken, seafood dishes, pastas, appetizers, salads, soups; food: entrees $6.50-12.50; drinks $2.75-6.50; individual tables; reserved tables

Reservations
Reserve at door, by phone

Location
On Fairfax between Beverly and Melrose

Parking
On street; municipal lot nearby

Y || (&)

LA SALA LOUNGE

Four Seasons Santa Barbara Biltmore
1260 Channel Drive
Santa Barbara, CA 93108
Info: (805) 969-2261   **Fax:** (805) 969-4212
Jazz club; seats 70; reservations not necessary; limited menu, complimentary hors d'oeuvres; non-smoking section; all ages.

The Four Seasons Biltmore Hotel is one of Santa Barbara's most beautiful spots. Both locals and tourists find its La Sala Lounge an elegant and comfortable respite. They come in black tie or designer jeans to sit back and listen to easy music. Five nights a week a solo pianist takes over. Jazz is featured one night a week, and Marimba music is played on weekends. The tunes can be heard from 5:30 to midnight each evening.

The music may not be the most adventurous, but the room is exquisite, the sounds are soft, and the hors d'oeuvres are free! There's also a low-key menu should you want more than appetizers. More inducements: La Sala has no cover charge, no drink minimum, and the valet parking is complimentary.

Performances
Mon-Sun 5:30 pm-midnight

Cost or Cover Charge
No cover; AE/Disc/MC/V

Dining
Complimentary hors d'oeuvres and light fare menu; food: $5-8; drinks: $4-6; individual tables

Reservations
Not necessary

Location
Off Hwy 101, Olive Mill Rd exit; on Channel Dr overlooking the Pacific

Parking
Valet, FREE; on street

Y || (&)

LAUGH FACTORY

8001 Sunset Boulevard
West Hollywood, CA 90046
Info: (213) 656-1336
Fax: (213) 656-2563
Comedy nightclub; seats 250 at tables; food served during sets; reservations necessary; 18 and over.

Laugh Factory has been manufacturing a good time on Sunset Boulevard for more than a decade.

Papier-mache celebrities smile at you from the club's Sunset Boulevard and Laurel Avenue location. You'll get ample time to study this artwork while you wait in line to be let in party-by-party. Don't expect to get off cheap on the two-drink minimum by ordering coffee or coke. These also cost several bucks.

The audience does have fun here. The Factory stamps out a fairly predictable lineup night after night, but has hosted the likes of Roseanne Arnold and Tim Allen. On the nights "Comic Strip Live" films for the Fox Television network, the lineup—and the audience—changes to the big time. The inside is pleasant enough and people dress up for a night out and often go in groups.

Street parking is no joke. Better to valet it for $2.75.

You can order finger foods and snacks at the club or else take advantage of the nearby eateries. The Gaucho Grill is just across the street, and Greenblatt's Deli sits right next door to the club. Or head further west on Sunset to the outdoor cafes at Sunset Plaza.

Performances
Mon-Thurs 8 pm, 10 pm; Fri and Sun 7:30 pm, 9:45 pm, 11:45 pm; Sat 7 pm, 9:45 pm, 11:30 pm; service during sets
Cost or Cover Charge
$8-10; 2 drink min, enforced if not dining; MC/V
Dining
Light dinner menu, finger foods; food: $4-6; drinks: $3-6; individual tables
Reservations
Reserve at door, by phone
Location
Between Fairfax and Crescent Heights
Parking
On premises, FREE; valet, $2.75; on street

LA VE LEE

12514 Ventura Boulevard
Studio City, CA 91604
Rsvn: (818) 980-8158
Restaurant/jazz nightclub; seats 75; reservations required for dinner only; food served during sets; all ages.

Much of what you'll hear in this pleasant Valley venue is Latin (or Brazilian), and sometimes some R&B. Poncho Sanchez is often on the calendar. Some nights the place sizzles, other nights are mellow. But whatever the night brings, this intimate spot is definitely worth a listen.

An enclosed patio off the main room is ideal for the less serious listener who wants his/her food first with music as a side order and in the background.

Dinners are Mediterranean. Or come for the show and drinks (two drink minimum). There's also a small bar.

Performances
Tues-Sun, 9 pm, 11 pm; service during sets
Cost or Cover Charge
FREE-$10; 2 drink min, enforced if not dining; AE/MC/V
Dining
Food: $11.95-14.95
Reservations
Reserve at door, by phone
Parking
Valet, $2; on street

LE CAFE See **The Room Upstairs at Le Cafe**

LIGHTHOUSE CAFE

30 Pier Avenue
Hermosa Beach, CA 90254
Info: (310) 376-9833   **Rsvn:** (310) 372-6911
Fax: (310) 372-0773
Cafe featuring world music and jazz; seats 130 at tables and 30 at bar; reservations not necessary; food served; separate non-smoking section; 21 and over.

With waves crashing steps from the front door to set the atmosphere, this is a fun listening spot for reggae, world beat, rock, blues, and jazz. A lively tavern highlighting local bands every week night plus Thursday through Sunday

Performances
Mon-Sat 6-8 pm, 9 pm-1:30 am; Sat noon; Sun 11 am, 2 pm, 8 pm
Cost or Cover Charge
$5 Fri/Sat; 2 drink min, enforced if not dining; AE/MC/V/Disc

days, this place never seems to die down. It's the kind of spirited pub where you "party hearty."

There's usually a $5 cover at the door with a two-drink minimum on Friday and Saturday. On Monday, beer's a buck, on Tuesday, it's twice that, and Wednesday, the well drinks and appetizers are all half price. Thursday and Friday there's a happy hour with price specials from 4 to 8 pm. On Thursdays, college students and Gold's Gym members (don't ask me why) get in free.

Dining
Giant burgers, pizza, sandwiches, assorted appetizers; full breakfast menu Sat-Sun; food: $5; individual tables; smoking/non-smoking

Reservations
Not necessary

Location
On Pier Ave 1/2 block from ocean; take the San Diego (405) Fwy to Rosecrans to Sepulveda (Pacific Coast Hwy) to Pier

Parking
Validated parking in city lots

LOBBY BAR AT LOEWS SANTA MONICA BEACH HOTEL

1700 Ocean Avenue
Santa Monica, CA 90201
Info: (310) 458-6700   **Fax:** (310) 458-6761
Jazz bar; seating for 40 at tables, 20 at bar; reserved tables available; food served during sets; 21 and over.

Surprisingly good jazz can be heard every night of the week at Loews, one of LA's only beachfront hotels. While the groups themselves perform in the Lobby Bar, you can relax in the pleasant, airy adjacent lobby and take in the sounds.

The elegantly appointed lounge is presided over by pianist Dan May and his bassist brother David. They usually play one night a week. The Mays draw from a pool of local instrumentalists and singers, like Stephanie Haynes, guitarist Ron Eschete, or pianist Pete Jolly, but they have been known to book the room in concert configuration with guitarist Joe Pass or pianist Walter Norris. When these shows occur (infrequently), you'll need reservations. Otherwise just drop in anytime after 7 pm to enjoy the ambiance, musical and otherwise.

The sound level is geared to accommodate conversation—not eliminate it. The sofas and armchairs in the lobby are comfortable and the lounge itself is intimate and relaxed. Most relaxing of all: no cover charge.

The full bar offers free hors d'oeuvres 5 to 7 pm weekdays. Or, order from a menu which includes Caesar salads, pizza, calamari, and quesadillas. If you work in Santa Monica, this is an ideal spot to escape to after a hectic business day. The $31 Sunday brunch (10:30 am to 2 pm), features the sweet sounds of a sax trio.

Performances
Mon-Sun evenings; Sun matinee; bands: Thurs-Sat evenings; service during sets

Cost or Cover Charge
No cover; AE/Disc/MC/V

Dining
Appetizers, pizza, quesadillas; food: $6-11; drinks: $4.50-6; individual tables; reserved tables

Location
Santa Monica (10) Fwy, 4th St exit, between Colorado and Pico

Parking
On premises, self or valet; on street

LA CABARET COMEDY CLUB

17271 Ventura Boulevard
Encino, CA 91316
Info: (818) 501-3737   **Fax:** (818) 501-3749
Comedy club; seats 220 at tables; food served; 16 and over.

LA Cabaret provides continuous stand-up comedy from 8:30 pm to midnight Sunday through Thursday. Weekend shows feature headliners, with two seatings on Friday, three on Saturday. There's even a 7:30 pm "No Smoking" show on Saturday night.

Performances
Sun-Thurs 8:30 pm; Fri 8:30 pm, 10:30 pm; Sat 7:30, 9:30, 11:30 pm

Cost or Cover Charge
$6-12; 2 drink min; check/AE/MC/V

Professional and amateur comics work out new material in the adjacent lounge. Lucky for you—a Karaoke Singing Machine is also on hand with over 200 selections!

A full continental menu comes with price tags of $10 to $23. Management suggests you get there an hour before showtime for "leisurely dining."

Dining
Continental menu, plus bar snacks; food: $9.95-22.95; individual tables

Reservations
Reserve at door, by phone, mail, fax

Location
Between Balboa and White Oak; at Ventura and Louise; near Ventura (101) Fwy

Parking
On premises, free; on street also available

LULU'S ALIBI

1640 Sawtelle Boulevard
West Los Angeles, CA 90025
Info: (310) 479-6007 **Fax:** (310) 575-9740
Coffeehouse; seats 50 at tables; no reservations necessary; food served; all ages.

It's multiple choice at Lulu's. This popular Westside cafe serves Brazilian specialty foods and books free readings and occasional live music and comedy shows. Lulu's has been known to host an after-hours *carnaval*, staying open all night and serving a traditional Brazilian breakfast. One Sunday afternoon salute to Brazil was a blend of bossa nova and Brazilian classics by guitar and voice, poetry readings, and the sounds of "Bongo Queen" Melanie Steele—plus special Brazilian menu items. Poetry readings have been hosted by radio station KCRW, and comedy nights are catered with an appropriate sense of humor.

European-style patio seating is available if you'd rather talk outside than hear the show. On the other hand, if you've come for the performance, avoid sitting at a table near the hectic entrance. You might be surprised at the modesty of the "stage" area, which consists only of a corner of the restaurant and a mike.

Original artwork adorns the walls and ceiling track lights shed the modern-art gallery feel. The place is chatty and trendy and attracts a Westside crowd. If you dine here, try the tasty Brazilian national dish, *feijoada* (available on selected days only).

There are no waiters or waitresses; you order at the register and cart your own meal. The management here is warm and welcoming.

Performances
Vary

Cost or Cover Charge
No cover; MC/V

Dining
Brazilian-Californian cuisine; homemade pastries, sugarless desserts; food: $5-12

Reservations
Not necessary

Location
East of the San Diego (405) Fwy; corner of Santa Monica Blvd and Sawtelle

Parking
On premises, FREE; on street

LUNARIA

10351 Santa Monica Boulevard
Los Angeles, CA 90025
Info: (310) 282-8870 **Fax:** (310) 282-0502
Restaurant and jazz lounge; seats 120 at tables in the lounge, 60 in bar; reservations suggested; food served during sets; non-smoking section in restaurant; 21 and over in lounge.

Someone did it right. Lunaria has actually separated its music space from its dining area. The pastel, art-filled dining room gives the feeling of being spacious because the tables aren't on top of each other. You can conduct a real conversation with your companions—a special phenomenon in an LA restaurant—while you dine on California French cuisine. When the music begins, behind a

Performances
Tues-Sat 9:30 pm-1:30 am

Cost or Cover Charge
$5; 2 drink min, enforced if not dining; AE/Disc/MC/V

Dining
Light salads, appetizers, pizza, desserts; food: $6 and up; drinks: $3.75 and up; individual tables

movable wall that is kept shut until showtime, the mood of the whole place either mellows or sizzles depending on who's playing. The Lounge remains intimate even when the dining room wall is opened. If you settle in the lounge, with its upholstered banquettes bordering the small stage and individual tables in the middle, avoid the end banquettes on either side of the stage, or you'll only be able to see the profiles of the performers.

Lunaria has one of the best jazz lineups in the city. A slot on this schedule bestows status in LA. Even better, the people who come here, come to listen.

Brazilian, straight ahead, mainstream, blues—there's a monthly schedule available by mail, or call directly. The staff is pretty helpful about who's on tap and what they're known for.

The cover runs around $12, and the two-drink minimum holds for all shows. There's no cover charge at the bar; although a half-wall obstructs much of the view, it obstructs none of the music. We've come late, ordered salad and delicious gourmet pizza at the bar and listened to hot Latin jazz through two sets.

The clientele runs the gamut from 20-and 30-something Westside singles to mature Beverly Hills couples. Everyone dresses up on the weekend.

Location
Off San Diego (405) Fwy 1 mile E on Santa Monica Blvd

Parking
On premises, $ 2; valet, $2; on street

MCCABE'S

3101 Pico Boulevard
Santa Monica, CA 90405
Info: (310) 828-8037 **Rsvn:** (310) 828-4497
Fax: (310) 457-4245

Guitar shop-cum-concert space with 150 makeshift seats; reservations recommended; snacks only; no alcohol, no smoking; all ages.

Do you prefer nightclubs frequented by black-garbed fashion worshippers? At a concert, do you revel in cutting-edge acoustics and dazzling light shows and backdrops? Do you expect beer and cigarettes to fuel your good time? If you answered yes to any, of the above, forget about McCabe's.

Folk music fans, on the other hand, know this place well for jazz, blues, country, Appalachian, pop, and gospel shows. More often than not, you'll see a sole performer with a guitar on stage and nothing else. Only the musicianship counts here. Plus a little old-fashioned salesmanship, as this unassuming, unaffected venue doubles as a guitar shop during the day. Walk to the rear of the store and you'll find the entrance to the "concert hall." The only effort made at creating any musical ambience is the crowded display of guitars, mandolins, and tambourines for sale on every wall.

But don't let the simplicity fool you. Celebrated, major artists show up and offer performance-of-a-lifetime sets here. Musicians like Elvis Costello and Joni Mitchell have walked in, spontaneously jumped on stage, and delivered impromptu concerts.

Concerts are offered most Fridays and Saturdays and sometimes on Sundays, but always call first for the schedule. Ask to be put on the mailing list for future events.

There's a no-smoking, no alcohol policy here. Cookies, tea and coffee are the only food served (by donation). The crowd that frequents McCabe's is as dressed-down as the sound, opting for comfort in T-shirts and jeans.

Performances
Fri-Sun

Cost or Cover Charge
$12.50-17.50; check/ AE/Disc/MC/V

Dining
Coffee, tea, cookies

Reservations
Reserve at door, by phone

Location
On corner of 31st and Pico Blvd; Centinela exit off Santa Monica (10) Fwy

Parking
On street

MALDONADO'S

1202 East Green Street
Pasadena , CA 91106
Info: (818) 796-1126 or (213) 681-9462
Cabaret; seats 55 at tables, 10 at bar; reservations recommended; food served; non-smoking section; all ages.

Forty-second Street crosses the Boulevard St. Germain in this setting of intimacy and elegance. Maldonado's entertains cabaret-style. Owner Bill Maldonado, accompanied by a half dozen performers, whips up musical reviews of Broadway shows. This is not just singing around a piano, mind you, but mini-casts performing the music of Andrew Lloyd Webber, Gershwin, Lerner and Loewe, Cole Porter, as well as opera and operetta selections.

There are special seating times, with performances beginning after dinner. The menu leans toward French cuisine. If you choose not to make an entire evening out of it, you can watch the show from the bar, where the cover is $3. Dress up for this evening out.

Performances
Tues-Wed 7:30 pm;
Thurs-Sat 6 pm,9 pm;
Sun 5 pm, 8 pm
Cost or Cover Charge
$10-12; min at bar;
AE/MC/V
Dining
Award winning
continental menu,
emphasis on French
cuisine; food: entrees
$25-28; drinks: $4 and
up; individual tables;
reserved tables;
smoking/non-smoking
Reservations
Reserve at door, by
phone
Location
Four blocks E of Lake
Ave; 1 mile S of the 210
Fwy
Parking
Valet, $2; on street

MANCINI'S/CLUB M

20923 Roscoe Boulevard
Canoga Park, CA 91304
Info: (818) 341-8503   **Rsvn:** (818) 341-7434
Fax: (818) 341-3393
Rock, blues, and alternative music; seats 200 at tables, 20 at bar; no reservations necessary; food served during sets; 18 and over.

For guaranteed good seats, a friendly clientele, and a relaxed, good time, check this place out when you're in the West Valley. Every night of the week, bands play rock, blues and alternative music on the surprisingly large stage.

The sounds of bluegrass fill the air from 3 to 7 pm on Sundays, while the $7 all-you-can-eat buffet amply fills you. Musicians are encouraged to sit in on-stage; children are welcome (in fact, kids 12 years old and under eat at half price, and those under 6 dine free). Most everyone in the 20- and 30-something crowd seems to know each other.

Performances
Mon-Sun 8 pm-2 am,
Sun 3 pm; service
during sets
Cost or Cover Charge
$3-up; 1 drink min,
enforced if not dining;
AE/Disc/MC/V
Dining
Italian foods: pizza,
pasta, sandwiches;
food: under $10; drinks:
$2-6; individual tables;
reserved tables
Reservations
Not necessary
Location
NW corner of Roscoe
and Desoto; near 118
and 101 Fwys
Parking
On premises, FREE; on
street

MARLA'S JAZZ AND SUPPER CLUB

2323 Martin Luther King Jr. Boulevard
Los Angeles, CA 90008
Info: (213) 294-8430   **Rsvn:** (213) 294-8430
Restaurant/jazz club; seats 144 at tables, 14 at bar; reservations not required; food served during sets; non-smoking section; age minimum depends on show (Sunday brunch none).

       Jazz in LA, like other American arts, is battling for its survival during the recession. A disastrous fire and the financial strain of the recession have kept jazz fans checking local listings for the latest word on this long-standing nightspot. The jazz landmark was known originally as the Memory Lane and has been lounging around since 1940. By 1981, the owner wanted to trade the place in for retirement in Hawaii. Actress Marla Gibbs ("The Jeffersons," etc.), wanting to preserve something of LA's jazz heritage, bought it. The going hasn't always been easy, but Gibbs has persevered. Through three name changes (Marla's Memory Lane, Marla's and now Marla's Jazz and Supper Club), the club has presented many established jazz artists (Linda Hopkins, Kenny Burrell, Arthur Prysock, Benny Powell come to mind), as well talented newcomers like Black/Note. Gibbs herself performs on occasion.

       Dinner packages are available; covers vary based on the performer—anywhere from $5 to $15. If you're into eggs benedict with your jazz, call about the Sunday jazz brunch.

Performances
  Mon, Fri-Sat 9 pm, 11 pm; Sun 11 am-4 pm; service during sets
Cost or Cover Charge
  $5-15; 2 drink min at bar, enforced if not dining; AE/Disc/MC/V
Dining
  Continental creole; food: $8.95 and up; reserved tables
Reservations
  Not necessary
Location
  Between Crenshaw and Western
Parking
  On premises, FREE; valet, $3; street

MAXWELL'S BY THE SEA

317 Pacific Coast Hwy
Huntington Beach , CA 92648
Info: (714) 536-2555
Fax: (714) 536-3157
Jazz club/seafood restaurant; seats 75 at tables; full meals served; no reservations; 21 and over at bar.

       Should you find yourself adrift in the South Bay and simultaneously in the mood for an afternoon or evening of live jazz by the sea, tie up at this Twenties spot at the base of the Huntington Pier. Maxwell's breezy seafood restaurant and club serves up three music sets on Friday and Saturday night and three on Sunday afternoon. The lineup usually highlights established jazz artists such as Jim De Julio (a veteran bassist for Frank Sinatra and Tony Bennett) and former "Tonight Show" trumpeter Conti Candoli.

       The cover varies, and there's an additional food and beverage minimum. Seating is first-come, first served. Those under 21 are entitled to all but alcohol.

Performances
  Fri-Sat 8 pm, 9:30 pm, 11 pm; Sun 3 pm, 4:30 pm, 6 pm; service during sets
Cost or Cover Charge
  $4; $7 drink min at bar, enforced if not dining; extra charge for extra sets; AE/Disc/MC/V
Dining
  Jumbo shrimp, oysters Rockefeller, nachos, lobster springrolls; food: $5-10; drinks: $3-5; individual tables
Reservations
  Reserve at door
Location
  On PCH, between Beach and Golden West off the San Diego (405) Fwy
Parking
  On premises, $2; valet, $2; on street

THE MINT

6010 West Pico Boulevard
Los Angeles, CA 90035
Info: (213) 937-9630
Blues club; seats 55 at tables, 10 at bar; reservations taken for parties of four or more; food served during sets; 21 and over.
      LA's premiere blues club is not a fancy affair, just a meat-and-potatoes bar with some tables and chairs. It's in a shoebox-size building, nestled inconspicuously in the Mid-Wilshire area. Only the mint-green neon sign on the otherwise gloomy street clues you in.
      Bookers Jed and Lance Ojeda have been serving up blues Monday through Saturday since 1937. The bands on the schedule are often led by featured players who stock the touring bands of big name artists. When they're off the road, they call their own bands together and work the Mint. Catfish Hodge, the Texicali Horns, William Clarke, Rod Piazza, and Debbie Davies are some of the name blues artists you'll hear. On occasion, the Ojedas will book visiting blues royalty from Chicago and elsewhere, such as Lefty Dizz or Magic Slim. The great local blues guitarist, Arthur Adams, is also a regular.
      Plan to sing the blues with a packed crowd—make those reservations. Sit anywhere you like or lean at the bar—the bandstand isn't hard to see, and you can usually hear the music three blocks away. Food is served here.

Performances
Mon-Sat 8 pm; Sun 6 pm; service during sets
Cost or Cover Charge
$4-10; AE
Dining
American; casual dining; food: nothing over $8; drinks: $3.25-4.50; individual tables; reserved tables
Reservations
Reserve at door, by phone for 4 or more
Location
N of Santa Monica (10) Fwy; between La Cienega and Fairfax
Parking
On street

MOLLY MALONE'S

575 South Fairfax Avenue
Los Angeles, CA 90036
Info: (213) 935-1577   **Rsvn:** (213) 935-2707
Bar; seats 45 at tables, 25 at bar; no reservations; no food; 21 and over.
      If you're crazy for Irish accents, this place'll mollify you. Open every night, the darkly lit, unpretentious rectangular pub with portrait-covered walls and small stage features mainly bluesy and acoustic lyricists, with some up-and-coming innovative bands thrown in. Both the bench seats and bar offer a fine view, except near the entrance. If the music so inspires you, a postage stamp dance floor is at your feet. Molly's is said to be a popular spot with worker bees from the music industry who order up gallons of "the best" Irish coffee in town and listen to the jukebox jammed with Irish groups between sets.
      Park in the lot at the corner of Fairfax or on the street at Fairfax and 6th. Most other street parking is reserved for permit holders. Defy the "permit only" signs around, and not even the luck of the Irish will save you from a ticket. Neighbors get understandably irked at noisy late night departers, so put a cork in it when you leave.

Performances
Mon-Sun 8 or 9 pm
Cost or Cover Charge
$3; 2 drink min at bar; MC/V
Dining
Everything under $5; individual tables
Reservations
None
Location
1 block N of Wilshire Blvd
Parking
On premises, FREE; on street

MOONLIGHT TANGO CAFE

13730 Ventura Boulevard
Sherman Oaks, CA 91423
Info: (818) 788-2000   **Fax:** (818) 784-7179
Supper club; seats 195; reservations recommended; food served during sets; non-smoking section; all ages.
      If you're too young to remember the supper club era of the 1930s and 1940s and to have Stardust memories of your own, this art-deco club will give you a good idea of what you missed. A bandstand, dance floor, conga lines,

Performances
Tues 8 pm, 9:30 pm; Wed-Sat 7 pm; Sun 6:30 pm; service during sets
Cost or Cover Charge
$9-13 Tues; $10 drink or food min, enforced if not dining; must order to attend performance; AE/MC/V

singing waiters, a cool sort of tropical deco decor—all the trappings of that bygone swing scene have found a home.

There's music and entertainment Tuesday through Sunday. Tuesday is the "Best of the Big Bands" night, featuring a different 18-to-20-piece band playing swing, Brazilian, or contemporary each week. Other nights, the Palm Beach Trio holds sway, with a featured male and female singer. The fun starts about 7 pm most nights.

Dinner is continental, and prices (strictly '90s in flavor) range from about $14 to $17 per entree. A cover is charged only on Tuesdays (although there is a minimum food charge, which decreases after 11 pm).

Dining
American regional cuisine: grilled and sauteed chicken, beef, lamb, fresh fish, seafood, pastas, salads; food: $13.50-17; drinks: $4.25; individual tables; reserved tables; smoking/non-smoking

Reservations
Reserve at door, by phone, mail, fax (818) 784-7179

Location
1/2 block W of Woodman, just off Woodman exit of Ventura (101) Fwy

Parking
Valet, FREE

NUCLEUS

7267 Melrose Avenue
Hollywood , CA 90046
Info: (213) 939-9023   **Rsvn:** (213) 939-8666
Fax: (213) 931-6545
Restaurant/jazz club; seats 150 in the dining room, 15 at bar; reservations recommended; food served during sets; all ages.

Remember what Hollywood supper clubs were like in the '40s? Neither do I. But if we did, we'd recognize the model in this intimate bistro.

The entertainment holds forth in the Club Room, a small facility away from the dining area. The Club Room has just 16 intimate tables. The bandstand isn't quite as small as a postage stamp (drummers often work elbow-to-elbow with bartenders), but the most important acreage is the modest-sized dance floor anyway. Management makes sure that everyone who plays at Nucleus makes music to dance by. That includes blues and jazz.

The cover is a modest $5 on Fridays and Saturdays. The minimum is two drinks.

Performances
Tues-Sun 7 pm, 9:30 pm, 11 pm, 12:30 am

Cost or Cover Charge
$5; 2 drink min at bar, enforced if not dining; AE/Disc/MC/V

Dining
California/continental cuisine; food: entrees $15-21; dinner till 11 pm, late night menu till 2 am; individual tables; reserved tables

Reservations
Reserve at door, by phone, fax

Location
2 blocks W of La Brea; between Poinsettia and Alta Vista; near Hollywood Fwy

Parking
Valet parking on premises, $3

ONYX SEQUEL

1802 Vermont Avenue
Los Angeles, CA 90027
Info: (213) 662-5820
Coffeehouse entertainment; seats 40; no reservations; food served during sets; no liquor; all ages.

Onyx is a great hangout—in the most positive sense of that word—in a "true" LA neighborhood. Its two combined storefronts share the block with a popular bookstore, a playhouse, a cinema, and various other shops.

In one Onyx space you can ingest coffee drinks, juices, soups, sandwiches, bagels, and desserts. This room even has tables and chairs, to which music is piped over the

Performances
Wed 8 pm, Sun 8:30 pm; Sun 4 pm; service during sets

Cost or Cover Charge
No cover

Dining
Soups, sandwiches, bagels, coffee; food: $4; drinks: $2; individual tables

speakers. Art work, changed every two months, covers the walls; there's a two year waiting list of eager artists waiting to show their work. During daylight hours, the regulars use this part of the cafe for lively conversations. Writers, readers, and others looking for simple peace and quiet gravitate to the room next door with its better light and fewer distractions. There are a few tables outdoors.

On Wednesday and Sunday evenings, the pace picks up in the "quiet room" where performance artists, musicians, and dramatists take over. It gets pretty loud and pretty crowded, but the 40-person limit is regularly monitored. If you show up late and can't get in, you'll happily discover you can usually hear just as well outdoors.

Park on one of the side streets in the evening and on weekends. The neighborhood is safe enough for strolling.

Reservations
None
Location
Between Franklin and Hollywood Blvds; between Hollywood (101) Fwy and Golden State (5) Fwy
Parking
Public parking lot in alley behind club; on street

OPEN DOOR

513 State Street
Santa Barbara, CA 93101
Info: (805) 965-6655
Jazz and contemporary acoustic soloists; seats 94; no reservations; limited menu served during sets; non-smoking section; all ages.

The sushi-bar-meets-1950s-cafeteria decor of this listening club on Santa Barbara's lower State Street doesn't seem to be a turn-off to anyone. Neon lights, pub mirrors, plastic chairs, red booths, and art posters coexists in Zen-like harmony. Weekends, though, are busy as locals stop by to hear the contemporary acoustic soloists and jazz trios.

Yards and half-yards of beer attract a lively beer-guzzling crowd. A brief appetizer menu offers pizza, ice cream bars, and popcorn. The weekend cover charge is a piddling $1 to $2 and there's no drink minimum.

Performances
Tues, Thurs, Fri, Sun 9 pm-1 am; service during sets
Cost or Cover Charge
$1-2; AE/MC/V
Dining
Small appetizer menu, Puck's pizzas, Haagen Daz ice cream bars, popcorn; food: $1.25-6.75; drinks: $1.75-11; individual tables; reserved tables; smoking/non-smoking
Reservations
None
Location
Between Cota and Haley
Parking
On premises, FREE

THE PALACE

1735 North Vine Street
Hollywood, CA 90028
Info: (213) 467-4571 and 462-3000 **Fax:** (213) 462-0579
Concert hall/cabaret; accommodates 850 to 1,100; reserve tickets in advance; food available; 18 and over.

Built in 1927, this Art Deco Hollywood landmark achieved national prominence when it was converted into a television studio for shows such as ABC-TV's long-running "Hollywood Palace" in the 1960s. This West Coast rival of the "Ed Sullivan Show" played host to the biggest mainstream entertainers of the century—Bing Crosby, Fred Astaire, Jimmy Durante, Frank Sinatra and Groucho Marx, as well as upstarts like the Rolling Stones.

The building has been revamped into a concert facility. The main floor is either taken up by nightclub tables or cleared entirely for standing or dancing. A bar with tables is located in back of the floor, and folding chairs are wedged in on the sides toward the rear. If the audience is standing, good luck trying to see anything from the chairs—and even in the best of conditions, it is difficult to see the entire stage over the drinkers who are standing at the bar tables. Upstairs, the balcony is bisected into two sections of seats

Performances
Vary
Cost or Cover Charge
$ varies; MC/AE/V
Reservations
Reserve by TicketMaster; concerts only
Location
Half block N Hollywood Blvd; the Hollywood (101) Fwy at the Vine or Hollywood Blvd exits
Parking
On premises, $5-7; on street

separated by a control booth that hogs the middle. The sightlines are distant and sometimes obstructed, particularly up front near the railings, and it can be sweltering up there in the summer. The amplified sound everywhere varies from acceptable to horrible from night to night.

In the 1980s, the Palace went on a roll, playing host to several top-flight jazz musicians such as Ornette Coleman, Sonny Rollins, John Scofield and Joe Zawinul, as well as rock iconoclasts like the Residents and Frank Zappa. Occasionally you can still catch such choice events as a rare summer 1992 gig by Stones drummer Charlie Watts' bebop quintet. On weekend nights, the Palace features dance parties hosted by two of LA's hot rock radio stations, KISS-FM on Fridays and KPWR-FM (or Power 106) on Saturdays.

Pay parking is available on either side of the theater and across the street by the Capitol Records Tower. Street parking on Vine Street can also be found if you're fortunate, but be leery of some of the poorly-lit side streets. Food is available in the Palace Cafe.

THE PALOMINO

6907 Lankershim Boulevard
North Hollywood, CA 91605
Info: (818) 764-4018   **Rsvn:** (818) 264-4010
Nightclub offering rock 'n' roll and country entertainers; seats 300 at tables, 40 at bar; reservations recommended; food served during sets; all ages.

This L-shaped room on a nondescript stretch of Lankershim Boulevard once was Los Angeles' world-famous country-western music headquarters. Local good-ole-boys, truck drivers on their ways up and down the state, and country music's greatest performers all loved this rough-hewn honky-tonk.

Founded in 1949 by the late country musician/comedian Hank Penny (he named the club after the label of a shirt he'd just bought), the Pal became the stuff of legend from 1952 into the mid-'80s under the ownership of the late Tommy Thomas. Before he became a superstar, Willie Nelson presided over marathon drunken evenings of Western swing (sometimes broadcast on the radio) that helped cement his outlaw image. On other nights, juiced to the gills, Jerry Lee Lewis would wail one tortured country ballad and rockabilly potboiler after another in between bouts of braggadocio.

The list of names who performed on the Pal's pint-sized stage is incredible—Hoyt Axton, Bobby Bare, Asleep at the Wheel, Ernest Tubb, Merle Haggard, Bob Wills, Marty Robbins, Lefty Frizzell, George Jones, Buck Owens, Charlie Rich—to name-drop just a few. Another club landmark was a hulking bouncer named Tiny, who became nearly as famous as the singing stars.

When Thomas died, some thought that the Pal would die with him. Yet the club is still kicking, albeit with a lower profile. Country's national boom was almost the Pal's bust as appearance fees skyrocketed, pricing most star country acts out of the club's reach. Nowadays, the fare is mostly little-known rock and rockabilly acts, with an occasional name like former Rolling Stone Mick Taylor, Eek-a-Mouse or The Radiators.

Yet a memorable event can still occur without warning—such as a late '80s February evening when George Harrison, Bob Dylan and John Fogerty got up onstage during a Taj Mahal gig and jammed into the night (an event preserved on a bootleg CD). Or you might happen upon a bells ringer like avant-garde jazz spaceman Sun Ra

Performances
Mon-Tues 8:30 pm;
Wed-Sun 9 pm; service
during sets
Cost or Cover Charge
$3-15; MC/V
Dining
Full meals of steaks,
chicken, burgers, and
ribs; individual tables
Reservations
Reserve by phone,
TicketMaster
Location
Between Van Owen and
Sherman Way
Parking
On premises, FREE

(he insists he was born on the planet Saturn). Local bands are often well-supported by a sold-out house.

In any case, the old barbecue restaurant is still there, as is the full bar. Parking is FREE and PLENTIFUL.

PARLOR PERFORMANCES

See press listings for performance locations.
Info: (310) 471-3979
Performances in private homes; reservations required.

A down-to-earth modification of intimate Renaissance performances, Parlor Performances were introduced several years ago as a way to enjoy the lively arts in a quiet, personal setting. Offering cabaret and variety acts in private living rooms donated for the evening, producer Jeannine Frank treats audiences to the most intimate of theater and music experiences. The best seats in the house here are literally in the house, so make reservations in advance.

Many of the performers have been hailed by local critics and entertain a loyal following. Audiences and artists mingle over complimentary coffee and desserts afterwards.

Call Jeannine Frank for a calendar. Tickets aren't cheap, but there's no line for the bathroom!

Performances
Mon, Wed, Sat, Sun, 7:30 pm; Sun 2 pm
Cost or Cover Charge
$12-25; includes dessert and coffee; check
Reservations
Reserve by mail (P.O. Box 49283, Los Angeles, CA 90049), or phone 9 am-9 pm; exchanges made with advance notice

PATRICK'S II

428 "F" Street
San Diego, CA 92101
Info: (619) 233-3077
Jazz, rock, and blues bar; seats 85; no reservations; no food served; 21 and over.

Patrick's is a tight little, right little 30-foot narrow bar that's packed when the music plays. It's a dark and sexy spot for blues, boogie, jazz, and rock. One look at the handwritten calendar of music and you'd think the joint's Irish, but it's as far from Irish as you can imagine. With one wall of banquettes and a bar, most people end up standing for the live jive. It's cheap—no cover charge and just a two-drink minimum.

Performances
Mon-Sun 9 pm-1:30 am
Cost or Cover Charge
No cover; 2 drink min, enforced if not dining; min at bar
Reservations
None
Location
F St and 5th Ave
Parking
On street

THE ROOM UPSTAIRS AT LE CAFE

14633 Ventura Boulevard
Sherman Oaks, CA 91403
Info: (818) 986-2662   **Fax:** (818) 783-1095
Jazz club; seats 60 upstairs; reservations strongly recommended; food served; all ages.

The careers of many notable jazz and pop musicians have been launched at the very small Le Cafe's Room Upstairs over the past dozen-plus years. Its ongoing commitment to spotlighting top Brazilian artists makes it one of the most important venues for hot Brazilian groups and soloists. Ivan Lins, Guiherme Verquero, and Cecilia Noel can all be heard here. Dale Jaffe, who books the room (and is the son of Lois Boileu, who makes an occasional appearance), keeps a grand piano as the only fixture in the intimate room for the occasional solo pianist such as Dick Hyman or Steve Kuhn.

Beware of the more pop-inflected bands who think that volume is a substitute for quality—they can pin you to the walls with their amplification.

While The Room Upstairs is cozy and intimate, downstairs is decidedly more open and airy and offers a feast for grumbling stomachs. You can order everything from spicy international specialty appetizers such as

Performances
Sun-Sat 9 pm,11 pm
Cost or Cover Charge
$6-15; 2 drink min; AE/MC/V
Dining
Served downstairs only, not in music room; food: $8-16
Reservations
Reserve at door, by phone
Location
1 1/2 blocks W of Van Nuys Blvd; very near the intersection of the San Diego (405) and the Ventura (101) Fwys
Parking
On premises, $2.50; valet, $2.50; on street

quesadillas and handmade tamales to fresh mahi mahi and numerous pasta dishes. Le Cafe serves up spa cuisine and American Heart Association approved meals. The bar and restaurant stay open until 2 am, and there's a late-night supper menu. Combining dinner with the show entitles you to preferred seating, and unless you want to stand in line for a spot in the tiny upstairs room, I'd strongly suggest popping for dinner.

Ask to be put on the mailing list; the newsletter not only offers a calendar, but profiles of the upcoming artists.

THE ROXY THEATRE

9009 Sunset Boulevard
West Hollywood, 90069
Info: (310) 278-9457   **Rsvn:** (310) 276-2222
Fax: (310) 278-2447
Nightclub; seats 400-500; advance ticket purchase recommended; food served; all ages.

The Roxy has undergone a nearly complete personality change since the '70s through mid-'80s when it was the record company showcase in town. In his pre-stadium days, Bruce Springsteen would rock at the Roxy for nights on end. Hardcore Brucites insist he was never more electrifying (the proof is on his epic multidisc live album). George Benson recorded his signature hit "On Broadway" here—not on the Great White Way; Andrew Lloyd Webber introduced Variations on Roxy's stage. Figures as diverse as rocker Frank Zappa, reggae giant Bob Marley, minimalist composer Philip Glass, popular jazz stars George Duke, Branford Marsalis, and a rusty kid named Harry Connick, Jr., would play and in some cases, cut vinyl at the Roxy.

There are still flashbacks to its starry past, as when Duke returned royally for one night in December 1992, but nowadays, the most newsworthy aspect of the Roxy is the fashion show. It's truly a sight to behold—hordes of heavy metal and rock fans lining Sunset Boulevard to get into the club. Hardly a Paris runway, but a fashion extravaganza none-the-less of ultra-miniskirts, cut-off T-shirts with expletives exploding across the front, strategically ripped Levi's and (that outlaw staple) black motorcycle jackets.

Top rock and punk-metal artists have indeed taken center stage here. The club is always packed and the greetings rowdy. It's fun if you like getting a little wild—but consider wearing armor, or at least knee pads. The club can also become suffocating thanks to the intense heat and smoke (paramedics have been called in to revive musicians and fans).

There's a one-drink minimum at the tables. No reservations accepted for seating, though, so arrive early if you don't want to stand the whole night. Burgers, chicken sticks, fried zucchini, frozen yogurt and the like fill the menu and are served only at the tables.

You can buy tickets for the show in advance through TicketMaster (the popular bands do sell out), or you can get on that punk fashion line and take your chances buying tickets at the door. Ticket prices vary.

If you can afford the $5 for valet parking, go for it. Street parking, especially on weekends, is a real hassle.

Performances
  Mon-Sun
Cost or Cover Charge
  $ varies
Dining
  Burgers, fries, fried zucchini, frozen yougurt, chicken sticks;
  food: $4 and up
Reservations
  Tickets through TicketMaster; at door
Parking
  Valet, $5; street permit parking only

ST. MARK'S

23 Windward Avenue
Venice , CA 90291
Info: (310) 452-2222
Club plays R&B and jazz; seats 135 at tables, 25 at bar; reservations recommended; food and drink served during sets; separate non-smoking section; 21 and over.

You'll dine and listen in an architecturally impressive spot set in the area that Orson Welles tried to pass off as Tijuana in the opening of *Touch of Evil.* Quaint arches span the outside, while glass, metal, and marble decorate the interior. St. Mark's is a paradox of LA's cultural extremes. It's situated on the inimitably funky Venice Beach boardwalk, yet was designed with upscale elegance. The sophisticated decor, complete with marble bathrooms, couldn't contrast more with the daily eccentric street scenes out front.

In addition to the local blues band fare, names like Ike Turner, Basia, and Poncho Sanchez take their turns here. The weekly visits from rhythm 'n' blues singer King Cotton are the pick of the crop. Cotton has a good band of capable players and the vocal aid of Three Cool Cats to back up his hip selection of authentic R&B. On the King Cotton night, the place is packed. The crowd isn't just off the beach—they dress for this scene. Jazz is back with the sounds of Sanchez plus Black/Note and others.

Since the room is kind of a two-tiered layout in a U-shaped configuration, not many seats will have prime views of the bandstand. Closed-circuit TV monitors feed those seated in outer Slobovia. If you like conversation with your dinner, be sure to eat before the show starts (unless you enjoy yelling). The California cuisine is good—as long as money is no object. A dinner for two can run $100 if you include drinks.

In a throwback to "ancient" times, women get in free every Wednesday night. Tuesday through Friday from 6 to 8 pm everyone gets a deal during the two-for-one well drinks special. In the bar, $5 covers you weeknights, $10 weekends.

Performances
Tues-Thurs 9 pm, Fri-Sat 9:30 pm, Sun 9 pm; service during sets
Cost or Cover Charge
$5-10; food min for dining patrons but no cover charge—$15 weekdays and $20 weekends; AE/MC/V
Dining
Casual California cuisine; seafood, pasta, pizza, chicken; food: $15; individual tables; reserved tables; smoking/non-smoking
Reservations
Reserve at door, by phone
Location
Between Windward and Pacific; right on Venice Beach, 1 block N of Venice Blvd
Parking
On premises, $2.50; valet, $2.50; on street

SIDEWALK CAFE

1401 Oceanfront Walk
Venice , CA 90291
Info: (310) 392-4687   **Fax:** (310) 399-4512
An indoor/outdoor cafe with nightly music; reservations not necessary; food served between sets; non-smoking section; all ages.

Located just blocks from the Venice Pier, you can drop into this breezy cafe after a boardwalk stroll. Original rock, acoustic, blues and reggae music emanate from the patio-stage. You probably won't recognize the artists—this is a local-band showcase. The music begins at 8:30 pm Thursday through Saturday, and Monday, Tuesday, Wednesday, and Sunday at sunset.

This easygoing hangout is not for the pompous or stuffy. Everything about it suggests "California casual." Dinner is segued in during the performers' breaks and includes an array of omelettes, pizza, and burgers (the cafe is also open for breakfast and lunch). There's a drink minimum for non-diners, and everyone pays a cover charge which varies daily.

Performances
Thurs-Sat 8:30 pm-9 pm (bands); Sun-Wed sunset out on the patio (acoustic)
Cost or Cover Charge
$ varies; drink min enforced if not dining; AE/MC/V
Dining
Pizza, burgers, omelettes, breakfast, lunch and dinner; food: under $10; drinks: $3; individual tables
Reservations
Not necessary

(More. . .)

Location
Between Horizon and Speedway; take the San Diego (405) Fwy to Venice Blvd W; 4 miles to Pacific; N 1/4 mile past Windward to Horizon; left 1 block

Parking
On premises, $1.50 evenings, varies during the day; on street

THE SIX GALLERY CAFE

8861 Santa Monica Boulevard
West Hollywood, CA 90069
Info: (310) 652-6040

Coffeehouse with weekend entertainment; seats 80; no reservations required; food served during sets; non-smoking area; all ages.

This West Hollywood cafe is an important meeting ground for the gay, lesbian, and bohemian political and cultural community.

Local and Bay Area performers present all varieties of music, poetry, drama, and performance art. Schedules at the Six are, typical of coffeehouses, unpredictable. There's no cover. Just drop in and check them out.

The Frank Gehry-style exposed steel, brick, concrete and wood slabs of the interior are juxtaposed with plush, plump sofas and chairs. Out front is a partially enclosed patio set up with tables and chairs, inhabited most often by the after-work crowd.

Sandwiches, soups, pastries, juices, and coffee drinks are dirt cheap. For more substantial fare, little cafes dot Santa Monica east and west

Parking can be a challenge.

Performances
Thurs-Fri

Cost or Cover Charge
No cover

Dining
Sandwiches, soups, pastries, coffee drinks, juices; food: $1.50-6; drinks: $1.50-3; individual tables; reserved tables; smoking/non-smoking

Reservations
Not required

Location
Between San Vicente and La Cienega

Parking
On street

SOHO

21 West Victoria Street
Santa Barbara, CA 93101
Info: (805) 965-5497

Jazz and reggae; seats 150; reservations not necessary; food served; no smoking in the restaurant; 21 and over.

Soho is considered a top Santa Barbara spot for nightly jazz and reggae since Sunday. Located in what was once a church parsonage, a half block off State Street next to the Victoria Street Theater, the wood-floor restaurant/bar is decorated with flowers and soft candlelight. A seat in the bar practically puts you in the musicians' laps. Or you can simply audit the cool sounds from any of the three dining rooms.

You can hear such top local talent as Dick Dunlap, Randy Tico, and Theo Saunders. Management also regularly books in good LA musicians. The cover is low, and the California cuisine is pretty good. Soho is crowded on weekends and pretty voluble in the bar. There's no cover if you dine in.

Performances
Mon-Sun 9 pm-midnight or 1:30 am

Cost or Cover Charge
$2-5; Check/AE/MC/V

Dining
California cuisine; food: appetizers $5-8, entrees $10-17; drinks: $3.25-25; individual tables; smoking/non-smoking

Reservations
Not necessary

Location
1/2 block off State St, next to the Victoria St Theater

Parking
On premises, FREE

THE STRAND

1700 South Pacific Coast Highway
Redondo Beach, CA 90277
Info: (310) 316-1700   **Rsvn:** (310) 316-1700
Fax: (310) 316-2815
Concert-hall-sized club for all types of music; seats 500; reservations necessary; before-show dinner, appetizers during show; 18 and over.

Well known throughout the Southland, the Strand fills the large capacity house with some big name artists. Jazz musicians like Sonny Rollins, *salseros* like Willie Colon, or bluesmasters like Bobby "Blue" Bland work this club. Past familiar names have included B.B. King., Miles Davis, Jimmy Cliff, Robert Townsend, Branford and Wynton Marsalis, Ray Charles, and Les Paul in a rare West Coast gig. All types of music are performed here except for metal or rap, and there's a different established attraction each night. There are no warm-up acts—performers just get up and do their concert-like thing. Top comedians appear as well.

The room is a sprawling affair with two bars, a flotilla of barstools, oceans of tables and chairs, and a gallery in back. Seating is first-come, first-served; thus reservations and an early arrival are important. With a room this big, the sound leaves something to be desired, but don't let that stop you.

The full kitchen accommodates everyone from vegetarians to carnivores. Priority seating accompanies dinner. The cover charge varies depending on the performers.

Performances
Vary
Cost or Cover Charge
$ varies; 2 drink min; AE/MC/V
Dining
7-8 entrees on any given night; vegetarian, steak, seafood, chicken, pasta; dinner section gets priority seating; individual tables; reserved tables
Reservations
Reserve by phone, Strand box office, TicketMaster
Location
At intersection of Pacific Coast Hwy and Palos Verdes Blvd; San Diego (405) Fwy to Hawthorne Blvd (S/W) to PCH, make a right, down 1 1/2 miles
Parking
On premises, free lot due west; valet, $2.50; on street

SYSTEM M CAFFE GALLERY

213 A Pine Avenue
Long Beach, CA 90802
Info: (310) 435-2525   **Rsvn:** (310) 435-2525
Fax: (310) 435-7804
Cafe/coffeehouse with entertainment; seats 70; reservations recommended; food served during sets; non-smoking section; all ages.

When I see something called "cafe/gallery" I immediately expect the usual coffee house-cum-art gallery. Which is just fine. But this place is unique.

Art isn't just plastered to the walls. The exhibition space is seriously conceived and laid out. But there's no "attitude" here. The philosophy seems to be, "Come, hang out, enjoy." And considering the club stays open until 2 am—in Long Beach—and gets followers from Orange County and LA, they must be doing something right.

The entertainment is eclectic, to say the least: a little jazz, a little blues, some Cambodian dance troupes, accordion/guitar duets, folk rock, performance art, readings—the whole nine yards.

This isn't a big place: Seating for 70, a bar, and a loft.

Naturally the food follows this eclectic theme—and the price is right. All entrees are under $10. Choose from Southwestern, Indian, Mediterranean, and California grill (I've never known exactly what that means!). Park on the street or with the valet. For anyone using the city's Blue Line service, note this place is only steps away.

Performances
Tues-Thurs 8 pm; Fri-Sat 9:30 pm, 11 pm; service during sets
Cost or Cover Charge
$5-10; extra charge for extra sets; AE/Disc/MC/V
Dining
Southwestern, Indian and Mediterranean influences, eclectic california grill; food: $5-9.50; drinks: $1.25-5; individual tables; reserved tables; smoking/non-smoking
Reservations
Reserve at door, by phone, mail, fax
Location
Broadway exit on Long Beach (710) Fwy; between Broadway and 3rd St
Parking
Valet, $2; on street

TROUBADOR

9081 Santa Monica Boulevard
West Hollywood, CA 90069
Info: (310) 276-1158   **Rsvn:** (310) 276-1158
Club; seats 300; food served; all ages.

   The Troubador's history is known, at least in part, by nearly anyone who knows the '60s music scene. Some of the greatest—or at least most well-known—names in music of that period performed here. Elton John's first performance took place on this stage. Arlo Guthrie, Carole King, Van Morrison, Miles Davis, and Neil Diamond each had their turn. You may not know, however, that the Troubador was first a folk music house in another location on La Cienega Boulevard. Triny Lopez, the New Christy Minstrels, and Phil Ochs were all part of that time. And it wasn't just the performers who were important here, the guests were equally as famous—John Lennon was one example, Frank Zappa another.

Performances
   Fri-Sun; Wed 9 pm;
   Tues 8 pm; Thurs 10 pm
Cost or Cover Charge
   $ varies; MC/V
Dining
   Sandwiches, burgers,
   salads; food: $3.50;
   drinks: $3; individual
   tables
Reservations
   Reserve at door,
   TicketMaster, not
   responsible for
   cancellations; if band
   reschedules, tickets will
   be accepted for
   rescheduled date
Location
   Between Robertson and
   Doheny
Parking
   On premises, $2.50-3;
   valet, $2.50-3; on street
   on the E side of Doheny
   Blvd

TROY CAFE

418 East First Street
Los Angeles, CA 90012
Info: (213) 617-0790
Cafe/coffeehouse; seats 70; reservations not required; food served during sets; all ages.

   If you find yourself in Little Tokyo a little short on taste for sushi but with a yen for a bite of the bohemian, pull up your Honda horses at the Troy. This informal coffeehouse-eatery-gallery-performance space attracts a cross-cultural clientele of performers, film people, artists, and anyone else who wants to watch and listen to some of the best Latino talent in town.

   What the Troy offers (besides a cup of good espresso) is a launching pad for Latino performers headed for success. With limited venues for this cultural category, Troy owners Sean Carrillo and Bibbe Hansen try to make up the slack by making room for the known and unknown. Performers like the comic trio Culture Clash and Chicano Secret Service, and the guitar duets of Guitarras have all appeared. As if the cappuccino and coffee specialties weren't art enough!

   Here are some Troy tips: the space is long and narrow, so sit by the door if you're a chatterer, by the stage if you want to listen. Don't be dissuaded by "unknown" talent—expect the best.

   This is one of downtown LA's few late night hangouts. They have their own parking lot, so steer clear of street parking. Emergency snacks like hamburgers and sandwiches are also on hand.

Performances
   Fri-Sat 10 pm; service
   during sets
Cost or Cover Charge
   $3-5
Dining
   Hamburgers,
   sandwiches; food: $5;
   drinks: $2
Reservations
   Not necessary
Location
   Between Central and
   Alameda; near
   Hollywood (101) Fwy
Parking
   On premises, FREE
   after 5 pm; on street

UPFRONT COMEDY SHOWCASE

1452 Third Street Promenade
Santa Monica, CA 90401
Rsvn: (310) 319-3477
Comedy club; seats 50; reserved seating available; no smoking; no alcohol; food served; all ages.
  The genesis of this establishment was itself suitably improvisational. The husband-and-wife owners, veterans of Chicago's famed Second City theater, moved out to LA a few years ago with no intention of establishing their own comedy club. Instead, Jeff Michalski and Jane Morris moved West to join the fledgling Santa Monica Second City. They soon found themselves out in the cold (figuratively speaking) when the operation self-destructed. Resilient and determined, M & M gathered funds and forces and opened Upfront in Second City's place.
  Other original Chicago troupe vets have joined up to bring us what they all do best: on-the-spot improvised shows. They create sketches, songs, and scenes based entirely on suggestions jettisoned from the audience. They also perform a clever ongoing lunchtime soap opera.
  Open every night, the lineup varies. Monday is novice night, with students of the major improv schools testing their wings on stage. On Thursday, Viola Spolin theater games are a crowd-pleaser, and there's more. Call for a calendar.
  Italian is the name of the food game, and it's served at cabaret-style tables. Both smoking and alcohol got the hook here from the get-go. If you're not amused by the eats, you're right on the Third Street Promenade with its plethora of full-size restaurants with full-size tables.

Performances
 Sun-Thurs 8 pm; Fri-Sat 6:30 pm, 8 pm, 10 pm
Cost or Cover Charge
 $7-12; check
Dining
 Italian food; no smoking
Reservations
 Reserve at door
Location
 Off Santa Monica (10) Fwy, exit 4th St, turn left on Broadway, on the Third St Promenade between Broadway and Santa Monica Blvd
Parking
 On street; nearby parking lots

VAN GO'S EAR, MAIN STREET

796 Main Street
Venice, CA 90291
Info: (310) 314-0022
Performance art, poetry readings, music; seats 60; no reservations; no reserved seating; food served; all ages.
  Artsy, off-beat, pseudo-bohemian coffeehouses have enjoyed such a renaissance over the last few years with cliques of "in" young people that their original countercultural essence has grown eerily conformist. So what's an iconoclast to do when insurgency becomes establishment and avant-garde becomes old hat?
  Get thee to Van Go's Ear, an arcane, freewheeling cafe where the front of a '50s Buick peers out from the counter and bikini-clad women dance in the window (granted, a bit exploitative, but nonconformist nonetheless).
  Even for Venice, this place is weird. The one-earlobed coffeehouse has a loft space devoted to presenting poetry readings and performance art, bands, a capella singers, and whatever else management feels like showcasing. On the reassuring side, there's hardly ever a cover charge, and sandwiches are served along with an array of gourmet coffees.
  There's no alcohol, but liquor would probably just inhibit these folks anyway. The cafe is open from 6 am to 4 am, but it's most fun after sunset.

Performances
 Fri-Sat
Cost or Cover Charge
 No cover; check
Dining
 Breakfast, lunch, dinner; food: $4-8; individual tables; smoking/non-smoking
Reservations
 No reservations
Location
 Just S of Rose, on Main; Santa Monica (10) Fwy heading W, exit 4th St, make a left on 4th St, right on Pico Blvd, left on Main St, 1 mile S to Van Go's Ear
Parking
 On street

VINE ST. BAR AND GRILL

1610 Vine Street
Hollywood, CA 90028
Info: (213) 463-4375   **Rsvn:** (213) 463-4050
Jazz club; seats 75; reservations required for dinner; food served during sets; non-smoking section; all ages.

Vine St. is a small, classy, well-respected art deco place holding scarcely more than 75 people. It's split into two sides—diners on the left, drinkers on the right. Tables and booths accommodate the former, two rows of barstools take care of the latter. (The rough-backed barstools are pretty hard on the backs of fans who stay for more than one set.) You can sit close enough to touch the performers, although this is not a recommended activity. The back of the room has the more romantic ambiance.

Bands with more than five pieces seldom work this room because there's no stage, per se—just a small area at the back. Singers and soloists with rhythm sections are the usual bill of fare here, and the intimacy of the club works to their advantage. The music runs the gamut from mainstream jazz, to pop, to down-and-dirty blues.

Audiences at Vine St. are generally attentive, and for this reason, a performer who can communicate with a crowd can pull off magic tricks here that would fall flat elsewhere. Anita O'Day and Mose Allison seldom work anywhere else in LA.

Northern Italian food is served and boasts good pasta, fish, and veal selections. You could, however, run up a tab of just under $100 for food and drinks. The desserts are pretty wonderful, too. Reservations are advised for dinner, but you'll still pay a cover if one is announced that night. Plan on a two drink minimum at the bar.

Vine Street is the choice stop for lots of folks who attend performances at the Doolittle Theater across the street. Park as close to the club as you can, if not at the reasonably priced lot on the corner.

Performances
Tues-Sat 9:15 pm; service during sets
Cost or Cover Charge
$ varies; 2 drink min at bar, enforced if not dining; MC/V
Dining
Italian cuisine; main courses: $9.50-18.50; drinks: $3.50 up; restaurant open for lunch; individual tables; reserved tables; smoking/non-smoking
Reservations
Reserve at door, by phone
Location
Between Hollywood Blvd and Sunset Blvd; Gower or Vine exit off Hollywood (101) Fwy
Parking
On street; 6 pay parking lots in surrounding area

THE WHISKY-A-GO-GO

8901 Sunset Boulevard
West Hollywood, CA 90069
Info: (310) 652-4205   **Rsvn:** (310) 652-4202
Fax: (310) 652-3238
Rock nightclub; seats 450; food served during sets; all ages.

Mention the Whisky to a rock historian or a Los Angeles baby boomer and watch their eyes mist over with nostalgic flashbacks.

Back in its heyday, the club was renowned for its go-go-dancers and as an incubator for some of the Sixties greatest acts. Johnny Rivers made the club nationally famous in mid-decade when he recorded album after hit album of handclapping Louisiana-flavored rock 'n' roll on its stage. The Doors were the house band for awhile in 1966 before they struck it rich, regularly trying to blow the headliners away (for that and other original sins, mostly on the part of one Jim Morrison, they were repeatedly fired and rehired).

And what headliners—The Who, Cream, The Byrds, The Young Rascals, The Animals, Buffalo Springfield, Them (with Van Morrison), the Paul Butterfield Blues Band and Otis Redding, among many others. Even an occasional jazzman like Herbie Mann tried to capture the flavor of the Whisky by recording an album there.

Despite periodic closings over the years, the Whisky is still around sporting and supporting acts like Sister Scream, Robitussin Buzz, and—heaven help the

Performances
Mon-Sun 8 pm-2 am; service during sets
Cost or Cover Charge
$3-15; MC/V
Dining
Salads, chicken, hamburgers, tacos, sandwiches, appetizers; food: $4-10; drinks $4-8; individual tables; reserved tables
Reservations
At door, TicketMaster
Location
At corner of Sunset and San Vicente
Parking
On premises, $5; valet, $5

retro-lovers—The Spin Doctors. Recently even Van Halen made its way back to the club that gave the group its beginnings to celebrate its 15th anniversary.

WINDOWS ON HOLLYWOOD

Holiday Inn Hollywood
1755 North Highland Avenue
Hollywood, CA 90028
Info: (213) 462-7181 **Fax:** (213) 962-9669
Restaurant/jazz club; seats 200; reservations recommended; food served; non-smoking section; all ages.

The music-and-brunch at this hotel venue is novel, as much for the setting as anything. Perched on top of the Holiday Inn in Hollywood, the circular room revolves slowly, allowing for a 360-degree skyline view of Southern California—smog permitting. The jazz brunch only jams on Sunday, when the music is provided by the Art Graham Trio, a polite outfit that favors standards.

The hub of the room houses the formidable buffet, which features every conceivable breakfast desire and then some. (Yes, even prime rib in the morning.) Graham and company's bandstand hugs one point of the room's circumference, thus giving new meaning to the term "swing band." If you want a shot at sitting at a booth or table nearby, arrive early (the brunch crunch hits at 11 am) The acoustics here carry well throughout the room, however.

Performances
Tues-Thurs 8:30 pm-12:30 am; Fri-Sat 9 pm-1:30 am; Sun brunch from 11:30 am-3 pm
Cost or Cover Charge
$3.75 drink min; AE/Disc/MC/V
Dining
French California cuisine; food: $12.95-21.95; individual tables; reserved tables; smoking/non-smoking
Reservations
Reserve by phone
Location
Off Hollywood (101) Fwy; at Higland Ave between Hollywood Blvd and Franklin Ave
Parking
Validate parking for 3 hours in restaurant; $5.50 max. per day; on street also available on Orchid St

ART FILMS

INTRODUCTION TO ART FILMS

By Ken Wlaschin

There are more film festivals and quality film events for movie-lovers in Los Angeles than in any other city in the world. There are numerous opportunities to see all manner of moving images from all periods and countries, new and old, avant-garde and classic, silent and talkie, celluloid or video. Many fine retrospectives of older Hollywood films are held on the assumption that when Hollywood films have aged for a few years, they are transmuted into "art films." So much for definitions. Like a particular director? You can pretty much assume you'll see a retrospective of that artist's films somewhere in town.

Festivals from Santa Barbara and Palm Springs down to San Diego specialize in Asian cinema, Latino cinema, African-American cinema, gay and lesbian cinema, women's cinema, environmental cinema, animated films, documentaries, archival and preservation work, and independent American films. Some fests focus on geographical areas (the European Community Film Festival and the Organization of American States' Americas Film Festival come to mind). There are large multi-faceted generalist festivals such as the American Film Institute's International Film Festival, the AFI Los Angeles Film Festival, and its video equivalent, the AFI National Video Festival.

Take, for example, what might seem the greatest of rarities and the most difficult "art films" to see, silent films, now over a half century old. If you live in the LA area and love the silent cinema and such memorable stars as Douglas Fairbanks or Mary Pickford, you have more opportunities to see them in Los Angeles than anywhere else. Silent films with full piano accompaniment are shown every weekend at the Silent Movie cinema, the only theater in the world totally devoted to films of the pre-sound period. Once a year, the Los Angeles Chamber Orchestra presents a silent film classic starring such greats as Chaplin, Keaton, and Garbo with full orchestral accompaniment, usually with new scores written and conducted by Carl Davis. Silent films are also shown regularly at the UCLA Film Archive theater, the Los Angeles County Museum of Art's Bing Theatre, and at festivals like AFI Fest.

If your preference is for new films in foreign languages or for classic sound films of any language, opportunities abound: UCLA Film and Television Archive theater, American Cinematheque, the Film forum, LACMA, and often at the Academy of Motion Picture Arts and Sciences and the Directors Guild of America theaters.

On the commercial theater scene, the Landmark (which has houses in other Southern California cities), the Goldwyn, and the Laemmle theaters regularly present the best of world cinema and the hottest new art house releases. They often host special events like the Laemmle Santa Monica's year-long presentation of films from Hong Kong. In Los Angeles, the Nuart is widely known for its eclectic and diverse film programs that include many great rarities as well as hits. The Los Feliz and its companion the Vista have become very good places to see new art film releases, while the New Beverly has an excellent repertory program. The Four Star often hosts important series of foreign films.

It might seem strange that the center of the commercially-oriented Hollywood film industry is so well served for viewing non-Hollywood movies. There are two important reasons for this: first, the Hollywood creative folk welcome the chance to see new ideas and faces from other countries and sectors. To keep on the cutting edge of filmmaking, they need to see what new techniques are being devised by others and what new ideas are being explored. The talent agencies are always on the lookout for new directors, writers, and actors. A low budget film or a foreign language film may not have great potential, but the people who made them may have a future in the commercial market.

Second, one needs to remember that Los Angeles is a multinational cultural melting pot with huge populations of nearly every ethnic and language group in the world. In addition to the dominant Spanish-speaking Angelenos, there are large groups from almost every Asian, Middle Eastern, and European country. Nearly every language group has its own newspapers which advertise films from the "homeland."

What this means for everyone who lives in Los Angeles is a wonderful diversity of moviegoing possibilities. The surrounding cities then reap the same benefits. Los Angeles is truly a cinematic window on the world.

Ken Wlaschin is currently director of Exhibition and Festivals for the American Film Institute. Previously he was the Program Director of the London Film Festival and National Film Theatre in England. He is the author of a number of books on cinema including The Faber Book of Movie Verse *and* The Encyclopedia of Great Movie Stars.

AMERICAN CINEMATHEQUE Also See CHILDREN

Directors Guild
7920 Sunset Blvd
Hollywood, CA 90046
Info: (213) 466-FILM   **Rsvn:** (213) 466-FILM
Fax: (213) 461-9737
Three to five-day monthly mini-film festivals presented at the Directors Guild's 150-seat theater.

    This non-profit, member-supported revival and art film organization screens all kinds of movies during monthly festivals at the Directors Guild. A *tres* comfortable way to view or review important works of cinematic art, you can usually catch the event on the second or third weekend of every month.

    Spotlighting a director, producer, actor or writer, or even a film making era or genre, the presentations are that rare double feature: informative and fun. Sometimes the featured film makers put in a live appearance.

    Retrospective tributes cover cinematic luminaries as diverse as Charlie Chaplin, Milos Forman, and Kirk Douglas. The next program might be on the "art of music video," followed by banned Czech films.

    Saturday children's matinees are presented on the same weekend as the main films. The 24-hour information line repeats schedules for both young and old.

    Aside from these weekend mini-fests, American Cinematheque occasionally presents concert-movies at the Hollywood Bowl in association with other arts organizations. Live music accompanies the moving pictures on the Bowl's huge screen. *Singin' in the Rain* and *The King and I* were both smashing past presentations. Book early.

    Regulars to the screenings make their dinner stop at the Gaucho Grill, a block west of the Director's Guild building, or the dependable Greenblatt's, a block further.

Screenings
    Fri-Sat 7 pm, 9 pm; Sun 3 pm, 8 pm
Tickets
    $6-13
Discounts
    Children
BO
    Phone 466-FILM
Location
    On Sunset Blvd in Hollywood; between Fairfax and Crescent Heights, near Hollywood (101) Fwy
Parking
    On premises; on street

AMERICAN FILM INSTITUTE LOS ANGELES INTERNATIONAL FILM FESTIVAL See FESTIVALS & SEASONAL EVENTS

AMERICAN INDIAN FILM FESTIVAL See FESTIVALS & SEASONAL EVENTS

ANNENBERG THEATER See THEATER

BEYOND BAROQUE See THEATER

CINEMA SOCIETY/ NORTH SAN DIEGO COUNTY

AMC Wiegand Plaza 8 Theatres
Encinitas, CA 92024
Info: (619) 454-7373   **Fax:** (619) 551-1048
Film preview club.

    This preview club gives cinema aficionados the jump on everyone for first-run films before critics can color their perceptions. All attempts are made to show only quality, tasteful fare.

    Membership in the Society means not having to endure long lines at the box office (often finding out the time slot you want is sold out). Instead, members get to meet those in the know at an exclusive reception held nearby before the show begins. What's more, you get to take part in a discussion with the filmmakers and other invited speakers following the movie. Andy Friedenberg, the head honcho of

Screenings
    Fall–spring; selected Tues and Wed
Tickets
    $160 per person for the season
Discounts
    Groups of 25+, call
BO
    Call, by mail

both regional branches, manages to book major actors and directors.

Two separate cinema societies are held on different weeknights and at different locations, but the protocol is basically the same. Screenings are held at the AMC Wiegand Plaza 8 Theaters (where you can buy popcorn with real butter and gourmet desserts) and in the Sherwood Auditorium at the San Diego Museum of Contemporary Art in La Jolla (see following entry). Members pay a hefty sum, but all the perks make it worth it. The success of the preview clubs in San Diego County has prompted Friedenberg to clone his idea nationwide.

Location
Hwy 5 to Encinitas Blvd, go E to El Camino Real, left 2 blocks, theater is on the left side of street
Parking
On premises; on street

CINEMA SOCIETY/ SAN DIEGO See **Cinema Society/North San Diego County**

COLORADO See **Laemmle Theaters**

COVE THEATRE See **Landmark Theatres**

DOCUFEST See **FESTIVALS & SEASONAL EVENTS**

ESQUIRE THEATRE See **Laemmle Theaters**

EZTV

8547 Santa Monica Boulevard
West Hollywood, CA 90069
Info: (310) 657-1532   **Rsvn:** (310) 657-1532
Fax: (310) 657-6558
Independently produced videos.

Even in today's Video Age, most of us aren't yet familiar with places like EZTV, which present alternative taped (as opposed to filmed) footage. All the videos played here are independently produced and dependably provocative, such as the disturbing anti-war short, *Pax Americana*, centering on Hollywood's Welcome Home Desert Storm Parade. Live artists often perform alongside their recorded works to produce a multi-media showcase.

The main entrance to the complex looks like a techno-art gallery. You walk in to the first floor network of editing rooms and performance spaces. Upstairs, a more conventional 100-seat theater environment awaits. The various environments allow artists to choose the milieu most conducive to their work.

There's no regular schedule of screenings, so call for times and days.

Screenings
Vary
Tickets
$5-7
Discounts
Seniors
BO
Call
Location
1 1/2 blocks W of La Cienega Blvd
Parking
On premises, FREE

FESTIVAL OF ANIMATION See **FESTIVALS & SEASONAL EVENTS**

FILMFORUM

LACE
6522 Hollywood Boulevard
Los Angeles, CA 90028
Info: (213) 663-9568
Weekly screenings of alternative films by independent filmmakers.

Southern California's only ongoing alternative cinema venue, 19-year-old Filmforum is committed to

Screenings
Vary
Tickets
$3-5 (regular shows)

promoting and presenting independent, experimental, and progressive movies. Weekly screenings, shown at LACE (Los Angeles Contemporary Exhibitions), have included a widely varied group of films. *Classics of African Cinema* beautifully explored the cultural myths of initiation to adulthood in Mali; *Splendors of Azatlan: A Quarter Century of Chicano Cinema* featured topics of social resistance and ethnic identity; and a Jack Smith retrospective included two of his notorious classics of American avant-garde cinema.

Regularly featured along with the films are panel discussions and lectures aimed at provoking the audience into debate over the ideas and themes presented. Filmforum passwords are diversity, defiance, and innovation. And in the threatening face of today's resurgent wave of art censorship, those are welcome themes.

Individual screenings are reasonably priced. The price goes down even further if you become a member. Call for a spot on the mailing list.

Discounts
Children/seniors/ students/groups; call Jon Stout for further information

BO
Reserve at door; Filmforum members reserve by phone

Location
Call for current screening location

Parking
Available; volunteer parking attendant oversees parking and provides security at LACE

THE FINE ARTS

8556 Wilshire Boulevard
Beverly Hills, CA
Info: (310) 652-1330   **Rsvn:** (310) 289-4AMC

Once a fairly comfortable, but old (1936) and worn, art film house, the Cecchi Gori Fine Arts theater has just been transformed to its original glory by the same man, Joe Musil, who redid the El Capitan in Hollywood. It's in a convenient location, and the parking is free across the street. Tickets can be purchased in advance by phone or at the box office.

Screenings
Vary

Tickets
$7.50, matinees $5.50, twilight $4.50

Discounts
Children/seniors/ students

Location
Two blocks W of La Cienega

Parking
FREE for four hrs at Great Western Bank, 8484 Wilshire

GOLDWYN PAVILION CINEMAS See Landmark Theatres

GRANDE 4-PLEX See Laemmle Theaters

HILLCREST CINEMAS See Landmark Theatres

IMAX THEATER/CALIFORNIA MUSEUM OF SCIENCE AND INDUSTRY

Corner of Exposition Boulevard and Figueroa Street
Los Angeles, CA 90037
Info: (213) 744-2014   **Rsvn:** (213) 744-2019
Fax: (213) 744-2364

Mostly documentaries projected on huge screen equipped with surround-sound.

Since the Fifties, 3-D has been getting even more three-dimensional (if that's possible). Now there are flight simulators at video arcades whose model aircraft turn you all-too convincingly into a pilot. Meanwhile, interactive movies have taken us to new one-dimensional lows in movie making.

And then there are IMAX movies at the California Museum of Science and Industry in Exposition Park. Neatly,

Screenings
Vary

Tickets
$4-6

Discounts
Children/seniors/ students/groups of 10+, call

BO
Reserve at door daily 9:30 am-9 pm; by phone, TicketMaster

simply and with great skill, IMAX movies suck you into the illusion of total participation—you become part of the movie. Each frame in the film is 10 times the standard size of movie film, so the clarity of the moving pictures is almost scary. The colossal size of the screen, reaching five stories high and seventy feet wide, is also intimidating—until you get used to it. Soon you'll get hooked on it. The number of seats are disproportionately small for a screen this size in order to minimize distractions, and the six-channel surround-sound adds the final touch to make you feel like you're part of the action.

IMAX shows some fine films that sweep you away emotionally. *Antarctica* was a big success, as was *Blue Planet*, *Mountain Gorilla*, and *The Fires of Kuwait*. I know people who go back to these same presentations over and over. Films change every four months, but several films are usually running at once, most 40 minutes in length (*At the Max* was IMAX's first feature-length film, but most presentations are shorter). Ticket prices are discounted if you opt for more than one show at a time. Most of the films are appropriate for children, although very young kids might be frightened by the scope and sound.

Location
Off Harbor Fwy, Exposition Blvd exit; corner of Exposition and Figueroa at California Museum of Science and Industry
Parking
On premises, $3

INTERNATIONAL FESTIVAL OF SHORT FILMS See FESTIVALS & SEASONAL EVENTS

KEN CINEMA See Landmark Theatres

LACE See Filmforum and THEATER

LAEMMLE THEATRES

See below for theatre locations.
General Info: (310) 478-1041
Family-owned art film theater chain established in 1938.

Laemmle theaters are the Louvres of art film houses. It all began a year before WWII, when Max Laemmle arrived from Paris to start this now-legendary chain. For half a century, the theaters have brought Los Angeles audiences intriguing, superb and often enigmatic features from every corner of the world.

If you don't dig subtitles, Laemmle theaters are not for you. Academy Award-winning foreign films make up most of the fare, although some local independent films do get screen time. The movie houses also screen documentaries, filmmaker retrospectives (sometimes with the filmmakers making house calls for after-show discussions), and the occasional festival—including those focusing on Shakespeare and animation. Eight bucks will put you on the mailing list for the comprehensive biweekly schedule of movies and events. Write: **Laemmle Theatres, 11523 Santa Monica Boulevard, West Los Angeles, CA 90025.**

Although the **Grande 4-Plex** at the downtown Sheraton Grande Hotel is the one Laemmle theater to play primarily Hollywood product, on occasion it hosts art films and special cinema festivals.

If you feel like a movie on LA's Westside but suffer from blockbuster blahs, the **"Monicas"** offer a treasure chest of fine art films and foreign releases. The four screening rooms are small enough to feel almost executive. The theater earned some notoriety years ago when its showing of *The Battle of Algiers* brought dozens of Black

Screenings
Vary
Tickets
$4-6.50
Discounts
Children/seniors/ students/groups of 20+, call
BO
Reserve at door; call 466-FILM for some locations
Location
Call individual theaters
Parking
Call individual theaters

Panthers (and subsequent cops) to watch it as a training film.

With its majestic, gilded arch atop the screen and the faux side balconies, the Westside's **Royal Theatre** is the grande dame of the chain, playing gracious host to delectable foreign treats and retrospectives.

The newest member of the Laemmle theater dynasty is the **Sunset 5-Plex.** How civilized: Evian water and juices are served up with your popcorn and M&Ms. Brand new, clean, and comfortable, the Sunset 5 is a "10" in the Laemmle chain.

Laemmle Theatres:

> **Colorado**
> 2588 East Colorado Boulevard
> Pasadena, CA 91107
> (818) 796-9704

> **Esquire Theatre**
> 2670 East Colorado Boulevard
> Pasadena, CA 91107
> (818) 793-6149

> **Grande 4-Plex**
> 349 South Figueroa
> Downtown LA, CA 90071
> (213) 617-0268

> **Monica 4-Plex**
> 1332 2nd Street
> Santa Monica, CA 90401
> (310) 394-9741

> **Music Hall Theatre**
> 9036 Wilshire Boulevard
> Beverly Hills, CA 90211
> (310) 274-6869

> **Royal Theatre**
> 11523 Santa Monica Boulevard
> West Los Angeles, CA 90025
> (310) 477-5581

> **Sunset 5-Plex**
> 8000 Sunset Boulevard
> West Hollywood, CA 90046
> (213) 848-3500

> **Town & Country Theatre 3-Plex**
> 17200 Ventura Boulevard
> Encino, CA 91316
> (818) 981-9811

LANDMARK THEATRES

See below for theater locations.
Info: (310) 473-6701   **Fax:** (310) 477-3066
A national string of 93 movie houses specializing in showing broad-appeal foreign films and new works by challenging directors, as well as of innovative rookie filmmakers.

The legacy of Landmark art film houses began in 1974 with the restoration of the Nuart on LA's Westside. An instant success among Angelenos, with its art deco decor and novel daily "calendar" format of cult films and classics, the Nuart served as the blueprint for clones throughout the country. But VCR's gradually erased the format, and by the

Screenings
Vary
Tickets
$4-7.50
Discounts
Children/seniors/groups
(call for information)
BO
Reserve at door
Location
Call individual theaters

1980s, Landmark changed its bookings to open-ended runs.

The Samuel Goldwyn company, with a history of distributing foreign and independent films, landed Landmark several years ago. The films shown still vary from foreign premieres to American classics, from filmmaker tributes to an array of enigmatic gems.

The Landmark chain offers a "frequent goer" discount: five admissions for $20—a landmark bargain in this day and age. A film calendar with profiles of the new movies is available via mail. Write: **NuWilshire & Nuart Theatres Mailing List, P.O. Box 24608, Los Angeles, CA 90024**, and enclose a check for $5. Totally dissatisfied with the show? You can get a refund within the first 15 minutes.

Landmark theaters are now too numerous to talk about individually, but here's some info about some of them:

The **Guild** in San Diego was the first Landmark to open without a "calendar" format and instead premiere open-ended engagements. The films screened here tend to be less obscure than at other art and foreign film houses.

The **Ken** sprang up in San Diego and remains one of only three Landmark movie houses still operating the daily-change model.

The first of Landmark's chain, the **Nuart** is the mother of cult films and independent programming. You can still catch the midnight screening of *The Rocky Horror Picture Show* here. The Nuart is an art-deco masterpiece and remains a hubbub of activity for knowledgeable moviegoers.

That the **NuWilshire** recently sprouted up from the remains of Mann's Wilshire Theater is sort of a happy fluke. Now Santa Monicans have another opportunity to see the arcane and controversial. A far cry from the multiplex, everything about this place is modest: the seats are not plush, the screening rooms get stuffy, and there's not much of a lobby area. One of its screening rooms is calendared like the Nuart. The other offers open-ended premieres.

Some folks aren't aware that LA's **Goldwyn Pavilion Cinemas** in the Westside Pavilion are art houses. In addition to showing the more commercial and the Saturday children's programs, they book foreign and independent releases.

Parking
Call individual theaters

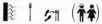

Landmark Theatres:

> **Cove Theatre**
> 7730 Girard Avenue
> La Jolla, CA 92037
> (619) 459-5404
>
> **Goldwyn Pavilion Cinemas**
> 10800 Pico Boulevard (Westside Pavilion)
> West Los Angeles, CA 90064
> (310) 475-0202, or 475-0301
>
> **Guild Theatre**
> 3827 5th Avenue
> San Diego, CA 92103
> (619) 295-2000
>
> **Hillcrest Cinemas**
> 3965 5th Avenue
> San Diego, CA 92103
> (619) 299-2100

Ken Cinema
4061 Adams Avenue
San Diego, CA 92116
(619) 478-6379

Nuart Theatre
11272 Santa Monica Boulevard
Los Angeles, CA 90025
(310) 473-8099, or 399-7875

NuWilshire Theatre
1314 Wilshire Boulevard
Santa Monica, CA 90403
(310) 394-6331

Park Theatre
3812 Park Boulevard
San Diego, CA 92103
(619) 294-9264, or 294-9265

Port Theatre
2905 East Coast Highway
Corona Del Mar, CA 92625
(714) 673-6260

Rialto Theatre
1023 Fair Oaks Avenue
South Pasadena, CA 91030
(818) 799-9567

LOS ANGELES ASIAN PACIFIC INTERNATIONAL FILM AND VIDEO FESTIVAL See
FESTIVALS & SEASONAL EVENTS

LOS ANGELES CONSERVANCY—LAST REMAINING SEATS SERIES

See press listings for performance locations
Info: (213) 623-CITY   **Rsvn:** (213) 466-1767
Series of classic films presented in original movie
houses.

Imagine seeing the Marx Brothers in *A Night at the Opera* in the oldest surviving Orpheum theater in the world, or the 1931 film *City Lights* in Chaplin's lavish and ornate Los Angeles Theater. How about an old fashioned matinee featuring two hours of *Our Gang* comedies in the Rialto Theater in South Pasadena? Well, true, some of the theaters are in stages of disrepair or are downright tacky. But if you can see past all of that and imagine these once *grande dames* of the cinema world, then you are in for a treat.

The Los Angeles Conservancy, the group dedicated to preserving and revitalizing great Los Angeles architectural resources, has been sponsoring this summer film series since 1987, when it was first presented as part of the Motion Picture Centennial. Founding member John Miller initiated the series naming it for the 15,000 seats that once existed in downtown LA theaters. Now there are fewer than 6,000.

The purpose of the program is twofold: First, to offer the classics to film buffs who know the best way to view cinema is on the big screen; and second, to make people aware of the Broadway Historic District and the effort the Conservancy has made to preserve the lavish motion picture palaces.

Tickets can be purchased individually or in a series, and are available by mail. Members of the Conservancy receive modest discounts on tickets. (P.S. If you can't make the film, but would like to tour the movie

Screening
Wed June
Tickets
$10-15 individual tickets;
$35-45 series
Discounts
Children/seniors
BO
Reserve by mail, at
door, call
Location
Varies
Parking
Varies

houses, the Conservancy provides Saturday tours at 10 am
for a donation of $5 by nonmembers. Call for reservations.)

LOS ANGELES COUNTY MUSEUM OF ART—BING THEATER

5905 Wilshire Boulevard
Los Angeles, CA 90036
Info: (213) 857-6010
Fax: (213) 936-5755
Variety of film series for members and nonmembers.

Each year more than 50,000 people attend
screenings in Los Angeles County Museum of Art's Leo S.
Bing Theater. On the one hand, being set in an art museum
lends the flick a little class; on the other, there's no popcorn
or Milk Duds.

The Bing Theater, with its $500,000 renovation
providing state-of-the-art sound and projection equipment,
refurbished seats, and safety equipment (for your protection
as well as for the nitrate film), is possibly one of the best
venues in LA to feature classic films. The projection systems
allow for the showing of 16mm, 35mm, and 70mm films, as
well as silent films, which call for specific frame speeds.

LACMA believes variety is the spice of classic film
life: retrospective tributes to writers, directors, stars,
producers, and even studios; plus festivals, including the
Museum of Television & Radio Festival, DocuFest
(International Documentary Association), and other special
programs.

The evening festival programs are usually held
weekends. Fridays in summer you might stop by early for
the free jazz performances on the plaza (5:30 to 8:30 pm).
Museum members are entitled to discounts.

One of life's secret pleasures is ducking out of
work in the afternoon for a movie. LACMA's Wednesday
afternoon screenings ease the guilt, as they only cost $1
($.50 for senior citizens). There's also the "By Popular
Demand" series of oldies like *Red River* and *The Sea Wolf.*
These films are screened at a variety of times during the
week.

Screenings
Vary
Tickets
$6 general admission;
$4 museum members;
$1 Wed matinee
Discounts
Seniors/students
BO
Reserve at door,
TicketMaster
Location
Off of the Santa Monica
(10) Fwy, Fairfax exit, N
to Wilshire, right onto
Wilshire; 2 blocks E of
Fairfax
Parking
On premises, $3.30-5;
street parking

LOS ANGELES INTERNATIONAL GAY & LESBIAN FILM/VIDEO FESTIVAL See FESTIVALS & SEASONAL EVENTS

LOS FELIZ CINEMAS

1822 North Vermont Avenue
Los Angeles, CA 90027
Info: (213) 664-2169
Three-screen house.

After 50 years on the scene, this theater has
evolved from a one-screen institution to a contemporary
three-screen house. The house runs first-run commercial
features as well as foreign films, classics, and films with
controversial themes.

The Los Feliz adjoins Chatterton's Bookstore
(another institution), while just down the block lies Onyx, a
funky coffeehouse popular with a mixed, but mostly young,
arty crowd. There are super restaurants in this area:
Farfalla, Katsu, Louise's on Hillhurst, or El Chavo on
Sunset.

Screenings
Vary
Tickets
$4-7.50
Discounts
Children/seniors
BO
Reserve at door
Location
Between Franklin Ave
and Sunset Blvd; near
Golden State (5) Fwy,
Hollywood (101) Fwy
Parking
On street

MONICA 4-PLEX See **Laemmle Theatres**

MUSIC HALL THEATER See **Laemmle Theatres**

NEW BEVERLY CINEMA

7165 Beverly Boulevard
Los Angeles, CA 90036
Info: (213) 938-4038
Revival house seating 300.

When it was built in the 1950s, what was then called the Beverly Cinema was LA's first art cinema. Thirtysomething years and various incarnations later (including a stint as a combo gay-straight porno theater—don't ask), the New Beverly is screening a variety of films from classic, to foreign, to cult. You can see Hitchcock, current documentaries, and deserving commercial re-releases.

Inside it's kind of "arty" (read: shabby). But with ticket prices at movie box offices soaring, it's a special treat to pay just $4.50 (general admission). The one drawback: no air conditioning.

The theater screens double features, usually of related subjects (or the same director, writer, genre, actors). Just down the street is The Revival Cafe. There's time between shows to take out coffee drinks (or a quick dessert, like their chocolate pizza).

Screenings
Vary
Tickets
$2.50-4.50
Discounts
Children/seniors/
students/groups (see
manager)
BO
Reserve at door
Location
1 block W of La Brea
Ave
Parking
On street

NUART THEATRE See **Landmark Theatres**

NUWILSHIRE THEATRE See **Landmark Theatres**

PARK THEATRE See **Landmark Theatres**

PIERSON PLAYHOUSE CLASSIC FILM SERIES

841 Temescal Canyon Road
Pacific Palisades, CA 90272
Info: (310) 454-8040

One Sunday night each month, join *Los Angeles Times* film critic Kenneth Turan for a classic Samuel Goldwyn Company film. Mr. Turan is on hand each screening night at 7:30 to introduce flicks such as "The Best Years of Our Lives" or "The Ghost Goes West." Popcorn is free, but tickets aren't. Pick them up for $5 at the door.

Screenings
Sunday 7:30
Tickets
$5
Location
Between Pacific Coast
Highway and Sunset
Blvd on Temescal
Canyon Rd at Haverford
Ave
Parking
Parking on premises or
street; FREE

PORT THEATRE See **Landmark Theatres**

RIALTO THEATRE See **Landmark Theatres**

ROYAL THEATER See **Laemmle Theatres**

SANTA BARBARA INTERNATIONAL FILM FESTIVAL See **FESTIVALS & SEASONAL EVENTS**

SILENT MOVIE THEATRE

611 North Fairfax
Los Angeles, CA 90036
Rsvn: (213) 653-2389   **Fax:** (213) 653-9161
Seats 250 for silent screen gems.
    In a nostalgic mood for pre-talkies-era Hollywood? If so, this place is the ticket. Originally established in 1942 (when ticket prices were a dime), and reopened in 1991, this cinema is the world's only operating silent movie theater. Delve into Hollywood's past and enjoy its bygone silent age. It's a hoot to see (and hear) films accompanied by live organ music. You'll be rendered speechless at the sight of yesteryear stars such as Charlie Chaplin (who used to visit the theater to gage audience reaction to his films), Buster Keaton, and Laurel and Hardy. Wednesday nights are slightly different: the night starts with a short, follows with an intermission, and finishes with the feature. There are nights set aside for comedy, and an annual Labor Day weekend film festival.
    The movie house was resurrected from a dozen years of darkness and is now run by Larry Austin, an old friend of the theater's founding family. Austin, himself a veteran of the movie industry, is the son of silent screen star William Austin. Today the younger Austin hunts for vintage reels and surviving film fragments to give modern audiences the chance to journey into movie history. The house fills with a wonderfully mixed bag of "artsy" cinema aficionados, young families, and seniors.
    Park across the street at Fairfax High School or on the street. You're within walking distance of falafel stands, Largo (The Pub), and Canter's 24-hour deli.

Screenings
  Wed, Fri-Sat 8 pm
Tickets
  $3-6
Discounts
  Children/students/
  groups of 100+, call
  manager
BO
  Reserve at door
Location
  Between Melrose Ave
  and Beverly Blvd
Parking
  On street and at high
  school across the street

SIMON WIESENTHAL CENTER, MUSEUM OF TOLERANCE FILM SOCIETY

9786 West Pico Boulevard
Los Angeles, CA 90035
Info: (310) 553-9036   **Rsvn:** (310) 553-9036 ext. 319
    The relatively new Los Angeles Museum of Tolerance has established a film program that screens at least 24 movies annually. These classic and contemporary movies are not only about the Holocaust—a formidable task in itself. The Society offers issues ranging from antisemitism to apartheid.
    The inaugural season's choices included Laura Z. Hobson's Academy Award-winning "Gentlemen's Agreement," "Faces," winner of the Venice International Film Festival, and the 1951 movie about apartheid, "Cry the Beloved Country."
    Movies are screened in the beautiful Peltz Theater on Tuesday evenings. Museum members are afforded discounts to the Society, and Film Society members receive advance notice and discounts for additional films not part of the calendar.

Screenings
  Tues, 7:30 pm
Tickets
  $5 members, $7.50
  nonmembers; $100 and
  $150 series
Location
  Between Beverly Dr and
  Roxbury, just S of
  Beverly Hills
Parking
  Parking on premises,
  FREE

SUNSET CINEMA FILM FESTIVAL See **FESTIVALS & SEASONAL EVENTS**

SUNSET 5-PLEX See **Laemmle Theatres**

TOWN & COUNTRY THEATRE 3-PLEX See **Laemmle Theatres**

UCLA FILM AND TELEVISION ARCHIVE AT MELNITZ THEATER Also See
FESTIVALS & SEASONAL EVENTS

Melnitz Theatre
1438 Melnitz Hall, 405 Hilgard Avenue
Los Angeles, CA 90024
Info: (310) 206-FILM, or (310) 206-8013
Fax: (310) 206-3129

The various ongoing movie, video, and TV series at UCLA's Melnitz Hall comprise a feast of little known art films and classic revivals, documentary shorts and featured filmmaker retrospectives year-round, all showcased in a well-equipped, comfortable theater with a new Dolby sound system.

In the past, these programs, sponsored by public and private grants, have included Women Make Movies, the UCLA African-American Filmmakers Festival, Swiss Classics, a Pier Paolo Pasolini retrospective, Asian Pacific Film and Video Festival, 40th Anniversary of Hallmark Hall of Fame (Hallmark donated its entire collection to the archive), Human Rights Watch Festival, and Fritz Lang in America.

Three monthly events to keep watch on: Archive Treasures, which presents a restored or preserved classic film; Critic's Choice, offered jointly with Los Angeles Film Critics Association; and Independent's Forum, a showcase of independent filmmakers. The annual Festival of Preservation, usually held in summer, presents all the films the archive has brought back from the dead throughout the year in its Hollywood preservation laboratory.

Tickets for all films presented by the UCLA Film and Television Archive are available at the Melnitz Theater box office one hour before show time (generally 7:30 pm).

For information, brochures, and mailing list particulars, call (310) 206-FILM.

Screenings
Vary
Tickets
FREE-$5
Discounts
Seniors/students
BO
Reserve at door
Location
NE corner of the UCLA campus; near Sunset Blvd and Hilgard Ave
Parking
On premises, Lot #3, $5

CHILDREN

Introduction to Children

By Carey Simon

Children are the next generation of arts patrons, and it's up to us to prepare them for their future roles by exposing them to the thrill of live entertainment as early as possible. The key to their immediate enjoyment and eventual appreciation is preparation.

Matinees are best for young children's attention and for grown-up pocketbooks. Let your kids know what they'll be seeing, and explain that if they have questions during the performance, they must whisper them to you. If the ballet or play you choose is based on a book, you might read it together beforehand.

Be prepared to leave the theater—or at least to take a walk in the lobby—if your child gets restless. Even in productions geared exclusively to children, it's not fair to others to disrupt the performance. Many of us couldn't wait to take our children to their first *Nutcracker Suite*. But let's face it, there are segments of that ballet that won't hold the attention of some youngsters.

Don't push your luck first time out with a full-length theater performance. Try inexpensive visits to Open House at the Hollywood Bowl in summer. If your child is over five years old, consider a subscription to the Junior Programs of California, a series which exposes youngsters to a variety of artists while teaching them good theater behavior. The Los Angeles Music Center's Saturday Symphony Series is a perfect way to introduce classical music, and the music is performed by one of the finest orchestras in the world. (It also gives *you* a crash course in a style of music you may not be familiar with.)

Festivals are usually an affordable and fun way to have a family outing and experience the talents of musicians and dancers from all over the world. Dance productions are wonderful experiences for kids—and not just ballet. The Jazz Tap Ensemble, for instance, offered a geared-to-families abridged performance at last year's "Summer Nights at the Ford" series.

In the **THEATER** chapter, you'll discover adult companies that devote a certain number of performances each year to children's plays. In the **CHILDREN** chapter, there are numerous options, including the Coronet Theatre's Serendipity theater company, one LA group that focuses solely on children's performances, as does the Actors Repertory Theatre company at the Santa Monica Playhouse. P.L.A.Y., formerly the Mark Taper Forum's Improvisational Theatre Project, has more than 22 years under its belt. The Odyssey's Glorious Players are highly respected in LA. The San Diego Junior Theatre has been training children for the stage since just after World War II. Two traveling companies should be noted, too: The Great American Children's Theater, and the Minnesota Children's Theater, each of which puts in annual appearances in the Southland. Most Saturdays or Sundays you can find children's theater performances scheduled somewhere in Southern California.

Taking a child to a play not specifically marketed for their age group (i.e., a Broadway musical) might seem potentially disastrous. But look for productions tagged "great family fare." My annual Christmas Eve visit to the Gem Theatre's *A Child's Christmas in Wales* established not only a special family tradition, but introduced my (then) eight-year-old to the lyrical prose of Dylan Thomas. She understood and appreciated it more and more each time she saw it performed. If you're not sure how your tyke will manage, check out the seating charts at the end of the **Applause Guide**, then request aisle seats when you purchase your tickets. Come armed with a baggie of Cheerios and be prepared to scoot out the door with your darling Samantha if she lets out a peep. You have to be willing to sacrifice the price of those tickets.

Many of the performing arts centers in this guide, such as the UCLA Center for the Performing Arts, offer separate family series often with internationally-known artists.

Expose your children to all the lively arts. Help create a generation that will make music, dance, theater, and art films a regular part of their lives.

Follow my prescription and you may end up like the parent I sat next to at *Les Miserables*—her seven-year-old daughter not only sat through that long performance and loved it, but had already seen it once before!

ABRAHAM LINCOLN CABIN THEATER See **THEATER**

AFTERNOON THEATER FOR CHILDREN See **Santa Monica College Concert Hall**

AMERICAN CINEMATHEQUE

Directors Guild Theatre
7920 Sunset Boulevard
Los Angeles, CA 90046
Info: (213) 466-FILM   **Rsvn:** (213) 461-9622
Fax: (213) 461-9737
Monthly Saturday afternoon film classics for children.
The Saturday movie matinee that many of us remember growing up is still alive and well at the Directors Guild Theater, albeit without the ubiquitous box of popcorn. The monthly series for children and their parents brings classic films to entire families. Flicks such as the original *Tom Sawyer*, *Music Man*, or *Bad News Bears* are specially chosen to please both the juvenile and his/her grown-up companion. Children are also exposed to outstanding foreign cinema, both live action and animation, such as a recent month of all-Russian animation films.

American Cinematheque, a nonprofit, viewer-supported organization, is dedicated to promoting and celebrating all forms of moving pictures. For information on its regular film and video programs, see the chapter on **ART FILMS**. To find out the schedule of family films, call (213) 466-FILM for recorded information. Films do sell out early; there is no late seating.

Performances
Sat 12 pm, 2 pm
Tickets
$3-6
Discounts
Children
BO
1 hr before performance; check/AE/MC/V/reserve by mail, fax, telephone
Location
W of Fairfax, on Sunset
Parking
On premises, FREE

AMERICAN INDIAN FESTIVAL AND MARKET See **FESTIVALS & SEASONAL EVENTS**

AMERICAN YOUTH SYMPHONY See **MUSIC**

ANNUAL LOS ANGELES COUNTY HOLIDAY CELEBRATION See **FESTIVALS & SEASONAL EVENTS**

ANNUAL SUMMER SOLSTICE FOLK MUSIC AND DANCE FESTIVAL See **FESTIVALS & SEASONAL EVENTS**

AT THE GROVE PRODUCTIONS See **THEATER**

BALLET PACIFICA See **DANCE**

BEVERLY HILLS LIBRARY AUDITORIUM See **THEATER**

BIRDCAGE THEATRE See **THEATER**

BLACKSTREET U.S.A. PUPPET THEATRE

4129 West Washington
Los Angeles, CA 90016
Info: (213) 936-6091   **Rsvn:** (213) 936-6091
Artistic Director: Bill Shaw
Performances in its Culver City theater.

      Gary Jones lives with 3-foot-tall Mr. Stomp, Sweet Georgia Brown, Purity, Judith and a host of others. Gary Jones is a master puppeteer who for more than 20 years has been entertaining children—and adults—with the antics and stories of his make-believe pals.

      It's particularly rewarding to watch someone so dedicated to a craft which often seems in danger of fading away entirely. The stories Jones creates are upbeat, and most of his puppets are African-American. He not only writes the stories and manipulates the rod puppets, he dances with them, talks to them, and basically becomes a member of the cast. (He even admits to talking to his puppets when there isn't an audience to eavesdrop!)

      Children ages 5 to about 12 will delight in these matinee performances for which the audience sits on folding chairs (the room seats up to 40) while the action unfolds on a small, raised platform stage. Birthday parties can be arranged; there's a question-and-answer period after the show as well as a short tour of the workshop where the puppets are made.

Performances
Sat matinee 2 pm; Sun matinee 3 pm
Tickets
$5 children; $8 adults
Discounts
Groups of 40, call
BO
Tickets are purchased at the door on the day of performance
Location
5 blocks E of La Brea; 3 blocks N of the Santa Monica (10) Fwy
Parking
On premises, free of charge; street parking

BLESSING OF THE CARS See FESTIVALS & SEASONAL EVENTS

BLUE PALM See DANCE

BOB BAKER MARIONETTE THEATRE

1345 West First Street
Los Angeles, CA 90026
Info: (213) 250-9995   **Rsvn:** (213) 250-9995
Theater in the half-round.

      Since 1963, the Bob Baker Marionette Theatre has been an LA institution. Like so many arts groups, it's had its ups and downs in terms of funding. Currently, it's up. Baker himself bought back the theater after having sold it in 1988.

      Children sit on the floor ("no feet over the line, please"), parents on the chairs. There's nothing glitzy or ultra-sophisticated here. The programs are simple, but the costumes and marionettes themselves are remarkable. The "performers" make their way all over the carpeted space within touching distance of the audience. After the show, children meet the puppeteers and their puppets.

      Admission includes refreshments. Birthday parties can bo arrangod.

      The area is pretty lousy, but the parking lot is adjacent to the building.

Performances
Tues-Fri 10:30 am; Sat-Sun 2:30 pm
Tickets
$10
Discounts
Seniors/groups
BO
Mon-Fri 9 am-5 pm; Sat-Sun 11 am-4 pm; check/reserve by mail, phone; no cash refunds, can exchange tickets due to illness
Location
Downtown at First and Glendale Blvd; near the Hollywood (101) Fwy and Harbor (110) Fwy
Parking
On premises, free of charge; street parking available

BREA CIVIC & CULTURAL ARTS CENTER

For more information about the Civic Light Opera performances and the Brea Theater League, both of which often offer family fare, and the Brea City Orchestra's holiday concerts for children, see **THEATER**.

BREA'S YOUTH THEATRE

Info: (714) 990-7727 **Rsvn:** (714) 990-7722
For specific information on ticket prices and show times, see THEATER.

The Curtis Theatre draws children from all over the county to be in the cast of these large-scale musicals. The organization, in association with the City of Brea and Stagelight Family Productions, produces two shows a year. Expect large casts ranging in age from age 4 to adult. More than 100 children, all amateurs, pay a registration fee for a six week program in dance, acting, and movement. The culmination of that training is a lavish production—*Annie, Peter Pan, Oliver* are examples—often presented to a sold-out house.

Children from ages 4 and up are accepted, and parents are encouraged to act with the kids, insuring that the adult parts are played by adults, and so on.

YOUTH ACTOR'S THEATRE

Casts consist of Orange County volunteer teenagers in productions geared accordingly, such as *West Side Story*. They usually produce one show a year.

BRIDGES AUDITORIUM See **THEATER**

CALIFORNIA YOUTH THEATRE See **THEATER**

CALTECH PUBLIC EVENTS—FAMILY FAIRE

Beckman Auditorium
Michigan Avenue one block south of Del Mar Boulevard
Pasadena, CA 91106
Info: (818) 356-3834 **Rsvn:** (818) 356-4652
Fax: (818) 577-0130
Annual series of family programs in Beckman Auditorium at California Institute of Technology.

The university's family fare is geared for audiences ages 7 to adult and packaged into a series of storytelling and/or music. Sample ingredients: the Robert Minden Ensemble, who perform "The Boy Who Wanted to Talk to Whales"; the marvelous local group We Tell Stories who are usually successful at their innovative storytelling; a puppet show or a magic show. Each series offers five such choices, some of which are ASL (American sign language) interpreted. The CalTech staff has even gone the extra mile to compile kiddie bibliographies of suggested background readings for each season's shows.

Series tickets are available at a considerable savings over single tickets, but all seats are unreserved. The afternoon programs in Beckman Auditorium are kept to a pragmatic 50 to 70 minutes. If you buy 20 or more tickets (this is a birthday party-appropriate activity!) you'll receive an extra pair complimentary.

Performances
Sat 2 pm
Tickets
$4.50-8.50, unreserved
Discounts
Children/groups of 20+, call BO
BO
Mon-Fri 10 am-4:30 pm; Sat 1 pm-4:30 pm; BO by phone Mon-Fri 10 am-4:30 pm; AE/Disc/MC/V/check/order by mail, fax, TicketMaster; subscription program
Location
S of Del Mar Blvd, between Wilson and Hill Aves; 1 mile S of the 210 Fwy
Parking
On premises, free; street parking

CARLSBAD YOUTH THEATRE

3557 Monroe Street
Carlsbad, CA 92008
Info: (619) 931-8709   **Rsvn:** (619) 931-8709
Performances are held at the Carlsbad Community Cultural Arts Center.

The Patrons of the Arts Foundation, a nonprofit, cultural organization of North County San Diego residents who subsidize, produce and promote cultural events, oversees the Carlsbad Youth Theatre.

Each year Patrons of the Arts offers a popular production of *A Christmas Carol,* usually with a special New Year's Eve performance at 10:30 pm. Following the show, kids get to party with nonalcoholic drinks, noisemakers, party hats, and snacks. Children are encouraged to come to the late show in their jammies.

The community theater offers young people ages 6 to 16 the chance to audition for productions, though they are required to take one of the organization's Actor's Workshop Series.

For hungry tummies, there's a snack bar in the community center, but Carlsbad has a fine selection of restaurants. Call ahead for suggestions of what's best for the ages of your children.

Parking is free outside the theater.

Performances
Vary
Tickets
$5-12
BO
24 hr answering machine; check/reserve by mail
Location
Between Carlsbad Village Dr and Chestnut Ave; near Int-5
Parking
On premises, free; street parking also available

CENTER STAGE THEATER See THEATER

CHILDREN'S CONCERTS IN HISTORIC SITES

See press listings for performance locations.
Info: (310) 440-1351   **Rsvn:** (310) 440-1351
Fax: (310) 440-1363

Da Camera Society director Dr. MaryAnn Bonino introduces youngsters to chamber music with the same flare and innovation she uses to entertain adults. This spin-off series, launched in 1992, became deservedly popular from the moment the initial flyers were mailed.

Bonino's aim is to make classical music accessible to young people by placing it in settings that relate to the music at hand. In that spirit, two young pianists from the Colburn School of the Performing Arts Discovery Center played Saint-Saens' "Carnival of the Animals" in the Natural History Museum during the series' opening season. Other concerts were held in the Museum of Flying and the Southwest Museum. At the close of the latter concert, with the Armadillo String Quartet, the children were given either a souvenir beaded necklace or an arrowhead.

A narrator guides the children through the music; performances are approximately 45 minutes, followed by a themed activity. And yes, parents are perfectly welcome, either through single tickets or a family package for two adults and two children. The society recommends the events for ages 4 and older.

Contact the Da Camera Society to be put on the mailing list.

Performances
Vary
Tickets
$18 adult, $10 children
Discounts
Family package/ students/groups of 10+, call BO
BO
By phone Mon-Fri 8:30 am-5 pm; check/MC/V/ reserve by mail; (12001 Chalon Rd, Los Angeles, CA 90049; add $4 per order for phone order), fax; no refunds or exchanges; subscription program
Location
Varies

CHILDREN'S DAY CELEBRATION

Japanese American Cultural & Community Center
244 South San Pedro Street
Los Angeles, CA 90012
Info: (213) 628-2725   **Rsvn:** (213) 680-3700
Fax: (213) 617-8576
Annual Japanese holiday celebrated in May at a variety of locations in Little Tokyo.

Kids think every day is "children's day"! Now those youngsters who have never known about this traditional celebration can boast *two* days just for them.

The Japanese community observes this May holiday—*Kodomo-no-hi*—with an annual festival held in several Little Tokyo locations. Festivals are a particularly wonderful way to expose children to new cultures. Though the fest emphasizes Japanese cultural traditions, it often combines customs of other countries and will engage children from all backgrounds.

The celebration is rich with traditional Japanese performing arts: dance and music, magic, puppetry, and the unique *taiko* (festival drums). Past celebrations have introduced theater and Japanese-language family films.

Additional features include numerous drop-in crafts booths, games, traditional food, exhibits, and cultural demonstrations. A big draw is the *Chibi K*, or Kids Fun Run, a noncompetitive quarter-, half-, and 1K "marathon" for ages 4 to 12. The registration fee is $20 plus a new toy, which is given to a charity. The fee entitles the kids to a T-shirt, pancake breakfast, and a "goodie" bag.

Call for this year's dates.

Performances
 May
Tickets
 $ varies
Discounts
 Children/seniors
 students/groups of 20+,
 call (213) 628-2725
BO
 Mon–Sun noon–5 pm
 MC/V/reserve by mail
Location
 Between San Pedro St
 and 2nd St; near
 Hollywood (101) Fwy
 and Harbor (110) Fwy
Parking
 On street

THE CHILDREN'S THEATRE COMPANY

See press listings for performance locations and times.
Info: (612) 874-0500   **Rsvn:** (612) 874-0500
Fax: (612) 874-8119

From their slick, color series brochures to their opulent settings, gorgeous costumes, and professional performances, the Minneapolis-based CTC has been at the forefront of children's theater for years. In fact, it's North America's largest theatre for young people and their families. Just to let you in on how popular it is, approximately 25% of CTC's total adult audiences come without their kids!

If you see them coming (in press announcements), rush to the McCallum in Palm Desert, Bridges Auditorium in Claremont, the Barclay in Irvine, or the Mandeville in San Diego, or hopefully, somewhere in Los Angeles—do not hesitate for a moment before calling for tickets.

CTC makes you realize that fine children's theater is possible—so why don't our communities here support it?!

CHRISTIAN COMMUNITY THEATER AND CHRISTIAN YOUTH THEATER See THEATER

THE COMEDY & MAGIC CLUB

1018 Hermosa Avenue
Hermosa Beach, CA 90254
Info: (310) 376-6914   **Rsvn:** (310) 372-1193
Fax: (310) 379-2806
300-seat comedy, magic, and variety club.

Head for the South Bay for a Sunday afternoon of great fun.

Performances
 Sun 12:30 pm
Tickets
 $12 overall; includes
 lunch

The club, which features well-known, familiar acts such as Garry Shandling and Dave Coulier (from ABC's "Full House") in the evening, books the same high-quality name performers for the kids during the day. Goldfinger & Dove, for example, well-known to magic-lovers who frequent the Magic Castle in Hollywood, are regulars both in the evening and for the kids.

Performers actively involve the children in the shows, whether during a magic act, or via conversations with the comedians. Although it's a big place, the sound system is great. Kids feel free to leave their seats at the beginning of the show and sit on the floor up front.

Shows are advertised for children ages 2 to 14. But know your child; $12 a person can seem like a big waste if your two-year-old can't sit still and you have to leave midway through the performance.

The box office opens at 12:15 with lunch from 12:30 to 1 pm. Shows run from 1 to 2 pm. Birthday parties are arranged all the time and average $14 to $16 per child; the birthday "person" is brought up on the stage for an introduction.

Turn to the **CLUBS** chapter for information on adult performances.

BO
Sun-Sat 10 am-6 pm
AE/MC/V;
nonexchangeable
Location
Off the 91 Fwy; also
accessible off the San
Diego (405) Fwy; major
intersection Pier Ave
Parking
On premises free; street
parking also available

CONCERTS IN THE PARK

Warner Park, 5800 Topanga Canyon Road
Woodland Hills, CA 91367
Info: (818) 704-1358
Shows scheduled at Warner Park in Woodland Hills.

This is the perfect family concert line-up—and not just because of the price. On summer Sundays, performances for the kids begin at 4 pm, and the adult concerts—which are appropriate for the entire family (see **FESTIVALS**)—kick in at 5:30. So bring the kids—all ages—for a picnic dinner and a chance to hear Dan Crow, Caren Glasser, Craig & Co., Pam Wood, or other performers the kids will either recognize or meet for the first time.

Parents are encouraged to bring the youngsters to the front of the stage so that they can interact with the artists. At the end of the kids' show, you can line up to purchase cassettes or get pictures autographed. Call for a schedule; children's concerts are *not* scheduled before each and every adult show.

Performances
Vary
Tickets
$1

CORONET THEATRE

366 North La Cienega Boulevard
Los Angeles, CA 90048
Info: (310) 652-9199   **Rsvn:** (310) 652-9199
Fax: (310) 657-1101
A 272-seat theater used most often for family theater productions. Sometimes booked for evening adult performances.

You'll find the Coronet just south of Trashy Lingerie and north of the Beverly Center. It's a nondescript building with a nondescript interior. But it is LA's only venue set aside specifically for family theater.

The sound is good from most any seat, although the noise of the humming air conditioner also carries well. There are only 12 rows of comfortable seats in the center, and all of them offer good sightlines—if you're an adult. If only Executive Director Jody Davidson would rope off the first five rows for "kids only" as does the staff of the Los Angeles Junior Programs, all the children could see. Avoid row 1 and even row 2 on the sides. There's no assigned seating, and the front fills up fast, especially when there's a birthday party in residence.

Candy, sodas, and bottled water are brought out for sale during intermission.

Watch for restricted parking signs on the side streets; park on La Cienega or use the valet.

Performances
Fri 7:30 pm; Sat 2 pm,
7:30 pm; Sun 1 pm, 4
pm
Tickets
$6 children 13 and
under; $12 adults
Discounts
Children/groups of 20+,
call BO
BO
Tues-Sun noon-5 pm;
check/MC/V/reserve by
mail; exchanges on
season tickets only;
subscription program
Location
Between Beverly Blvd
and Melrose Ave; just N
of the Beverly Center
Parking
Valet, $4; street parking

SERENDIPITY THEATRE COMPANY—Resident Co.

The valiant efforts of this company results in entertaining productions for kids. Davidson produces seven plays each season for an optimum age range of 7 to 12 year-olds. Usually four of these selections are designed to captivate 4-year-olds and up. Everything from *The Diary of Anne Frank* to a stage adaptation of *Angelina Ballerina*, has found a place on the marquee.

The actors meet up with the kids in the courtyard after each performance to sign autographs and answer questions. The first Saturday evening performance of each show is sign-language interpreted. There is a subscription series available.

Attending plays here is an excellent way to introduce your children to live theater, and an excellent site in which to begin to teach them theater etiquette.

DANCE KALEIDOSCOPE See FESTIVALS & SEASONAL EVENTS

DANISH DAYS FESTIVAL See FESTIVALS & SEASONAL EVENTS

DEAF WEST CHILDREN'S THEATRE

660 North Heliotrope Drive
Hollywood, CA 90004
Info: (213) 660-0877 **Rsvn:** (213) 660-4673
TTY: (213) 660-8826 **Fax:** (213) 660-5016
99-seat theater in what was the Heliotrope Theatre.

Deaf West is the only resident company of deaf theater artists in the Western United States. Its adult theater is award-winning, compelling, and original. Now, lucky for us, a grant from the United States Department of Education will support its children's plays for at least three years.

The first presentation opened with a new production of *Cinderella* performed by students from TRIPOD (a private junior high school) and from the John Muir Middle School. Actors were deaf, hard of hearing, and hearing students, and some signed and spoke their own roles.

The community looks forward to future presentations guided by this solid, creative theater.

Performances
  Thurs-Sat 7 pm, Sat-Sun 2 pm
Tickets
  $10-12
Discounts
  Previews/children/groups of 25+, call
BO
  24 hr answering machine; MC/V/exchanges made with 48 hr notice; reserve tickets by mail; fax
Location
  Just S of Melrose between Normandy and Vermont.
Parking
  On premises, $1.50

FOLLOWS CAMP FAMILY BLUEGRASS FESTIVAL See FESTIVALS & SEASONAL EVENTS

THE GREAT AMERICAN CHILDREN'S THEATRE

See press listings for performance locations and schedules.
Info: (414) 276-4230 **Rsvn:** (800) 852-9772
Fax: (414) 276-2214
National touring company performing at the Pantages and Wilshire Theatres in LA, selected theaters in San Diego and San Bernardino.

Although as a rule, this book doesn't include touring companies based outside of Southern California, there's so little large-scale children's theater in Los Angeles I've included two important exceptions: the Children's

Performances
  Vary
Tickets
  $6-16.50
Discounts
  Seniors/students/groups of 10+, call (800) 852-9772

Theatre Company (of Minneapolis) and this, the Great American Children's Theatre.

These two companies are both based in the Midwest—America's heartland—in communities which support them well.

The Great American is coming close to 20 years of production, not all of them spent touring. Its artistic statement is simple, and one every theater—and parent—should take to heart: "The future of theatre in America is largely dependent on the development of the young audience."

In short, the GACT produces shows that respect their young audience. Whether it's *Charlotte's Web*, *Charlie and the Chocolate Factory*, *The Secret Garden*, or *Wind in the Willows*, founder and producer Teri Solomon Mitze is adamant about producing a high-quality show in terms of script, director, actors, costumes, and sets. As a result, children are treated to polished, well-staged performances.

The shows are best for ages 4 through 14. Children under age 4 aren't admitted. Kids get to talk to the performers, the director, and even the stagehands at the end of the show.

BO
By phone Mon-Fri 7 am-5:30 pm; MC/V/check/reserve by mail, TicketMaster; no exchanges
Location
Varies
Parking
Varies with location

GUILD OPERA COMPANY

See press listings for performance locations.
Info: (213) 463-6593

If we had a dollar for every Los Angeles school child who saw their first opera through the auspices of Guild Opera, we could build our own opera house—almost.

For decades after the Guild's founding in 1949, children were bused down to the Shrine Auditorium once a year in order to see Guild productions such as *The Magic Flute*, *Hansel and Gretel*, and *The Bartered Bride*. Back in the good old days, you could even hear future stars like Marilyn Horne—a local girl herself—Mary Costa, and Ken Remo gaining experience. No other company has ever devoted all of its resources to building audiences among children. The Guild deserves credit for creating the base of local public support that finally gave birth to the major-league Music Center Opera.

Guild Opera remains the second oldest surviving opera company in the state after San Francisco Opera. Though no longer at the Shrine, the company still puts on fully-staged, fully-costumed productions for kids at various locales in the LA area such as UCLA's Royce Hall, the Terrace Theatre in Long Beach, and El Camino College's Marsee Auditorium. The repertoire still includes the above-named works, plus standard favorites like *The Barber Of Seville*, *The Mikado*, and *Cinderella*—always sung in English.

The performances are held during school hours, usually starting at 10:30 am. With school funds being cut all over California, it's possible your child's school will not be attending. Should that be the case, there are evening performances open to the public, although the kids won't have had the benefit of the customary preparation of the school tours.

Performances
March through April; Fri 8 pm; Mon-Fri 10:30 am (for school children)
Tickets
$8-25
Discounts
Children/seniors/students/groups of 20+, call
BO
Only by mail or phoning office; check/reserve by mail
Location
Varies

HANS CHRISTIAN ANDERSON FAIRY TALE FESTIVAL

Solvang, CA 93463
Info: (805) 688-5575
Fax: (805) 688-8620

Solvang's spring festival celebrates the great author's work. Storybook characters come alive at children's theater presentations, and musicians, magicians, and storytellers dressed in traditional costumes join the parade of children outfitted in their Easter finery and accompanied by their favorite pets. The Solvang Village Dancers recall 19th-century Denmark, a country with which many folks in this Scandinavian-style town have family ties. The annual Easter Egg Hunt takes all comers.

The two-day event takes place a week before Easter Sunday and is a treat for youngsters and parents alike.

Performances
1 week before Easter Sunday
Tickets
FREE
Location
Corner of Atterdag Rd and 1st St
Parking
On street

HAUGH PERFORMING ARTS CENTER AT CITRUS COLLEGE See **Junior Programs of California**

IMAGINATION CELEBRATION

See press listings for performance locations.
Info: (714) 556-ARTS   **Rsvn:** (714) 556-ARTS
Nine-day County Festival.

Orange County is the lucky recipient of this countywide nine-day festival of arts for children and their families. Spanning five days and two weekends, dozens of live performances, hands-on workshops, and exhibits take place at more than 20 sites throughout the county. From malls to museums, parks and libraries, children sample some fine entertainment and visual arts. More than 150,000 people attend the various shows and displays.

Recent highlights included performances by the Pacific Symphony, the Kankouran West African Dance Company, and the Pacific Chorale. You don't have to look for the entertainment here—you can't miss it. There are street fairs, performances by local artists, storytelling, technical workshops, and puppetry. Most events are free, and even paid events don't cost more than $5.

In 1986, the Orange County Performing Arts Center and the Orange County Department of Education founded this program in cooperation with a similar program inaugurated by the Kennedy Center in Washington, D.C.

Watch for announcements about this spring celebration in the local papers, or call the Orange County Performing Arts Center.

Performances
  Vary
Tickets
  FREE-$5
BO
  Call

IMAGINATION STATION

Burbank Little Theater
1100 West Clark Avenue
Burbank, CA 91510
Info: (818) 954-9858
Free performances at the Burbank Little Theater.

Free noon-on-Saturdays readings are offered by The Actors Company at the Burbank Little Theater. Different members of the regular company take over each week and decide what will happen, and children are often invited to participate. The first Saturday of each month is unique—the kids get to concoct the story, while an on-hand professional animator is present to illustrate the "work in progress." You may attend on a day of sing-a-longs or storytelling.

The only chance you take at the Station is that your child might be too young or too old for a particular piece. But even when the age match is off, most children will be happily amused. And what do you have to lose— performances are free!

Performances
  Sat noon
Tickets
  FREE
Location
  On Olive, near Victory
  and Olive; Olive exit off
  Int-5
Parking
  On premises, FREE;
  street parking

IMAX THEATER See **ART FILMS**

IMPROVISATIONAL THEATER PROJECT—MARK TAPER FORUM THEATRE FOR YOUNG PEOPLE See **P.L.A.Y. (Performing for Los Angeles Youth)**

INTERNATIONAL FESTIVAL OF MASKS See **FESTIVALS & SEASONAL EVENTS**

IRVINE BARCLAY THEATRE See **MUSIC**

JAPAN AMERICA THEATRE See THEATER

JIM GAMBLE PUPPETS

See press listings for performance locations.
Info: (310) 541-1921
Fax: (310) 541-2195
A touring puppet show appearing in schools or at a variety of festivals.

Jim Gamble and his merry band of puppets have been a part of the Los Angeles family scene for more than 30 years. You may even have had them at your birthday party and are now hiring them for your kids! (At modern prices, of course.)

Gamble's shows can be seen at festivals all through the Southland. He puts on a variety of productions such as "The Adventures of Peer Gynt," using his marionettes, or "Peter and the Wolf," performed with rod puppets.

The shows are geared for children from ages 3 through 12. Birthday parties are his specialty (as long as you provide the space).

JUNIOR PROGRAMS OF CALIFORNIA

This marvelous annual theater series encompasses a variety of communities. There are separate programs for Los Angeles, Long Beach, La Mirada, and San Gabriel Valley. The programs are listed separately below, as each has different ticket information. Junior Programs presents a variety of children's theater groups and entertainers, all carefully selected with an eye toward entertaining theater and good solid plots for children ages 6 through 12. In addition to presenting local groups such as Golden State Children's Theatre, Jim Gamble Puppet Productions, Little Broadway Productions, and Cerritos College Children's Theatre, the series also brings in out-of-state artists such as Theatreworks/USA out of New York.

Children under 5 are not admitted at the Los Angeles and La Mirada programs (in Long Beach and San Gabriel Valley, the cut-off is age 4), thus reducing the chance of crying babies and toddlers with short attention spans roaming the aisles. Children are encouraged to use "proper theater etiquette."

The one-hour programs are available with a series subscription or by purchasing single tickets. Some of the locations have snacks for sale out front before the performance, but none allows snacks inside. Often the performers come outside after the show to sign autographs.

The seating at these venues is not reserved. Call the individual program for a current brochure and ticket ordering form.

KEY TO SYMBOLS

Air conditioning (Only in ART FILMS)		Hearing device available	
Snack bar		Binoculars availabe	
Full bar		All OK for kids	
Restaurant on premises		Some OK for kids	
Restaurant nearby		See seating plans	
Fully handicap accessible		Obituary—entity no longer exists or is no longer in operation	
Handicap seats only			

LOS ANGELES JUNIOR PROGRAMS

P.O. Box 24572
Los Angeles, CA 90024
Info: (310) 276-2769   **Rsvn:** (310) 825-9261
    This three-play series is held at the Wadsworth Theater (on the grounds of the Veterans Administration in West LA, which is just north of Wilshire Boulevard and west of the San Diego (405) Freeway. The one-time only performances take place on Sundays in the winter. The front center section of the Wadsworth is allocated to children only—no parents to block the view. If your child will sit alone, this is the place to put her. If not, kids and parents can sit together behind the front section and on the sides.

Performances
  Sun 1 pm
Tickets
  $4-6 (individual tickets)
  $11-15 (series)
BO
  Day of performance;
  check/reserve by mail;
  no exchanges
Location
  W of San Diego (405)
  Fwy; and N of Wilshire
  Blvd
Parking
  On premises, $5

LA MIRADA JUNIOR PROGRAMS

14900 La Mirada Boulevard
La Mirada, CA 90638
Info: (714) 994-6150 **Rsvn:** (714) 994-6310
Fax: (714) 994-5796
    La Mirada Theatre Foundation sponsors this five-performance series at the La Mirada Theatre for Performing Arts at 14900 La Mirada Boulevard on Saturdays or Sundays in the fall and winter. There are often two performances on each scheduled day.

Performances
  Sat-Sun 1:30, 3:30
Tickets
  $5
BO
  Mon-Thurs 10 am-5 pm;
  Fri 10 am-8 pm; Sat-Sun
  noon-5 pm; 1 hr prior to
  performances; check/
  Disc/MC/V/reserve by
  mail
Location
  Santa Ana (5) Fwy to
  Rosecrans exit
Parking
  Street parking

JUNIOR PROGRAMS OF LONG BEACH

P.O. Box 15744
Long Beach, CA 90815-0744
Info: (310) 496-4595   **Rsvn:** (818) 914-4403
    Long Beach features a six-performance season from winter through spring at the Lakewood High School Auditorium, 4400 Briercrest in Lakewood.

Performances
  Sun 2:30 pm
Tickets
  $4; $15 season
Discounts
  Groups of 10+, call
  (310) 496-4595
BO
  Open day of
  performance only;
  check/reserve by mail;
  no exchanges, no
  refunds; subscription
  program
Location
  Harvey Way and
  Briercrest Ave off
  Bellflower Blvd
Parking
  On premises, FREE;
  street parking

SAN GABRIEL VALLEY JUNIOR PROGRAMS

1290 Hillcrest Drive
Pomona, CA 91768
Info: (818) 914-4403 **Rsvn:** (818) 914-4403

The six-performance schedule runs from fall through winter, with one spring performance. Shows are at Citrus College in the Haugh Performing Arts Center, 1000 West Foothill Boulevard, Glendora. At this venue, children must sit with an adult.

Performances
Sat 2 pm
Tickets
$4; $14/season
Discounts
Groups of 10+, send to Group Orders, 739 S Bender, Glendora, CA 91740
BO
Open 1/2 hr before performance; check/ reserve by mail; no refunds or exchanges
Location
Foothill Blvd and Citrus Ave off the Foothill (210) Fwy
Parking
On premises

KATJA BIESANZ/DANCE THEATER See DANCE

KID'S CABARET See LA Cabaret Comedy Club

KID'S KONCERTS AT WILL GEER THEATRICUM BOTANICUM

1419 North Topanga Canyon
Topanga, CA 90290
Info: (310) 455-2322 **Rsvn:** (310) 455-3723
For directions and ticket information, see Will Geer Theatricum Botanicum in THEATER.

Kids' favorite entertainer Peter Alsop has put together a summer series of musical entertainers that most youngsters will love. 1993 saw J.P. Nightingale and Dan Crow, plus Melora Marshall and Dave Kinnoin. There are only five performances, most on Sundays at 11 am. Series tickets are available. Don't forget "tushy" cushions; picnics are okay, too. It's sunny up in these hills, so be sure to bring along sunscreen. Call for an order form.

Performances
Sat 2 pm; Sun 11 am
Tickets
$5
BO
2 hrs prior to curtain; check; ticket good for any performance; subscription program
Location
(From coast) Pacific Coast Hwy to Topanga Cyn Blvd; (from Valley) Ventura Fwy to Topanga Cyn S exit
Parking
On premises, FREE; street parking

LA CABARET COMEDY CLUB

17271 Ventura Boulevard
Encino, CA 91316
Info: (818) 501-3737   **Rsvn:** (818) 501-3737
Fax: (818) 501-3749
Encino adult comedy club with Sunday family shows.

The kids' version of this adult club happens on Sunday afternoons when comics, jugglers, ventriloquists, and magicians invade the stage. For your $12 each, you get a show, pizza, and a beverage. A great idea for birthday parties or special events. Shows are geared for ages 3 and up. If you trust your kids alone, you can hide out in the lounge with the big screen TV.

Performances
Sun 1:30, 3:30
Tickets
$12
BO
Mon-Sun 11 am-midnight; check/AE/MC/V
Location
On Ventura Blvd between Balboa and White Oak; take Balboa exit off the Ventura (101) Fwy
Parking
On premises, FREE; street parking

LA CONNECTION—COMEDY IMPROV FOR KIDS BY KIDS

13442 Ventura Boulevard
Sherman Oaks, CA 91423
Info: (818) 784-1868   **Rsvn:** (818) 784-1868
Fax: (818) 710-8666
The young set's version of an improv theater.

If you want your child to be the next Chevy Chase or Jane Curtin, cough up about $200 for 10 lessons with the pros at LA Connection. No doubt at the end of the class, the kids'll be begging for an agent. But if you just want to take them to watch the class perform what it's learned, your costs will be substantially lower. You can catch these gutsy kids every other Sunday at 3:30 pm.

This Valley spot has been around for more than 20 years. See **THEATER** for information about the adult connection.

Performances
Sun 3:30 pm (alternate Sundays)
Tickets
$7
Discounts
Groups, call
BO
Prior to curtain; MC/V/check/reserve by mail, fax, TicketMaster; exchanges accepted
Location
2 1/2 blocks E of Woodman
Parking
On premises, FREE; street parking

LAGUNA PLAYHOUSE YOUTH THEATRE

The Laguna Playhouse
606 Laguna Canyon Road
Laguna Beach, CA 92651
Info: (714) 497-9244   **Rsvn:** (714) 494-8021
Children's performances at the Laguna Playhouse.

The youth division of the Laguna Playhouse welcomes all children from the community to auditions for children's roles; we older folks get a shot at adult roles.

Three plays a year are aimed at children ages 4 and up, with one for youngsters over 8. Seating is unreserved so come early. Four- and three-play series tickets may be had at a slight discount.

This is a wonderful place to expose even your very young children to live theater.

This is also the site for Ballet Pacifica's annual *Nutcracker* presentation.

A Disabled Youth program was created to teach disabled children the basics of theater. They write and

Performances
Fri-Sat 7:30 pm; Sat-Sun 2 pm
Tickets
$4-8
Discounts
Children/students/groups of 20+, call
BO
Tues-Sat noon-5 pm; MC/V/check/reserve by mail; exchanges for subscribers only; subscription program
Location
Off Laguna (133) Fwy, Int-5, San Diego (405) Fwy or Pacific Coast Hwy

perform their own productions, often about the experience of being disabled.

Parking
On premises FREE; street parking available

LITTLE BROADWAY PRODUCTIONS

See press listings for performance locations.
Info: (818) 894-4222   **Rsvn:** (800) 527-8747
Fax: (818) 891-1813

This traveling troupe sets up its stage for school children all over California and Nevada. They also perform (usually musicals) for the general kiddie public on occasional weekends and holidays. Catch them at a Junior Programs series, LA Valley College, or Orange Coast College among other area venues.

Performances
Vary
Tickets
$4.50-8
Discounts
Children/students/ groups of 25+, call BO
BO
Call; check/reserve by mail (P.O. Box 5008, Mission Hills, CA 91395 0008); fax; exchanges made for different date or time

LOBERO THEATRE FAMILY SERIES See **THEATER**

LONG BEACH CARNAVAL See **FESTIVALS & SEASONAL EVENTS**

LONG BEACH CIVIC LIGHT OPERA See **Terrace Theatre** in **THEATER**

LOS ANGELES CHAMBER BALLET See **DANCE**

LOS ANGELES CHAMBER ORCHESTRA—Family Concert Series

See press listings for performance locations.
Info: (213) 622-7001   **Rsvn:** (213) 622-7001
Fax: (213) 955-2071

If you thought chamber music was just for the serious, think again. The Los Angeles Chamber Orchestra has come up with an innovative way to introduce children (and adults who have never heard a chamber orchestra) to classical music. Alas, this annual program is limited to one event, but the Chamber Orchestra is hoping to expand that to three events in the near future.

In the first year, the "Bach to the Future" program offered the event in two languages with music performed by the full chamber orchestra. The most recent undertaking took advantage of Southern California's outdoors with "Bach Hits the Beach." The mini-festival was held at the Beach Club in Santa Monica, where families picked up picnic baskets (adult and children's meals available) upon arriving, and were encouraged to swim and play in the sand. All the music-oriented events were geared to entertain and introduce classical music. The Petting Zoo allowed the kids to try out the wonderful instruments; the evening ended with the "Toy Symphony." It wasn't cheap, though—$55 for adults and $20 for children, but that included a three-hour event, dinner, and the excellence of the full chamber orchestra.

Spokespeople don't know yet what's on tap for next season. Be sure to call for current information.

Performances
Sat
Tickets
$20-55
Discounts
Children
BO
Mon-Fri 10 am-4 pm; AE/MC/V/reserve by mail (315 W Ninth St, Ste. 801, Los Angeles, CA 90015), fax; exchanges accepted
Location
Varies
Parking
Varies with location

LOS ANGELES CHILDREN'S MUSEUM

310 North Main Street
Los Angeles, CA 90012
Info: (213) 687-8800 **Rsvn:** (213) 687-8225
Fax: (213) 687-0319
Louis B. Mayer Performance Space seats 99.

Most parents are familiar with our city's downtown children's museum and its hand-on, interactive displays, workshops, and educational programs. What they may not be familiar with are the performances that go on in the Louis B. Mayer Performance Space.

You can find something going on almost any weekend during the year. In the spring, you might even see Shakespeare Festival LA's Shakespearean puppet show; in December, "Celebrate the Light" depicts holidays celebrated by numerous cultures.

The 24-hour information telephone number will keep you up-to-date on Monday through Sunday activities. Most performances are appropriate for children ages 2 to 12; some may suit kids over 4.

Bring lunch and eat on the plaza outside, or eat before you arrive. There is fast food sold on the level below. Parking is discounted in the City-operated lot for museum patrons, or park on the street on weekends.

Performances
Sat-Sun 12 pm, 2 pm; weekdays during summer and school holidays
Tickets
$5 (this is the entrance fee to the museum; performances FREE)
Discounts
Groups of 10+, call
BO
Check/MC/V
Location
Downtown LA; across from City Hall between Aliso and Temple Sts
Parking
On premises, $3.30 per hr, not more than $6.60 week days and $3.30 weekends; nearby lots; street parking also available

&

LOS ANGELES CHOREOGRAPHERS & DANCERS See DANCE

LOS ANGELES JEWISH FESTIVAL See FESTIVALS & SEASONAL EVENTS

LULA WASHINGTON CHILDREN'S JAZZ DANCE ENSEMBLE

5179 1/2 West Adams Boulevard
Los Angeles, CA 90016
Info: (213) 936-6591
Fax: (213) 671-4572
Quake damage has closed the studio temporarily. Be sure to call for an update.

In an age of increased television-watching and a decade of funding cutbacks in the public schools, Lula Washington's work with children isn't a luxury (see **Lula Washington Contemporary Dance Theatre** in **DANCE**); rather, it's essential to the survival of an art form, not to mention the well-being of any number of kids who otherwise might have nowhere to go if not for Washington's dance classes. With high marks for her outstanding ability to impart both dance technique and self-esteem to her young charges, Washington makes a star of any young girl or boy lucky enough to make her way into the ensemble. And those stars shine, especially when they strut their stuff at the many in-house recitals, local festivals, or the popular Black History Month shows. Call for a schedule of events.

Performances
Vary
Tickets
$5-10
BO
Check; no exchanges
Parking
Street

THE MAGIC MIRROR PLAYERS

Third Stage Theatre
2811 West Magnolia Boulevard
Burbank, CA 91505
Info: (818) 508-4780   **Rsvn:** (818) 842-4755
Fax: (818) 508-8588
Performances generally at the Third Stage Theatre.
      Lost in the lore of the magic mirror, five children shouted out answers to an actor's questions. The rest wiggled in their seats, giggled, and were generally excited about the program in front of them. The Magic Mirror Players were working their improvisational skills on kids averaging in age from 5 to 10.
      Producer Bunnie Strassner's actors rotate and present a fresh show each week, asking all the children for suggestions for each skit. Best of all, they get the children involved immediately so they feel part of the making of each segment. The show runs indefinitely at the tiny Third Stage Theatre, where the kids are so close to the actors they can actually touch them. Also ask about other venue dates, as the company is exporting its talents to other parts of town.
      Prepare your youngsters in advance. Some kids, who are used to attending "regular" theater where they're not supposed to make a peep, are hesitant to get involved with the show. Let them know that in improv, it's okay.
      This kind of theater is best for the 5- to 11-year-olds. The performances last one hour. There's no snack bar—just a soda machine—and no lobby to speak of. Nor are there many places to eat nearby. Speak to Strassner about renting out the theater for birthday parties.

Performances
  Sat-Sun noon
Tickets
  $5
Discounts
  Groups of 12+, call
BO
  Sat-Sun noon; call for reservations
Location
  Between Hollywood Way and Buena Vista; near Ventura (134) Fwy
Parking
  On street

MAGNIFICENT MOORPARK MELODRAMA & VAUDEVILLE THEATRE See THEATER

MCCALLUM THEATRE OF THE PERFORMING ARTS See THEATER

MOJO ENSEMBLE—FAMILY THEATRE
MOJO ENSEMBLE—YOUTH THEATRE

1540 North Cahuenga Boulevard
Hollywood, CA 90028
Info: (213) 957-0690   **Rsvn:** (213) 960-1604
      The Family Theatre targets children 12 and under with Sunday afternoon matinees of adventure and music provided by adult actors in original or West Coast premieres. *Por Quinley* by Quincy Long, for instance, originally premiered at the Sundance Festival. Performances run an hour to an hour and a half.
      Youth Theatre is theater with a message, and my message to you is, "fasten your seat belts." These performances are rap/musical operas! The Youth Theatre company consists of teenager actors from throughout Los Angeles aiming at their peers and everybody's parents.
      These two new matinee programs are the ambitious offspring of Michele Martin, the artistic director of the Family Theatre project, and Lanyard Williams, who heads up the Youth Theatre Department.

Performances
  Family Theatre Sat-Sun 2 pm; **Youth Theatre** Sat-Sun 4 pm
Tickets
  FREE-$8
Discounts
  Children/groups of 10+, for **Family Theatre** only
BO
  Open 45 minutes prior to show; 24 hr message machine for reservations; check/AE/ reserve by mail
Location
  On Cahuenga between Sunset and Selma
Parking
  On premises, $2.50 (Sundays only); street parking

MUSIC IN THE LA ZOO

Griffith Park
5333 Zoo Drive
Los Angeles, CA 90027
Info: (213) 664-1100
Summer program of evening music.
What do you do at the zoo after dark? Well, in summer you listen to music. Each July the Los Angeles Zoo offers selected nights of live music and entertainment from 6:15 to 9 pm to soothe the savage and not-so-savage beast alike. Most selections suit any age or species; even if the kids get restless during classical and jazz night, lots of animals are still on the howl and the prowl until about 8.

Each evening has a different theme: one night might be country and western, another world music. Several concerts fitting the theme can be found throughout the zoo on the scheduled evening, with sets repeated two or three times to allow you to migrate from site to site to catch it all. Individual performers and costumed characters perform on the routes to the entertainment areas.

Bring your own picnic dinner, or take advantage of the special adult and children's meals that can be ordered ahead of time or on site. Call the zoo's Special Events Department for information on this year's dates and advance tickets.

Performances
July
Tickets
$7-10
Discounts
Children
BO
MC/V/check/reserve by mail, fax (213) 662-6879
Location
Off the Ventura (134) Fwy or Golden State (5) Fwy; Griffith Park
Parking
On premises, FREE

NANETTE BRODIE DANCE THEATRE See DANCE

NATIONAL WOMEN'S THEATRE FESTIVAL See FESTIVALS & SEASONAL EVENTS

THE NEW IVAR THEATER/INNER CITY CULTURAL CENTER See Inner City Cultural Center in THEATER

NORRIS THEATRE FOR THE PERFORMING ARTS See THEATER

ODYSSEY THEATRE ENSEMBLE

2055 South Sepulveda Boulevard
Los Angeles, CA 90025
Info: (310) 477-2055   **Rsvn:** (310) 477-2055
Fax: (310) 444-0455
Make a beeline for the Odyssey's Saturday family shows performed by the highly professional, creative troupe, The Glorious Players. Its track record is great: *The Island* impressed children for more than three years, as did the popular *Cirque Du LA: Working Without Annette! Opossum Tails* has been beguiling the young set for quite a while and is sure to join the ranks of the previous shows. The regular programming for adults at the Odyssey is so respected and professional, it stands to reason it will be the same for children!

Artistic Director of the Glorious Players, Debbie Devine, and her troupe involve children in the performances, making theater intimate and experiential. While the kids are being entertained, they don't realize they're also being taught to read or are being exposed to current social issues (such as "what is a family" in *Opossum Tails*). No matter what the subject, the children aren't talked down to.

The three theater spaces here are so great that, no matter which one the performance is scheduled in, everyone will be able to see and hear. As an added introduction to theater, the actors greet the kids in the lobby

Performances
Usually Sat noon, 2 pm
Tickets
$6.50
Discounts
Groups of 20+, call BO
BO
Tues-Sat 10 am-6 pm; Sun 2 pm-6 pm AE/MC/ V/check/reserve by mail; no refunds, no exchanges; subscription program
Location
On Sepulveda Blvd between Santa Monica Blvd and Olympic Blvd in West LA; near the San Diego (405) Fwy, exit Santa Monica Blvd
Parking
On premises, FREE; street parking

and do "warm ups." Once everyone is led into the theater, the children are usually seated down in front and the adults in back and on the sides.

Birthday parties are a big deal at the Odyssey. For a fee, you get the show and a party which includes a creative dramatics workshop, plus all the party supplies (not the cake) and a staff of adults to serve and supervise. There is only one party per show, which allows the actors to really pay attention to your group. Call (818) 989-7655. A mailing list will keep you up-to-date on all the family programs.

It's hard to specify age appropriateness here—it really depends on the play. When you call for tickets, ask the staff what age range the current show fits.

OPEN HOUSE AT THE HOLLYWOOD BOWL

1301 North Highland Avenue
Hollywood, CA 90078
Info: (213) 850-2077   **Rsvn:** (213) 850-2000
Fax: (213) 851-5617
Summer program on the grounds of the Bowl.

Open House at the Hollywood Bowl, under the auspices of the Los Angeles Philharmonic, recently hit the 25-year mark. This summer festival offers children 3 to 12 an introduction to the music, storytelling, mime, puppetry, and theater of many countries. The festival takes place for six weeks beginning in July, and each program is performed twice a day for a week. Monday's 10 am performances are signed for the hearing-impaired.

Children are treated to performers and groups such as Lula Washington Children's Jazz Dance Ensemble, J.P. Nightingale, the South Bay Ballet, and Magical Moonshine Theatre. An optional workshop, themed to that day's performance, follows each show. Kids are divided into age groups for the activities, which might include mask-making, musical instrument making, or dancing.

The performance area is outdoors, shaded from the sun. However, because of our hot July and August weather, I still recommend the cooler early show. Kids are packed into the performance area on grass mats near the stage, while the adults sit on chairs behind them. The space gets quite congested with little children running back and forth to check on Mom and Dad. Volunteers do a good job of making sure eager youngsters stay seated so everyone can see. If your children can stand waiting in line, queue up early for the best seating.

The literature recommends the performances for the 3 to 12-year-olds, but I'd say kids 5 (with good concentration skills) to 9 or 10 will enjoy them the most.

The best part of the visit is listening to the Philharmonic rehearse in the morning (9:30 am to noon except Wednesdays and some Mondays) free of charge. Plop yourselves down in box seats (which can rarely be booked during the regular season), and feel quite privileged. After the workshops, grab your picnic lunches and wander the grounds for awhile. The Hollywood Bowl Museum is open (free of charge) for anyone interested. Parking is free and easy.

Although you can purchase tickets the day of the concert, I'd suggest ordering them in advance to avoid that line. You can place an order for one or more performances by mail. Adults may observe the workshops free. Call (213) 850-2000 for a schedule of events.

Performances
Summer Mon-Fri performances 10 am and 11:15 am; Mon-Fri workshops 11 am and 12:15 pm
Tickets
$1-3
Discounts
Groups of 15+, call
BO
Mon-Sun 10 am-6 pm; check/reserve by mail; no exchanges or refunds
Location
Off of the Hollywood (101) Fwy, Highland exit
Parking
On premises, FREE

OPEN HOUSE AT THE MUSIC CENTER

Music Center
Dorothy Chandler Pavilion
135 North Grand Avenue
Los Angeles, CA 90012
Info: (213) 850-2000   **Rsvn:** (213) 850-2000
Fax: (213) 955-2071

     This open house is the Music Center's Saturday program geared to 3-to-5-year-old budding Stravinskys. The season of three 30-minute concerts introduces them to symphonic music as well as the instruments of the orchestra. Even Philharmonic Music Director Salonen has gotten into the act, leading the musicians in a "Music All Around" program. The kids get to sit on the floor close to the musicians. The program begins at 11:30 am. Tickets are pint-size, too, at $3 each, but order well ahead as only a limited number of tickets are made available to ensure that everyone can see. See **Music Center of Los Angeles County** in **THEATER** for directions.

Performances
  Sat 11:30 am
Tickets
  $4
Discounts
  Groups call (213) 972-0703
BO
  Mon-Sat 10 am-6 pm; check/reserve by mail,TicketMaster; no exchanges, no refunds; subscription program
Parking
  On premises, $5; city lots, $3; street parking

  ♿

PCPA THEATERFEST See THEATER

PACIFIC ISLANDER FESTIVAL See FESTIVALS & SEASONAL EVENTS

PASADENA COMMUNITY ORCHESTRA See MUSIC

PEARSON PARK AMPHITHEATRE

400 North Harbor Boulevard
Anaheim, CA 92805
Info: (714) 254-5274   **Rsvn:** (714) 635-3751
Summer outdoor family performances.

     Each summer, beginning in June, the Anaheim Parks and Recreation department sponsors three nights of family performances each week at the 2,100-seat Pearson Park Amphitheatre. The Thursday night series, "Just for Kids," is designed for very young children and their families. The amateur performances usually feature audience participation. Friday and Saturday evenings are for band concerts and variety shows, but even these shows are geared for families with children of all ages.

Performances
  Summer Thurs-Sat 7:30 pm and 8 pm
Tickets
  $1-5
Discounts
  Children/seniors/groups of 20+, call BO
BO
  Open 1 hr before performance; check/reserve by mail
Location
  2 miles S of Riverside (91) Fwy near Harbor Blvd and Lincoln Ave
Parking
  On premises, FREE; street parking

PERFORMANCE/RIVERSIDE See THEATER

P.L.A.Y. (Performing for Los Angeles Youth)

Mark Taper Forum
135 North Grand Avenue
Los Angeles, CA 90012
Info: (213) 972-7662

     For more than 22 years, P.L.A.Y. (until recently known as ITP—Improvisational Theater Project) has been bringing creative, cutting-edge theatrical performances to

Performances
  Vary
Tickets
  FREE or minimal $

young people locally, nationally, and internationally. Social issues are the essence of these productions, which, rather than being pedantic, are fast-paced, contemporary works, most often including music and stylized movement. The age appropriateness depends on the production.

But you have to watch for the announcement of these performances—there's no real season, nor is there a regular performance space. The actors tour the schools as well as venues such as the Natural History Museum and the New Ivar Theatre. Sometimes shows are free, sometimes there is a charge—it depends on the venue. Call the Audience Services line at the Taper for more information: (213) 972-0700.

BO
Vary from venue to venue; reserve by mail, TicketMaster

R.D. COLBURN SCHOOL OF PERFORMING ARTS See MUSIC

REDONDO BEACH CITY THEATER GROUP

1935 Manhattan Beach Boulevard
Redondo Beach CA 90278
Info: (310) 318-0610   **Rsvn:** (310) 318-0610
Fax: (310) 316 6467
Community theater with performances at Aviation Auditorium, 1935 Manhattan Beach Boulevard, and at Perry Park Playhouse, 2301 Grant Avenue, both in Redondo Beach.

This community-based group gives its neighbors an annual series of children's performances in both the large Aviation Park Auditorium and the smaller Perry Park Playhouse. Call for their newsletter with performance schedule and audition information.

Performances
Fri-Sat 8 pm, Sun 2 pm
Tickets
$5-10
Discounts
Previews/children/ seniors/students/groups of 20+, call BO
BO
Mon-Fri 8 am-5 pm; check/MC/V/call for order form; subscription program; exchanges prior to performance
Location
Off San Diego (405) Fwy at Inglewood; W on Manhattan Beach Blvd to Aviation Blvd
Parking
On premises, FREE

RIO HONDO SYMPHONY ASSOCIATION See MUSIC

SAN DIEGO INTERNATIONAL CHILDREN'S FESTIVAL

Mariner's Point
Mission Bay Park
San Diego, CA 92640
Info: (619) 234-5031   **Rsvn:** (714) 636-7213
Fax: (714) 539-2651

For the past five years, this lively outdoor festival has taken place at Mariner's Point, Mission Bay Park. For five days, usually Wednesday through Sunday, children from preschool through grade school are treated to music, mime, puppet shows, storytelling, and other arts. The 4-and-under crowd get their own roped-off arts and crafts area, as well as their own mini-festival.

The performers have been local, well-known groups and individuals: storytelling by a native American, music from a Latin American, and an ethnomusicologist explaining the world's music to the children. Chairs and mats are set up for the stage performances. The stage show changes every hour on the half hour.

Bring a picnic or purchase hot and cold food and drinks at the location. Rest rooms are nearby.

Performances
Wed-Sun
Tickets
$5
Discounts
Groups of 10+, call
BO
MC/V/check/reserve by mail (call for mailing address), phone; no exchanges; subscription program
Location
Take Sea World Dr to West Mission Bay Dr
Parking
On premises, FREE; nearby lot

Watch for news about the festival in the local press or call to be put on a mailing list. Remember: the location and month may change (although it will always be in spring—usually May).

SAN DIEGO JUNIOR THEATRE

Casa del Prado, Room 208
Balboa Park
San Diego, CA 92101
Info: (619) 239-1311 **Rsvn:** (619) 239-8355

That little person ushering you to your seat at the San Diego Junior Theatre is probably a member in good standing of the San Diego Junior Theatre program—just like the actors on stage and the prop people behind the scenes.

San Diego Junior Theatre, which began operation just two years after the end of World War II, trains children from 8 to 18 in theater, taking them from classes to performances at the Casa del Prado Theatre stage in Balboa Park. In the process, it has molded countless San Diegans into theater performers and patrons. For some children in the audiences, it's their first exposure to live theater.

The Casa del Prado Theatre is more auditorium than theater house, but the floor is raked, so viewing is not a problem. The acoustics are another story, but people generally don't go to San Diego Junior Theatre for the ultimate in sound. They go to catch the kids and their infectious enthusiasm and pride in what they're doing. The group puts on six mainstage performances each year, which draw total audiences of as many as 35,000 people—not a bad turn out in a 650-seat theater!

Like the performers, ticket prices are pint-sized, ranging from $5 to $7 an admission, though that's not counting the discounts available to seniors, groups, and military families. There are also reasonably priced season subscriptions.

Some final dress rehearsals are open to the public gratis. There's also a chance to meet the actors; theater tours can be arranged. Age-appropriateness varies according to the play.

Performances
Fri 7 pm; Sat-Sun 2 pm
Tickets
$5-7
Discounts
Children/seniors/
students/groups of 15+,
call BO
BO
Tues-Fri 12:30 pm-4:30
pm; plus 1 1/2 hours
prior to show; check/AE
MC/V/reserve by mail;
exchanges for
subscribers only;
subscription program
Location
Off Park Blvd, on Village
Place, one street South
of San Diego Zoo
Parking
On street and in parking
lots in Balboa Park

SAN DIEGO MINI-CONCERTS See MUSIC

SAN DIEGO REPERTORY THEATRE See THEATER

SANTA MARIA SYMPHONY SOCIETY See MUSIC

SANTA MONICA ARTS FESTIVAL See FESTIVALS & SEASONAL EVENTS

SANTA MONICA COLLEGE CONCERT HALL

1900 Pico Boulevard
Santa Monica, CA 90405
Info: (310) 452-9396 **Rsvn:** (310) 452-9396
Concert Hall seats 250 for adult, family, and children's performances.

Concert Hall presents an Afternoon Theater for Children series with performances by a variety of companies and performers including the popular children's songwriter Dan Crow, puppeteer Jim Gamble, the Imagination Theatre company, magician Dick Barry, and Max's Playhouse.

Performances
Sat 1 pm, 3 pm
Tickets
$5-6
Discounts
Groups of 15+, call BO
BO
Check/MC/V/reserve by
mail; no exchanges

While the staff feels children ages 2 to 14 will enjoy this series, I'd definitely ask what age a show is geared toward before ordering tickets. Ticket prices are quite reasonable. Shows usually last one hour.

Seating is first-come, first-served, and doors open a half hour before show time. Seats can be roped off for birthday parties; make arrangements by phone.

Location
At Pico Blvd and 19th St; Cloverfield exit off Santa Monica (10) Fwy
Parking
On premises, FREE

SANTA MONICA PLAYHOUSE

1211 4th Street
Santa Monica, CA 90401
Info: (310) 394-9779   **Rsvn:** (310) 394-9779 ext. 2
Also see THEATER Chapter.

This is a very popular spot for children's birthday parties, when it becomes a "play" house in earnest. Take a group of 10 or more, and the theater takes over from there by providing party favors, cookies, candies, and punch. They even set up and clean up! The birthday child gets to appear on stage for a Happy Birthday greeting.

Performances
Sat-Sun 1 pm, 3 pm
Tickets
$7-8
Discounts
Groups of 25+, call BO
BO
Mon-Sun 11 am-6 pm; check/reserve by mail
Location
4th St exit off of the Santa Monica (10) Fwy
Parking
Near premises, $.50 per hr; street parking

ACTORS' REPERTORY THEATRE COMPANY—Resident Co.

In the Family Theatre Series, classic stories, musical adaptations of fairy tales, and Christmas shows crowd the weekend matinee schedule. Most of the plays are appropriate for children two and older.

Discussions between cast and kiddies generally prove entertaining and can be specially pre-arranged to follow the 3 pm performance.

Grumbly tummies can be "fixed" at nearby Fama or several spots on the Third Street Promenade including Johnny Rockets.

SCANDINAVIAN FESTIVAL See FESTIVALS & SEASONAL EVENTS

SERENDIPITY THEATRE COMPANY See Coronet Theatre

SOUTH COAST REPERTORY See THEATER

SPRECKELS ORGAN PAVILION See MUSIC

STARLIGHT MUSICAL THEATRE See THEATER

SUMMER SOLSTICE CELEBRATION See FESTIVALS & SEASONAL EVENTS

SUNDAY CONCERTS IN THE PARK See FESTIVALS & SEASONAL EVENTS

SUNDAY MORNINGS AT THE IVAR THEATRE See Inner City Cultural Center in THEATER

SUNDAYS AT THE MUSEUM

Los Angeles County Museum of Art
5905 Wilshire Boulevard
Los Angeles, CA 90036
Info: (213) 857-6139 or (213) 857-6000

    This Los Angeles County Museum of Art family program takes place once a month in summer. Storytellers, dancers, musicians, and writers entertain youngsters ages 5 to 12. The mailing list gives advance notice about who is on the schedule. Some programs are participatory, others are stage programs for the entire family. Shows last about an hour. Meet at 11 am at the top of the stairs, Wilshire Boulevard entrance.

    The only caveat: open registration begins at 11 am and is first-come, first-served. Sometimes things can get a bit chaotic. Get there early.

Performances
    May-Dec; last Sunday of each month
Tickets
    Museum admission (members FREE, adults $6)
Discount
    Children/seniors/ students
BO
    Wed-Thurs 10 am-5 pm, Fri 10 am-9 pm, Sat-Sun 11 am-6 pm; check/AE/ MC/V
Location
    Off Santa Monica (10) Fwy, Fairfax exit, 2 blocks E of Fairfax Ave
Parking
    $4 on premises, street parking

SYMPHONIES FOR YOUTH

Dorothy Chandler Pavilion
135 North Grand Avenue
Los Angeles, CA 90012
Info: (213) 850-2000   **Rsvn:** (213) 850-2000
LA Philharmonic's music series for children.

    Want your 6-to-12-year-olds to recognize the sounds of Debussy, Beethoven, Mendelssohn, or Prokofiev? You can't get much better instructors than the musicians of the Los Angeles Philharmonic. An annual program of five performances is offered at the Dorothy Chandler Pavilion. The 45-minute concerts are just the right length to hold a child's attention and maybe even have her coming back for more. The portions may be kid-sized, but the performances are not. In fact, in 1993 Music Director Esa-Pekka Salonen himself led the way.

    Each concert has a theme (animals, music from around the world, etc.), and an hour before the performance the children can join in activities and demonstrations geared to the day's musical theme.

    Concerts are handicapped-accessible as well as signed for the hearing impaired. It's strongly suggested you do not bring children under the age of 6. (See **Open House at the Music Center** for information on programs geared to the younger kids.) Tickets go fast, so order in advance.

    A new series of family-oriented concerts have been added to the Saturday line-up. Series N is geared, though, for children and teens who can sit through a full (usually two hour) performance. The premiere season had Salonen conducting one of three concerts. Adult subscriptions cost $25, while seniors and students pay $12.50. Don't overlook this as a way for your older children to be introduced to the classics, and for the entire family to enjoy an activity together.

Performances
    Sat. 10:15 am
Tickets
    $5-7.50
BO
    Mon-Sat 10 am-6 pm check/MC/V/reserve by mail, TicketMaster; no exchanges; subscription program
Location
    See **Music Center** in **THEATER**
Parking
    On premises, $5; city lots, $3; street parking

SYNTHAXIS THEATRE COMPANY See **THEATER**

TAFFY FESTIVAL (THEATER ARTS FESTIVAL FOR YOUTH)

Peter Strauss Ranch
30,000 Mulholland Highway
Agoura, CA 91306
Info: (818) 998-2339 **Rsvn:** (818) 998-2339
Fax: (818) 709-1461

    Los Angeles children have their own arts festival in this annual fall program, which has been entertaining families since 1985. Set at Peter Strauss Ranch in Agoura, the October weekend event encompasses a kaleidoscope of shows for all ages. John Wood and his wife, Pam, both better known to your kids as J.P. Nightingale, produce the event and give performances.

    They are masters at knowing what kids want. Theater, music, dance, puppetry, and mime are performed on four stages simultaneously by talented artists such as Peter Alsop, Dan Crow, the Banana Slug String Band, and the Japanese dance troupe Fujima Kansuma Kai. Workshops, games, and arts and crafts booths abound. There's even a special area just for toddlers under 3.

    Attendance at the festival has grown, not surprisingly, from 800 to more than 6,000 attendees. There are plenty of food booths and drinks to assuage LA's notorious October heat, or you can bring your own picnic and spend the day.

    Funding cuts are threatening to prevent the festival from reaching its 10th birthday. Watch the papers for notices, or call to be put on the mailing list.

Performances
  Fall (October)
Tickets
  $7-10
Discounts
  Groups of 10+
BO
  Check/reserve by mail (P.O. Box 2665, Canoga Park, CA 91306) TicketMaster; buy at door
Location
  Ventura Fwy (West) Canan Rd exit, left (over Fwy), go 2.8 miles to Troutdale, left, 1/2 mile dead end into Peter Strauss Ranch
Parking
  On premises, FREE

TGIF NOONTIME CONCERTS See FESTIVALS & SEASONAL EVENTS

THEATRE IN OLD TOWN See THEATER

THEATRE PALISADES KIDS See Pierson Playhouse in THEATER

THEATRE WEST—STORYBOOK THEATRE

3333 Cahuenga Boulevard West
Los Angeles, CA 90068
Info: (213) 851-4839 **Rsvn:** (818) 761-2203
Theatre West's children's theater. 180 seats.

    On the stage of this nondescript theater in this fairly nondescript part of Cahuenga Boulevard, children's fairy tales come to life. The Storybook people present simple tales such as "Aladdin and His Lamp" and "Princess and the Frog" with adult actors. Take your kids ages 2 to 8.

Performances
  Sat 1 pm
Tickets
  $6
Discounts
  Groups of 25+, call BO
BO
  24 hours taped message; check
Location
  Just W of the Hollywood (101) Fwy between Barham and Lankershim
Parking
  Across street, FREE; street parking also available

UCLA CENTER FOR THE PERFORMING ARTS (Family Series) See THEATER

VALLEY CULTURAL CENTER See **Concerts in the Park**

VIVA LA! See **FESTIVALS & SEASONAL EVENTS**

WALNUT/DIAMOND BAR THEATRE See **THEATER**

WILL & COMPANY See **THEATER**

WONDERWORLD PUPPET THEATER

See press listings for performance locations.
Info: (310) 532-1741   **Rsvn:** (310) 532-1741
Ric Morton and wife Julee have been taking their troupe of hand and rod puppets on tour since 1974. Formerly appearing at the Torrance Community Theater, they now perform intermittently at the Palos Verdes Players Theater at 2433 Moreton in Torrance, and at numerous malls around the Southland. You can call the Mortons to find out their current schedule of performances.

Performances
Sat 11 am
Tickets
$4-5
BO
1/2 hr before showtime

FESTIVALS &
SEASONAL EVENTS

Festivals & Seasonal Events

By Adolfo V. Nodal

Los Angeles' cultural diversity is known the world over. Because of this richness of resources, festivals play an important role and are an integral part of the cultural expression of our city. The various ethnic communities in Los Angeles have distinct cultural traditions that include music, dance, fine arts, crafts, and food. Festivals are a good way to preserve and express these traditions and also provide an excellent opportunity for Angelenos to learn about each other.

Experimental and avant-garde artists are also creating new images, new music, and new traditions, and these young artists and artisans need to share their visions. Festivals are one important forum for the current cultural voice as well as cultural heritage.

LA's cultural festival program, the responsibility of the Cultural Affairs Department, is committed to the exploration and celebration of traditions, philosophies, and arts of the various diverse communities in our city. We hope that a spirit of harmony and peace will enjoin people of diverse and similar backgrounds to come together to celebrate and promote cultural sharing and understanding.

Adolfo V. Nodal is the General Manager, City of Los Angeles Cultural Affairs Department. Although Mr. Nodal represents LA, there's no doubt that he includes all the Southland cities in his quest to encourage residents and visitors alike to sample the rich diversity offered by our varied communities.

AMERICAN INDIAN FESTIVAL AND MARKET

Natural History Museum of Los Angeles
900 Exposition Boulevard
Los Angeles, CA 90007
Info: (213) 744-3488   **Rsvn:** (213) 744-DINO
Fax: (213) 746-4803
Folk art and performing arts festival sponsored by the Natural History Museum.
    This March celebration is as much a Native American folk art event as a performing arts festival. American Indian dancers such as the Inter-Tribal Dancers of Los Angeles perform their traditional, intricate dances over the course of the three-day festival. Dressed in authentic garb, the artists display a variety of traditional and sacred pieces such as the Apache Mountain Spirit Dance, meant to cast off evil and invoke blessings on the world.
    In addition to the dance concerts, 40 American Indians from Canada and the U.S. meet up at the Natural History Museum to show, sell, and discuss their fine arts and folk crafts. This market, which has been thriving for over two decades, is the largest of its kind on the West Coast, nearly doubling its size in recent years.
    You might want to take advantage of one of the many educational programs offered, such as beadwork or North American Indian Music. Children love listening to stories in front of the three Cheyenne and Blackfoot tepees set up on the lawn.
    Food is served in the museum cafeteria. Festival tickets are free to museum members.

Performances
March
Tickets
$2-5; free to museum members
Discounts
Children/seniors/students/groups of 20+, call (213) 744-3426
BO
Tues-Sun 10 am-5 pm; check/reserve by mail, fax, TicketMaster; checks accepted for groups only
Location
Between Figueroa and Exposition; near the Harbor (110) Fwy, exit Exposition
Parking
On street

BLESSING OF THE CARS

Arroyo Seco Park
5568 Via Marisol
Los Angeles, CA 90042
Info: (213) 485-2437   **Fax:** (213) 485-6835
Homage to the automobile.
    More curses are hurled at the automobile in LA than any place else on earth. Perhaps its only appropriate then, that a day be put aside to put those curses in reverse. Three stages are set up in the Arroyo Seco Park each spring to provide a day of puppet shows, rap and salsa bands, children's activities and other performing arts that pay homage to "the Car as Art." Craft workshops include doll making and, of course, paper car cutouts. Food is for sale. Greatest blessing of all—parking is free and plentiful.

Performances
One day, spring
Tickets
FREE
Location
Pasadena (110) Fwy, exit Marisol
Parking
FREE lot; street

CALARTS SPRING MUSIC FESTIVAL

See press listings for performance locations.
Info: (805) 255-1050 ext. 2116   **Rsvn:** (805) 253-7800
Fax: (805) 254-8352
Performances at a variety of LA locations.
    This freewheeling two-week April orgy of concerts is really an amalgam of several once-separate events, encompassing world music, jazz, and contemporary music.
    The Contemporary Music Festival, for instance, once was the most stimulating and important showcase for new music on the West Coast. Launched in 1977 by the California Institute of the Arts in Valencia (back when it was an isolated island in the barren hills just off Int-5), the Contemporary Music Festival was little more than an in-house secret in the '70s. World premieres of important electronic music played to a total house of just six people!
    But starting in 1980, word began to spread about this wonderful, zany new music festival in which the public

Performances
Spring
Tickets
$3-20 depending on venue
Discounts
Seniors/students
BO
Hrs vary; MC/V/check
Location
Varies

could rub shoulders with some of the most famous composers of the day. The national press began to take notice. A new young audience was attracted to events like the pulsing, theatrical Harry Partch Ensemble, the boiling sound cauldrons of Iannis Xenakis, the dada pronouncements of John Cage, and the Dionysian minimalist mechanisms of Steve Reich and Terry Riley.

At its peak—1983 and 1984—the festival sprawled out to six days with a non-stop marathon of concerts. Even the Los Angeles Philharmonic got in on the act by linking their new music events with CalArts. There were masterpieces, duds, and outrages, but no one could ever accuse CalArts of being dull.

Alas, the Olympic Arts Festival later in 1984 and New Music America in fall 1985 (with heavy CalArts participation) knocked the festival off its annual March rhythm. Funding began to dry up, the schedule was cut back, famous composers stopped coming, and so did the audience.

Around 1984, CalArts began to develop a World Music Festival later in the spring, where music from all over the globe—fueled by CalArts excellent ethnomusicology department—along with food from the regions of origin—could be sampled. Intrepid music explorers heard Balinese gamelan music, Indian sounds, African ensembles, and other exotic forms without leaving the county.

In 1991, the shrunken Contemporary Music Festival and World Music Festival were absorbed into a new umbrella event, the CalArts' Spring Music Festival. By 1992, they would no longer be separate entities; rather, they would be components of a new concept for the CalArts Spring Festival. Now, instead of being confined to weekends, the Spring Music Festival runs consecutively for two weeks, with a few days off. No longer are there segregated blocks of time for each idiom; an exploration of the classical avant-garde on a Monday might be followed by a jazz gig on Tuesday or a gamelan ensemble on Wednesday.

Audience response to the unified Spring Music concept was immediate; they sold out the Mod Theatre every night for the first time in many years. Noted visiting composers returned (Frederic Rzewski, Robert Ashley, Lou Harrison). And the popular ethnic food feature of the World Music Festival has been continued.

Thankfully, the marvelous sense of informality at the early new music festivals and the peak years still prevails today. Whenever they feel like it, CalArts may just hold a concert out in the hallway (officially known as the Main Gallery). Otherwise they repair to the starkly modern Modular Theatre, a studio-like black box space where the stage and the seating can be rearranged in any number of ways.

But now the festival is expanding off the campus in a more ambitious way than ever before. The New Century Players' (formerly the Twentieth Century Players) Green Umbrella dates at the Japan America Theatre are deemed part of the festival, reigniting a practice from the mid-'80s. There are also concerts in Barnsdall Park in Hollywood, jazz events in the Watts Towers Art Center, and an alliance with the LA Cultural Affairs Department.

CHAMBER MUSIC/LA FESTIVAL

Japan America Theatre
244 South San Pedro Street
Los Angeles, CA 90012
Info: (213) 850-8064 **Rsvn:** (213) 680-3700
Fax: (213) 882-6814
Artistic Director: Yukiko Kamei
Performances are co-produced with and held at the Japan America Theatre.

In May, when most concert series are winding down for the summer siesta, Chamber Music/LA is just coming to life.

Yukiko Kamei, the Festival's founder, artistic director and participating violinist, credits the Sitka Summer Music Festival in Alaska—which was populated by musicians who had studied with the late Gregor Piatigorsky and Jascha Heifetz at USC—for the inspiration. Using the Sitka musicians as a core, Kamei has evolved a five-concert mid-May festival at the acoustically satisfying Japan America Theatre.

Though the repertoire is not likely to stretch your ears, the individual programs are often quite inventive. The festival is commonly centered around a single theme, with intriguing subsets within the concerts made possible by the festival format.

The instrumental and sometimes vocal forces may vary within each concert since there are no featured stars or star groups who dominate a whole evening. Nevertheless, in a given year, you can sample such standout regulars as cellists Nathaniel Rosen and Jeffrey Solow, pianist Jerome Lowenthal, French hornist Richard Todd, and flutist James Walker. As such, the festival is remarkably faithful to the original spirit of chamber music— friends getting together in ad hoc groups to explore the literature.

Three rehearsals are open to high school students. KUSC-FM broadcasts the concerts through American Public Radio, reaching an impressive five million pairs of ears nationwide. What a way to push aside the May doldrums!

Performances
May, Wed 8 pm and
Sun 3 pm
Tickets
$18-20
Discounts
Seniors/students
BO
Mon-Sun 1 pm-5 pm;
check/AE/V/reserve by
mail
Location
Japan America Theatre;
downtown LA, near the
Hollywood (101) Fwy
and Harbor (110) Fwy
Parking
On premises, $3; on
street
Special Features
Open rehearsals for
high school students.

CHILDREN'S DAY CELEBRATION See **CHILDREN**

DEAFESTIVAL

See press listings for performance locations.
Info: (213) 485-2437 **Fax:** (213) 485-6835
Sponsored by the Los Angeles Cultural Affairs Department.

This annual event highlights works of deaf artists, including storytelling, mime, theater, dance, and fine arts. Everyone is welcome at the series, which is produced in segments throughout the year, each program taking place in a different location. Activities are presented in American Sign Language, with hearing members of the audience accommodated by sign-to-voice interpreters. The free celebration is sponsored by The City of LA Cultural Affairs Department in cooperation with the Deaf Studies Program of Cal State Northridge and the Deaf Communications Foundation.

Poetry, storytelling, and comedy constituted the last festival with guest performers Mary Beth Miller and Evon Black.

Performances
Spring and fall
Tickets
FREE

FESTIVAL OF PHILIPPINE ARTS & CULTURE

See press listings for festival location.
Info: (213) 485-2437   **Fax:** (213) 485-6835

This lively all-day event takes place in LA during May's Asian Pacific Heritage Month. More than 60 arts organizations and individual artists from LA's vital Filipino community, representing the diverse regions of the Philippines, present folk, traditional, and contemporary arts. The free cultural fair celebrates Filipino dance, music, poetry, storytelling, martial arts, and a crafts exhibits. Renowned Filipino performers such as World Kulintang Institute's gong and drum music and the Bibak Dance ensemble also drop by. Children are invited to special workshops and events like fan-making and face-painting.

The festival is sponsored by the City of LA Cultural Affairs Department and the Festival of Philippine Arts and Culture Advisory Committee. Last year's event took place at LA City College, but the location changes.

Performances
May
Tickets
FREE

HANS CHRISTIAN ANDERSON FAIRY TALE FESTIVAL See CHILDREN

LONG BEACH CARNAVAL

Downtown Long Beach
Long Beach, CA 90802
Info: (310) 436-7794   **Rsvn:** (310) 436-7794
Fax: (310) 495-8398
Annual celebration from Pine to Long Beach Boulevard, and from Third to First Streets.

It may not be Rio, but this annual street fair is still pretty hot. Third to First Streets, and Pine to Long Beach Boulevard are gated off to make way for this Memorial Day rite. A colorful parade opens the two-day event, while an electric light parade closes it the next night. Five stages handling up to 50 bands a day blare out Afro-Cuban, reggae, steel drum, folk, calypso, jazz, salsa, R&B, country, oldies, and you name it. Carnaval has drawn performers as diverse as Poncho Sanchez, Tiny Tim, and Jose Feliciano.

One stage devoted to kids is a kaleidoscope of hip hop dancers and rap artists; puppet and magic shows; fire-eaters and folk dancers.

The parade kicks off 10 am Saturday; the festival then runs till 10 pm; Sunday hours are 11:30 am to 10.

Area restaurants often cater their menus to the event and offer exotic and ethnic foods. On Saturday morning, there's usually a celebrity breakfast at nearby Birdland West from 7 am to 9. Event tickets are priced reasonably, while kids under 12 get in gratis. You'll have to valet park or search the side streets. Don't forget that sunscreen.

Performances
Spring
Tickets
$5
Discounts
Children
BO
Mon-Sat 10 am-6 pm, (310) 436-7794; AE/MC/V; TicketMaster; no refunds
Location
Streets of downtown Long Beach are sectioned off into a contained area
Parking
Valet, $1.50; on street

LOS ANGELES ASIAN PACIFIC FILM & VIDEO FESTIVAL

See press listings for performance locations.
Info: (310) 206-8013   **Rsvn:** (310) 206-FILM
Fax: (310) 206-3129
Annual spring film festival presented in a variety of local venues.

In a grand celebration of Asian and Asian Pacific American filmmaking, this comprehensive series includes the works of some of the finest Canadian and U.S. filmmakers, and South Asian, Pacific Island, and Southeast Asian media artists.

Festival-goers are presented with a unique opportunity to learn about and live the Asian experience

Performances
May
Tickets
$5-10
Discounts
Children/seniors/students/groups

thanks to this annual ten-day long jubilee of dramas and documentaries. The most recent festival showcased more than 100 movies. Screenings are held at different venues such as the Japan America Theater, UCLA's Melnitz Theater, and the Laemmle's Sunset 5. There's usually a festival symposium worth sitting in on, and, recently, performance art paralleled some of the presentations.

BO
  Festival passes/reserve by mail; call festival office for individual box offices

LA FIESTA BROADWAY

See press listings for performance location.
Info: (818) 793-9335
Downtown festival.
  Arrrriba! Come join the fiesta at this Cinco de Mayo party ("5th of May" to all you gringos)—which, by the way, doesn't always take place on May 5th! The block party lines 36 city streets on downtown's Broadway corridor. Last year a quarter of a million revelers converged on this predominantly Latino neighborhood in the country's largest outdoor Cinco de Mayo festival.

  The free, family-oriented event features top Latino entertainers occupying more than a dozen stages. The lineup of big stars shadows the smaller names, but all the bands are worth an audience. More than 100 music acts perform on the two main stages. It can get so packed that a band only has time to play one song. As a result, there's lots of intermission time between sets. Audiences complain that their favorite groups may only sing to tapes rather than live back-up bands. But the smaller stages scattered around the area play longer sets. The whole gamut of Latin music gets air time here.

  The festival site encompasses Hill, Spring, and Broadway from Temple to Olympic.

Performances
  Last Sun in April, prior to Cinco de Mayo Sun
Tickets
  FREE
Location
  From Temple to Olympic, including Broadway, Spring and Hill streets
Parking
  On streets outside of festival area

LOS ANGELES JEWISH FESTIVAL

See press listings for festival location.
Info: (213) 857-0036 ext.2221   **Fax:** (213) 937-9426
Outdoor festival of entertainment, Arts, Crafts, information booths, special exhibits, cultural and varied.
  Los Angeles is home to the third largest Jewish community in the world after Israel and New York, so it's only appropriate that the city hold one of the largest annual celebrations of Jewish culture anywhere. This spring exhibition is free of charge, and attracts about 40,000 people of all ages and backgrounds.

  In addition to strolling musicians and continuous folk dancing and lessons, international and local Jewish and multiethnic entertainers perform on three stages. This is truly a family day, with special entertainment and rides for kids. For the "Gimmee a break, mom, I'm too old for carnivals" youth, there are organized activities and information booths about trips to Israel specially catered to teenagers and young adults.

  Depending on where the festival is held, parking can be a real problem. The staff usually sets up free continuously-running shuttle buses from major parking lots. The festival is co-sponsored by the office of the Consulate General of Israel, the Jewish Community Centers Association, and more than 500 schools, synagogues and centers.

Performances
  Late spring
Tickets
  FREE
Location
  Varies

MUSEUM OF TELEVISION & RADIO LOS ANGELES FESTIVAL

Los Angeles County Museum of Art
5905 Wilshire Boulevard
Los Angeles, CA 90036
Info: (212) 621-6600   **Rsvn:** (213) 857-6110
The festival salutes television's diversity and rich heritage. Each evening during the 18-day festival a different program or individual is saluted with a screening and discussion.

New York City's Museum of Television & Radio has held this festival in LA for a decade. For about three weeks in March, the Bing Theater at the Los Angeles County Museum of Art screens and stages TV retrospectives and tributes. Often, the creators of the shows and original cast members lead discussions after the airings.

Tickets come two ways: screenings with celebrity attendants and screenings only. Seating is not reserved.

Performances
  March
Tickets
  $15 per event
BO
  Call Museum BO;
  TicketMaster
Discounts
  Members of Museum of
  TV & Radio, LACMA;
  students/seniors
Location
  At LACMA; near the
  Santa Monica (10) Fwy,
  Fairfax exit; between
  Fairfax and La Brea on
  Wilshire Blvd
Parking
  Metered parking on
  premises; metered
  parking on street;
  parking lot

THE OJAI FESTIVAL

Libbey Bowl, Libbey Park, Ojai Avenue
Ojai , CA 93023
Info: (805) 646-2094   **Fax:** (805) 646-6037
Spring fest of classical music held at Libbey Bowl in Ojai.

Once a year, like Brigadoon, sleepy Ojai comes to cultural life, playing host to one of the most musically sophisticated yet wonderfully informal festivals on the globe.

On a long weekend in late May or early June, the music Establishment and music lovers from Southern California (and often elsewhere) drive about 80 miles from the smog and congestion of Los Angeles to this little town, pop. 7,613. The annual pilgrimage has been going on since the Ojai Festival premiered in 1947 under music director Thor Johnson.

In those early days, the concerts took place in a local school building, Nordhoff Auditorium. But 1954 saw the opening of the Libbey Bowl, a lovely rustic amphitheater shaded by the twisting sycamores and peaceful oaks of Libbey Park, where birds frequently trill along with the music.

The 1950s also saw the coming of Lawrence Morton as artistic director. Morton promptly used his connections to bring in 20th-century giants like Igor Stravinsky and Aaron Copland, along with major figures like Pierre Boulez, Lukas Foss, Robert Craft, and Ingolf Dahl—even young upstarts like Michael Tilson Thomas, Andre Previn, and James Levine. Morton's bold example has been generally followed by his successors, who have brought in major composers like Elliott Carter, Olivier Messiaen, and Peter Maxwell Davies to supervise performances of their own music.

As a result, Ojai became a testing ground for daring, imaginative programming quite unlike anything one would expect in a small isolated town. One fondly remembers a 1979 film night in which Foss led music from the 1920s as accompaniment to silent films, or the wide-ranging 1982 Stravinsky Centennial programs led by Craft, the composer's associate. Nor is Ojai afraid of controversy;

Performances
  The weekend after
  Memorial Day
Tickets
  $12 lowest single ticket,
  $125 for a full "A
  category" series
Discounts
  Groups of 15+, call
BO
  Mon-Fri 9 am-5 pm;
  check/MC/V/reserve by
  mail, TicketMaster; no
  exchanges
Location
  At Libbey Bowl in Libbey
  Park on Ojai Ave
Parking
  On street

as recently as 1992, professional provocateur Peter Sellars unveiled his own version of Stravinsky's *L'Histoire du Soldat,* set in riot-torn South-Central LA.

The "premium" seats in the Bowl are little more than wooden park benches, while to the rear stretches a lawn often packed with picnicking young couples and families. The amplified sound is shockingly good for a quirky outdoor amphitheater. Other concerts are sometimes held in smaller nearby (and indoor) facilities such as the tiny yet acoustically splendid Ojai Presbyterian Church.

But even Shangri-la changes. In place of the endearing thrown-together booths and card tables now stands a permanent wooden structure where tickets, T-shirts, seat cushions, drinks, Ojai's famous lentil soup, and homemade cookies and "killer brownies" are sold. Gridlocked traffic has become more of a problem on Ojai's main drag, so be prepared to walk a little further from your parking spot. (Here's an idea: splurge if you can on a room for the weekend at the Ojai Valley Inn and Country Club within bicycling distance of the Libbey Bowl.)

To the delight of everyone who loves the interludes at Ojai, musical standards remain sky-high, and the festival organizers are still able to present world-class musicians on a regular basis. Indeed, Boulez returned in 1992 to preside over a mostly triumphant Festival, while composer/conductor John Adams, the Los Angeles Chamber Orchestra, and the New Music Group of the Los Angeles Philharmonic were on tap in 1993, and Michael Tilson Thomas is penciled in for 1994. Don't miss 'em.

PACIFIC ISLANDER FESTIVAL

Harbor City Regional Park
25820 Vermont Avenue
Harbor City, CA 90710
Info: (310) 926-6707

Performances
May
Tickets
FREE
Location
Off the Harbor (110)
Fwy on Pacific Coast
Hwy
Parking
On street

The melting pot of Los Angeles celebrates the heritages of our transplanted Pacific Islanders in this two-day festival.

Bring your own mats or blankets and spend the day—or both days—enjoying the continuous lineup of drama, dance, and music representing the Samoan, Hawaiian, Tongan, Maori, Chamorro/Guamanian, Marshallese, Belau, Tahitian, and Cook Islands cultures. Dancing from each Island group goes on all day. (P.S.: this is a wonderful way to introduce children to an unfamiliar culture.)

Around the lake at Harbor City Regional Park, little island villages offer demonstrations of the rich customs and ceremonies of the groups. Naturally, there are crafts for sale, as are food specialties from each island group.

The free festival is usually held in May, but that can change. Call for this year's dates.

SAN DIEGO INTERNATIONAL CHILDREN'S FESTIVAL See CHILDREN

SAN DIEGO MAINLY MOZART FESTIVAL

Spreckels Theatre, 121 Broadway
San Diego, CA 92101
Info: (619) 233-4281   **Rsvn:** (619) 235-9500
Fax: (619) 233-4524
Two-week spring festival held at Spreckels Theatre.

Performances
Late spring, early
summer
Tickets
$15-32

The festival's repertoire generally includes 18th-century gems by Mozart and his contemporaries and early 19th-century Romantic works. Mozart, mainly. But Bach,

Beethoven, Brahms, Telemann, Tchaikovsky and many others are celebrated at this spring concert. Classical music favorites and music rarely performed are the norm.

Respected musicians from orchestras and ensembles around the country gather in San Diego in late spring to form an expert chamber orchestra and perform under the baton of maestro David Atherton.

Atherton, former music director of the Hong Kong Philharmonic and San Diego Symphony, has also conducted extensively in Great Britain and has won numerous awards for recordings. His Mainly Mozart programs have gained critical acclaim over the festival's four years.

Performances are held in the Spreckels Theatre, notable for its Baroque decor and for being the oldest theater in San Diego, dating back to 1912. Each evening there's a pre-concert lecture at 7 pm. Subscription tickets can be purchased for as few as two concerts or for all performances. Single tickets are also available.

Discounts
Seniors/students/groups of 15+, call Group Sales Coordinator, (619) 487-7968
BO
Call for current hours; check/AE/MC/V/reserve by mail, fax, TicketMaster
Location
Spreckels Theatre; downtown San Diego, on Broadway between 1st and 2nd Sts; near Int-5, 8 and 163
Parking
On premises, $5; valet, $5; street parking also available
Special Features
Pre-concert lectures at 7 pm performance days

SANTA BARBARA INTERNATIONAL FILM FESTIVAL

1216 State Street
Santa Barbara, CA 93101
Info: (805) 963-0023   **Fax:** (805) 965-0557
Santa Barbara's annual film fair injects a revitalizing shot of adrenaline in the cultural and recreational life of the town. Every spring for the past eight years, the charming beach city has screened dozens of internationally culled films in a 10-day jubilee.

The festival features various premieres, American independent features, foreign shorts, and Oscar-nominated documentaries, as well as special panel discussions with industry insiders and filmmakers, actors from some of the films, and celebrity guest speakers. The festival's "Evenings With" series has spotlighted stars such as Louis Gossett, Jr., Charlton Heston, Dean Stockwell, Rod Steiger and Kim Novak in discussions and audience-participation question-and-answer formats. All special events at the festival are interpreted for the hearing impaired.

Recent festivals have culminated in world and U.S. premieres of featured films, and eventual Oscars for Best Foreign Film and best Documentary Short.

If you've never been, Santa Barbara is a lovely beachside getaway. Consider spending the weekend. The Four Seasons Biltmore offers a tempting hotel and entertainment package. One price gets you a ready-made combo of passes to screenings, dinner, and overnight accommodations (call the Biltmore at (805) 969-2261 for details). A variety of other special festival passes are available through the SBIFF office. Advance tickets can be ordered by mail or by phoning one of the ticket agencies. A limited number of single tickets for screenings are sold at the box office 15 minutes before show time, space permitting. Take heed: many events get sold out; advance ticket purchases are the way to go.

Performances
Spring
Tickets
$7-250
Discounts
Previews/children/groups of 20+, call
BO
Arlington Ticket Agency Mon-Sat 9 am-5:30 pm; Sun noon-5 pm; check/MC/V/reserve by mail, TicketMaster; no refunds or exchanges
Location
Downtown Santa Barbara, between Sola and Cota Sts
Parking
On street
Special Features
Workshops, "Evening With" film luminaries, youth program, signed for the hearing impaired, parties, receptions

SPRING MUSIC FESTIVAL See **CalArts Spring Music Festival**

TOPANGA BANJO/FIDDLE CONTEST, DANCE & FOLK ARTS FESTIVAL

Paramount Ranch
3230 Cornell Road
Agoura Hills, CA 91301
Info: (818) 594-1742
Usually held spring or summer at Paramount Ranch in Agoura.

Fearless and fierce fiddle, banjo, guitar, and mandolin players, plus singers from all over the state have been competing at this annual festival for over 32 years. Families come from all around to spend the day listening to the tunes of the fiddles, square dancing to the instructions of a professional call leader, listening to cowboy storytelling, or just chowing down on barbecue beef.

Amateurs and professionals play one after the other at one of the three music stages. But anyone is welcome to bring his or her musical instrument and just start jamming. A replicated Old Western town is filled with wagonloads of arts and crafts for sale. There's lots of shade and plenty of places to sit around the storytelling and songwriting stage near the back of the "town." And when folks get tired of the crowds, they head out for the nearby hiking trails meandering throughout the ranch.

It can be pretty hot out at Paramount Ranch, even when the festival is held in April or May. I suggest you bring your own water and even a cooler with drinks. Picnic paraphernalia would be useful; definitely bring along sunscreen and hats (ten-gallons preferably), especially for the kids.

There's a big dirt parking lot not far from the festival grounds—bring that four-wheel if you have one.

Performances
First Sun of May
Tickets
$6
Discounts
Children/seniors
Tickets
Sold at the event only; 9 am-3:30 pm; check
Location
Off Ventura (101) Fwy, Kanan Rd exit, S to Cornell Rd, turn left
Parking
On premises, free; street parking is sometimes not allowed

UCLA SCHOOL OF THE ARTS SPRING WORLD MUSIC FESTIVAL

Schoenberg Hall
405 Hilgard, UCLA
Info: (310) 825-4761   **Rsvn:** (310) 825-2101

Each spring at the end of May, the departments of ethnomusicology (world music) and dance fall in step to put on the ethnically diverse five-day Spring World Music Festival. Most of the musicians are students who've been studying the music of different countries and learning to play the national instruments. Student dancers accompany the music with ethnic footwork. One festival feature is a free outdoor concert, usually in the afternoon on the patio at Schoenberg Hall. Families bring food and pillows and enjoy a festive afternoon.

For other department events throughout the year and a quarterly pocket calendar, "The Arts at UCLA," call the Department of Dance Information (310) 825-3951 or the Department of Music Information (310) 825-4761.

Performances
Spring
Tickets
FREE-$5
Discounts
Seniors/students
BO
Mon-Fri 9 am-6 pm; Sat 9 am-1 pm; Sun 10 am-3 pm; reserve by mail, phone
Location
Hilgard and Westholme entrance
Parking
On premises, $5

UCSB NEW MUSIC FESTIVAL

University of California, Santa Barbara
Santa Barbara, CA 93106
Info: (805) 893-3261
Fax: (805) 893-7194
Held on the UCSB campus.

William Kraft, Corwin Professor of Composition at UCSB and the original spark behind the Los Angeles Philharmonic New Music Group, had plugged the idea of an annual spring new music festival here for some time. So when composer Milton Babbitt trekked out to UCSB in May 1992 for a residency, Kraft built a three-day festival around him, incorporating three concerts, a composers panel and

Performances
Spring
Tickets
$7-10
BO
At the door; check
Location
At UCSB; off of Ventura (110) Fwy or 217 Fwy; UCSB exit

lectures by Babbitt, composer Robert Morris, pianist Robert Taub, and Kraft himself. The festival was already in high gear.

The 1993 festival was similarly structured around a mini-residency by composer Charles Wuorinen, with supplemental appearances by fellow composers Mel Powell and Henry Brant. Among the scheduled performers were the Southwest Chamber Music Society, New Music diva Phyllis Bryn-Julson, and UCSB's Ensemble for Contemporary Music. The festival also squeezed in compositional tutorials by Powell and Wuorinen, a lecture by Brant, master classes by the performers, and a composers' panel with Powell and Kraft. UCSB Festivals take place in April so as not to compete with the Ojai Festival (at the beginning of June).

Kraft says that the 1994 edition will forego the residency feature and sport a Pacific Rim theme, "Dialogues in National Styles," with composer Chou-Wen Chung as co-artistic director. The festival will spotlight Asian composers who integrate Western techniques with their native roots.

Most of the concerts take place in the campus' 468-seat Lotte Lehmann Concert Hall, while others can be heard in smaller campus spaces and occasional off-campus locales. Coffee and modest refreshments are available.

Parking
On premises, FREE

AMERICAN FILM INSTITUTE LOS ANGELES INTERNATIONAL FILM FESTIVAL

See press listings for screening locations.
2021 North Western Avenue
Los Angeles, CA 90027
Info: (213) 856-7707 **Fax:** (213) 462-4049
Exhibition of International and U.S. Independent Film.

This is the mother, or at least aunt, of foreign and independent film expos in the city. It is a "don't miss" if you're a die-hard movie fan. But don't feel you have to be able to drop names like Wajda or Makavejev to attend. This fest gives everyone something to see. Either come for the more familiar, or expand your cinematic experience.

The most recent annual festival, which featured more than 100 films from 40 countries, was a feast of full-length flicks (the Hollywood biggies as well as those from foreign filmmakers), shorts, documentaries, special tributes, and seminars. Screenings have included Bergman, Chaplin, Fellini, and Truffaut classics, alongside a dizzying number of new works by known and unknown American and international directors. Many of America's independent films get noticed here first and go on to broad distribution. Filmmakers sometimes visit to discuss their work.

Over the past seven years, the festival has presented nearly a thousand films from 60 countries. That's a lot of subtitles to read, but it's worth the eye strain to catch as many of these offerings as possible.

Some of the films will sell out; it's a good idea to purchase seats ahead of time through Theatix. The last festival was arranged so that filmgoers could see just about every flick. Call for this year's dates and locations. Information becomes available in May.

Performances
June
Tickets
$7
BO
MC/V/check/Theatix; exchanges only if a show is cancelled
Location
Changes annually
Special Features
Seminars, panels, tributes

ANNUAL SUMMER SOLSTICE FOLK MUSIC AND DANCE FESTIVAL

See press listings for festival locations.
Info: (818) 342-7664 **Fax:** (818) 609-0106

Folk music fans, this is the weekend you've been waiting for. On the weekend following Father's Day each June, the California Traditional Music Society presents this outdoor festival (held at Soka University in Calabasas in 1993) of Irish and Scottish music. The event has also included a storytelling concert, the folk dancing of Bulgaria, Greece, and France, traditional Contra dancing, folklore workshops, and children's events. There's plenty of folksy food, too. Back-to-nature folks should inquire about the camping facilities.

For complete festival details and other music events the society presents throughout the year, call for a free catalogue.

Performances
June
Tickets
$4-20
BO
Check/reserve by mail
Location
Varies

BEVERLY HILLS LIVE!

Courtyard Greystone Mansion
905 Loma Vista
Beverly Hills, CA 90210
Info: (310) 550-4654

Tucked away in Greystone Park's inner courtyard is a summer classical music concert now in its third decade. The Beverly Hills Symphony, under the musical direction of Bogidar Avramov, has the permanent parking spot here. A recent season offered an evening of Vivaldi, serenades of Mozart, Elgar, and Tchaikovsky, and the Santa Cecilia Opera performing excerpts from *The Marriage of Figaro* and *La Traviata*.

There's open seating for about 300 people; snacks and refreshments are for sale. Early ticket buyers

Performances
June-Sept
Tickets
$15-20
BO
Open day of performance only; check/reserve by mail (Recreation and Parks Dept., 9268 W Third St, Beverly Hills, CA 90210); exchanges made only if concert is cancelled

can join the tour of the park grounds. But come prepared: you'll need comfortable, low-heeled shoes for the hills and stairways. The concert seating, however, is accessible to people in wheelchairs.

Location
Sunset Blvd to Foothill Rd, N to Doheny Rd, E to Loma Vista, left into driveway
Parking
On premises, FREE
Special Features
Free tours of park grounds for advance ticket purchases only

CALIFORNIA PLAZA

300 South Grand Avenue
Los Angeles, CA 90071
Info: (213) 687-2190   **Rsvn:** (213) 687-2159
Fax: (213) 687-2191
Eclectic arts on the stages of downtown LA's California Plaza.

This is one of LA's secret entertainment bargains—until now, of course. During summer months, this spot is an enjoyable—and economical—daytime escape from the office if you work downtown. Unfortunately, budget cuts have forced the cancellation of a regular evening schedule, although occasional nighttime performances are scheduled.

The Spiral Court, Marina Pavilion and the brand-new Waterstage collectively make up the three outdoor stages of the Plaza located on Bunker Hill. Each amphitheater features a rich agenda of dance and music concerts as well as an array of hard-to-classify "other" arts. And every concert is free! (Bargains don't get any better than that!)

Examples of recent performances here include LA's *Phantom of the Opera* cast singing Rodgers and Hammerstein; Huayucaltia, a group of South American musicians; Amy Hill, LA's well-known Asian-American comedian; and Mzwakhe Mbuli, South African musician and poet.

Most daytime concerts start at noon on Wednesday and Friday. The performing season generally stretches from May to September. Just show up and take a seat. If you want to grab a quick meal before or after the show, there are several Plaza restaurants dispensing gourmet coffees and fast food.

Downtown visitors: note that California Plaza is on DASH Route B.

Performances
May-Sept; Wed, Fri noon
Tickets
FREE
Location
On Grand Ave at Third St, on Bunker Hill
Parking
On premises; street parking

CHILDREN'S DAY CELEBRATION See CHILDREN

CONCERTS IN THE PARK

Warner Park
5800 Topanga Canyon Boulevard
Woodland Hills, CA 91367
Info: (818) 704-1358   **Fax:** (818) 704-1604
Outdoor concerts in Woodland Hills, at Warner Park.

The Lettermen, Fabian, The Kingston Trio—who could ask for anything more? Well they were just three oldies-but-goodies at one season's Concerts in the Park at Warner Park in Woodland Hills.

Nowadays several thousand people attend this annual series of free concerts on Sundays at 5:30 from June

Performances
Every Sun from 5:30-7:30, June through mid-Sept; announced in March
Tickets
FREE
Location
Take Ventura Fwy to Topanga Canyon off ramp

through September. The festival lineups have also included reggae, samba, Scottish and Spanish folk, jazz and classical, folk-pop and country-western, and children's rhymes and fairy tales. (See the chapter on **CHILDREN** for further information.) Have we left anyone out? A brand new, $1 million outdoor concert facility has been built, but it hasn't taken away the sense of casual, summertime fun. Bring a folding chair or a blanket. Pre-concert picnics are popular, but concession stand standards are available at a Rotary Club stand.

Parking
Parking in a structure available with $1 donation; street parking available; also handicap drop off area

Special Features
Seating area for members/sponsors in front of stage, all concerts; rehearsals usually just before concert begins

CONCERTS IN THE PARK

Info: (619) 437-8788
Sunday evening band concerts at Spreckels Park in Coronado.
These one-hour family-friendly concerts, also known as Coronado Promenade Concerts, are held Sunday evenings in summer. The free performances usually recruit military bands, although sometimes there's a jazz concert. Bring a picnic dinner. Don't confuse this with the Spreckels Organ Pavilion or Spreckels Theatre; this is in Coronado.

Performances
During summer; Sun 6 pm-7 pm
Tickets
FREE
Location
On Orange Ave, between 6th and 7th Sts
Parking
Street parking

DANCE KALEIDOSCOPE

California State University, Cal State Playhouse
5151 University Drive
Los Angeles, CA 90035
Info: (213) 343-5124 **Rsvn:** (213) 343-4118
Fax: (213) 343-2670
Annual festival of dance held for one week in July at the Cal State LA Playhouse.
This summertime festival stands nearly alone in its commitment to Southern California's smaller professional companies and individual dancers. You're guaranteed a valuable introduction to an impressive array of artists if you catch even one or two offerings. All areas of the discipline—from jazz to ballet, modern to folk, traditional ethnic to performance art—are represented over the six-day period.
Under the dedicated leadership of artistic director Donald Hewitt, who roused this event in 1988 from a three-year hibernation, the festival usually schedules a healthy dose of premieres from familiar groups. You'll also get the chance to see performers who seldom dance for so-called general audiences.
Many folks bring dinner and picnic on the campus grounds before performances. Some matinees are perfect for the whole family. Seating is not reserved and the space often fills to capacity, so arrive early. Some performances are offered at the John Anson Ford Theatre.

Performances
July, Fri-Sat 8 pm, Sun 2:30 pm
Tickets
$15
Discounts
Previews/seniors/ students/groups of 50+, call
BO
Daily 10 am-5 pm check/reserve by mail, Theatix; exchanges with 24 hrs notice
Location
San Bernardino (10) Fwy E, Eastern exit, follow signs to Cal State
Special Features
Picnic areas

DANCE ROOTS: ETHNIC DANCE FESTIVAL

See press listings for performance locations.
Info: (213) 485-2437 **Rsvn:** (213) 485-2437
Sponsored by the City of LA Cultural Affairs Department.
This free summer event celebrates dance from many countries, many styles. One year offered an introduction to African, Eastern, Middle Eastern, Eastern

Performances
Summer
Tickets
FREE, first come first serve

European, and Caribbean dance with well-respected dance companies such as AVAZ and Aisha Ali Dance Company on stage. The third, and most recent festival focused on traditional and contemporary dance. For two days the Los Angeles Theatre Center was filled with flamenco, jazz, modern, tap, classical, and even drum dance. The celebration of movement from ethnic communities around the world is presented by the City of LA Cultural Affairs Department in association with Collaborative Arts.

The fest was expanded last year to include two full days of engrossing performances; the seats were filled and the audiences fulfilled. The venue and month change each year.

FESTIVAL OF ARTS AND PAGEANT OF THE MASTERS

650 Laguna Canyon Road
Laguna Beach, CA 92651
Info: (714) 494-1145   **Rsvn:** (800) 487-3378
Fax: (714) 494-9387
Exhibit of artwork by artists and craftsmen of the area in a six acre park in Laguna Beach.

The Pageant of the Masters defies a standard "performing art" description. Trust me, there isn't anything like it anywhere. The pageants, which have been presented annually since 1933 (except during World War II), are recreations of well-known artworks using live models in a form known as *tableaux vivante*. Following me so far?

Hundreds of local volunteers help recreate paintings, sculptures, photographs, and—yes—ceramic artwork. Great care goes into the costumes and backgrounds. The volunteers—adults, children, seniors—pose in the dark "in" the famous artworks on the amphitheater stage. Once the lights go on, the cast members freeze into position like some giant human jigsaw puzzle. It is a remarkable spectacle. Everything on stage is meticulously set to scale, and the illusion of brush strokes and innate figures on canvas boggles the mind. The entire pageant lasts two hours.

A Laguna Beach tradition, the human gallery boasts sell-outs, especially the better seats in the loges and first two terrace areas. If you sit too far back or on the side, you may be left out of the full picture.

The Festival grounds are open daily with the Pageant proper taking place after nightfall in the Irvine Bowl. Don't bring alcohol, cameras, sound recording equipment, cigarettes—or easels. Convenient parking information is available by phone.

By the way, the daytime portion of this annual Laguna Beach attraction is a visual art exhibition and sale of sculpture, ceramics, jewelry and drawings.

Food is available on site with concession stands scattered throughout the area.

Performances
   July through August
Tickets
   $9-38
BO
   Check/MC/V/reserve by phone, mail; no exchanges or refunds
Location
   Irvine Bowl Park; near downtown Laguna Beach
Parking
   Street parking available nearby
Special Features
   A variety of special entertainment held on the Festival grounds

FESTIVAL OF N.O.T.E.

Info: (213) 666-5550
Anthology of original short works.

Take note. The New One-Act Theatre Ensemble was founded in 1981 as a forum for original one-act plays and other short-form theater. The annual festival presents its Anthology of Short Works—ten-minute plays selected from N.O.T.E.'s Playwriting Workshops and commissioned from affiliated playwrights. In the past, the short pieces hit the small stage usually late summer through early fall. Because of the quake damage, the theater is closed. Call for an update on this year's location.

Performances
   Thurs-Sat, summer
Tickets
   $5-10
BO
   Call BO for reservations
Location
   To be determined

FOLLOWS CAMP FAMILY BLUEGRASS FESTIVAL

Follows Camp
23400 East Fork Road
Azusa, CA 91702
Info: (818) 700-8288   **Rsvn:** (818) 910-1100
  If you like bluegrass, you'll love this biannual weekend festival at the Follows Camp in Azusa. The nonstop music and entertainment blowout jumps from Friday through Sunday with top artists and guest bands, banjo, fiddle, mandolin and guitar contests, gospel and special children's events.

  Located on grounds that hark back to the great California Gold Rush, the Follows Camp is an original gold mining expanse with modern facilities for overnight camping. People from all walks of life come here, many with tents and sleeping bags, to enjoy a full weekend of outdoor activities like fishing and panning for gold, as well as the nonstop jam sessions. Supervised children's activities continue throughout the festival and include a fishing derby, clown shows, and music workshops. Bring your own folding chairs if you plan to sit during the concerts.

  Breakfast, lunch, and dinner are served at an outdoor BBQ and grill and at the Fort Restaurant. Or you can buy groceries at the General Store. Prices vary according to the number of days you plan to stay and whether you plan to camp overnight. Overall, it's a hoot for the whole family.

Performances
 1st weekend in June
 and Oct
Tickets
 $11-14 per day/$40-48
 for 3 days
Discounts
 Children
BO
 Check/MC/V/
 reserve by mail
Location
 Off 210 Fwy, to 39 Hwy
Parking
 On premises, $3
Special Features
 Special child area

GRAND SUMMER NIGHTS AT SANTA MONICA COLLEGE

1900 Pico Boulevard
Santa Monica, CA 90405
Info: (310) 452-9350   **Rsvn:** (310) 452-9396
Fax: (310) 452-9385
  This eclectic performing arts series of music, dance, and opera draws hundreds of entertainment seekers to the amphitheater each summer. A special Independence Day celebration with fireworks takes place the weekend before the 4th.

  A troupe from Tibet touted colorful costumes and dances on stage one past season, and a symphony-accompanied performance of *Faust* was staged by SMC's Opera Theatre. The series provided a great way to see Opera A La Carte's *The Magic of Gilbert & Sullivan*.

  Coffee, popcorn, and candy are available, though a better choice might be your own picnic basket, Hollywood Bowl-style, minus the wine (no alcohol on campus).

  Series passes offer a serious discount but must be purchased early. Seating for amphitheater events is unreserved. "Celebrate America," the Independence Day program, which has featured celebrity performers like Glenn Campbell and Maynard Ferguson, is held on the University's Corsair Field. Bring blankets and sand chairs (low beach chairs) for this free event.

Performances
 Summer
Tickets
 $10-16
Discounts
 Groups of 20, call BO
BO
 Mon-Fri 9 am-5 pm;
 event days 6 pm-8:30
 pm MC/V/check/reserve
 by mail
Location
 Santa Monica (10) Fwy,
 Cloverfield exit, S to
 Pico
Parking
 On premises, $3; on
 street

HOLLYWOOD BOWL SUMMER FESTIVAL

2301 North Highland Avenue
Los Angeles, CA 90078
Info: (213) 972-7300   **Rsvn:** (213) 850-2000
Fax: (213) 851-5617
Los Angeles' best-known summer music series.

The venerable Hollywood Bowl Summer Festival (fast approaching its 75th anniversary) traditionally signals the beginning of summer when you can pack that picnic dinner—along with candlesticks, candles, and a bottle of your favorite bubbly—and head for the Hollywood Hills.

For those of you living in a cave—or if you are a visitor (and thus excused from not knowing about the Bowl)—the Bowl is an outdoor amphitheater built in the 1920s and set on 120 acres. There is seating for about 18,000 people in boxes and on benches. The bandshell is unique, and you may indeed have seen photos of the big round sound balls that "decorate" it. Its place on the LA landscape is so entrenched that during its season, large, commercial airplanes are diverted from flying over the basin so as not to disturb the subtle sounds of a violin, or the rhythm of the drums. (Helicopters and small planes, however, continue to buzz the Bowl. Director Peter Sellars, during a spiritual LA Festival music performance, suggested to the audience that they imagine the helicopters as angels.)

The Los Angeles Philharmonic and the relatively new Hollywood Bowl Orchestra are the main players during this summer program. See **Los Angeles Philharmonic** in **MUSIC** for detailed information on the variety of musical series offered at the Bowl. Generally, though, there's everything from jazz, classical, contemporary, and Broadway show tunes. Special performances include the 4th of July Fireworks Spectacular, the only night for which you might, if you mark your calendar early enough, be able to purchase box seats. Otherwise you'll have to settle for the wooden benches.

Subscriptions and single tickets are available, and there are a certain number of $1 seats put on sale for the Tuesday, Thursday and Sunday night concerts.

Picnics can be ordered in advance and picked up before the show. You can also bring your own cooler and food. Each year more and more local restaurants offer to prepare picnic dinners for take out. Some folks get very elaborate, bringing in luxurious tablecloths, silver candlesticks, and crystal champagne glasses. Anything goes at the Bowl—as long as you're willing to schlep it. There are concession stands throughout the area for those who skip the baskets. Folks picnic at tables set up on Cahuenga Boulevard just across from the entrance, or in their boxes, at the picnic tables (you'll really have to arrive early for one), or right on the walkways loading up to the seats (the best people-watching spots if you haven't inherited a box seat). Be sure to bring jackets, blankets, and cushy pillows (or rent one).

The sound at the Bowl—a major point of dispute among critics here—is widely variable from night to night and even from seat to seat, given atmospheric conditions and human adjustments of the controls. The lower boxes give you the most natural sound, while above the 1200 level of boxes, the sound is mostly amplified. Generally, the fidelity ranges from that of a good component stereo system downstairs to a one-dimensional mono radio up in sky country.

Have patience for parking. On some nights I've dreamed about a limousine dropping me off and picking me up at the bottom of the hill. If no black-stretch number shows

Performances
Summer
Tickets
$1-73.50
Discounts
Children/seniors/ students/groups of 10+, call Hollywood Bowl's Group Sales Office
BO
During the summer season: Mon-Sat 10 am-6 pm; Sun 12 pm-6 pm; and through intermissions on all concert nights; check/AE/MC/V/reserve by mail,TicketMaster; exchanges at least 24 hrs in advance on full priced tickets only; subscription available
Location
Off Hollywood (101) Fwy, Highland Ave exit
Parking
On premises, $4-20; valet
Special Features
Morning rehearsals by the LA Philharmonic and some guest artists and ensembles are open and free to the public; picnic grounds open

up for you, you're best off utilizing the Bowl's Park-and-Ride bus service from 14 locations throughout the Southland. There are also four parking lots closer to the Bowl from which you can take a shuttle bus. There is a nominal fee for these services, but it's worth it. The stops and schedules are detailed in the Bowl brochure.

If you get into the Bowl parking lot (subscribers can get this reserved parking on a limited basis), you'll wonder whether your Volvo will come out without a scratch. Autos are "stacked"—parked very tightly in a line. Many a night I've ended up stuffed between the cars of patrons who stay behind for that last glass of wine ignoring the possibility that they're blocking someone's car. Valet parking is at a premium. There are parking lots near the Bowl—some of which are equally hard to leave; others are hard to find.

The season is announced around March. If you're not a subscriber, you'll need to call to be put on a mailing list for annual brochures.

IRVINE MEADOWS AMPHITHEATRE See MUSIC

JAZZ LIVE AT THE HYATT

1107 Jamboree Road
Newport Beach, CA 92660
Info: (714) 729-1234
Newport Beach summer jazz series.

Orange County's summer jazz scene has been building a head of steam in Newport Beach lately, thanks to this rapidly rising concert series.

When the Hyatt Newporter underwent renovation a few years ago, an outdoor amphitheater was added to the hotel grounds, prompting the start of a regular jazz series. After a tune-up year, Jazz Live at the Hyatt proper got rolling in 1991, and shows every sign of becoming a major jazz player for the entire Southern California area.

In its first season, the series was able to attract the likes of saxophonist Flip Phillips, bass legend Milt Hinton, Louie Bellson's Big Band, and the team of vibraphonist Terry Gibbs and clarinetist Buddy De Franco. Since then, the lineup has included a lot of big-league saxophone talent—Gerry Mulligan, Frank Morgan, Phil Woods, Harold Land, Supersax—as well as a rare local appearance by pianist Jay McShann and the return of Bellson's band.

The accent is mainstream, heavily influenced by listener requests, but the Hyatt says its ultimate goal is to also present major artists who have never before performed together.

Jazz Live at the Hyatt now regularly sells out every Friday night in the 1,100-seat amphitheater, located on a bluff above Pacific Coast Highway and overlooking Newport's Back Bay. The series consists of at least a dozen concerts, tuning up on Memorial Day weekend (May 28) and running through September 10. The sound is first-rate for an outdoor facility. If you miss the concerts, you can catch delayed broadcasts the following Thursdays on KLON-FM (88.1).

Portable seating is set up on the lawn, but concertgoers are welcome to bring blankets and other portable furniture. Rotating food selections such as hamburgers, hot dogs, pizza, ravioli and desserts ("Things easy to eat on your lap") are sold, plus there's a complete bar. Thankfully, parking is free (or shell out the bucks for valet parking).

Performances
May- Sept; Fri evenings
Tickets
$8-12
BO
Fri 6 pm-10 pm
AE/Disc/MC/V;
TicketMaster
Location
San Diego (405) Fwy to Jamboree Rd, W on Jamboree Rd, 5 miles to entrance of hotel
Parking
On premises, complimentary; valet, $4
Special Features
Broadcast on Jazz 88.1 KLON radio

J. PAUL GETTY MUSEUM SUMMER CONCERT SERIES

17985 Pacific Coast Highway
Malibu, CA 90265
Info: (310) 458-2003

    Away from the roar of the freeway traffic and noise of the city exists a paradise of sorts. The world-renowned J. Paul Getty Museum, which sits atop a hill overlooking the Pacific, presents Saturday evening summer concerts. The programs are set outside in the lush gardens near a pond surrounded by Roman and Greek statues. Each season's concerts revolve around one theme and open with a short lecture about the composer, that evening's music, and how it relates to the theme. Last year, the concerts were called Music and Mythology and were performed by a variety of classical musicians and ensembles, including the Los Angeles Baroque Orchestra and the Los Angeles Vocal & Instrumental Ensemble.

    After each concert there are refreshments to enjoy at no charge. As you will be sitting across the road from the ocean, it's wise to bring a warm jacket. Although the musicians are dressed in tux and gown, casual clothes are the norm (but no shorts, please!). Along with the beautifully printed programs, worth saving, you'll be given a suggested bibliography relating to the concerts' theme.

    Tickets sell out very quickly. Get to the garden about 15 minutes early to stake out a good seat.

Performances
  July-August
Tickets
  $15
BO
  TicketMaster
Location
  1 mile N of Sunset Blvd
Parking
  On premises, FREE
  (reservations required)

LONG BEACH JAZZ FESTIVAL

211 Pine Avenue
Long Beach, CA 90802
Info: (310) 436-7794   **Rsvn:** (310) 436-7794
Fax: (310) 495-8398
Held at Rainbow Lagoon Park, next to the Hyatt Regency Hotel, Shoreline Drive at Linden Avenue.

    The Long Beach Jazz Festival is the soulful survivor of a number of attempts to jump-start a regular special jazz weekend in this city.

    Al Williams, of nearby jazz club Birdland West, started a Queen Mary Jazz Festival on board the mother ship in 1978, suspended it after 1980 and then restarted it in mid-May 1985 in the parking lot alongside the historic liner. The following year, Williams left the Queen Mary Festival to other operators and resurfaced in 1988 with the Long Beach Jazz Festival in beautiful Rainbow Lagoon Park near the Convention Center. The Queen Mary Festival packed up and moved to Orange County, where it soon passed from the scene.

    The various Long Beach festivals have had a reputation for leaning toward electric jazz acts—or fusion or jazz lite or whatever you want to call them (George Howard, The Rippingtons, et al.) —with a sprinkling of mainstream or soul-jazz artists like Les McCann and Eddie Harris.

    Nowadays the festival takes up Friday night and all day Saturday and Sunday on the second full weekend in August. There are VIP seats close to the stage, with box seating and lawn seating near and around the lagoon bringing up the rear. The VIP boxes also come with All Access passes, allowing backstage visits. But these seats go quickly, and you have to be on Birdland West's mailing list just to get a crack at them.

    The setting can be idyllic on a lucky August weekend—with the ocean breezes blowing and the Long Beach skyline soaring. The cylindrical Convention Center and ultramodern Hyatt Regency Hotel counterpoint the peaceful lagoon and gently rolling lawn. But it can get very warm in Long Beach even near the water, so bring your

Performances
  August
Tickets
  $20-100
BO
  Mon-Sat 10 am-6 pm
  (310) 436-7794
  AE/MC/V/reserve by
  mail, TicketMaster; no
  refunds
Location
  Off the Long Beach
  (710) Fwy S, exit on
  Shoreline Dr between
  Pine Ave and Linden
  Ave
Parking
  On premises, $5; street
  parking also available

sunscreen, and something to keep you cool besides the jazz.

LOS ANGELES AFRICAN MARKETPLACE & CULTURAL FAIRE

Rancho Cienega Park
5001 Rodeo Road
Los Angeles, CA 90016
Info: (213) 237-1540   **Fax:** (213) 485-1610

This seven-year-old festival evolved from a modest one stage, three performing groups, and five vendors, to a mega-festival of six stages, numerous performing groups, and 300 vendors.

For three weekends from the mid-August to Labor Day, Rancho Cienega Park is transformed into an African marketplace. Africa's influence around the world is represented in dance and music performed by numerous ensembles. There are children's events, and, of course, the visual arts. You'll enjoy cuisine from Africa, the Middle East, the Caribbean, and Latin America. More than 70 countries are represented by the vendors who sell everything from clothing and fabrics to musical instruments and jewelry.

Be prepared for huge crowds and hot weather. There's a parking lot and street parking. The event is free; however, some venues within the festival do charge from $3 to $10.

Performances
August-Sept
Tickets
FREE; some venues within the festival charge $3-10
Location
Rodeo Rd at La Brea; near the Santa Monica (10) Fwy
Parking
On premises, $3.50; on street

LOS ANGELES COUNTY MUSEUM OF ART—SUMMER BIG BAND JAZZ

5905 Wilshire Boulevard
Los Angeles, CA
Info: (213) 857-6010

Sunday is the day to come out for this free summer event. From 1:30 to 3:30 on eight summer Sundays, the museum presents the sounds of big bands such as Frank Capp and the Juggernaut Big Band, Roger Neumann's Rather Large Band, and Med Flory Big Band with the LA Voices. These concerts, which have been presented for more than six seasons, are performed on the Times Mirror Central Court.

Friday evenings from 5:30 to 8:30 pm, the sounds of jazz played by local musicians can also be heard on the Court.

Sundays at Four concerts, also free, are presented in the museum's Leo S. Bing Theater and broadcast live on KUSC, 91.5 FM. See **MUSIC** for more information.

Performances
Sun, 1:30-3:30; summer
Tickets
FREE
Location
Between Fairfax Ave and La Brea Blvd
Parking
On premises; street

LOS ANGELES FESTIVAL

This triennial blowout was intended to be Los Angeles' cultural calling card to the world, the equivalent of world-class events such as the Holland Festival or the Edinburgh Festival. And it was supposed to bring creative forces within and outside the city together in one glorious multi-week shout. Many agree it succeeded and has even begun to erode the idea that LA is little more than a glossy, superficial, culturally backward company town.

It was the 1984 Olympic Arts Festival, an adjunct to the Olympic Games, which ran its own kind of grueling arts marathon from the beginning of June through the middle of August, that gave birth to the Los Angeles Festival and its ideals. Robert Fitzpatrick, then the president of CalArts, was engaged to run the Olympic festival and the risk it entailed. He insisted upon booking many performers and companies either unknown to the American public or on the cutting edge of their crafts. Accordingly, he launched the festival with a hotly controversial performance of Stravinsky's *The Rite of Spring* by the extreme avant-garde Pina Bausch Wuppertaler Dance Theatre Company of Germany.

Fitzpatrick's vision was declared an immediate success by the hypesters—this, mind you, before the festival had run a quarter of its initial course. By the end of the run, however, Los Angeles had been inundated by a cultural feast it had never seen before, or since. Once the festival was over and the Olympic Games showed a profit, it was decreed that the surplus should go to finance future sports events, while a runner-up one-time-only grant was doled out to create the 1987 Los Angeles Festival.

Plenty of complaints had been aired over the '84 extravaganza at the time: the shortage of music programs in comparison with the embarrassment of riches in dance and theater; the paucity of work by (and support by) Los Angeles artists; letting the most ambitious project of all, Robert Wilson's gigantic theater piece *the CIVIL warS,* get away due to lack of funds (the work still has yet to be performed); the cancellation of a giant rock concert in the Rose Bowl because producer Stevie Wonder couldn't get his act together.

But with the hindsight of nearly a decade since the Olympian year, Fitzpatrick's achievement now looms larger than ever. Few will forget such milestones as the Royal Shakespeare Company's outstanding productions at UCLA, intuitively communicative Shakespeare in French by Le Theatre du Soleil, and the dizzyingly eclectic assortment of international dance companies. In music, three unforgettable productions by the Royal Opera of London, Covent Garden, the world premiere of electronic composer Morton Subotnick's trailblazing *The Double Life of Amphibians,* and the joyously mainstream Olympic Jazz Festival all glow in retrospect. Most of all, the Olympic festival gave local artists a surge of adrenaline as they envisioned a Los Angeles that at last could be a major, innovative cultural rival to the Big Bad Apple.

Fitzpatrick was asked to do it all over again for 1987—but this time with a non-Olympian budget, only three-and-a-half weeks of time in September, and a new name, the Los Angeles Festival. Again Fitzpatrick acted boldly, leading off with an obscure circus troupe that had never performed outside Canada. This was Le Cirque du Soleil, a young, energetic company that injected snazzy elements of Broadway, Las Vegas, and pop music into their death-defying acrobatic show. Their immediate LA success catapulted them to world fame.

Again, the cutting edge was honed by Canada's slam-dancing La La La Human Steps and another mesmerizing Subotnick multimedia piece, *Hungers.* Peter Brook's nine-hour marathon, *The Mahabharata,* became the '87 fest's theatrical hit. Once more, music was shortchanged in comparison to dance and theater, revolving mostly around an alternately tedious and fun week-long John Cage 75th birthday party and three existing productions by the new Los Angeles Music Center Opera.

Perhaps most encouragingly, in the three years between the first and second festivals, the local community of artists and arts organizations, led by a vanguard of theater producers, galvanized into action, or reaction, around the idea of a parallel festival, or "Fringe" as in Edinburgh, to showcase Los Angeles artistic achievements. Using the Edinburgh model, any group could participate so long as it produced itself. The Fringe was established as an alternative to the imported work in the Los Angeles Festival. With seed money from the Los Angeles Festival, Aaron Paley, Director of Fringe Festival/Los Angeles, organized the local community to produce over 400 events in 500 sites.

The first Los Angeles Festival amounted to a long encore to the original Olympic blowout. Understandably, it didn't receive as much overall acclaim as its predecessor. Fitzpatrick, his work done, promptly departed Los Angeles to become president of Euro-Disneyland in France.

Fitzpatrick's successor, Peter Sellars, the *enfant terrible* stage director, faced with an even smaller budget and 17 days of time slots, decided that the 1990 Festival would be confined to an overall Pacific Rim theme. Since the 1987 Festival was criticized for being too heavily concentrated downtown, Sellars spread the 1990 edition all over the city down to the tip of San Pedro.

Reacting to charges that the 1987 festival was too elitist in subject matter and pricing, Sellars proclaimed that the majority of events would be free and often loosely scheduled. As a result, the main festival threatened to become the Fringe, and the Fringe was now a 400-event Open Festival. Sellars even joked about telling people to come to a specific event and then switching it to something else when they arrived.

The final mix (or mixup) was a bewildering collection of events from South and Central America, Asia, Australia, Oceania and the West Coast, a confusing melange symbolized by the illegibly printed program booklet. There was theater from Chile, dance from Java and Cambodia, cinema from Japan and the Philippines, genuine Chinese opera and Sellars' own production of John Adams' opera *Nixon In China*, and hundreds of other combinations of idiom and nation. Sellars promised to beef up the music end, and he did so with a wave of ethnic esoterica and progressive jazz that made even free-jazz pioneer Ornette Coleman sound conventional.

Unlike the first two festivals, it's now difficult to recall highlights—which may have been the subliminal idea. But there was no cultural melting pot; each ethnic group tended to attend their own events. Reviews from the mainstream press were often non-existent since much of what went on was so new, no one knew how to approach it. The festival also ran up a large deficit which wasn't retired until 1992.

For the 1993 Los Angeles Festival, the ever-resilient Sellars promised an overall theme of "Home, Place and Memory," centering upon African, African-American, Middle Eastern, and Middle-Eastern-American artists. What was announced as an eight-week festival was finally pared down to four. The international stars that were named could not be scheduled because of political and monetary problems, so the focus was on U.S. and LA-area artists (with some foreign artists sponsored by different organizations)—another Fringe festival? Instead of spreading itself thin, the '93 fest concentrated much of its programming in Leimert Park's Vision Complex in the Crenshaw area.

Nine years after the Olympic Arts Festival, one still encounters a condescending LA-equals-Tinseltown attitude in the Eastern press, LA artists remain scattered and isolated from each other, and the concept of multiculturalism was dealt a shattering blow by the spring 1992 "unrest." But the festival goes on, an exciting break from the normal cultural routine and a chance to immerse oneself in diverse and perhaps stimulating new experiences. It remains to be seen what 1996 will bring.

LOS ANGELES INTERNATIONAL GAY & LESBIAN FILM/VIDEO FESTIVAL

Director's Guild of America
7720 Sunset Boulevard
Los Angeles, CA 90046
Info: (213) 650-5133   **Fax:** (213) 650-2226

    This popular festival runs for about ten days in July in three screening rooms at the Directors' Guild. The recent fest brought more than 200 features, documentaries, shorts, and videos to town. The presentations are truly international in scope coming from over a dozen countries around the world.

Performances
  July
Tickets
  $5-30 (opening night)
BO
  AE/MC/V/check/reserve by mail
Location
  On Sunset just W of Fairfax
Parking
  On premises, $1; street parking also available

MCCABE'S ANNUAL VARIETY DAY SUMMER FESTIVAL

Lincoln Park
Lincoln & Wilshire Boulevards
Santa Monica, CA
Info: (310) 828-4497

    These free concerts have been coproduced for the past 17 years by the well-known club McCabe's and the City of Santa Monica. The setting is Lincoln Park, at Lincoln and Wilshire. The annual event, scheduled on the third Sunday in July, from 11 am to 4 pm, attracts friends of McCabe's, music lovers and neighborhood residents for a day of al fresco music.

    The festival is a "best of"—performers are standouts from McCabe's popular open mike and variety nights. Most musical tastes are addressed here, whether acoustic guitar, alternative, jazz, or classical compositions. Singer/songwriter Christina Olsen, known for her bluesy folk style, is a festival regular. Lots of humorous songs are performed throughout the day.

    No food is served, although sometimes apple juice is on hand; picnic lunches, blankets, and lawn chairs are welcome. Street parking is available. Children who can't sit still can climb and play on McCabe's fire truck, a 1961 fully operational rig. Sunscreen is a must.

Performances
  July
Tickets
  FREE
Location
  Lincoln Park; off of Santa Monica (10) Fwy; Lincoln exit; head N towards Wilshire; at the corner of Lincoln and Wilshire Blvds
Parking
  On street

MALIBU STRAWBERRY CREEK MUSIC FESTIVAL

Smothers Theatre
Pepperdine University
24255 West Pacific Coast Highway
Malibu, CA 90265
Info: (310) 393-3378   **Rsvn:** (310) 456-4522

    Conductor Yehuda Gilad has created a flurry of fanfare on LA's music scene with this wonderful 3-week summer classical music concert series, now approaching its 11th season. The chamber music, chamber orchestra, and full orchestra concerts take place in an inspiring setting overlooking the ocean at the Smothers Theatre on the Pepperdine campus.

    The high levels of professionalism and artistry have established this festival as a major classical music event. Innovative and impressive lineups have come to be expected. With performances by artists such as violinist Glenn Dicterow, clarinetist Mitchell Lurie, cellist Ofra Harnoy, pianist Jeffrey Kahane, and Soprano Juliana Gondek, such expectations are well-met.

    The festival orchestra is composed of festival faculty and gifted students from the top schools nationally and internationally, and led by master performers. The event

Performances
  July- August
Tickets
  $20
Discounts
  Children/seniors/ students; based on availability
BO
  Mon-Fri 10 am-5 pm; check/AE/MC/V/reserve by mail; exchanges subject to a service charge
Location
  Primarily at Smothers Theatre, Pepperdine University, Malibu; N of Malibu, E of the Pacific Coast Hwy;

350

serves as a training institute for university-level musicians while offering the public a first-rate festival.

The Smothers Theatre seats 450 in a comfortable, steeply raked auditorium. Coffee, tea and light refreshments are offered during intermission.

The Strawberry Creek Festival also offers an "In Town" outreach series of free public concerts, including a special "Young People's Concert," performed at various city venues.

Parking
On premises of Pepperdine University, FREE; on street

Special Features
The Festival offers free outreach concerts in Los Angeles, open to the public, in addition to its evening concerts at Pepperdine University.

MOONLIGHT AMPHITHEATRE AND MOONLIGHT WINTER PLAYHOUSE See **THEATER**

MUSIC IN THE LA ZOO See **CHILDREN**

NATIONAL WOMEN'S THEATRE FESTIVAL

See press listings for performance locations.
Info: (310) 453-6042   **Rsvn:** (310) 825-2101
Fax: (310) 453-4347

A new LA arts festival aimed at promoting women's issues through theatrical expressions ranging from drama to dance to multimedia performance art, this six-day series of concerts and shows speaks eloquently for women around the world. It is a festival with a calculated agenda. However like so many other arts festivals, this one also depends on grants, which were not forthcoming this year. We hope the fest comes back, even if it's on a smaller scale.

Past highlights have included a one-woman show about poet Edna St. Vincent Millay starring Marion Ross; the Split Britches play, *Lesbians Who Kill,* a "butch-femme" comedy; Nobuko Miyamoto, a member of the Asian dance company, Great Leap, in a performance exploring ethnic identity; and the 12th Night Repertory Company portraying stories of famous American women "in an effort to even the historical score."

The festival philosophy is decidedly broad in political and social scope, but bonds cohesively as a platform of women's expression. As ambitious as it is long overdue, the National Women's Theatre Festival promises to be a powerhouse of feminism in art—if it can remain on the scene.

The venue changes with the year. It has been open to children over six years old, and has even featured a special children's matinee. Dates and venues will be known approximately six to eight months in advance. It's best to call the office.

Performances
July

Tickets
$8-12

Discounts
Children/seniors/ students/groups of 10+

OPEN HOUSE AT THE HOLLYWOOD BOWL See **CHILDREN**

PCPA THEATERFEST See **THEATER**

PASADENA JAZZ FESTIVAL

Ambassador Auditorium
300 West Green Street
Pasadena, CA 91129
Info: (818) 304-6166   **Rsvn:** (818) 304-6161
Fax: (818) 356-0522

The Ambassador Foundation has been trying to jazz up its agenda the last few years. This new festival will do nicely.

Launched in 1991, the Pasadena Jazz Festival unfolds over one summer weekend in Ambassador Auditorium. Already it's received acclaim for its tasteful lineups. The 1992 edition was comfortably balanced between such acts as the versatile electric jazz guitarist Lee Ritenour; the high-wire trumpeter from Cuba, Arturo Sandoval; and mainstream vibraphonist (and MJQ member) Milt Jackson. The latest version welcomed Dave and Don Grusin, the Clayton-Hamilton Jazz Orchestra, Diane Schuur, and Dori Caymmi.

As far as indoor locales go, it's hard to beat Ambassador for its comfortable seating, easy freeway access, and generally good vibes, sound-wise (even taking the variables of amplification into account). Food and drink is also easily accessible, courtesy of local gourmet restaurants. Parking, ranging from $2 to $7, can be found in a variety of outdoor lots and structures, as well as on nearby streets, gratis.

Performances
Summer
Tickets
$25-35
Discounts
Children/seniors/ students/groups of 20; call 1 (800) CONCERT
BO
Mon-Thurs 9 am-5 pm; Fri 9 am-4 pm; selected Sundays; AE/MC/V/ reserve by mail
Location
Between Orange Grove and Fair Oaks; Green St and Del Mar; near Foothill (210), Ventura (134), Pasadena (110) Fwys
Parking
On premises, $2-7; on street

PASADENA POPS See MUSIC

PEARSON PARK AMPHITHEATRE See CHILDREN

PLAYBOY JAZZ FESTIVAL

Hollywood Bowl
2301 North Highland Avenue
Los Angeles, CA 90078
Info: (310) 659-4080   **Rsvn:** (310) 450-9040
Fax: (310) 659-4093
Always at the Hollywood Bowl Father's Day weekend.

The Playboy Jazz Festival may be the best jazz fest in the West—or at least in Southern California. It sells out well in advance of its Father's Day weekend date each year and brings together many of the artists off the Billboard charts.

If you're a Spyro Gyra fan from way back, or view Mel Torme as your jazz vocalist idol, you're gonna meet Daddy on Father's Day. There's a little something for all tastes: Buddy Guy and Dorothy Donegan were on tap recently, as were the big band sounds of McCoy Tyner's ensemble, and saxophonist Charles Lloyd. Wynton Marsalis was a hit, of course, as was New Orleans' Dr. John. The ubiquitous Poncho Sanchez stirred things up, and even Washington's Preparatory High School Jazz Ensemble was represented *en masse*. The fest was well-received, but for those whose tastes run to the more avant-garde, experimental, or at least challenging, there isn't much to choose from.

The Hollywood Bowl is the setting. Because the boxes sell out before the lineup is even announced, if you're not on that Hollywood Bowl subscriber list (is there anyone who isn't?), forget it. Watch the papers early in the year to write in for other tickets or risk a close shave from the scalpers.

Performances
June
Tickets
$10-60
BO
Check/reserve by mail, TicketMaster after April 17, if still available
Location
At the Hollywood Bowl near the Hollywood (101) Fwy
Parking
On premises, $9-10
Special Features
A month long series of free events prior to the 2-day Playboy Jazz Festival

One way to get in on the musical action is to attend one of the six-week-long traditional series of *free* pre-festival community events that take place six weeks prior. There may be a concert in the San Fernando Valley, a big band jazz competition in Hermosa Beach, in-school jazz concerts, a senior citizens performance in south central LA, and a noontime downtown concert at City Hall.

If you plan to attend the Bowl, remember it may be warm in the daytime then cool off at night. A pre-Bowl picnic lunch or dinner is *de rigueur*. The usual hot dog-style food is available at the stands. If you're lucky and Uncle Wilbert just willed you box seats, celebrate by ordering a gourmet dinner from the Bowl to be delivered to your box (around $25 each). Best bet for parking is in nearby lots. Or, take a bus, or even a taxi.

SAN DIEGO SUMMERPOPS ORCHESTRA

5th and Marina Way
San Diego, CA 92118
Info: (619) 699-4200 **Rsvn:** (619) 699-4205
Fax: (619) 699-4237
Nine week summer concert festival, downtown San Diego.

One of the wildest sonic experiences in San Diego happens at SummerPops. It's not the music (which bubbles more than it pops). The wild thing erupts at the end of the concert. Fireworks boom and reverberate with battleship force off giant high rises on the bay. San Diego's famous Navy ships aren't near enough to be jealous (or to fire back), though. Instead, harborside with the Pops is a seascape of bobbing yachts and sailboats at sunset and, later, under the stars.

Outdoors, under a big bonnet, pops fans bring their blankets to counter the cool night air or to sit and picnic during Sousa marches and Gershwin tunes played by San Diego Symphony regulars. For closer views of guest artists such as Diane Schuur and the Romeros, for example, some families sit at the cafe tables where servers discreetly whisper offers of light dinners and desserts, wine, and hot cocoa.

The season runs for nine weeks beginning in late June. In addition to the usual series tickets, there are Grass Passes for the entire season allowing you to picnic with unlimited entry, and Tickets for Ten—a book of 10 tickets (a couple could attend five times, or 10 people all at once).

In addition to its SummerPops schedule, the San Diego Symphony presents a Summer Extras! series of concerts by stars such as Whitney Houston and Art Garfunkel; this series, which takes place at the outdoor Pops site, was recently expanded from five concerts to 12. Grass Passes cannot be used.

Performances
June-August; Wed-Sun
7 pm
Tickets
$10-24
Discounts
Previews/seniors/
students/groups of 15+,
call BO, ask for Group
Sales Coordinator
BO
Mon-Tues noon-5 pm;
Wed-Sun noon-
performance
intermission; AE/MC/V/
reserve by mail,
TicketMaster exchanges
for season subscribers
only; subscription
program
Location
At 5th Ave and Marina
Way in downtown San
Diego; directly behind
the San Diego
Convention Center
Parking
On premises (San Diego
Convention Center lot),
$4

SANTA MONICA COLLEGE AMPHITHEATRE See **Santa Monica College** in **MUSIC**

SANTA MONICA INDEPENDENCE ARTS FESTIVAL

Third Street Promenade between Broadway and Wilshire
Santa Monica, CA 90401
Info: (310) 393-9825

For the past four years, Santa Monica's bustling Third Street Promenade has played host to this mixed-arts Fourth of July celebration (which, for some reason, was held in September this year!).

Come stroll the length of the promenade at the

Performances
July; Sat and Sun
closest to the 4th of July
Tickets
FREE
Location
4th St exit off of the
Santa Monica (10) Fwy

free all-day event, and listen to the sounds of back-to-back bands on three separate platforms. It's a good ol' country-folk-fare birthday party for the U.S. of A.—no matter what the month. The music varies; just don't expect heavy metal—or a full symphony.

More than 60 artists exhibit their fine artistry, and you may well catch an impromptu performance artist commandeering the crowds with mime or a juggling show. The small shops and cafes that line the walk cater to the event.

The festival donates 10 percent of all proceeds from artwork sold to the Santa Monica-Malibu Unified School District. So feel good about partying here.

Metered parking is available at six area structures. Don't forget to mind your meter or you're bound to find an unwelcome birthday present from the city on your windshield. Call for more event information.

Parking
On premises (6 public parking structures); on street

SANTA MONICA PIER TWILIGHT DANCE SERIES

200 Santa Monica Pier
Santa Monica, CA 90401
Info: (310) 458-8900   **Fax:** (310) 393-1279

As the sun sets, the energy heats up on the Santa Monica Pier. One of the summer's best free musical events, this annual series always delivers on its promise of a good time. The musicians hug the end of the pier with the sunset and ocean as backdrop. An often romantic, mellow night ensues.

Top international music artists play along with lesser-known, miscellaneous acts. It was worth the struggle to see over all the heads in front of me to get a look at and hear legendary Latin jazz artist Tito Puente. Poncho Sanchez is another star who's played to the sound of lapping waves. But jazz isn't the only offering. Fifties rockers Sha Na Na have entertained, as have the Drifters and The Marvelettes, the gospel-singing Five Blind Boys of Alabama, and Terrance Simien and the Mallet Playboys performing zydeco from the Louisiana Bayou.

Everyone from every walk of life makes his way to this free outdoor fest. Come right off the beach in your bathing attire, or join the flood from the nearby office buildings. The two-hour concerts begin Thursday at 7:30 during the summer months. You can pay the $6 parking charge at the beach; but if you don't mind the stroll, park free in the nearby garages on 2nd Street. Before or after, try dinner at any of the restaurants on the Third Street Promenade, or try one of three full-service restaurants on the pier.

Performances
July-August; Thurs 7:30 pm
Tickets
FREE
Location
Off the Santa Monica (10) Fwy, 4th St exit; at Ocean and Colorado; the SW end of the Santa Monica Pier
Parking
On premises, $6; street parking and FREE city lots

SHAKESPEARE-BY-THE-LAKE See **Octad-One Productions** in **THEATER**

SHAKESPEARE FESTIVAL/LA

See press listings for performance locations.
Info: (213) 489-1121   **Fax:** (213) 489-7850

This annual event is one of the best entertainment deals the city has to offer. Every summer, thanks to Artistic Director and Good Samaritan Ben Donenberg, you have the privilege of witnessing professionally staged and acted Shakespeare absolutely gratis. Thou art a fool if thou dost not partake!

The non-profit group charges only canned food donations for the homeless as admission. (One year, the festival brought in $100,000 worth of tins.) A can of beans will never bring you more delight!

Performances
Summer
Tickets
FREE—canned food donations requested
Discounts
Some group arrangements available through office
BO
Mon-Fri 9:30 am-6 pm, call

The plays tend to be imaginative and accessible versions of Shakespeare. This is Shakespeare how it's meant to be: for *everyone*, not just English majors and the cultural elite. In an effort to begin enlarging the festival, artistic director Ben Donenberg expanded to two plays this past summer. *Romeo and Juliet* played at the John Anson Ford, and *The Two Gentlemen of Verona* was free at Citicorp Plaza. Admission was charged at South Coast Botanic Gardens.

Nearing a decade of success, the company has consistently delivered fully staged, union-contracted productions to its audiences.Performances are mounted five nights a week for approximately two weeks at each location.

More Will Power to this company!

SHAKESPEARE TILL YOU DROP See **Will & Company** in **THEATER**

SUMMER NIGHTS AT THE FORD

John Anson Ford Theatre
2850 Cahuenga Boulevard
Hollywood, CA
Info: (213) 974-1343　**Rsvn:** (213) 466-1767
Fax: (213) 625-1765
Series scheduled at the John Anson Ford Theatre.

The County of Los Angeles made a smart move in the Summer of '93: it threw open the gates to the little John Anson Ford Amphitheatre, across from the Hollywood Bowl, and in no time created a welcome addition to the summer arts scene with 14 professional groups giving 34 performances of music, dance, theater, and opera.

The inaugural season, which ran from the end of May to the second week in September, enjoyed a schedule that included Euterpe Opera Theatre producing Mozart's Zaide, Lynn Dally's Jazz Tap Ensemble, the chamber music ensemble Ima, the Los Angeles Philharmonic's "Chamber Music Under the Stars" series, and Collage Dance Theatre, among the players.

The 1,200-seat outdoor theater was the scene of the first performance of the *Pilgrimage Play* in 1920 (in fact, the theater was named the Pilgrimage Playhouse). Lucky for us it was rebuilt after being destroyed by fire in 1929. Today it is an intimate space in which to enjoy excellent groups that may not have the big bucks to rent entertainment spaces. You see, they don't pay any rent! But, they must submit proposals and be chosen by the County's Music and Performing Arts Commission.

When a special family show of Lynn Dally's Jazz Tap Ensemble was forced to cancel because of rain (it never rains here!), Theatix, the Ford's ticket agency, managed to call all the ticket-holders to tell them of the cancellation and offer refunds! With service like that, the Summer Nights at the Ford series should have no trouble commencing a second season.

Performances
　May-Sept
Tickets
　$10-60
Discounts
　Previews/children/
　groups of 20, call BO
BO
　Tues-Sun 11 am-7 pm;
　noon day of the
　performance; rush
　tickets 1/2 hr prior to
　performance; AE/Disc/
　MC/V/check/ reserve by
　mail (c/o Los Angeles
　Philharmonic, 135 N
　Grand Ave, LA, CA
　90012), fax (213) 466-
　6972, Theatix;
　exchanges made
Location
　Near Hollywood (101)
　Fwy in the Cahuenga
　Pass across from the
　Hollywood Bowl
Parking
　On premises, $4

SUMMER SOLSTICE CELEBRATION

Info: (805) 965-3396　**Fax:** (805) 683-3337
A Santa Barbara Festival held in the downtown area.

You'll wish this day would never end—and it nearly doesn't! At noon on the Saturday closest to the summer solstice, downtown Santa Barbara is transformed into a lively celebration of the arts. Larger-than-life puppets parade down its streets with people-powered floats and celebrants in fantastic costumes. Alameda Park is the end— of the parade, not the festivities. Families are entertained by

Performances
　On the Saturday closest
　to the Summer solstice
Tickets
　FREE

drummers, dancers, storytellers, and clowns. At dusk, following the festival, everyone gathers at Santa Barbara Courthouse's Sunken Gardens for an evening of music, light, sound, and dance.

The popular festival was kicked off in 1974 by artist and mime Michael Gonzales to celebrate his own birthday. The scope has broadened somewhat into a major theatrical celebration of the dawn of summer. The event now predictably attracts 1,000 participants and 80,000 attendees to the streets.

The parade is truly a community-inspired effort. Each year a workshop is offered for Santa Barbarans who'd like to get involved in constructing the festival floats and costumes, puppets, and banners.

Food is always available; park in the numerous downtown lots and garages. Out-of-towners should book hotel reservations in advance. Call the Summer Solstice Hotline for information: (805) 965-3396.

Location
The parade begins on lower State St (at Cota) and continues N to Micheltorena where the parade turns E and enters Alameda Park where the festival begins

Parking
Street parking is available as well as public parking garages

SUMMER SOUNDS (AT THE PACIFIC DESIGN CENTER)

8687 Melrose Avenue
West Hollywood, CA 90069
Info: (310) 854-7471   **Fax:** (310) 652-8314

This little known summer concert series adorns the Pacific Design Center's outdoor amphitheater. The annual lineup consists of six free concerts ranging from jazz, Native American, and Jewish folk to new age music. Only an hour and a half long, the 5 pm Sunday concerts usually run June through August.

The City of West Hollywood and the Musicians Union Local #47 sponsor the program. A fusion of musical styles brings a mix of people, including PDC patrons, seniors, families, and bargain seekers to the professional-quality shows. Occasionally light snacks and drinks are served, with all proceeds going to the homeless. Look for announcements about the series at the PDC or at civic centers around town, or call the West Hollywood Human Services office for info: (310) 854-7471.

Performances
June-August; Sun 5 pm
Tickets
FREE
Location
At the Pacific Design Center: Melrose Ave and San Vicente Blvd
Parking
On premises, FREE

SUNDAY CONCERTS IN THE PARK

Peter Strauss Ranch
Lake Enchanto
30000 Mulholland Highway
Malibu, CA 90265
Info: (818) 597-9192   **Fax:** (818) 597-8357

Another blissful LA concert site, the Peter Strauss Ranch (a.k.a. Lake Enchanto) boasts a tree-shaded amphitheater nestled in the Santa Monica Mountains. From May to September, bands play the gamut of folk music, from traditional Hawaiian sounds to bluegrass in this free family-oriented annual concert series.

Actor Peter Strauss purchased this tract of land in 1977 after filming a television mini-series here. He lived on the grounds until 1983, then sold the land to a state conservancy. In 1987, the National Park Service bought the expanse for a public recreational area. The concerts are also made possible by the Theatre Arts Festival for Youth and the Topanga Banjo Fiddle Contest corporation.

Bring your own nibbles—no food is available. For handicap access, call ahead.

Performances
May-Sept
Tickets
FREE
Location
Off of Mullholland Hwy, end of Troutdale at Mulholland Hwy
Parking
On premises, FREE

SUNSET CINEMA FILM FESTIVAL

See press listings for performance locations.
Info: (619) 454-7377   **Fax:** (619) 551-1048
Sponsored by Visual Arts Foundation and San Diego Unified Port District.

Attend a screening at this festival and you'll come away with sand in your shoes—sort of. Welcome to cinema with a capital sea. This novel film festival annually sails into a handful of bayside parks to offer a series of films under—and with—the stars. Movie-fans in the San Diego area shouldn't miss it. The movies are projected from an anchored barge, and you can watch the 30-foot rear-projection screen (with a good sound system) from your beach blanket. A new age "drive-in" movie, perhaps? (But without that back seat.) You'll have to make do without a concession counter, however. Picnic dinners are highly recommended.

The lineup of classics is eclectic and includes commercial hits of the '70s and '80s. Beach-cum-moviegoers recently confronted *Jaws* uncomfortably near the shore. Marilyn Monroe and Tony Curtis movies have also been featured, along with Oscar-winning animated shorts from the '40s.

Sponsored by the San Diego Unified Port District and Visual Arts Foundation, the event is absolutely free and lots of fun. Call to get this year's confirmed show times and locations. (I wonder what Gidget, Frankie, and Annette would have made of this!)

Performances
  Summer
Tickets
  FREE
Location
  At various bayside parks in San Diego
Parking
  On premises, free; street parking also available

TOPANGA BLUES FESTIVAL

Will Geer Theatricum Botanicum
1419 North Topanga Canyon Boulevard
Topanga, CA 90290
Info: (714) 594-1841   **Rsvn:** (714) 594-1841
Fax: (714) 594-7033

Blues fans will have a blast at this all-day annual music jubilee at the Will Geer Theatricum Botanicum in Topanga. The fest spans the weekend after Memorial Day and for 11 years has highlighted local R&B acts. The 1993 line-up included the soul/R&B/jazz voice of Brenda Burns; jump pianist/vocalist Floyd "Hey Bartender" Dixon with his band, Port Barlow and the Full House; and pianist Steve F'Dor and Friends.

If you've never been to the Will Geer, you're in store for a treat. The outdoor theater is shrouded in a rough rustic setting and the natural canyon acoustics can astound.

This is a summertime good time if this kind of music is your cup of tea—or, rather, mug of beer—handmade beer, that is. Local breweries offer samples of their popular brews between sets—free. The food menu varies from year to year, but the moderate prices endure.

Exclusive on-stage seating (for 20 people) is available at a higher price. Proceeds from these VIP tickets go to a different charity fund each year. Parking is plentiful and free. No coolers, lawn chairs, or personal alcohol can be brought in.

Performances
  May or June—the weekend after Memorial Day
Tickets
  $20-40
Discounts
  Children under 5 FREE; children under 12 $5
BO
  Mon-Sun 9 am-5 pm check/MC/V/reserve by mail, fax, TicketMaster; Lamar's Records (Long Beach), Rhino Records (West LA)
Location
  On Topanga Canyon Blvd; accessible from the Ventura (101) Fwy or Pacific Coast Hwy
Parking
  On street

UCLA FESTIVAL See **UCLA** in **THEATER**

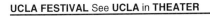

UCLA FILM AND TELEVISION ARCHIVE AT MELNITZ THEATER

See ART FILMS UCLA Film and Television Archive for further information.
Info: (310) 206-8013

    Several worthwhile film festivals return each year for encore engagements at Melnitz Hall. One example is the Contemporary Documentary Series, a survey of recent work in the documentary field. Admission is free to these diverse and provocative movies.

    The annual Festival of Preservation, featuring recently-restored beloved and forsaken oldies has been inspiring cinema fans for five years. Preserving our rich movie heritage from obscurity and extinction is the aim of the series, so the Archive shows only mint-quality, uncut and uncolorized copies of old and nearly forgotten classics.

    The dates of some of the series vary with the year, so call the Archive for scheduling details.

YOUNG ARTISTS PENINSULA MUSIC FESTIVAL

Norris Theater for the Performing Arts
27570 Crossfield Drive
Rolling Hills Estates, CA 90274
Info: (310) 377-8891 **Rsvn:** (310) 544-0403

    Since 1977, pianist/teacher Erika Chary has been running this mid-June weekend festival for aspiring musicians up to age 25. The wunderkinds, some as young as seven, are selected during spring auditions (or in special cases, audio tapes), then are awarded modest honorariums, housing in private homes, and up to 20 minutes of performing time come June. The repertoire ranges all over the lot from the 18th to the 20th centuries.

    Appearances are also put in by orchestras such as the Southwest Youth Symphony Orchestra and the Temple Emanuel Chamber Orchestra (with former County Supervisor Ed Edelman in the cello section). All concerts take place in the Norris Theatre for the Performing Arts on the Palos Verdes Peninsula. Admission is free, regardless of age.

Performances
  July
Tickets
  FREE
BO
  10 am-noon; reserve by mail, fax, TicketMaster;
Location
  Palos Verdes Peninsula; off Hawthorne Blvd and Indian-Peak at Crossfield Dr
Parking
  On premises, FREE; street parking

DANISH DAYS FESTIVAL

Atterdag Street to Alisal Road
Solvang, CA 93463
Info: (805) 688-0701   **Fax:** (805) 688-8620

For more than half a century, folks have been celebrating Solvang's Scandinavian heritage with a two-day free festival of dance and music the third weekend of September at a variety of midtown locations. The storytelling, dancing, accordion and band music, crafts demonstrations, and a parade add up to an enchanting experience of Danish old world customs and pageantry. Delectable food from old-world and new-world recipes can be sampled throughout the town.

Not far from Santa Barbara, Solvang can be round-tripped from LA or Orange County in a day.

Performances
3rd weekend of Sept
Tickets
FREE
Location
Atterdag St to Alisal (closed off)
Parking
On street

DOCUFEST

See press listings for performance locations.
Info: (310) 284-8422
Sponsored by the International Documentary Association.

A distinguished lineup of documentary films (on video as well as celluloid) is assembled for this day-long festival with International Documentary Association prize winners the featured players. Provocative, dark, and sometimes very funny films are routine here.

The venue changes each autumn, so make sure to get a calendar update.

Performances
Fall
Tickets
$7 single tickets; all day pass
Discounts
Children/seniors/ students/IDA member
BO
Call; TicketMaster

FESTIVAL OF ANIMATION

See press listings for festival locations.
Info: (916) 444-2266   **Fax:** (916) 444-2373
A collection of animated short films from around the world.

Animation buffs get more than their fill with this smorgasbord of every imaginable (and imaginative) kind of animated film. You won't just see the Saturday morning cat-chases-mouse-and-learns-a-cruel-lesson genre, but everything from the truly depraved to the erotic to archival World War II recruitment cartoons. Plus, there's a separate showing of really perverse cartoons during the "Extra Sick and Twisted" animated festival held at a different time each year by the same folks.

While animation fests are nothing new to Europe and Japan, the United States knew no such thing until the First International Animation Celebration in Los Angeles a few years ago. Luminaries of the animated world such as Jim (Muppet-master) Henson's company and "The Simpsons" creator Matt Groening have been past sponsors. Artists from countries such as Germany, Denmark, and Japan are represented by their animated works. A competition among the entries dishes out big cash prizes.

Although the regular animation fest is usually held in the fall and spring and the extra "gross" films in the winter, exact dates are uncertain until about three months ahead of showtime.

Performances
Spring and fall
Tickets
$7
Discounts
Children/groups of 20+, call office for arrangements

FESTIVAL OF NEW WORKS See **Mojo Ensemble** in **THEATER**

INTERNATIONAL FESTIVAL OF MASKS

Hancock Park
Corner of Wilshire Boulevard and Curson Avenue
Los Angeles, CA 90036
Info: (213) 937-5544   **Fax:** (213) 937-5576
Sponsored by the Los Angeles Craft and Folk Art Museum.

One of LA's most interesting festivals takes place each fall on the grounds of the George C. Page Museum/La Brea Tar Pits.

Everything revolves around the theme of the mask: First there's a parade, then all sorts of multicultural performing arts (dance, theater, singing, storytelling), creative workshops, vendors, a cornucopia of ethnic food booths, demonstration booths, and, of course, mask-making.

Los Angeles' Craft and Folk Art Museum sponsors, while Community Arts Resources (CARS) produces the colorful free fest, which has been going on for over 15 years. The best part is watching the community come together for this. (Even the elephant family stuck in the gooey tar seems to like it!)

Parking isn't easy, but you can usually count on the lots behind the Wilshire Boulevard office buildings.

Performances
  Oct
Tickets
  FREE
Location
  Hancock Park, at corner of Wilshire Blvd and Curson Ave; near the Santa Monica (10) Fwy, exit Fairfax, go N to Wilshire Blvd, right to Curson Ave
Parking
  Street parking available; public parking available nearby in public lots
Special Features
  Pre-Festival programming: mask-making workshops, lectures, satellite exhibitions of masks in various public spaces in Los Angeles

JOHN COLTRANE FESTIVAL

See press listings for performance locations.
Info: (818) 888-5571   **Fax:** (818) 888-3657

This floating festival has been carrying on for the past six years without a permanent gig. It surfaces in autumn—whenever possible in September, Coltrane's month of birth—and operates under the aegis of his widow, Alice. So far, it's been held at the Wiltern, the Wilshire-Ebell, and, recently, at Royce Hall.

The festival is a living legacy of Coltrane's lasting impact on jazz through the many artists he touched during his lifetime (1926-1967). The musical centerpiece has always been Alice herself, accompanied by her sons, saxophonists Oran and Ravi. Guest artists have included tenor saxophonist Joe Henderson, bassists Reggie Workman, Art Davis, and Charlie Haden, drummer Tootie Heath and Elvin Jones, and many other standouts. The one-day celebration usually runs from afternoon into evening.

The main goal, though, is to promote young musicians. Days prior to the fest is a competition for junior, high school, and college-aged kids called the YMAC (Young Musicians and Artists Competition). The winner gets to open the main concert. Mrs. Coltrane is also attempting to get funding to hire kids to work at the competition, and eventually to find the festival a permanent home.

In the meantime, scan the papers for this one.

Performances
  Usually Sept
Tickets
  $18-25
Discounts
  Children/seniors/ students
BO
  At venue; TicketMaster

LONG BEACH BACH FESTIVAL

See press listings for performance locations.
Info: (310) 438-4356

Though the festival is named after Bach, it's not Back-to-Back Bach. The 1992 edition, for example, was dominated by Bach influenced works, with pieces as diverse as Rossini's *Streetabat Mater* and even Copland's *In The Beginning*. Mozart was the sole focus of 1991's opening concert. At least one concert per festival is devoted to a

Performances
  Call
Tickets
  $9-12
Discounts
  Students/seniors

large choral work, surrounded by less-populated pieces such as cantatas, chamber ensembles and solo recitals.

The core group is the Camerata Singers of Long Beach, a 50-voice chorus with format flexibility. Backing is provided by well-prepared 15-to-18-piece orchestras, though on occasion the LA Baroque Orchestra is called in for that authentic instrument touch.

Most of the festival takes place at the Covenant Presbyterian Church, though some concerts go out to the Los Altos United Methodist Church and other locales. Up until 1991, the Long Beach Bach Festival had been held in the first weeks of May. However, region-wide urban unrest postponed the 1992 festival to late-September/early October. Festival president John Wills says there's a chance that the Fall switch will be permanent, depending upon audience size. Sometimes pre-concert lectures are scheduled 45 minutes prior to downbeat.

It's best to eat before the concert, as there's no on-site food service. (Sometimes, however, receptions with refreshments follow.)

BO
Reserve by mail; no exchanges, but any festival ticket is good at any festival concert
Location
Varies

LONG BEACH BLUES FESTIVAL

California State University Long Beach Campus
1250 Bellflower Boulevard
Long Beach, CA 90815
Info: (310) 985-5566   **Rsvn:** (310) 985-5566
Fax: (310) 598-5729
Held at California State University, Long Beach.

Originally conceived as a local musician's showcase, the Long Beach Blues Festival is now one of America's top blues festivals, even sponsoring a nationwide talent search for an unknown (but deserving) opening act.

Past headliners include: Big Joe Turner, Eddie "Cleanhead" Vinson, John Lee Hooker, Ruth Brown, Koko Taylor, Otis Rush, B.B. King, Robert Cray, and Alter King. One of the great strengths of this fest is the uncompromising booking policy. The rock and pop elements are kept to a bare minimum and are, in any case, all blues-related. You'll always find some of the finest living country blues exponents on the festival bills.

Each year this two-day fest is held in mid-September. It can get pretty warm outside on the Cal State Long Beach athletic field. As seating is "festival style," you'll need to bring your own chairs, blankets, and sun covering. Food is sold, and some of the ethnic dishes are great. Or you can bring your own picnic provisions. And be sure to bring plenty of liquid reinforcements if you plan to spend the day. The lineup runs from about 1 to 11 p.m.

Performances
Sept
Tickets
$25 per day in advance; $30 at the gate
Discounts
Students/groups of 25+, ask when placing the advanced ticket order
BO
Mon-Fri 8:30 am-5:30 pm; check/AE/MC/V/ reserve by mail, fax, TicketMaster; no refunds or exchanges
Location
Shoreline Aquatic Park, Shoreline Dr and Pine Ave in Long Beach; Long Beach (710) Fwy, exit Broadway, take to Pine Ave, turn right
Parking
Near premises, FREE; street parking
Special Features
Pre-festival special events, check with BO

LOS ANGELES BACH FESTIVAL

540 South Commonwealth Avenue
Los Angeles, CA 90020
Info: (213) 385-1341   **Rsvn:** (213) 385-1345
Fax: (213) 487-0461
Concerts are held at the First Congregational Church on South Commonwealth Avenue in the mid-Wilshire district.

Here is a real oldie but still goodie, founded way back in 1934, and now running strong under the direction of Thomas Somerville.

The festival continues to celebrate at the austerely impressive First Congregational Church (founded

Performances
Usually in the third week of Oct
Tickets
$10-17
Discounts
Seniors/students/groups of 10+, call to make arrangements
BO
Mon-Fri 10 am-4 pm check/reserve by mail

in 1868) for ten days in October, either in the main church or smaller spaces like the Shatto Chapel. Of course, the focus is on the music of Johann Sebastian Bach, whose exhaustive catalogue can keep many a festival supplied in perpetuity. But the agenda is not necessarily limited to Bach; one solo cellist, not long ago, strayed as far as Rachmaninoff.

The format can be as intimate as a harpsichord recital, or as grandiose as a full-scale performance of Bach's mighty *St. Matthew Passion* or *B-minor Mass,* authoritatively led by Somerville himself. The Bach Festival also benefits from the presence of the church's two huge, splendid pipe organs—among the best in the city—played by world-class organists like Michael Murray, Peter Hurford, and James Walker.

Performances are on a high professional level, and the festival usually concludes with a big choral work. In addition to the formal evening performances, there is a noon concert series that presents half an hour of music free to the public.

Location
First Congregational Church located at the corner of 6th St and Commonwealth Ave in the mid-Wilshire area; 1 block N of Wilshire between Alvarado and Vermont
Parking
On premises, no charge; street parking available nearby

LOS ANGELES CLASSIC JAZZ FESTIVAL

Los Angeles Airport Marriott
5855 West Century Boulevard
Los Angeles, CA 90045
Info: (310) 391-6435   **Fax:** (310) 390-3677
Labor Day weekend bash presented by the Jazz Clubs of Southern California.

Each Labor Day weekend this traditional jazz and Dixieland festival takes over the LA Airport Marriott and, recently, the Westin at the Airport for three nights and four days of revelry. You needn't worry about special seating, because there are always simultaneous shows in different rooms; the recent program saw 300 musicians working more than 200 events. One ticket each day will do.

When eight of the most active area jazz clubs banded together to form The United Jazz Clubs of Southern California, they decided to put on a festival to encourage and interest young people in "real" jazz. Although the first festival in 1984 was a financial disaster, the group has bounced back and now operates a successful, well-attended program that even auditions young musicians and dispenses cash prizes.

You really need to study the Classic schedule; there's so much going on you could miss what you most want to hear. Some of the best local traditional players (such as Dick Cary, Betty O'Hara, Dick Cathcart and others) are always on hand, while out-of-towners like Dave McKenna, Ruby Braff, or Kenny Davern might just stop by to sit in. But you'll have to dig them out—these fine players will be buried in an avalanche of amateur Dixieland groups from all corners of the globe.

The two hotels, which offer special jazz festival rates, book up early. Dance floors are set aside for those who can't sit still when the music is jumping. You'll even find some attendees moving to the tunes in the swimming pool! Don't worry about going hungry: to bolster the hotel restaurants, the festival organizers set up ramps loaded with barbecue treats.

One price admits you to all events except the Patron's Brunch. One-day badges can be purchased, too.

Performances
Labor Day weekend
Tickets
$15-35; $65 all events; $160 patrons badge
Discounts
Groups of 20+
BO
Check/reserve by mail, TicketMaster; full credit on next year's festival or refund in case of emergency
Location
Near LAX
Parking
On premises

LOS ANGELES POETRY FESTIVAL

See press listings for performance locations.
Info: (213) 660-4306

With the popularity of poetry having climbed to new heights in LA, it's only poetic justice that the most recent Los Angeles Poetry Festival garnered so much press time. The week-long festival plays out in numerous locations around town, normally taking place towards the end of October.

Almost anyone will connect with a lyrical mind that appeals especially to them: a sensibility that stretches the imagination, or reminds them of the classical poetry they packed away with their diploma. If need be, this is a wonderful way to introduce yourself to poetry, as the attitude is casual and positive. Recent presentations included staged dramatic readings of Beckett and Wordsworth at the Los Angeles Theatre Center, poetry by 28 of the entrants in last year's poetry contest at Midnight Special Bookstore in Santa Monica, and readings by new poets at the Burbage Theatre.

Sponsored by the Cultural Affairs Department and produced by poet Suzanne Lummis, the festival also collaborates with other arts groups to present poetry readings and even storytelling.

Some of the events beg a nominal charge, but most are on a free verse basis. Check press listings for dates, locales, and times. After May call the Festival office.

Performances
End of Oct
Tickets
$2-5/but often FREE
BO
Reserve by mail, fax, TicketMaster
Location
All around the city

MULTI-CULTURAL SPOKEN WORD FESTIVAL

See press listings for festival location.
Info: (310) 288-6898   **Fax:** (310) 829-4128

This annual event celebrates the kaleidoscope of peoples and the arts which represent our ethnically diverse city.

Inaugurated at the 1990 Los Angeles Festival, the Spoken Word Festival was created to reflect that Festival's multi-cultural theme. Artists from African-American, Asian, Native American, and Latino communities perform together in a cross-section of art and spoken literary forms. The festival visits Watts Towers Arts Center, Olvera Street, and neighborhoods in downtown and East LA, as well as other often overlooked sites for performing arts concerts as part of its important outreach program. Residents from our mecca of mixed cultures are encouraged to participate in this theatrical/literary exhibition featuring rappers, poets, monologists, singers, and musicians.

The dates of the festival vary, but are announced a few months ahead of time.

Performances
Sept-Oct
Tickets
Most events FREE
Locations
Vary

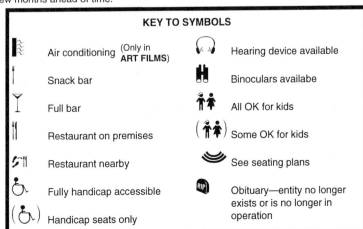

KEY TO SYMBOLS	
Air conditioning (Only in **ART FILMS**)	Hearing device available
Snack bar	Binoculars availabe
Full bar	All OK for kids
Restaurant on premises	Some OK for kids
Restaurant nearby	See seating plans
Fully handicap accessible	Obituary—entity no longer exists or is no longer in operation
Handicap seats only	

SAN DIEGO THANKSGIVING DIXIELAND JAZZ FESTIVAL

Info: (619) 297-5277
Held at Town and Country Hotel, 500 Hotel Circle West, San Diego.

Three days each fall, more than 25 U.S. and Canadian bands jam (and jam in) San Diego's Town and Country Hotel, 500 Hotel Circle N., San Diego, CA 92108.

There's plenty of food and refreshments, dance floors, and even RV accommodations. Write the festival at P.O. Box 82776, San Diego, CA 92138, or call for this year's schedule.

Performances
Nov
Tickets
$15-20 daily; or festival pass $50 and $60
Discounts
Children/students
BO
Thurs-Sun check/reserve by mail; exchanges made with other festivals
Location
Mission Valley off Int-8 and Hotel Circle
Parking
On premises, FREE; street parking

SANTA MONICA ARTS FESTIVAL

Santa Monica Pier
Info: (310) 458-8350   **Fax:** (310) 398-7063

A popular free happening, the Santa Monica Arts Festival takes advantage of the city's pier as backdrop for this day-long event, usually held in September. Planned by the City of Santa Monica, the annual fest stresses the multicultural. Drawing talent from LA's diverse ethnic groups, the celebration features dance, music, performance art, comedy, and children's programming. There are often programming and sponsorship changes, but whatever the alterations, newspaper listings provide current information. Beach parking is available for $5, and food vendors and restaurants line the pier.

Performances
Fall and throughout the year
Tickets
FREE
Location
Colorado Blvd and Ocean Ave

SCANDINAVIAN FESTIVAL

Colorado Place
2425 Colorado Avenue
Santa Monica , CA 90404
Info: (213) 661-8137

Estonian and Finnish folk dancers and a parade of national costumes highlight this all-day annual celebration of matters Nordic. The event joyously renews the cultural traditions of Denmark, Iceland, Finland, Norway, and Sweden to the American melting pot. You'll hear ongoing accordion, fiddle, and violin concerts to placate any Viking. And tyke Vikings should enjoy the special children's booths and events (kids get in free).

This Scandinavian outdoor fair occurs each October at Colorado Place in Santa Monica. It's sponsored by The American Scandinavian Foundation of Los Angeles, a nonprofit organization promoting the traditions and artistry of a small but vital LA Scandinavian community.

And speaking of melting pots, the Scandinavian food specialties at this fair are worth a pot of gold: authentic meatballs, sausages, pancakes, and baked goods from each country will transport you to Valhalla.

Parking is free in the lot.

Performances
Oct
Tickets
$3
Discounts
Children
BO
At entrance day of the event, 10 am-6 pm
Location
N of the Santa Monica (10) Fwy exit 26th St
Parking
On premises, free

SIMON RODIA WATTS TOWERS MUSIC & ARTS FESTIVAL

Watts Towers Art Center
1727 East 107th Street
LA, CA 90002
Info: (213) 485-2437 or 569-8181
Sponsored by the Cultural Affairs Department.
     A tribute to jazz, gospel, and rhythm and blues has livened up Watts Towers for more than 15 years. Two stages host a continuous lineup of music and dance, and there are plenty of arts and crafts and food booths. Sponsored by the Cultural Affairs Department, the one-day free festival usually takes place in September.

Performances
  End of Sept
Tickets
  FREE
Location
  Harbor (110) Fwy, exit
  Century Blvd, E to
  Central, S to 103rd, E to
  Graham, follow signs to
  Watts Towers
Parking
  On premises, FREE;
  street parking

TAFFY FESTIVAL See CHILDREN

TAPER LAB NEW WORK FESTIVAL

John Anson Ford Cultural Center
2580 Cahuenga Boulevard East
Hollywood Hills, CA 90068
Info: (213) 972-7372   **Rsvn:** (213) 972-7372
Fax: (213) 972-0746
     "New work" is the key phrase for this annual festival. As part of an effort to create and assist new artists, the Taper offers the opportunity to submit new material that can then be developed and read without the pressures of critical reviews and production requirements. Plays are accepted and read beginning (usually) in June. After approximately two weeks of rehearsal, they're presented as public workshops, usually in fall and sometimes spilling over into winter. But that can change, so it's best to call the audience services line at (213) 972-0700 for current dates.

Performances
  Oct-Nov
Tickets
  FREE
BO
  Call for reservations
Location
  Off the Hollywood (101)
  Fwy; either Barham Blvd
  or Cahuenga Blvd exits
Parking
  On premises, FREE

TGIF NOONTIME CONCERTS

Los Angeles Music Center Plaza
135 North Grand Avenue
Los Angeles, CA 90012
Info: (213) 972-7211
Sponsored by the Los Angeles Music Center.
     What lunchtime sound bites could be better? Free, one hour noon concerts at the Music Center Plaza every Friday in September and October, May and June. There is truly something for almost everyone when the Music Center brings in musicians—from Tower of Power to Poncho Sanchez, even "stringers" from the venerable Philharmonic.

Performances
  Fridays, Sept-Oct
Tickets
  FREE
Location
  Los Angeles Music
  Center Plaza
Parking
  On premises; street

VIVA LA!

Los Angeles Music Center
135 North Grand Avenue
Los Angeles, CA 90012
Info: (213) 972-7211
Sponsored by the Los Angeles Music Center.
     September sets off a number of area celebrations honoring Mexican Independence Day. The Music Center sponsors a free one-day festival that extends from Hope Street to the Music Center Plaza. More than a dozen bands

Performances
  Sept
Tickets
  FREE
Location
  Music Center Plaza
Parking
  On street; on premises

horn in, and there are all sorts of game and food booths. Call for this year's date, then bring the whole family.

WATTS TOWERS DAY OF THE DRUM FESTIVAL

Watts Towers Arts Center
1727 East 107th Street.
Los Angeles, CA 90002
Info: (213) 485-2437 or 569-8181

     The Cultural Affairs Department sponsors this upbeat, megawatt festival annually at Watts Towers. It's a pure celebration of drums and drummers, past and present, locally and internationally. Two stages are filled with music continuously. This all-day free affair is held the day before the Simon Rodia Watts Towers Music and Arts Festival. Food is plentiful.

Performances
  End of Sept
Tickets
  FREE
Location
  Watts Towers Arts Center; exit Harbor (110) Fwy at Century Blvd, E to Central, S to 103rd, E to Graham, then follow the signs to the Watts Towers; Blue Line stop-103rd and Grandee Sts
Parking
  On premises, FREE; street parking

THE ACTORS' FESTIVAL

Info: (619) 299-6475
Sponsored by the San Diego Actor's Alliance.

The San Diego-based Actor's Alliance sponsors this annual festival of work selected by its members. Programs are usually presented over one or two weekends at St. Cecelia's Theater, 1620 Sixth Avenue at Cedar. The best of the bare-bones productions is then extended.

The audience gets the opportunity to see original and sometimes not-often-performed material conceived, acted, and directed by the actors. Rather than working within the vision of the director, the actors are able to directly express their own personal conception of a work.

Contact the Actors Alliance for this year's dates and location.

Performances
Feb-March
Tickets
$10; Festival Pass $28
Discounts
Previews/children/
seniors/students/groups
of 10+
BO
Tues-Sat 10 am-7 pm;
MC/V/check; Art Tix

AMERICAN INDIAN FILM FESTIVAL

Southwest Museum
234 Museum Drive
Los Angeles, CA 90065
Info: (213) 221-2164   **Rsvn:** (213) 221-2164
Fax: (213) 224-8223
Sponsored by the Southwest Museum.

The wonderful Southwest Museum hosts this series of four films highlighting the cinematic works of and about Native Americans. In previous screenings, you might have seen an intimate piece on how one person adjusts to the integration of reservation and contemporary urban life. Other films present customs and cultural ceremonies of the rich American Indian heritage. The festival runs in late January.

Performances
Late Jan
Tickets
$3-5
Discounts
Children/seniors/
students
BO
Call for reservations;
check/reserve by phone
Location
At the corner of
Marmion Way and
Museum Dr in Highland
Park area of Los
Angeles; near the
Pasadena (110) Fwy
(Ave 43 exit, turn W,
follow signs up the hill)
Parking
On premises, FREE;
street parking

ANNUAL LOS ANGELES COUNTY HOLIDAY CELEBRATION

Dorothy Chandler Pavilion
135 North Grand Avenue
Los Angeles, CA 90012
Info: (213) 974-1343

The Los Angeles County Music and Performing Arts Commission sponsors this three-decades-old tradition at the Music Center. The area's diverse communities come together with dance companies, symphonies, and chorales. Most of the events take place at the Dorothy Chandler Pavilion, where audiences come and go at will. No reservations necessary; no seats reserved; admission and parking(!) are free. (Now there's something to celebrate.)

Past offerings have included a sneak preview of the Kirov Ballet's *Nutcracker,* as well as performances by Rhapsody in Taps, Lula Washington's Los Angeles Contemporary Dance Theatre, choirs from various local communities, the Los Angeles Mozart Orchestra, and numerous other performers.

Call the Commission for a schedule of events.

Performances
Dec 24th
Tickets
FREE
Parking
On premises, FREE;
street parking

CHINESE NEW YEAR CELEBRATION

Info: (213) 617-0396
Celebrated on the streets of Chinatown.

Each year in February this festival of the Lunar New Year showers spectators with color and excitement, tradition and symbolism. Participants celebrate it with dinners, contests, and carnivals.

Especially exciting is the Dragon Dance performed during the Golden Dragon Parade. Once a year the spectacular, powerful dragon comes out to wish good fortune to everyone. The Lion Dances are next in popularity, performed to symbolize the banishment of evil.

Contact the Chinese Chamber of Commerce for information on this year's celebration dates.

Performances
Feb
Tickets
FREE
Location
Los Angeles Chinatown on N Broadway and N Hill Sts, between Sunset Blvd and Bernard St
Parking
Parking lots; street parking

INTERNATIONAL FESTIVAL OF SHORT FILMS

See press listings for performance locations.
Info: (619) 497-0911   **Hotline:** (800) 925-CINE
Fax: (619) 497-0811
Runs in Santa Barbara, San Diego, Long Beach, and Los Angeles. Call for locations and dates.

Andalusian Pictures Ltd. is circulating this funky new film festival committed to bringing short live-action pictures to wider audiences. The first and second years proved successful and eclectic. Shorts from France, Belgium, and New Zealand joined several from the U.S. and together they saluted Edwin S. Porter's *The Great Train Robbery*—a mere 90 years young!

Screenings have taken place at the Four Star Theatre and Cal State Long Beach.

Performances
April in Santa Barbara, Nov in San Diego, Jan-Feb in Los Angeles, Feb in Long Beach
Tickets
$5 bargain weekend matinee; $6 in advance; $7 at the door
Discounts
Call
BO
TicketMaster and other outlets
Location
In Santa Barbara: Victoria Street Theatre; San Diego: San Diego Museum of Contemporary Art Theatre; in Los Angeles: The Four Star Theatre; in Long Beach: Cal State Long Beach
Parking
Varies with location

OPERA ON THE CONCOURSE

San Diego Civic Center Theatre
Third Avenue at B Street, San Diego
Info: (619) 232-7636
Free noontime concerts performed winter through spring.

The concourse in front of San Diego's Civic Theatre is the setting for this series of free lunch-hour concerts. Local and visiting opera stars, accompanied by piano, sing for their lunch (and yours) selections from opera, operetta, and musical comedy. You'll see business people balancing take-out containers and taking in the music, as well as subscribers and benefactors from the opera guild. The one-hour concerts begin at noon and are performed eight times during opera season, January through April.

Performances
Jan-April
Tickets
FREE
Parking
On street

PALM SPRINGS INTERNATIONAL FILM FESTIVAL

See press listings for performance locations.
Info: (619) 322-2930   **Rsvn:** (619) 778-8979
Fax: (619) 322-4087

Who says the desert doesn't bloom? This 10-day long annual festival of international movies has flourished handsomely in arid Palm Springs, and by all indications promises to flower into a world-class film event. Former Mayor Sonny Bono laid the groundwork for this expo in spring of 1989 (and is currently chairman of the board). The premier festival ran for five days in January of the following year and closed to thunderous applause from tourists, critics and filmmakers alike.

Since many or all of the selected pictures won't be familiar to you, you'll have to gamble a bit. Many films go on to broader distribution after debuting here. If you can't afford Cannes, this festival makes a good consolation prize.

There are special galas and receptions, retrospectives and lectures in addition to the assortment of screenings. You can buy passes for a single screening, a limited series, or the "platinum pass," admitting you into every movie and seminar except the closing and opening night galas (which you must pay for separately). Theater locations are close to each other so that you can practically walk from screening to screening. Call the festival office to get the current schedule and dates, and ask them whether there are any hotel and/or restaurant discounts being offered this year.

Performances
Jan
Tickets
Festival passes and single tickets; $6-200
Discounts
Seniors
BO
To be determined; MC/V/reserve by mail
Locations
At the Plaza Theatre, Courtyard Theatres and Annenberg Theatre
Parking
On premises, FREE; street parking
Special Features
Opening and Closing Night Gala and Screenings; Desert Palm Achievement Award Presentation Black Tie Gala

FREE EVENTS

Free THEATER Events and Venues

Free MUSIC Events and Venues

Free DANCE Events and Venues

Free ART FILMS Events and Venues

Free CHILDREN Events and Venues

Free FESTIVALS & SEASONAL EVENTS Events and Venues

SEATING
PLANS

AMBASSADOR AUDITORIUM

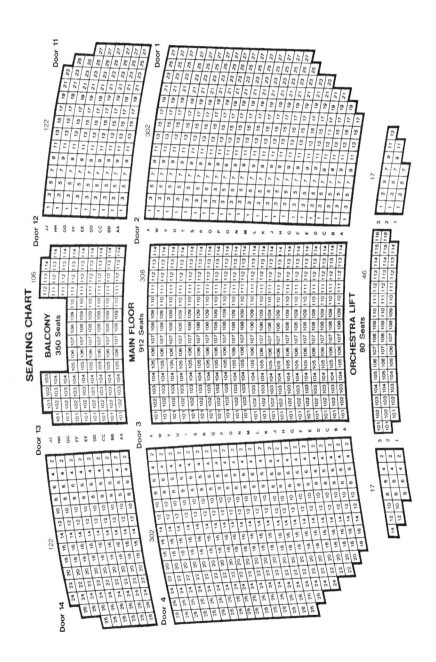

SEATING CHART

BALCONY
350 Seats

MAIN FLOOR
912 Seats

ORCHESTRA LIFT
80 Seats

Door 11 · Door 12 · Door 13 · Door 14
Door 1 · Door 2 · Door 3 · Door 4

ANNENBERG THEATER

Right   Left

Stage

BREA CIVIC & CULTURAL CENTER
Curtis Theatre

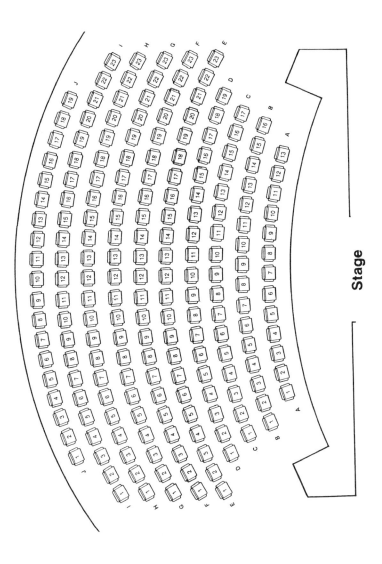

Stage

CALTECH PUBLIC EVENTS
Beckman Auditorium

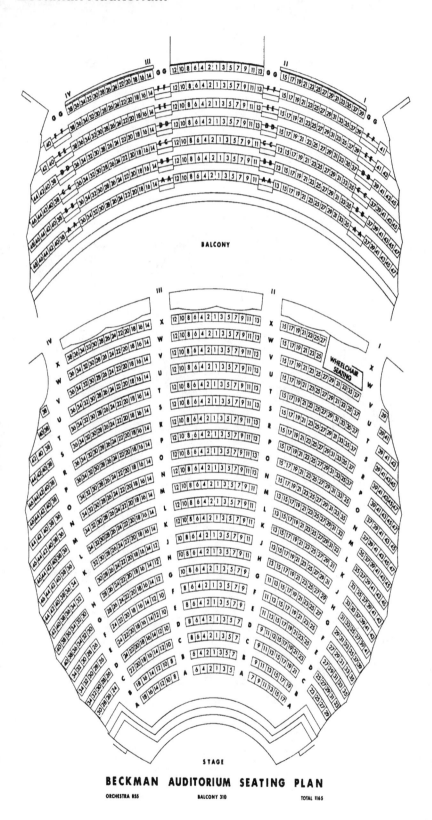

BECKMAN AUDITORIUM SEATING PLAN

ORCHESTRA 855   BALCONY 310   TOTAL 1165

CALTECH PUBLIC EVENTS
Ramo Auditorium

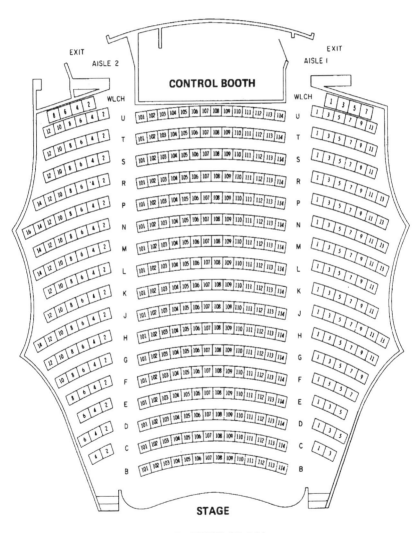

STAGE

SEATING PLAN

THE CANDLELIGHT PAVILION

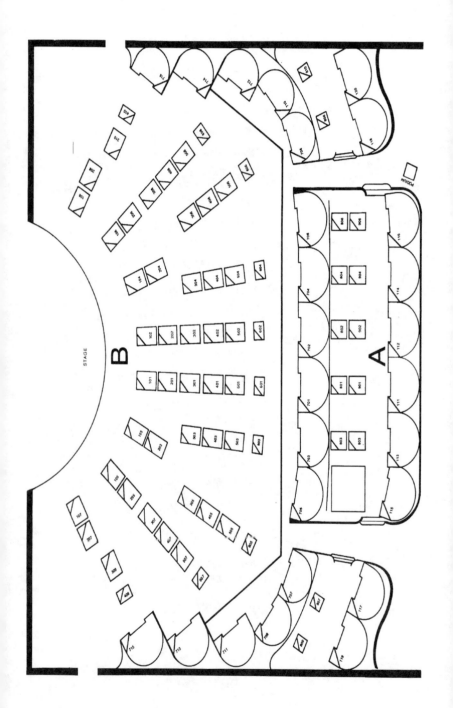

CARLSBAD CULTURAL ARTS CENTER

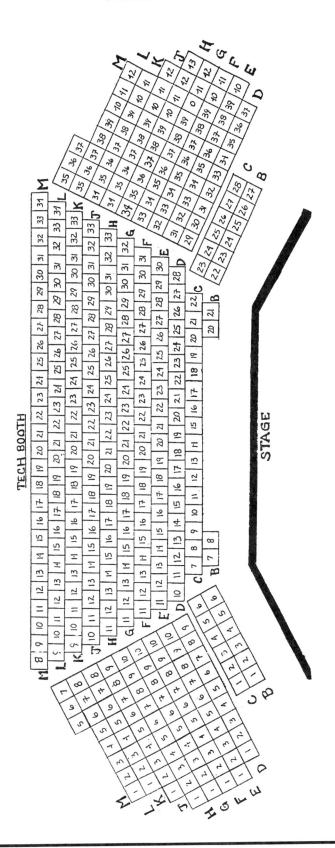

CELEBRITY THEATRE
Full House

FULL HOUSE

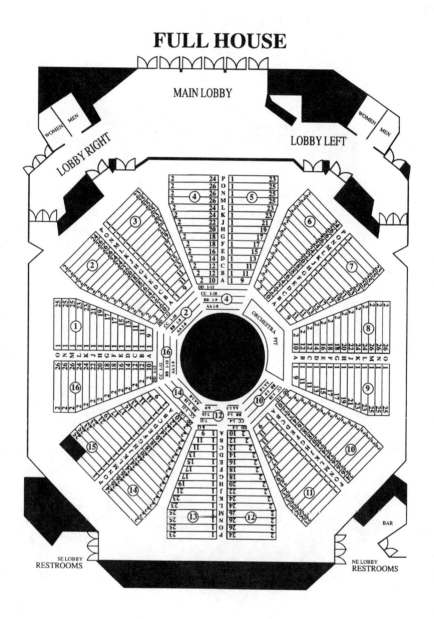

CELEBRITY THEATRE
Half House

HALF HOUSE
Aisle 5 & 12 are not obstructed views for all shows.

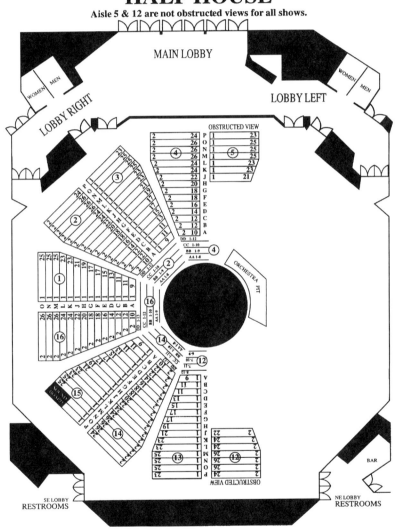

CENTER THEATER

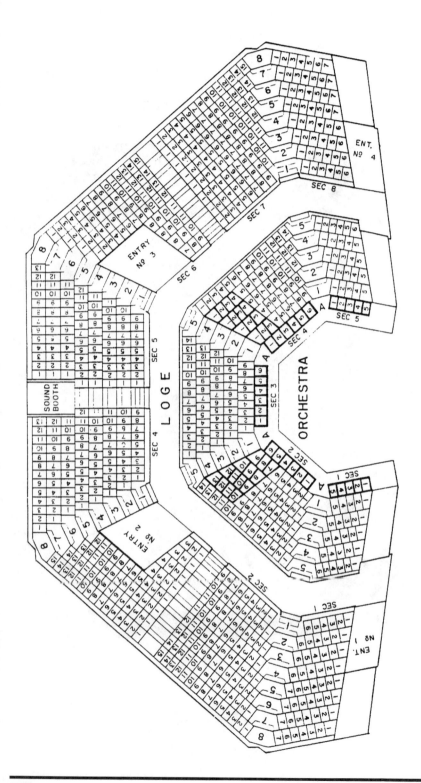

CERRITOS CENTER FOR THE PERFORMING ARTS
Arena & Concert Configurations

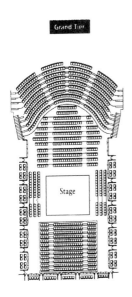

Grand Tier

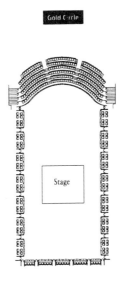

Gold Circle

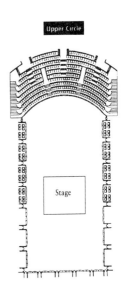

Upper Circle

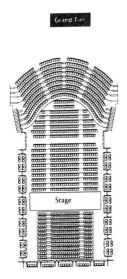

Grand Tier

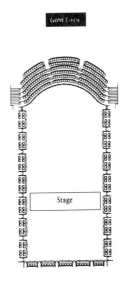

Gold Circle

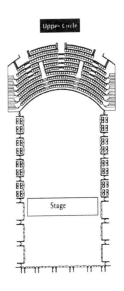

Upper Circle

CERRITOS CENTER FOR THE PERFORMING ARTS
Lyric, Drama & Flat-Floor Configurations

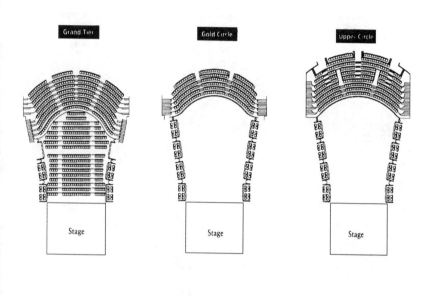

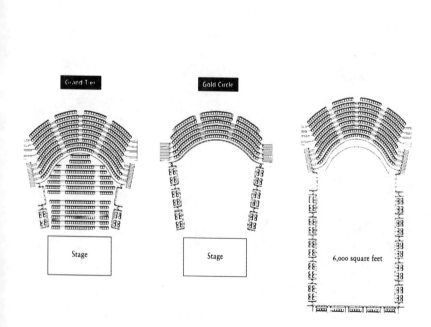

CHRISTIAN COMMUNITY THEATER
Kit Carson Park

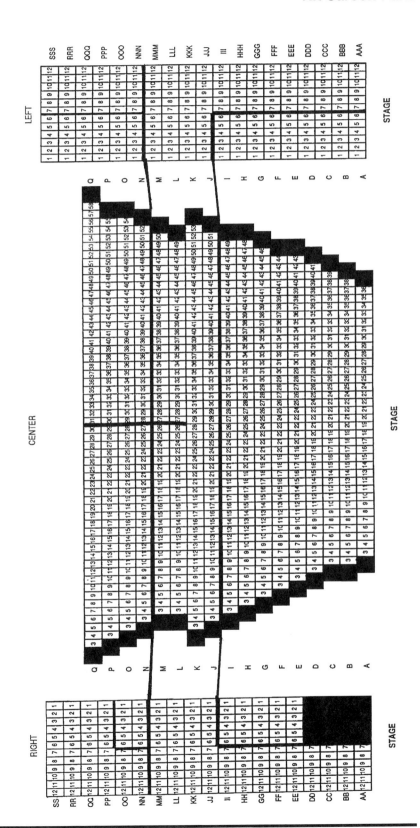

CHRISTIAN COMMUNITY THEATER
Mount Helix

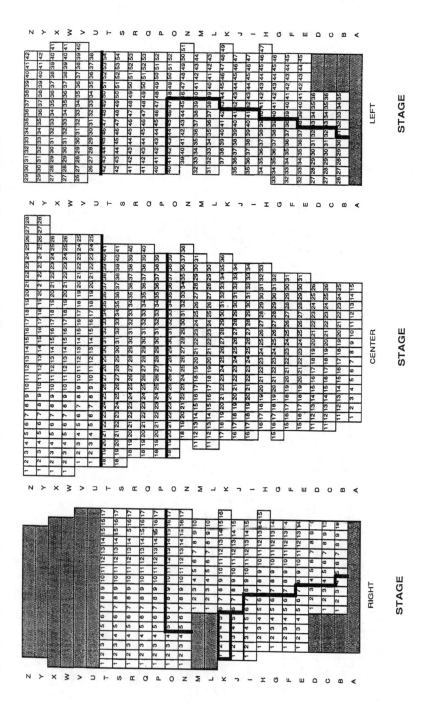

DOWNEY THEATRE

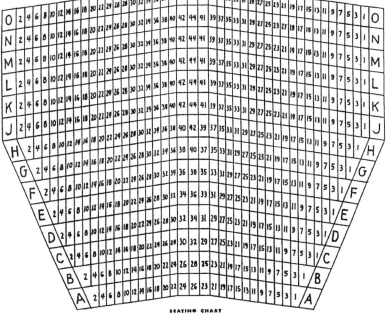

SEATING CHART

FULLERTON CIVIC LIGHT OPERA
Plummer Auditorium

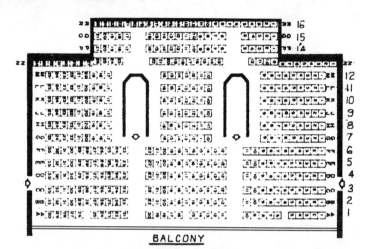

BALCONY

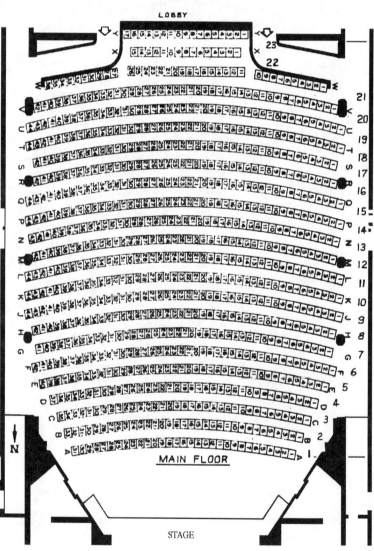

MAIN FLOOR

STAGE

GINDI AUDITORIUM AT THE UNIVERSITY OF JUDAISM

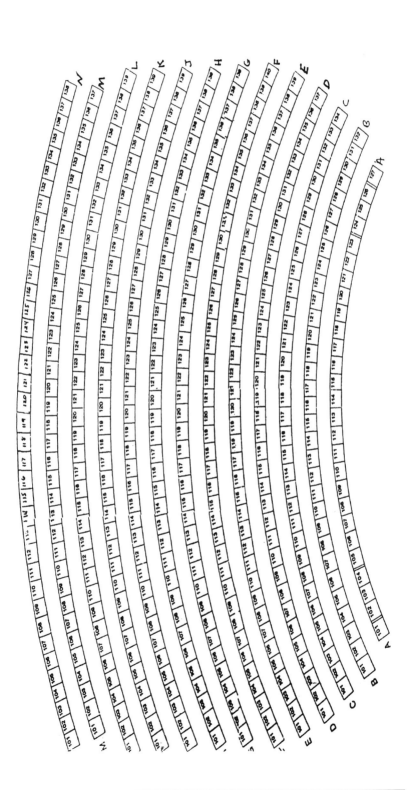

THE GREAT WESTERN FORUM
End Stage Set-Up

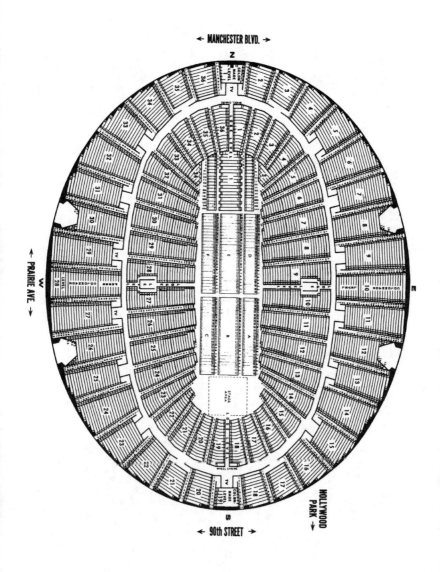

THE GREAT WESTERN FORUM
Basketball Set-Up

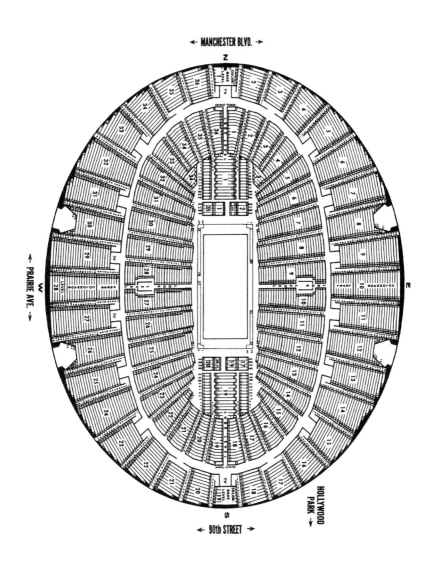

THE GREAT WESTERN FORUM
Hockey Set-Up

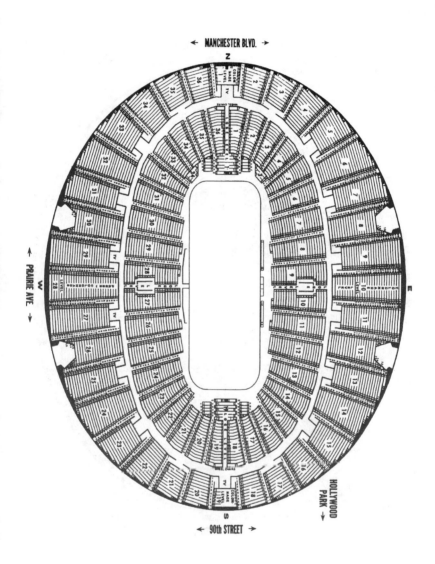

THE GREEK THEATRE

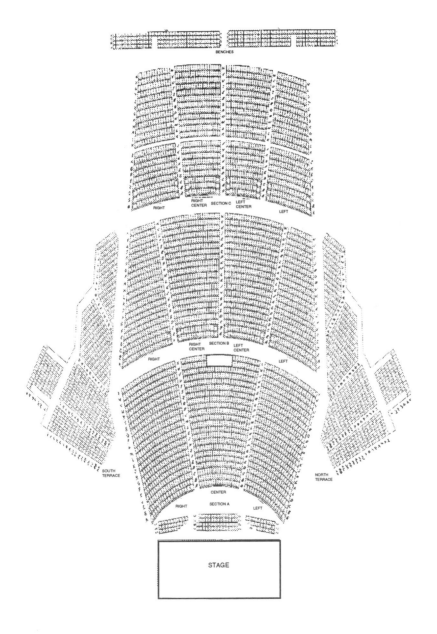

HAHN COSMOPOLITAN THEATRE

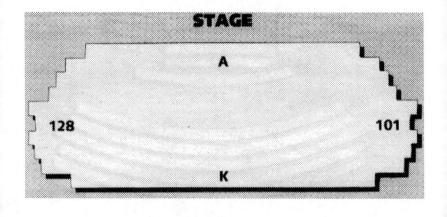

HAUGH PERFORMING ARTS CENTER

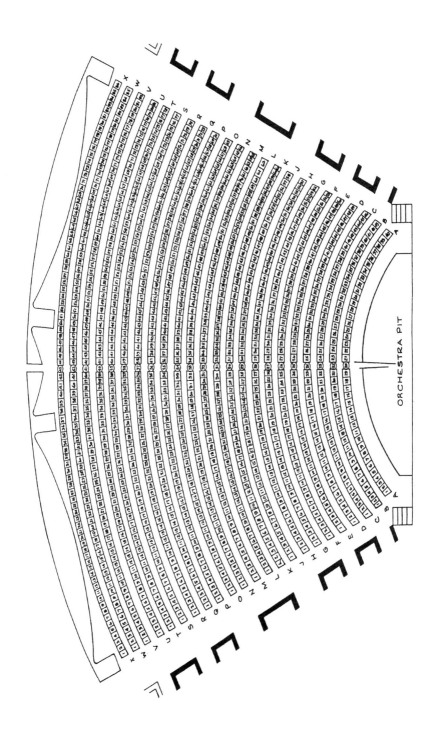

ORCHESTRA PIT

HENRY FONDA THEATRE

BALCONY

ORCHESTRA

HERMOSA CIVIC THEATRE

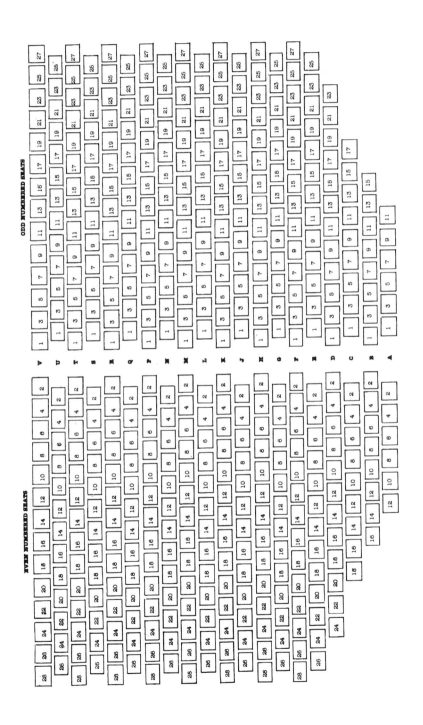

HOLLYWOOD BOWL

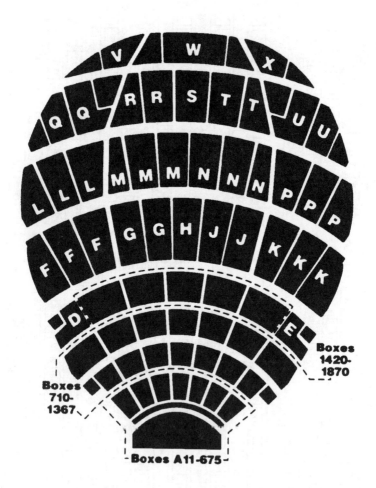

HOLLYWOOD PALLADIUM

THEATRE STYLE

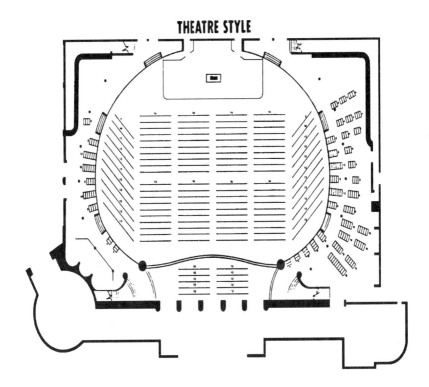

IRVINE BARCLAY THEATRE
Orchestra

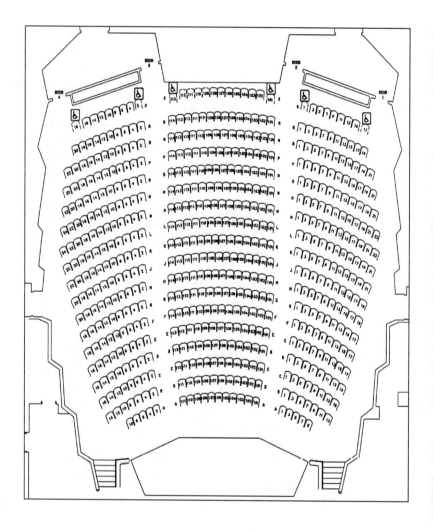

IRVINE BARCLAY THEATRE
Balcony

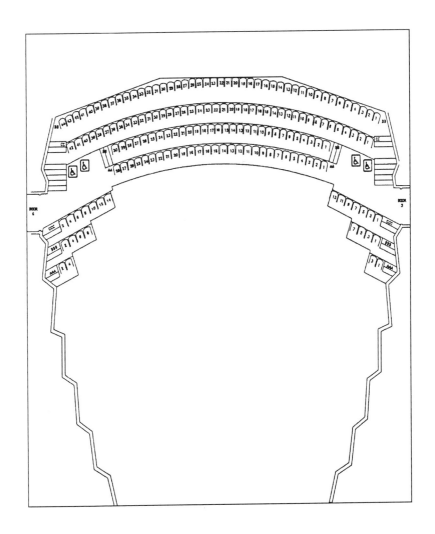

LAGUNA PLAYHOUSE

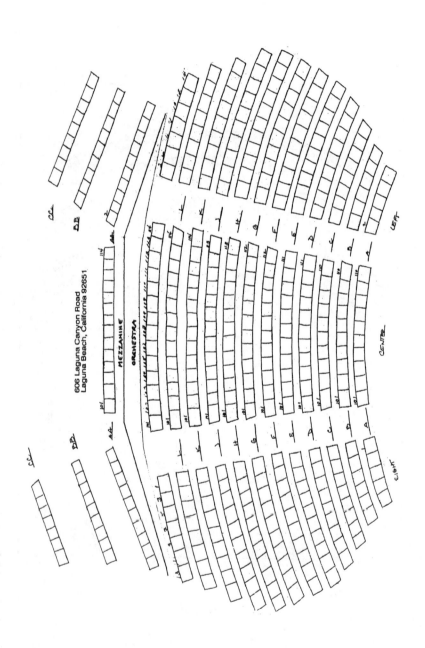

606 Laguna Canyon Road
Laguna Beach, California 92651

LA JOLLA PLAYHOUSE
Mandell Weiss Forum

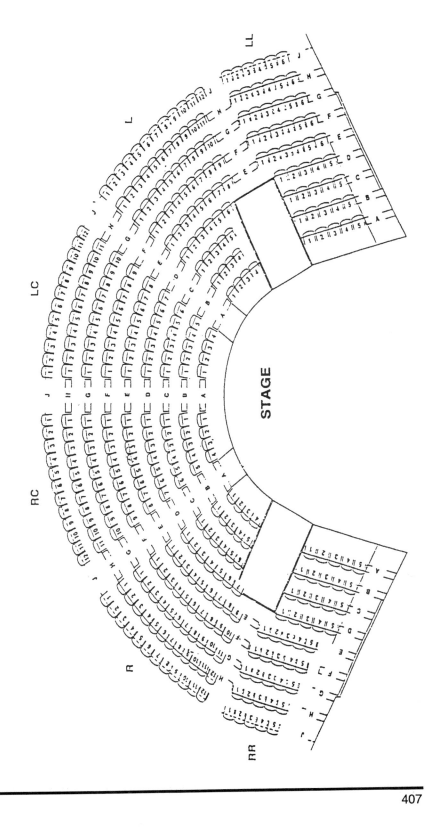

STAGE

LA JOLLA PLAYHOUSE
Mandell Weiss Theatre

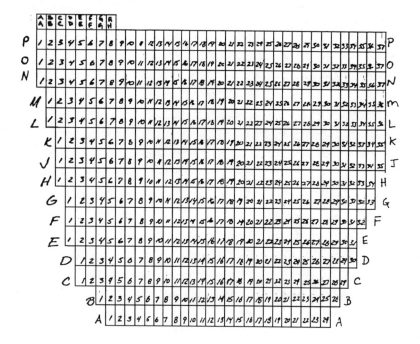

LA MIRADA THEATRE FOR THE PERFORMING ARTS

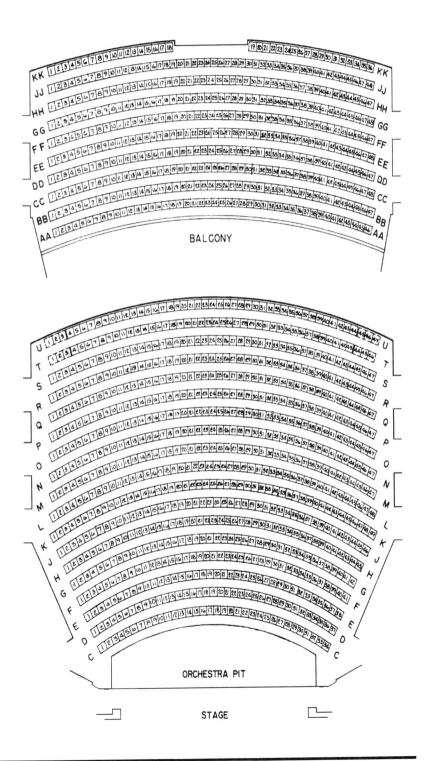

BALCONY

ORCHESTRA PIT

STAGE

LANCASTER PERFORMING ARTS CENTER

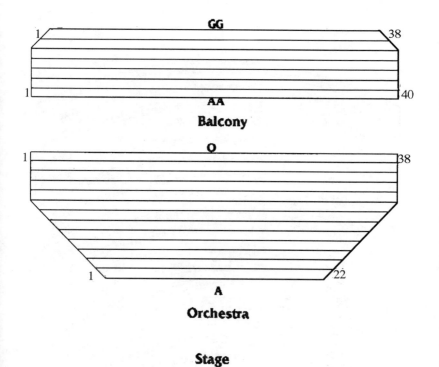

GG
1   38
1   40
AA
Balcony

O
1   38
1   22
A
Orchestra

Stage

LANDIS AUDITORIUM

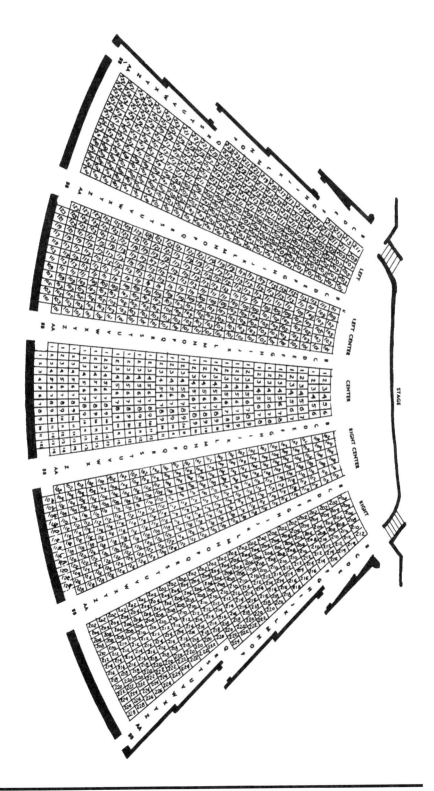

LAWRENCE WELK RESORT THEATRE

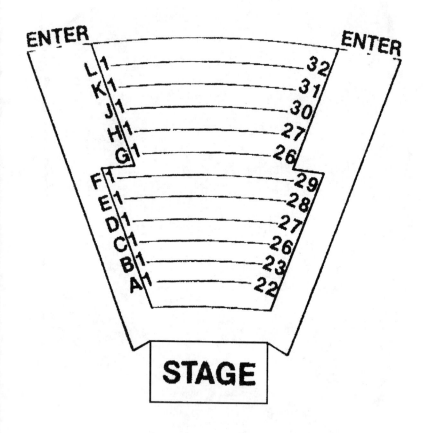

ENTER ENTER

L 1 — 32
K 1 — 31
J 1 — 30
H 1 — 27
G 1 — 26

F 1 — 29
E 1 — 28
D 1 — 27
C 1 — 26
B 1 — 23
A 1 — 22

STAGE

LOBERO THEATRE

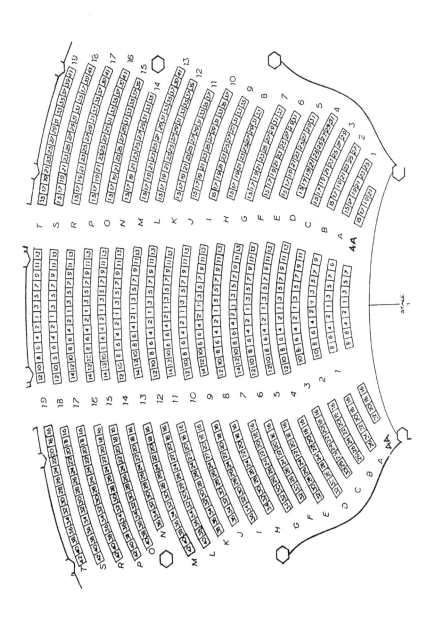

LONG BEACH ARENA

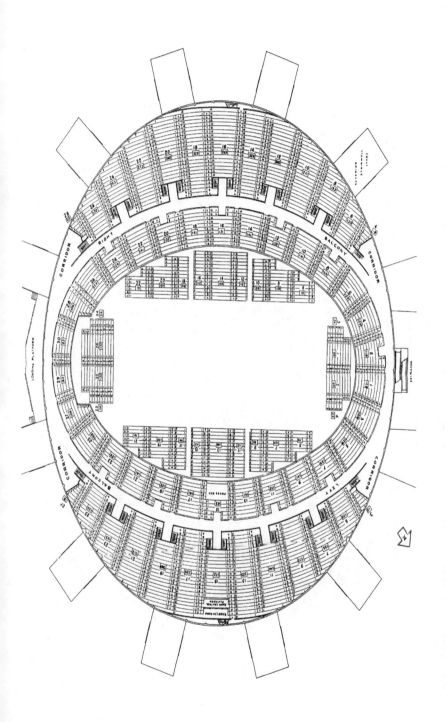

LONG BEACH COMMUNITY PLAYHOUSE
Main Stage

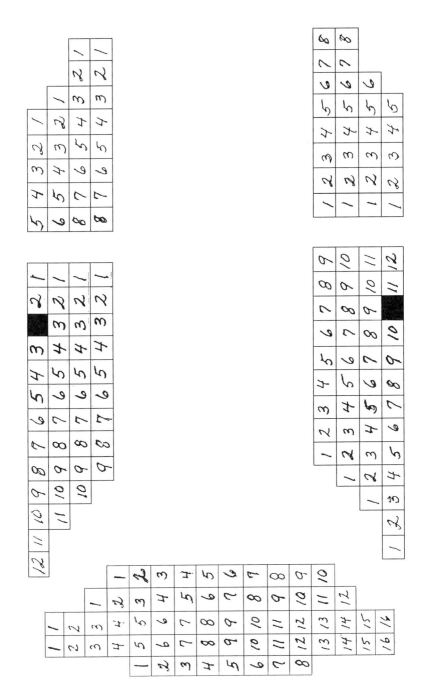

LONG BEACH COMMUNITY PLAYHOUSE
Studio Theatre

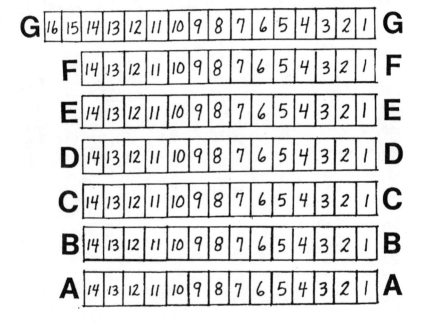

LOS ANGELES PIERCE COLLEGE PERFORMING ARTS BUILDING

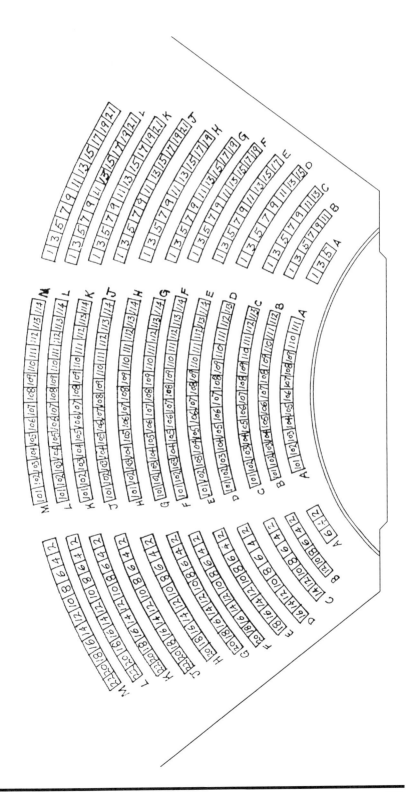

LOS ANGELES THEATRE ACADEMY
Camino Theater

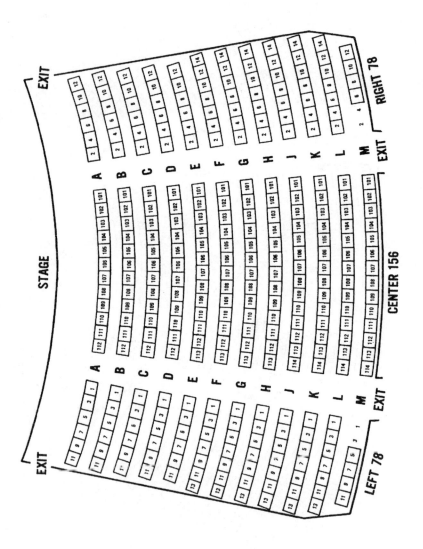

LOS ANGELES THEATRE CENTER
Tom Bradley Theatre

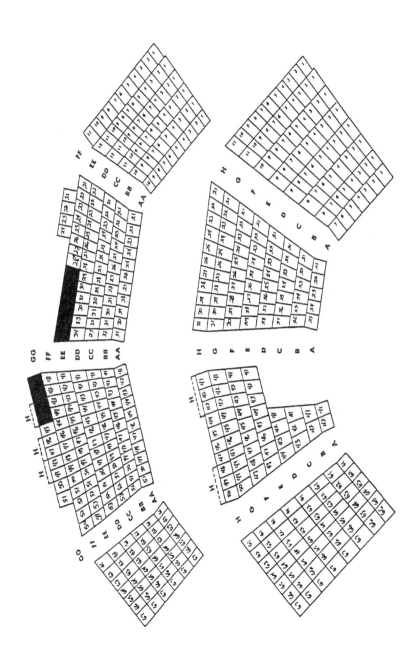

THE MCCALLUM THEATRE FOR THE PERFORMING ARTS AT THE BOB HOPE CULTURAL CENTER

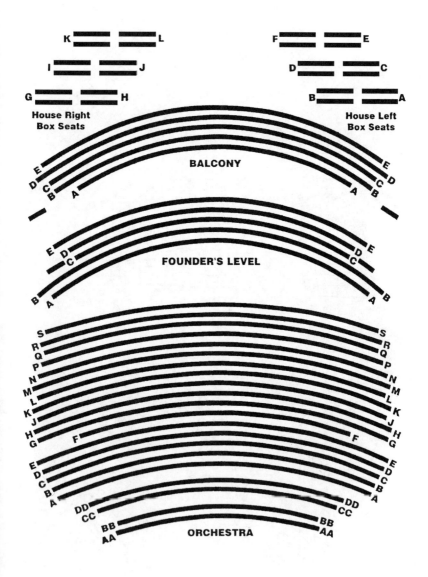

House Right Box Seats

House Left Box Seats

BALCONY

FOUNDER'S LEVEL

ORCHESTRA

MUSIC CENTER OF LOS ANGELES COUNTY
AHMANSON THEATRE
Orchestra

ORCHESTRA
(FIRST LEVEL)
977

MUSIC CENTER OF LOS ANGELES COUNTY
AHMANSON THEATRE
Parquet Terrace

MUSIC CENTER OF LOS ANGELES COUNTY
AHMANSON THEATRE
Balcony

MUSIC CENTER OF LOS ANGELES COUNTY
DOROTHY CHANDLER PAVILION
Orchestra

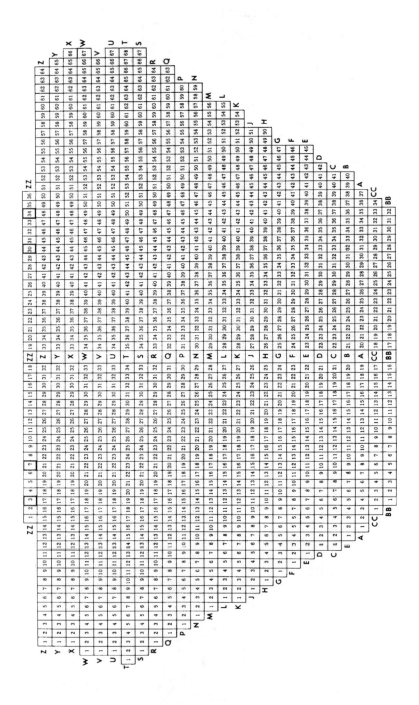

MUSIC CENTER OF LOS ANGELES COUNTY
DOROTHY CHANDLER PAVILION
Loge & Founders Circle

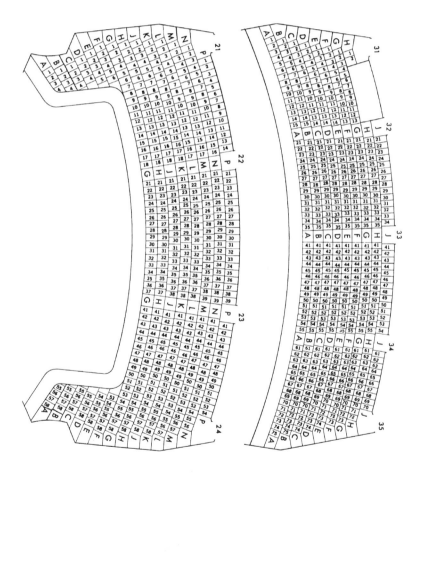

MUSIC CENTER OF LOS ANGELES COUNTY
DOROTHY CHANDLER PAVILION
Balcony

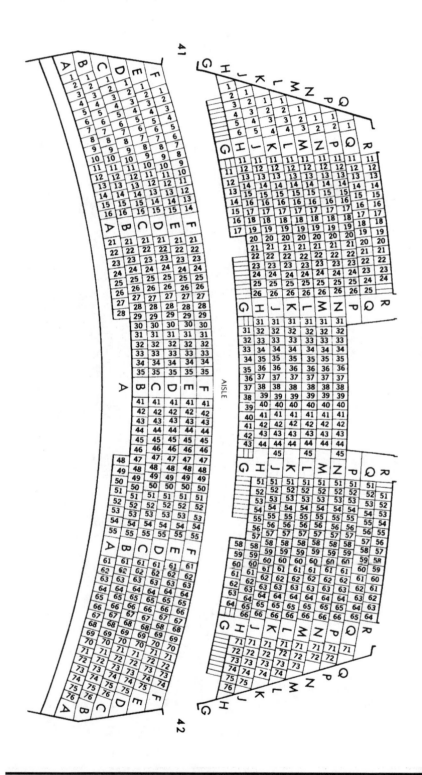

MUSIC CENTER OF LOS ANGELES COUNTY
JAMES A. DOOLITTLE THEATRE

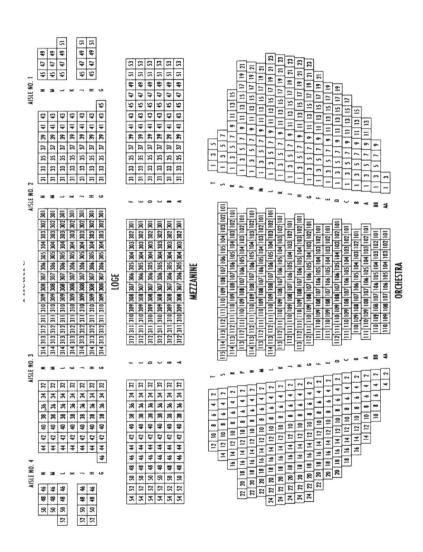

MUSIC CENTER OF LOS ANGELES COUNTY
MARK TAPER FORUM

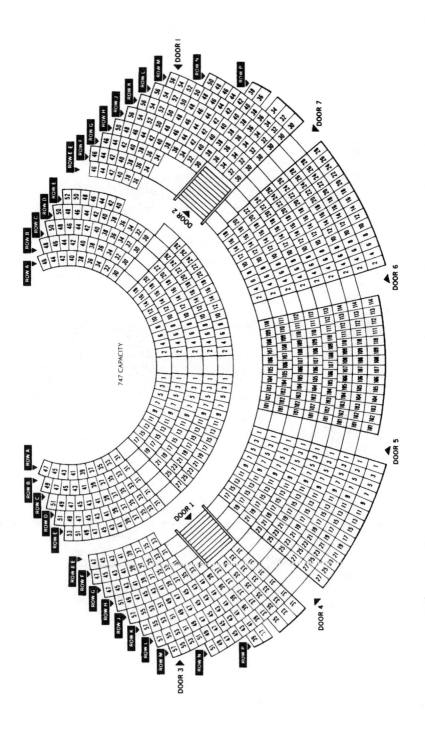

747 CAPACITY

NORRIS THEATRE FOR THE PERFORMING ARTS

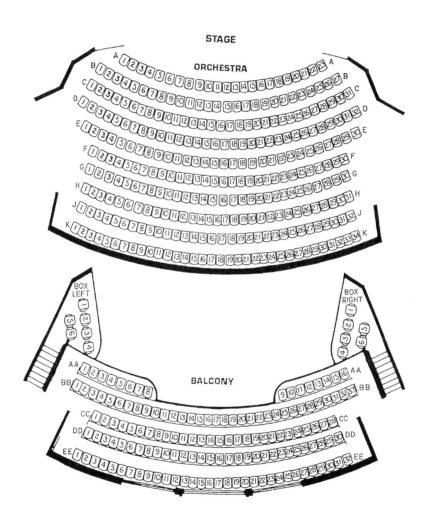

STAGE

OCCIDENTAL COLLEGE PERFORMING ARTS SERIES
Thorne Hall

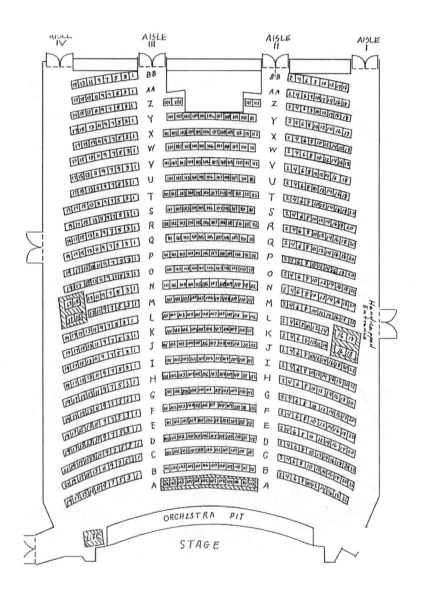

ORANGE COUNTY PERFORMING ARTS CENTER
Orchestra Level

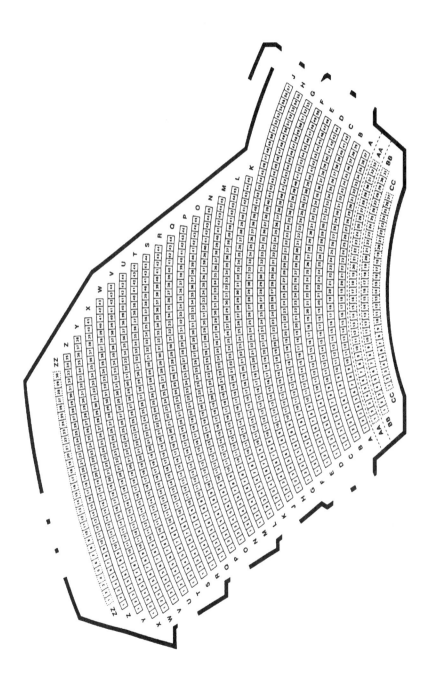

ORANGE COUNTY PERFORMING ARTS CENTER
First Tier

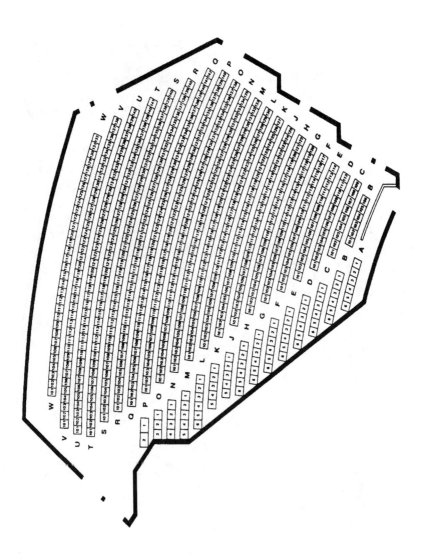

ORANGE COUNTY PERFORMING ARTS CENTER
Second Tier

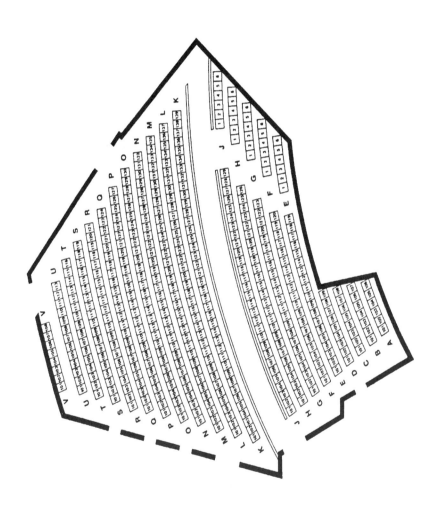

ORANGE COUNTY PERFORMING ARTS CENTER
Third Tier

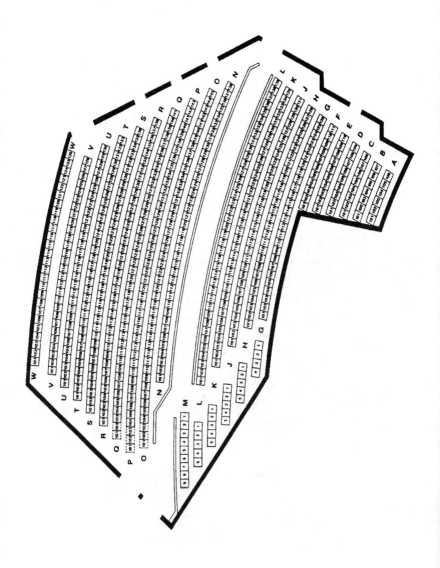

PACIFIC AMPHITHEATRE
Loge

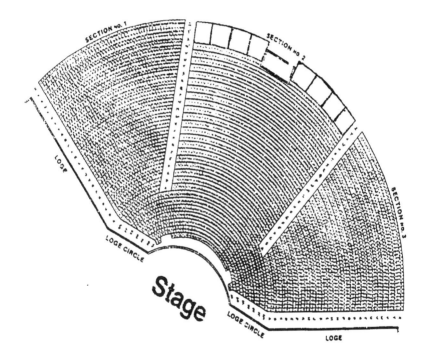

PACIFIC AMPHITHEATRE
Terrace

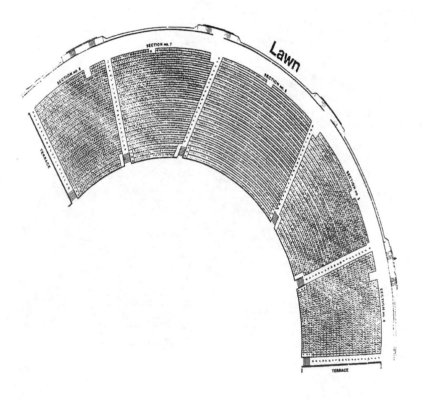

Lawn

PANTAGES THEATER

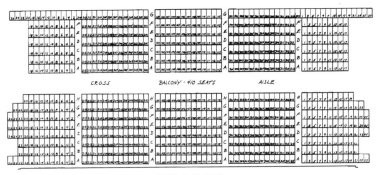

CROSS   BALCONY · 410 SEATS   AISLE

MEZZANINE · 504 SEATS

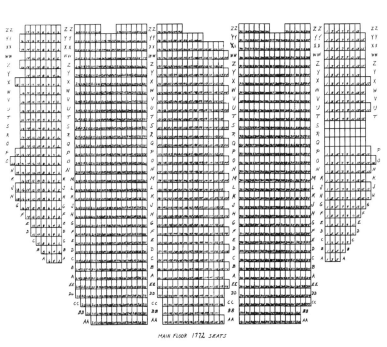

MAIN FLOOR 1772 SEATS

PASADENA CIVIC AUDITORIUM
Loge

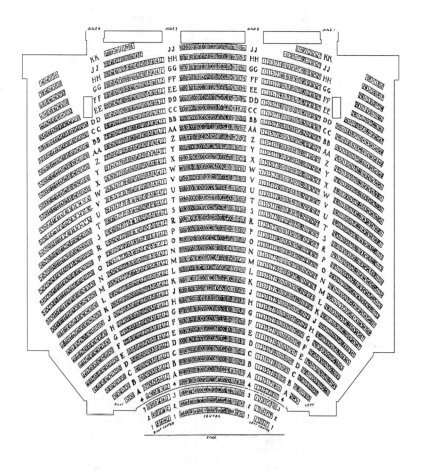

PASADENA CIVIC AUDITORIUM
Balcony

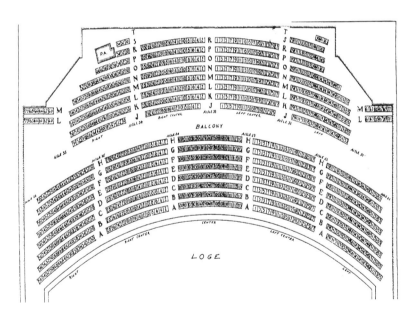

PEPPERDINE UNIVERSITY CENTER FOR THE ARTS
Smothers Theatre

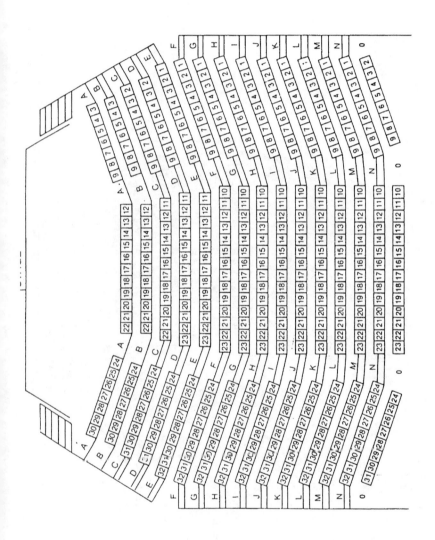

POWAY CENTER FOR THE PERFORMING ARTS
Orchestra

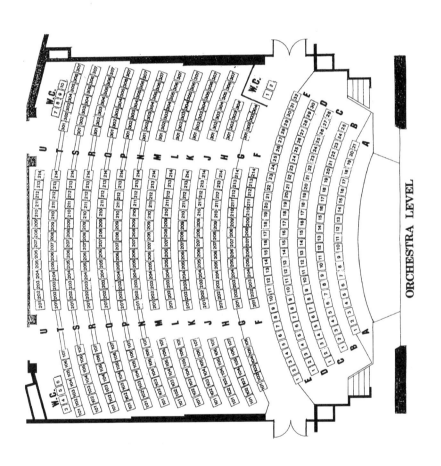

POWAY CENTER FOR THE PERFORMING ARTS
Mezzanine

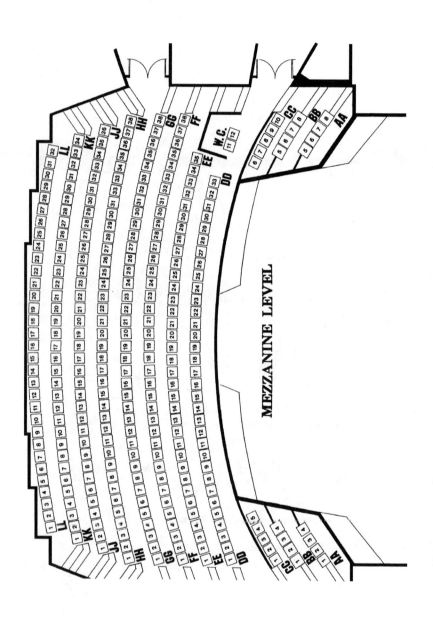

REDONDO BEACH CITY THEATER GROUP
Aviation Park Auditorium

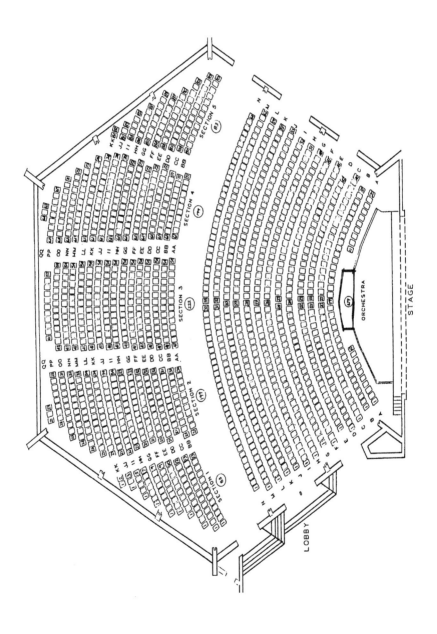

SAN DIEGO STATE UNIVERSITY DEPARTMENT OF DRAMA
Don Powell Theatre

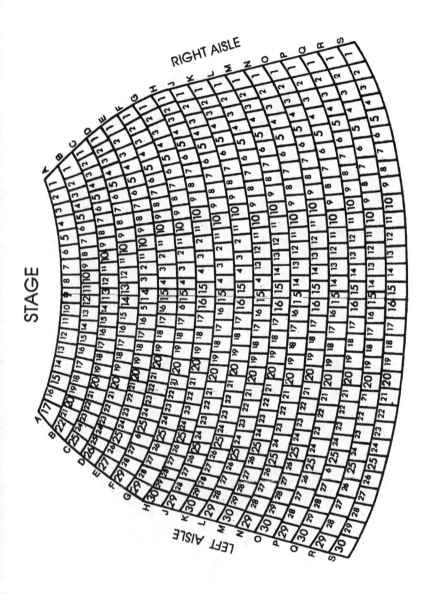

SAN DIEGO SYMPHONY ORCHESTRA
Copley Symphony Hall

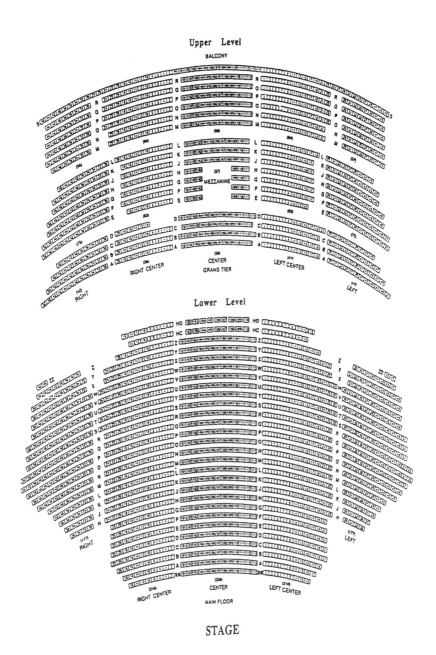

Upper Level
BALCONY

MEZZANINE

RIGHT CENTER

CENTER
GRAND TIER

LEFT CENTER

RIGHT

LEFT

Lower Level

RIGHT

LEFT

RIGHT CENTER

CENTER
MAIN FLOOR

LEFT CENTER

STAGE

SAN GABRIEL VALLEY CIVIC AUDITORIUM

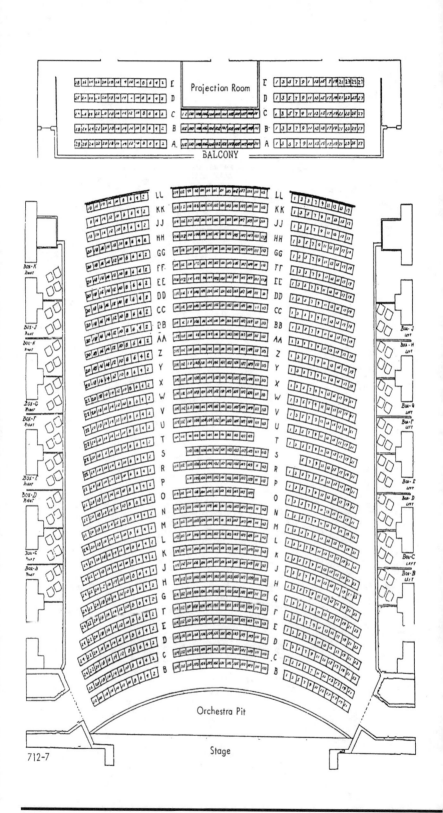

Projection Room

BALCONY

Box-K Right
Box-J Right
Box-H Right
Box-G Right
Box-F Right
Box-E Right
Box-D Right
Box-C Right
Box-B Right

Box-J Left
Box-H Left
Box-G Left
Box-F Left
Box-E Left
Box-D Left
Box-C Left
Box-B Left

Orchestra Pit

Stage

712-7

SANTA MONICA PLAYHOUSE

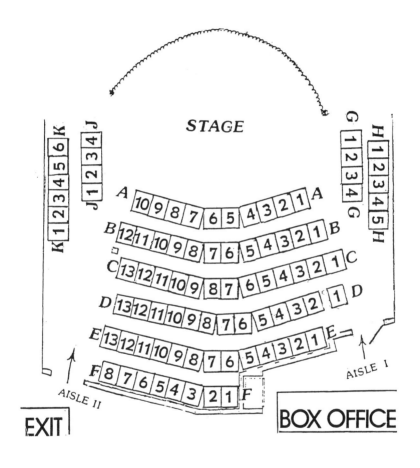

SHRINE AUDITORIUM
Mezzanine

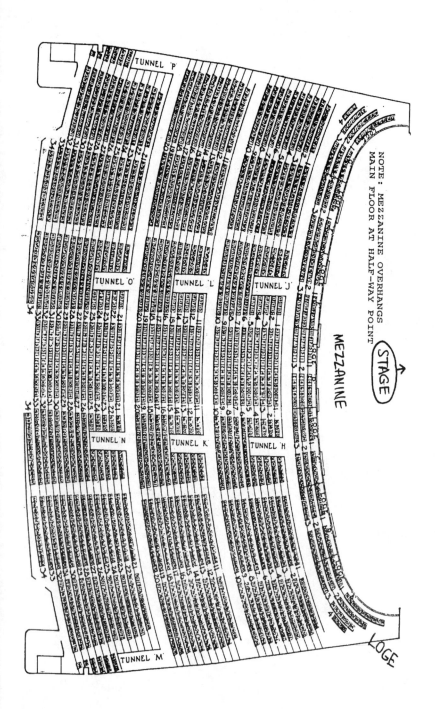

SHRINE AUDITORIUM
Orchestra

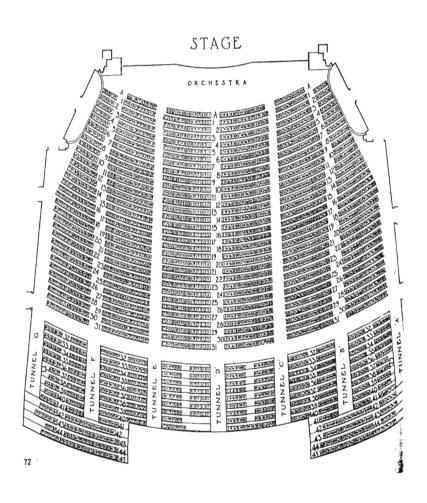

72

SOUTH BAY CENTER FOR THE ARTS
Marsee Auditorium

```
OOOOOOOOOOOOOO T    OOOOOOOOOOOOOO T    T OOOOOOOOOOOOOO    T OOOOOOOOOOOOOO
OOOOOOOOOOOOOO S    OOOOOOOOOOOOOO S    S OOOOOOOOOOOOOO    S OOOOOOOOOOOOOO
OOOOOOOOOOOOOO R    OOOOOOOOOOOOOO R    R OOOOOOOOOOOOOO    R OOOOOOOOOOOOOO
OOOOOOOOOOOOOO P    OOOOOOOOOOOOOO P    P OOOOOOOOOOOOOO    P OOOOOOOOOOOOOO
OOOOOOOOOOOOOO N    OOOOOOOOOOOOOO N    N OOOOOOOOOOOOOO    N OOOOOOOOOOOOOO
OOOOOOOOOOOOOO M    OOOOOOOOOOOOOO M    M OOOOOOOOOOOOOO    M OOOOOOOOOOOOOO
OOOOOOOOOOOOO  L    OOOOOOOOOOOOO  L    L OOOOOOOOOOOOO     L OOOOOOOOOOOOO
OOOOOOOOOOOOO  K    OOOOOOOOOOOOO  K    K OOOOOOOOOOOOO     K OOOOOOOOOOOOO
OOOOOOOOOOOOO  J    OOOOOOOOOOOOO  J    J OOOOOOOOOOOOO     J OOOOOOOOOOOOO
OOOOOOOOOOOOO  H    OOOOOOOOOOOOO  H    H OOOOOOOOOOOOO     H OOOOOOOOOOOOO
OOOOOOOOOOOOO  G     OOOOOOOOO    G    G  OOOOOOOOO       G OOOOOOOOOOOOO
OOOOOOOOOOOOO  F     OOOOOOOOO    F    F  OOOOOOOOO       F OOOOOOOOOOOOO
OOOOOOOOOOOOO  E     OOOOOOOOO    E    E  OOOOOOOOO       E OOOOOOOOOOOOO
4A OOOOOOOOOOO D  3A OOOOOOOOO    D    D  OOOOOOOOO 2A    D OOOOOOOOOOO 1A
OOOOOOOOOOO    C     OOOOOOOOO    C    C  OOOOOOOOO       C OOOOOOOOOOO
OOOOOOOOOOO    B     OOOOOOOOO    B    B  OOOOOOOOO       B OOOOOOOOOOO
OOOOOOOOOO     A     OOOOOOOO     A    A  OOOOOOOO        A OOOOOOOOOO
10        1       8        1                1        8     1        10

                        B A L C O N Y
------------------------------------------------------------------
54                                    5
W.C.                                                W.C.
  58 OOOO    OOOOOOOOOOOOOOOOOOOOOOOOOOOOOOOOOOOOOOOOOOOOOOOOOOO  OOOO 1 Z
   59 OOOOOOOOOOOOOOOOOOOOOOOOOOOOOOOOOOOOOOOOOOOOOOOOOOOOOOOOOOO 1 Y
   60 OOOOOOOOOOOOOOOOOOOOOOOOOOOOOOOOOOOOOOOOOOOOOOOOOOOOOOOOOOO1 X
   61 OOOOOOOOOOOOOOOOOOOOOOOOOOOOOOOOOOOOOOOOOOOOOOOOOOOOOOOOOOO 1 W
   60 OOOOOOOOOOOOOOOOOOOOOOOOOOOOOOOOOOOOOOOOOOOOOOOOOOOOOOOOOOO 1 V
   59 OOOOOOOOOOOOOOOOOOOOOOOOOOOOOOOOOOOOOOOOOOOOOOOOOOOOOOOOOO 1 U
   58 OOOOOOOOOOOOOOOOOOOOOOOOOOOOOOOOOOOOOOOOOOOOOOOOOOOOOOOOOO 1 T
   57 OOOOOOOOOOOOOOOOOOOOOOOOOOOOOOOOOOOOOOOOOOOOOOOOOOOOOOOOO 1 S
   58 OOOOOOOOOOOOOOOOOOOOOOOOOOOOOOOOOOOOOOOOOOOOOOOOOOOOOOOOOO 1 R
  55 OOOOOOOOOOOOOOOOOOOOOOOOOOOOOOOOOOOOOOOOOOOOOOOOOOOOOOOO 1 Q
  54 OOOOOOOOOOOOOOOOOOOOOOOOOOOOOOOOOOOOOOOOOOOOOOOOOOOOOOO 1 P
  53 OOOOOOOOOOOOOOOOOOOOOOOOOOOOOOOOOOOOOOOOOOOOOOOOOOOOOO 1 O
  52 OOOOOOOOOOOOOOOOOOOOOOOOOOOOOOOOOOOOOOOOOOOOOOOOOOOOO 1 N
  51 OOOOOOOOOOOOOOOOOOOOOOOOOOOOOOOOOOOOOOOOOOOOOOOOOOOO 1 M
  50 OOOOOOOOOOOOOOOOOOOOOOOOOOOOOOOOOOOOOOOOOOOOOOOOOOO 1 L
  49 OOOOOOOOOOOOOOOOOOOOOOOOOOOOOOOOOOOOOOOOOOOOOOOOOO 1 K
  46 OOOOOOOOOOOOOOOOOOOOOOOOOOOOOOOOOOOOOOOOOOOOOOOO 1 J
  43 OOOOOOOOOOOOOOOOOOOOOOOOOOOOOOOOOOOOOOOOOOOO 1 H
  42 OOOOOOOOOOOOOOOOOOOOOOOOOOOOOOOOOOOOOOOOOOO 1 G
  41 OOOOOOOOOOOOOOOOOOOOOOOOOOOOOOOOOOOOOOOOOO 1 F
  38 OOOOOOOOOOOOOOOOOOOOOOOOOOOOOOOOOOOOOOOO 1 E
  37 OOOOOOOOOOOOOOOOOOOOOOOOOOOOOOOOOOOOOO 1 D
  34 OOOOOOOOOOOOOOOOOOOOOOOOOOOOOOOOOOO 1 C
  33 OOOOOOOOOOOOOOOOOOOOOOOOOOOOOOOOO 1 B
  30 OOOOOOOOOOOOOOOOOOOOOOOOOOOOO 1 A
  25 OOOOOOOOOOOOOOOOOOOOOOOO  1 BB (Pit)
  25 OOOOOOOOOOOOOOOOOOOOOOOO  1 AA (Pit)

                    S T A G E
```

SOUTH COAST REPERTORY
Mainstage

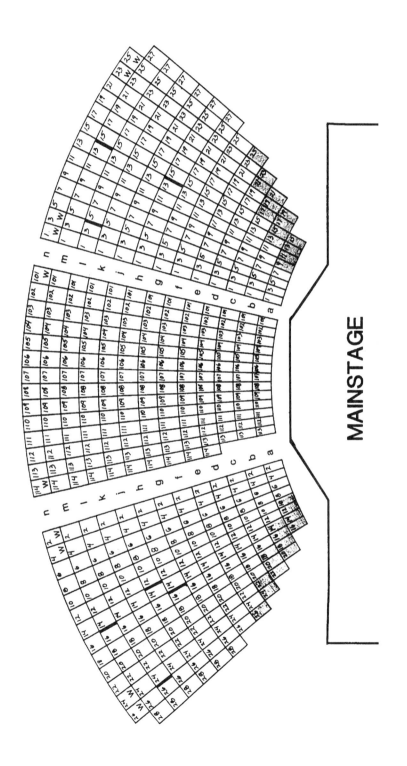

MAINSTAGE

SOUTH COAST REPERTORY
Second Stage

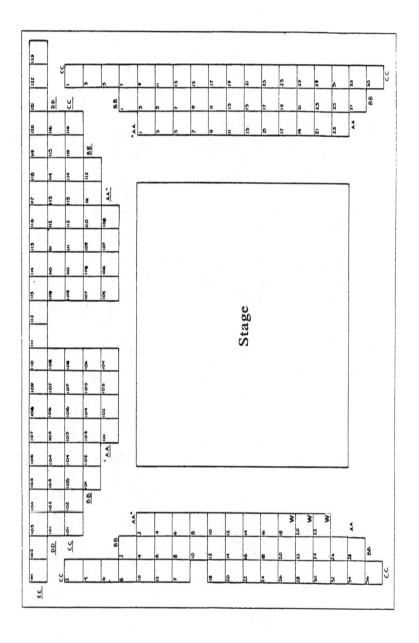

SPRECKELS THEATRE

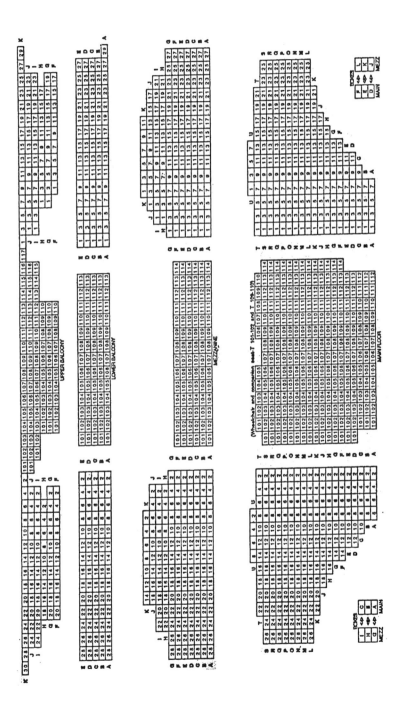

NEW STARLIGHT THEATER
Starlight Bowl

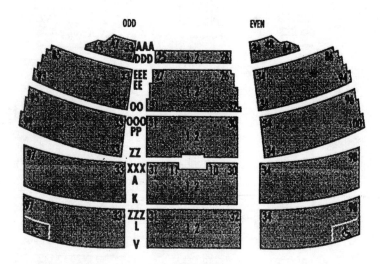

TERRACE THEATER

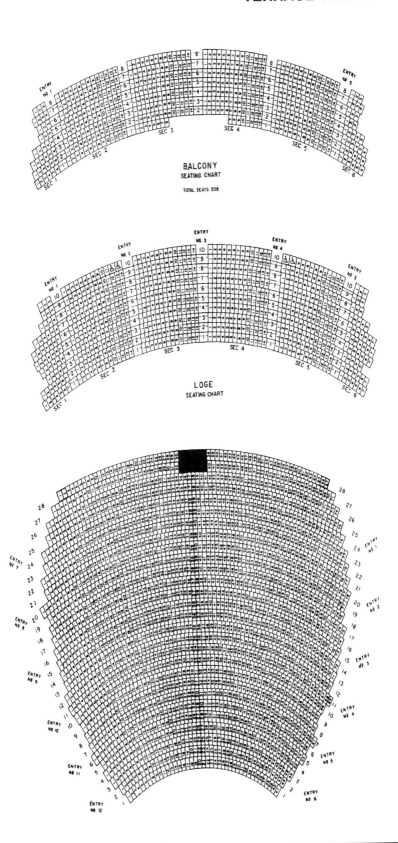

BALCONY
SEATING CHART

TOTAL SEATS: 508

LOGE
SEATING CHART

UCLA
Royce Hall

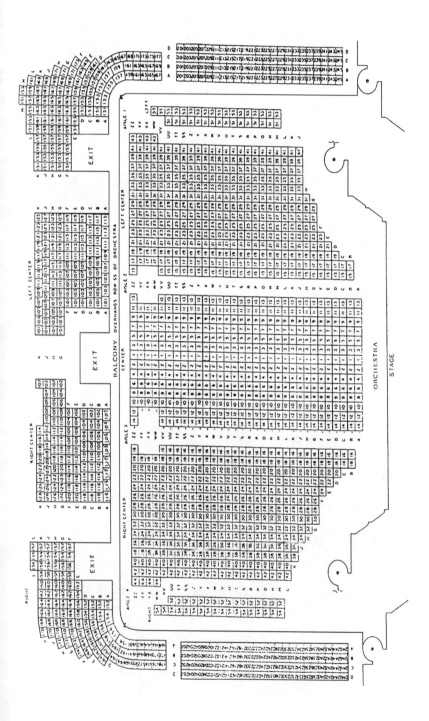

UCLA
Schoenberg Auditorium

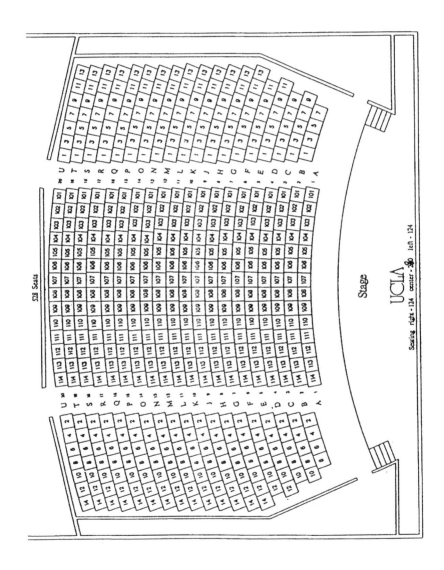

UCLA
Wadsworth Theater

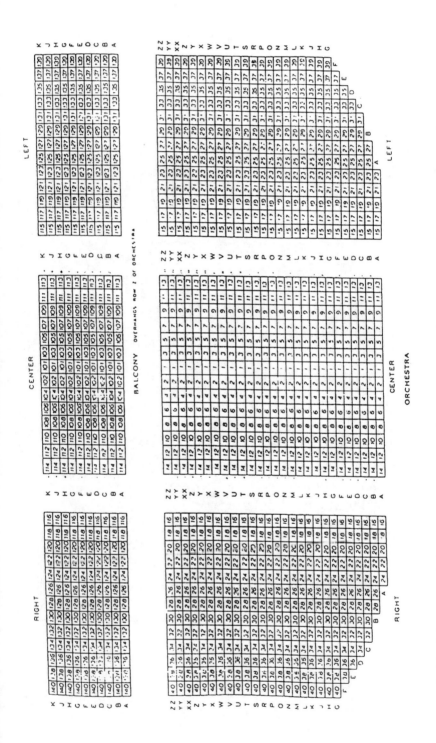

UC SAN DIEGO UNIVERSITY
Mandeville Auditorium

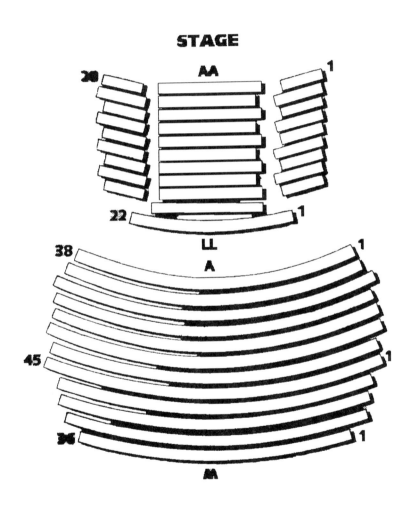

UNIVERSAL AMPHITHEATER

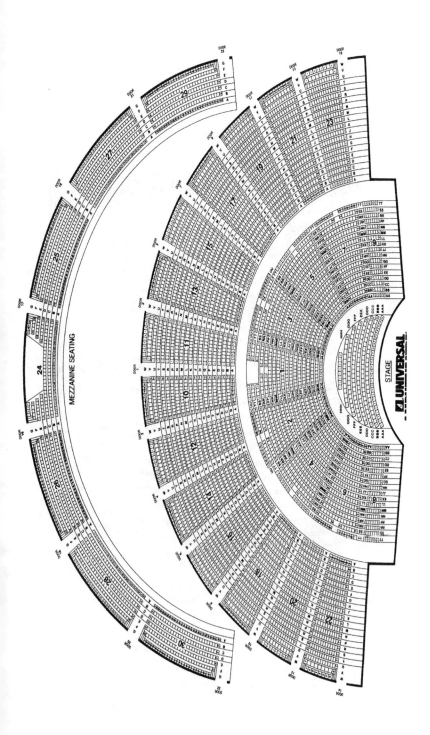

WESTWOOD PLAYHOUSE

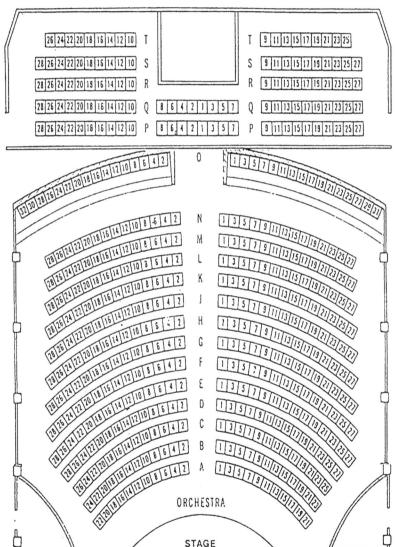

MEZZANINE

ORCHESTRA

STAGE

WILSHIRE EBELL THEATRE

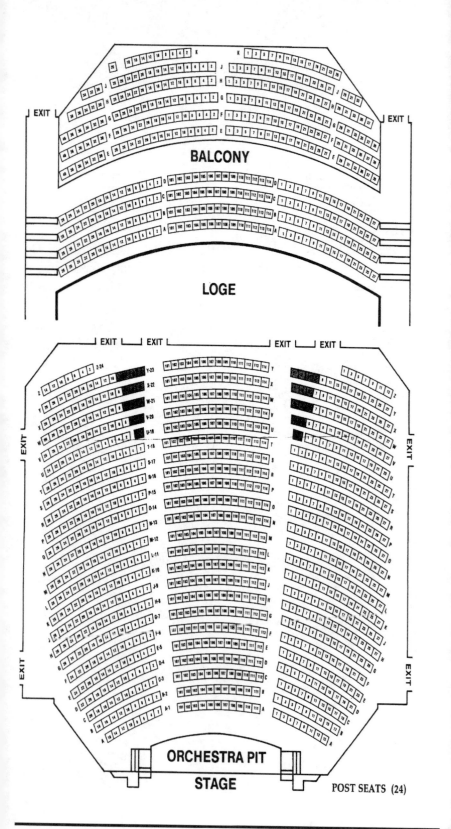

BALCONY

LOGE

ORCHESTRA PIT

STAGE

POST SEATS (24)

WILSHIRE THEATRE

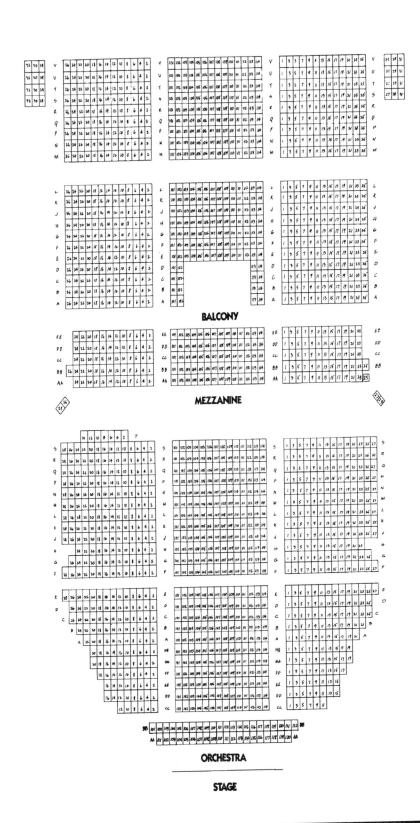

BALCONY

MEZZANINE

ORCHESTRA

STAGE

WILTERN THEATRE

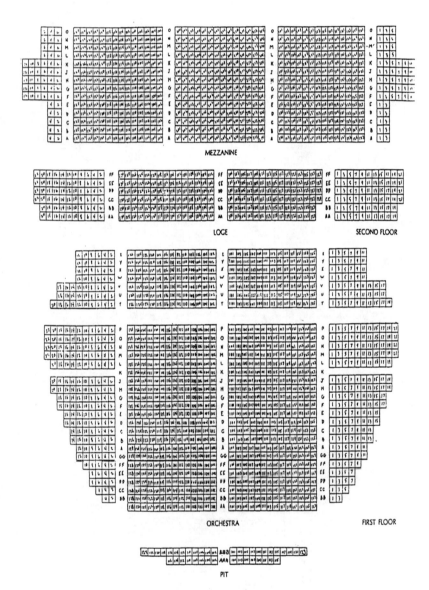

MEZZANINE

LOGE

SECOND FLOOR

ORCHESTRA

FIRST FLOOR

PIT

ABOUT THE AUTHOR

Carey Simon has been writing and editing guidebooks for more than a decade. She is the co-author of the award-winning *Frommer's California with Kids*, currently in its 3rd edition, as well as *Frommer's Los Angeles with Kids* and *San Francisco with Kids*. Her travel commentary, parenting articles, and stories on the performing arts have appeared in *Los Angeles Magazine*, *The Los Angeles Times*, *San Francisco Examiner*, *Westways*, *Child Magazine*, and *Publisher's Weekly*. She is also a frequent contributor to *Family Fun* magazine.

Ms. Simon is practically considered a native of Los Angeles, having lived there nearly 20 years.

INDEX

INDEX

This index lists entries for all chapters in alphabetical order. Page numbers in **boldface type** refer to seating plans.

INDEX

APPLAUSE: NEW YORK'S GUIDE TO THE PERFORMING ARTS
by Ruth Leon

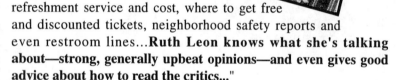

"A MUST FOR ANYONE WHO VENTURES TO NEW YORK ON OR OFF BROADWAY... It will make life a lot easier. It gives the practical lowdown on 1,000 performing arts spaces—for dance, classical music, jazz, as well as theater—in all five boroughs. Here is **SOLID INFORMATION** about subway and bus directions, parking availability, wheelchair access, refreshment service and cost, where to get free and discounted tickets, neighborhood safety reports and even restroom lines...**Ruth Leon knows what she's talking about—strong, generally upbeat opinions—and even gives good advice about how to read the critics...**"

—**Frank Rich**

"**THE APPLAUSE GUIDE** talks to you like a New Yorker: straight from the shoulder, pulling no punches, telling no lies. Just the companion you want to the city's performing arts scene."

—**Mary Holloway,** Executive Director,
ASSOCIATION FOR A BETTER NEW YORK

"I've never seen anything like it ! **THE APPLAUSE GUIDE** is **THE *ZAGAT'S* FOR ANYBODY WHO DEVOURS CULTURE.**"

—**Thomas Wolfe,** Concierge Manager,
THE PLAZA

"Even for the initiated, **THE APPLAUSE GUIDE** will be a constant revelation."

—**Mary Schmidt Campbell,** Commissioner
NEW YORK CITY DEPT. OF CULTURAL AFFAIRS

ISBN 1-55783-096-7 $15.95 US £8.99 UK